THE JAZZ STANDARDS

ALSO BY TED GIOIA

The Imperfect Art: Reflections on Jazz and Modern Culture

West Coast Jazz: Modern Jazz in California 1945–1960

The History of Jazz

Work Songs

Healing Songs

Delta Blues

The Birth (and Death) of the Cool

THE
JAZZ
A GUIDE TO THE REPERTOIRE
STANDARDS

TED GIOIA

OXFORD
UNIVERSITY PRESS

OXFORD
UNIVERSITY PRESS

Oxford University Press, Inc., publishes works that further
Oxford University's objective of excellence
in research, scholarship, and education.

Oxford   New York
Auckland   Cape Town   Dar es Salaam   Hong Kong   Karachi
Kuala Lumpur   Madrid   Melbourne   Mexico City   Nairobi
New Delhi   Shanghai   Taipei   Toronto

With offices in
Argentina   Austria   Brazil   Chile   Czech Republic   France   Greece
Guatemala   Hungary   Italy   Japan   Poland   Portugal   Singapore
South Korea   Switzerland   Thailand   Turkey   Ukraine   Vietnam

Copyright © 2012 by Ted Gioia

Published by Oxford University Press, Inc.
198 Madison Avenue, New York, NY 10016

www.oup.com

Oxford is a registered trademark of Oxford University Press

Library of Congress Cataloging-in-Publication Data
Gioia, Ted.
The jazz standards : a guide to the repertoire / Ted Gioia.
    p.   cm.
Includes bibliographical references, discographical references, and index.
ISBN 978-0-19-993739-4
1. Jazz—Bibliography. 2. Jazz—Discography.
3. Jazz—Analysis, appreciation. I. Title.
ML128.J3G56   2012
016.78165—dc23   2011042921

19

Printed in the United States of America
on acid-free paper

For my siblings: Dana, Greg, and Cara

CONTENTS

ACKNOWLEDGMENTS

I have been learning about these songs for most of my life, and could never list the many people who have helped to shape my understanding of the jazz repertoire. But a handful of individuals gave me valuable advice and input during the actual course of writing this work, and I want to thank them by name. I have greatly benefited from the contributions of Duck Baker, Kenny Berger, Uri Caine, Breaux Castleman, Paul Combs, Thomas Cunniffe, Ronan Guilfoyle, John Edward Hasse, Ethan Iverson, Todd Jenkins, Bill Kirchner, David McGee, John McNeil, Stuart Nicholson, Lewis Porter, Ricky Riccardi, Jeff Sultanof, Terry Teachout, Scott Timberg, Rob van der Bliek, and Carl Woideck. However, I must absolve them of any blame for the limitations or excesses of the present work. I am also deeply indebted to Suzanne Ryan and her colleagues at Oxford University Press, including Joellyn Ausanka, Woody Gilmartin and Caelyn Cobb—without their support this book would not have been possible. Finally, I offer public thanks to my wife, Tara, and our two sons, Michael and Thomas, for their love, patience, and understanding.

NOTE

Each entry is accompanied by a list of recommended recordings. I have made these selections on the basis of their historical importance, influence on later artists, inherent quality, and originality of conception. At the same time, I also tried to highlight a range of interpretive styles. Most of the listed tracks are from the jazz idiom, but I have occasionally included a performance from outside the jazz world if I felt it particularly worthy of attention. For tracks recorded after the early 1950s, I have typically provided the name of an album or CD on which the music can be found. The earlier tracks, predating the era of long-playing albums, are often available on a wide range of reissues and compilations, which frequently go in and out of print—for these, I have simply listed a date and location for the recording. In a few instances, I list the track under the name of the best-known artist rather than the original bandleader, since this reflects how these works are typically packaged and sold.

When I was learning how to play jazz during my teenage years, I kept encountering songs that the older musicians expected me to know. I eventually realized that there were around 200 or 300 of these compositions, and that they served as the cornerstone of the jazz repertoire. A jazz performer needed to learn these songs the same way a classical musician studied the works of Bach, Beethoven, or Mozart.

In fact, I soon learned that knowledge of the repertoire was even more important to a jazz musician than to a classical artist. The classical performer at least knows what compositions will be played before the concert begins. This is not always the case with jazz. I recall the lament of a friend who was enlisted to back up a poll-winning horn player at a jazz festival—only to discover that he wouldn't be told what songs would be played until the musicians were already on stage in front of 6,000 people. Such instances are not unusual in the jazz world, a quirk of a subculture that prizes both spontaneity and macho bravado. Another buddy, a quite talented pianist, encountered an even more uncooperative bandleader—a famous saxophonist who wouldn't identify the names of the songs even *after* the musicians were on the bandstand. The leader would simply play a short introduction on the tenor, than stamp off the beat with his foot . . . and my friend was expected to figure out the song and key from those meager clues. For better or worse, such is our art form.

I had my own embarrassing situations with unfamiliar standards during my youth—but fortunately never with thousands of people on hand to watch. I soon realized what countless other jazz musicians have no doubt also learned: in-depth study of the jazz repertoire is hardly a quaint historical sideline, but essential for survival. Not learning these songs puts a jazz player on a quick path to unemployment.

But no one gave you a list. Nor would a typical youngster of my (or a later) generation encounter many of these songs outside the jazz world—most of them had been composed before I was born, and even the more recent entries in the repertoire weren't part of the fare you typically heard on TV or mainstream radio. Some of these tunes came from Broadway, but not always from the hit productions—many first appeared in obscure or failed shows, or revues by relatively unknown songwriters. Others made their debut in movies, or came from big bands, or were introduced by pop singers from outside the jazz world. A few—such as "Autumn Leaves" or "Desafinado"—originated far away from jazz's land of origin. And, of course, many were written by jazz musicians themselves, serving as part of the legacy of Miles Davis, Thelonious Monk, Duke Ellington, John Coltrane, Charlie Parker, and other seminal artists.

My own education in this music was happenstance and hard earned. Eventually "fake books" appeared on the scene to clear up some of the mystery, but I never saw one of these (usually illegal) compilations until I was almost 20 years old. When I first encountered *The Real Book*—the underground collection of jazz lead sheets that began circulating in the 1970s—even the table of contents served as a revelation to me. And, I'm sure, to others as well. Aspiring musicians today can hardly imagine how opaque the art form was just a few decades ago—no school I attended had a jazz program or even offered a single course on jazz. Most of the method books were worthless, and the peculiar culture of the art form tended to foster an aura of secrecy and competitiveness. Just knowing the names of the songs one needed to learn represented a major step forward; getting a lead sheet was an unwonted luxury.

A few years later, when I started teaching jazz piano students, I put together a brief guide to the repertoire, listing the songs my pupils needed to learn and the keys in which they were normally played—a rudimentary forerunner to the work you now have in your hands. Still later, as I began writing about jazz, I continued to study these same songs, but from a different perspective. I now tried to unravel the evolution of these compositions over time, understand how different jazz artists had played them, and what changes had taken place in performance practices.

Over the years, I often wished I had a handbook to this body of music, a single volume that would guide me through the jazz repertoire and point me in the direction of the classic recordings. A few books were helpful in my early education into the nuances of this body of music, especially Alec Wilder's *American Popular Song* (1972), but even the best of these books invariably focused on only a small part of the repertoire—mainly Broadway and Tin Pan Alley songs—and dealt very little with this music as it related to jazz. The book I needed didn't exist when I was coming up, and still doesn't. I wanted to delve into these songs as sources of inspiration for great jazz performances—a perspective that often took one far afield from what the composer might have originally intended. I wanted a guide to these works as building blocks of the jazz art form, as a springboard to improvisation, as an invitation to creative reinterpretation.

This book aims to be that type of survey, the kind of overview of the standard repertoire that I wished someone had given me back in the day—a guide that would have helped me as a musician, as a critic, as a historian, and simply as a fan and lover of the jazz idiom. To some degree, this work represents the fruition of all my experiences with these great songs over a period of decades. The compositions that were once mysterious and even foreboding have now become familiar friends, the companions of countless hours, and I have relished the opportunity to write about these songs and discuss my favorite recordings. Certainly those readers familiar with my other books will note a more personal tone here, a more informal approach—one that felt natural to me as I delved into a body of work that has become, by now, such a vital part of my life.

Let me share a few final words about the selection process involved in picking the songs highlighted here. I chose songs based on their significance in the jazz repertoire of the current era. I have picked the compositions that a fan is most likely to hear—and a musician is most frequently asked to play—nowadays. This approach has led me to pass over some songs that might have once held sway in the jazz world—"The Sheik of Araby," "Some of These Days," etc.— while including others that have, perhaps, been recorded on fewer occasions *in toto*, but have been performed more often in recent years. In short, my choices reflect the jazz idiom as a vibrant, present-day endeavor.

Even so, I am troubled by how few recent compositions are discussed in these pages. If I were writing a book about my favorite jazz songs or the jazz composers I most admire, a somewhat different list of songs would be highlighted here—but that is a task for another day. The jazz repertoire is not as fluid as it once was, and the same process of codification that resulted in works such as *The Real Book* has also made it difficult for newer songs to enter the standard repertoire. And though a number of jazz artists have tried to champion more recent material—works by Radiohead, Björk, Pat Metheny, Kurt Cobain, Maria Schneider, etc.—these songs still haven't received enough traction to justify inclusion here. I lament this state of affairs, even as I respect its harsh reality. I would welcome a more expansive and adaptive repertoire, and would happily embrace the very changes in the art form that might make the song selection in this book obsolete.

In the interim, here is an assessment of the cornerstones of the jazz repertoire as it exists today—songs that have formed the soundtrack of my own life. As such, this book is my tribute to them, to the compositions and the creative minds that not only wrote them, but those others who have reinterpreted and refreshed them over the years, inspiring me by taking old songs to new places.

THE JAZZ STANDARDS

After You've Gone

Composed by Turner Layton, with lyrics written by Henry Creamer

In a reversal of the more typical formula for jazz standards, "After You've Gone" was composed by African-American songwriters but popularized by white performers. The song is almost as old as recorded jazz itself, introduced in 1918, and made famous by Al Jolson, Sophie Tucker, and Marion Harris—none of them pure jazz artists, but each borrowing some aspects of their individual styles from the hot music of the day.

The story of composer Turner Layton is a fascinating one, a tale of social mobility and success that few African-Americans born in the nineteenth century could match. Raised by parents who took pride in education and community service—his father had been a music professor and Civil War veteran, and his mother also a teacher—Layton studied at Howard University's dental school, then switched to a music career, gaining renown as both a performer and songwriter. In partnership with lyricist Harry Creamer, he composed for Broadway and the Ziegfeld Follies and enjoyed a series of hits, including "Way Down Yonder in New Orleans," "Dear Old Southland," and his most famous composition, "After You've Gone." In 1924, Layton took his act to England where, along with Clarence "Tandy" Johnstone, he enjoyed fame as a cabaret performer, allegedly selling some ten million records—a number hard to believe but, even if we cut it by half, testifies to his remarkable drawing power. Layton's legacy is still felt in Britain, where royalties from his estate have funded the Great Ormond Street Hospital for Children in London.

Alec Wilder, a connoisseur of classic popular music, has called "After You've Gone" an "American-sounding song"— not a technical term vetted by musicologists, but I can hear what he means. A boisterous, emphatic quality, marked by the repeated short, ascending phrases, jumps out at the listener, furthered by the rapid pace of harmonic activity: at least one chord change takes place every bar throughout the unconventional 20-bar form. The words, in which the singer talks about being left crying and in ruin, seem transplanted from a different, more despairing tune—the melody tells a different story: after you've gone, I'll be partying, not brooding.

Nowadays this song is typically played in a sprightly up-tempo manner, but the earliest recordings tend to be slower and much darker in tone. Marion Harris's successful recording from 1918 lopes along at under 80 beats per minute, while Bessie Smith's performance from 1927 adopts a similar pulse, and is so angst-ridden that the song sounds akin to the downhearted blues that made up most of her repertoire, although the stellar jazz band on hand (which included Fletcher Henderson and Coleman Hawkins) does an admirable job of swinging the beat even at this lugubrious pace. Sophie Tucker's version, recorded a few weeks later, is only slightly more energetic, and Johnny Dodds's treatment, also from 1927, is very similar in conception to Smith's.

But around this same time, the California Ramblers and the Charleston Chasers—the latter group drawing on the talents of Miff Mole, Jimmy Dorsey, and Red Nichols—doubled the tempo and proved that "After You've Gone" could be an effective vehicle for hot jazz. When Coleman Hawkins recorded the song in Holland in 1935, he kept close to Bessie Smith's approach, not surprisingly, since he had participated on that performance. But most of the other leading jazz players who had recorded the song during the intervening years—including Louis Armstrong, Art Tatum, Fletcher Henderson, Paul Whiteman (with an arrangement by William Grant Still), and Django Reinhardt—preferred a faster and looser interpretation.

"After You've Gone" remained popular with improvisers during the Swing Era, and no one left behind more recordings of the composition than Benny Goodman—more than 40 if you include all the bootlegs, radio broadcasts, and film clips. The most popular would prove to be his trio rendition, alongside Teddy Wilson and Gene Krupa, which was a top 20 hit in 1935. Goodman's sidemen also took a liking to the song, with Lionel Hampton enjoying a hit with his vocal rendition from 1937. Trumpeter Roy Eldridge also made a compelling claim to "After You've Gone," recording it under his own leadership and as a sideman with Gene Krupa, Benny Goodman, and others.

Bebop and "cool school" players were far less likely to play this song. Charlie Parker, Thelonious Monk, Dizzy Gillespie, Miles Davis, Bud Powell, and most of their fellow travelers never brought it to a studio session (although Parker left behind a memorable live rendition as part of a Jazz at the Philharmonic jam). Sonny Stitt proved an exception, recording the song on several occasions during the 1950s, while Sonny Rollins borrowed the chords for "Come, Gone" on his

Way Out West album. Art Pepper did the same with his composition "Straight Life," which became both one of his trademark tunes and the title for his later tell-all autobiography.

The composition has continued to be widely performed in more recent decades, with everyone from Woody Allen to Wynton Marsalis trying their hand at "After You've Gone." As many as a dozen or more new jazz versions are released on the market each year, and with more than a thousand already available, fans have no shortage of choices. Most of these mimic the jazz sensibilities of a bygone age, with fresh new treatments very much a rarity. Yet Nicholas Payton's performance from his 1995 *Gumbo Nouveau* project, which reconfigures both the harmonies and rhythmic sensibility, shows that this venerable song from 1918 is still capable of taking on new guises.

RECOMMENDED VERSIONS

Marion Harris, Camden, New Jersey, July 22, 1918

Charleston Chasers, New York, January 27, 1927

Bessie Smith, New York, March 2, 1927

Louis Armstrong, New York, November 26, 1929

Benny Goodman (with Teddy Wilson and Gene Krupa), New York, July 13, 1935

Roy Eldridge, Chicago, January 28, 1937

Gene Krupa (with Roy Eldridge), New York, June 5, 1941

Jazz at the Philharmonic (with Charlie Parker), Los Angeles, January 28, 1946

Sonny Stitt, from *The Hard Swing*, Los Angeles, February 9, 1959

Nicholas Payton, from *Gumbo Nouveau*, November 28–30, 1995

Ain't Misbehavin'
Composed by Fats Waller and Harry Brooks, with lyrics by Andy Razaf

Most jazz historians point to Louis Armstrong's Hot Five and Hot Seven recordings from the 1920s as the key turning point in establishing the trumpeter as a star. But Armstrong himself saw his performance of "Ain't Misbehavin" in Fats Waller's 1928 Broadway show *Hot Chocolates* as his big breakthrough moment. "I believe that great song, and the chance I got to play it, did a lot to make me better known all over the country," he later asserted. Armstrong's success was all the more remarkable, given that he didn't appear onstage. He merely sang and played the song from the orchestra pit during intermission.

The New Yorker carped that *Hot Chocolates* had "no good new music," but the *New York Times* reviewer countered that "one song, a synthetic but entirely pleasant jazz ballad called 'Ain't Misbehavin''' stands out, and its rendition between the acts by an unnamed member of the orchestra was a highlight of the premiere." Armstrong's role didn't remain anonymous for long—his name was soon added to the show's program and his performance featured onstage.

Armstrong recorded the song in July of the following year, and he took great liberties with the written melody—as was his modus operandi at the time. Fats Waller performed "Ain't Misbehavin'" in the studio two weeks later and, though he, too, could mess around with his own songs, he delivered a no-nonsense solo stride piano version that provides us with our clearest sense of how the composer originally approached his most famous piece. Many others were getting into the act, and more than 20 versions of "Ain't Misbehavin'" were recorded in 1929 alone.

Yet the song was mostly forgotten by the following year, and only gradually returned to the jazz repertoire in the mid-1930s, helped along by the advocacy of some influential parties. Duke Ellington recorded "Ain't Misbehavin'" during his 1933 London visit—a track that makes an unusual use of five-against-two rhythm midway through Barney Bigard's solo, perhaps the first time that atypical phrasing showed up in a written horn arrangement on a jazz recording. Paul Whiteman's 1935 recording benefits from a vocal and solo contribution by Jack Teagarden. Django Reinhardt recorded "Ain't Misbehavin'" in Paris in 1937, and the following year Jelly Roll Morton performed it at a Library of Congress session for Alan Lomax—one of the few times that this New Orleans pioneer deigned to offer a cover version of a song composed by a jazz player of a later generation. He even concluded with a choice scat singing chorus that made clear Morton's often underappreciated skills as a vocalist.

A few big bands embraced "Ain't Misbehavin'" during the Swing Era, but the song's pronounced two-beat sensibility marked it as a carryover from an earlier day. Even fewer beboppers felt the call of Waller's piece, and a handful of recordings—by Sonny Stitt (1950), Dizzy Gillespie (1952)—show how difficult it was to make this composition sound sufficiently progressive during the post–World War II years. The bop-era pianist Hank Jones eventually earned a gig as pianist and conductor of the hit 1978 Broadway show *Ain't Misbehavin'*—winner of the Tony Award for Best Musical—and made a noteworthy recording of the song that same year, but needed to adopt a far more traditional style than he typically employed in order to pull it off.

Modern jazz singers have tended to have an easier time with Waller's composition, as demonstrated on recordings by Sarah Vaughan (1950), with Miles Davis in the band, and Johnny Hartman (1955). In truth, Razaf's words are an essential part of the experience of this "Ain't Misbehavin'"—the nursery rhyme allusions to Jack Horner in his corner are both witty and appropriate, perfectly matched to the whimsical tone of the tune. But the harmony and bassline movement in the bridge are equally fascinating, a surprisingly modern touch in such an old-school anthem.

"Ain't Misbehavin'" is not quite as important a part of the jazz repertoire nowadays as it once was. But for any pianist who wants to learn the Harlem stride keyboard tradition, it remains an essential composition, an important milestone in that idiom. Few can match, and none surpass, Art Tatum's robust two-handed performance style, and he left behind a number of recordings of the Waller classic, but my favorite by far is a little-known live performance from 1944, in which Tatum has the audience gasping and laughing at his pyrotechnics.

RECOMMENDED VERSIONS

Louis Armstrong, New York, July 19, 1929

Fats Waller, Camden, New Jersey, August 2, 1929

Duke Ellington, London, July 13, 1933

Paul Whiteman (with Jack Teagarden), New York, July 9, 1935

Django Reinhardt (with the Quintette du Hot Club de France), Paris, April 22, 1937

Jelly Roll Morton, Washington, D.C., May–June 1938

Art Tatum, New York, Fall 1944

Sarah Vaughan (with Miles Davis), New York, May 18, 1950

Johnny Hartman (with Howard McGhee), from *Songs From the Heart*, New York, October 1955

Hank Jones (with Teddy Edwards), from *Ain't Misbehavin'*, Berkeley, California, August 5–6, 1978

Dick Wellstood, from *Live at the Sticky Wicket*, live at The Sticky Wicket, Hopkinton, Massachusetts, November 9, 1986

Airegin
Composed by Sonny Rollins

The song title is "Nigeria" spelled backwards, and Sonny Rollins was only one of several leading modern jazz composers who played this kind of word game with his listeners. Dizzy Gillespie had already given us "Emanon" ("No Name" spelled backwards) back in 1946. In 1952, Horace Silver had recorded "Ecaroh" (his first name spelled backwards). Miles Davis would do the same years later with "Selim" and "Sivad." Thelonious Monk was credited with

"Eronel" ("Lenore" in reverse, the name of an old girlfriend of Sadik Hakim who, along with Idrees Sulieman, wrote most of the piece).

Some may see these titles as signs of the playfulness and informality of the jazz world, while others, looking for deeper reasons, may point to the long history of African-American performers relying on coded and hidden significations in their work. In this instance, the linguistic games proved a hurdle for Jon Hendricks when he tried to match words to Rollins's melody while still keeping the title in mind. For his 1958 version, included on the Lambert, Hendricks & Ross 1958 release *The Swingers!*, he opens with "Wait'll y'dig it on the map; Airegin spelled backwards"—for which his rhyme is the neologism "gone fac'wards." No, Mr. Rollins did not make it easy for future collaborators.

The song first came to prominence via the 1954 Miles Davis project *Bags' Groove*, an album that is far less well known than the trumpeter's work from later in the decade. Even so, the album presented several songs destined to become standards, including three of Rollins's best compositions: "Airegin," "Doxy," and "Oleo." "Airegin" offers the most interesting conception of the batch, with an opening that hints at a minor blues at the outset, then morphs into a lopsided 36-bar form—an oddity, with 20 bars elapsing before the repeat, but then running only 16 bars before coming back to the top of the form—all packed with plenty of harmonic movement to keep things interesting for the soloists. The opening chords look back to "Opus V," a piece by J. J. Johnson that Rollins had recorded back in 1949, while the second eight bars are reminiscent of the bridge to Billy Strayhorn's "Day Dream." But the whole as constructed by Rollins is distinctive and the work ranks among the most intricate of the saxophonist's better known pieces. Certainly "Airegin" showed that in an era when other jazz players were expanding their audience by moving toward either a cool melodicism or an earthy funkiness, Rollins was intent on writing songs that would appeal to other horn players rather than patrons at the jukebox.

"Airegin" did just that. Two years later, Davis resurrected the song for another Prestige session, and this time featured John Coltrane, Rollins's leading rival as reigning tenor titan of modern jazz. Davis made a surprising choice to substitute an 8-bar vamp over an F minor chord for Rollins's original chord changes during the second A theme; by doing so, he anticipated the modal approach that would come to the fore in his music later in the decade. The tempo is faster here, and the mood much more aggressive, with Trane serving notice that he could play this composition just as well as Rollins himself.

Other prominent soloists followed suit. Phil Woods recorded "Airegin" on his 1957 session with Gene Quill, and periodically returned to the song in various settings over the years. Art Pepper tackled it on his *Art Pepper Plus Eleven* date from 1959, and in the early 1960s, Stan Getz, Chet Baker, and Maynard Ferguson, among others, could be heard performing the Rollins standard.

The song has kept its place in the standard repertoire, although it is less often heard than the same composer's "Oleo" or "St. Thomas." Yet this may simply reflect the fact that these other songs are easier to play, relying in the former instance on familiar "rhythm" changes while the latter is simple enough to perform by ear without a rehearsal. But probing soloists still find sustenance in "Airegin." For two invigorating examples, check out the treatments by Chris Potter and Michael Brecker, both from 1993.

RECOMMENDED VERSIONS

Miles Davis (with Sonny Rollins), from *Bags' Groove*, Hackensack, New Jersey, June 29, 1954

Miles Davis (with John Coltrane), from *Cookin'*, Hackensack, New Jersey, October 26, 1956

Art Pepper (with arrangement by Marty Paich), from *Art Pepper Plus Eleven*, Los Angeles, March 14, 1959

Wes Montgomery (with Tommy Flanagan), from *The Incredible Jazz Guitar of Wes Montgomery*, New York, January 26, 1960

Phil Woods (with Jaki Byard), from *Musique du Bois*, New York, January 14, 1974

Maynard Ferguson, from *New Vintage*, New York, July 10, 1977

Michael Brecker and David Friesen, from *Two for the Show*, Portland, April 25, 1993

Chris Potter, from *Sundiata*, New York, December 13, 1993

Alfie
Composed by Burt Bacharach and Hal David

It is a bit of mystery why Burt Bacharach's songs aren't played more often by jazz musicians. He is a fine craftsman, but also much more. The radical touches in his songs—changing meters, surprising harmonic shifts, and other interesting twists—are married to memorable melodies in a way that might seem perfectly suited for jazz performance. Yet though some of his hit songs have enjoyed occasional attention by various jazz artists, few have become entrenched as standards.

Perhaps this derives from the widespread reluctance of jazz musicians to draw on popular material of any sort after the rise of rock, or maybe it's attributable to the sometimes unappetizing arrangements in which Mr. Bacharach's compositions were first presented to the public. Then again, perhaps the idiosyncrasies of Bacharach's charts scare away would-be performers: in truth, they can appear more suited to a careful arrangement rather than a carefree jam. Even so, the more than 70 hit songs to his credit, as well as lesser known works such as the lovely "name" songs "Nikki" and "Lisa," represent a body of work that jazz players ought to know better. I especially like how Donald Fagen, of Steely Dan, once characterized Bacharach's style: Ravel-like harmonies married to street-corner soul. How apt!

"Alfie" has secured a modest, but well-deserved, place in the jazz repertoire. And this despite its convoluted formal structure and a melody that, after the catchy opening phrase, becomes exceedingly baroque. Sometimes the performances are perfunctory or peculiar—for example, Maynard Ferguson's attempt to transform this tune into a high note show-off exercise for trumpet, or a curio from 1969, which finds the Ellington band tackling "Alfie" with unexpected guest Wild Bill Davis dominating the proceedings on organ. Another surprise comes from Stevie Wonder, who enjoyed a modest hit with "Alfie" in 1968 via a pop-oriented harmonica instrumental—released under the pseudonym Eivets Rednow (spell it backwards to crack the code). But more often the song serves as a springboard for a heartfelt jazz probing of its emotional essence, as in the several live performances by Bill Evans from the late 1960s and early 1970s. As more recent recordings by Pat Metheny, Patricia Barber, and John Scofield testify, the song continues to elicit distinguished interpretations in the new millennium.

By the way, jazz fans should not confuse this song with "Alfie's Theme," performed by Sonny Rollins, also from the soundtrack to the film *Alfie*. Although Rollins's mid-tempo groove tune is more overtly jazzy than Bacharach's ballad, it has rarely been covered by other jazz players. How odd to think that the contribution of a genuine jazz legend to a movie would be surpassed by the Bacharach theme, sung by Cher for the film, in an arrangement by another Sonny . . . namely Sonny Bono, whose behind-the-scenes work on this track helped put it on the charts.

RECOMMENDED VERSIONS

Carmen McRae, from *Second to None*, New York, August 1964

Rahsaan Roland Kirk, from *Now Please Don't You Cry, Beautiful Edith*, Englewood, New Jersey, May 2, 1967

Bill Evans, from *Montreux II*, live at the Montreux Jazz Festival, Montreux, Switzerland, June 19, 1970

Art Farmer (with Cedar Walton), from *The Summer Knows*, New York, May 12–13, 1976

Patricia Barber, from *Nightclub*, Chicago, May 15–19, 2000

John Scofield, from *En Route*, live at the Blue Note, New York, December 2003

Pat Metheny, from *What's It All About*, New York, February 2011

All Blues
Composed by Miles Davis

Miles Davis's *Kind of Blue* album—the best-selling jazz recording of all time, by most accounts, with its quadruple platinum status validated by the Recording Industry Association of America in 2008—is famous for its scale-driven modal song structures. But this frequently played piece from the album has no modal component, and instead follows a modified blues structure. Yet, the work is anything but conventional, given its 6/8 meter—unusual for a blues song—as well as its distinctive piano vamp and surprising shift up a half step from the dominant chord before moving into the turnaround.

Despite its boldness, "All Blues" is fairly easy to play and will not tax even a student soloist too strenuously. By the way, I've noticed that jazz performers—a prolix bunch, in most circumstances—tend to underplay on this song. I suspect this is due to the momentum of the piano vamp, which tends to push the song forward even if the soloist stays mum. This is in line with some hoary jazz lore that has been validated by my experience: namely, if the rhythm section is swinging, the horn players don't need to use as many notes. And the vamp on this song almost swings by itself.

The original recording is difficult to top, but if anyone could it was Miles himself. It's a toss-up, from my perspective, in deciding between the *Kind of Blue* version and Davis's live performance, captured at Lincoln Center in 1964. The latter is faster and constantly feels as if the musicians are pushing too hard, that the underlying structure will collapse into chaos. Yet somehow the whole thing coheres, due to the sheer collective willpower of all the parties on stage, albeit without achieving the meditative translucency of the 1959 original.

A song this iconic invites radical reworkings, and "All Blues" is no exception. Three progressive reinterpretations have impressed me with their boldness: first, a 5/4 version, for the *Miles from India* project, which matches Davis alums Jimmy Cobb and Ron Carter with sitar and ghatam in an East-meets-West rhythm section that backs a front line of Rudresh Mahanthappa and Gary Bartz; second, Vince Mendoza's daring postmodern chart for an international all-star band, commissioned for the 2007 Traumzeit Festival in Duisburg, Germany; and, finally, the 1998 free-for-all-blues romp by the World Saxophone Quartet in which Davis's original 6/8 is supplanted by an Africanized duple beat.

Sad to say, these provocative attempts to reorient a familiar standard are the exceptions rather than the rule. Most recordings treat this song with museum reverence, even replicating the original rhythm section groove. One can understand the attraction of the urtext—Davis's initial conception deserves our admiration—yet given the trumpeter's own willingness to shake things up, perhaps a little infidelity is in order when paying tribute to his oeuvre.

Oscar Brown Jr. later added words to this composition, which work better than most after-the-fact jazz lyrics, and persuasively match the emotional temperament of Miles's song. For an especially effective vocal rendition, track down Mark Murphy's performance from his 1990 *Bop for Miles* project.

RECOMMENDED VERSIONS

Miles Davis, from *Kind of Blue*, New York, April 22, 1959

Miles Davis, from *My Funny Valentine*, live at Philharmonic Hall, New York, February 12, 1964

Mary Lou Williams, from *Live at the Cookery*, New York, November 1975

Mark Murphy, from *Bop for Miles*, live at an unidentified location in Vienna, May 10, 1990

World Saxophone Quartet, from *Selim Sivad: The Music of Miles Davis*, New York, March 2–3, 1998

Vince Mendoza, from *Blauklang*, live in Duisburg, Germany, July 7, 2007

Rudresh Mahanthappa, Gary Bartz, and others, from *Miles from India*, no date or location given (CD released in 2008)

All of Me

Composed by Gerald Marks and Seymour Simons

"All of Me" is the only song by Gerald Marks and Seymour Simons to find its way into the standard jazz repertoire. From the start, vocalists embraced the song, and two different versions, by Louis Armstrong and Mildred Bailey (fronting the Paul Whiteman Orchestra), rose to the top of the charts in 1932. Louis Armstrong was especially fond of "All of Me," and he frequently performed it in later years, but I can't help hearing a mismatch between the lyrics, which describe romantic surrender, and the triumphal attitude of his delivery, which is more befitting a conqueror than supplicant. Bailey stays closer to the spirit of the words in her interpretation, although the support from Paul Whiteman's orchestra is far too dainty for either the song or the singer.

The definitive version of "All of Me" wouldn't appear for another decade, but when Billie Holiday recorded the song, with tenor saxophonist Lester Young on hand, she staked a claim of ownership that no one has managed to dislodge in subsequent years. (And not just on the version issued on the 78—if you can track it down, listen to the rejected third take recorded that day, which is a masterpiece in its own right.) Instead of Armstrong's confident sense of conquest, Holiday describes a more complicated romance, one just as likely to end in heartbreak as in a happily-ever-after. This type of equivocal mood is often hard to capture at the bouncy mid-tempo rhythm at which this song is usually played, but Holiday offers a textbook example of how it's done.

The emotional knots described in the song allow a singer a wide range of interpretive stances, from the flirtatious to the fatalistic. Frank Sinatra, who recorded "All of Me" on several occasions, took different approaches over the years. My favorite is an early version, from 1946, which finds him at his most vulnerable. Sinatra helped introduce many outside the jazz world to "All of Me," as did Willie Nelson, who included a touching interpretation on his enormously successful *Stardust* album, which stayed on the *Billboard* chart for an entire decade—from 1978 until 1988. The song has also appeared in a number of motion pictures (*Lady Sings the Blues, All of Me, Bird*) and on some unlikely television programs (*Sanford & Son, The Sopranos, The Muppet Show*).

The melody, for its part, combines the contradictory possibilities of the song. The downward thrusts of the opening phrases hint at emotional despair while the closing line, with its repeated high notes, seems almost jubilant. The chords are simple enough, but not without their interest. Warne Marsh later borrowed them for his composition "Background Music" and Lennie Tristano did the same for his piece "Line Up." But the lyrics are the main draw here, and remain the key reason why this song is still a vibrant part of the jazz repertoire so many decades after it was composed.

RECOMMENDED VERSIONS

Paul Whiteman (featuring Mildred Bailey), Chicago, December 1, 1931

Louis Armstrong, Chicago, January 27, 1932

Billie Holiday (master take and rejected third take), New York, March 21, 1941

Frank Sinatra, Hollywood, November 7, 1946

Charlie Parker (with Lennie Tristano), New York, August 1951

Duke Ellington, from *Jazz Party*, New York, February 19, 1959

Earl Hines, from *An Evening with Earl Hines*, New York, 1972

Willie Nelson, from *Stardust*, Southern California, December 1977

Dee Dee Bridgewater, from *In Montreux*, live at the Montreux Jazz Festival, Montreux, Switzerland, July 18, 1990

Luciana Souza, from *North and South*, 2003

All of You
Composed by Cole Porter

These lyrics must seem tame stuff indeed to listeners raised on today's radio fare. But Hollywood's inclusion of this song in the movie version of *Silk Stockings*, the musical that spawned "All of You," made the censorship screeners at the Motion Picture Association of America (MPAA) queasy. When Cole Porter said he loved "all of you," he apparently meant *all* of you; the MPAA found the references to making a "tour of you" with a rest stop at the "south of you" potentially offensive to American sensibilities. These phrases made it through the final cut and onto the silver screen, but Fred Astaire's hand gesture to Cyd Charisse during the "south of you" line was about as edgy as a Hollywood musical could get, circa 1957.

The Broadway show had opened two years earlier, and enjoyed considerable success, running for 478 performances. The plot relied on a predictable Cold War scenario: Soviet comrades come to the West and fall under the sway of capitalism in general, and wine, women, and song in particular. Yet the story line actually dates back to the 1939 Greta Garbo film *Ninotchka*. The 1955 show aimed to be cuttingly current—the Broadway production featured a song on "Stereophonic Sound," and the film version added "The Ritz Roll and Rock." The collaboration of 57-year-old Astaire and 66-year-old Porter on the latter rock tune, which we hope was intended as parody, belongs on any short list of the low points of either's career. "All of You" was the only song from *Silk Stockings* to find its way into the standard jazz and cabaret repertoire.

Jazz musicians quickly picked up on the tune, even before Astaire's movie performance. Ahmad Jamal recorded it three months after the musical's debut on Broadway, and Miles Davis—who often followed Jamal's lead in selecting songs during this era—added "All of You" to his repertoire in 1956, and continued performing it in concert for the next decade. A 1955 rendition by the Modern Jazz Quartet on their well-known *Concorde* album further solidified the song's emerging reputation as a vehicle for cool school melodic musings. Ella Fitzgerald, Sarah Vaughan, and Billie Holiday each recorded "All of You" during the second half of the decade, and they all took it at the same ambling medium tempo, trying to swing the melody but not too aggressively. Bill Evans, who had played "All of You" during his stint with Miles Davis, featured the Porter standard in his 1961 trio recording at the Village Vanguard, and his interpretation was even more introspective than these subdued precedents.

"All of You" actually works quite well at a faster tempo and when played with considerably more bite, although it is rarely showcased in that manner. Hear McCoy Tyner's performance at Newport in 1963 for a revealing example. Even vocal versions can stand the heat. After all, the lyrics fall into the familiar category of the list song—the lover enumerates the various aspects of the beloved that he wants to get to know, and no angst-ridden pauses or moments of self-reflection are required in the delivery. Yet this song seems permanently stamped with the label of low-key chamber jazz, and it rarely gets pushed into unfamiliar directions. For a refreshing version by a trio that is not afraid to manhandle the Porter standard, check out Makoto Ozone's 1995 performance with John Patitucci and Peter Erskine from the album *Nature Boys*.

RECOMMENDED VERSIONS

Ahmad Jamal, from *Chamber Music of the New Jazz*, Chicago, May 23, 1955

Modern Jazz Quartet, from *Concorde*, Hackensack, New Jersey, July 2, 1955

Miles Davis (with John Coltrane), from *'Round About Midnight*, New York, September 10, 1956

Sarah Vaughan, from *After Hours at the London House*, live at the London House, Chicago, March 7, 1958

Bill Evans (with Scott LaFaro and Paul Motian), from *The Complete Village Vanguard Recordings, 1961*, live at the Village Vanguard, New York, June 25, 1961

McCoy Tyner, from *Live at Newport*, live at the Newport Jazz Festival, Newport, Rhode Island, July 5, 1963

Shelly Manne (with Tom Scott), from *Hot Coles*, Los Angeles, 1975

Makoto Ozone, from *Nature Boys*, Los Angeles, October 4–5, 1995

Buster Williams (with Gary Bartz), from *Somewhere Along the Way*, Englewood Cliffs, New Jersey, November 11–12, 1996

Denny Zeitlin, from *Denny Zeitlin Trio in Performance*, live at the Outpost Performance Space, Albuquerque, New Mexico, December 2004

All the Things You Are
Composed by Jerome Kern, with lyrics by Oscar Hammerstein II

I am tempted to say that "All the Things You Are" is my favorite jazz standard. But I would need to immediately clarify my statement. Frankly, I am not especially entertained by the song as written by Jerome Kern—the melody, with its predictable whole notes and chord tones, moves with an austere, quasi-mathematical precision that leaves me cold—but the piece represents, to my mind, an exciting set of possibilities as a springboard for jazz improvisation. I love this song less for what it *is*, than for what it can *be*.

In my twenties, I would play "All the Things You Are" almost every day, often at great length, and I found constant solace in constructing melodic variations over its chord changes. I'm sure I'm not alone in this regard: many jazz artists have returned to this song, over and over again, during the course of their careers. I recall talking to saxophonist Bud Shank a few months before his death at age 82, when he noted that he never felt he had exhausted the possibilities of this specific song, which he had first recorded almost 60 years earlier. Pianist Lennie Tristano and his acolytes have also demonstrated a quasi-obsessive fixation on this composition, apparently finding in it a zen-like inspiration for higher-order creative improvisation—an attitude I must admit to sharing.

There is some heavy irony here. Jerome Kern was notoriously hostile to jazz musicians who took liberties with his songs; and in his mind, almost anything a jazz musician might want to do was considered a liberty. Yet the improvisers persisted despite this antagonism and have worked tirelessly over the years to showcase—and keep vital—the legacy of this composer, born back in the nineteenth century before jazz even existed. In the last decade alone, more than 300 jazz versions of "All the Things You Are" have been recorded—testimony to the fact that this piece, once a Broadway show tune, is now primarily a jazz composition, more likely to be heard wherever improvisers congregate than on TV or radio.

"All the Things You Are" first appeared in the 1939 musical *Very Warm for May*, an unsuccessful show that closed after seven weeks, a victim of such nasty reviews that, on the second night, only 20 people purchased tickets. (However, nine-year-old Stephen Sondheim saw one of the 59 performances, and later credited it as a reason for his interest in a career as a Broadway composer.) Yet jazz players quickly took a liking for Kern's song, and both Tommy Dorsey and Artie Shaw scored top 10 hits with "All the Things You Are" in February 1940.

After 1940, this song would never again show up on the pop charts, and for good reason: the salient virtues of this piece may well be lost on the general public. To the uninitiated listener, the second eight bars may sound identical to the first eight bars, yet musicians will appreciate the unusual modulation that brings the same melody down four scale steps, a shift that appeals to me as a deepening of the underlying mood of the song. Throughout most of the form, the bassline moves through the circle of fifths with such zeal, that when Kern departs from the pattern, at the end of the bridge and in the elongated final A theme, it imparts added piquancy to the proceedings. Kern himself reportedly felt that the composition was too complex to ever become a lasting hit, and Alec Wilder, mulling over this verdict, offers the intriguing suggestion that if the opening bars of a song are catchy enough, the public will put up with the most labyrinthine constructions later on in the form.

"All the Things You Are" has weathered the passing fads and styles of the jazz world with admirable endurance and adaptability. The song stayed in the big band repertoire during the early 1940s and was taken up by the beboppers almost from the start. Dizzy Gillespie recorded it with Charlie Parker in an influential 1945 track (incorporating a much imitated intro—perhaps initially intended as a parody of Rachmaninoff's *Prelude in C-Sharp Minor*), and the duo revisited the Kern standard at their Massey Hall concert from 1953. Parker, for his part, frequently included this song on his set list, and it also served as the basis for his "Bird of Paradise," recorded with Miles Davis in 1947. But the cool jazz and West Coast players of the 1950s were equally attuned to "All the Things You Are," and it shows up in recordings of this period by the Modern Jazz Quartet, Stan Getz, Chet Baker, Art Pepper, and indeed almost every significant improviser associated with these movements. Nor did the rise of hard bop, free, fusion, and other contrary styles do much to dislodge the song from its prominent place in the standard repertoire.

This song's cross-generational familiarity and popularity have made it a frequent choice when musicians of different eras collaborate on projects. The results can be both strange and exhilarating. Sonny Rollins delivers some of the most avant-garde playing of his career (ably assisted by Paul Bley) in his 1963 pairing with Coleman Hawkins, an odd time to explore the limits of tonality. Equally fascinating is the daring combination of Dave Brubeck, Anthony Braxton, Lee Konitz, and Roy Haynes on a 1974 session, in which Brubeck, the oldest man in the studio, digs into his polytonal bag in an attempt to show that he can push the changes with as much prickly insistence as any of his younger compatriots.

This piece has hardly exhausted its potential—a remarkable claim given the frequency with which this warhorse from the 1930s has been dissected and deconstructed. Brad Mehldau's 13-minute trio performance from 1999 finds him delivering "All the Things You Are" in a very fast 7/4—a recording that did much to popularize the playing of familiar standards in unexpected time signatures among the younger generation of jazz improvisers. Yet this song can also generate excitement in a simple jam, as demonstrated on the heated give-and-take by Phil Woods, Vincent Herring, and Antonio Hart from their *Alto Summit* recording from 1995, Woody Shaw's match-up with Bobby Hutcherson from the 1982 *Night Music* album, and Johnny Griffin's 1957 all-star confrontation (including John Coltrane and Lee Morgan) from *A Blowing Session*.

RECOMMENDED VERSIONS

Tommy Dorsey (with Jack Leonard), Chicago, October 20, 1939

Artie Shaw (with Helen Forrest), New York, October 26, 1939

Dizzy Gillespie (with Charlie Parker), New York, February 28, 1945

Johnny Griffin (with John Coltrane and Lee Morgan) from *A Blowing Session*, Hackensack, New Jersey, April 6, 1957

Sonny Rollins and Coleman Hawkins (with Paul Bley), from *Sonny Meets Hawk!*, New York, July 15, 1963

Dave Brubeck (with Anthony Braxton and Lee Konitz), from *All the Things We Are*, New York, October 3, 1974

Woody Shaw (with Bobby Hutcherson), from *Night Music*, live at Jazz Forum, New York, February 25, 1982

Keith Jarrett (with Gary Peacock and Jack DeJohnette), from *Standards, Vol. 1*, New York, January 11–12, 1983

Gonzalo Rubalcaba (with Charlie Haden and Paul Motian), from *Discovery: Live at Montreux*, live at the Montreux Jazz Festival, Montreux, Switzerland, July 15, 1990

Phil Woods, Vincent Herring, and Antonio Hart, from *Alto Summit*, New York, June
    4–5, 1995

Brad Mehldau, from *Art of the Trio 4—Back at the Vanguard*, live at the Village
    Vanguard, New York, January 5–10, 1999

Alone Together
Composed by Arthur Schwartz, with lyrics by Howard Dietz

At 14, Arthur Schwartz played piano accompaniment to silent films in his native
Brooklyn, and from an early age he showed a knack for writing his own songs.
At his father's urging, though, Schwartz put music on the back burner and
pursued a career in law. With degrees from NYU and Columbia in hand, he was
admitted to the New York bar in 1924, and practiced law for four years before
turning his back on the legal profession to work full-time as a songwriter.
Around that same time Schwartz met up with lyricist Howard Dietz, another
Columbia University alum (where Dietz had been a classmate of Lorenz Hart
and Oscar Hammerstein), and the following year they launched their first
Broadway production, the successful revue *The Little Show*.

Like Schwartz, Dietz was multitalented, pursuing a day gig as a marketing
exec for Samuel Goldwyn Productions and MGM. One of his brainstorms was
the roaring lion at the start of the studio's movies (another Columbia connection there: Dietz had seen this as a personal tribute to his alma mater's mascot).
Dietz had already worked with Jerome Kern and briefly with George Gershwin—filling in on the show *Oh, Kay!* after Ira Gershwin was sidelined following
an emergency appendectomy—and was initially skeptical about moving from
these Broadway icons to a partnership with a little-known attorney with musical
leanings. Yet Dietz and Schwartz would become one of the most successful
songwriting duos of the middle decades of the twentieth century, eventually
collaborating on 11 musicals over a period of 34 years.

"Alone Together" made its debut in the 1932 show *Flying Colors*, which
closed as a financial failure after 188 performances, weighed down by the extravagant sets of Norman Bel Geddes. These included a filmed background
vista and a moving stage that drew the dancers back into darkness at the conclusion of "Alone Together." The song fared better than the show, however, and Leo
Reisman enjoyed a top 10 hit with his recording that same year.

"Alone Together" has an unusual form, with a 14-bar A theme that resolves
surprisingly in the tonic major, but in the last restatement is truncated to 12 bars
that conclude in the minor. The form can confuse the uninitiated, and don't be
surprised if you hear the pianist at the cocktail bar try to squeeze "Alone Together"
into a standard 32-bar AABA form. Yet I suspect that the very peculiarities in the

composition, especially the major-minor ambiguity, account for much of the appeal to improvisers.

Artie Shaw played the key role in establishing "Alone Together" as a jazz standard, recording it with his band in 1939, performing it on a *Symphony of Swing* film clip that was distributed to movie theaters around this same time, and then making another studio version in 1941 with a string-enhanced ensemble. When Dizzy Gillespie recorded "Alone Together" in 1950, he followed the Shaw playbook with a somber rendition over string accompaniment. Miles Davis adopted a far more modernistic approach in his 1955 recording, with the countermelodies and shifting rhythms bearing more the stamp of Charles Mingus (who was bassist on this date) than the trumpeter.

The personality of this song would change gradually over the years, as it lost its exotic, mood music origins and emerged as a dark, minor-key song in a straight swing rhythm. In the right arrangement, "Alone Together" can sound like a hard bop chart written for a Blue Note session. In fact, given the dark, brooding quality of the tune, I'm surprised it didn't show up on more Blue Note dates, but when it did (as on Stanley Turrentine's 1966 session with McCoy Tyner for the *Easy Walker* date), it fit perfectly with the grit and groove of the proceedings. Sonny Rollins takes a similar tack on his 1958 performance for the Contemporary label.

The composition is still typically performed at a medium tempo, not much different from what Leo Reisman offered back in 1932—although usually more medium-fast than medium-slow nowadays. But fast, aggressive versions are increasingly common—hear, for example, Brad Mehldau's tumultuous take on the song from 2000. For another interesting reworking of the composition, check out Chris Anderson's 1997 duet with bassist Charlie Haden. Anderson, little known among jazz fans, was a mentor and teacher to Herbie Hancock, and possessed one of the best harmonic minds of his generation, as demonstrated on this inventive track.

RECOMMENDED VERSIONS

Artie Shaw, New York, January 31, 1939

Dizzy Gillespie, Los Angeles, October 31, 1950

Miles Davis (with Teddy Charles and Charles Mingus), from *Blue Moods*, New York, July 9, 1955

Sonny Rollins, from *Sonny Rollins and the Contemporary Leaders*, Los Angeles, October 20–22, 1958

Ray Charles and Betty Carter, from *Ray Charles and Betty Carter*, Los Angeles, June 13, 1961

Paul Desmond (with Jim Hall), from *Take Ten*, New York, June 12, 1963

Stanley Turrentine (with McCoy Tyner), from *Easy Walker*, Englewood Cliffs, New
    Jersey, July 8, 1966

Pepper Adams (with Kenny Wheeler and Hank Jones), from *Conjuration: Fat
    Tuesday's Session*, live at Fat Tuesday's, New York, August 19–20, 1983

Mal Waldron, from *No More Tears (for Lady Day)*, Munich, November 1–3, 1988

Wallace Roney, from *Obsession*, Englewood Cliffs, New Jersey, September 7, 1990

Charlie Haden and Chris Anderson, from *None But the Lonely Heart*, New York, July
    5–7, 1997

Brad Mehldau, from *Progression: Art of the Trio, Vol. 5*, New York, September 22–24,
    2000

Angel Eyes
Composed by Matt Dennis, with lyrics by Earl Brent

The 1953 film *Jennifer*, starring Ida Lupino, is little known today, but Matt Dennis's theme music from the movie has become a popular jazz standard. The
tune itself dates back to the mid-1940s, and was even recorded—by Herb Jeffries and the composer—years before its movie debut. But with its haunting,
noir-ish quality, this song seemed destined for the cinema. Dennis recorded it
himself for the movie soundtrack.

    The song is explicitly jazzy, with a heavy reliance on the blues notes in the
melody line—and not just in passing tones. The opening phrase of the melody
lingers on the flat five of the tonic key for a full beat and a half. Even more exotic
is the flat nine in the bar three. The shock of these notes is softened by the
chord changes—even so, effects of this sort rarely found their way into the popular music of the period. The shift into a major key for the bridge only amplifies
the tenebrous quality of the final eight bars. With so much bluesiness written
into the score, this composition seems custom built for jazz interpretation.
Even so, Dennis and Brent might have torpedoed its success had they stuck
with the original title they had considered: "Have Another Beer on Me."

    Earl Brent's words add to the late night mood—I especially like the almost flip-
pant closing line: "Excuse me while I disappear"—the attitude sounds very up-to-
date even now, and I could imagine someone posting the phrase as a final Twitter
or Facebook update of the day before retiring to bed. When Frank Sinatra performed a series of "farewell concerts" in 1971—launching a supposed retirement
that actually proved to be a short absence from the stage—he used this number as
a closer, and the concluding line made for an emotionally charged finale.

    Ella Fitzgerald was among the first jazz artists to embrace "Angel Eyes," and
by some accounts it was her favorite standard. She eventually left behind more

than a half-dozen recordings, and other jazz divas followed on her heels. Sinatra also kept "Angel Eyes" in his repertoire for many years, and added a new twist by starting the song with the bridge ("So drink up, all you people . . .") on his well-known 1958 recording. But the appeal of "Angel Eyes" goes beyond jazz, with artists as diverse as Sting, Willie Nelson, Ray Charles, Roberta Flack, and k.d. lang offering up their personal interpretations on record.

If the song has a weakness, it may be the ease with which it invites a soloist to pull out every stale minor blues cliché—a temptation many are unable to resist, judging by the various jazz recordings of "Angel Eyes" I have heard over the years. The chords make few demands on the soloist, and even an amateur musician can construct a passable improvisation without much strain. But if "Angel Eyes" invites glibness, it is also capable of profundity in the hands of the right artist.

RECOMMENDED VERSIONS

Matt Dennis, from *Matt Dennis Plays and Sings Matt Dennis*, live at Tally-Ho, Hollywood, circa 1954

Benny Carter, from *Cosmopolite*, New York, September 14, 1954

Ella Fitzgerald, from *Ella in Rome—The Birthday Concert*, live at the Teatro Sistina, Rome, April 25, 1958

Frank Sinatra, from *Frank Sinatra Sings for Only the Lonely*, Los Angeles, May 29, 1958

Sonny Criss (with Barry Harris), from *Saturday Morning*, Los Angeles, March 1, 1975

McCoy Tyner (with big band), from *The Turning Point*, New York, November 19–20, 1991

Joe Lovano, from *Rush Hour*, New York, April 6, 1994

Karrin Allyson, from *In Blue*, New York, February 11–14, 2002

April in Paris
Composed by Vernon Duke, with lyrics by E. Y. Harburg

Vernon Duke was having a meal with friends, when one lamented, "Oh, to be in Paris now that April's here." This complaint—which was a paraphrase of a line from a famous Robert Browning poem about England, *not* Paris—was transformed into a song when Duke was enlisted to write music for *Walk a Little Faster*, a Broadway revue from 1933 that closed after 119 performances. Freddy Martin enjoyed the first hit recording of "April in Paris" that same year, but his tepid version of the composition gives little hint of its jazz potential. The Sauter-Finegan Orchestra brought the song back to the charts in 1952, at the same time that Hollywood released a Doris Day movie inspired by the tune, but this arrangement, with its wordless female vocal, is stronger on exoticism than swing.

In truth, this song struggled for years to find its true jazz personality. Too many big band versions by name leaders—including Artie Shaw, Tommy Dorsey, and Glenn Miller—stay safely ensconced in the realm of mood music. Even when the more progressive beboppers embraced this work, they seemed to have modest ambitions, as witnessed by Charlie Parker's chardonnay-and-brie rendition with icky string accompaniment. Coleman Hawkins also delivered a forgettable version with strings, and even in his 1947 combo performance of the song, where Hawk is accompanied by several top-notch modernists, he rarely strays far from the melody and the sidemen are far too deferential for my tastes. Fortunately for us, a former Hawkins accompanist, Thelonious Monk, took a different tack around this same time, squeezing the romanticism out of "April in Paris" for a more eccentric spring itinerary in the City of Lights.

Yet the most celebrated jazz version of "April in Paris" remains Count Basie's extravagant performance from the summer of 1955. This hit single is remembered for the novelty of its fake-out ending, but the entire track is a charmer, from arranger Wild Bill Davis's horn writing to Thad Jones's "Pop Goes the Weasel"-ish solo. I'm not surprised that Basie kept this song in his set list for the rest of his career; it was even reprised on film in a memorable scene from *Blazing Saddles*.

Performers today could learn a thing or two from Basie, but most later versions I have heard of "April in Paris" are too complacent. However, Wynton Marsalis inserts some brisk polyrhythms into his 1986 version from the first volume of *Marsalis Standard Time*; Kurt Elling gets a nice incantatory groove happening on his performance, a decade later, from *The Messenger*; and Cindy Blackman gives "April in Paris" a radical makeover on her *Works on Canvas* project from 1999.

RECOMMENDED VERSIONS

Thelonious Monk, New York, October 24, 1947

Bud Powell, New York, February 1950

Sauter-Finegan Orchestra, from *New Directions in Music*, New York, July 1, 1952

Count Basie, from *April in Paris*, New York, July 26, 1955

Erroll Garner, from *Concert by the Sea*, live at the Sunset Auditorium, Carmel, California, September 19, 1955

Louis Armstrong and Ella Fitzgerald, from *Ella and Louis*, Los Angeles, August 16, 1956

Frank Sinatra, from *Come Fly With Me*, Los Angeles, October 3, 1957

Wynton Marsalis, from *Marsalis Standard Time, Vol. 1*, New York, May 29–30, 1986
    and September 24–25, 1986

Kurt Elling, from *The Messenger*, Chicago, July 1994–December 1996

Cindy Blackman (with JD Allen), from *Works on Canvas*, New York, April 9, 1999

Autumn in New York
Composed by Vernon Duke

During the course of his career, composer Vernon Duke worked with the most talented lyricists of the period—including Johnny Mercer, Ira Gershwin, Sammy Cahn, Yip Harburg, and Ogden Nash—but for this song he contributed his own words. The circumstances were happenstance, but the results enduring. Unlike most of his other well-known works, this tune was written without a commission or show in mind, inspired merely by the composer's longing for New York during a stay in Westport, Connecticut, in the late summer of 1934. Yet this orphan tune would prove to be one of Duke's most popular works, and until John Kander and Fred Ebbs raised the bombast level with their song "New York, New York" in 1977, it would stand as the definitive Big Apple standard.

Yet I can't give Duke all of the credit here. Earlier in 1934, he had enjoyed a huge hit with "April in Paris," and his new song imitated the same "city and season" concept as well as the nostalgic imagery that lyricist Yip Harburg had contributed to the prior work. Even so, Duke gets kudos for the daring of his wordplay. How many tunesmiths, seeking a rhyme for "inviting," would settle on the syntactically challenged "thrill of first-nighting"? Or, with New Yorkers in mind, envision "dreamers with empty hands" sighing for "exotic lands"?

Vernon Duke also doubled as a serious composer, and this piece, more than any of his other popular efforts, seems to straddle the divide between conservatory ambitions and commercial considerations, especially in its unusual harmonic movement. When the song eventually resolves into F minor, you can look back and contemplate the intricacy and misdirection of a structure that never states that chord at any point in its first 24 bars. The melody, with its alternation of downward-stepping and upward-sweeping phrases, perfectly matches the emotional arc of the words.

"Autumn in New York" found a home in Murray Anderson's 1934 revue *Thumbs Up*—Duke offered it when he learned the producer was looking for a song celebrating Manhattan in the fall. But the show, which opened in December 1934, never made it to autumn, closing in early May after 156 performances. Little fanfare greeted "Autumn in New York" at the time, and the song languished for 15 years, before Frank Sinatra turned it into a hit record with his

1947 interpretation. Sinatra, whose renditions remain the measuring rods for all other versions of "Autumn in New York," would return to it again during two fall sessions: an October 1957 date for *Come Fly with Me*, and, finally, on an autumn day in New York itself, at his celebrated Madison Square Garden concert from October 1974.

The song has inspired more than a few outré reconfigurations. Bud Powell's Birdland performance from 1953, where he is joined by Charles Mingus and Art Taylor, is both eloquent and disturbing, with jarring cross-rhythms and a tonal palette that occasionally seems more suited for a horror film soundtrack than a modern jazz trio. On his 1954 recording, Shelly Manne dispenses with bass and harmony instruments entirely, instead engaging in an avant-garde musical conversation with Shorty Rogers and Jimmy Giuffre. And for his solo piano performance at the Maybeck Recital Hall, from 1990, Steve Kuhn does occasionally insert a chord or two, but they typically bear no obvious relation to those Vernon Duke provided in his sheet music. This is a stream-of-consciousness version of "Autumn in New York," which eventually gets us to Manhattan, but only after many detours.

RECOMMENDED VERSIONS

Frank Sinatra, New York, December 4, 1947

Billie Holiday, Los Angeles, May 1952

Bud Powell (with Charles Mingus), live at Birdland, New York, May 30, 1953

Modern Jazz Quartet, from *Django*, June 25, 1953

Dexter Gordon, from *Daddy Plays the Horn*, Hollywood, September 18, 1955

Shelly Manne, Jimmy Giuffre, and Shorty Rogers, from *The Three & The Two*, Hollywood, September 10, 1954

Steve Kuhn, from *Live at Maybeck Recital Hall, Vol. 13*, live at Maybeck Recital Hall, Berkeley, California, November 18, 1990

Mark Turner, from *Mark Turner*, New York, December 7, 1995

Autumn Leaves

Composed by Joseph Kosma, with lyrics by Jacques Prévert (English lyrics by Johnny Mercer)

Few things are rarer in the jazz pantheon than a standard composed by a Frenchman. The French may have invented the jazz discography (courtesy of Charles Delaunay), published jazz magazines (*Le Jazz Hot*, founded in 1935) before Americans did, and in general acknowledged the importance of jazz as an art form when few in the United States bought in to the concept, but they rarely get their songs covered by the name bands. Yet US jazz musicians and pop singers eventually embraced "Autumn Leaves" as if it were one of their own. By the way, the British also own a share of this song, or at least Sir Paul McCartney does: his MPL Communications controls the publishing rights.

The geographical lineage gets even more complex. The composer Joseph Kosma was born in Budapest before moving to Paris in 1933. There he met poet Jacques Prévert, who would contribute lyrics to this song, which was composed for the 1946 film *Les portes de la nuit* and first took life under the name "Les feuilles mortes." The title might be more accurately translated as "The Dead Leaves," which sounds to me like a better name for punk rock band than a jazz ballad. But lyricist Johnny Mercer, a native son of Savannah, Georgia, fixed this by adding the final *pièce de résistance*. After mulling over the song and its original words for several months in 1951, he finally turned out "Autumn Leaves"—a song that, he later admitted, made more money for him than any of his other works.

Jazz musicians probably associate this song with Cannonball Adderley, Bill Evans, and Miles Davis, but schlocktail-cocktail pianist Roger Williams made it into a hit. His 1955 recording reached the top of the *Billboard* chart, a rare piano instrumental hit during the early days of rock-and-roll. That same year, Mitch Miller, Jackie Gleason, and Steve Allen also released well-received recordings of "Autumn Leaves." I would prefer to say that jazz musicians paid little attention to such kitschy precedents, but the popularity of this tune in the jazz world increased in the aftermath of these successes. And when one hears Erroll Garner's florid intro to his version from his famous *Concert by the Sea* recording from late 1955, it is hard not to be reminded of Roger Williams's recording, which was released around the same time as this now seminal jazz performance.

Ahmad Jamal's interpretation, recorded a few weeks after Garner's, reveals a more modern, streamlined approach to "Autumn Leaves." Cannonball Adderley did even more to entrench this song as a jazz standard with his much-admired 1958 performance on his album *Somethin' Else*—helped along by the unusual appearance of Miles Davis as a sideman on a Blue Note recording. Miles, for his part, adopted the song and played "Autumn Leaves" frequently with his various ensembles, leaving behind a number of top-notch recordings. And on a personal note, I still recall fondly the day I was able to purchase an LP featuring Miles's sideman Wynton Kelly's swinging version of "Autumn Leaves" (whose intro I stole for my own performances) at a Salvation Army store in Petaluma for just 25 cents.

The song has shown up in many surprising places. It inspired a movie (with the song performed by Nat King Cole over the title credits), and today serves as a signature song of the Bluecoats Drum and Bugle Corps. And, just think, it all helps to support Sir Paul in his golden years.

RECOMMENDED VERSIONS

Erroll Garner, from *Concert by the Sea*, live at the Sunset Auditorium, Carmel,
    California, September 19, 1955

Ahmad Jamal, from *The Ahmad Jamal Trio*, New York, October 25, 1955

Cannonball Adderley (with Miles Davis), from *Somethin' Else*, Hackensack, New
    Jersey, March 9, 1958

Bill Evans, from *Portrait in Jazz*, New York, December 28, 1959

Wynton Kelly, from *Wynton Kelly!*, New York, July 20, 1961

McCoy Tyner, from *Today and Tomorrow*, Englewood Cliffs, New Jersey, June 4, 1963

Miles Davis, from *Miles Davis in Europe*, live at the Antibes Jazz Festival, Antibes,
    France, July 27, 1963

Jim Hall and Ron Carter, from *Alone Together*, live at the Playboy Club, New York,
    August 4, 1972

Chet Baker (with Paul Desmond), from *She Was Too Good to Me*, Englewood Cliffs,
    New Jersey, 1974

Keith Jarrett (with Gary Peacock and Jack DeJohnette), from *Still Live*, live at
    Philharmonic Hall, Munich, July 13, 1986

Eva Cassidy, from *Live at Blues Alley*, live at Blues Alley, Washington, D.C., January
    2, 1996

Bags' Groove

Composed by Milt Jackson

For many jazz aficionados of the 1950s and 1960s, Milt Jackson not only stood out as the leading modern jazz vibraphone player, but for many he was the *only* modern jazz vibraphone player. True, Jackson was neither the first nor the last significant jazz musician to play this unconventional mallet instrument—similar to the xylophone, but with aluminum instead of wooden bars and motor-driven resonators that impart a vibrato effect to the tones—but he did more than anyone to assert its relevance in the midst of the rapidly evolving post-World War II jazz scene. Jackson always seemed to be ahead of the game, working alongside leading beboppers just as bop started its ascendancy, then establishing himself as a major exponent of the "cool school" of the 1950s alongside his colleagues in the Modern Jazz Quartet (MJQ), a popular and long-lived chamber jazz ensemble that worked steadily from 1952 to 1974 and sporadically in later years.

Yet many of Jackson's most fervent fans lamented his association with the MJQ, preferring to hear the vibraphonist stretch out on a simple jam tune rather than navigate through the often Byzantine compositions of the band's musical director, John Lewis. Jackson kept these supporters happy with songs such as "Bags' Groove," a simple 12-bar blues that was a mainstay of the quartet's repertoire—as documented by more than a dozen surviving recordings of the MJQ performing this song. Except for a simple canonic exchange between Lewis and Jackson during the melody statement, the band put aside its chamber music aspirations when performing this catchy tune, almost a throwback to the Swing Era in its riff-based construction. Listen to the audience at Avery Fisher Hall clapping on the backbeat in tandem with the final melody statement on the quartet's celebrated *The Last Concert* from 1974, and you will get a sense of how the combo relied on "Bags' Groove" to provide needed contrast to its more tightly structured offerings.

The song's title comes from the composer's nickname. The "bags" in question were those under the musician's eyes, not a sign of aging—Jackson wrote "Bags' Groove" when he was still in his twenties—but a legacy of a late-night and liquor lifestyle. The song itself actually predates the formal launch of the MJQ—its first appearance on record features Jackson as bandleader, joined by his future MJQ colleagues and alto saxophonist Lou Donaldson. But the most famous recording of "Bags' Groove" finds Jackson in a much different setting: sideman on the famous Miles Davis Christmas Eve date from 1954 when the trumpeter told pianist Thelonious Monk to abstain from playing behind his solos. "Monk never did know how to play behind a horn player," Davis later recounted in his autobiography. Rumors later circulated of the two musicians exchanging heated words or possibly even coming to blows—somewhat exaggerated accounts, but the session was, by any measure, rife with tension. Yet Miles and Monk delivered impressive solos on "Bags' Groove," and both the controversy and peculiar chemistry of their pairing helped raise the visibility of Jackson's trademark composition.

Usually signature songs of this sort fade from view after the artist has retired from the stage. But "Bags' Groove" continued to find a place in the standard repertoire even after Jackson's death in 1999. Sometimes it figures as a vibes feature or tribute to Jackson (as on Gary Burton's 2000 rendition), but I suspect its longevity is mostly due to its lasting appeal to audiences, who nowadays may not even know who "Bags" is or what he did, yet still are drawn to clap along with his best-known song.

RECOMMENDED VERSIONS

Milt Jackson (with Lou Donaldson), from *Wizard of the Vibes*, New York, April 7, 1952

Miles Davis (with Thelonious Monk and Milt Jackson), from *Miles Davis and the Modern Jazz Giants*, Hackensack, New Jersey, December 24, 1954

Hank Mobley (with Lee Morgan), from *Monday Night at Birdland*, live at Birdland, New York, April 21, 1958

Modern Jazz Quartet (with Sonny Rollins), from *The Modern Jazz Quartet at Music Inn, Vol. 2*, live at Music Inn, Lenox, Massachusetts, September 3, 1958

Modern Jazz Quartet, from *The Last Concert*, live at Avery Fisher Hall, New York, November 25, 1974

Gary Burton, from *For Hamp, Red, Bags, and Cal*, New York and Boston, May–June 2000

Ron Carter, from *Dear Miles*, New York, February 2006

Basin Street Blues
Composed by Spencer Williams

When this song was published in 1926, tourists would have been unable to find Basin Street on a map of New Orleans. That thoroughfare in the French Quarter had been renamed North Saratoga after the Secretary of the Navy shut down the Storyville red light district in 1917. Only when the traditional jazz revival of the 1940s cast attention on the historical significance of Basin Street did the city reconsider its decision. In January 1945, Louis Armstrong, Sidney Bechet, and Bunk Johnson gave a celebratory concert at the Municipal Auditorium in New Orleans to commemorate the return of the original name to the now-famous street.

Armstrong first recorded the song back in 1928 in a peculiar track that featured Earl Hines on celesta for part of the performance and the band providing backing vocal harmonies. Armstrong eventually left behind around 50 recordings of the song, and his influence hovers over most later jazz interpretations of the composition. Hear Cab Calloway's recording of "Basin Street Blues" from 1931 and try to count the Armstrong-inspired elements, both in the vocal and instrumental parts—and this was back when the trumpeter was still in his twenties and had not yet achieved his full dose of fame. The song was so closely associated with Armstrong that, when Ella Fitzgerald released her version in 1949, she incorporated an uncanny imitation of him into her final chorus, and Decca even released the record under the name "Ella 'Satchmo' Fitzgerald."

Yet other musicians have put their own stamp on "Basin Street Blues." Benny Goodman enjoyed a modest hit with the song as a member of the Charleston Chasers in 1931—a recording he later cited as the first time he presented his own distinctive musical vision on record—and again when the track was re-released under his own name in 1934. Jack Teagarden handled vocal duties on this performance, and he, too, frequently returned to the composition in later years, even rivalling Armstrong for ownership of the tune. Indeed, when Teagarden was a member of Armstrong's combo, he was often featured as singer on "Basin Street Blues"—either in conjunction with the bandleader or on his own. For an example of their collaboration, track down the version the duo recorded for the soundtrack to the 1951 Mickey Rooney film *The Strip*.

Another high-powered duo, Bing Crosby and Connee Boswell, enjoyed a top 20 hit with the song in 1937. That same year, Fats Waller recorded a solo piano version of "Basin Street Blues," which didn't get the same radio airplay as Bing's or Benny's treatments, but ranks among the finer examples of Harlem stride piano from the period. In the postwar years, jazz bands continued to rely on "Basin Street Blues," but one must search long and hard for examples of beboppers, hard-boppers, or cool school exponents performing this composition. Yet the growing popularity of trad jazz ensembles during this period gave "Basin Street Blues" a new lease on life. Sidney Bechet's recording from 1949, in company with Wild Bill Davison and Art Hodes, showcases this distinctively retrograde approach to Spencer Williams's standard.

When interesting renditions were released in later years, they often came from outside of the jazz idiom. Sam Cooke's treatment, with altered words, graces the flip-side to his hit single "Good News" from 1964, and introduced the song to a new generation of R&B fans. When Wynton Marsalis revived "Basin Street Blues" in 2007, more than 80 years after its first appearance, he successfully updated it—but with the help of Willie Nelson, who proved that this now venerable song was still capable of fresh reinterpretation. But the most disjunctive recent recording of "Basin Street Blues" comes to us from DJ Kid Koala, who stitched together various bits and pieces in coming up with his crazy-quilt version of the song in 2003. He distorts the pitches with such vehemence that the result sounds like an intoxicated band of New Orleans musicians who failed to tune their instruments before taking the stage.

RECOMMENDED VERSIONS

Louis Armstrong (with Earl Hines), Chicago, December 4, 1928

The Charleston Chasers (with Benny Goodman and Jack Teagarden), New York, February 9, 1931

Cab Calloway, New York, July 9, 1931

Fats Waller, New York, June 11, 1937

Bing Crosby and Connee Boswell, Los Angeles, September 25, 1937

Sidney Bechet and His Blue Note Jazzmen, New York, March 23, 1949

Ella Fitzgerald (with Sy Oliver's Orchestra), New York, September 20, 1949

Louis Armstrong and Jack Teagarden, from the soundtrack to the film *The Strip*, Hollywood, December 26–29, 1950

Louis Armstrong, from *The Great Chicago Concert 1956*, live at the Medina Temple, Chicago, June 1, 1956

Sam Cooke, from *Keep Movin' On*, California, December 21, 1963

Dave Brubeck and Gerry Mulligan, from *Live at the Berlin Philharmonie*, live at the Philharmonie, Berlin, November 7, 1970

Keith Jarrett (with Gary Peacock and Paul Motian), from *At the Deer Head Inn*, live at Deer Head Inn, September 16, 1992

Kid Koala, from *Some of My Best Friends Are DJs*, no location provided, circa 2003

Wynton Marsalis and Willie Nelson, from *Two Men with the Blues*, live in the Allen Room at Frederick P. Rose Hall, New York, January 12–13, 2007

Beale Street Blues
Composed by W. C. Handy

W. C. Handy had visited Beale Avenue—the popularity of his song eventually spurred the change to the name Beale *Street*—during his youth, and later established his Pace & Handy Music Co. there in 1913. Sad to say, the very success of songs such as "Beale Street Blues" put an end to his Memphis residency, fueling Handy's ambition to move his business to New York, which he did in 1918. The thoroughfare itself has changed markedly since the composer published "Beale Street Blues" back in 1917, but unlike so many other former centers of African-American entertainment, this street still boasts a vibrant nightlife. Pride of place, however, still belongs to W. C. Handy: a statue of him, with avuncular mien and horn in hand, looks over Beale Street today.

The song had the good fortune of making its debut at the same time as the first jazz recordings. Handy was no doubt stunned when his company received payment of $2,857 in royalties from the sales of a successful recording of "Beale Street Blues" by an all-white ensemble—Earl Fuller's Famous Jazz Band, which featured the "laughing trombone" of Harry Raderman. Recording technology was viewed with such indifference, or perhaps suspicion, among black musicians at the time that, when Handy secured an offer to make his own recordings that same year, most of the sidemen he tried to hire refused to make the requisite trip to New York. Handy never became a major recording star, but as Fuller's success with "Beale Street Blues" made clear, he didn't need to appear personally in the studio to take advantage of the economic opportunities presented by this new medium.

The 1921 recording of "Beale Street Blues" by Marion Harris, a vampish white singer who had helped popularize Handy's "St. Louis Blues," was a top 10 hit in December of that year. But, for the most part, jazz players adopted this song as an instrumental number in the early days. When blues diva Alberta Hunter recorded it with Fats Waller in 1927, most of the track was devoted to Waller's pipe organ with the vocal arriving only in the final 24 bars; a second take recorded that same day dispensed with the singing entirely. The following month, Jelly Roll Morton recorded "Beale Street Blues" at a Chicago session, and delivered the most moving jazz performance of the song to that date—but again he played it as an instrumental. A few years later, Jack Teagarden adopted the song as a vocal feature, and recordings from the 1930s and early 1940s find him singing it in a half-dozen different ensembles—hear, for example, his performance as a member of the Joe Venuti–Eddie Lang band from 1931, with Benny Goodman providing clarinet obbligato and an impassioned solo.

Like Handy's even more famous "St. Louis Blues," this song juxtaposes the 12-bar blues form with an 8-bar counter-theme, the latter more akin to ragtime in the case of "Beale Street Blues." Yet the song adapted easily enough to the stylistic demands of the big band era, as demonstrated on recordings by Tommy Dorsey and Duke Ellington. Even so, few other name bandleaders followed their lead, and the modern jazz players of the era evinced no interest in "Beale Street Blues."

Since the early 1950s, "Beale Street Blues" has been claimed by the trad jazz bands, with few others disputing their ownership. Even the song's inclusion in a 1958 biopic starring Nat King Cole as W. C. Handy, with Ella Fitzgerald delivering the number in a very up-to-date manner, failed to change the general perception that this was an old-fashioned song. One invariably encounters Handy's standard nowadays among those jazz bands that so strenuously avoid the cutting edge they have learned to live happily on the dull side of the blade. As a result, this song, like the statue on Beale Street, earns our respect as a homage to the past rather than as a harbinger of the future. I'm hardly surprised that the most interesting recording of this song in recent years comes from Carl Wolfe, on his 2002 album *W. C. Handy's Beale Street: Where the Blues Began*, where he aims to replicate how Handy's own band might have played this song during the composer's Memphis days.

RECOMMENDED VERSIONS

Earl Fuller's Famous Jazz Band (with Harry Raderman), New York, August 13, 1917

Marion Harris, New York, March 2, 1921

Fats Waller and Alberta Hunter, Camden, New Jersey, May 20, 1927

Jelly Roll Morton, Chicago, June 10, 1927

Joe Venuti and Eddie Lang (with Jack Teagarden and Benny Goodman), New York, October 22, 1931

Tommy Dorsey, New York, May 26, 1937

Duke Ellington, Hollywood, August 26, 1947

Louis Armstrong, from *Louis Armstrong Plays W. C. Handy*, Chicago, July 12, 1954

Earl Hines, from *Live at the Crescendo, Vol. 2*, live at the Crescendo Club, Los Angeles, March 13, 1956

Bobby Gordon and Dave McKenna, from *Clarinet Blue*, New York, May 17–18, 1999

Carl Wolfe, from *W. C. Handy's Beale Street: Where the Blues Began*, Memphis, circa 2002

Bemsha Swing

Composed by Thelonious Monk and Denzil Best

Most jazz fans probably assume that "Bemsha" is just one more fanciful word invented by Monk—akin to "Epistrophy" or "Misterioso" and those other colorful song titles the pianist concocted over the years. But the copyright application for the song, filed a few days before its debut recording in 1952, uses the title "Bimsha Swing"—drawing on a common nickname for Barbados, which natives often call Bimshire, Bimsha, or just Bim. The co-composer, Denzil Best, had Barbadian roots, and this song aimed to capture a quasi-Caribbean sensibility, albeit one sufficiently Monkified for modern jazz fans.

I find Monk's initial recording appealing in its conceptual daring, but the piano sounds tinny and out-of-tune, which gives me some pause before recommending it. But Monk left no shortage of other versions behind for posterity, allowing fans to compare, contrast, and choose. My preferred treatment comes from a 1956 session for Monk's *Brilliant Corners* LP, where tenorist Sonny Rollins joins the composer for an extended exploration of "Bemsha Swing."

Few jazz artists would cover this song during the 1950s, but the first two treatments following Monk's initial trio recording are significant ones. Miles Davis featured both the song and its composer at his Christmas Eve session for Prestige in 1954, and the trumpeter plays with an uncharacteristic edge and angularity to his phrases—it's clear that in this matchup of two of the most confident and distinctive jazz personalities of the day, Davis was the one who blinked first, Miles adapting more to Monk than vice versa. But if edginess is the goal, the next artist to bring this song into the studio trumps all comers: Cecil Taylor delivered a splintered, unsettling rendition of "Bemsha Swing" for his aptly named *Jazz Advance* album of 1956. As the opening track, it signaled the arrival of a pianist who would soon push beyond Monk's dissonance into full atonality.

These high-profile performances had little effect in popularizing "Bemsha Swing." Only a dozen or so jazz artists would make recordings of this song over the next two decades, but they included some of the leading artists of the day. John Coltrane drew on the Monk song for his 1960 collaboration with trumpeter Don Cherry. Bill Evans, who rarely played Monk's compositions, recorded three of them for his 1963 *Conversations with Myself* project—although "Bemsha Swing" and "Blue Monk" were left off the initial LP release (both are now part of the CD reissue). Bud Powell, Max Roach, and J. J. Johnson also offered up their interpretations during this period.

Finally, in the late 1980s, "Bemsha Swing" started showing up more frequently on bandstands and record dates. The song deserved this long-denied acceptance. The melody sounds like a surreal riff-tune from an alternative jazz universe, but is catchy enough to leave you still humming its off-center phrases hours after you've left the nightclub. When the chords and riff move up a fourth, the effect is reminiscent of blues form—track down Houston Person's 1990 duet with Ron Carter if you want to hear how soulful this song can get—yet "Bemsha Swing" avoids the 12-bar structure and standard blues changes. The end result is that appealing combination of the familiar and unexpected that characterizes Monk's best pieces.

RECOMMENDED VERSIONS

Thelonious Monk, New York, December 18, 1952

Miles Davis (with Thelonious Monk), from *Miles Davis and the Modern Jazz Giants*, Hackensack, New Jersey, December 24, 1954

Cecil Taylor, from *Jazz Advance*, Boston, September 14, 1956

Thelonious Monk (with Sonny Rollins), from *Brilliant Corners*, New York, December 7, 1956

John Coltrane and Don Cherry, from *The Avant-Garde*, New York, July 8, 1960

Bill Evans, from *Conversations with Myself*, New York, February 20, 1963

Steve Lacy and Gil Evans, from *That's the Way I Feel Now*, New York, 1984

Houston Person and Ron Carter, from *Now's the Time*, Englewood Cliffs, New Jersey, January 6, 1990

Chico Freeman (with Arthur Blythe and George Cables), from *Focus*, Berkeley, California, May 16, 1994

Billie's Bounce
Composed by Charlie Parker

The bebop revolution spearheaded by Charlie Parker in the 1940s was a radical movement with markedly traditional roots. Even at his most daring, this iconic and iconoclastic artist never strayed far from the musical values of his native Kansas City, where a swinging 4/4 time and a blues sensibility were ever present on the bandstand—a lasting legacy that was especially noticeable whenever Parker delved into a 12-bar blues progression. On "Billie's Bounce," Parker mixes in modernistic elements—the passing chords in bar nine, for example, which allows for a major seventh in the melody—with more traditional syncopations and blues notes. Unlike some other progressive forays in the history of jazz music, there is nothing subversive or tentative here, no open renunciation of the past. Parker instead built his modernism on the most stable of foundations, namely his careful assimilation and reframing of the preexisting jazz heritage.

The song, dedicated to agent Billy Shaw (whose name was misspelled "Billie" on initial release, with the error retained on future recordings), dates from Parker's debut session as a bandleader for the Savoy label. A number of personnel oddities turned this occasion into a discographer's nightmare. Apparently Bud Powell had originally been slated for the session but was in Philadelphia that day, and a second pianist, Sadik Hakim, was enlisted, yet caused concern at the studio because he lacked a union card. On "Billie's

Bounce," Dizzy Gillespie took over the keyboard—but was listed as "Hen Gates" on the release because he was under contract to the Guild label.

Bop fans of the day would no doubt have preferred to hear the great Gillespie on trumpet, but instead that honor fell to 19-year-old Miles Davis. At this stage in his career, Davis lacked the poise that he would demonstrate a decade later, but—perhaps due to the sobering presence of Gillespie—he showed more control and restraint here than on other tracks from the period, delivering a surprisingly cogent solo for a young performer with little studio experience thrown into a high-pressure setting. But the star attraction is Parker, who rises above the disorganization of the date and problems with his horn, and contributes four incomparable blues choruses—choruses that have been transcribed and studied by many later musicians.

Only a few cover versions were recorded in the 1940s, but during the course of the 1950s "Billie's Bounce" gradually gained traction as a jazz standard. The song's popularity was fueled by high-profile renditions, such as John Coltrane's 1957 performance alongside Red Garland and Stan Getz's live recording with J. J. Johnson from that same year. Even after bop moved from center stage in the jazz world, this song retained its appeal. Cover versions in later decades would often come from artists associated with Parker, either personally or stylistically, but even musicians with little or no allegiance to the bebop idiom—Keith Jarrett, George Benson, David Murray, Bob Wilber, and others—have also turned to this composition, which remains one of the most commonly played modern jazz blues pieces. Singers have also adopted this bop anthem—both Eddie Jefferson and Jon Hendricks have added their lyrics to Bird's line.

The original recording was inducted into the Grammy Hall of Fame in 2002. But the influence of this track has transcended the jazz idiom, serving in some quarters as a talisman of hipness. As such, "Billie's Bounce" shows up in the fiction of Donald Barthelme and the beat poetry of David Meltzer. Artist Jean-Michel Basquiat has even made a painting out of the discographical information from the original Parker session scrawled graffiti-style across his canvas.

RECOMMENDED VERSIONS

Charlie Parker (with Miles Davis), New York, November 26, 1945

Stan Getz and J. J. Johnson (with Oscar Peterson), from *Stan Getz and J. J. Johnson at the Opera House*, live at Shrine Auditorium, Los Angeles, October 25, 1957

Red Garland (with John Coltrane), from *Dig It!*, New York, December 13, 1957

Eddie Jefferson (with Johnny Griffin), from *Letter from Home*, New York, January 12, 1962

George Benson (with Herbie Hancock), from *Giblet Gravy*, New York, February 1967

Keith Jarrett (with Gary Peacock and Jack DeJohnette), from *Still Live*, live at Philharmonic Hall, Munich, July 13, 1986

Jerry Granelli, from *A Song I Thought I Heard Buddy Sing*, Seattle, January–February 1992

David Murray, from *Saxmen*, New York, August 19, 1993

Blue Bossa
Composed by Kenny Dorham

"Blue Bossa" is an "insider's" jazz standard, familiar to musicians but virtually unknown among the general public. When I was learning the ropes, this tune was frequently called at jam sessions. One of the simplest songs in *The Real Book*, that famous and notoriously illegal fake book that every jazz player owns, "Blue Bossa" follows a repeating 16-bar form, and improvisers can get by, in a pinch, with just a handful of licks. Hence, student musicians can tackle it without too much preparation or perspiration. I suspect that for many current day players this was one of the first jazz compositions they learned to play.

Trumpeter Kenny Dorham, the song's composer, introduced "Blue Bossa" at a session under Joe Henderson's leadership in 1963—the bossa nova craze was in full swing, and even the hard bop players associated with the Blue Note label were looking for a chance to participate. Yet, despite the title, the song is not a blues and does not necessarily need to be played as a bossa. The rhythm section on the debut recording never really settles into a Brazilian groove. When McCoy Tyner, the pianist on the Henderson date, returned to "Blue Bossa" for his Latin All-Stars date 35 years later, he goes for the full-blown Afro-Cuban treatment, with no bossa elements whatsoever. Dorham, for his part, never recorded it again, but Henderson kept the song in his repertoire and would play it on four later albums.

Trumpeter Art Farmer was one of the first to embrace "Blue Bossa." He added it to his repertoire in the mid-1960s and was still performing it 30 years later. But the dissemination of *The Real Book* in the early 1970s played the key role in establishing "Blue Bossa" as a bandstand staple. Some of my favorite versions come from that decade. Check out Eddie Daniels's duet with Bucky Pizzarelli from 1973; the trio performance by Milt Jackson, Joe Pass, and Ray Brown from 1975; Art Pepper's fiery rendition from 1978; and Dexter Gordon's workout alongside Barry Harris from 1979.

Despite these precedents, this song is more likely to be performed at casual gigs than on recording sessions—probably due to its association with beginners. A quick check of YouTube shows dozens of versions of "Blue Bossa," but most of them uploaded by students, amateurs, and music teachers. So it's a safe bet that jazz pedagogy will keep this simple and still obscure song alive, even as standards that were once jukebox hits fall by the wayside.

RECOMMENDED VERSIONS

Joe Henderson (with Kenny Dorham), from *Page One*, Englewood Cliffs, New Jersey, June 3, 1963

Eddie Daniels (with Bucky Pizzarelli), from *A Flower for All Seasons*, Sea Cliff, New York, January 2, 1973

Milt Jackson, Joe Pass, and Ray Brown, from *The Big Three*, Los Angeles, August 25, 1975

Art Pepper, from *Among Friends*, Hollywood, September 2, 1978

Dexter Gordon (with Barry Harris), from *Biting the Apple*, New York, November 9, 1979

Art Farmer (with Harold Land), from *Live at Stanford Jazz Workshop*, live at Dinkelspiel Auditorium, Stanford, California, August 5, 1996

McCoy Tyner, from *McCoy Tyner and the Latin All-Stars*, New York, July 29–30, 1998

Blue in Green
Composed by Miles Davis

I greatly admire this piece, but don't really consider it a song. It's more a meditation, or—to borrow a term that didn't exist at the time Davis recorded "Blue in Green"—a type of improvised *ambient music.* Yes, the composition does have a precise structure and set chorus length, unlike Davis's "Flamenco Sketches" from the same *Kind of Blue* project, but a few unconventional elements in the work tend to obscure the underlying blueprint. Indeed, the casual listener could be forgiven for thinking that the work is just a free-form improvisation, without clear beginning or end.

The composition is ten bars long, which is quite unusual for jazz, an idiom that tends to thrive in 8-, 12-, or 16-bar increments. As a result, the ear is deceived when it reaches the end of the form of "Blue in Green." It is expecting another two or four bars, but instead the composition slides back to the start. The absence of a dominant chord here adds to the aural ambiguity of the turnaround. The result is a flowing musical reverie that doesn't seem to have clear borderlines between its choruses.

Although "Blue in Green" is usually credited to Miles Davis, pianist Bill Evans claimed that he did most of the compositional work, albeit relying on two chords—G minor and A augmented—that the trumpeter had asked him to develop into a piece. A short while before the *Kind of Blue* sessions, you can hear Evans working with this concept during his piano intro to "Alone Together" on the Chet Baker album *Chet.* Certainly Evans showed a greater allegiance to "Blue in Green" than Davis did in later years, keeping it in his repertoire for the next two decades, and leaving behind a number of memorable recorded performances. Miles, in contrast, never recorded it again.

For many years, few jazz artists other than Evans performed this work. When Gary Burton drew on "Blue in Green" for a project with Stéphane Grappelli a decade after *Kind of Blue*, the idea of covering this composition was still something of a novelty—its charm, in this instance, furthered by the presence of a violinist associated with prewar swing tunes and not this kind of music. The following year, John McLaughlin recorded "Blue in Green" for his *My Goals Beyond* album—a performance worth hearing, but you are also advised to track down his longer live version from 1989. All in all, only a dozen or so jazz artists recorded "Blue in Green" during the 1970s. Then more than 40 versions were made in the 1980s, and the song's popularity continued to increase in later years. Nowadays this composition is a familiar component of the standard jazz repertoire, its position enhanced by its fresh, cliché-free chords and melody, which sound just as contemporary today as they did when Davis first presented "Blue in Green" to the public.

Despite its popularity, musicians need to be brave to call this song at a gig. "Blue in Green" has no catchy hooks or flamboyant interludes, and unless you have earned a chamber music reverence from the audience, you run the risk of losing their attention. I would keep it under wraps at a noisy nightclub, but in the right setting with listeners who are willing to participate in a collective meditation, this work can be a springboard to an experience that almost transcends jazz.

RECOMMENDED VERSIONS

Miles Davis, from *Kind of Blue*, New York, March 2, 1959

Bill Evans, from *Portrait in Jazz*, New York, December 28, 1959

Gary Burton and Stéphane Grappelli, from *Paris Encounter*, Paris November 4, 1969

John McLaughlin, from *My Goals Beyond*, New York, 1970

Richie Beirach, from *Elegy for Bill Evans*, New York, May 12, 1981

Fred Hersch, from *Sarabande*, New York, December 4–5, 1986

John McLaughlin, from *Live at the Royal Festival Hall*, live at the Royal Festival Hall, London, November 27, 1989

World Saxophone Quartet, from *Selim Sivad: The Music of Miles Davis*, New York, March 2–3, 1998

Cassandra Wilson (recorded under the title "Sky and Sea"), from *Joy*, New York, May and September 1998

Blue Monk
Composed by Thelonious Monk

Thelonious Monk composed some dauntingly difficult jazz pieces, but *those* songs are rarely called on the bandstand. In contrast, the melody to the jam session staple "Blue Monk" could be taught to a beginning piano student, and the form couldn't be more straightforward: a basic 12-bar blues in B flat. The song, helped along by these user-friendly attributes, gained the support of jazz players at a time when few Monk songs found advocates—helped, no doubt, by the zeal of the composer, who left behind more than 30 recorded or filmed performances. The only song he recorded more often was his oft-requested "'Round Midnight."

Monk usually took great care in constructing his songs, but "Blue Monk" was hastily composed. Bob Weinstock of Prestige Records, perhaps unsettled by the difficulty in recording the more complex Monk compositions, griped that the pianist never played the blues. The accusation was unfair—at this point, Monk had already written some classic blues lines, including "Straight, No Chaser" and "Misterioso"—but rather than debate the point, the artist sought to assuage his producer. Drawing part of his melody from Charlie Shavers's tune "Pastel Blue," Monk quickly put together this now well-known song without leaving the studio.

At its debut recording in 1954, Monk stretched out for more than seven minutes. His solo encompasses 14 choruses, and the performance would serve as a useful introduction to any student trying to come to grips with Monk's through-composed approach to improvisation. Instead of running the licks and phrases that other modern jazz players happily dished out, Monk conceives each new chorus as an integrated structure with its own motivic development and personality. Some of these choruses, in particular the ninth and the fourteenth, could serve as stand-alone pieces, so persuasive is the logic with which they are constructed.

In my opinion, the song loses its character unless the melody is played in moving thirds, as Monk originally conceived it. For this reason, "Blue Monk" often works best as a piano feature or with at least two horns on hand—but you wouldn't guess that from the typical lead sheets for the song, such as the one included in *The Real Book*, which presents the melody as a monophonic line. In any event, keyboardists have taken the lead as advocates for "Blue Monk." Many of the leading jazz pianists of the last half-century have tackled this piece at one time or another, as demonstrated on recordings by McCoy Tyner, Chick Corea, Hank Jones, Mal Waldron, Fred Hersch, Cedar Walton, Muhal Richard Abrams, Kenny Barron, Marcus Roberts . . . even Earl Hines and Bill Evans, two fellows who rarely covered Monk compositions but tried their hands at this one.

I don't write off the horn players completely, but too many treat this song as just one more blues, a simple blowing tune to fill up a set or session time. As a result, more than a few lackluster recordings of this standard can be found at your local (or virtual) record store. "Blue Monk" is better served by reed players who have demonstrated their affinity for this composer's worldview, such as Steve Lacy or, strangely enough, trad jazz stylist Pee Wee Russell, whose whimsical collaboration with Monk from 1963 at Newport ranks among the most successful pairings of (supposed) opposites in the festival's long history.

RECOMMENDED VERSIONS

Thelonious Monk, from *Thelonious Monk*, Hackensack, New Jersey, September 22, 1954

Thelonious Monk (with John Coltrane), from *Thelonious Monk Quartet with John Coltrane at Carnegie Hall*, live at Carnegie Hall, New York, November 29, 1957

Abbey Lincoln, from *Straight Ahead*, New York, February 22, 1961

McCoy Tyner, from *Nights of Ballads & Blues*, Englewood Cliffs, New Jersey, March 4, 1963

Thelonious Monk (with Pee Wee Russell), from *Miles Davis & Thelonious Monk Live at Newport 1958 & 1963*, live at the Newport Jazz Festival, Newport, Rhode Island, July 4, 1963

Earl Hines, from *Honor Thy Fatha*, Los Angeles, 1978

Marcus Roberts, from *The Truth Is Spoken Here*, New York, July 26–27, 1988

Steve Lacy and Mal Waldron, from *Communiqué*, Milan, March 8–9, 1994

Chick Corea, from *Solo Piano Standards, Part 2*, live at Club Fasching, Stockholm, November 17, 1999

Chick Corea and Bobby McFerrin, from *Rendezvous in New York*, live at the Blue Note, New York, December 2001

Blue Moon
Composed by Richard Rodgers, with lyrics by Lorenz Hart

This is an odd tune to come from the pen of Richard Rodgers, with its sing-song melody, more suitable for a nursery rhyme than a Broadway production. Yet Rodgers explains the anomaly in his autobiography *Musical Stages*: he originally wrote the composition for the 1934 movie *Hollywood Party*, where the music was intended to match the mood of "an innocent young girl saying—or rather singing—her prayers." But the scene was discarded from the final cut of the film, and the music was recycled, with new lyrics, for the Clark Gable movie *Manhattan Melodrama*.

This latter film is famous in the history books less for its cinematic excellence but rather as the movie watched by the notorious bank robber John Dillinger immediately before being gunned down by the FBI on the way out of the theater on July 22, 1934. How fitting that the Rodgers and Hart song was known, at this point, as "The Bad in Every Man"! But the songwriters were not yet through with their 32-bar tune, and perhaps felt it needed to be purified of the taint of blood-shed and lawlessness. The piece underwent more tinkering when Hart, at the prodding of the studio, turned the song—now on its third incarnation—into the hit "Blue Moon."

The original mood of innocent prayerfulness remains even after the trans-formation into a love song. Or at least it does when "Blue Moon" is played at a stately tempo. In contrast, if you accelerate the underlying pulse too much, this song is better suited for spurring on the horse on the merry-go-round with a hot calliope than advancing the cause of romance and courtship. Back when the Casa Loma Orchestra enjoyed a number one hit with "Blue Moon" in 1934, the romance still prevailed, and Benny Goodman's hit recording from this same period is equally chastened. But by the time Tommy Dorsey interpreted "Blue Moon" at the close of the decade, a more playful, deconstructive attitude has prevailed, with a corny ensemble response undercutting the plausibility of Jack Leonard's lead vocal. A similar contrast can be heard between Coleman Hawkins's 1935 performance alongside Django Reinhardt and the tenorist's 1944 recording alongside Cozy Cole, with "Blue Moon" becoming faster and less of a lover's lament over time.

By the time we get to the postwar years, "Blue Moon" has turned into a *ve-hicle*, popular with jazz players due to its adaptability rather than for the power of its original inspiring vision. When the young Dave Brubeck performed it with his 1949 trio it served as a plaything for his most experimental tendencies, and if you want to know why this pianist was considered an iconoclast and a progressive at this stage in his career, this track is a good place to begin. When Dizzy Gillespie featured "Blue Moon" in his session with Roy Eldridge, it turned into a platform for trumpet jousting. And if you still had doubts about how far this tune could be pushed, you need only hear the recording of "Blue Moon" by Elvis Presley, made a few weeks earlier, which is poised midway between coun-try-and-western and pop-rock.

Ella Fitzgerald tackled "Blue Moon" at her celebrated 1961 performance at the Crescendo Club in Los Angeles, but rather than take this standard back to its original conception—which she could have easily done, given Ella's incom-parable skill in imparting wide-eyed innocence to a love song—she instead par-odies the doo-wop version that the Marcels had pushed to the top of the *Billboard* chart the previous month. Yet Ella can't do it with a straight face, and toward the conclusion of her performance she starts adding words never vetted by Lorenz Hart: "They asked us to sing this request, and so we tried our best . . . it's a pity to take a pretty, pretty tune like Blue—ooooh-oooh Moon, and mess up such a pretty tune like this. . . ." And she wraps up with a hilarious imitation of the Marcels' most famous doo-wop lick. Score one for Fitzgerald, the comedienne!

Occasionally a performer will sing this song straight—hear, for example, Mel Tormé's heartfelt versions, where this vocalist, so often given to excess, submerges his ego into a pristine and unabashedly beautiful interpretation of the standard. Tormé enjoyed a top 20 hit with his 1949 recording of "Blue Moon" for Capitol, and he kept the song in his repertoire in later years. I suspect that Tormé's encounter with the composer, while working on the 1948 film *Words and Music*, may have had something to do with the integrity of his approach to the song. When he started his performance of "Blue Moon," Richard Rodgers interrupted the proceedings, shouting out, "No, no, no, no, no! Not like that, Mel! Not like that!" before storming off the soundstage. I am not sure how much the singer took this criticism to heart, yet listening to Tormé's 1960 performance, backed by Russ Garcia's arrangement, I find it hard to believe that the composer could be anything other than gratified by the end result.

RECOMMENDED VERSIONS

Casa Loma Orchestra, New York, November 16, 1934

Coleman Hawkins (with Django Reinhardt), Paris, March 2, 1935

Cozy Cole (with Coleman Hawkins and Earl Hines), New York, February 22, 1944

Dave Brubeck, San Francisco, September 1949

Dizzy Gillespie and Roy Eldridge, from *Roy and Diz*, New York, October 29, 1954

Mel Tormé, from *Swingin' on the Moon*, Los Angeles, August 3, 1960

Ella Fitzgerald, from *Ella in Hollywood*, live at the Crescendo Club, Los Angeles, May 11–12, 1961

Erroll Garner, from *That's My Kick*, New York, November 17, 1966

The Bad Plus, from *Motel*, Minneapolis, December 28, 2000

Blue Skies
Composed by Irving Berlin

Belle Baker was unhappy with the solo numbers composed for her by Rodgers & Hart for the 1926 show *Betsy*, so she decided to find a better tune on her own. Irving Berlin came to the rescue with "Blue Skies," only half-finished at the time, but he hastily composed a bridge to meet the pressing deadline. The song demonstrated its appeal at its very first performance, with the audience demanding some two dozen encores. After so many renditions, the flustered and gratified singer finally bungled the lyrics, and producer Flo Ziegfeld had the spotlights put on the composer, who stood up from the audience and told her the correct words. I would have loved to have seen the expression on Richard Rodgers's face.

Betsy ran for only 39 performances, but "Blue Skies" had legs, and showed up the next year in the first talking film *The Jazz Singer*—a last-minute replacement again, this time substituting for "It All Depends on You." The new sound technology brought Berlin's song to audiences who would never see a Broadway show. Half of the first dozen documented jazz recordings of "Blue Skies" were made in Berlin, and I can't help suspecting that Al Jolson's immense popularity in that city (more than 300,000 Berlin residents came to see him on the screen in 1928 alone) had something to do with this transatlantic success. A surviving German newspaper ad for the film depicts the scene where Jakie Rabinowitz (played by Jolson) sings "Blue Skies" at the piano for his mother, showing off how he can jazz it up, only to be sent packing when his shocked father, a cantor at the synagogue, arrives on the premises.

Present at the birth of the "talkies," "Blue Skies" has found itself recruited again and again by Hollywood. It appeared in *Alexander's Ragtime Band*, nominated for Best Picture in 1938, and served as the title song for another hit movie, starring Bing Crosby and Fred Astaire, from 1946—no surprise, then, that two jazz versions, by Benny Goodman and Count Basie, reached the top 10 on the charts that same year. The song showed up again in *White Christmas*, the biggest grossing film of 1954 and a perennial television classic. When "Blue Skies" made its intergalactic debut in *Star Trek: Nemesis* (2002), Trekkies might have been bewildered, but Irving Berlin fans had, by that time, grown accustomed to encountering this song in the strangest places.

A simple and catchy main melody with lots of whole notes and half notes offset by a klezmer-ish bridge, "Blue Skies" is a song you could teach a toddler—I used to sing it as a lullaby to my son when he was a baby—or bring to the nightclub, cabaret, or (as Benny Goodman did) Carnegie Hall. But don't underestimate the lyrics, with their crisp naturalistic imagery closer to a traditional folk song or populist poetry than to Tin Pan Alley fare. Even today, "Blue Skies" is more likely to be called on the gig by a vocalist rather than an instrumentalist, and many of the most formidable versions feature the defining singers of modern times—Ella Fitzgerald (hear her extended scat excursion from 1958); Frank Sinatra, who sang it with Tommy Dorsey in 1941 and again as a leader in 1946; Willie Nelson, who had a number one country hit with "Blue Skies" in 1978 . . . all the way to Cassandra Wilson and Dr. John in more recent years.

I fear that the melody does not sound half so convincing when played on piano—you need to be able to sustain and bend those long, held notes to extract the maximum amount of emotion from this song. But I still give the nod to versions by Art Tatum and Mary Lou Williams. Among big band performances, Benny Goodman's rendition of Fletcher Henderson's arrangement at Carnegie Hall in 1938 is well known, but six years later Duke Ellington presented a very hot chart of the Berlin song to conclude the program of his own Carnegie Hall concert, and it also deserves a close hearing.

RECOMMENDED VERSIONS

Benny Goodman (with arrangement by Fletcher Henderson), live at Carnegie Hall, New York, January 16, 1938

Mary Lou Williams, New York, August 10, 1944

Duke Ellington, live at Carnegie Hall, New York, December 19, 1944

Count Basie (featuring Jimmy Rushing), Hollywood, October 9, 1945

Frank Sinatra, Hollywood, July 30, 1946

Art Tatum, Los Angeles, September 29, 1949

Ella Fitzgerald, from *Ella Fitzgerald Sings the Irving Berlin Songbook*, Los Angeles, March 18, 1958

Willie Nelson, from *Stardust*, Southern California, December 3–12, 1977

Cassandra Wilson, from *Blue Skies*, New York, February 4–5, 1988

Dr. John, from *Afterglow*, Hollywood, February 7–9, 1995

Susannah McCorkle, from *From Broken Hearts to Blue Skies*, New York, October 27–29, 1998

Bluesette
Composed by Toots Thielemans, with lyrics by Norman Gimbel

Toots Thielemans, a much-beloved jazz artist, is best known for bringing the chromatic harmonica from the fringes of the jazz world and into the mainstream. In my late teens, I taught myself how to play jazz on this instrument, and developed to the point where I could perform the chromatic harmonica on a bandstand without quite embarrassing myself. My biggest inspiration, and source of sweet phrases, was Mr. Thielemans, and I still recall my first reaction on hearing him. It was sheer astonishment that what he did on the harmonica was even possible, given the inherent limitations of the human mouth and Hohner's creation.

Yet the harmonica was a late career move for this artist, who started playing accordion at age three in his native Belgium and later served as guitarist alongside many major jazz artists. But "Bluesette" became Thielemans's most famous song and an international hit due to another skill of this multitalented artist—namely his uncanny knack for whistling. The hook of the song, in its original version, derives from the preternatural fluidity of Thielemans's whistled melody line and its perfect meshing with his guitar notes. The song had humble origins: Thielemans started humming backstage one day while tuning his guitar. Violinist Stéphane Grappelli, who was sharing a dressing room with Thielemans, was struck by the melody and urged him to "Ecrivez tout de suite!" ("Write it down immediately!")

I could give you many reasons why this song should never have become a jazz standard. The song doesn't sand bluesy (although it is based on Charlie Parker's substitute blues changes). Although jazz waltzes had started to enter the repertoire in the early 1960s, when this song was first recorded, they were still outliers and many bands happily went months on the road without playing a single song in 3/4 time. But the biggest strike against this song was its obvious novelty quality, whistling tunes typically gravitating to vaudeville rather than the Village Vanguard.

But the darn thing is catchy, and I can't blame jazz players for latching on to "Bluesette," despite all these warning signs. Even so, who could have foreseen so many major singers, the ones you know on a first-name basis (Ella, Sarah, Mel, Anita, Blossom, etc.) finding inspiration in "Bluesette"? Norman Gimbel's lyrics are not much to consider, and sometimes the vocalist merely scats along (as does Ella Fitzgerald in her 1983 live performance with Joe Pass). And even when a singer gives the words their due, as does Mel Tormé in his 1978 recording with Buddy Rich, I sense that this is merely an appetizer and that the ensuing wordless vocal is the main course.

In time, Thielemans took his whistling-and-guitar song and adapted it to the harmonica. And if you can deal with the idea of multiple harmonicas, track down the widely available Internet video featuring Thielemans playing this song in concert when Stevie Wonder strolls onstage and dishes up some wondrous give-and-take.

RECOMMENDED VERSIONS

Toots Thielemans, from *The Whistler and His Guitar*, Stockholm, June 1963

Sarah Vaughan, from *Jazzfest Masters*, live at the New Orleans Jazz Festival, New Orleans, June 1969

Mel Tormé and Buddy Rich, from *Together Again—For the First Time*, New York, January 25, 1978

Hank Jones, from *Bluesette*, London, July 22, 1979

Stevie Wonder and Toots Thielemans, video from the Polar Prize Music Award ceremony, Stockholm, 1999

Body and Soul
Composed by Johnny Green, with lyrics by Edward Heyman, Robert Sour, and Frank Eyton

This is the granddaddy of jazz ballads, the quintessential torch song, and the ultimate measuring rod for tenor sax players of all generations. Even in the new millennium, this 1930 composition continues to serve as a cornerstone of the repertoire. Yet "Body and Soul" could easily have missed the mark, fallen out of favor and never established itself as a standard, let alone achieved this pinnacle of success. Coleman Hawkins, who did more than anyone in validating the composition's jazzworthiness and will forever be associated with the song, expressed puzzlement over its popularity. "It's funny how it became such a classic," he later mused. "Even the ordinary public is crazy about it. It's the first and only record I ever heard that all the squares dig as well as the jazz people, and I don't understand why or how. . . . I didn't even bother to listen to it afterwards."

The whole history of this song marks it as an unlikely jazz classic. "Body and Soul" was written by an unproven songwriter—Johnny Green was a former stockbroker with an economics degree from Harvard and an approach to the piano more akin to novelty players such as Zez Confrey than to jazz. Green was working on a tight deadline for a British actress, Gertrude Lawrence, who didn't even bother to make a recording of the song she commissioned. Part of the composition was a retread: the bridge had been rejected as a section in a work Green had written for Guy Lombardo, arguably the least jazzy bandleader of the era. Edward Heyman and Robert Sour continued to tinker with the lyrics after the song was copyrighted, and even the title was problematic—the word "body" was considered edgy by NBC radio, whose announcers initially refused to mention the song's name on the air or broadcast any vocal version.

Although Louis Armstrong made a recording at the time of the song's release, "Body and Soul" most often showed up in the repertoire of white dance bandleaders, such as Paul Whiteman (who had a number one hit with the song in the fall of 1930), Leo Reisman, and Jack Hylton. But a few cover versions from the mid-1930s gave notice of the song's potential as a springboard for improvisation. Henry Allen, Benny Goodman, and Art Tatum all enjoyed top 20 hits with "Body and Soul" before Hawkins's celebrated recording.

Hawkins was late to the party, and didn't start playing the song until toward the end of the decade, sometimes using "Body and Soul" as an encore, or stretching out with chorus after chorus—ten-minute performances unsuitable for 78 rpm records, then limited to roughly three minutes before all the available "disk space" was exhausted. Or so the saxophonist thought. RCA exec Leonard Joy had a different opinion, and prodded Hawkins to record a shorter version of "Body and Soul." The result was an astonishing success—a surprise hit record that caught on with the public in February 1940. The tenorist barely hints at the melody, and instead plunges into an elaborate improvisation, heavily reliant on tritone substitutions and built on phrases that are anything but hummable. The intellectual component here was daunting, yet for once the general public rose to the challenge.

Just a few months after Hawkins's performance, Charlie Parker was captured playing a solo sax version of "Body and Soul" on an amateur recording made in Kansas City. Parker seems to have found more inspiration in Roy Eldridge's solo on this song from a 1938 recording with Chu Berry, than in Hawk's hit version. But by the time Parker recorded "Body and Soul" with Jay McShann's band in November 1940, he had clearly assimilated Hawkins's solo and quoted directly from it. Another amateur recording of Parker playing this song, made in Chicago, in 1943, also reflects Hawkins's influence, but by now the bebop elements are far more pronounced—Parker now transcending his influential predecessor even as he shows deference to him.

With the rise of bebop, cool jazz, hard bop, and other styles, "Body and Soul" retained its central place in the repertoire. During the 1950s and 1960s, the song was recorded by a who's who of the most influential players of the day, including John Coltrane, Thelonious Monk, Charles Mingus, Sonny Rollins, Stan Getz, the Modern Jazz Quartet, Freddie Hubbard, Wayne Shorter, Bud Powell, Dave Brubeck, Gerry Mulligan, Art Pepper, Sonny Stitt, Dexter Gordon, and many others. But the song was just as likely to show up in the set list of Louis Armstrong, Benny Goodman, Earl Hines, Jack Teagarden, or another representative of the music's past. In a period during which different schools of jazz were often depicted as being at war, "Body and Soul" was a meeting ground where the generations could converse on friendly terms.

The song has hardly lagged in popularity in more recent years. Certainly its appeal among saxophonists is well documented, and one could easily chart a history of the tenor sax through the various recordings of "Body and Soul" over the decades. Yet pianists have been almost as enthusiastic as the horn players. Art Tatum left behind around 20 recorded versions, and virtually every significant later jazz pianist, of whatever persuasion, has taken it on. But many other options present themselves to jazz fans, and whether your tastes turn to trumpet, vocals, harmonica, violin, accordion, or marimba (to name a few options), you will find an arrangement of "Body and Soul" to suit your predilection.

For all that, something cold and almost clinical comes across in many performances of this piece. I suspect this may be the lingering after-effect of Coleman Hawkins's transformation of "Body and Soul" from a romantic ballad to a showpiece for advanced saxophony. Soloists nowadays often tackle "Body and Soul" with something to prove—and that proof may have little to do with exploring the emotional insides of the song Johnny Green bequeathed to us. For better or worse, this ballad has become more than a ballad, rather a testing ground where aspirants to the jazz life prove their mettle. In this regard, "Body and Soul" is likely to be around for a long, long time, and its own rise and fall linked to the health of the jazz idiom as a whole.

RECOMMENDED VERSIONS

Louis Armstrong, Los Angeles, October 9, 1930

Benny Goodman (with Teddy Wilson and Gene Krupa), New York, July 13, 1935

Chu Berry and Roy Eldridge, New York, November 10, 1938

Coleman Hawkins, New York, October 11, 1939

Billie Holiday, New York, February 29, 1940

Art Tatum, live at Gee-Haw Stables, New York, July 26, 1941

Charlie Parker, Chicago, February 28, 1943

John Coltrane (with McCoy Tyner), from *Coltrane's Sound*, New York, October 24, 1960

Thelonious Monk, from *Monk in Italy*, live at Teatro Lirico, Milan, April 21, 1961

Freddie Hubbard (with Wayne Shorter), from *Here to Stay*, Englewood Cliffs, New Jersey, December 27, 1962

David Murray, from *Morning Song*, New York, September 25–30, 1983

Joe Lovano (with Michel Petrucciani), from *From the Soul*, New York, December 28, 1991

Jason Moran, from *The Bandwagon*, New York, November 29–30, 2002

Keith Jarrett and Charlie Haden, from *Jasmine*, Oxford, New Jersey, March 2007

But Beautiful
Composed by Jimmy Van Heusen, with lyrics by Johnny Burke

Jimmy Van Heusen led one of those glorious reinvented lives that were hardly possible outside of America in the twentieth century. Where else could Edward Chester Babcock of Syracuse turn himself into Jimmy Van Heusen of Hollywood? In his teens, Chester (as he was then known) was already writing songs and broadcasting his own show on a small radio program in his hometown—at which point he took on his new name, borrowed from the famous shirt company. Not many lads would adopt a fashion brand for an identity, but Van Heusen apparently knew that a glamorous life was his for the taking. And he did just that: first securing work at Harlem's posh Cotton Club, later earning the support of the hottest bandleaders of the Swing Era, and eventually taking his act to the West Coast and the movie industry.

He flourished in this new setting, serving as a test pilot for Lockheed, enjoying the Los Angeles nightlife—despite having composed the song "Love and

Marriage," Van Heusen spent most of his life as a bachelor, and was known to take full advantage of the opportunities it presented—and, yes, writing songs. But Van Heusen did more than provide material for the stars; he hung out with them as well, counting Frank Sinatra and Bing Crosby among his closest friends; and when John F. Kennedy adopted a theme song for his presidential campaign, even he turned to Van Heusen and was soon barnstorming the country to the sound of "High Hopes."

"But Beautiful," written with Van Heusen's longtime partner Johnny Burke, resulted from the songwriter's ties to Bing Crosby. Crosby's collaborations with Bob Hope in a series of "road" movies—starting with *Road to Singapore* in 1940 and ending with *Road to Hong Kong* in 1962—ranked among the most popular comedies of the era, and Van Heusen provided music for six out of the seven in the series. "But Beautiful" made its debut in *Road to Rio*, which opened on Christmas Day in 1947 and became the highest-grossing film of the following year. The song is first performed with an ersatz Brazilian beat during the title credits, later shows up as a ballroom-style waltz—both versions giving little indication of its future as a jazz ballad—and finally takes center stage as a love song delivered by Crosby to his recurring road partner Dorothy Lamour.

The song failed to earn an Oscar nomination—unlike the 14 other Van Heusen songs so honored over the years—but recordings by the songwriter's buddies Sinatra and Crosby were modest hits in early 1948. Jazz artists also took notice, with Mel Tormé and Eddie "Lockjaw" Davis recording "But Beautiful" around this same time. The song stayed in the jazz repertoire during the 1950s, covered by Stan Getz and Lionel Hampton, and gained the support of a number of leading vocalists during the closing years of the decade, as demonstrated on recordings by Nat King Cole, Billie Holiday, Lena Horne, Betty Carter, and Johnny Hartman. In later years, Bill Evans was a persistent champion of "But Beautiful," featuring it with his own trio as well as on all-star collaborations with Tony Bennett and Stan Getz. I especially like the less known version, recorded by Evans alongside Eddie Gomez and Marty Morrell in 1974 at the Village Vanguard, from the album *Since We Met*—Evans's solo here captures a relaxed, conversational way of phrasing, almost as if some private lyrics known only to the pianist are in his mind as he constructs melodic lines to match them.

The song follows a simple enough recipe: a short motif is stated, then repeated starting on a different note, then tried out a third time in a still higher register. The mood is contemplative and probing, as if the melody is attempting to find the right pathway to resolution; and when it arrives at the title phrase, it pulls up short and places a firm emphasis on the word *beautiful*. This is our destination, the moment the whole song has been anticipating. And the same word is a fitting description of the song itself, a standout even in the hit-filled oeuvre of Mr. Van Heusen.

RECOMMENDED VERSIONS

Bing Crosby, Los Angeles, November 13, 1947

Eddie "Lockjaw" Davis, New York, circa 1948

Lionel Hampton (with Oscar Peterson), from *The Complete Lionel Hampton Quartets and Quintets with Oscar Peterson*, New York, September 15, 1954

Billie Holiday, from *Lady in Satin*, New York, February 19, 1958

Freddie Hubbard (with Tina Brooks), from *Open Sesame*, Englewood Cliffs, New Jersey, June 19, 1960

Bill Evans, from *Since We Met*, live at the Village Vanguard, New York, January 11–12, 1974

Tony Bennett and Bill Evans, from *The Tony Bennett/Bill Evans Album*, Berkeley, California, June 10–13, 1975

Paul Bley, from *Tango Palace*, Milan, May 21, 1983

Kenny Garrett, from *Garrett 5*, New York, September 21–23, 1988

Chick Corea, from *Solo Piano: Standards*, live at Minato Mirai Hall, Yokohama, Japan, November 28, 1999

But Not for Me

Composed by George Gershwin, with lyrics by Ira Gershwin

One of George Gershwin's most beloved standards, "But Not for Me" seems to find a new crossover audience every decade. Film makers love it—not only did the original Broadway musical (Gershwin's *Girl Crazy* from 1930) inspire three movie adaptations, but "But Not for Me" has regularly appeared in later hit films, including Woody Allen's *Manhattan* (1979), Rob Reiner's *When Harry Met Sally* (1989), and Mike Newell's *Four Weddings and a Funeral* (1994). The song even inspired its own movie, Walter Lang's *But Not for Me* (1959), which was one of Clark Gable's final efforts. The latter movie showcased Ella Fitzgerald's version of the familiar standard, and the film's debut coincided with the release of the vocalist's massive Gershwin songbook, the most ambitious recording project of Fitzgerald's career, spanning 5 LPs and an EP encompassing 59 performances, including "But Not for Me."

Ella delivers a finely etched vocal and a convincing realization of the lyrics, but the sensibility here is more pop-oriented than jazzy, largely due to Nelson Riddle's mawkish arrangement. If you want to hear Ella sing this standard in a more intimate and jazzier setting, check out the lesser known Gershwin theme album she made a quarter of a century later—*Nice Work If You Can Get It*, a collaboration with André Previn. Here, on "But Not for Me," Previn offers a clever reharmonization during his solo, reminding us of why he once had a sizable following among jazz fans, while Fitzgerald, for her part, is in top form.

The song gained some traction with jazz players during the 1940s—Harry James even enjoyed a modest hit with his 1941 recording, which featured vocalist Helen Forrest—but Gershwin's composition was better suited for the cool jazz stars of the 1950s. Chet Baker may have lacked Ella's technique and range, but his 1954 recording of "But Not for Me" ranks among his finest moments in the studio, both for its quintessentially cool vocal and his lyrical trumpet solo. Four months later, Miles Davis recorded the song for his *Bags' Groove* album, and his two released takes find him playing it initially in a medium tempo similar to Baker's approach, while the second take is faster, and a better setting for his front-line bandmate Sonny Rollins. Ahmad Jamal delivered an appealingly understated piano performance on his live recording from the Pershing from 1958, which was one of the best-selling jazz albums of the period. The Modern Jazz Quartet and Kenny Burrell offered similarly subdued interpretations around this same time.

Most later jazz renditions of "But Not for Me" have kept to the cool ethos. But Coltrane offered a dissenting view with his 1960 recording from his *My Favorite Things* album. He incorporates his "Giant Steps" chord substitution scheme into the Gershwin piece, and the result is a case study in the advanced harmonic concepts of the time, worthy of inclusion in the curriculum of any jazz educational institution. Dexter Gordon dispenses with the Coltrane chord changes but achieves a similar energy level on his 1967 recording in Copenhagen, an intense 15-minute outing on "But Not for Me"—including nine full tenor choruses that persuasively demonstrate why this saxophonist was such a formidable combatant at a jam session.

RECOMMENDED VERSIONS

Harry James (with Helen Forrest), New York, December 30, 1941

Modern Jazz Quartet, from *Django*, New York, June 25, 1953

Chet Baker, from *Chet Baker Sings*, Los Angeles, February 15, 1954

Miles Davis (with Sonny Rollins), from *Bags' Groove*, Hackensack, New Jersey, June 29, 1954

Kenny Burrell, from *Introducing Kenny Burrell*, Hackensack, New Jersey, May 30, 1956

Red Garland, from *Red Garland's Piano*, Hackensack, New Jersey, March 22, 1957

Ahmad Jamal, from *But Not for Me*, live at the Pershing Lounge, Chicago, January 16, 1958

Ella Fitzgerald, from *Ella Fitzgerald Sings the George and Ira Gershwin Songbook*, Los Angeles, January 5–8, 1959

John Coltrane, from *My Favorite Things*, New York, October 26, 1960

Dexter Gordon, from *Take the A Train*, live at Montmartre, Copenhagen, July 20, 1967

Ella Fitzgerald (with André Previn), from *Nice Work If You Can Get It*, New York, May 23, 1983

Harry Connick Jr. from the soundtrack to *When Harry Met Sally*, New York, June 1989

James Moody (with Kenny Barron), from *Moody 4B*, New York, July 21–22, 2008

Bye Bye Blackbird
Composed by Ray Henderson, with lyrics by Mort Dixon

I still remember my surprise when I learned that this song had first been a hit in 1926—I had assumed it was of more recent vintage. The lyrics, with their laments about "cares and woe," seem more aligned with the Great Depression or perhaps the Cold War than the Roaring Twenties, and the plaintive, mostly diatonic melody reminds me more of the pop-folk fare of the 1960s than the speakeasies of the Jazz Age. Yet no fewer than four versions of "Bye Bye Blackbird" were hits in 1926, and Gene Austin's sprightly rendition, which was the biggest seller of them all, climbed all the way to the top of the chart.

Austin is mostly forgotten in the new millennium, but he was one of the first popular singers to adapt his style to take advantage of the close-miked approach made possible by the new recording technology of the era. The crisply articulated, conversational style of his delivery influenced a range of more famous artists, including Bing Crosby and Frank Sinatra. Nonetheless, listeners today are likely to dismiss Austin's approach to "Bye Bye Blackbird" as quaintly vaudevillian, and prefer the faster tempo and sassier attitude of Josephine Baker's Paris recording from 1927.

The song was destined to have a strange future. In the years leading up to World War II, it was more popular in Europe than in the United States—perhaps due to Baker's advocacy—but who would have expected Nazi propagandist Joseph Goebbels to sponsor the recording of an alternative version of "Bye Bye Blackbird," with new lyrics designed to demoralize the British soldiers with exhortations of "bye bye" to the British Empire.

The Yankees are still out of sight
I can't make out wrong from right
Empire, bye, bye

The arrangement is surprisingly nuanced, but the pervasive German accent of the lead singer Karl Schwedler is a giveaway that this broadcast wasn't coming from the Cotton Club or Roseland. Meanwhile, few jazz versions of this song were recorded in the United States during World War II and the early postwar period.

The song made a comeback in the 1950s, but had a little help from Hollywood. It appeared in the 1954 film *The Eddie Cantor Story* as well as the 1955 movie *Pete Kelly's Blues*, and was recorded by Peggy Lee, who received an Oscar nomination for her performance in the latter film (but, contrary to many accounts, did not sing it on screen). The Henderson-Dixon standard received an even bigger boost in jazz circles the following year when "Bye Bye Blackbird" was recorded by Miles Davis—who had been born a few days before the song first topped the chart—in a gripping combo version that also featured John Coltrane.

In the aftermath of these fresh interpretations by Lee and Davis, more jazz cover versions were made in the three following years than had appeared in the previous three decades. For the most part, Miles's relaxed medium-tempo approach has served as the template for later performances, but if you want to see how far a soloist can push this old song, you are advised to track down Albert Ayler's 1963 recording of "Bye Bye Blackbird." Coltrane would also revisit the composition in later years and interpret it in an expansive manner, as demonstrated by his 1962 live performance in Stockholm, which would result in his first Grammy Award—albeit one granted posthumously in 1981.

The song requires a very modest range and, given the mostly stepwise motion of the melody, "Bye Bye Blackbird" stands out as one of the easiest jazz standards for vocalists and would-be vocalists. But the *meaning* of the words is far more problematic, and Mort Dixon's lyrics have puzzled many commentators over the years. For some, "blackbird" potentially signifies an antebellum slave or—according to one popular view—the customer of an overworked prostitute. The song's early association with Eddie Cantor, well known for performing in blackface, may have convinced others that pejorative minstrel associations are hidden in the phrases. Then again, one listener recalls his father insisting that the song was about a Jewish landlord in New York who was tired of dealing with his black tenants and decided to sell his properties and move to Florida. A separate verse that is rarely sung these days also refers to a bluebird—which convinces me that a straightforward ornithological interpretation of the title phrase is the most plausible.

RECOMMENDED VERSIONS

Josephine Baker, Paris, January 1927

Peggy Lee, from *Songs from Pete Kelly's Blues*, Los Angeles, May 10, 1955

Miles Davis, from *'Round About Midnight*, New York, June 5, 1956

Ben Webster and Oscar Peterson, from *Ben Webster Meets Oscar Peterson*, New York, November 6, 1959

John Coltrane (with McCoy Tyner and Elvin Jones), from *Bye Bye Blackbird*, live at Koncerthuset, Stockholm, November 19, 1962

Albert Ayler, from *My Name Is Albert Ayler*, Copenhagen, January 14, 1963

Rahsaan Roland Kirk, from *The Case of the 3 Sided Dream in Audio Color*, New York, May 14, 1975

Patricia Barber, from *Nightclub*, Chicago, May 15–19, 2000

C Jam Blues

C

Composed by Duke Ellington, with lyrics by Bill Katz, Ruth Roberts, and Bob Thiele

The Smithsonian claims to have documentation of 4,700 compositions by Duke Ellington or his frequent collaborator Billy Strayhorn in its archives. But "C Jam Blues" must be the simplest of all. The melody uses only two notes, and the chart sticks to a basic blues progression. Some people claim that Ellington got the idea for the song from clarinetist Barney Bigard, but I'm not sure anyone can stake a claim on an interval leap. When you add the lyrics (which are almost as bare bones as the melody, yet apparently required a committee of three to concoct), the song becomes known as "Duke's Place." The definitive vocal version, unlikely to be topped, comes from a 1961 studio encounter between the composer and Louis Armstrong, fittingly released under the title *The Great Summit*.

Ellington's debut recording of "C Jam Blues" was actually a music video—or what was known as a "soundie" back in the day. During a West Coast visit shortly before Pearl Harbor, Ellington performed "C Jam Blues" on camera at the Fine Arts studios in Hollywood. This movie clip finds Duke and company gigging at the "Harlem Cats Eatery," where a group of enthusiastic ladies show up to admire the musicians and their stylish hats. The premise is a bit goofy, but the band is one of Ellington's finest units, and many of the players on hand—including Ben Webster, Rex Stewart, Sonny Greer, Barney Bigard, and Duke himself—get a chance to solo.

Perhaps because it is so user-friendly, "C Jam Blues" has been a popular number with jazz musicians. And despite its simple pretensions, the song has retained its capability to surprise over the years. Who would believe that, the day before the recording session for *A Love Supreme*, McCoy Tyner would be in the studio to perform a very cool and relaxed version of this song for his *McCoy Tyner Plays Duke Ellington* album? It hardly sounds like the same piano player on these two dates. Charlie Parker's jam session performance, captured live in Washington, D.C., in 1948, is just as intriguing, with Buddy Rich trying to move the beat into a Swing Era groove, and Wild Bill Davison attempting to shift the music in a Dixieland direction—the latter musician finally forcing the performance to end prematurely when he walks offstage in a huff. But Rahsaan Roland Kirk tops them all, with the masterful game of one-upmanship he plays against George Adams during the course of a 24-minute workout on "C Jam Blues," under Charles Mingus's leadership, happily captured on tape at Carnegie Hall in 1974.

RECOMMENDED VERSIONS

Duke Ellington (recorded as "Jam Session"), Hollywood, late November or early December 1941

Charlie Parker, live at Washington Music Hall, Washington, D.C., May 23, 1948

Louis Armstrong and Duke Ellington (recorded as "Duke's Place"), from *The Great Summit*, New York, April 3, 1961

Oscar Peterson, from *Night Train*, Los Angeles, December 16, 1962

McCoy Tyner (recorded as "Duke's Place"), from *McCoy Tyner Plays Duke Ellington*, Englewood Cliffs, New Jersey, December 7–8, 1964

Joe Venuti and Zoot Sims, from *Joe and Zoot*, New York, September 27, 1973

Charles Mingus, from *Mingus at Carnegie Hall*, live at Carnegie Hall, New York, January 19, 1974

Cantaloupe Island
Composed by Herbie Hancock

When jazz players want to poke fun at rock and roll musicians, they ridicule their "three-chord" songs. But, here, Herbie Hancock constructs a taut composition built on just three chords, and no one will demean this gem. (And to prove it wasn't a fluke, Hancock almost did it again the following year with a brilliant four-chord song—the title track to his classic *Maiden Voyage* release.)

Occasionally a bandleader feels compelled to enhance the stark harmonic structure. Poncho Sanchez, who uses this song as the opening track for his 2009 release *Psychadelic Blues*, adds in passing chords and unexpected modulations. Or, in the most famous case, a rap group, Us3, founded in London in 1991 superimposed their chants and musical overdubs onto a cut-and-paste sample of Hancock's original. The result was a million-copy seller and the first Blue Note release to go platinum.

I don't dismiss this Us3 recording as many jazz purists do. It is effective, even if parasitical on the original track. But I also give the nod to some lesser known covers, especially a fine version by Milton Nascimento with the composer on piano and Pat Metheny joining in on guitar, and a very spacey, 14-minute Hancock solo electric keyboard interpretation from an obscure 1974 album (*Dedication*) that was released in Japan and all but unknown in other markets.

That said, it's hard to top the original recording. Hancock's piano vamp is the key hook here—and also the reason, in my opinion, for Us3's success. But Freddie Hubbard's trumpet solo is just as compelling, and one of his career highlights. If you compare tempos, you will note that Hancock took this song much slower than most of the cover versions, and this gave Hubbard the chance to start out in a pensive mood before superimposing his syncopated double-time licks in the second chorus.

Because of the simple chord structure and slow pace of harmonic movement—the chords each last for at least four bars—this is a suitable song to teach student musicians. It allows them to develop some funk and hard bop phraseology on an unthreatening chart that can be taken down to a very slow tempo without losing the groove.

RECOMMENDED VERSIONS

Herbie Hancock (with Freddie Hubbard), from *Empyrean Isles*, Englewood Cliffs, New Jersey, June 17, 1964

Herbie Hancock, from *Dedication*, Tokyo, July 29, 1974

Mark Murphy, from *Mark Murphy Sings The Red Clay, Naima and Other Great Songs*, New York, June 17–19, 1975

Herbie Hancock, Freddie Hubbard and Joe Henderson, from *One Night with Blue Note Preserved*, live at Town Hall, New York, February 22, 1985

Us3 (recorded as "Cantaloop (Flip Fantasia)"), from *Hand on the Torch*, London, no date given (CD released in 1993)

Milton Nascimento (with Herbie Hancock and Pat Metheny), from *Pietà*, New York, no date given (CD released in 2005)

Poncho Sanchez, from *Psychadelic Blues*, Los Angeles, no date given (CD released in 2009)

Caravan
Composed by Juan Tizol and Duke Ellington, with lyrics by Irving Mills

The popularity of this song has been steadily on the rise in the jazz world during the last several decades, so much so that "Caravan" is now one of the most commonly covered "Ellington" songs. I attribute this state of affairs to the composition's adaptability to a modernistic, modal-based approach. The main theme relies on a vamp that is well suited for a wide gamut of post-bop and Coltrane-esque performance styles. A horn player who has been working over modal licks and scales all day in the practice room can call this at the gig and immediately try out all of the tricks of the trade, in a way that just wouldn't be possible with, say, "Sophisticated Lady" or "Mood Indigo."

The main theme of this composition was contributed by Juan Tizol, not Ellington, nor was Duke the first bandleader to record it. "Caravan" first shows up as a small combo feature for Barney Bigard and His Jazzopators, with Ellington on piano—one of a series of tracks released during this period under the ostensible leadership of sidemen in Duke's ensemble. Tizol himself did not appreciate the commercial potential of his song, at least at first. He sold his rights to Irving Mills for a flat fee of $25—although when he complained after the tune became a hit, Mills gave him a cut of the royalties. Ellington, for his part, understood the appeal of "Caravan" almost from the start, especially since it fit perfectly with the musical exoticism that patrons were demanding at his regular gig at the Cotton Club in Harlem. A few months after the Bigard recording, the song shows up on a radio broadcast from that establishment in March 1937, and Duke brought it to the studio for a New York recording session in May. Both the combo and big band version were top 20 hits, and Ellington kept "Caravan" in the band's book for the rest of his life. He left behind more than 100 recordings of it, including one made just a few weeks before his death in 1974.

Fans of this work will find no shortage of outstanding renditions. Mid-1950s recordings from Thelonious Monk, Art Tatum, Willie "The Lion" Smith, and Nat King Cole indicate the wide range of interpretative stances available to a performer. Art Blakey's 1962 hard bop treatment served as the title track of an outstanding release for the Riverside label, which showcases what is arguably the finest lineup in the history of the Jazz Messengers: Wayne Shorter, Freddie Hubbard, and Curtis Fuller in the front line, and Cedar Walton and Reggie Workman joining Blakey in the rhythm section. Two years later, Wes Montgomery relied on "Caravan" as the opening track for his *Movin' Wes* album, which became the biggest selling release to date in the guitarist's career. In 1974, when Dizzy Gillespie and Oscar Peterson teamed up in London to record their Grammy-winning duet album, "Caravan" was also their choice for an opening track. Three years later, Art Pepper unleashed a blistering 14-minute rendition, with Elvin Jones in the rhythm section, on his much-admired live recording at the Village Vanguard. Wynton Marsalis's performance from 1986 ranks among the finest tracks from his mid-career oeuvre.

I don't anticipate the popularity of this song to fade any time soon. It works as a loose jam session song, and is also adaptable to very stylized arrangements evoking any number of moods. The changes are easy enough for even intermediate players to handle, and the melody still sounds modernistic so many decades after it was composed. Certainly audiences respond to it, but the musicians are even more devoted to the song, assuring it a prominent place in set lists for the foreseeable future.

RECOMMENDED VERSIONS

Barney Bigard and His Jazzopators (with Duke Ellington and Juan Tizol), Hollywood, December 19, 1936

Duke Ellington, New York, May 14, 1937

Art Tatum, Los Angeles, April–July 1940

Dizzy Gillespie (with Stuff Smith), October 25, 1951

Thelonious Monk, from *Thelonious Monk Plays Duke Ellington*, Hackensack, New Jersey, July 27, 1955

Nat King Cole (with Juan Tizol), from *After Midnight*, Los Angeles, September 14, 1956

Art Blakey (with Freddie Hubbard and Wayne Shorter), from *Caravan*, New York, October 23, 1962

Wes Montgomery, from *Movin' Wes*, New York, November 16, 1964

Dizzy Gillespie and Oscar Peterson, from *Oscar Peterson & Dizzy Gillespie*, London, November 28–29, 1974

Art Pepper, from *Friday Night at the Village Vanguard*, live at the Village Vanguard, New York, July 29, 1977

Wynton Marsalis, from *Marsalis Standard Time, Vol. 1*, New York, May 29–30, 1986, and September 24–25, 1986

Medeski, Martin, and Wood, from *Notes from the Underground*, New York, December 15–16, 1991; and Hoboken, January 23, 1992

Michel Camilo, from *Rendezvous*, New York, January 18–20, 1993

Gonzalo Rubalcaba, from *Inner Voyage*, New York, November 23–25, 1998

Chelsea Bridge
Composed by Billy Strayhorn

During its first decade, "Chelsea Bridge" found few advocates except for the composer's employer, Duke Ellington, who gave the song its debut in 1941. But Ben Webster, who was tenor soloist with that illustrious edition of the Ellington orchestra, recorded the song several times during the 1950s and 1960s and even delivered an ethereal performance on television. His appearance on *Jazz from Studio 61* took place on the same day that Miles Davis, then in the midst of re-cording *Kind of Blue*, visited the same CBS studio to perform "So What" for TV viewers. "Chelsea Bridge" stayed in Webster's repertoire for the rest of his career, and he must be given credit for doing even more than Ellington to estab-lish it as a widely played jazz standard.

The song was a perfect match for Webster's musical persona, starting from its lazy opening phrase with the slow triplet before the first downbeat, and remains an ideal vehicle for tenorists of his school, well suited to their predilec-tion for lingering behind the beat. Strayhorn is rather daring in dwelling so long on the flat fifth in the melody, used here less as a blue note and more as an impressionistic color tone, with appropriate harmonies to accentuate this quality. The result is a distinctively modern-sounding art song, with very little in common with the typical pop ballads of its era.

I doubt this piece could have been turned into a hit record, even back in the 1940s when popular music often incorporated advanced harmonic thinking, but I am hardly surprised that the song (like several other Strayhorn ballads) became so popular with jazz musicians in subsequent decades. Jazz composers and big band arrangers of the postwar years have cited this composition as an important influence. "From the moment I heard 'Chelsea Bridge,' I set out to try to do that," Gil Evans has commented. "That's all I did—that's all I ever did—try to do what Billy Strayhorn did."

Chelsea Bridge, located on the Thames in North London, might seem an unusual landmark to commemorate in song for a composer best known for celebrating the A Train in Harlem. But Strayhorn had apparently been inspired by a painting of Battersea Bridge—probably the Whistler on display at the Tate in London, although some have suggested a Turner canvas served as impetus for the song—and successfully managed to convey a comparable misty impres-sionism via his languorous melody and the soft edges of his harmonies.

Lyrics were added in 1958 by Bill Comstock, later a member of the Four Freshmen, but the song is more often favored by saxophonists and pianists than by vocalists; even when singers tackle it, many (such as Ella Fitzgerald and Cassandra Wilson) have performed it as a wordless vocal, relying on breathy oohs and ahs. The composer himself rarely led recording sessions, but did perform a moving solo piano version in 1961 for *The Peaceful Side of Billy Strayhorn*.

RECOMMENDED VERSIONS

Duke Ellington (with Billy Strayhorn replacing Ellington on piano), Hollywood, December 2, 1941

Ben Webster, for the CBS television show *Jazz from Studio 61*, New York, April 2, 1959

Gerry Mulligan and Ben Webster, from *Gerry Mulligan Meets Ben Webster*, Los
Angeles, November 3, 1959

Billy Strayhorn, from *The Peaceful Side of Billy Strayhorn*, Paris, May 1961

David Murray, from *Tenors*, New York, January 1988

Cassandra Wilson, from *She Who Weeps*, Brooklyn, October–December 1990

Joe Lovano (unaccompanied saxophone), from *Rush Hour*, New York, June 12, 1994

Keith Jarrett (with the Standards Trio), from *Whisper Not*, live at Palais de Congrès,
Paris, July 5, 1999

Jim Hall and Bill Frisell, from *Hemispheres*, New York, September 9, 2008

Cherokee
Composed by Ray Noble

During the 1940s, "Cherokee" became a show-off piece for beboppers. The song, which had previously served as a medium tempo interlude of bogus world music for the Charlie Barnet band—sort of an ersatz Native American counterpart to Duke Ellington's "Caravan" or Tommy Dorsey's "Song of India"—had now morphed into an up-tempo sparring number for jazz progressives. Even so, the song never had much connection with America's first residents, and the fact that it was composed by British-born Ray Noble (for his 1938 "Indian Suite") did little to enhance its authenticity as an anthem for the Cherokee Nation.

The lyrics, which express deep passion for a sweet Indian maiden, are best left unheard, and in any case are a mismatch with the extremely fast tempo at which this song is usually played nowadays. Barnet certainly managed to succeed without them, parlaying "Cherokee" into an instrumental hit that reached as high as number 15 on the pop charts in 1939. Even earlier, Count Basie had recorded the song in a two-part version that may not have sold as well as Barnet's but more closely anticipates the future evolution of the song into a virtuoso solo vehicle.

The melody is simple enough, mostly whole and half notes, but the rapid modulations of the chords in the bridge present a serious challenge to a soloist, especially when the tempo goes beyond 300 beats per minute. I've heard bands tackle this song at even faster paces, sometimes approaching the 400 beats per minute mark, at which speed "Cherokee" becomes more of a test for the rapid repetition of rote licks than a platform for creative improvisation.

An early recording of Charlie Parker from his Kansas City days finds him showing off his newfound musical maturity in three full choruses of "Cherokee." Although Parker is closely associated with this song—he once claimed that he achieved a breakthrough in improvising off the "higher intervals of the chord" after working over this song during a Harlem jam session in December 1939—he didn't play it very often in public. He never recorded it during any of his studio dates as a bandleader. The closest he came was with "Ko-Ko," a blistering workout over the chord changes to "Cherokee," which he recorded alongside Dizzy Gillespie at a session for the Savoy label in 1945. A few live versions of Parker performing "Cherokee" in concert have survived, but usually when he was playing with musicians outside his typical cadre of sidemen.

Most of the leading modern jazz stars of the postwar years tackled this song at one time or another. Bud Powell's 1949 rendition, with its clever descending passing chords and assertive solo, ranks among his very best recordings. Lennie Niehaus is known for his film scores nowadays, but his extroverted 1955 outing on "Cherokee" while with the Kenton band will remind listeners why his saxophone work caused such a stir when he first arrived on the West Coast scene. Clifford Brown's studio recording of "Cherokee" from that same year is a standout performance by the trumpeter, but his fans may also want to track down a more obscure curio: a practice tape that captures him working over the chords to the Ray Noble standard. The sound quality is poor but this homemade effort provides a fascinating glimpse into how musicians of the era employed "Cherokee" as part of their behind-the-scenes development.

Lee Konitz, who never recorded this song until his mid-forties but then went on to release around 20 different versions, has also shared with us a long solo version of "Cherokee" that, despite its appearance on a commercial album, captures the spirit of a practice-room workout. In that capacity, "Cherokee" still plays an important role in the jazz world, and though you will continue to hear it on record and in concert, I suspect it shows up even more often in the rehearsal rooms at Berklee and other jazz spawning grounds.

RECOMMENDED VERSIONS

Count Basie (with Lester Young), New York, February 3, 1939

Charlie Barnet, New York, July 17, 1939

Charlie Parker, Kansas City, Missouri, probably September 1942

Don Byas, New York, May 17, 1945

Bud Powell, New York, January–February 1949

Clifford Brown, from *A Study in Brown*, New York, February 25, 1955

Stan Kenton (featuring Lennie Niehaus), from *Contemporary Concepts*, July 20, 1955

Johnny Griffin, from *Way Out!*, New York, February 26–27, 1958

Lee Konitz, from *Lone-Lee*, Copenhagen, August 15, 1974

Art Pepper, from *Saturday Night at the Village Vanguard*, live at the Village Vanguard, New York, July 30, 1977

Wynton Marsalis, from *Marsalis Standard Time, Vol. 1*, New York, May 29–30, 1986, and September 24–25, 1986

A Child Is Born
Composed by Thad Jones, with lyrics by Alec Wilder

Thad Jones started writing arrangements at age 13—for his uncle's band—and continued doing so for the next half-century. For this precocious youngster, just getting out of the shadow set by his siblings (older brother Hank and young brother Elvin both became famous jazz stars) presented no small challenge. But Thad Jones would earn his own share of renown, first as performer and arranger with Count Basie, and then as co-leader of his own much admired big band, the Thad Jones–Mel Lewis Orchestra.

Many assume that the band's 1970 treatment of "A Child Is Born," from the album *Consummation*, marked the first recording of the song. But Richard Davis and Roland Hanna can be heard performing it at a session in Germany six months earlier. Hanna even claimed to have been the originator of the piece, which by his account started as a piano interlude he inserted between numbers by the big band—Jones later transforming it into a chart for the orchestra. Yet Hanna undercuts his own authorship claim on his 1969 debut recording, where he can be clearly heard stating into the microphone before playing the song (probably for the benefit of those in the recording booth): "A Child Is Born . . . Thad Jones."

On the *Consummation* version, Jones adopts a chamber jazz attitude for most of the track—opening with just solo piano from Hanna, then adding bass and drums after bar eight. Following the melody statement, Jones enters on flugelhorn and turns the trio into a quartet, but instead of soloing, opts to play the melody one more time. Only then, well over the halfway mark of the track, does the orchestra enter—yet again, they play the melody, in a rich, textured arrangement that brings the song to its conclusion. No improvisation takes place here, yet the performance is perfectly realized.

The song quickly spread through the jazz world, and one can almost track the path of dissemination from the personnel on the early recording dates. A few months after the Thad Jones–Mel Lewis recording, Oscar Peterson featured the song on a solo piano date, and a short while later he played it at a collaborative date with the Singers Unlimited. In 1971, Kenny Burrell delivered a memorable performance amid a large orchestra on his *God Bless the Child* album; Burrell later recorded it with Bill Evans, while Evans in turn would showcase it at his session with Tony Bennett. Several members of the Thad Jones–Mel Lewis band would record "A Child Is Born" on their own albums. One of my favorites finds drummer Lewis leading a small combo on his 1976 date for A&M, where he is without Thad (relying instead on Freddie Hubbard), but with Thad's brother Hank on piano. Hank Jones would eventually record "A Child Is Born" on at least a dozen occasions, including projects with Benny Carter and Joe Lovano. The former, a duet recorded for a Christmas theme album, turns "A Child Is Born" into a nativity song—a connection that others have made, with the result that this ostensibly secular song frequently shows up on holiday season playlists.

The composition is a gem, a 30-bar waltz that builds off a simple motif for the entire piece. What an unpromising formula: a held note in the first bar followed by three upward-moving, on-the-beat notes in the next one. And then the composer relies on the same melodic rhythm in the next two bars . . . and again and again, with few exceptions, for the entire duration of the song. Yet the effect is quite soothing and unlabored—if only childbirth were this relaxing!—and the harmonic movement is satisfying without becoming too predictable. Soon after the song's debut, Alec Wilder contributed lyrics, which are as moving as the music.

RECOMMENDED VERSIONS

Richard Davis and Roland Hanna, from *Muses for Richard Davis*, Villingen, Germany, December 9, 1969

Thad Jones–Mel Lewis Orchestra, from *Consummation*, New York, May 25, 1970

Kenny Burrell, from *God Bless the Child*, New York, April–May 1971

Oscar Peterson and The Singers Unlimited, from *In Tune*, Villingen, Germany, July 5–13, 1971

Bill Evans (with Kenny Burrell and Harold Land), from *Quintessence*, Berkeley, California, May 27–30, 1976

Mel Lewis (with Freddie Hubbard and Hank Jones), from *Mel Lewis and Friends*, New York, June 8–9, 1976

Tony Bennett and Bill Evans, from *Together Again*, San Francisco, September 27–30, 1976

Stanley Turrentine (with George Benson and Jimmy Smith), from *Straight Ahead*, New York, December 7, 1984

Benny Carter and Hank Jones, from *A Jazz Christmas: Hot Jazz for a Cool Night*, New York, June 17, 1992

Joe Lovano and Hank Jones, from *Joyous Encounter*, New York, September 8–9, 2004

Come Rain or Come Shine
Composed by Harold Arlen, with lyrics by Johnny Mercer

This melody couldn't possibly produce a hit, could it? Composer Harold Arlen delivers the same note—flogging an A natural until it is bloody—13 times in a row to start out "Come Rain or Come Shine." And, as if that isn't enough, he tosses out a half-dozen more of the same note in bar five, and another six over the next two bars. This isn't a melody; it's a musical starvation diet.

By the time Arlen lays out 13 Bs in a row in the second ending, you are worried what will happen when he finally gets to C and D. You're now begging for rain, shine, flooding, or typhoon, anything to cut short this exercise in frustrated phraseology. Could this meteorologically-minded composer really be the same tunesmith who gave us the sweeping melodies of "Over the Rainbow" and "Stormy Weather"? Yet—amazingly!—Arlen offers enough harmonic movement to keep me interested. No, this will never be my favorite Harold Arlen song, but he earns my grudging respect as a craftsman who can work with so few notes, such a constrained range, and so few intervallic leaps . . . and still land a spot in the jazz standard repertoire.

Arlen composed "Come Rain or Come Shine" for the 1946 musical *St. Louis Woman*, a controversial Broadway production that some praised for showcasing African-American performers in a story based on a novel by a black author (Arna Bontemps's *God Sends Sunday*). Yet *St. Louis Woman* was also castigated by the NAACP for its stereotyping. The show closed after 113 performances, but left behind this now-famous song, which was quickly embraced by the swing bands of the day.

Given the paucity of melodic material and the richness of the harmonic underpinnings, this composition tends to resist grandstanding, and instead appeals to the more introspective improviser. Recordings by Bill Evans, Stan Getz, and Ralph Towner testify to the pastoral qualities of Arlen's tune. Only a few hard bop players—Art Blakey, Clifford Brown, Sonny Clark—have delivered top-notch versions. But I am even more surprised by the soulful interpretations by Ray Charles and James Brown, which take this song to places I never thought it would visit. But the strangest performance of "Come Rain or Come Shine," hands down, comes from the beatnik bard Jack Kerouac, who garbles the lyrics but actually holds a tune better than most hipster poets in his little-known recording. For once, I was glad that this song was written with such modest demands on the singer.

RECOMMENDED VERSIONS

Tommy Dorsey, New York, January 31, 1946

Clifford Brown, "Take 2," from *The Clifford Brown Quartet in Paris*, Paris, October 15, 1953

Sonny Clark (with John Coltrane), from *Sonny's Crib*, Hackensack, New Jersey, September 1, 1957

Art Blakey (with Lee Morgan), from *Moanin'*, Hackensack, New Jersey, October 30, 1958

Ray Charles, from *The Genius of Ray Charles*, New York, May 6, 1959

Bill Evans (with Scott LaFaro and Paul Motian), from *Portrait in Jazz*, New York, December 28, 1959

Peggy Lee, from *I'm a Woman*, Hollywood, January 5, 1963

James Brown, from *Cold Sweat*, New York, 1964

Stan Getz, from *Pure Getz*, San Francisco, January 29, 1982

Ralph Towner, from *Time Line*, Austria, September 7–8, 2005

Claudio Roditi, from *Impressions*, Rio de Janeiro, January 15, 2006

Come Sunday
Composed by Duke Ellington

In anticipation of his debut concert at Carnegie Hall, Ellington cultivated grand plans for what would prove to be the most ambitious composition of his career, a three-movement work that would be, in his words, "a tone parallel to the history of the Negro in America." On January 23, 1943, Ellington gave *Black, Brown and Beige* its premiere in front of a star-studded audience, which included the First Lady Eleanor Roosevelt, Leopold Stokowski, and reporters from most of the major news outlets. Ellington was already a star, and many fans no doubt realized he also had artistic aspirations that went beyond making hit records, but never before had the bandleader aimed so high and challenged his audience with such a long and complex piece.

Nor would he again. After the Carnegie Hall concert, Ellington would only perform *Black, Brown and Beige* in its entirety once more—five days later in Boston. When one counts the preview performance, held at a high school the day before the Carnegie Hall event, the total complete public renditions by Ellington of this important composition stand at only three. The critics' mixed appraisals—filled with opinions on what Ellington *ought* to do, and less skilled at comprehending what he had actually done—clearly gave him pause. He would never produce such a big work again, and even when he recorded *Black, Brown and Beige* it would be after extensive pruning and trimming. Sometimes sections of the work would find their way into one of his performances or albums, but for the most part only one snippet of this daring work would have a robust life outside of the longer work and enter the ranks of jazz standards.

That would be "Come Sunday," built on a typical AABA song form, and originally featured in the opening "Black" movement of the longer work. At Carnegie Hall, Johnny Hodges's alto was showcased during this interlude—a rare moment for an individual band member to stand out in this mostly ensemble-oriented magnum opus—and he takes a full two minutes just to state the 32-bar melody. Jazz critic Leonard Feather, in attendance at the concert as well as at rehearsals, would later remark that Hodges's contribution here ranked among "the most exquisite moments of music ever heard on a concert stage."

Ellington was obviously pleased with "Come Sunday," even as he reconsidered *Black, Brown and Beige* as a whole. He recorded it as a stand-alone track for the Victor label in December 1944, and during this period he often featured the song in performance—not in dance halls, where he probably felt "Come Sunday" would be out of place, but on occasions when his band was hired for a concert-hall engagement. It can be heard on live recordings from the Philharmonic Auditorium in Los Angeles, the Hollywood Bowl, and the Civic Opera House in Chicago and other similarly highbrow venues. When Ellington was asked to perform a memorial concert to honor Franklin Delano Roosevelt, which was broadcast on the radio two days after the president's death, he again drew on "Come Sunday."

In 1958, Ellington relaunched a streamlined *Black, Brown and Beige*, and gave "Come Sunday" a prominent place—both as an instrumental and as a vocal feature for gospel singer Mahalia Jackson. Trumpeter Ray Nance claimed he cried the first time he heard Jackson sing this piece, while Ellington, who had expressed doubts about the adequacy of the lyrics he had penned for the song, was so moved after his first session with Jackson, that he asked her to repeat her performance the following day, not for the record but as a favor for him—which she proceeded to do, with the lights dimmed in the studio and the band members serving as hushed audience.

Ellington later noted, in a passing aside in his autobiography, "This encounter with Mahalia Jackson had a strong influence on me and my sacred music." Given the growing importance of religious themes in Ellington's work during the final years of his life, one should not underestimate the significance of this moment in his career. "Come Sunday" would be transformed as a result. The song that was originally featured when he wanted to impress serious listeners at his concert-hall engagements now became a work for Ellington to play at church. Few were surprised when this prayerful piece turned up on the program for Ellington's first Sacred Concert, which took place at San Francisco's Grace Cathedral in October 1962.

Given the history of this song—which Ellington seemed intent to keep out of nightclubs and dance halls—you might think that it would never make much headway as a jazz standard. And, true, it took a long time before jazz players embraced "Come Sunday." Around 1946, Gerald Wilson added "Come Sunday" to his band's repertoire at a time when, as far as I can tell, no other big band, except for Ellington's, was performing it. Yet the inherent beauty of the melody and the satisfying development of the harmonic progression would eventually gain adherents. Ellington's recording with Mahalia Jackson finally gave the song the nudge it needed, and over the next few years, a number of jazz stars of varying styles and generations—including Dizzy Gillespie, Joe Zawinul, Eric Dolphy, Abbey Lincoln, Oscar Peterson, Carmen McRae, and Stan Getz—began performing it.

Most subsequent recordings follow in the footsteps of Ellington's example of how "Come Sunday" should be performed. And if Duke's songs, especially the slow moody ones, inspire reverential interpretations, this quasi-spiritual tends to be treated with more decorum than most. But renditions by Eric Dolphy, Eric Reed, and Randy Weston show that you can push at the edges of "Come Sunday" while still respecting Ellington's original vision of a piece that connects with both our aesthetic and spiritual sensibilities.

RECOMMENDED VERSIONS

Duke Ellington (from *Black, Brown and Beige*), live at Carnegie Hall, New York, January 23, 1943

Gerald Wilson, Hollywood, circa April 1946

Duke Ellington (with Mahalia Jackson), from *Black, Brown and Beige*, Los Angeles, February 1958

Abbey Lincoln, from *Abbey Is Blue*, New York, March 25, 1959

Dizzy Gillespie, from *A Portrait of Duke Ellington*, New York, April 27–28, 1960

Eric Dolphy (with Richard Davis), from *Iron Man*, New York, July 1, 1963

Joe Zawinul, from *Nippon Soul* (a Cannonball Adderley album, but Adderley does not appear on this track), live at Sankei Hall, Tokyo, July 15, 1963

Andrew Hill, from *Live at Montreux*, live at the Montreux Jazz Festival, Montreux, Switzerland, July 20, 1975

Randy Weston from *Ancient Future*, New York, June 2001

Eric Reed, from *Mercy and Grace*, New York, October 29, 2001

Con Alma
Composed by Dizzy Gillespie

The beboppers of the 1940s frequently borrowed chord changes from older songs for their new compositions. Dizzy Gillespie did just this on many occasions, taking the harmonies for his "Groovin' High," first recorded in 1945, from "Whispering," a hit for Paul Whiteman back in 1920, and relying on changes from "I Got Rhythm" (1930) for the solo sections in "Salt Peanuts" and "Dizzy Atmosphere," first recorded in 1944 and 1945, respectively.

Yet Gillespie did not need hand-me-downs in order to compose some of his most characteristic works. "Con Alma" is smartly constructed, with no borrowings from previous songs. I could envision this elegant, compact work studied by aspiring composers: the melody line is simple enough, much of it built on repeated half notes, but Gillespie shows great ingenuity in the textures he uses to support and enliven these bare-bones phrases. Long before he wrote "Con Alma," Gillespie had relied on descending basslines when trying to capture a Latin or exotic mood, as he had demonstrated in pieces such as "Night in Tunisia" and "Tin Tin Deo." But in the former composition, this device is restricted to an intricate interlude that is not intended for soloing, while in the latter work the harmonic movement is fairly conventional. "Con Alma," in contrast, offers a more complex workout for improvisers over a taut structure.

In the debut recording from 1954, the Latin groove is very much dominant throughout the performance—Gillespie is the only non-Hispanic member of the band, and though his trumpet solo is first rate, even the sound balance seems to favor the percussion. Three and a half years later, the composer brought "Con Alma" back into the studio for an exciting matchup with Sonny Stitt, and this version is looser and more focused on the soloists. Sad to say, Sonny Rollins was in the studio for the session but did not join in on this track: I would have enjoyed hearing him in this context. Gillespie continued to record "Con Alma" in various settings, from intimate duets to big band blowouts, for the rest of his career—one of the better late-career interpretations find him in a London studio with just Oscar Peterson as accompanist.

In truth, "Con Alma" does not need to be played with a Latin beat in order to be effective. Listen to Stan Getz's excellent recording with Chick Corea from 1967, and pay attention to the contrasting and evolving rhythmic conceptions of the different members of the band. Drummer Grady Tate shows a fleeting allegiance here to an Afro-Cuban sensibility, but pianist Corea sounds as if he wants to push the band into a more open 6/8 rhythm. Ron Carter, for his part, plays some of the same games he had mastered as a member of the Miles Davis quintet, moving back and forth from triple to duple conceptions of time. Getz thrives in this labyrinth, delivering a poised, fluid solo, yet before the performance concludes the beat has changed so markedly that the tenorist is exchanging fours with Tate in a straight swing rhythm.

Charles McPherson takes an even odder approach on his 1965 recording of "Con Alma." At times the rhythm section falls into an on-the-beat march, elsewhere a two-beat strut, but the one thing the band clearly avoids is the slightest hint of a Latin rhythm. When George Shearing tackled "Con Alma" on his 2004 record *Like Fine Wine*, he adopted an almost classically baroque sensibility, and the beauty of Gillespie's composition is that it adapts easily to this conception, just as it does to the hotter approaches of Tito Puente or Randy Weston. It's a real treat to hear the latter's forceful piano interpretation of this song, supported by African percussion played by his son Azzedin "Niles" Weston and Anthony "Reebop" Kwaku Baah.

In addition to test-driving this song with different underlying pulses, advanced students will find this a useful piece for developing their transposition skills. For a practice-room exercise, I would suggest starting "Con Alma" in the original key, and then transposing down a half-step after every chorus. The turnaround naturally lends itself to this modulation and such an approach could even enliven a public performance.

RECOMMENDED VERSIONS

Dizzy Gillespie, from *Manteca*, New York, June 3, 1954

Dizzy Gillespie (with Sonny Stitt), from *Duets*, New York, December 11, 1957

Charles McPherson (with Clifford Jordan and Barry Harris), from *Con Alma*, Englewood Cliffs, New Jersey, August 6, 1965

Stan Getz (with Chick Corea), from *Sweet Rain*, Englewood Cliffs, New Jersey, March 30, 1967

Randy Weston, from *African Cookbook*, Paris, June 1969

Oscar Peterson and Dizzy Gillespie, from *Oscar Peterson and Dizzy Gillespie*, London, November 28–29, 1974

Tito Puente, from *Salsa Meets Jazz*, San Francisco, January 27–28, 1988

George Shearing, from *Like Fine Wine*, New York, October 27–28, 2003

Karrin Allyson (recorded as "Something Worth Waiting For (Con Alma)"), from *Footprints*, New York, September 24–29, 2005

Confirmation
Composed by Charlie Parker

Most compositions by Charlie Parker either borrow their chord changes from familiar popular songs or follow a 12-bar blues pattern. But "Confirmation," as with "Con Alma" above, is a wholly original work. Don Maggin, for his part, has called it Parker's "most beautiful composition." I am not sure that "beauty" is the first word I would reach for—it's more a slap in the face than a gentle caress—but I would call attention to its ingenuity, especially in its exposition of Parker's approach to ii–V substitute changes, and his melody, which balances conventional motivic development with the free flow of bop improvisation.

I marvel at a piece that can sound so highly structured and spontaneous at the same time. In the last half of the bridge, the song almost seems ready to depart from any written chart and leap into the solos right there—that's the moment at which you will be forced to stop humming along with the tune, because the speed and intervals involved will leave even seasoned bop fans tongue-tied—before settling down for a final repeat of the A theme. This is heady stuff, and especially so given the context of Swing Era riff songs and more hook-driven pop tunes of the period in which it was written.

Because Parker didn't bring this song to a commercial session until 1953, many fans assume that it is one of his later works. In fact, the piece must date from almost a decade earlier. Dizzy Gillespie (using the alias "Gabriel" for contractual reasons) made the debut recording of "Confirmation" back in February 1946, when he fronted a band that also showcased vibraphonist Milt Jackson playing one of his earliest recorded modern jazz solos. Producer Ross Russell very much wanted to feature Parker at this session, but the altoist had gone AWOL from his West Coast band by then—another vanishing act during an especially unstable period of the artist's career. Yet even this Parker-less performance, little known nowadays, is well worth hearing. It is likely that "Confirmation" was in the regular repertoire of the band that Parker and Gillespie brought to Los Angeles in 1945–46, and the song shows up again on their playlist for the duo's September 1947 Carnegie Hall concert, where Bird contributes his finest recorded solo on this number. Finally, in the summer of 1953, Parker brought "Confirmation" to a New York studio date for Norman Granz, where the altoist delivered the studio performance of this piece that is probably best known among jazz fans today.

I especially enjoy covers of this song made by artists who had played with Charlie Parker. Less than a year after Parker's studio rendition, Art Blakey recorded a dramatic version live at Birdland, featuring Clifford Brown, Lou Donaldson, and Horace Silver—all playing at peak form. I also call attention to *The Bop Session*, a 1975 project that finds Sonny Stitt—in my opinion, the saxophonist of the era most capable of taking on the mantle of Parker—working alongside Dizzy Gillespie, John Lewis, and Max Roach, and staking his own claim to this bop standard.

John Coltrane relied on "Confirmation" as the inspiration for his piece "26-2" recorded in 1960. Here Coltrane incorporates some of the harmonic innovations he was exploring, around this same time, in his compositions "Giant Steps" and "Countdown." I suspect that Parker would have been delighted by this tribute. As a final curio, I point you in the direction of Michael Brecker's workout on "Confirmation" from the 1981 session for Chick Corea's *Three Quartets* release—a track left off the initial LP release but included in the CD reissue. At first hearing you might think that Corea does not appear on this piece, because no piano or keyboard is featured, but he is playing drums on this informal and very hot duet performance of Parker's tune.

This song is less frequently played in recent years, as the once transformational bebop movement becomes more and more a historical relic or dim memory for the current crop of players. Yet if a young musician were interested in studying Charlie Parker at close hand, and wanted to learn a few of his songs, I would put "Confirmation" and "Donna Lee" at the top of the list. They encapsulate many of the innovations of bop in their compact 32-bar forms and can almost serve as a primer in modern jazz phrase construction.

RECOMMENDED VERSIONS

Dizzy Gillespie, Glendale, California, February 6, 1946

Charlie Parker and Dizzy Gillespie, live at Carnegie Hall, New York, September 29, 1947

Charlie Parker, New York, July 28, 1953

Art Blakey (with Clifford Brown), from *A Night at Birdland*, live at Birdland, New York, February 21, 1954

Dizzy Gillespie and Sonny Stitt, from *The Bop Session*, New York, May 19–20, 1975

Hank Jones, from *Bop Redux*, New York, January 18–19, 1977

Eddie Jefferson, from *The Main Man*, New York, October 9, 1977

Michael Brecker (with Chick Corea on drums), from *Three Quartets*, Los Angeles, January/February 1981

Billy Hart (with Mark Turner and Ethan Iverson), from *Quartet*, Easton, Connecticut, October 2005

Corcovado
Composed by Antonio Carlos Jobim (English lyrics by Gene Lees)

"Corcovado," which translates as "hunchback," is the name of the mountain overlooking Rio de Janeiro, a 700-meter peak capped by an almost 40-meter statue of Jesus Christ—*Cristo Redentor*, or Christ the Redeemer, a symbol of the city and a defining landmark of modern-day Brazil. But when Gene Lees wrote English lyrics to Jobim's song, he decided that hit songs need something other than a mountain, hunchback, or Jesus Christ in the title, and renamed "Corcovado" as "Quiet Nights of Quiet Stars," often shortened to "Quiet Nights."

The new title is an apt one. The song evokes a tranquil mood, driven by a series of calming phrases that move down and up a whole step. All in all, "Corcovado" could work as a lullaby, even the two big interval leaps in bars 25 and 27 hardly disturb the quiescent ambiance. Perhaps the mood was too understated for radio listeners. This serene song only had modest success on the airwaves, with Andy Williams stalling out at number 92 on the *Billboard* chart in December 1965.

Jobim wrote a lovely six-bar intro that performers often leave out—especially singers, perhaps because the composer did not provide lyrics for this section of the piece. Yet a lot of feeling is compacted into these bars, and they effectively set the emotional temperature for the rest of the song. If you have any doubts about how much the composer liked this passage, listen to the initial recording of "Corcovado," made under Jobim's supervision and featuring singer João Gilberto, where the opening section shows up again at the end of the track—and, in aggregate, accounts for almost half of the performance. Jobim also stretches out the form, with an elongated coda that serves both as a path back to the A minor that opens the work or, in a surprising conclusion employed in most jazz arrangements of this song, to C major for a final resolve at the end of the performance. The resolution in major was a later addition, not present on the debut recording, but an effective twist nonetheless.

Although "Corcovado" never had much traction as a single, Stan Getz's version is featured on his best-selling *Getz/Gilberto* album, and is no doubt the best-known treatment of this song. Miles Davis also featured the composition as the title track of his 1963 *Quiet Nights* collaboration with Gil Evans. The trumpeter was unhappy with the release of what he felt was an unfinished project, yet this version of "Corcovado" ranks among the finest jazz realizations of bossa nova material, lyrical yet avoiding the saccharine qualities that turn so many Jobim covers into kitschy easy listening music.

The song has been frequently recorded in later years, but with few performances that live up to these precedents. Two of the better versions feature the composer as accompanist. Frank Sinatra included "Quiet Nights" on his *Francis Albert Sinatra & Antonio Carlos Jobim* album from 1967, but a better (albeit too brief) performance, with just voice and guitar, can be heard on the singer's 1967 TV special. Elis Regina, for her part, is hardly as well known as Sinatra, but she is a legend in her native Brazil, and her 1974 collaboration with Jobim is a much-beloved classic of bossa nova music.

RECOMMENDED VERSIONS

João Gilberto, from *The Legendary João Gilberto*, Rio de Janeiro, March 30, 1960

Miles Davis (with Gil Evans), from *Quiet Nights*, New York, July 27, 1962

Cannonball Adderley (with Sérgio Mendes), from *Cannonball's Bossa Nova*, New York, December 7, 1962

Stan Getz (with João Gilberto), from *Getz/Gilberto*, New York, March 18–19, 1963

Frank Sinatra (with Antonio Carlos Jobim), from the NBC-TV special *A Man and His Music + Ella + Jobim*, taped October 1–3, 1967, Burbank, California, broadcast on November 13, 1967

Elis Regina and Antonio Carlos Jobim, from *Elis & Tom*, Los Angeles, February–March 1974

Cotton Tail
Composed by Duke Ellington

This is both one of Duke Ellington's finest compositions and also perhaps his most uncharacteristic. Honestly, "Cotton Tail" has more in common with the songs that would be composed during the 1940s by the young revolutionaries of the bebop generation—Charlie Parker, Dizzy Gillespie, Thelonious Monk, Bud Powell—than with the Swing Era stylings of Ellington and his contemporaries. So much so, that if someone had told me that the Duke had been inspired to compose this piece after spending an evening at Minton's (the epicenter of the new bop movement) in the company of his bop-leaning bassist Jimmy Blanton, I could be convinced of the genealogy. But since this piece was recorded a few months *before* Thelonious Monk & Co. radicalized the house band at Minton's, I am forced to conclude that the Duke came up with this gem without any help from the younger generation.

Yet here are all the usual bebop ingredients. We have a fast jam-oriented song based on chord changes from "I Got Rhythm." We have an intricate melody line, drenched in chromaticism—in particular, check out the progressivism of bars seven and eight—and, in toto, more reminiscent of Parker's "Moose the Mooche" (1946) than "Solitude" or "In a Sentimental Mood." Given the prickly modernism of the melody, I am not surprised that this piece, unlike the other Ellington standards featured in this volume, never found much favor as a vocal number, even though the composer added his own lyrics (as did, years later, Jon Hendricks). This song is best realized as a showpiece for instrumentalists, and any attempt to turn it into another Ellington mood number for singers is swimming against the current.

And the improvisers have risen to the occasion. Ben Webster's tenor outing on Ellington's debut recording from May 1940 is his most famous solo of the era, studied by other saxophonists as a model for working through "Rhythm" changes. Webster returned to the song on a number of later occasions, and it continued to inspire him—as demonstrated at Carnegie Hall in 1943, on his 1953 *King of the Tenors* project, or his collaboration with Ella Fitzgerald from her Ellington songbook project. Other worthy performances include Terry Gibbs's hard-swinging workout on an Al Cohn chart with his "Dream Band" from 1959, Wes Montgomery's combo performance with Hank Jones from 1961, and a pull-out-the-stops jam by Wayne Shorter and Herbie Hancock from 1998.

RECOMMENDED VERSIONS

Duke Ellington, Hollywood, May 4, 1940

Duke Ellington, live at the Crystal Ballroom, Fargo, North Dakota, November 7, 1940

Duke Ellington, live at Carnegie Hall, New York, January 23, 1943

Ben Webster (with Oscar Peterson), from *King of the Tenors*, New York, May 21, 1953

Terry Gibbs (with arrangement by Al Cohn), from *Dream Band*, live at the Seville, Hollywood, March 17–19, 1959

Wes Montgomery (with Hank Jones), from *So Much Guitar!*, New York, August 4, 1961

Herbie Hancock (with Wayne Shorter), from *Gershwin's World*, New York and Los Angeles, March–June 1998

Darn That Dream

D

Composed by Jimmy Van Heusen, with lyrics by Eddie DeLange

Blame it on Shakespeare! The 1939 show *Swingin' the Dream*, based on *A Midsummer Night's Dream*, closed after only 13 performances and lost $100,000—serious money back in the 1930s. You certainly can't blame the jazz. Check out the talent: Louis Armstrong as Bottom; Maxine Sullivan as Titania; Butterfly McQueen as Puck; the Dandridge Sisters as fairies; onstage music by Benny Goodman and his sextet (including Lionel Hampton and Fletcher Henderson), as well as a second group featuring Bud Freeman, Pee Wee Russell, and Eddie Condon; and the creative team behind the show counted Agnes De Mille and Walt Disney in its ranks. And it closed within two weeks? Lord, what fools these audiences be!

Maybe the public wasn't ready for a fully integrated cast or a Shakespeare story set in nineteenth-century New Orleans. Yet the precedents of *The Boys from Syracuse*, a 1938 hit based on Shakespeare's *The Comedy of Errors; The Hot Mikado*, an African-American take on Gilbert and Sullivan, which proved to be a big attraction at the New York World's Fair in 1939 and 1940; and, of course, *Porgy and Bess* (1935), would have suggested a more receptive audience for this ambitious show. But Brooks Atkinson, writing in *The New York Times*, dismissed *Swingin' the Dream* as a "hodge-podge of Shakespeariana," and other first-hand accounts stress the incoherence and disorganization of the whole, rather than any problem with the individual parts.

Only a small fragment of the script has survived, but one of the songs has enjoyed an illustrious post-show history. Who would have guessed that the most lasting success of this star-studded musical would come from one of its least known contributors? Just a year before, Jimmy Van Heusen had been working as a staff pianist for Tin Pan Alley publishers, and had only shown the slightest hints of the talent that would eventually garner him 14 Academy Award nominations and four Oscars. But "Darn That Dream" has become more popular with jazz performers than any of these film hits.

Even before the show closed, two leading swing bands—Benny Goodman's and Tommy Dorsey's—recorded "Darn That Dream." Both versions sold well, and Goodman's, featuring Mildred Bailey on vocals, reached the top of the chart. The song fell out of circulation during the 1940s, but Miles Davis later revived it for his *Birth of the Cool* band and it has stayed in the jazz repertoire ever since. Ahmad Jamal, who often influenced Davis's choice of songs, followed the trumpeter's lead in this instance; he recorded "Darn That Dream" in 1955 and 1962, and a 1959 video clip of Jamal performing the song for a CBS television show, widely available on the Internet, is one of my favorite examples of jazz on film. Other memorable renditions of the standard include recordings by Billie Holiday, Thelonious Monk, and Dexter Gordon.

I've recorded it myself, and was attracted to the song because of Van Heusen's skill in building sturdy harmonic structures with minimal reliance on conventional circle-of-fifths movement. The melody, filled with spacious interval leaps that move up in thirds and fourths, effectively matches the yearning sentiments of the words. The bridge is a bit of a letdown after such a lively main theme, but works well in context as a sedate interlude before the finale, in which the lyrics both bless and curse dreamtime visions of romantic bliss.

Even song connoisseur Alec Wilder, who had good reasons to hate Van Heusen's tune—Wilder had written an entire score for the same show, but it was never used—praises the spirit of "sophistication and chance-taking" this song represents, and suggests that it was only the pervasiveness of jazz in American culture at the time that allowed listeners to accept such a daring composition. By the same token, I find it almost inconceivable that a song this complex could receive significant airplay or sales nowadays.

RECOMMENDED VERSIONS

Benny Goodman (with Mildred Bailey), New York, November 22, 1939

Miles Davis, from *Birth of the Cool*, New York, March 9, 1950

Ahmad Jamal, from *Chamber Music of the New Jazz*, Chicago, May 23, 1955

Dexter Gordon, from *Daddy Plays the Horn*, Hollywood, September 18, 1955

Billie Holiday, from *Body and Soul*, Los Angeles, January 7, 1957

Ahmad Jamal, for the CBS television show *Jazz from Studio 61*, New York, April 2, 1959

Stan Kenton (with arrangement by Lennie Niehaus), from *Sophisticated Approach*, Hollywood, July 5, 1961

Thelonious Monk, from *Solo Monk*, New York, March 2, 1965

Charles McPherson (with Mulgrew Miller), from *Come Play with Me*, New York,
    March 2, 1995

Days of Wine and Roses
Composed by Henry Mancini and Johnny Mercer

This Oscar-winning song, from the 1962 movie of the same name, reached the
Billboard charts twice in 1963, with separate versions by Henry Mancini and
Andy Williams making brief appearances in the top 40. Around this same time,
Perry Como added his own cloying, string-enhanced version, and "Days of
Wine and Roses" seemed destined for permanent enshrinement in the angst-
pop hall of fame.

But the song was too well written for such an abject fate. "Days of Wine and
Roses" proved especially popular among jazz guitarists, with Joe Pass, Barney
Kessel, and Laurindo Almeida recording early cover versions. Yet Wes Montgomery's light swinging performance on his *Boss Guitar* LP probably did the
most to legitimize "Days of Wine and Roses" as a popular jazz standard. Before
the year was over, Dizzy Gillespie, Sarah Vaughan, Milt Jackson, Art Farmer,
and Bill Evans had each recorded their interpretations of the Mancini tune.

I've enjoyed playing this song over the years. The harmonies have a satisfying sense of completeness to them, and it's easy to miss the rigorous logic of
the melody in the languorous mood of the music. But make no mistake, this is
one of Henry Mancini's most eloquent compositions, bereft of the ersatz-jazz
tricks he often used as building blocks for his soundtrack themes. Jazz musicians have found in it a versatile platform for improvisation, and have performed it in a wide range of tempos and styles. Yet though it works as a fast
jam—hear Mark Turner's 1998 recording with Brad Mehldau for an example—
I think it reveals its most intimate secrets when brought down to a slow or
medium-slow pace.

One of the most moving versions you will hear of this song comes from
guitarist Lenny Breau, who spent much of his all-too-brief and troubled life
battling addiction before his death at age 43. He is not a household name, even
in jazz circles, but retains a cult following among guitarists who prize his harmonic inventiveness and poetic conception of the guitar. His ten-minute version of "Days of Wine and Roses," released posthumously on the *Cabin Fever*
recording, is one of his finest performances and perfectly aligned with the spirit
of Mancini's song—which came, it may be worth noting, from a film that dealt
bravely with the subject of addiction and the ways it destroys lives. Bill Evans, in
the final days before his drug-fueled demise at age 51, also featured this song at
almost every performance.

RECOMMENDED VERSIONS

Wes Montgomery, from *Boss Guitar*, New York, April 22, 1963

Art Farmer (with Jim Hall), from *Interaction*, July 25, 1963

Tony Bennett and Bill Evans, from *The Tony Bennett/Bill Evans Album*, Berkeley, California, June 10–13, 1975

Lenny Breau, from *Cabin Fever*, Killaloe, Ontario, early 1980s

Michel Petrucciani, from *Days of Wine and Roses: The Owl Years 1981–1985*, Zuid-broek, Holland, April 3–4, 1981

Mark Turner (with Brad Mehldau), from *In This World*, New York, June 3–5, 1998

Maria Schneider (featuring Tim Ries and Rich Perry), from *Days of Wine and Roses*, live at the Jazz Standard, New York, January 2000

Bill Frisell, from *East/West*, New York, December 9–12, 2003

Desafinado
Composed by Antonio Carlos Jobim, with lyrics by Newton Mendonça

I had the opportunity to perform this song with Stan Getz who, when a bossa nova tune was expected, preferred calling "Desafinado" at gigs rather than the better-known "The Girl from Ipanema." In truth, "Desafinado" was also a huge seller in its own right, reaching as high as number 15 on the *Billboard* pop chart in 1962, but this success was obscured when "Ipanema" helped Getz win four Grammy Awards—including "Best Record of the Year"—three years later. Most jazz players, however, would side with Getz and opt for "Desafinado" or another Jobim composition rather than the overplayed "tall and tan, young and lovely" alternative.

Getz would sometimes poke gentle fun at the song onstage, calling it "Dis Here Finado"—an inside jazz joke that slyly referenced the popular funk numbers "Dis Here" and "Dat Dere" performed by Getz's contemporary, altoist Cannonball Adderley. In other instances, he introduced it as the song that would pay his kids' way through college (and I would hope that, by now, enough is left for the grandkids too). Yet when he put the horn in his mouth and played, Getz left the humor behind and took these Brazilian tunes very seriously. His tone and conception were perfectly suited to Jobim's characteristic *saudade* (a Portuguese word that loosely translates as a melancholy and almost fatalistic nostalgia). If you didn't know the history of this song, you might think it had been written with Getz's tenor saxophone sound in mind.

João Gilberto had introduced the song back in 1958 as part of the Brazilian studio sessions with Jobim that established the bossa nova style. Few outside of

Brazil were paying attention at the time, but this song would eventually become a global hit. Legal wranglings would later lead to the removal of these early recordings from the marketplace and many bossa nova fans have never heard them. What a shame! Even with the over-produced arrangements, Gilberto's delivery is mesmerizing, and his guitar work remains the starting point for anyone who wants to master the bossa groove.

Despite Getz's famous association with "Desafinado," Dizzy Gillespie adopted the song even earlier and presented it as part of a "musical safari" program at the 1961 Monterey Jazz Festival. "We'd like to play a number that we picked—that we stole—in Brazil," was how Gillespie jokingly introduced Jobim's song that day. But someone else would soon steal it from Dizzy in turn. Gillespie's Monterey band kept closer to a two-beat samba pulse, and it is hard envisioning his interpretation generating the airplay that Getz later enjoyed. Dizzy's own comments suggest that he saw Jobim as a samba composer, not as originator of the new, lighter 4/4 bossa style: "We had a lot of samba music and Stan Getz used to bug me to death trying to get some of those tunes. I meant to give them to him; it wasn't that I was trying to withhold the music, but he was here while I was there all the time. He finally got ahold of it and made a big hit with it."

The song is masterfully written. The lyrics refer to singing "out of tune" but the discordant notes are just the old blues flat fifth, albeit softened by its incorporation into Jobim's impressionistic harmonies. English-language lyrics, both those by Gene Lees as well as a different set by Jon Hendricks, are suitable enough, but I prefer hearing the Jobim classics performed in the original Portuguese. Long before Paul Simon sang about Nikon cameras and Kodachrome film, Gilberto set a stylish tone here by referring here to his Rolleiflex camera, and the words in general adopt a clever stance on the connection between harmony in music and human relationships. But the chord changes are the real treat in "Desafinado." During the late 1950s and 1960s, popular songs were getting simpler and simpler, but no one apparently told Mr. Jobim, who packs more modulations and melodic shifts into his 64-bar form than many rock bands employ in an entire career.

After Getz's success, almost every member of Local 802 jumped on to the bossa nova bandwagon. Even so, some fans must have been shocked to hear Coleman Hawkins, who had revolutionized the role of the tenor sax with his performances from the 1930s, record "Desafinado" as the title track to a Brazilian theme album. The accompaniment here is too close to lounge music for my taste, but Hawk plays with conviction. In truth, this has been one hit that improves with age and benefits from an artist's maturity—I don't think I am alone in preferring Getz's later version with João Gilberto over his hit single with Charlie Byrd. But my favorite rendition is a new millennium revisiting by Gilberto, relying on just solo guitar and voice, for his release *João Voz e Violao.*

RECOMMENDED VERSIONS

João Gilberto, from *The Legendary João Gilberto*, Rio de Janeiro, November 10, 1958

Dizzy Gillespie, from *A Musical Safari*, live at the Monterey Jazz Festival, Monterey, California, September 23, 1961

Stan Getz and Charlie Byrd, from *Jazz Samba*, Washington, D.C., February 13, 1962

Coleman Hawkins, from *Desafinado: Coleman Hawkins Plays Bossa Nova and Jazz Samba*, Englewood Cliffs, New Jersey, September 17, 1962

Stan Getz with João Gilberto, from *Getz/Gilberto*, New York, March 18–19, 1963

Antonio Carlos Jobim (with Pat Metheny and Joe Henderson), from *Carnegie Hall Salutes the Jazz Masters*, live at Carnegie Hall, New York, April 6, 1994

João Gilberto, from *João Voz e Violao*, Rio de Janeiro, 2000

Dinah
Composed by Harry Akst, with lyrics by Sam M. Lewis and Joe Young

A chance intervention led to the addition of the song "Dinah" to the successful musical *Kid Boots*, which opened on Broadway on the last day of 1923, and enjoyed a run of 489 performances before closing in February 1925. Harry Akst was working for Irving Berlin, and it was only after he failed to interest the show's star Eddie Cantor in a song by his boss that Akst sat down at the piano and noodled out his own melody. Cantor loved the tune, which became the basis for "Dinah," and he phoned Berlin the next day to say that he wanted the plugger's song, not the one by the famous tunesmith. Sam Lewis and Joe Young contributed strange, if unforgettable, lyrics, built on a series of corny rhymes—no one is *finer* in Caro*lina* than *Dinah*, but if she went to *China* you'd need an ocean *liner*, etc., etc. The resulting song was a perfect match for Cantor's comedic talents, but hardly timeless material destined for jazz immortality.

Ethel Waters, who replaced Florence Mills at the Plantation Club around this same time, put her personal stamp on the Cantor song, and enjoyed a top 10 hit in early 1926—a release also noteworthy for showcasing the new electronic recording technology of the day. Her interpretation downplays the humorous elements, and succeeds due to the expressive qualities of Waters's voice. More than anyone, she transformed this novelty song into a supple jazz vehicle, even imparting a judicious dose of sensuality to a tune that would seem to resist this kind of treatment. Other African-American performers followed in Waters's wake, adding "Dinah" to their repertoires. Her former accompanist Fletcher Henderson enjoyed one of his most popular recordings with the song, which features Coleman Hawkins, still in the process of developing his horn style, contributing a chorus on bass sax.

The song maintained its appeal during the Great Depression, returning as a hit for Bing Crosby who, in tandem with the Mills Brothers, delivered some hokum in a recording that was one of the most popular releases of 1932. "Dinah" also served up hit recordings for the Boswell Sisters in 1935 and Fats Waller in 1936. Waller is especially effective, and extracts maximum jocularity from the absurdity of the lyrics. In general, "Dinah" has been best matched with jazz artists who take pride in their skill as entertainers—figures such as Waller, Louis Armstrong, and Cab Calloway, who can make the most of the fanciful qualities of the song.

In a much different vein, Django Reinhardt recorded "Dinah" as the first song at the debut recording session for his Quintette du Hot Club de France in December 1934. This performance helped validate the unusual concept (even today) of a jazz band made up entirely of string instruments. Equally unconventional was Reinhardt's recording from September 1937, which finds his guitar supporting a violin battle between Stéphane Grappelli and Eddie South.

The range of these various early interpretations is striking. Yet "Dinah," for the most part, has remained in the jazz repertoire as a jaunty, traditional tune. If you weren't aware of the song's history, and only knew it from jazz recordings of recent decades, you might assume that "Dinah" originated in New Orleans or on the riverboats traveling the Mississippi. Even Thelonious Monk, who performed the song on his *Solo Monk* release for Columbia, was unable to establish this composition among jazz progressives. But "Dinah" continues to be favored by Dixieland ensembles, stride pianists, and nostalgia acts of various lineages and flavors.

RECOMMENDED VERSIONS

Ethel Waters, New York, October 20, 1925

Fletcher Henderson (with Coleman Hawkins), New York, January 6, 1926

Louis Armstrong, New York, May 4, 1930

Cab Calloway, New York, June 7, 1932

Django Reinhardt (with the Quintette du Hot Club de France), Paris, December 28, 1934

Fats Waller, Camden, New Jersey, June 24, 1935

Pee Wee Russell, New York, August 31, 1938

Thelonious Monk, from *Solo Monk*, Los Angeles, November 2, 1964

Ralph Sutton and Ruby Braff, from *Ralph Sutton & Ruby Braff Duet*, New York, October 29, 1979

Django
Composed by John Lewis

Those who hear this song for the first time today may struggle to reconcile the somber colorings of this music with the flamboyant guitar stylings of the artist for whom it was named. But listeners need to remember that the piece was composed shortly after Django Reinhardt's death, on May 16, 1953, and is John Lewis's lament for the loss of a friend.

The dissemination of this song in jazz circles has probably been hindered by the incorrect lead sheets that still circulate among many musicians. The original edition of *The Real Book*, which introduced many performers to this composition, only includes the chords for the 20-bar dirge that Lewis used to open and close the piece. But if you listen to Lewis's own debut performance, recorded with the Modern Jazz Quartet seven months after Reinhardt's passing, you will hear that he had a much more ambitious song structure in mind.

After the mournful introduction, the song moves into an unconventional 32-bar form for the solos. The A section, repeated twice, is only six bars long—usually eight bars would be expected in this kind of piece. The B section does last eight bars, but shifts into an unusual pedal point over the tonic. Then at the moment one would anticipate a return to the A section chords, Lewis introduces a new 12-bar segment of the song, with a surprising boogie bass motif tossed in at the end. By the standards of jazz composition, this whole work is an oddity, but to add a further twist, Lewis draws on elements of the opening dirge to serve as an interlude between solos, only now played in double time. The end result is more an obstacle course than a blowing tune, but indicative of the formalist tendencies that set Lewis apart from other jazz combo performers of his day.

"Django" sounds deceptively simple to the casual listener: indeed, there is a certain innocent, childlike quality to this composition that contrasts markedly with its arcane structural underpinning. The work is not quite a *tabula rasa*, but performers have a wide range of options open to them. Consider the lyrical approach of the young Wynton Marsalis and compare it with the electric reworking by John McLaughlin and Jeff Beck, much of it in 6/8, or the straight swing treatment of Joe Pass, or the hot-and-heavy approach of Sonny Rollins feeding off the energy of Herbie Hancock.

Each of these concepts brings out a different facet of "Django," although none bears much similarity to how the composer played the song himself. And for a version that builds additional levels atop John Lewis's already intricate work, go no further than Gunther Schuller's three-movement reconfiguration of the composition, recorded with an all-star band in 1960 under the title "Variants on a Theme of John Lewis."

RECOMMENDED VERSIONS

Modern Jazz Quartet, from *Django*, New York, December 23, 1954

Gunther Schuller (under the title "Variants on a Theme of John Lewis"), from *Jazz Abstractions*, New York, December 20, 1960

Sonny Rollins (with Herbie Hancock), from *The Complete RCA Recordings*, New York, January 24, 1964

Joe Pass, from *For Django*, Los Angeles, October 1964

Bill Evans (with Eddie Gomez), from *Montreux III*, live at the Montreux Jazz Festival, Montreux, Switzerland, July 20, 1975

Wynton Marsalis, from *Hot House Flowers*, New York, May 30–31, 1984

John McLaughlin (with Jeff Beck), from *The Promise*, London, 1995

Gary Burton (with Mulgrew Miller), from *For Hamp, Red, Bags, and Cal*, New York and Boston, May 11–June 3, 2000

Do Nothin' Till You Hear from Me
Composed by Duke Ellington, with lyrics by Bob Russell

I am put off by the words, which turn this tune into an anthem for cheatin' lovers. We get admissions of infidelity (*yes, I've been seen with someone new*), hints of how exciting other lovers can be (*other lips, other arms hold a thrill*), and then a vague promise . . . no, not to stop fooling around, but never to talk about it again. Does anyone really find this convincing, let alone romantic? The whole attitude is just a step above Groucho Marx's brazen alibi: "Who are you going to believe, me or your lying eyes?"

Fortunately, Ellington saves the day with an insinuating melody that makes even these excuses and rationalizations sound persuasive. The song, as was often the case with this composer, started out as a big band instrumental, with words added after the fact. "Concerto for Cootie," as the piece was originally named, was quite self-sufficient without all the guile and evasions of the lyrics, and I prefer trumpeter Cootie Williams's warm, relaxed melody statement and solo on the 1940 recording, which demonstrate his skill with both plunger mute and open horn, over later vocal versions.

Yet many jazz fans had a different opinion. With the addition of Bob Russell's lyrics, and a new title, the song gained recognition via Ellington's radio broadcasts from the Hurricane Restaurant in 1943. The American Federation of Musicians strike prevented Ellington from making a new recording with the now-popular lyrics, but Woody Herman and Stan Kenton were not under similar restrictions. Their labels, Decca and Capitol, had already reached agreement with the union and both enjoyed big hits with "Do Nothin' Till You Hear from Me" in early 1944. Ellington's label reissued his earlier instrumental under the new name, and it did even better, staying atop the R&B charts for eight weeks. Finally, Ellington recorded a vocal performance, featuring Al Hibbler, at a studio session for the Columbia label in 1947—a release that many mistakenly assume was the composer's hit recording of this song, but that honor belongs to the Cootie Williams instrumental.

By this time, the modern jazz revolution was under way in the music world. But the beboppers mostly ignored "Do Nothin' Till You Hear from Me."— although, in a rare broadcast appearance with Cootie Williams's band from 1945, Charlie Parker can be heard in the sax section on this tune. Swing Era veterans, however, kept the song in their set lists, and Ellington alums continued to perform and record it even after leaving the band. Two of them, Ben Webster and Clark Terry, can be heard in fine form on their 1964 rendition, captured on *The Happy Horns of Clark Terry*. Cootie Williams engages in playful give-and-take with Coleman Hawkins when he revisits his signature song on the 1957 session for *The Big Challenge*, and various studio and concert recordings find Jimmy Hamilton, Lawrence Brown, Johnny Hodges, and other of Duke's men playing this song in bands under their own direction.

Alas, "Do Nothin' Till You Hear from Me" is often delivered as glibly as the two-timing tales told in the lyrics. Yet the up-and-down interval movement in the opening phrases of the melody imparts a distinctly modernistic touch—it reminds me of the kind of practice-room pattern a Coltrane acolyte might play—and Duke's progression moves with an irresistible force through the form. Certainly this composition deserves better than a staid rendition in an Ellington tribute album, yet these days that is the most likely place where you will encounter this song.

RECOMMENDED VERSIONS

Duke Ellington (recorded as "Concerto for Cootie"), Chicago, March 15, 1940

Woody Herman, New York, November 8, 1943

Duke Ellington, New York, November 18, 1947

Hampton Hawes, from *All Night Session, Vol. 3*, Los Angeles, November 13, 1956

Cootie Williams (with Coleman Hawkins), from *The Big Challenge*, New York, April 30, 1957

Clark Terry (with Ben Webster), from *The Happy Horns of Clark Terry*, Englewood Cliffs, New Jersey, March 13, 1964

Rahsaan Roland Kirk and Al Hibbler, from *A Meeting of the Times*, New York, March 31, 1972

Hank Jones, from *Satin Doll*, Tokyo, January 24, 1976

Diana Krall, from *Stepping Out*, North Hollywood, October 18–19, 1992

Ahmad Jamal, from *I Remember Duke, Hoagy & Strayhorn*, New York, June 2–3, 1994

Do You Know What It Means to Miss New Orleans?
Composed by Louis Alter, with lyrics by Eddie DeLange

The New Orleans jazz tradition as it stands today is an odd gumbo made up of authentic local ingredients mixed in with peculiar anachronisms, impositions from afar, and a generous dose of romanticized and mythologized concepts of dubious validity but suitable for tourist consumption. This song is very much part of that ersatz history of New Orleans, representing not so much the authentic aural legacy of the Crescent City, but rather the way the heritage has been reconstructed along certain familiar lines.

So don't look for any recordings of this tune by Buddy Bolden, Jelly Roll Morton, and King Oliver. They were dead by the time it was composed, and it bears little resemblance to the kind of music they once performed. Instead, "Do You Know What It Means to Miss New Orleans?" came to prominence in the corny 1947 movie *New Orleans*, a piece of fluff built around the exploits of white characters who gape at the creativity of well-known African-American performers situated in stereotypical roles—much like what the Blues Brothers would do with James Brown and Aretha Franklin years later—and features historical incongruities, such as the Woody Herman big band performing in 1917. The song itself, wrongly referred to in the film as a blues, was written by Louis Alter, who hailed from Massachusetts, and New York–born Eddie De Lange, both well schooled in the needs of the movie industry but hardly folks who miss New Orleans.

Yet this film retains its historical value, not because of its insights into early New Orleans (where it will do more to mislead than enlighten) but due to the producer's wise decision to cast Billie Holiday and Louis Armstrong and give them a chance to showcase their talents onscreen. They infuse much-needed vitality into a superficial film, and also helped validate this song as something more than a Disneyfied take on the birthplace of jazz. Holiday delivers a very poised performance in *New Orleans*—a sharp contrast to her predictable casting as a servant (at one point she delivers this song while wearing a maid's uniform). You can offer your own opinion on why she showed little interest in performing this tune in later years. Certainly it wasn't because she didn't sing it convincingly. Armstrong, in contrast, embraced "Do You Know What It Means" with as much fervor as if he had heard it as a kid at Funky Butt Hall.

The release of the film roughly coincided with the rise of the New Orleans jazz revival movement. Many of the new trad bands springing up, often with only the loosest personal connections to the music's early history, adopted the song, as did the surviving stars who had actually helped shape the course of jazz in the 1920s. In addition to Armstrong, a number of his former sidemen and contemporaries—including Earl Hines, Kid Ory, Sidney Bechet, and Jack Teagarden—also took to the piece, whether they hailed from New Orleans or elsewhere. Stéphane Grappelli, with no personal connections to the city, state or nation, left behind more than a half-dozen recordings.

The song itself, for all its contrivances, is well crafted and actually far more suitable for crossover audiences than most of the genuine repertoire of early New Orleans jazz bands. The lyrics are loaded to the brim with potent images— magnolias in bloom, tall sugar pines, moonlight on the bayou—and the melody strikes just the right nostalgic tone to make it all sound plausible. For the most part, performers play along with the game, delivering the song with a sweet sound and leisurely beat. But, once in a Bayou moon, you encounter a risk-taker probing different aspects of the song. Hear, for example, Stefano Bollani's inventive solo piano rendition from 2005 and, perhaps most outré of all, Jerry Granelli's solo drum version from 2008, where you will not only miss New Orleans, but also the melody and chords.

RECOMMENDED VERSIONS

Billie Holiday, from the film *New Orleans*, Culver City, California, September 1946

Louis Armstrong, Los Angeles, October 17, 1946

Louis Armstrong, from *The Great Chicago Concert*, live at Medina Temple, Chicago, June 1, 1956

Kid Ory and Henry "Red" Allen, from *Kid Ory & Red Allen in Denmark*, live at K. B. Hallen, Copenhagen, November 13, 1959

Stéphane Grappelli, from *Vintage 1981*, San Francisco, July 1981

Wynton Marsalis, from *Live at Blues Alley*, live at Blues Alley, Washington, D.C., December 19–20, 1986

Harry Connick Jr. and Dr. John, from *20*, New York, May–June 1988

Stefano Bollani, from *Piano Solo*, Lugano, Switzerland, August 2005

Take 6 (with Aaron Neville), from *The Standard*, no recording information provided (CD released in 2008)

Jerry Granelli (drum solo), from *Vancouver '08*, Vancouver, October 20–21, 2008

Donna Lee
Composed by Charlie Parker

Although Charlie Parker is listed as the composer of this classic bop workout over the chord changes from "Indiana," Miles Davis claimed that he actually wrote the song. "Donna Lee" was "the first tune of mine that was ever recorded," Davis later asserted. "But when the record came out it listed Bird as the composer. It wasn't Bird's fault, though. The record company just made a mistake."

The melody line of "Donna Lee"—named after the daughter of bassist Curly Russell—is drenched in chromatic tones and bop mannerisms, and is so much in the spirit of Parker's style of constructing phrases, that I find it hard to imagine Davis, then a 20-year-old trumpeter still struggling with the bebop idiom, coming up with this piece. No other Davis composition sounds anything like "Donna Lee," and judging by the recording, Parker was much more comfortable playing the song at its debut. The trumpeter never recorded it on his own—in contrast, Parker performed it on many occasions without Davis in attendance. My only way of reconciling Davis's claim with the personality of the song itself is to imagine that he composed it almost as a student exercise, trying to capture the sound of his mentor Charlie Parker as closely as possible. Certainly he succeeded, if that was, in fact, his aim.

The pronounced modernism of the composition caught the attention of those trying to come to grips with the new sound in jazz. A transcription recording made only a few months after Parker's version finds Claude Thornhill performing Gil Evans's stirring chart of "Donna Lee"—a departure from the impressionistic approach associated with both this bandleader and the arranger. Perhaps even more surprising is Benny Goodman's performance of "Donna Lee" alongside tenorist (and former Charlie Parker sideman) Wardell Gray, which dates from the King of Swing's brief fling with modern jazz—although Gray and the rhythm section take on the bop heavy lifting here.

This is one of the hardest bebop lines to play, so "Donna Lee" is more likely to show up at a gig by a polished pro than at a casual jam. Even so, it served as a feature number at the well-known jam session recording of Clifford Brown at the Music City club in Philadelphia. For many years, this amateur tape was believed to have been made a few hours before Brown's death in a car accident in the early hours of June 26, 1956—imparting an aura of tragic grandeur to the music making. Yet a persuasive case has been made that the Philly session took place a full year earlier. In any event, it is a commanding performance, and presents Brown at the peak of his abilities.

The song has had an unusual post-bop history. Anthony Braxton has performed it, and his "Opus 23B" from 1974 is an atonal reconfiguration of the Parker standard. But an equally unusual and more influential adaptation took place a few months later when fusion icon Jaco Pastorius recorded "Donna Lee" with just percussion accompaniment for his debut leader date. This track was much admired at the time by electric bassists and fans of jazz-rock music, and probably introduced the song to more people than the efforts of all the boppers put together.

Those seeking sheer virtuosity, however, will find it hard to top the guitar and bass duet from Joe Pass and Niels-Henning Ørsted Pedersen, preserved on video in 1979 and widely available on the Internet. This version is taken much faster than either Bird's or Jaco's recordings and is exhilarating to hear. In modern-day interpretations, as presented by artists such as Wynton Marsalis and Gonzalo Rubalcaba, "Donna Lee" has become something of a bop étude, played as a showpiece and crowd-pleaser—hear the audience cheering Marsalis on during his solo for validation that this 1940s masterwork has not lost its mojo with the passing years. Joe Lovano, for his part, departs from the usual practice and turns "Donna Lee" into a ballad on his 2010 recording in an arrangement that changes the tempo, melody, and chords so markedly from the original that Lovano might have been justified in taking composer credit.

RECOMMENDED VERSIONS

Charlie Parker (with Miles Davis), New York, May 8, 1947

Claude Thornhill (with arrangement by Gil Evans), New York, December 17, 1947

Benny Goodman (with Wardell Gray), live at the Clique, Philadelphia, June 3, 1948

Clifford Brown, from *The Beginning and the End*, live at Music City, May 31, 1955

Anthony Braxton (recorded as "Opus 23B"), from *The Complete Arista Recordings of Anthony Braxton*, New York, September–October 1974

Jaco Pastorius, from *Jaco Pastorius*, New York, October 1975

Joe Pass with Niels-Henning Ørsted Pedersen, video filmed in Juan-les-Pins, France, July 26, 1979

Gonzalo Rubalcaba, from *Diz*, Toronto, December 1993

Wynton Marsalis, from *Live at the House of Tribes*, live at the House of Tribes, New York, December 15, 2002

Joe Lovano, from *Bird Songs*, New York, September 7–8, 2010

Don't Blame Me
Composed by Jimmy McHugh, with lyrics by Dorothy Fields

Producer Lew Leslie made his reputation staging all-black entertainment for white audiences—first at the Cotton Club and later on Broadway—but with his 1932 project *Clowns in Clover* he aimed to prove that he could achieve equal success with an all-white production. For songs, he turned to Jimmy McHugh and Dorothy Fields, who had contributed "I Can't Give You Anything but Love" to his *Blackbirds of 1928*, and "Exactly Like You" and "On the Sunny Side of the Street" to his *International Revue* from 1930. But the new show never made it to Broadway, stalling out after a trial run in Chicago.

But when McHugh and Fields were enlisted to write music for the 1933 Hollywood film *Meet the Baron*, they recycled their *Clowns in Clover* song "Don't Blame Me" for the movie score. This screwball comedy, which featured the

Three Stooges, Jack Pearl, and Jimmy Durante among its stars, was an unlikely staging ground for a melancholy love ballad. "Don't Blame Me" shows up in the background of a Durante comedy bit, and the placement here would hardly convince anyone of the tune's hit potential. The song is also frequently mentioned in books and articles as part of the soundtrack to the 1933 Jean Harlow movie *Dinner at Eight*, but is not evident in the version of that film that has survived—nor are McHugh or Fields mentioned in the credits to that movie.

Ethel Waters, who had enjoyed previous successes with songs by McHugh and Fields, stepped in to record "Don't Blame Me" with the Dorsey brothers— and her intervention took what might have otherwise become one more forgotten pop song and gave it a much-needed dose of street cred as a jazz song. Teddy Wilson's much-admired solo piano performance from 1937 added to the song's luster, and helped set the stage for its later popularity as a jazz keyboard feature—as demonstrated in recordings over the next decade by Nat King Cole (who relied on it both as an instrumental and vocal number), Mel Powell, Erroll Garner, and others.

The song clearly deserved the attention. The hook comes at the very beginning, with an angular three-note phrase, each tone carried along by its own chord change. The lyrics, for their part, rank among Dorothy Fields's finest. She takes a title phrase that is almost a banal, throwaway line and draws out new meanings and implications. By the time Fields arrives at the conclusion, one of the most memorable closing phrases to any pop song of the period—"Blame all *your* charms that melt in my arms, but *don't blame me*"—she has played this blame game like a pro and turned the fault on the all-too-alluring and elusive lover. Touché!

For all its virtues, this song must have seemed an unlikely platform for the bebop movement. Yet Charlie Parker delivered one of the finest ballad performances of his career on his recording of "Don't Blame Me" from his November 1947 session for Dial. A few months earlier, Lennie Tristano had recorded a solo piano version in Chicago full of dissonant-laden chord voicings that few jazz keyboardists of the day would have dared to bring into the studio. Some years later, Thelonious Monk would find similar inspiration in "Don't Blame Me" for his own idiosyncratic approach. J. J. Johnson relied on this song at his 1949 Savoy session to showcase his fluid trombone technique. That same year, Charlie Parker's former drummer, Roy Porter, recorded "Don't Blame Me" with his L.A.-based modern jazz big band, and the alto saxophonist in the ensemble, Eric Dolphy, would resurrect the song years later as an extended flute feature.

These probing performances have coexisted with many more staid renditions of "Don't Blame Me" over the years. This song adapts just as easily to the demands of a cabaret revue or cocktail lounge as to the requirements of jazz improvisers. It's worth remembering that the first artist to enjoy a hit with "Don't Blame Me" was that maestro of anti-jazz Guy Lombardo—the fellow who billed his band as "The Sweetest Music This Side of Heaven." But if this tune is accessible as low-rent mood music or as easy listening for the complacent, its history shows that it also can serve as a platform for the ambitious and experimental.

RECOMMENDED VERSIONS

Ethel Waters (with the Dorsey Brothers Orchestra), New York, July 18, 1933

Teddy Wilson, New York, November 12, 1937

Coleman Hawkins (with Teddy Wilson), May 29, 1944

Nat King Cole, Los Angeles, May 19, 1945

Lennie Tristano (sometimes issued under the title "Blame Me"), Chicago, circa
     1945–46

Charlie Parker, New York, November 4, 1947

J. J. Johnson, New York, May 11, 1949

Eric Dolphy, from *Eric Dolphy in Europe*, live at Berlingske Has, Copenhagen,
     September 6, 1961

Thelonious Monk, from *Criss Cross*, New York, February 27, 1963

Steve Grossman (with Michel Petrucciani), from *Steve Grossman Quartet with Michel
     Petrucciani*, Paris, January 23–25, 1998

Terence Blanchard (with Cassandra Wilson), from *Let's Get Lost*, New York, January–
     February 2001

Don't Get Around Much Anymore
Composed by Duke Ellington, with lyrics by Bob Russell

Many listeners over the years have assumed this song was called "Mister Saturday Dance" based on a common mishearing of the opening lyrics ("Missed the Saturday dance . . ."). But my favorite garbling of the title came from an inebriated regular at a bar where I once played the piano. He stumbled up to the keyboard late one night, after another evening striking out with the ladies, and asked me if I knew how to play "Don't Get Much Around Here Anymore."

The song originated as a counter-melody composed for "I Let a Song Go Out of My Heart" that got recycled into "Never No Lament," which Ellington recorded with one of his finest bands in 1940. This peculiar version leaves out the B theme and final A theme recapitulation in the opening statement. Ellington frequently broke the rules of song form during this period, but this particular "innovation" will sound quite odd to anyone familiar with the way this song is typically played. There are compensating factors, however: the melody serves as an ideal vehicle for alto saxophonist Johnny Hodges—who, according to Rex Stewart, may have provided the riff that originally inspired the song—while Cootie Williams also contributes an outstanding solo.

By 1942, lyrics by Bob Russell were added, and the song had been rechristened as "Don't Get Around Much Anymore." Yet the world-weary words seem at odds with the merry-making music. When Ellington presented the composition at Carnegie Hall, at the famous concert that also saw the debut of his magnum opus *Black, Brown and Beige*, he announced it under the new name but retained the anomalous opening half-chorus from the studio recording. The lyrics are not featured, and the melody is still assigned to Hodges, who plays it with, if anything, even more passion here than on the 1940 recording.

In March of that same year, an understated cover version by the Ink Spots, brandishing their sweet barbershop harmonies, reached the top of the R&B chart. This success gave Ellington a stunning, if pleasant, surprise soon afterward, when he strolled into the William Morris Agency office, hoping to borrow a few hundred dollars. While he was waiting, an office boy gave him a letter that had been sitting around for him. Duke opened it to find a check for $22,500—all due to "Don't Get Around Much Anymore" and fueled by the Ink Spots' big hit.

The ASCAP strike prevented Ellington from seizing the opportunity with a vocal version of his own; he wouldn't release one until 1947. But his label reissued his 1940 recording under the new name, and it also reached the top of the R&B chart in late May. The song never left his repertoire in later years. Given its popularity, "Don't Get Around Much Anymore" was demanded by audiences when Duke performed, but he often slipped it into the dreaded (at least by many Ellington devotees) "medley" that he frequently used to get such requests out of the way.

If any vocalist owned this song, it was Al Hibbler, who joined Ellington's band in 1943 and stayed on for eight years. He recorded "Don't Get Around Much Anymore" on many occasions, but my favorite, hands down, is the version he made with Rahsaan Roland Kirk in 1972. For this project, Hibbler engages in his trademark hemming and hawing, which makes it sound as if he is making up the lyrics as he goes along. Kirk, for his part, acts as if he is auditioning for some demonic R&B band. Even Duke must have been envious.

Like many Ellington hits, this one shows up in surprising places. Paul McCartney performed an old time rock-and-roll arrangement of the song on his 1987 "Soviet" album *Снова в СССР*, and his version is quite endearing. After hearing this track, one might almost think that Little Richard or Chuck Berry had written the tune. Other unexpected covers of this song include a rendition by Harry Connick Jr. for the soundtrack for *When Harry Met Sally* and Willie Nelson's heartfelt performance on his platinum *Stardust* release from 1978.

Yet for all its popularity—and it does get around much, the title notwith-standing—this song is devilishly hard to update into a modern jazz version. The melody almost demands a conventional swing rhythm and the harmonic sequence does not rank among Ellington's most inspired. For that reason, this standard is rarely performed by the younger generation of progressive players who probably find it easier to relate to Duke's ballads than to such dance-oriented numbers.

RECOMMENDED VERSIONS

Duke Ellington (recorded as "Never No Lament"), Los Angeles, May 4, 1940

The Ink Spots, July 28, 1942

Duke Ellington, live at Carnegie Hall, New York, January 23, 1943

Duke Ellington (with Al Hibbler), New York, December 20, 1947

Ella Fitzgerald, from *The Duke Ellington Songbook*, Los Angeles, September 4, 1956

Mose Allison, from *Young Man Mose*, New York, January 24, 1958

Johnny Hodges (with Billy Strayhorn), from *Soloist*, New York, December 11, 1961

Rahsaan Roland Kirk and Al Hibbler, from *A Meeting of the Times*, New York, March 30, 1972

McCoy Tyner, from *Solar*, live at Sweet Basil, New York, June 14, 1991

Dr. John (with Ronnie Cuber), from *Duke Elegant*, New York, 2000

East of the Sun (and West of the Moon)   E
Composed by Brooks Bowman

Many jazz standards arrive on the bandstand via Broadway or Hollywood, but how many were written for a student stage production by a college undergraduate? Brooks Bowman was a student at Princeton when he was enlisted to compose songs for the 1934 musical *Stags at Bay*, produced by the Princeton Triangle Club. Perhaps an old Norwegian fairy tale entitled "East of the Sun and West of the Moon" inspired the young composer. In any event, the results were impressive—F. Scott Fitzgerald proclaimed the Princeton production the "best in ten years," and "East of the Sun" was a hit even before Bowman graduated. This promising songwriter might have enjoyed many more successes, but he died in a car accident four days before his twenty-fourth birthday.

A second boost to "East of the Sun" came more than a dozen years later, when Frank Sinatra recorded it during his stint with Tommy Dorsey. In the years following World War II, the song became a frequently played standard, showing up in the repertoires of everyone from Louis Armstrong to R&B artist Earl Bostic. Charlie Parker recorded it with strings. Lester Young relied on it for one of his best postwar ballad performances, and his former studio mate Billie Holiday delivered a definitive rendition at her 1952 session for Norman Granz. When Stan Getz made his *West Coast Jazz* album for the same producer three years later, "East of the Sun" was his opening track—and I would not be surprised if the choice of an "East" song for a "West" LP was his way of quietly protesting a theme project imposed by his label.

Despite these endorsements, I find the melody a little too predictable and the lyrics too vague—built on sentimental generalities almost too akin to those of the fairy tale that may have set this whole song in motion. Yet the composition has more flexibility than most jazz standards, and its very malleability somewhat compensates for its cardboard qualities. Although it is typically taken at a medium swing tempo, it can be gentle enough to serve as a lullaby or boisterous enough to bring the house down. But an autopilot performance doesn't work here, and musicians who tackle "East of the Sun" are advised to impose their own personality on the song or even rough it up a bit.

RECOMMENDED VERSIONS

Tommy Dorsey (featuring Frank Sinatra and Bunny Berigan), New York, April 23, 1940

Lester Young, New York, December 29, 1947

Billie Holiday, from *Billie Holiday Sings*, Los Angeles, May 1952

Stan Getz, from *West Coast Jazz*, Los Angeles, August 15, 1955

Wynton Marsalis, from *Standard Time, Vol. 2: Intimacy Calling*, New York, September 1987 and August 1990

Kenny Barron, from *Confirmation*, live at the Riverside Park Arts Festival, New York, September 1, 1991

Diana Krall, from *Live in Paris*, live at the Olympia, Paris, November–December 2001

Easy Living
Composed by Ralph Rainger, with lyrics by Leo Robin

As was the case with many other songwriters, Ralph Rainger was prodded by his family to choose some other, more respectable career. He left the Institute of Musical Art, a forerunner of Juilliard, after only a year, to study at Brown University's law school. But on graduation Rainger decided to make his living as a pianist, bandleader, and arranger. In time he was writing songs for Broadway revues, and teamed up with another one-time law school student, lyricist Leo Robin—a partnership that would produce dozens of hit songs and last until Rainger's death in a plane crash in 1942.

In the 1930s, the duo were under contract to Paramount and wrote songs for a number of Hollywood features, including Preston Sturges's 1937 screwball comedy *Easy Living*, for which this song was composed. Around this same time, Teddy Wilson recorded the song as a feature for Billie Holiday. Although the recording was a top 20 hit, few other jazz musicians adopted the song over the next decade, but Holiday recorded it again in 1947, and gradually other performers picked up on "Easy Living." Ballad treatments, from the late 1940s and early 1950s, by Clifford Brown, George Shearing, Peggy Lee, and Wardell Gray did much to establish the composition in jazz circles.

Between 1955 and 1957 more jazz cover versions of "Easy Living" were recorded than during the entire preceding period. The song proved especially popular with the up-and-coming performers of the era: Bill Evans featured the song on his initial leader date for Riverside Records, Hampton Hawes did the same on his first album for Contemporary, while Rahsaan Roland Kirk showcased "Easy Living" on his debut for the King label. Miles Davis plays it on a stimulating 1955 session that took him away from his working band and found him backed by an unconventional rhythm section of bassist Charles Mingus, drummer Elvin Jones, and vibraphonist Teddy Charles.

Despite the allegiance of many jazz modernists, I find the main theme a bit old-fashioned. The recurring use of diminished chords to push the progression up by half-steps, similar to what rag-stride pianist Eubie Blake did with his song "Memories of You" a few years before, is the kind of effect you would put into a composition to make it sound like a period piece. Even so (and to my surprise) the trad jazz players have never paid much attention to "Easy Living" while some of the finest versions of recent years find it recast in appealing, uncluttered—and definitely nostalgia-free—treatments by modern-minded players such as Steve Coleman, Greg Osby, and Enrico Rava.

RECOMMENDED VERSIONS

Teddy Wilson (with Billie Holiday and Lester Young), New York, June 1, 1937

Billie Holiday, New York, February 13, 1947

Clifford Brown, New York, August 28, 1953

Bill Evans, from *New Jazz Conceptions*, New York, September 27, 1956

Rahsaan Roland Kirk, from *Third Dimension*, New York, November 9, 1956

Lee Morgan, from *Expoobident*, Chicago, October 13, 1960

Paul Desmond (with Jim Hall), from *Easy Living*, New York, September 9, 1964

Sarah Vaughan (with Oscar Peterson), from *How Long Has This Been Going On?* Hollywood, April 25, 1978

Frank Morgan (with Cedar Walton), from *Easy Living*, Glendale, California, June 12–13, 1985

Ann Hampton Callaway (with Wynton Marsalis), from *Easy Living*, New York, 1999

Steve Coleman, from *Resistance Is Futile*, live at Le Jam Club, Montpellier, France, July 12–13, 2001

Marc Copland and Greg Osby, from *Round and Round*, New York, November 30, 2002

Enrico Rava (with Stefano Bollani), from *Easy Living*, Udine, Italy, June 2003

Easy to Love
Composed by Cole Porter

Cole Porter referred to "Easy to Love" as a "Jewish song," no doubt finding an ethnic hook in the shifting sensibility of the harmonies, which open in a minor mode but eventually reach resolution with a resounding major cadence. Porter may have been (that rarity in the American songwriting pantheon) an Episcopalian, but even earlier—back in 1926—he had confided to Richard Rodgers that in order to create hit compositions, "I'll write Jewish tunes." Rodgers thought that this was a joke, and only later realized that Porter was dead serious.

Porter had originally written "Easy to Love" for the 1934 show *Anything Goes*, but dropped it when actor Billy Gaxton complained that he couldn't hit the high notes. The song was introduced in the 1936 film *Born to Dance*, with Jimmy Stewart and Eleanor Powell serving as unlikely vocalists. Porter could hear the limitations in Stewart's singing but thought he played the role to perfection, and the scene is quite effective—apparently Stewart never realized that the song was too high for his range, and somehow pulled it off with his characteristic aw-shucks nonchalance. But the sensitivity of Hollywood to the risqué can be seen in the censoring of the lyrics—the rhyme about "sweet to waken" and "sit down to eggs and bacon" was nixed apparently due to concerns about the scurrilous implications of a shared breakfast.

The other hook for jazz musicians (as well as listeners) is a melody built mostly on half and quarter notes, which allows them to deliver the phrases in a leisurely manner even at a fast tempo. Jimmy Dorsey, the first jazz artist to record "Easy to Love," does not take full advantage of this potential on his 1936 side, which was primarily a feature for vocalist Frances Langford, with no instrumental solos and an unassuming chart. But ten weeks later, Billie Holiday went into the studio, as part of Teddy Wilson's band and, adopting a much quicker pulse, showed how Porter's melody could allow her to superimpose a probing and unhurried vocal on top of a hot, swinging rhythm section. Holiday, more than anyone, established the jazz credentials of "Easy to Love" with this memorable track.

For a time, "Easy to Love" seemed destined to serve as a vehicle for lady singers, as testified by versions by Maxine Sullivan, Mildred Bailey, and Lee Wiley. But this song is a fitting platform for an up-tempo instrumental jam, and it was only a matter of time before more horn players embraced it. Artie Shaw enjoyed great success with Cole Porter songs throughout his career—his version of "Begin the Beguine" was one of the biggest hits of the Swing Era—and he recorded Dean Jones's elegant arrangement of "Easy to Love" in 1945. Taking a much different tack, Charlie Parker recorded the standard in the studio and in live performances during his "Bird with Strings" phase, and though I find the arrangement far too bland, he had a real affinity for the composition—his 1950 performance at Carnegie Hall is a good setting to hear his mastery of it.

"If ever there was a song that shouldn't have a note changed, it's 'Easy to Love,'" Alec Wilder has proclaimed. Certainly the composition has aged well. While many tunes from the 1920s and 1930s survive mostly as nostalgia pieces, prized for the quaint old-fashioned qualities, "Easy to Love" is open to a wide range of interpretative stances, including very modern ones. Compare the versions listed below by Sun Ra, Patricia Barber, and Adam Makowicz for a sense of this flexibility.

RECOMMENDED VERSIONS

Jimmy Dorsey (with Frances Langford), Los Angeles, August 3, 1936

Teddy Wilson (with Billie Holiday), New York, October 21, 1936

Maxine Sullivan, New York, October 22, 1937

Mildred Bailey, New York, January 15, 1940

Lee Wiley, New York, April 15, 1940

Artie Shaw, Hollywood, June 7, 1945

Charlie Parker (with strings), live at Carnegie Hall, New York, September 16, 1950

Ella Fitzgerald, from *Ella Fitzgerald Sings the Cole Porter Songbook*, Los Angeles, February 7, 1956

Sun Ra (with John Gilmore), from *Standards*, New York, late 1962 or early 1963

Adam Makowicz, from *Live at Maybeck Recital Hall, Vol. 24*, Berkeley, California, July 19, 1992

Susannah McCorkle, from *Easy to Love*, New York, September 6–8, 1995

Roberta Gambarini, from *Easy to Love*, Los Angeles, June 18–19, 2004

Patricia Barber, from *The Cole Porter Mix*, Chicago, December 15–22, 2007

Embraceable You

Composed by George Gershwin, with lyrics by Ira Gershwin

This is one of Gershwin's most consummately constructed songs. The melody dovetails nicely with the harmonic structure and builds from the gentle musings of its opening phrases to its declamatory conclusion with confidence and plausibility.

How odd, then, to consider that the most influential jazz recording of this song dispensed with the melody in favor of the inspiration of the moment. Charlie Parker makes only the most fleeting acknowledgment of Gershwin's

original line in bar 21 of his alto workout, but the rest of his performance is a
tautly constructed, thematic improvisation that has been closely studied by
other saxophonists. At a pace of just 70 beats per minute, this was a very slow
ballad tempo for the era—by comparison, when Judy Garland had performed
this song in the film *Girl Crazy* four years earlier, she had taken it at 130 beats
per minute. Parker is usually remembered for his fast tempos, but this recording was very influential in popularizing the extremely slow ballad among
modern jazz players.

The song dates back to 1928, when Gershwin was working on the Ziegfeld
production *East Is West*. A musical sketchbook from this period, which includes
an early version of "Embraceable You," recently sold at auction for $116,250, but
the financial returns were hardly so promising back in 1928. Gershwin abandoned *East Is West* but managed to recycle the song in his 1930 Broadway musical *Girl Crazy*, where Ginger Rogers performed "Embraceable You" in a dance
number choreographed by Fred Astaire. This landmark show not only made
Rogers into a star but also featured the Broadway debut of Ethel Merman (who
sang "I Got Rhythm"). No other Gershwin production introduced more future
jazz standards in its score. Even the pit orchestra boasted top-notch jazz talent,
with Benny Goodman, Glenn Miller, Tommy Dorsey, Jack Teagarden, and Gene
Krupa within its ranks.

Despite these promising connections, few jazz renditions of this song were
recorded until the 1940s. Hazel Scott released a version in 1942, and an amateur recording made by Bob Redcross in room 305 of Chicago's Savoy Hotel the
following year finds a young Charlie Parker playing along with Scott's 78. In
November of 1943, the film version of *Girl Crazy* was released, and Garland's
performance with Tommy Dorsey's orchestra played a key role in establishing
"Embraceable You" as a favorite with audiences. A few weeks after the film's
release, Nat King Cole recorded the song in a memorable version of his own,
and over the next year a host of jazz stars—Billie Holiday, Glenn Miller, Erroll
Garner—would issue their own interpretations. Holiday's 1944 recording is the
version of "Embraceable You" inducted in the Grammy Hall of Fame, but I
think this same artist's 1957 track for producer Norman Granz compares favorably, and offers far better recording quality to boot.

In deciding between Ella Fitzgerald and Billie Holiday, most jazz critics
would probably give Ella the nod on fast numbers and Lady Day on the ballads.
But the gentle, introspective nature of the lyrics here made this a perfect song
for Fitzgerald—who was always better at singing about prim courtship than
sultry lovemaking—and I am not surprised to learn (via Amazon.com) that her
recording, from the ambitious *Ella Fitzgerald Sings the George and Ira Gershwin
Songbook* project, is the retailer's most downloaded version of this standard. Her
interpretation cuts to the heart of this standard, but Nelson Riddle's arrangement will probably strike many jazz fans as too syrupy.

The following year, Ornette Coleman offered a much more unconventional version of "Embraceable You." The fact that Coleman recorded this tune at all is something of an anomaly, given his antipathy to popular song material and conventional chord progressions. Yet his rendition is quite moving, and leaves one wondering what this artist might have accomplished if he had tried to put his personal stamp on more old standards.

Most later versions have been far more deferential. The song is probably more popular with cabaret singers than jazz artists these days. Yet whenever a Gershwin tribute album comes out, "Embraceable You" is typically one of the selections. I especially like Herbie Hancock's introspective reworking from his 1998 *Gershwin's World,* which showcases this pianist's knack for reharmonization and ability to take this song, seventy years after it was written, and make it sound convincingly up-to-date.

RECOMMENDED VERSIONS

Judy Garland (with Tommy Dorsey), Hollywood, early 1943

Nat King Cole, Los Angeles, December 15, 1943

Billie Holiday, New York, April 1, 1944

Charlie Parker, New York, October 28, 1947

Billie Holiday, from *Body and Soul,* Los Angeles, January 3, 1957

Ella Fitzgerald, from *Ella Fitzgerald Sings the George and Ira Gershwin Songbook,* Los Angeles, January 5–8, 1959

Ornette Coleman, from *This Is Our Music,* New York, July 26, 1960

Herbie Hancock, from *Gershwin's World,* April–June 1998

Geri Allen, from *Timeless Portraits and Dreams,* New York, March 16–17, 2006

Emily
Composed by Johnny Mandel, with lyrics by Johnny Mercer

Hollywood movies would change dramatically during the course of the 1960s, with outsiders and edgier fare increasingly countering the studio system's historical focus on entertaining mainstream America with films that shared, rather than confronted, traditional values. In just a few years, we went from *My Fair Lady* (winner of the Oscar for Best Picture in 1964) to the X-rated *Midnight Cowboy* (recipient of the same honor in 1969), and nobody—at least in Hollywood—ever looked back.

Movie music needed to change in this same environment, and a few years later the team of Johnny Mandel and Johnny Mercer, a dream matchup when they collaborated on this song from the 1964 film *The Americanization of Emily*, would no longer fit so easily into the film industry. To get a sense of this shift, just look at the Academy Award nominees for best song. Mandel won the Oscar in 1965 (for "The Shadow of Your Smile") and was nominated the following year for "A Time for Love," but he would never get another nomination, although he was only 41 years old at the time of the latter honor. He didn't change, and continued to do quality work during the five ensuing decades, but the film industry did.

Given this history, I tend to look at "Emily" as an end-of-an-era kind of song, a late blossoming from an all-too-brief period when someone like Mandel could step out of the big band jazz world and into the movie business with an ease that can hardly be imagined nowadays. Mandel had very deep jazz roots before making his name as a film composer. As a trombonist, he had played with Count Basie, Buddy Rich, Jimmy Dorsey, and other name bandleaders, while continuing to develop his skills in composing and arranging. A referral from André Previn led to his first movie scoring project, for the 1958 film *I Want to Live*. Yet, by his own admission, "Emily" was Mandel's first serious attempt to compose a song—not an instrumental or theme or background music, but a genuine pop tune with lyrics.

Mandel tried to create a song that matched Julie Andrews's character in the film, and his melody is as changeable as her on-screen persona. The modulation after bar eight is as sublime as it is unexpected, and when the song enters what appears to be the second ending of the A theme, the resolution is so unusual and extended that it almost seems tantamount to a bridge placed incongruously at the end of the form. The studio allowed Mandel to choose his own lyricist, and he decided to aim high, looking to secure the services of Johnny Mercer, who agreed to the project. Although the melody had clear hit potential, adding words was problematic—the title "Emily" was dictated by the film, yet the name offers no perfect rhymes with any serviceable word, although I give the lyricist credit for taking a chance on "dreamily" and "family." Moreover, Mandel's melody, built on three-note phrases with an accent on the last tone, forced Mercer to exercise all his ingenuity in finding words and phrases ("silver bells. . . . coral shells . . . carousels") that fit this almost maddening constraint. The fact that the finished song sounds so effortless is testimony to the craftsmanship involved.

This composition was quickly adopted by jazz musicians—helped along, no doubt, by the growing interest in jazz waltzes during the 1960s. Bill Evans, who probably did more for 3/4 time signatures in jazz than anyone else, first recorded "Emily" in 1966 and kept it in his repertoire until the end of his life. He left behind a number of trio recordings of the song from various live dates, but I would also call attention to his collaboration with Stan Getz on "Emily" from 1974 and his over-dubbed piano arrangement from his 1967 *Further*

Conversations with Myself project for Verve. Other noteworthy interpretations include Paul Desmond's 1968 performance from his *Summertime* album, and Lenny Breau's extended excursion on "Emily" (probably chosen in tribute to his daughter of that name) from his late 1970s work captured on *The Complete Living Room Tapes.*

RECOMMENDED VERSIONS

Bill Evans, from *Further Conversations with Myself,* New York, August 9, 1967

Paul Desmond, from *Summertime,* New York, October 16, 1968

Eddie Daniels and Bucky Pizzarelli, from *A Flower for All Seasons,* Sea Cliff, New York, January 2, 1973

Bill Evans and Stan Getz, from *But Beautiful,* live at the Middelheim Jazz Festival, Antwerp, August 16, 1974

Richard Davis (with Joe Henderson and Stanley Cowell), from *Fancy Free,* Berkeley, California, June 30–July 1, 1977

Oscar Peterson, from *The London Concert,* live at Royal Festival Hall, London, October 21, 1978

Lenny Breau, from *The Complete Living Room Tapes,* Maine, circa 1978–79

Bill Watrous, from *A Time for Love,* Hollywood, 1993

Epistrophy
Composed by Thelonious Monk and Kenny Clarke

This song appears as early as 1941 in amateur recordings made at Minton's, the foremost breeding ground for the young modern jazz players of the period. You can even hear Jerry Newman, a Columbia University student at the time, introducing the band and mentioning "a guy named Monk on piano," then adding, "I'm sorry I haven't found out his last name." Ignorance or irreverent humor?

"Epistrophy" was copyrighted around this same time. Back then, it was simply known as "The Theme." Drummer Kenny Clarke, a Minton's regular who is credited as co-composer along with Monk, referred to the song as "Fly Right" or "Fly Rite," and for a time the piece was also known as "Iambic Pentameter," before settling into its current identity. Clarke claims that he wrote the melody, helped along by some fingering patterns that Charlie Christian showed him on the ukulele, while Monk's contribution was restricted to the chord changes. The account is plausible, yet the melodic development here is very much in keeping with the kinds of phraseology and rhythmic displacements Monk would employ in other compositions.

Strange to say, this song was familiar to Swing Era dancers at the Savoy Ballroom before it earned its reputation as a paragon of the new thing in jazz. Trumpeter Cootie Williams played regularly at the celebrated Harlem dance-hall, and for a time adopted "Epistrophy" as a theme song for his band. Williams was far more open to modern sounds than most established bandleaders of the day, and two years later he would make the debut recording (and claim co-composer credits) on Monk's most famous piece, "'Round Midnight." But his choice of "Epistrophy" was even more daring. The song is 32 bars long but does not follow a typical AABA form—bars 9–12 are a repeat of bars 5–8, and bars 13–16 are a repeat of bars 1–4. It's a peculiar structure, but a casual listener will hardly notice the deviation from standard practice. Indeed, "Epistrophy" bears a superficial resemblance to other riff-based swing tunes of the era, but the melodic material is both more eccentric and insistent than in other such tunes. Monk's chromatic progression, moving up and down a half-step at two-beat intervals, can present challenges to the soloists unused to this kind of song. Williams made a recording of "Epistrophy"—under the name "Fly Right"—on April Fools' Day in 1942, but it remained unreleased for many years. It's a fascinating track: Williams somehow manages to transform this very modernistic number into a fast, danceable big band chart—without much in common with Monk's approach to his song, but effective in its own way.

Monk would not make a commercial recording of "Epistrophy" until 1948, when he performed it at his fourth session for the Blue Note label, which featured the pianist in the company of vibraphonist Milt Jackson. This composition remained a part of Monk's core repertoire for the rest of his career, often filling the role of set closer, and shows up on a number of live recordings of his band— at Carnegie Hall, the Five Spot, the Black Hawk, and other locales—from the late 1950s and early 1960s. More than 50 recordings of Monk performing this song have survived.

For a while, Monk was almost the only jazz artist promoting "Epistrophy." Few cover versions were recorded in the 1960s, although Eric Dolphy left behind two recordings from the final month of his life, and I could imagine him continuing to play this song, and other Monk compositions, had he lived longer—the angularity and unconventionality of the horn player's phrasing seem a perfect match for this music. After Monk's death in 1982, "Epistrophy" gradually gained the allegiance of other improvisers as part of a wider reassess-ment of a player once seen as too quirky for assimilation into the mainstream.

Even so, I advise caution before musicians jump into "Epistrophy." This song has a strong personality, so much so that you may find that it plays you, rather than the other way around. It's a rarity to hear a performer take this song and put such a stamp on it that it becomes an individual statement rather than another homage to the originator. Three good examples: Max Roach's recording with his percussion ensemble M'Boom from 1979; Paul Motian's trio performance, with

Joe Lovano and Bill Frisell, captured live at the Village Vanguard in 1995; and Charlie Hunter's Latin-tinged guitar outing from 2000.

RECOMMENDED VERSIONS

Cootie Williams (recorded as "Fly Right"), Chicago, April 1, 1942

Thelonious Monk (with Milt Jackson), New York, July 2, 1948

Thelonious Monk (with John Coltrane), from *Thelonious Monk Quartet with John Coltrane at Carnegie Hall*, live at Carnegie Hall, New York, November 29, 1957

Eric Dolphy, from *Last Date*, Hilversum, the Netherlands, June 2, 1964

Max Roach (with M'Boom), from *M'Boom*, New York, July 25–27, 1979

Paul Motian (with Joe Lovano and Bill Frisell), from *Sound of Love*, live at the Village Vanguard, New York, June 7, 1995

Charlie Hunter, from *Charlie Hunter*, New York, December 19–26, 2000

Everything Happens to Me
Composed by Matt Dennis, with lyrics by Tom Adair

Tommy Dorsey had heard about composer Matt Dennis via singer Jo Stafford, and flew both the songwriter and lyricist Tom Adair out to New York, where he set them up in his penthouse office in the Brill Building. Here the duo was expected to churn out material for Dorsey's band, which turned "Everything Happens to Me" into a top 10 hit. But in this instance, as in a few others, Dorsey rode the coattails of his prized singer, Frank Sinatra, who had a special knack for interpreting Dennis's works. In his later years, Sinatra would probably have played up the campier elements in the lyrics of "Everything Happens to Me," and maybe added a few new jokes à la Dennis himself, but his 1941 recording is pure and pristine, and goes straight to the heart.

This is a very well-crafted song, which Dennis and Adair built out of the simplest of ingredients. The bassline of the main theme runs through variations on one of the most predictable patterns in popular music—an almost vaudevillian vamp that, in its most basic form, moves from II to V to III to VI, and then starts all over again. But Dennis tinkers with the progression, and inserts some choice jazz-oriented substitutions. Even better, he draws on some of the color tones in these chords in shaping an affecting melody.

Adair, a lyricist who prized cleverness almost to an extreme, took a gamble with the words. He adopts a coy, at times comic tone, and uses Dennis's melody as the basis for a list song—in this instance, relating all the unlucky and incongruous things that have happened in a jinxed life. This type of approach is

usually better suited to a medium-tempo or fast patter song, and the few popular jazz ballads that rely on lists (for example, "These Foolish Things") usually
steer away from humor. But Adair delivers less-than-zinging zingers in one of
the oddest love songs in the jazz repertoire—I can almost imagine Henny
Youngman or Milton Berle grabbing on to some of these concepts on a bad
night in Peoria (*I try out everything that comes around. . . . like the measles*).

But somehow, the song works, and an emotionally sensitive vocalist can
deliver these lines in a way that even amplifies the pathos of the final bars. The
stance here is actually a familiar one: a person is telling a painful and revealing
personal story, and though the humor may be awkward, it allows for a degree of
self-revelation that could not take place with a more serious demeanor. Even so,
you can push the comedy too much here: Dennis, a fine singer in his own right,
performed this song with an additional chorus about the travails of playing
piano in a cocktail lounge, with references to the bartender turning on the
blender, loud conversations, and people blowing their noses. Such additions
may get a few chuckles, but undercut the power of what can be a very intense,
revelatory song. To hear the profundity in this composition, listen instead to
Billie Holiday's interpretation, where no laugh track is needed or intended.

A few jazz bands covered this song in the months leading up to America's
entry into World War II, but it soon fell out of the repertoires of the big bands
and didn't emerge as a popular standard until embraced by a number of modern jazz artists after the war. Bud Powell recorded a trio version, with Curly
Russell and Max Roach, in 1947, and Charlie Parker adopted the song for his
string orchestra project from 1949. Thelonious Monk selected it for his solo
piano session with the Riverside label in 1959, and then chose it again when
Columbia had him do a solo session five years later. The song was perhaps even
more popular with the cool school and West Coast players, and shows up on
recordings by Stan Getz, Gerry Mulligan, Chet Baker, Paul Desmond, Art
Pepper, Shelly Manne, and Lee Konitz, among others.

"Everything Happens to Me" remains one of the core ballads in the jazz
repertoire. I have been playing it for decades, and there are few standards that I
return to more often or with greater satisfaction. Certainly there is no shortage
of tunes aiming to capture a similar woe-is-me attitude, but many of them seem
to overshoot with theatrical angst or never get beyond glib clichés. Yet Dennis
and Adair found a very convincing and human angle on this ancient theme, and
their song shows no signs of going out of date or out of fashion.

RECOMMENDED VERSIONS

Tommy Dorsey (with Frank Sinatra), New York, February 7, 1941

Bud Powell, New York, January 10, 1947

Charlie Parker (with strings), New York, November 30, 1949

Billie Holiday, from *Stay with Me*, New York, February 14, 1955

Thelonious Monk, from *Thelonious Alone in San Francisco*, San Francisco, October 21, 1959

Scott Hamilton, from *Scott Hamilton 2*, Hollywood, January 7, 1978

Art Pepper (with George Cables), from *Roadgame*, live at Maiden Voyage, Los Angeles, August 15, 1981

Branford Marsalis, from *Bloomington*, live at Indiana University Auditorium, Bloomington, Indiana, September 23, 1991

Lee Konitz (with Brad Mehldau and Charlie Haden), from *Another Shade of Blue*, live at the Jazz Bakery, Culver City, California, December 21–22, 1997

Paolo Fresu and Uri Caine, from *Things*, Pernes-les-Fontaines, France, December 2005

Evidence
Composed by Thelonious Monk

Did you notice the pun in the song's title? No? Well, this is the world of Thelonious Monk, where you need to probe a little under the surface. Here's your crib sheet: the composition is based on the chord changes to the 1929 song "Just You, Just Me," which translates into "Just Us," which leads, naturally enough, to "Justice." And everyone knows that for justice you need evidence. Voilà!

The song is as elusive as its name. I can't think of any other jazz piece from the late 1940s that was so prickly—a composition without phrases, only isolated notes and clusters, most of them off the beat and surrounded by rests. Indeed, the opening gambit of Monk's debut recording from 1948 may be the most avant-garde moment in the artist's career, presenting a foreboding sequence of 11 tones and chord fragments that give little indication of tonality, tempo, or bar lines. Yet Monk is merely playing a variant of the "melody." It's something of a letdown (although perhaps a relief for first-time listeners) when this fusillade is followed by the bass and drums supporting a vibes solo in conventional 4/4 time. Only Monk is unaffected, continuing to extend his series of strident sounds, which are transformed into comping chords.

Monk's now-lauded compositions were slow in establishing themselves as jazz standards, but "Evidence" was more of a laggard than most. Over a decade elapsed before any bandleader other than Monk recorded the song—with the exception of Art Blakey, who featured the piece at a 1957 session . . . but probably only because Monk was guest pianist on the date. During the remainder of the decade, Blakey would occasionally perform "Evidence" with his working unit, but few followed this bold example. Throughout the 1960s, your best chance of hearing this work would be at a Thelonious Monk concert: it was a regular in the pianist's set list, and more than 20 live recordings of him playing it have survived from the decade. When pianist Jaki Byard showcased "Evidence" on his uninhibited 1968 collaboration with Rahsaan Roland Kirk, released as *The Jaki Byard Experience*, the piece was still something of a curio in the jazz world. The 1970s weren't much better for Monk's tune. "Evidence" never made the cut for *The Real Book*, the work that helped define the standard repertoire for the musicians of that period, nor does it show up in most of the other fake books of the era.

As with so many Monk pieces, "Evidence" only gained traction as a standard in the aftermath of the composer's death from a stroke on February 17, 1982. By coincidence, the band Sphere, featuring pianist Kenny Barron and Monk's erstwhile sideman Charlie Rouse on sax, recorded the song on that same day for their album *Four in One*. "Evidence" reached additional listeners through the many Monk tribute concerts and projects that followed. More cover versions were recorded between 1983 and 1987 than during the previous two decades combined.

This foreboding song from 1948 had finally gone mainstream, even if it had taken several decades. Yet it remains one of Monk's least accessible works and an unlikely candidate for crossover success of any sort. Even so, a handful of players have specialized in this piece and will serve as indispensable guides to its riches. Pianists Mal Waldron and Jessica Williams have offered up "Evidence" so often, they may well qualify as expert witnesses. But saxophonist Steve Lacy trumped them all, recording "Evidence" almost as many times as Monk himself, as documented on around 20 recordings made over a period of four decades.

RECOMMENDED VERSIONS

Thelonious Monk (with Milt Jackson), New York, July 2, 1948

Art Blakey and Thelonious Monk, from *Art Blakey's Jazz Messengers with Thelonious Monk*, New York, May 15, 1957

Thelonious Monk (with Johnny Griffin), from *Thelonious in Action*, live at the Five Spot, New York, July 9, 1958

Steve Lacy (with Don Cherry), from *Evidence*, Hackensack, New Jersey, November 14, 1961

Jaki Byard (with Rahsaan Roland Kirk), from *The Jaki Byard Experience*, New York, September 17, 1968

Sphere (with Charlie Rouse and Kenny Barron), from *Four in One*, Englewood Cliffs, New Jersey, February 17, 1982

Steve Lacy and Elvin Jones, from *That's the Way I Feel Now*, New York, 1984

Paul Motian (with Bill Frisell and Joe Lovano), from *Monk in Motian*, New York, March 1988

Mal Waldron, from *Evidence*, Toronto, March 14, 1988

Wynton Marsalis, from *Marsalis Plays Monk: Standard Time, Vol. 4*, New York, September 17–18, 1993, and October 3–4, 1994

Jessica Williams, from *Jazz in the Afternoon*, live at Chemekata College, Portland, Oregon, February 8, 1998

Ev'ry Time We Say Goodbye
Composed by Cole Porter

The stars were out at the December 1944 gala opening night for Cole Porter's *Seven Lively Arts*. Joe DiMaggio, Judy Garland, Ethel Merman, and other celebrities were on hand, helping to imbibe the 300 cases of champagne that producer Billy Rose dispensed to the patrons to commemorate the occasion. Drawings by Salvador Dalí adorned the lobby, and the audience had been entreated by Rose to come dressed in fine attire. Porter, for his part, needed to share some of the acclaim with Igor Stravinsky, who provided ballet music for the production, dancer Alicia Markova, and Benny Goodman, who performed with his combo. Did all these ingredients mix? No, not at all—at least judging by reviews and box office receipts. Bea Lillie, who starred in the show, would later refer to it as the *Seven Deadly Arts*, a not-inappropriate label for a production that closed a few months later with a $150,000 loss.

But one piece of music managed to survive the failure and become a hit, and it wasn't composed by Stravinsky. Porter's "Ev'ry Time We Say Goodbye" would rank among his most popular and frequently recorded pieces in later years. In contrast to the grandiose ambitions of *Seven Lively Arts*, Porter's composition succeeds through its small touches, which transform this elegiac song into a classic. The melody starts tentatively, almost shyly, with its gentle repeated notes, before expanding dramatically in the final eight bars—a powerful contrast that gives shape and substance to performances of this work. That sweet comparison of the lover's farewell to the change from "major to minor," with the music mimicking the lyrics, is sublimely realized—a brief moment, yes, but one of the finest in the American popular song repertoire. The music editor and composer Albert Szirmai wrote Porter a letter mentioning how this song brought him to tears whenever he heard it, and I wouldn't be surprised if it was this juncture in the composition that he found most heartrending.

Not everyone was so pleased with the song. Journalist Danton Walker accused Cole Porter of plagiarism, asserting that "Ev'ry Time We Say Goodbye" was lifted from the French song "Chanson de l'adieu" as well as from "Each Time You Say Goodbye (I Die a Little)" composed by Phil Ohman and Foster Carling for the 1939 film *Lady of the Tropics*. I've tracked down both the movie song and the French chanson, and am willing to exonerate Porter of all charges. In truth, a melody so dependent on repeated notes—in the opening bars, the major third is played eight times in a row, while other chord tones enjoy a similar treatment later in the form—is likely to remind listeners of many other songs. Just try it with your friends in a round of "Name That Tune" and see for yourself.

Benny Goodman recorded Porter's song even before opening night. Teddy Wilson, who played piano on this track, recorded "Ev'ry Time We Say Goodbye" under his own leadership one month later, and imparted a much jazzier sensibility to the composition, aided by Maxine Sullivan's relaxed vocal. Only a handful of jazz cover versions were recorded in the years following World War II, but Ella Fitzgerald delivered a deeply moving rendition as part of her Cole Porter songbook project from 1956—an album that reportedly inspired the composer to remark, "My, what marvelous diction that girl has." Over the next few years, many of the leading jazz artists of the day recorded the piece, and it has remained a very popular ballad ever since.

This is a song that is easy to play but hard to play well. There is nothing flashy in the written chart, and the piece resists glibness. I have heard well-known artists try to double the tempo and swing this standard with a bouncy beat—and it falls flat when played in that manner. Perhaps the best guide to how to approach "Ev'ry Time We Say Goodbye" comes from John Coltrane, whose performance on his best-selling *My Favorite Things* LP may be the most frequently heard jazz rendition of the work. Coltrane, often tempted to extreme gestures, takes no solo here but instead lays bare the emotional center of the song with a plaintive melody statement. A number of live recordings of Coltrane performing this song in Europe have surfaced over the years, and even in these settings, where he has plenty of room to stretch out, the saxophonist prefers to present a taut, introspective interpretation. Among more recent renditions, I call particular attention to the solo recording by Chris Potter from 1994 and Theo Bleckmann's ethereal performance with Ben Monder from 1996, for their similar sensitivity to the psychological depths of Porter's piece.

RECOMMENDED VERSIONS

Benny Goodman, New York, November 16, 1944

Teddy Wilson (with Maxine Sullivan), New York, December 18, 1944

Ella Fitzgerald, from *Ella Fitzgerald Sings the Cole Porter Songbook*, Los Angeles, February 7, 1956

John Coltrane, from *My Favorite Things*, New York, October 26, 1960

Ray Charles and Betty Carter, from *Ray Charles and Betty Carter*, Los Angeles, June 13, 1961

John Coltrane, from *The Paris Concert*, live at the Olympia, Paris, November 17, 1962

Bill Evans (with Warne Marsh), from *Crosscurrents*, Berkeley, California, February–March 1977

Chris Potter, from *Pure*, New York, June 14–15, 1994

Theo Bleckmann and Ben Monder, from *No Boat*, Stamford, Connecticut, August 30–31, 1996

Kurt Elling, from *This Time It's Love*, Chicago, December 1997–January 1998

Roy Hargrove (with Roberta Gambarini), from *Emergence*, Hollywood, June 16–17, 2008

Diana Krall, from *Quiet Nights*, Hollywood, 2009

Exactly Like You
Composed by Jimmy McHugh, with lyrics by Dorothy Fields

"Gaudy and vulgar." With those words, *Time* magazine dismissed *Lew Leslie's International Revue*, the 1930 show that introduced this classic song by Jimmy McHugh and Dorothy Fields. The critics' hostile reaction may have contributed to the show's short run—it folded after fewer than 100 performances—but didn't stop two of the songs from the revue from becoming mega-hits. (The other was "On the Sunny Side of the Street.")

Even so, the acceptance of this song in jazz circles was not immediate. Although Louis Armstrong and the Casa Loma Orchestra recorded versions when the tune was still fresh, not many jazz artists followed their lead. For more than five years—from January 1931 to August 1936—not a single jazz musician performed this song at a studio session.

Benny Goodman, then at the peak of his popularity, broke the unofficial ban when he turned to "Exactly Like You" as a feature number for Lionel Hampton—but with Hampton as a vocalist! In fact, Goodman had only met Hampton the previous week, and though he was fascinated by the latter's vibraphone playing, he was clearly assessing his new hire's skills as a singer. Goodman had no doubt heard the 1930 recording by Casa Loma Orchestra (a role model for his swing band), with Jack Richmond's vocal, and was trying to capture a similar ambiance. Hampton, for his part, shows how much his singing style is indebted to Louis Armstrong, and listening to his version of "Exactly Like You," I can't help but recall Hamp's boast about going around without an overcoat during the winter, hoping he would get laryngitis and capture a grit-in-the-throat sound like Satchmo.

On the heels of Goodman's success, many of the leading jazz bands added "Exactly Like You" to their repertoires. In 1937, Count Basie recorded a hard swinging version, at almost double the speed of Goodman's interpretation, for his second session with the Decca label. The track includes a memorable Jimmy Rushing vocal—if Hampton channels Armstrong, then Rushing sounds here as if he has fallen under the influence of Billie Holiday, who was singing with Basie around this time—and a half-chorus from Lester Young. A month later, Django Reinhardt recorded a more wistful interpretation of "Exactly Like You" in Paris.

The versatility of the song helped ensure its staying power. It works as a vocal feature at a range of tempos, as a swing dance number, or as a jam session workhorse. A few years after Basie's recording, the piece showed up at Minton's Playhouse in Harlem, then emerging as a launching pad for the bebop movement—an amateur recording made at that locale in 1941 finds Thelonious Monk backing Don Byas on "Exactly Like You."

The tune sounds deceptively simple, yet the placement of the rests and the spacious range required makes this more difficult to sing than your typical pop song—which hasn't, of course, stopped a host of iconic singers (Frank Sinatra, Louis Armstrong, Willie Nelson, Aretha Franklin, among them) from tackling this ever popular standard. The lyrics are oh-so-cute, but the double internal rhyme (dream I'm dreaming / scheme I'm scheming) that builds up to the climax provides a very powerful hook and is matched so perfectly with the melody that it is hard to imagine which came first. Every once in a while I run into an example of "songwriting twin birth" (as I call it), in which the words and music are so ideally matched that it seems as if they must have come into existence simultaneously. "Exactly Like You" is a stellar example, and I'm sure I'm not the only fan who, even when listening to an instrumental version, can't help hearing the words or even singing them *sotto voce*.

RECOMMENDED VERSIONS

Casa Loma Orchestra, New York, April 15, 1930

Louis Armstrong, New York, May 4, 1930

Benny Goodman (with Lionel Hampton), Hollywood, August 26, 1936

Count Basie, New York, March 26, 1937

Django Reinhardt (with the Quintette du Hot Club de France), Paris, April 21, 1937

Don Byas (with Thelonious Monk), live at Minton's New York, 1941

Dizzy Gillespie and Stan Getz, from *Diz and Getz*, Los Angeles, December 9, 1953

Sun Ra, from *New Steps*, Rome, January 2 and 7, 1978

Dave McKenna, from *Live at Maybeck Recital Hall, Vol. 2*, recorded live at Maybeck Recital Hall, Berkeley, California, November 1989

Diana Krall, from *From This Moment On*, Los Angeles, Spring 2006

Falling in Love with Love

Composed by Richard Rodgers, with lyrics by Lorenz Hart

Back when Richard Rodgers and Lorenz Hart composed this song, for the 1938 musical *The Boys from Syracuse*, jazz waltzes were rarities. Two years earlier, Benny Carter had recorded his "Waltzing the Blues" in London, and four years later Fats Waller would debut his "Jitterbug Waltz." Yet these were curios during the Swing Era, and a typical jazz fan of the era could go night after night to clubs and dance halls without hearing the band perform a single piece in 3/4 time.

Richard Rodgers, to his credit, did his best to provide suitable waltz material for jazz performers. Back in 1932 he composed "Lover" for the movie *Love Me Tonight*, destined to become a jazz standard; yet the big bands ignored it for a long time, and when stars such as Gene Krupa and Stan Kenton finally embraced it, they changed the beat to a fast 4/4. Almost 30 years later, Rodgers was still at it, serving up "My Favorite Things" in *The Sound of Music*, which would become a vehicle for John Coltrane's modal explorations, although with more of a 6/8 feeling to the pulse than Rodgers's original 3/4.

"Falling in Love with Love" encountered a similar response. It failed to find jazz advocates for many years, and then often showed up in arrangements that substituted a 4/4 meter. Sinatra kept to the original time signature for his 1944 V-disc recording, but few others followed this path. Clifford Brown opts for 4/4 on his 1953 Stockholm recording, and again on his recording of this same song with Helen Merrill from the following year, as does Cannonball Adderley in his outing with strings, Coltrane alongside Mal Waldron from 1957, and the vast majority of other jazz musicians who have played this tune over the decades. Oddly enough, *The Real Book* presents the chart in waltz time—suggesting that, in this instance at least, the de facto bible of jazz charts took its lead from the original sheet music instead of the better-known jazz recordings.

In truth, there are bigger challenges here than the time signature. The phrases are heavily dependent on held tones and repeated notes, and the chord changes are not among the most inspired of Richard Rodgers's creations. Even Alec Wilder, who found things to admire in the piece, noted its "considerable monotony." My experience is that this standard works best when the band tinkers with the sheet music—adding a descending counterline to the melody (as Art Blakey does on his 1981 recording with Wynton Marsalis), or spicing up the chord changes (as Buddy Montgomery does on his recording with his brother Wes from 1959).

Yet the song has one big advantage, albeit an intangible one. The tune seems to fall almost effortlessly into a groove and has produced a series of very swinging jazz performances over the years. I'm not quite sure what credit Richard Rodgers deserves for this, but I can't figure out who else might have put the pixie dust into his composition. In this regard, the song works well as a medium- or up-tempo 4/4 tune, and when listening, say, to Hank Mobley's or Jimmy Smith's 1957 recordings of the standard, both made for the Blue Note label, one might be forgiven for thinking that this piece was a hard bop original.

RECOMMENDED VERSIONS

Frank Sinatra, Hollywood, July 8, 1944

Clifford Brown, from *Memorial*, Stockholm, September 15, 1953

Helen Merrill (with Clifford Brown), from *Helen Merrill*, New York, December 24, 1954

Elmo Hope, from *Meditations*, New York, July 28, 1955

Jimmy Smith, from *A Date with Jimmy Smith*, New York, February 11, 1957

Mal Waldron (with John Coltrane and Jackie McLean), from *The Dealers*, Hackensack, New Jersey, April 19, 1957

Hank Mobley, from *Hank Mobley*, Hackensack, New Jersey, June 23, 1957

Wes Montgomery (with Buddy Montgomery and Monk Montgomery), from *Montgomeryland*, Los Angeles, October 1, 1959

Gene Ammons and Dodo Marmarosa, from *Jug & Dodo*, Chicago, May 4, 1962

Sheila Jordan, from *A Portrait of Sheila*, Englewood Cliffs, New Jersey, September 19, 1962

Art Blakey (with Wynton Marsalis), from *Straight Ahead*, live at the Keystone Korner, San Francisco, June 1981

Sonny Rollins, *Falling in Love with Jazz*, New York, September 9, 1989

Fascinating Rhythm

Composed by George Gershwin, with lyrics by Ira Gershwin

Aaron Copland lavished high praise on this song shortly after its debut, lauding Gershwin's composition as "rhythmically not only the most fascinating, but the most original jazz song yet composed." The assertion is a bit extravagant: Copland, in all fairness, probably hadn't paid much attention to the King Oliver or Jelly Roll Morton compositions recorded around the same time that Gershwin wrote this tune—yet the claim is not far off the mark. With "Fascinating Rhythm," Gershwin had tapped into something stirring and wholly up-to-date.

In the early 1920s, the jittery rhythms of jazz were starting to show up in popular songs but generally in very rudimentary forms. "The Charleston" was a hit around this time, and built its hook on a syncopation so easy to feel that you could teach kindergarten students to clap along with it. Other popular songs of the era, such as "Limehouse Blues" (written by British theatrical composer Philip Braham) and "Toot, Toot, Tootsie, Goodbye" (composed by Ted Fio Rito, the Newark-born son of Italian immigrants), showed that tunesmiths of all lineages were now borrowing jazz phrasing for their pop melodies.

But no one moved more aggressively in mixing popular song with a jazz sensibility than George Gershwin. Yet also give credit to his brother Ira—indeed, a strong case can be made that jazz slang entered the mouths of the masses primarily via song lyrics and that Ira Gershwin thus had an even more pervasive influence than, say, F. Scott Fitzgerald or Ernest Hemingway in shaping American diction. That, however, is a subject for another day.

In any event, the brothers' efforts for the 1924 show *Lady Be Good*, the first major Broadway collaboration by these songwriting siblings, include some of the jazziest songs they would ever write. "Fascinating Rhythm," a hit song from the production, builds its hook from a metric displacement—the fascinating rhythm of the title, I would suggest—that is very much out of the jazz playbook. In fact, I could easily imagine this melody having come from a New Orleans cornet player or a Chicago school clarinetist, so perfectly does it match the sound of hot jazz of the era. The song was, in turn, easily adapted to the needs of jazz bands. In many ways, its melody construction anticipates the riff-based charts that would usher in the Swing Era.

What a change from the popular songs of an earlier day! A composition of this sort was almost a signature for the sophisticated, with the less-than-stylish left behind. Even the composers' father struggled to keep up—although proud of his children's achievement, he garbled the title into "Fashion on the River." And I can only imagine how well Vernon Duke's translation of the lyrics into Russia for exportation to the USSR—where he thought they might serve as effective anti-Soviet propaganda—went over with the proletariat.

Cliff "Ukulele Ike" Edwards, who sang "Fascinating Rhythm" in the Broadway production, helped further the popularity of the song with his December 1924 recording. Both this version and Sam Lanin's were hits during the spring of 1925. But a far more exciting rendition from April 1926, made a few days after the London opening of *Lady Be Good*, finds Edwards's costars Fred and Adele Astaire singing "Fascinating Rhythm" with the composer at the piano. Gershwin sounds a bit heavy-handed during the verse, but once he is into the main theme his keyboard work reveals a real natural feeling for jazz, and his solo might fool listeners in a blindfold test into thinking they were hearing one of the better Harlem stride pianists of the day.

Often songs so closely associated with the zeitgeist are the first to fall out of fashion when the public's tastes shift to the next new thing. But this composition has managed to stay relevant over the years. Bill Russo turned it into an outstanding modern jazz big band chart for Stan Kenton—which was in turn adopted for voices by the Swingle Singers. In the mid-1950s, Tal Farlow showed the song's potential as a bebop virtuoso guitar feature, Jimmy Giuffre transformed it into an avant-garde-ish clarinet piece, and Mel Tormé drew on it as a vehicle for his scat singing. Over the year, the song has enjoyed considerable popularity among violinists—as testified by numerous recordings by Stéphane Grappelli (who recorded "Fascinating Rhythm" in four separate decades), Joe Venuti, Mark O'Connor, the Turtle Island String Quartet, and other string players. And Billy Childs contributes an ingenious arrangement of "Fascinating Rhythm" for Dianne Reeves's project *The Calling*, which makes Gershwin's piece sound like a new millennium groove tune.

RECOMMENDED VERSIONS

Fred and Adele Astaire (with George Gershwin on piano), London, April 19–20, 1926

Stan Kenton (with arrangement by Bill Russo), from *Sketches on Standards*, Hollywood, January 30, 1953

Tal Farlow, from *The Interpretations of Tal Farlow*, Los Angeles, January 17, 1955

Mel Tormé (with the Marty Paich Dek-Tette), from *Mel Tormé with the Marty Paich Dek-Tette*, Hollywood, January 16–18, 1956

Stéphane Grappelli, from *Improvisations*, Paris, February 6, 1956

Jimmy Giuffre, from *The Jimmy Giuffre Clarinet*, Los Angeles, March 22, 1956

Art Pepper (with Carl Perkins), from *The Art of Pepper*, Hollywood, April 1, 1957

Sarah Vaughan, from *Gershwin Live!* live at the Dorothy Chandler Pavilion, Los Angeles, February 1–2, 1982

Dianne Reeves (with arrangement by Billy Childs), from *The Calling*, Burbank, California, September 9–11, 2000

Jamie Cullum, from *Catching Tales* (not included on the US release), London, circa 2004–5

Fly Me to the Moon
Composed by Bart Howard

Musing over the success of this work, composer Bart Howard later noted that it took him 20 years to learn how to compose a hit song in 20 minutes. "Fly Me to the Moon" exemplifies the paradox of this revealing quip. The song opens with a pattern of descending phrases—in essence, the hook of the song—presented with a soothing predictability, almost as if the future direction of the melody is dictated by the opening five notes. The harmonic progression, for its part, rarely departs from the circle of fifths. Put them together on the bandstand, and this song almost seems to play itself. I can easily imagine that composing "Fly Me to the Moon" was almost as effortless.

But this tune has traveled far since then. It has been translated into Spanish ("Llévame a la Luna"), has been a hit in Germany ("Schiess mich doch zum Mond"), employed as a theme in a Japanese anime series (*Neon Genesis Evangelion*), and has—yes, literally!—flown to the moon, brought there by the Apollo 11 mission. That's a long way from where Howard started a music career that, at first, showed little potential for *that* kind of truly astronomical stardom. Born in 1915 as Howard Joseph Gustafson in Burlington, Iowa, the future songwriter first went on the road as part of a band backing the Siamese twins Daisy and Violet Hilton. A later gig found him working with female impersonator Rae Bourbon. Needless to say, these are hardly the kind of engagements that serve as a springboard to fame and fortune. In 1951, Howard found himself as master of ceremonies and pianist at the Blue Angel in New York, where he was an accompanist rather than a headliner, and seemingly destined for permanent second-tier or third-tier status in the musical life of Manhattan.

But "Fly Me to the Moon"—then known as "In Other Words"—was sung at the Blue Angel by Felicia Sanders, and other vocalists picked up on the catchy tune. Nancy Wilson recorded it in 1959, but the turning point came the following year when Peggy Lee performed the song on *The Ed Sullivan Show*, then the most popular variety program on TV. Others jumped on the bandwagon. Among the many cover versions, Frank Sinatra's 1964 recording with Count Basie (and a chart by Quincy Jones), must rank as the best-known version of "Fly Me to the Moon"—and was the rendition that Buzz Aldrin brought along as a personal soundtrack for his lunar visit. Sinatra also established that this song works just as well in 4/4 as in the original waltz time envisioned by the composer.

I am not immune to the appeal of this piece, and it possesses a satisfying sense of forward movement that makes it fun to play. Yet an ineradicable Las Vegas showroom quality permeates the tune, the cumulative result of recordings by Sinatra, Tony Bennett, Louis Prima, Doris Day, Connie Francis, and other singers with varying degrees of jazz credibility, but each the kind of artist your great aunt used to talk about after returning from her vacation in Sin City. Rich Little has done a devastating take-off, offering impressions of various celebrities swapping stories of their sexual prowess while a big band plays "Fly Me to the Moon" in the background. Little pauses every once in a while to encourage the musicians ("Hit it, Count, hit it!"), and you could hardly pick a better song for such a put-on. The exaggerations of the lyrics—do we really need to know what love is like on Jupiter and Mars?—contribute to the effect.

As a result, this song seems to invite campy or shallow performances from even the most sober-minded artists. Wes Montgomery is saddled with a corny baroque chart for his 1968 recording, but overcomes it through the sheer cutting power of his guitar lines. Nat King Cole and George Shearing are hardly so successful on their 1961 collaboration, where they battle desperately against the strings and are hopelessly outnumbered. Then again, this song almost begs for parody or even ridicule, and its inescapable history will always make deconstruction an inviting path for a jazz player.

But you can also play it without an attitude and just let it fall into a groove—in either 3/4 or 4/4 time—which seems to happen quite naturally when this song is called on the bandstand. For suitable examples, listen to three especially moon-worthy performances from the Apollo program years: Roy Haynes's 1962 version with Rahsaan Roland Kirk, Vince Guaraldi's trio recording from 1964, and Hampton Hawes's spirited treatment from 1965.

RECOMMENDED VERSIONS

Peggy Lee (recorded as "In Other Words"), from *Pretty Eyes*, Hollywood, February 15 and 18, 1960

Roy Haynes (with Tommy Flanagan and Rahsaan Roland Kirk), from *Out of the Afternoon*, Englewood Cliffs, New Jersey, May 16, 1962

Frank Sinatra and Count Basie, from *It Might as Well Be Swing*, Los Angeles, June 9, 1964

Vince Guaraldi, from *Jazz Impressions of a Boy Named Charlie Brown*, San Francisco, 1964

Hampton Hawes, from *Here and Now*, Los Angeles, May 12, 1965

Wes Montgomery, from *Road Song*, Englewood Cliffs, New Jersey, May 7, 1968

Ray Brown (with Benny Carter), from *Some of My Best Friends Are . . . Sax Players*, New York (November 20–22, 1995), and Los Angeles (February 13, 1996)

Diana Krall, from *Live in Paris*, live at the Olympia, November–December 2001

Joey DeFrancesco, from *Snapshot*, live at the Kerr Cultural Center, Scottsdale, Arizona, March 5, 2009

A Foggy Day
Composed by George Gershwin, with lyrics by Ira Gershwin

One night early in 1937, Ira Gershwin was sitting up late reading when his brother George returned from a party, removed his jacket, sat down at the keyboard, and proposed that they get to work on another song for *A Damsel in Distress*, the Fred Astaire movie that was the siblings' current project. Within an hour, the pair had finished all of "A Foggy Day" except for the verse. The following day, Ira suggested a verse in an Irish vein—so much for old London town!—and George responded with something suitably wistful.

The end result was a strange variant on the familiar "city song" theme. Generally these tunes sing the praises of the metropolis in question—the "my kind of town" routine—but here the lyrics try to make London seem as drab and dreary as possible, until the final bars, when "A Foggy Day" morphs into a love song, with all of the brightness and splendor coming from the damsel in distress. Yet Londoners are still justified in using this song in their tourism campaigns: it features one of the composer's most inspired melodies, especially noteworthy for the quirky final bars, reminiscent of a military fanfare—with echoes of the English folk tune "Country Gardens"—where the concluding phrase relies heavily on chord tones and a perky doubling in the pace of the chord changes. The contrast with the preceding buildup, constructed with static phrases that follow the pattern of what commentators have called Gershwin's "repeated note songs," could hardly be starker. This passage also forces the form beyond the 32 bars that listeners may have been expecting. If I hadn't heard the unimpeachable results, I would have doubted that such a dramatic change in temperament—encompassing both the words and the music, including harmony, rhythm and melody—at the finish line of a song could work so well.

A Damsel in Distress is based on P. G. Wodehouse's novel of the same name, about the British escapades of a young American composer of musical comedies named George Bevan. One might assume that the character was based on George Gershwin—except for the fact that the book was published in 1919 when the songwriter was at the very start of his career. But Gershwin took a liking to the story and suggested it as a vehicle for Fred Astaire's first RKO film without Ginger Rogers as co-hoofer. Gershwin did not live to see the film's release, but almost from the moment of its debut, at Radio City Music Hall in November 1937, "A Foggy Day" became a popular hit, with recordings by Fred Astaire and Bob Crosby enjoying particular success. Even so, jazz musicians were slow to embrace the song, which did not enjoy much currency on the bandstand until almost a decade and a half had elapsed.

Frank Sinatra featured the composition on his *Songs for Young Lovers*, released in 1954, and the next several years proved to be a jazz high point for the Gershwin standard. More versions of "A Foggy Day" were recorded by major jazz stars in 1956 than at any point in the song's history, and many of my favorite interpretations were made around this time. Some have become well known, such as Louis Armstrong's endearing give-and-take on the Gershwin tune with Ella Fitzgerald. Others deserve to be better known. Baritone saxophonist Lars Gullin is not a familiar name to most jazz fans today (although he is much revered in his native Sweden), but his 1956 recording of "A Foggy Day" will reveal to the uninitiated why many rank him among the finest cool school improvisers. A few weeks earlier, Art Tatum and Buddy DeFranco engaged in some decidedly uncool jousting on the same song, and the clarinetist's intrepidity in countering the florid pianist note for note makes for some queasy excitement. I am fascinated to hear Tatum, roused for combat, stepping on DeFranco's toes at the end of the latter's solo by playing a loud, flamboyant lick that overpowers the horn player's conclusion. Hey, perhaps Tatum conveniently forgot that this song does not follow a 32-bar form; then again this virtuoso pianist had a long history of making life on the bandstand difficult for those who challenged him head-on, and this session is a case in point.

Charles Mingus typically preferred to perform his own compositions rather than standards, but he recorded "A Foggy Day" both on his December 1955 live date with Mal Waldron and again on his *Pithecanthropus Erectus* album from the following year. The former track is interesting mostly for its querulous introduction, with its anticipations of the avant-garde sensibility that Cecil Taylor would bring to his debut leader date the following year—but this jarring moment, no doubt a musical evocation of a traffic jam in London town, lasts but a few seconds before being replaced by a conventional workout over the changes. Mingus's follow-up performance, made just a few weeks later, pushes this subversive conception of the Gershwin tune even further, with sound effects intruding on the soloists. I suspect many Gershwin aficionados were less than pleased, but this track is a good example of how jazz standards never sounded very . . . well, let's say, *standard* . . . after being taken on board by this fervidly creative artist.

At the close of this fog-happy year, pianist Bill Potts was informed by his boss at Olivia Davis's Patio Lounge in Washington, D.C., that she had hired "a guy named Lester Young" to join the band during the slow holiday season. We are fortunate that Potts thought to record the results, which despite (or perhaps because of) the informal setting, stand out as Prez's finest late-career efforts. A few days later, Young's frequent collaborator Billie Holiday made her sole recording of "A Foggy Day," and if the optimism of her interpretation comes across as somewhat forced, the solo contributions of Ben Webster and Jimmy Rowles make this a track also well worth hearing.

RECOMMENDED VERSIONS

Frank Sinatra, from *Songs for Young Lovers*, Hollywood, November 5, 1953

Benny Carter (with Oscar Peterson), from *Cosmopolite*, Los Angeles, November 12, 1954

Charles Mingus, from *Pithecanthropus Erectus*, New York, January 30, 1956

Art Tatum and Buddy DeFranco, from *The Tatum Group Masterpieces, Vol. 7*, Los
    Angeles, February 6, 1956

Lars Gullin, from *Baritone Sax*, Stockholm, April 25, 1956

Louis Armstrong and Ella Fitzgerald, from *Ella and Louis*, Los Angeles, August 16,
    1956

Lester Young, from *Lester Young in Washington, D.C. 1956, Vol. 1*, live at the Patio
    Lounge, Washington, D.C., December 7–8, 1956

Billie Holiday (with Ben Webster), from *Songs for Distingué Lovers*, Los Angeles,
    January 3, 1957

Red Garland, from *Red Garland at the Prelude*, live at the Prelude Club, New York,
    October 2, 1959

George Benson (with Ronnie Cuber), from *It's Uptown*, New York, February 9, 1966

Sarah Vaughan, from *Live in Japan*, live at Sun Plaza Hall, Tokyo, September 24, 1973

Wynton Marsalis (with Marcus Roberts), from *Marsalis Standard Time, Vol. 1*, New
    York, May 29–30, 1986, and September 24–25, 1986

Bill Charlap, from *Plays George Gershwin: The American Soul*, New York, February 7,
    2005

Footprints
Composed by Wayne Shorter

"Footprints" served as a core part of Miles Davis's repertoire in the final months
before he moved from acoustic to electric music. During this tumultuous period for the jazz world, Davis felt compelled to break new ground but was un-
willing to move into the free jazz camp, then shaking up the scene by abandoning
tonality, barlines, scalar improvisation, and most other guiding structures of
the jazz craft. In this environment, Davis sought to establish different rules of
engagement, ones that allowed him to find new creative spaces at the limits
of—but still within—conventional structures.

Increasingly he turned to the loose, oblique compositions of Wayne Shorter,
the saxophonist in his seminal mid-1960s band. These pieces stayed within
somewhat familiar terrain—they followed song forms and relied on (mostly)
familiar chord changes. Yet, when played by Davis's crack combo—where, along
with Shorter, the trumpeter fronted a rhythm section of Herbie Hancock, Ron
Carter, and Tony Williams—these songs could sound more freeform than they
actually were. Casual listeners would often fail to hear the underlying structures,
which the combo worked hard to subvert and hide. In many ways, the "footprints"
they left on these kinds of songs—which probed at the boundaries between formalism and freedom—set a path preferred by many progressive players of a later
generation, who often opted for edginess over sheer musical anarchy.

The song bears a superficial similarity with "All Blues," a well-known track from Davis's much-lauded *Kind of Blue* album from 1959. Both rely on blues progressions but are adapted to an unusual meter—in the case of "All Blues" we have 12 bars of 6/8 each while "Footprints," as it is typically notated, encompasses 24 bars of 3/4. Yet it all adds up to the same number of beats. But the minor blues sound of "Footprints" imparts a darker feel to the proceedings, while the piano vamp that grounds "All Blues" so comfortably in the groove is nowhere to be found on the more sinuous Shorter composition.

Miles takes the song faster than Shorter did on his Blue Note leader date, *Adam's Apple*, where "Footprints" made its debut in 1966. But faster still is Shorter's return visit to "Footprints" some 35 years later, on a live recording from Spain, which finds the saxophonist reconfiguring some of his early compositions alongside pianist Danilo Pérez, drummer Brian Blades (neither of them born when Shorter first recorded this song) and bassist John Patitucci. Shorter's young sparring mates also impose a much different rhythmic sensibility on the song, sometimes hinting at Afro-Cuban elements nowhere evident on the 1960s-era recordings.

Yet this malleability is the very reason that Davis found "Footprints" so appealing when it was first composed. More than most jazz standards, this song invites radical reconceptualization. Even more extreme examples can be found in Blay Ambolley's 2001 recording of "Footprints," which mixes hard bop with the West African highlife style of his native Ghana, or the Zappa-esque electric version by Anthony Jackson and Yiorgos Fakanas from their 2009 project *Interspirit*.

RECOMMENDED VERSIONS

Wayne Shorter (with Herbie Hancock), from *Adam's Apple*, Englewood Cliffs, New Jersey, February 24, 1966

Miles Davis (with Wayne Shorter and Herbie Hancock), from *Miles Smiles*, New York, October 25, 1966

Pat Martino, from *The Visit*, New York, March 24, 1972

David Liebman (with Randy Brecker and Richie Beirach), from *Pendulum*, live at the Village Vanguard, New York, February 4–5, 1978

Ahmad Jamal, from *Digital Works*, Dallas, August 1985

Wayne Shorter (with Danilo Pérez), from *Footprints Live!* live at Festival De Jazz, Vitoria-Gasteiz, Spain, July 20, 2001

Blay Ambolley, from *AfriKan JaaZZ*, Ghana, Los Angeles, and Brooklyn, 2001

Anthony Jackson and Yiorgos Fakanas from *Interspirit*, Athens and Woodland Hills, California, November 2008–August 2009

Gee, Baby, Ain't I Good to You?

G

Composed by Don Redman, with lyrics by Andy Razaf

"Gee, Baby, Ain't I Good to You?" dates from the early days of the Great Depression—it was first recorded a week after the stock market crash of 1929—a era when, in a possible sign of mass denial, the public's tastes turned toward songs about good times and extravagant spending. Among the incongruous hits of the period, one finds "Happy Days Are Here Again," "We're in the Money," and "Life Is Just a Bowl of Cherries." Andy Razaf's lyrics to "Gee, Baby, Ain't I Good to You?"—with their courtship commitment of a new Cadillac, fur coat, and diamond ring—were especially well suited to the tenor of these times, when hit records were enlisted as implements of financial wish fulfillment.

Composer Don Redman offers a touching semispoken vocal on the debut recording, and his chart, which borrows on the sensibility of the blues while actually following a 32-bar song form with a fairly sophisticated harmonic progression, is equally affecting. One might predict great things for this song on the basis of such a launch, but more than a decade would elapse before another major jazz star would bring this composition to a studio session. Chu Berry's 1941 recording serves as a vocal feature for Hot Lips Page, a dynamic trumpeter who was making more of a splash as a singer at the time—five days later Page would record "Blues in the Night," destined to be a top 10 hit. But it would be left to another singer to establish the Redman song as a jazz standard. Nat King Cole's understated performance, recorded in November 1943, became a number one R&B hit the following year, and inspired a host of cover versions, from jazz, rhythm-and-blues, and pop artists.

Count Basie never took actual legal ownership of this song, but from the mid-1940s onward many fans probably assumed that "Gee, Baby, Ain't I Good to You?" had come out of Kansas City, so closely was it linked to various Basie-ites. In 1944, Basie featured singer Jimmy Rushing on a V-disc version as well as on a Jubilee recording for Armed Forces Radio and at another transcription session for the National Guard. Rushing would keep the song in his repertoire for the rest of his career. Basie also continued to favor it, and even after Rushing departed, it served as a feature for Joe Williams, O. C. Smith, Mary Stallings, and other singers. The band's horn players also got into the act, and some of the most characteristic performances of this work can be found on leader projects by Buddy Tate, Harry "Sweets" Edison, Joe Newman, and others who had honed their craft in the Basie band.

Jazz players with more progressive leanings—Dizzy Gillespie, Art Blakey, Paul Bley—would occasionally turn to this song in later years, but Redman's standard showed up more often in the repertoires of artists who favored traditional fare, especially those with a sensibility for bluesy mood pieces. The song is especially well suited for a pulse somewhat faster than a ballad, but not rapid enough to qualify as a medium tempo. Many artists falter in just that range, which allows for neither ambling swing nor gentle musings. But for two impressive examples, check out Cassandra Wilson's performance from her *Blue Skies* album and Hank Crawford's version alongside Jimmy McGriff from *On the Blue Side*.

RECOMMENDED VERSIONS

McKinney's Cotton Pickers (with Don Redman), New York, November 5, 1929

Chu Berry (with Hot Lips Page), New York, August 28, 1941

Nat King Cole, Los Angeles, November 30, 1943

Count Basie (with Jimmy Rushing), New York, May 27, 1944

Joe Newman, from *I Feel Like a Newman*, New York, September 1955

Kenny Burrell, from *Midnight Blue*, Englewood Cliffs, New Jersey, January 8, 1963

Harry "Sweets" Edison and Oscar Peterson, from *Oscar Peterson & Harry Edison*, Los Angeles, December 21, 1974

Cassandra Wilson, from *Blue Skies*, New York, February 1988

Hank Crawford and Jimmy McGriff, from *On the Blue Side*, Englewood Cliffs, New Jersey, April 4 and 9, 1989

Georgia on My Mind
Composed by Hoagy Carmichael, with lyrics by Stuart Gorrell

Saxophonist Frankie Trumbauer gave Hoagy Carmichael the prod that resulted in "Georgia on My Mind." "Why don't you write a song called 'Georgia'?" he suggested one day. "Nobody lost much writing about the South." To start the process along, Trumbauer even offered an opening phrase: "It ought to go 'Georgia, Georgia . . .'" To which the composer sarcastically replied: "That's a big help."

But with this impetus, Hoagy Carmichael worked out a tune over the next few days, with some help on the lyrics from his roommate, Stu Gorrell. Gorrell, who later became a vice president at Chase Bank, was not officially credited on the copyright filing, but Carmichael sent him periodic checks as a share of royalties. Gorrell, for his part, never made another excursion into songwriting, except for his role in suggesting the title for "Star Dust"—but he may be the most remarkable dabbler in pop song history. He only contributed to two songs, but they became two of the biggest hits of the century.

"Georgia on My Mind" is a wonderful song, even if there isn't any real connection to the Peach State here. Trumbauer hailed from Illinois, and Carmichael was from Indiana, as was Gorrell. The song was written in Queens, New York, and the first recording featured Carmichael along with Iowa-born cornetist Bix Beiderbecke. But, fortunately, Ray Charles, born in Albany, Georgia, exactly 90 days before "Georgia on My Mind" was copyrighted, eventually stepped in to add some authentic local color. His version of "Georgia on My Mind" wouldn't show up on the airwaves for some 30 years, but it would rise to the top of the *Billboard* chart—and it remains today the best-known version of Hoagy Carmichael's standard.

By that time, the song had been well picked over by jazz players. Within 18 months of the debut recording, "Georgia on My Mind" had been recorded by Louis Armstrong, Coleman Hawkins (with the Mound City Blue Blowers), Mildred Bailey, and—the man who set the whole thing off in the first place—Frankie Trumbauer. Later in the decade, the composition was showcased by Fats Waller, Django Reinhardt, and Ethel Waters, but "Georgia on My Mind" had an added boost with the rise of the Swing Era, as a host of big band artists recorded it—including Artie Shaw, Glenn Miller, the Casa Loma Orchestra, and Gene Krupa (whose version featuring Anita O'Day was a top 20 hit in June 1941).

"Georgia on My Mind" has never fallen out of favor with jazz musicians. Although the song failed to make the same inroads among the boppers and cool school as it had among the big band generation, purveyors of soul jazz and funk soon stepped in to fill the breach. Saxophonists with strong blues leanings—Eddie Harris, David "Fathead" Newman, Plas Johnson—have often found inspiration in these chord changes.

Jazz musicians may have set "Georgia on My Mind" in motion, but they haven't been able to hold on to it. The biggest chart successes in the history of this song belong to Ray Charles, Willie Nelson, Jerry Lee Lewis, and Michael Bolton. The song has also been performed by James Brown, Coldplay, Dean Martin, and a host of other artists of various genres and allegiances. When

Rolling Stone magazine picked the greatest songs of all time in 2003, they placed "Georgia on My Mind" in the 44th spot, the highest ranking of any jazz standard on the list . . . but one wonders how many of the magazine's readers had ever heard a jazz band perform it.

The appeal of "Georgia on My Mind" comes from its plaintive, timeless quality, and one could almost imagine that it dated back to the nineteenth century, or perhaps had no true composer—ranking among those mysterious pieces attributed to "traditional"—instead springing up spontaneously in the fields and backwoods of Georgia. The biggest surprise may be that the same person who composed the convoluted and archly modern melody to "Star Dust" was also responsible for this melancholy lament, which is infused so deeply with elements of the blues and spirituals.

RECOMMENDED VERSIONS

Hoagy Carmichael (with Bix Beiderbecke), New York, September 15, 1930

Mound City Blue Blowers (with Coleman Hawkins), New York, June 30, 1931

Louis Armstrong, Chicago, November 5, 1931

Gene Krupa (with Anita O'Day), New York, March 12, 1941

Ray Charles, from *The Genius Hits the Road*, New York, March 25, 1960

Clark Terry, from *Clark After Dark*, London, September 9–12, 1977

Gerry Mulligan, from *Dream a Little Dream*, New York, April 14–29, 1994

Eddie Harris (with Jacky Terrasson), from *Freedom Jazz Dance*, New York, June 18, 1994

David "Fathead" Newman, from *I Remember Brother Ray*, Englewood Cliffs, New Jersey, August 14, 2004

John Scofield, from *That's What I Say: John Scofield Plays the Music of Ray Charles*, New York, December 2004

Ghost of a Chance
Composed by Victor Young, with lyrics by Ned Washington and Bing Crosby

As with many composers who gravitated to Hollywood during the 1930s and 1940s, Victor Young boasted a European pedigree, having studied at the Warsaw Conservatory and played violin with the Warsaw Philharmonic. Yet unlike the others, Young had actually been born in Chicago, and only went to Poland, to live with a grandfather, after becoming an orphan around his tenth birthday. When Young returned to the States following World War I, he was already a skilled classical performer, but now he made his mark in the commercial music world, where he earned a living as a violinist, arranger, musical director for record labels and radio programs, and ultimately as a songwriter and film composer of some distinction. Young received 22 Academy Award nominations but never won an Oscar during his lifetime—his sole victory came posthumously, four months after his death, for his score to *Around the World in Eighty Days*.

This song's full title is "I Don't Stand a Ghost of a Chance," but jazz players invariably shorten it to "Ghost of a Chance." Bing Crosby introduced the tune to the American public with his 1932 recording, a rendition more bellowing than relaxed—Crosby sounds as if he would be more comfortable if the chart were transposed up a few steps. But his vocal is eerily penetrating, and the public responded to the heartfelt performance, rewarding the crooner with a top 10 hit.

The melody builds effectively from a compact opening—it stays within the range of a minor third during the first half of the A theme—before reaching its highest note in bar six to coincide with the word "ghost" in the title phrase, then descending a full octave into the turnaround. The effect is melancholy and languorous, offset by the momentary optimism of the four ascending phrases in the bridge. Other standards offer more dramatic effects, but few do a better job of matching the emotional flow of the words to the development of the musical line.

Only a few jazz artists paid attention to the song during the 1930s, and when they finally did, an instrumentalist rather than a singer served as catalyst. Chu Berry's saxophone performance on "Ghost of a Chance," recorded with Cab Calloway's band in 1940, stirred up interest among other horn players, and stands out as one of the most influential tenor solos of the period. Much like Coleman Hawkins's recording of "Body and Soul" made a few months earlier, this track serves as a sax feature from start to finish—bandleader Calloway doesn't even figure in the arrangement—and Berry is tinkering with the melody almost from the outset, remaining in total command until the lingering coda. Berry would be killed in a car accident the following year, at age 33, and this performance is the best place to start for those who wish to understand why his name is often mentioned in the same breath as Coleman Hawkins, Lester Young, and Ben Webster in discussions of the great jazz tenorists of the era.

In the middle years of the decade, a number of other sax players made recordings of "Ghost of a Chance," including Lester Young, Dexter Gordon, Illinois Jacquet, and Charlie Ventura. The lyrics by Ned Washington and Bing Crosby are simple but effective, and in later decades many well-known jazz singers (Billie Holiday, Ella Fitzgerald, Diana Krall) would also embrace this composition. It especially rewards vocalists who respect the value of nuance and understatement. That said, saxophonists have been the most loyal advocates for "Ghost of a Chance," many of them retaining it as a featured ballad in their repertoire for decades. Arnett Cobb, Eddie "Lockjaw" Davis, Zoot Sims, Lew Tabackin, Lee Konitz, and others have each recorded the song on multiple occasions. Although it remains less well known than "Body and Soul," especially among the general public, this song continues to serve as a benchmark by which horn players are measured—both among their peers and against exemplary performers from the past.

RECOMMENDED VERSIONS

Bing Crosby, New York, October 14, 1932

Chu Berry (with Cab Calloway's orchestra), Chicago, June 27, 1940

Lester Young (with Count Basie), New York, May 1, 1944

Charlie Ventura, Los Angeles, March 1, 1945

Clifford Brown and Max Roach, from *Brown and Roach, Incorporated*, Los Angeles, August 3, 1954

Billie Holiday, from *Music for Torching*, Los Angeles, August 23, 1955

Thelonious Monk, from *Thelonious Himself*, New York, April 5, 1957

Arnett Cobb (with Bobby Timmons), from *Movin' Right Along*, New York, February 17, 1960

Lennie Tristano, from *Concert in Copenhagen*, live at Tivoli Gardens Concert Hall, Copenhagen, October 31, 1965

Yusef Lateef, from *The Golden Flute*, New York, June 15–16, 1966

Diana Krall, from *Love Scenes*, New York, 1997

Joe Lovano (with Dave Holland and Elvin Jones), from *Trio Fascination*, New York, September 16–17, 1997

Giant Steps
Composed by John Coltrane

"Giant Steps," first recorded by John Coltrane for his 1959 Atlantic album of the same name, quickly became famous in jazz circles—but more as an obstacle course than a favored jam session tune. The song "Cherokee" had played a similar role for the boppers of the early 1940s, weeding out the wannabes not ready for the demands of modern jazz. Think of "Giant Steps" as "Cherokee" on steroids.

True, "Giant Steps" was not as revolutionary as some of the more avant-garde offerings of the day. Coltrane's song stayed in 4/4 time, followed a 16-bar form, and did not veer outside the conventional boundaries of tonality. The chord progression borrowed many elements used previously by jazz players—listen to Richard Rodgers's bridge to the 1937 standard "Have You Met Miss Jones?" for an important predecessor. Yet at Coltrane's brisk tempo and with a few of his own ingenious harmonic twists added to the mix, this musical steeplechase presented a stiff challenge to an unprepared soloist, circa 1959.

Ah, Coltrane was quite prepared (although his pianist on the date, Tommy Flanagan, sounds a bit flummoxed—but give him credit, he recorded "Giant Steps" several times in the 1980s and showed he had it under his fingers by then). The saxophone titan, for his part, had developed some handy improvisational patterns to employ on the song, most notably a repeated phrase that draws on the opening four notes of the pentatonic scale. Coltrane relies on this motif repeatedly in his solo, and close study of his improvisation reveals a certain rote quality to it. Yet the overall effect is nonetheless impressive, perhaps even a bit unsettling. I tend to view "Giant Steps" less as a song, and more an exercise Coltrane developed as part of his own intense self-imposed musical education—one that he left behind after he had mastered it. Although this ranks among his most famous compositions, the saxophonist rarely played it in later years—no recording of him performing "Giant Steps" after his 1959 studio versions has been released (although an unreleased tape of a 1960 rendition exists).

But the jazz world did not forget "Giant Steps." Every serious jazz musician ought to learn and master it—not just because it might be called at the next gig, but simply for the mind-expanding lessons it imparts. Pianist Jaki Byard was the first to cover the song, and his 1961 version moves from solo to trio and reveals some original tricks of the pianist's own invention. His embrace of the song was rare at the time. "Giant Steps" wasn't widely performed by other jazz artists until the 1970s, when it started showing up on a wide range of recording projects, including albums by James Moody, Tete Montoliu, Phineas Newborn, and Woody Herman. Toots Thielemans even proved that one could solo persuasively over these changes on a chromatic harmonica—a sign, perhaps, that the radical innovation of 1959 had finally become somewhat tamed and mainstreamed. By the mid-1970s, when Dick Wellstood was playing it as a stride piano number and Rahsaan Roland Kirk added lyrics, the process of assimilation had seemingly been completed.

But this song will never really fit into any crossover formula, and a number of later artists have tried to reclaim its progressive origins. The World Saxophone Quartet turned "Giant Steps" into a free-for-all in its 1993 arrangement. A few years later, Anthony Braxton showed us what it sounds like when sax and guitar take a solo on "Giant Steps" at the same time. Leroy Jenkins, for his part, demonstrated that this composition could serve as inspiration for an avant-garde solo violin performance. All in all, Coltrane's étude has held up well. Even today, anyone who wants to add it to a set playlist needs to take some baby steps in the practice room before trying "Giant Steps" on the bandstand. I don't anticipate that changing any time soon.

RECOMMENDED VERSIONS

John Coltrane, from *Giant Steps*, New York, May 5, 1959

Jaki Byard, from *Here's Jaki*, New York, March 14, 1961

Woody Herman, from *Giant Steps*, New York, April 9–12, 1973

Toots Thielemans, from *Captured Alive*, Sea Cliff, New York, September 16, 1974

Rahsaan Roland Kirk, from *Return of the 5000 Lb. Man*, New York, 1976

World Saxophone Quartet, from *Moving Right Along*, New York, October 18–19, 1993

Kenny Garrett, from *Pursuance: The Music of John Coltrane*, New York, 1996

Pat Metheny, from *Trio Live*, unidentified location, 1999–2000

Anthony Braxton, from *23 Standards*, Brussels, February 22, 2003

The Girl from Ipanema

Composed by Antonio Carlos Jobim, with lyrics by Vinicius de Moraes (English lyrics by Norman Gimbel)

This song still hasn't recovered from its early success. After "The Girl from Ipanema" took over the airwaves during the summer of 1964, it soon started showing up at all the least cool locales. You heard it emanating from the wedding reception down at the American Legion Hall, at tacky tiki bars in landlocked cities, indeed anyplace where the unhip congregated for tame, inhibited fun. Comedy films soon learned to play on this chronic squareness, and thus "The Girl from Ipanema" shows up as elevator music in *The Blues Brothers*, in a dentist's waiting room in *Finding Nemo*, and as background music while Kim Basinger seduces hapless Dana Carvey in *Wayne's World 2*. By now, everyone from Monty Python to *The Simpsons* has taken potshots at it, and it's hard for any of us to remember when this tune, which once could swing so cool and sway so gently, wasn't a cliché.

Heloísa Pinheiro would later make a mini-career out of her connection to the song, parlaying it into everything from TV appearances to her own chain of boutiques (named, appropriately enough *Garota de Ipanema*). Back in 1962, this teenage carioca regularly strolled past the Bar Veloso, a block off the beach at Ipanema in Rio de Janeiro. Dressed sometimes in a school uniform or occasionally a two-piece bathing suit, she caught the attention of songwriter Antonio Carlos Jobim, who frequented the Veloso. Jobim already enjoyed considerable local fame—a short while later his "Desafinado" would become a hit in the United States—and he was working with Vinicius de Moraes on a musical comedy. When Moraes came to the Veloso, Jobim made sure his friend saw the graceful young lady, and soon they had crafted a sprightly bossa nova song inspired by her Ipanema strolls.

The legend has been stretched a wee bit over the years. Despite what you may have heard to the contrary, the songwriters didn't sketch out the song on the back of a napkin while girl-watching at the Veloso. Jobim actually composed the music in his home on Rua Barão da Torre, while Moraes wrote the words an hour's drive north in Petropolis. The song didn't even mention Ipanema in its original title—its name was "Menina que Passa" ("The Girl Who Passes By"). But more changes would be imposed on this song before it became a hit. When Stan Getz suggested that Astrud Gilberto sing the lyrics in English on the record, both Jobim and Astrud's husband, João, the star vocalist on the date, objected. After all, she wasn't a professional singer and, with all due respect, her delivery of Norman Gimbel's translation of the lyrics wouldn't make anyone forget Sarah or Ella.

But the very unaffected, conversational delivery of the words, combined with the undercurrent of a Brazilian accent to her voice, captivated listeners, and helped propel "The Girl from Ipanema" on to the charts at a time when most had assumed the bossa nova fad was over. Within weeks, the cover versions started proliferating, and in time even the least likely jazz players had added it to their repertoires—Louis Armstrong, Earl Hines, Benny Goodman, Count Basie, and others who were once trendsetters, but hardly the proper endorsers to give a mid-1960s song the right coolness quotient. Yet the real damage was done outside the world of jazz, with Eartha Kitt doing heavy breathing on her rendition, Jackie Gleason lending his name to a corny easy listening arrangement, and the innumerable karaoke versions, a technology for which this song is—alas!—all too well suited.

Even Getz eventually decided this song was best left off his set lists, and in later years he rarely performed it in public—standing out as that grand anomaly, the artist who doesn't play his biggest hit in concert. Who could blame him? Perhaps if a 20-year moratorium on public performance were implemented, "The Girl from Ipanema" could recapture some of its initial freshness, and I wouldn't be surprised if, at some distant point in time, this song even became a hit once again. In the meantime, jazz fans looking for the best recordings are advised to exercise caution in their purchases, if only because so many uninspired versions of "The Girl from Ipanema" clog up the marketplace.

Safe places to start are Archie Shepp's irreverent treatment of the song from 1965, João Gilberto's solo rendition from the 1985 Montreux Jazz Festival, and Eliane Elias's 1997 performance from her *Sings Jobim* release. Jobim, often a fine interpreter of his own songs, is not so trustworthy on this piece. I would pass on his versions from *The Composer of Desafinado Plays* (1963), *Tide* (1970), and *Terra Brasilis* (1976). A far better place to start is his less well-known live performance in Belo Horizonte from 1981 and his televised duet with Frank Sinatra from 1967.

RECOMMENDED VERSIONS

Stan Getz (with João Gilberto and Astrud Gilberto), from *Getz/Gilberto*, New York, March 18–19, 1963

Oscar Peterson, from *We Get Requests*, New York, October 19, 1964

Archie Shepp (with Ted Curson and Marion Brown), from *Fire Music*, New York, February 16, 1965

Frank Sinatra (with Antonio Carlos Jobim), from the NBC TV special *A Man and His Music + Ellas + Jobim*, taped October 1–3, 1967, Burbank, California, broadcast on November 13, 1967

Zoot Sims (with arrangement by Bill Holman), from *Hawthorne Nights*, New York, March 23, 1973

Antonio Carlos Jobim, from *Live at Minas*, live at the Palace of the Arts, Belo Horizonte, Brazil, March 15, 1981

João Gilberto, from *Live in Montreux*, live at the Montreux Jazz Festival, Montreux, Switzerland, July 18, 1985

Eliane Elias (with Michael Brecker), from *Sings Jobim*, New York, 1997

Diana Krall (recorded as "The Boy from Ipanema"), from *Quiet Nights*, Hollywood, circa 2008–2009

Pat Metheny, from *What's It All About*, New York, February, 2011

God Bless the Child

Composed by Billie Holiday and Arthur Herzog Jr.

In an attempt to extract higher payments from radio stations, the American Society of Composers, Authors, and Publishers (ASCAP) went on strike at the end of 1940. As a result, most of the leading songwriters of the day were kept off the airwaves, and for the next ten months the music industry struggled to adjust to this disruptive constraint. The power play backfired on ASCAP—by the time it settled with the broadcasters in October 1941, the organization was forced to accept lower fees from radio, and the move had also immeasurably strengthened its leading competitor, Broadcast Music, Inc. (BMI).

Yet this situation created opportunities for songwriters not affiliated with ASCAP. Arthur Herzog seized the moment, approaching Billie Holiday and suggesting that they collaborate on a song. "One night I met Holiday when she was off from work. . . . I said to Billie, this is the idea that I've got, and I want you to give me an old-fashioned Southern expression that we can turn into a song." At first, the singer came up blank, but soon she was recounting an anecdote—either about Billie borrowing money from her mother, or vice versa, depending on whether you rely on Herzog or Holiday's account—during which the singer muttered "God bless the child." Herzog asked her to explain what the phrase meant. "She said, 'You know. That's what we used to say—your mother's got money, your father's got money, your sister's got money, your cousin's got money, but if you haven't got it yourself, God bless the child that's got his own.'"

With just a little work, Herzog turned these thoughts into a song, and offered half of the royalties to Holiday if she would record it. She did just that in May 1941, and the song achieved exactly what Herzog had anticipated. Broadcasters played it frequently over their airwaves, and in the final days of the ASCAP strike, Billie Holiday enjoyed one of the last radio hits of her career. This version of "God Bless the Child" would gain induction into the Grammy Hall of Fame 35 years after its release.

For a song with such an unpromising lineage—coming from two unheralded composers trying to game the system—"God Bless the Child" turned out surprisingly well. There are a thousand love songs composed for every tune written about financial distress, and even when tunesmiths address the ticklish subject of money, they usually do so in a coy, ironic way. But the raw honesty and apparent autobiographical overtones to this song set "God Bless the Child" apart from your typical pop or jazz fare. Holiday had already differentiated herself from the other jazz divas of the big band era by tackling controversial and socially conscious themes in her songs—most notably in "Strange Fruit" first recorded two year earlier—and the new piece built on her reputation for probing matters other singers avoided.

The music does not match the incisiveness of the lyrics—the melody is a bit too sing-song for my taste—but the piece does open itself up to updating and reconfiguration. In the hands of the right artist, "God Bless the Child" can be an effective vehicle even as an instrumental. But for the most part, the song owes its longevity to its inherent drama as a vocal feature.

Few jazz musicians recorded this song while Holiday was still alive, probably because it seemed such a personal statement from her—less a song than a declaration of core beliefs. A notable exception came from trombonist J. J. Johnson, who delivered a moving ballad reading of "God Bless the Child" a few weeks before Lady Day's death at the March 1959 session for his *Really Livin'* album. The song found more advocates in the early 1960s and showed up in some surprising places. Eric Dolphy performed it as a solo piece for bass clarinet on the bandstand of the Five Spot in 1961; Sonny Rollins brought it to the studio for his return-from-semi-retirement LP *The Bridge*, where he was joined by guitarist Jim Hall; Eddie Harris garnered airplay with "God Bless the Child" in the fall of 1961 as he tried to follow up on his success with the theme to the movie *Exodus*, which had been a huge hit for him a few months earlier. The song also traveled far outside the jazz world, appearing on recordings by Sam Cooke, Aretha Franklin, Harry Belafonte, and Stevie Wonder.

For a song that deals with some very sticky subjects—family strife, poverty, and God—it works surprisingly well in commercial settings. Perhaps you've heard of the pushback Brian Wilson encountered back in 1966 when he was advised to nix his song title "God Only Knows." The conventional wisdom was that inserting a reference to the deity in the title of song was a recipe for disaster, unless you were Kate Smith singing "God Bless America." Well, it didn't hurt Brian and hasn't done much to keep the Holiday–Herzog creation off of slick recordings. Creed Taylor dishes up one of his oh-so-sweet orchestral settings for Kenny Burrell's only CTI release, suitably named *God Bless the Child*, but Burrell's soulful guitar lines rise above the waves of sappy strings. Diana Ross relied on "God Bless the Child" as the flip side to her hit single "Good Morning Heartache"—both given new prominence through her successful Holiday biopic *Lady Sings the Blues* (1972). And Blood, Sweat and Tears' reworking of "God Bless the Child" for the band's eponymous 1968 release, which would earn double platinum status, presents a rare example of a rock-oriented fusion band of the era putting a fresh spin on old jazz material. Even advertisers have latched on to the song: Billie Holiday's recording has been used by Volkswagen to sell automobiles. But the most extreme example of commercialization of "God Bless the Child" comes from the video game BioShock, which includes a creepy "remix" of the Holiday track by Moby and Oscar the Punk.

RECOMMENDED VERSIONS

Billie Holiday (with Eddie Heywood), New York, May 9, 1941

J. J. Johnson (with Nat Adderley), from *Really Livin'*, New York, March 19, 1959

Carmen McRae, from *Sings Lover Man and Other Billie Holiday Classics*, New York, June 29, 1961

Eric Dolphy, from *Here and There*, live at the Five Spot, New York, July 16, 1961

Julie London, from *For the Night People*, Los Angeles, 1966

Blood, Sweat and Tears, from *Blood, Sweat and Tears*, New York, 1968

Kenny Burrell, from *God Bless the Child*, New York, April–May 1971

Keith Jarrett (with the Standards Trio), from *Standards, Vol. 1*, New York, January 1983

Lester Bowie, from *Serious Fun*, Brooklyn, April 4–6, 1989

Etta Jones, from *Sings Lady Day*, New York, June 21, 2001

Gone with the Wind

Composed by Allie Wrubel, with lyrics by Herb Magidson

No, this 1937 song was not in the film *Gone with the Wind* (1939)—the biggest movie box office success of the era. But it did take advantage of the tremendous excitement generated by Margaret Mitchell's novel, which inspired the movie and sold a million copies within a few months of its publication in 1936, despite the soft economy and unprecedented cover price of $3 a copy (at a time when $5 per day was a typical salary).

The popularity of Mitchell's book carried over to the song, which was a number one hit for Horace Heidt in July 1937, and also a top 20 success for Guy Lombardo and Claude Thornhill a few weeks later—the latter recording featuring a nuanced vocal by Maxine Sullivan. Art Tatum recorded a solo piano version in November of that year, but after that, the song disappeared from the jazz repertoire for almost a decade. Even the film's release two years later did little to resuscitate the song with the same name.

In truth, the Wrubel-Magidson composition would have been a poor fit with the movie—its bouncy, lighthearted spirit fits better on a nightclub bandstand than backing scenes from the Civil War. Make no mistake, this song was no period piece. With its repeated ii-V-I progression in the opening four bars, which modulates up a major third for the next four bars, and a taut melody line, "Gone with the Wind" captured a streamlined, modernistic sensibility that would be out of place in the company of either Rhett Butler or Scarlett O'Hara— and certainly would not provide as good a match as Max Steiner's magisterial movie score.

The song itself seemed "gone with the wind" during the World War II years, but its comeback was helped along by its inclusion among a series of recordings by honorees in *Esquire* magazine's 1946 All-American Jazz poll, where it served as a feature number for alto saxophonist Johnny Hodges. He takes the song at a slower tempo and in a more reflective manner than had Thornhill or Tatum. Mel Tormé did the same in his renditions around this time. The song now seemed to have been reborn as a dreamy mood piece.

But the tempo picked up considerably during the course of the next decade. When Stan Getz recorded "Gone with the Wind" in 1950, he interpreted it as a romantic ballad in the spirit of Hodges's 1946 rendition, but when he tackled the same song three years later, in the company of Chet Baker, "Gone with the Wind" had returned to its earlier role as a jaunty medium-tempo number. Other well-known recordings of the song from the decade—Clifford Brown in 1954, Jackie McLean in 1956, Dave Brubeck in 1959—are even faster and more assertive.

The song has, for the most part, retained this extroverted personality in more recent years. It's typically played at a brisk pace, with few frills or fancy touches. "Gone with the Wind" doesn't show up on set lists as frequently as it did a few decades back, and not many fans in the audience will recognize it when it's played. But the song, which easily falls into an in-the-pocket groove, hardly sounds dated and can still serve as interesting fare for a jam session or live performance.

RECOMMENDED VERSIONS

Claude Thornhill (with Maxine Sullivan), New York, June 14, 1937

Art Tatum, New York, November 29, 1937

Esquire All-American Award Winners (with Johnny Hodges), New York, January 11, 1946

Mel Tormé, Hollywood, November 15, 1947

Chet Baker and Stan Getz, live at the Haig, Los Angeles, June 12, 1953

Clifford Brown (with Zoot Sims), from *Jazz Immortal*, Los Angeles, August 12, 1954

Jackie McLean, from *McLean's Scene*, Hackensack, New Jersey, December 14, 1956

Dave Brubeck (with Paul Desmond), from *Gone with the Wind*, Hollywood, April 22, 1959

Wes Montgomery (with Tommy Flanagan), from *The Incredible Jazz Guitar of Wes Montgomery*, New York, January 26, 1960

Bill Evans (with Eddie Gomez), from *Eloquence*, Berkeley, California, November 7–10, 1976

Charles McPherson (with Steve Kuhn), from *But Beautiful*, New York, July 24–25, 2003

Good Morning Heartache

Composed by Irene Higginbotham and Dan Fisher, with lyrics by Ervin Drake

This exquisite song, first recorded by Billie Holiday in 1946 but put on the charts by Diana Ross in 1973, is far better known than its composer, Irene Higginbotham (1918–1988). Given how few women managed to make a mark in the male-dominated songwriting industry during the first half of the twentieth century, and the almost total exclusion of African-American women from the field, one would think that curiosity alone might have given some notoriety to Higginbotham's career. Yet so little was published about her during her lifetime that the songwriter was later confused with Irene Kitchings, wife of pianist Teddy Wilson, and years would pass before anyone tracked down the details to prove they were two separate people.

We still know all too little about Higginbotham. She may have also written songs under the pseudonym Glenn Gibson—record industry exec Joe Davis (who had published some of Higginbotham's work) apparently used that name to earn royalties for songs written by others, and even attached it to some works in the public domain. And the composer's connection with trad jazz trombonist J. C. Higginbotham, who was her uncle, is also confirmed by a number of parties. But few other facts have come to light. Nonetheless, with almost 50 songs registered with ASCAP under her name, Higginbotham clearly was an experienced tunesmith, although few of her works are remembered today.

Billie Holiday adopted "Good Morning Heartache" during the post–World War II period, when the singer's jazz roots were often downplayed on her recordings—the musicians on her dates were not up to the caliber of her accompanists from the 1930s or 1950s, and her repertoire tended toward torch song originals. A few years later, Holiday shifted her emphasis to proven jazz standards, but throughout the 1940s she was more intent on finding fresh new material, a process that was hit-or-miss, with more misses than hits as the decade progressed. After "Lover Man," which was a success on the airwaves in May 1945, she enjoyed no more crossover hit recordings during her lifetime. Yet "Good Morning Heartache," which Holiday recorded seven months later, is one of her finest songs, and jazz fans have a right to lament that Diana Ross generated far more sales for her imitation of Holiday singing it in the film *Lady Sings the Blues* than Lady Day did herself.

Jazz musicians were no doubt paying attention to Hollywood, too, and "Good Morning Heartache" started showing up on their records and set lists with increasing frequency after the success of the Diana Ross film. Virtually no cover versions were made during the late 1960s, but in 1973 alone the song was showcased at studio sessions by Kenny Burrell, Lou Donaldson, Sonny Rollins, and Hank Crawford, as well as featured at the Newport Jazz Festival by Ella Fitzgerald. The song has retained its place in the jazz repertoire in ensuing decades, drawn on for Billie Holiday tributes, on disk or in concert, and also favored for its inherent virtues as a springboard for improvisation.

Like many of Holiday's signature pieces, this one is a perennial favorite among vocalists, and the words provide much of the magic here. I'm especially moved by the unexpected closing line, where the singer admonishers her heartache to "sit down," a turn of phrase that comes across as mundanely colloquial and eerily poetic at the same time. But horn players have plenty to chew on here too, and saxophonists have programmed this song just as often as vocalists. Among the many exemplary tenor sax interpretations made of "Good Morning Heartache," I would point listeners toward Joe Henderson's combo treatment from 1975, George Coleman's tour-de-force reworking from 1987, Houston Person's 1989 duet with bassist Ron Carter, and Paul Motian's 1995 trio date alongside Joe Lovano and Bill Frisell.

RECOMMENDED VERSIONS

Billie Holiday, New York, January 22, 1946

Carmen McRae, from *Torchy!* New York, December 29, 1955

Billie Holiday, from *Lady Sings the Blues*, New York, June 6–7, 1956

Diana Ross, from the soundtrack to *Lady Sings the Blues*, Hollywood, 1972

Joe Henderson, from *Black Narcissus*, Berkeley, California, April 1975

George Coleman, from *At Yoshi's*, live at Yoshi's, Oakland, August 1987

Houston Person and Ron Carter, from *Something in Common*, Englewood Cliffs,
New Jersey, February 23, 1989

McCoy Tyner, from *Infinity*, Englewood Cliffs, New Jersey, April 14, 1995

Paul Motian (with Joe Lovano and Bill Frisell), from *Sound of Love*, live at the Village
Vanguard, New York, June 7–10, 1995

Goodbye Pork Pie Hat
Composed by Charles Mingus

In jazz circles, a certain mystique surrounds the year 1959, a 12-month period that produced many of the most beloved masterpieces in the art form. In recounting the key events of the year, however, even knowledgeable jazz fans are liable to forget the death of tenor sax icon Lester Young, who passed away on March 15, 1959, at the age of 49. But Charles Mingus was deeply impacted by the loss, and on the night he learned of Young's death, he offered a musical tribute to the departed tenorist during a gig at the Half Note. The resulting minor blues served as the impetus for "Goodbye Pork Pie Hat"—the title was a reference to Young's distinctive headgear.

Mingus often forced musicians to learn his compositions by ear rather than give them written charts, and though band members often grumble at such an imposition, "Goodbye Pork Pie Hat" validates this technique. The chords on this 12-bar form bear no resemblance to a standard blues progression, but the improviser who keeps a minor blues scale in mind throughout the form is better able to navigate through them than one who tries to adapt to the implied scales of each written change. The result is magical: a composition that sounds both pointedly progressive and deeply traditional.

Two months after Young's death, Mingus recorded the piece for his seminal *Mingus Ah Um* album. "Goodbye Pork Pie Hat" would ultimately prove to be one of Mingus's most popular works—but not immediately. Few cover versions appeared until the 1970s, and it was probably the inclusion of the chart, with its unconventional changes, in *The Real Book* that brought the song into the standard repertoire. The piece took on surprising popularity with guitarists around this period—no guitar is featured on the original Mingus recording—with John McLaughlin recording it in 1970, Ralph Towner delivering a memorable performance with Gary Burton in 1974, and Mingus himself re-recording it in 1977 alongside guitarists Larry Coryell and Philip Catherine for his *Three or Four Shades of Blues* album.

This latter project sold 50,000 copies in the first few months—a major commercial success by Mingus's standards. But an even larger audience was exposed to "Goodbye Pork Pie Hat" via crossover cover versions by rock-pop performers, first by Jeff Beck, who included the song on his 1976 *Wired* album, and three years later by Joni Mitchell, who featured it on her 1979 *Mingus* project. Mitchell added her own lyrics, transforming this piece, originally a tribute to a departed saxophonist, into a celebration of Mingus as well. And just as Mingus's original recording was released shortly after Lester Young's death, Mitchell's reinterpretation appeared in the wake of Mingus's death in January 1979.

RECOMMENDED VERSIONS

Charles Mingus, from *Mingus Ah Um*, New York, May 12, 1959

John McLaughlin, from *My Goals Beyond*, New York, 1970

Ralph Towner and Gary Burton, from *Matchbook*, Ludwigsburg, Germany, July 26–27, 1974

Rahsaan Roland Kirk, from *Return of the 5000 Lb. Man*, New York, 1976

Jeff Beck, from *Wired*, London, 1976

Charles Mingus, from *Three or Four Shades of Blues*, New York, March 9, 1977

Joni Mitchell, from *Mingus*, Hollywood, Spring 1979

Gil Evans and Steve Lacy, from *Paris Blues*, Paris, November 30–December 1, 1987

Oliver Lake, from *Kinda' Up*, Paramus, New Jersey, August 1999

Paul Motian, from *Garden of Eden*, New York, November 2004

Groovin' High
Composed by Dizzy Gillespie

One day during his childhood, John Birks Gillespie—the artist subsequently known as Dizzy—attended a movie matinee, where he was captivated by an action-packed serial featuring the heroics of stuntman and actor Yakima Canutt. But the background music, as he later recalled, made an even more lasting impact on him. The song he heard that day, "Whispering," had been a huge hit for Paul Whiteman in 1920, selling two million copies and topping the charts for 11 weeks. A quarter of a century after Whiteman's success, Gillespie would borrow the chord changes from "Whispering" for "Groovin' High," which would become a well-known bebop anthem.

Despite Whiteman's reputation during the 1920s as the "King of Jazz," the jazz content in "Whispering" is negligible—the featured solo is played on the "bosun's-pipe-slide-trombone-whistle," an instrument that has yet to show up in any *Downbeat* poll, and the band plays as though auditioning for a parade rather than a nightclub gig. Yet Gillespie takes the underlying structure and harmonic movement and transforms "Whispering" into a showpiece for the new modern jazz sounds of the mid-1940s. His melody has a beguiling start-and-stop quality, in which short phrases alternate with longer bebop construc-tions, rich in chromaticism and skipping interval leaps.

Singer Billy Eckstine later claimed that Dizzy wrote "Groovin' High" while the trumpeter was with his big band. The initial recordings, however, feature small bop compos. Gillespie first recorded the song on February 9, 1945, with Dexter Gordon joining him in the front line. But the Guild label didn't issue the side immediately; as a result, the first version to reach the market was Gil-lespie's recording of "Groovin' High" made with Charlie Parker later that same month. A major difference between the two is the trumpeter's decision to use a cup mute at the second session. The trumpet solo is superior on the earlier date with Dexter Gordon, but Parker's presence makes the follow-up perfor-mance a must-hear record as well. Eckstine never recorded "Groovin' High," but Gerald Wilson deserves credit for comprehending almost immediately the potential for translating this song into the big band idiom—less than a year after the debut recording, Wilson had adapted "Groovin' High" for his West Coast big band.

Gillespie held on to this song as one of his signature pieces. It is revealing that when the trumpeter was invited to play at the White House in 1982, as part of a jazz gala event, he chose to play "Groovin' High" (joined by Stan Getz). But others who worked with Gillespie over the years showed almost equal loyalty to "Groovin' High." Charlie Parker left behind more than two dozen recorded ver-sions, although many of them are poorly recorded and, in the case of those made by Dean Benedetti, Bird-watcher par excellence, mere snippets of solos separated from the rest of the performance. Milt Jackson, who first came to prominence as a member of Gillespie's band, recorded "Groovin' High" on later occasions—including a memorable performance with Cannonball Adderley from 1958. Another former Gillespie collaborator, James Moody, is also worth hearing on this song—check out, in particular, his 1995 live recording from a birthday con-cert at the Blue Note, where the saxophonist is joined by Arturo Sandoval and Mulgrew Miller in a lengthy romp on "Groovin' High."

RECOMMENDED VERSIONS

Dizzy Gillespie (with Dexter Gordon), New York, February 9, 1945

Dizzy Gillespie (with Charlie Parker), New York, February 28, 1945

Gerald Wilson, Los Angeles, December 10, 1945

Cannonball Adderley and Milt Jackson, from *Things Are Getting Better*, New York, October 28, 1958

Booker Ervin (with Carmell Jones), from *Groovin' High*, Englewood Cliffs, New Jersey, June 30, 1964

James Moody (with Arturo Sandoval and Mulgrew Miller), from *Moody's Party*, live at the Blue Note, New York, March 23–26, 1995

Keith Jarrett (with the Standards Trio), from *Whisper Not*, live at the Palais des Congrès, Paris, July 5, 1999

Jon Irabagon, from *Outright!*, Brooklyn, March 2, 2007

H

Have You Met Miss Jones?

Composed by Richard Rodgers, with lyrics by Lorenz Hart

Richard Rodgers bragged that *I'd Rather Be Right* from 1937 might have been "the most eagerly awaited musical of all times." But it was the political satire of the production—which starred George M. Cohan as President Franklin D. Roosevelt—that spurred the public's interest and helped generate record advance ticket sales. George S. Kaufman, who wrote the book for the musical along with Moss Hart, even boasted to the composer that this was a musical in which the script was more important than the songs.

I'd Rather Be Right was a modest success, running for eight months. But the public and critics seemed mostly enamored with Cohan's evocation of FDR, and only one song survived the show as a popular hit. "Have You Met Miss Jones?" briefly showed up in the repertoires of a few swing bands, but the composition didn't make much headway on the bandstand until after World War II. George Shearing recorded a much-admired version in 1947, which finds him playing in an aggressive bop-oriented style that might surprise fans only familiar with the more staid block chord approach that would earn him a crossover audience two years later. The song's progressive credentials were further assisted by an ethereal performance recorded by Red Norvo's pioneering trio with Charles Mingus and Tal Farlow in 1950, while renditions by Stan Getz and Art Tatum from 1953 put the final stamps of approval on the tune. In the 18 months following the Tatum session, more jazz versions of "Have You Met Miss Jones?" were recorded than during the previous 18 years combined.

But the real modern jazz apotheosis for "Miss Jones" came at the close of the decade, when John Coltrane began using the chords from the bridge of the standard in various other settings—most notably as part of the framework for his well-known composition "Giant Steps." This sequence uses a series of ii-V chords to modulate down a major third every other bar, resulting in a growing sense of aural uncertainty over where the tonal center resides. Within the context of "Have You Met Miss Jones?" the progression hardly sounds radical, but when expanded beyond an eight-bar bridge it can impart a queasy, unsettling quality to the musical proceedings. Steve Kuhn, who worked briefly with Coltrane during this period, recalls mentioning the connection with the Rodgers and Hart song to the tenorist, but the saxophonist's response left it unclear whether he had consciously imitated the earlier piece.

Of course, even ingenious original harmonies are themselves susceptible to reharmonization, and for an especially daring approach to an old song, listen to George Coleman's 1998 primping of "Miss Jones" from his album *I Could Write a Book*. Given his time as saxophonist for Miles Davis in between the more celebrated stints of John Coltrane and Wayne Shorter, Coleman often gets lost in the shuffle in accounts by critics and historians, but he is one of the most adept masters of modulation and substitution of his generation, as this reconfiguration of an old standard makes clear.

Oddly enough, another fictional Miss Jones brought this song back to the public's attention in the new millennium. The song is delivered by Robbie Williams for the 2001 movie *Bridget Jones's Diary*. Here the tune is given a decidedly retro spin, showcased in an old school big band chart full of Swing Era clichés. One can only puzzle over the process by which a song that can still captivate progressive jazz players for its modernistic sounds becomes an exercise in quaint nostalgia among the general public.

RECOMMENDED VERSIONS

Benny Goodman (with Teddy Wilson and Gene Krupa), from a *Camel Caravan* radio broadcast, New York, December 7, 1937

George Shearing, New York, February 3, 1947

Red Norvo (with Charles Mingus and Tal Farlow), Chicago, October 13, 1950

Stan Getz (with Bob Brookmeyer), from *The Artistry of Stan Getz*, New York, May 16, 1953

Art Tatum, from *The Art Tatum Solo Masterpieces, Vol. 1*, Los Angeles, December 29, 1953

McCoy Tyner, from *Reaching Fourth*, Englewood Cliffs, New Jersey, November 14, 1962

Ahmad Jamal, from *At the Top: Poinciana Revisited*, live at the Village Gate, New York, 1969

Joe Pass, from *Virtuoso*, Los Angeles, November 1973

George Coleman, from *I Could Write a Book*, New York, January 8–9, 1998

Ethan Iverson, from *Deconstruction Zone (Standards)*, Paramus, New Jersey, April
     4–5, 1998

Here's That Rainy Day
Composed by Jimmy Van Heusen, with lyrics by Johnny Burke

Harold Arlen was supposed to compose the score for *Carnival in Flanders*, a 1953
musical financed primarily by Bing Crosby, but the songwriter bowed out and
allowed Jimmy Van Heusen to take the gig. The musical was a flop, closing after
only six performances, yet earned a Tony for actress Dolores Gray, the only time
a performance in a run that short was so honored. Today the production is
remembered for the song Gray performed, the standard-to-be "Here's That
Rainy Day."

In truth, this tune is more popular with performers than audiences. The
radical harmonic movement in the first few bars is more suited to art song than
pop hit, and serves as an inspiring underpinning for melodic improvisation.
Van Heusen would enjoy bigger sellers, but if jazz soloists were voting, this
song might come out as their favorite. I especially admire the way the composer
unfolds his surprising progression with only occasional use of dominant
chords, thus imparting an impressionist sheen to the proceedings.

Even so, the song was virtually unknown to jazz players during the 1950s,
and only Frank Sinatra's intervention put "Here's That Rainy Day" on the map.
No tunesmith enjoyed more support from Sinatra—who would eventually
record 85 of Van Heusen's songs. The composer once quipped that he deserved
a higher share of royalties given the countless hours he spent fraternizing with
Sinatra while convincing the star vocalist to record his various pieces. And the
two colleagues are still hanging out together: Van Heusen is buried in the Sinatra family plot in Cathedral City, California. Sinatra resurrected "Here's That
Rainy Day" for his *No One Cares* project from 1959. He also featured the song
on *The Frank Sinatra Timex Show: An Afternoon with Frank Sinatra* later that
same year. Unflagging in his favor for the tune, the vocalist turned to it again in
1973 for another TV special, *Ol' Blue Eyes Is Back*, and continued to perform it in
later years.

During the course of the 1960s, this song gradually established itself as a
part of the standard repertoire. Much of its appeal came, no doubt, from its
mutability. In its early days, "Here's That Rainy Day" was incorporated into the
bossa nova movement and was given a Brazilian treatment by Wes Montgomery, Sérgio Mendes, and others—the surprising outlier here being Stan Getz,
who recorded the song during the height of his bossa nova flirtation, yet

preferred to take the song at a slow swing tempo. In later years, "Here's That Rainy Day" served as a dramatic ballad showpiece for Freddie Hubbard and Bill Evans. In contrast, Richard "Groove" Holmes turned it into a medium-tempo funk feature, Dick Hyman transformed it into a stride piano piece, while Philly Joe Jones took the Van Heusen standard at a fast clip in a boppish vein. All these treatments work and bring out different facets in the composition.

Yet the harmonic structure may be even more adaptable than the rhythmic context. Few jazz pieces are better suited for reharmonization than "Here's That Rainy Day," and over the years I've taken great pleasure in tinkering with the chord changes in various ways, finding myself deeply engaged by the range of moods and emotional stances this song can support. Good examples of this aspect of the song can be heard on Denny Zeitlin's trio performance from 1967 and Martial Solal's duet with Dave Douglas from 2005.

RECOMMENDED VERSIONS

Frank Sinatra, from *No One Cares*, Los Angeles, March 25, 1959

Wes Montgomery, from *Bumpin'*, Englewood Cliffs, New Jersey, March 16, 1965

Denny Zeitlin, from *Zeitgeist*, Hollywood, March 18, 1967

Bill Evans, from *Alone*, New York, Septembr–October 1968

Gary Burton and Stéphane Grappelli, from *Paris Encounter*, Paris, November 4, 1969

Freddie Hubbard, from *Straight Life*, November 16, 1970

Dorothy Donegan, from *Makin' Whoopee*, Paris, March 16, 1979

Michel Petrucciani, from *Pianism*, New York, December 20, 1985

Martial Solal and Dave Douglas, from *Rue de Seine*, Paris, July 6–7, 2005

Honeysuckle Rose
Composed by Fats Waller, with lyrics by Andy Razaf

Anecdotes tell of Fats Waller writing songs off the cuff, in the taxi, at the recording studio, or in the publisher's office, where just a few minutes would suffice for the maestro to put everything in order. Even if such accounts are embellished, the historical record is clear on the cavalier attitude that Waller took toward these works once they were written—selling them for a song (or, to be precise, less than the value thereof). Or even forgetting them. "You don't remember the melody?" lyricist Andy Razaf reportedly berated Waller when he presented the pianist with the newly written words to "Honeysuckle Rose." "Lord man! Good thing *I* do." Waller had seen this tune as a negligible item, a soft-shoe piece for *Load of Coal*, a 1929 revue at Harlem's Connie's Inn. He had hardly sat down at the piano and tossed off a few notes for Razaf before running off to another appointment.

Shortly after the song's debut, "Honeysuckle Rose" was featured on Paul Whiteman's *Old Gold Show* in a vocal version by Mildred Bailey. A last-minute decision to double the tempo resulted in an uninspired performance. Harry Link, a publisher and sometime Waller collaborator present that day, later griped that this botched opportunity set the song back some 15 years. But the historical record tells a different story—"Honeysuckle Rose" was widely adopted by jazz bands during the 1930s. McKinney's Cotton Pickers recorded it in 1930, Frankie Trumbauer in 1931, and Fletcher Henderson in 1932—each of these preceding Fats Waller's first studio recording of the song in 1934. The Henderson version was a well-known hit, as was Waller's own 1934 rendition. A recorded jam session from 1937 that features the composer alongside Tommy Dorsey and Bunny Berigan also sold well. Red Norvo, in another integrated recording session from 1935, presents the song in a successful collaboration with Teddy Wilson, Chu Berry, Bunny Berigan, and Gene Krupa, while Norvo's then wife Mildred Bailey made her competing 78 later that same year.

Hollywood gave "Honeysuckle Rose" an additional boost in the 1940s. It showed up as a song-and-dance feature for Betty Grable in the 1940 film *Tin Pan Alley*—incurring the anger of Razaf with its depiction here as the creation of an oddball white songwriter in jail, who composes "Honeysuckle Rose" on the harmonica. Waller brushed off Razaf's concerns, claiming that any publicity was good publicity. Jazz fans were more pleased with the song's inclusion in *Thousands Cheer* (1943), where Lena Horne performed it, backed by Benny Carter's band.

Charlie Parker had even more influence in keeping the Waller song current among younger jazz players during this period. An amateur recording of Parker practicing over the chord changes to "Honeysuckle Rose" and "Body and Soul" gives us our earliest glimpse into techniques that he would use to shake up the jazz world a short while later. The dating of this recording is uncertain, with some claiming it was made as early as 1937 and others placing it as late as 1940. But Parker's melodic lines appear to reference a 1938 Chu Berry–Roy Eldridge recording as well as the melody of Jimmy Van Heusen's 1939 song "I Thought about You"—implying a recording date toward the end of this period. The performance itself is portentous, revealing both Parker's emulation of Lester Young but also the new melodic ideas the young saxophonist was then in the process of developing. An early indicator of where these efforts would lead can be heard on the recordings Parker made with Jay McShann's band in Wichita, Kansas, in November 1940. Here Parker again plays "Honeysuckle Rose," and his solo is crammed full of modernistic phraseology, so busy with activity that one suspects Bird was unhappy to have only a single 32-bar chorus to display all his musical ideas. Parker would later borrow chords from "Honeysuckle Rose" to serve as the basis for the A theme of his own frequently played composition "Scrapple from the Apple."

During the 1930s and 1940s, Waller's standard managed to transcend the stylistic barriers that divide the jazz world. Around the same time Parker made his amateur recording of "Honeysuckle Rose," both Lester Young and Coleman Hawkins were featured on disk with their diverging interpretations, Jelly Roll Morton recorded the song with a Baltimore combo, Benny Goodman performed the piece (in Fletcher Henderson's arrangement) with his swing band, and Louis Jordan gave the piece an R&B-ish treatment with his Tympany Five. Fats Waller also continued to record and perform the song in a wide range of settings. Dan Morgenstern has suggested that the composer "must have played this tune every working day of his life." Certainly he came to think more highly of it than when he had tossed it off as a throwaway tune to meet a pressing deadline.

In later years, "Honeysuckle Rose" appeared less often in the repertoire of modern jazz players—when they worked over these chords, it was often in the guise of Charlie Parker's "Scrapple from the Apple." But Thelonious Monk's 1956 recording of "Honeysuckle Rose" offers a fresh updating, as did the unusual pairing of Bill Evans and Bob Brookmeyer on a two-piano treatment from 1959. But, sad to say, the composition that once produced so many classic recordings has typically shown up in rote versions during more recent years. In the closing decades of the twentieth century, the best-known recordings of "Honeysuckle Rose" were typically by artists in their seventies and eighties—Lionel Hampton, Stéphane Grappelli, Benny Carter, etc.—who had first performed it before World War II. Even when younger players cover "Honeysuckle Rose," they rarely move beyond the approaches pioneered by these past masters. Occasionally an ambitious performer pushes against the confines of "Honeysuckle Rose"—hear, for example, Uri Caine's two takes from his 1997 album *Blue Wail*—but, for the most part, this once flexible song has become far too stiff and unyielding.

RECOMMENDED VERSIONS

McKinney's Cotton Pickers, New York, February 3, 1930

Fletcher Henderson (with Coleman Hawkins), New York, November 9, 1932

Fats Waller, New York, November 7, 1934

Red Norvo (with Chu Berry and Teddy Wilson), New York, January 25, 1935

Mildred Bailey, New York, December 6, 1935

Count Basie (with Lester Young), New York, January 21, 1937

Fats Waller, Tommy Dorsey, Bunny Berigan, and others, New York, March 31, 1937

Fats Waller, New York, April 9, 1937

Coleman Hawkins, Paris, April 28, 1937

Charlie Parker, Kansas City, circa 1939

Jay McShann (with Charlie Parker), Wichita, Kansas, November 30, 1940

Thelonious Monk, from *The Unique*, Hackensack, New Jersey, April 3, 1956

Bill Evans and Bob Brookmeyer, from *The Ivory Hunters*, New York, March 12, 1959

Mary Lou Williams, from *Solo Recital*, live at the Montreux Jazz Festival, Montreux, Switzerland, July 16, 1978

Stéphane Grappelli, from *Vintage 1981*, San Francisco, July 1981

George Shearing, from *In Dixieland*, New York, February 1989

Uri Caine (two takes, "Honeysuckle Rose #1" and "Honeysuckle Rose #2"), from *Blue Wail*, New York, December 1–2, 1997

Hot House
Composed by Tadd Dameron

Most jazz fans possess at least a few Dizzy Gillespie albums in their collections, yet these are typically the mid- and late-career projects the trumpeter recorded for producer Norman Granz. In contrast, the tracks Gillespie made as a young man are less often heard—especially nowadays when many listeners tend to avoid music recorded before the advent of high-fidelity audio quality. But these spirited Gillespie efforts from the 1940s redefined the role of the trumpet in modern jazz and ought to be the starting point in anyone's studies in Gillespi- ana. The early tracks have the added benefit of featuring, in many instances, altoist Charlie Parker at the top of his game.

Even Gillespie recognized this fact. Musing on his work with Parker, he later noted: "There was never anybody who played any closer than we did on those early sides like 'Groovin' High,' 'Shaw Nuff' and 'Hot House.'" French critic André Hodeir went even further. Discussing the session that produced the latter track, he enthused: "I believe that the history of jazz will remember as an essential date the point in May 1945 when five black musicians recorded 'Hot House' and 'Salt Peanuts.'" 'Tis an extravagant prediction but not an unjust one. These performances deserve that kind of recognition although, with the inexorable historical erosion that turns all modernist advances into rearguard skirmishes when viewed in retrospect, they rarely receive it in the new millennium.

Gillespie made "Hot House" into an oft-imitated bop standard—so much so that many fans, I suspect, assume he wrote the song. Yet Tadd Dameron gets the credit for the piece, which superimposes a new, serpentine melody on to the familiar chords of Cole Porter's "What Is This Thing Called Love?" The composer himself never recorded the song at a studio session (although he can be heard on a private tape made at Birdland, in 1950, performing "Hot House" amidst an all-star band). But Dameron helped Gillespie in his advocacy, contributing an arrangement for the trumpeter's 1947 big band. Gillespie and Parker, for their part, frequently relied on this song in their live encounters over the years, and it shows up on the surviving recordings of their 1945 Town Hall concert, their 1953 Massey Hall concert in Toronto, and on a rare film clip of the duo from 1952.

Other progressive players of the day were quick to follow the lead of these bop titans. John Coltrane, who performed "Hot House" at a 1946 studio session in Hawaii, where he was stationed with the U.S. Navy, was the first horn player to record "Hot House" after Parker and Gillespie, and one can easily understand the appeal this piece held for a saxophonist himself destined to shake things up a few years later. A live recording from 1947 finds Wardell Gray, Howard McGhee, and Sonny Criss working over "Hot House" at the Pasadena Civic Auditorium—testifying to the spread of the bebop ethos to the West Coast. Before the close of the decade, Max Roach, James Moody, and others can be heard performing the song during European sessions. Even jazz critics got into the act: "Hot House" is featured at a session, ostensibly under Hodeir's leadership from 1948, and a few years later a version was released under scribe Leonard Feather's name—in neither case do the critics play a note, but they both happily associated themselves with a progressive work of this sort.

Many bop charts were built on the foundations of older standards, but "Hot House" is one of the more effective examples. I especially admire the unexpected twist, starting in bar nine, where Dameron inserts an ardent new melody when one expects a repetition of the first theme. The chart is drenched in chromatic color tones, and the altered higher extensions of the chords are more than just passing notes here. Jazz fans and even other musicians must have been unsettled, back in 1945, to hear a melody where phrases ended on flat fives and flat nines.

"Hot House" is no longer a song to lead a musical revolution, but it still can generate excitement in performance. For three gripping late twentieth-century treatments, hear Paul Motian's Electric Bebop Band, with Joshua Redman and Kurt Rosenwinkel, from 1992; Anthony Braxton's trample-on-the-changes rendition from 1993; and Arturo Sandoval's Grammy-winning matchup with Michael Brecker, on the *Hot House* album, from 1997.

RECOMMENDED VERSIONS

Dizzy Gillespie (with Charlie Parker), New York, May 11, 1945

Miles Davis, Tadd Dameron, and others (sometimes released as "Miles' Midnight Breakaway"), live at Birdland, New York, June 20, 1950

Charlie Parker, Dizzy Gillespie, and others, from *Jazz at Massey Hall*, live at Massey
   Hall, Toronto, May 15, 1953

Eric Dolphy, from *The Berlin Concerts*, live at Jazz-Saloon, Berlin, August 30, 1961

Charles McPherson (with Barry Harris), from *Bebop Revisited*, Englewood Cliffs,
   New Jersey, November 20, 1964

Paul Motian (with Joshua Redman and Kurt Rosenwinkel), from *Paul Motian and
   the Electric Bebop Band*, New York, April 1992

Anthony Braxton, from *Charlie Parker Project 1993*, live at Rote Fabrik, Zurich,
   October 21, 1993

Arturo Sandoval (with Michael Brecker), from *Hot House*, Florida, 1997

How Deep Is the Ocean?
Composed by Irving Berlin

Irving Berlin recycled some of the lyrics from his earlier songs in crafting "How
Deep Is the Ocean?" but the end result is anything but second-hand rags. In
fact, this is one of the composer's most sophisticated tunes, both for the elaborate comparisons of the words and the careful construction of the chords, which
go on a long journey before finally resolving into the tonic key. The melody is
smartly developed, saving its grand effects and high notes for the final phrases.

Irving Berlin was at a low point, both financially and psychologically, when
he wrote this song. The death of his infant son, Irving Berlin Jr., on Christmas
Day in 1928, came during a period of creative stagnation for the composer. The
following year, Berlin lost millions of dollars in the stock market crash that announced the beginning of the Great Depression. Both Tin Pan Alley and Broadway suffered from the economic malaise, but even in better circumstances
Berlin would have felt out of touch with the new plot-driven musicals that followed in the wake of Jerome Kern and Oscar Hammerstein's *Show Boat* (1927).
He turned his attention to Hollywood instead, but found a cold welcome
there—four of the five Berlin songs contributed to *Reaching for the Moon* (1930)
were cut from the film before its final release. In desperation, Berlin looked to
radio, despite his doubts about a medium that gave away music for free, playing
a promising song endlessly for a couple of weeks until, in his opinion, it became
stale and then discarded by the public.

Thus, without the benefit of a musical or movie to give it momentum, "How
Deep Is the Ocean?" was launched on the airwaves in 1932. Disproving Berlin's
skepticism, his song not only spurred four hit recordings that year—including
Paul Whiteman's version, the biggest seller of this group—but had hardly lost
its appeal more than a decade later. Benny Goodman had a top 20 hit in 1945

with his version of "How Deep Is the Ocean?" featuring vocalist Peggy Lee, and the following year Hollywood finally took notice and included the song in *Blue Skies*, where it was performed by Bing Crosby.

Certainly jazz musicians paid attention to these renditions, but Coleman Hawkins's recording of "How Deep Is the Ocean?" from 1943 may have had equal influence in convincing other improvisers to take on this composition. Hawkins later remarked that this was one of his favorites among his own performances, and expressed surprise that it never enjoyed the commercial success that his version of "Body and Soul" achieved. Yet the cumulative impact of Hawkins, Goodman, and Crosby ensured that, by the second half of the decade, Berlin's song had become a staple of the jazz repertoire.

In the late 1940s and early 1950s, "How Deep Is the Ocean?" was recorded by Charlie Parker, Miles Davis, Nat King Cole, Billie Holiday, Stan Getz, Artie Shaw, and other jazz stars of the era. A fascinating curio from 1956 finds John Coltrane paired up with three other tenor saxophonists—Al Cohn, Zoot Sims, and Hank Mobley—in a 15-minute treatment of the song at a ballad tempo. Most of the early recordings showcased the Berlin composition in a similarly dreamy mood, but I note a gradual acceleration in tempos over the years. Billie Holiday delivers it in a bouncy and sassy manner in her 1954 version, and some of the most interesting renditions from later decades—such as Wynton Marsalis's treatment alongside Art Blakey and Kenny Barron's outing with Roy Haynes—present harder swinging interpretations. On the opposite extreme, pianist Fred Hersch offers a poignant and languorously slow treatment on his highly recommended *Night and the Music* album from 2006.

RECOMMENDED VERSIONS

Paul Whiteman, New York, September 26, 1932

Benny Goodman (with Peggy Lee), New York, October 8, 1941

Coleman Hawkins, New York, December 8, 1943

Nat King Cole, Los Angeles, April 25, 1946

Charlie Parker, New York, December 17, 1947

Billie Holiday, from *Recital by Billie Holiday*, New York, April 14, 1954

John Coltrane, Al Cohn, Zoot Sims, and Hank Mobley, from *Tenor Conclave*,
    Hackensack, New Jersey, September 7, 1956

Art Blakey (with Wynton Marsalis), from *Straight Ahead*, live at the Keystone Korner,
    San Francisco, June 1981

Chet Baker and Paul Bley, from *Diane*, Copenhagen, February 27, 1985

Roy Haynes (with Kenny Barron), from *Love Letters*, New York, May 23–24, 2002

Fred Hersch, from *Night and the Music*, Pipersville, Pennsylvania, December 4–5,
    2006

How High the Moon
Composed by Morgan Lewis, with lyrics by Nancy Hamilton

This song became a famous bebop anthem in the early 1940s. The boppers clearly liked the chord changes better than the melody, and when Charlie Parker composed his also oft-played song "Ornithology," he kept the former and discarded the latter. I have often heard jazz musicians interpolate the opening phrase of "Ornithology" into their solos on "How High the Moon," but I would advise against this now hackneyed conflation of standards. I recall an evening when a soloist quoted Parker's melody one time too many, and a group of musicians in the audience, less than impressed with this predictable motif, immediately started singing along with the riff—not because they liked it but merely to show that they found this choice of notes all too banal.

The song, which originated in the 1940 Broadway production *Two for the Show*, was the sole jazz standard composed by Morgan Lewis—a double threat who could choreograph dance numbers as well as write songs—with the assistance of lyricist Nancy Hamilton, better known for her clever wordplay than poetic nuance. For my part, I don't find this song convincing as a lover's declaration; the rigorous patterns pursued by the harmony and melody undermine the passion. That said, I can comprehend the appeal of this piece for improvisers, but more as a type of puzzle to solve than a source of emotional catharsis.

Benny Goodman was the first to appreciate the jazz potential of "How High the Moon," and enjoyed the first hit recording in a version that featured Helen Forrest on vocals. Stan Kenton also placed on the charts with his treatment of "How High the Moon" in July 1948, relying on a Neal Hefti chart that showcased June Christy and offered a half-chorus solo spot to Art Pepper. But Les Paul and Mary Ford achieved the biggest success of all with this song, reaching a huge crossover audience with a hard-swinging over-dubbed recording—a technological marvel at the time that allowed Ford to sing in harmony with her own voice—which stayed on top of the chart for nine weeks. Their version of "How High the Moon" was later inducted into the Grammy Hall of Fame.

The beboppers could not match the sales of these recordings, but ultimately they put a lasting stamp on how this song would be played by later generations. "How High the Moon" might have been originally conceived by its composer as a ballad, and found acceptance with swing bandleaders as a vocal feature. But its destiny was to become a jam session workhorse, a meeting ground for battling soloists, and a springboard for virtuosic displays. Guitarist Charlie Christian, who was a member of Goodman's band when the latter had his hit with "How High the Moon," is the likely linchpin, the person who brought the song from the dance halls to the Harlem late night jams where the bebop vocabulary was refined. Virtually all of the leaders of the "new thing" in 1940s jazz left behind recordings of the song (or of variants based on the same harmonies) in the years following World War II.

Yet Ella Fitzgerald did more than anyone to put a stamp of ownership on "How High the Moon." More than 15 surviving recordings testify to her lasting fascination with the song, which she typically employed as a vehicle for her scat-singing chops. Given the number of times she tackled the song, we can perhaps forgive the Grammy judges who in 2002 decided to put her recording of "How High the Moon" in their Hall of Fame, alongside the Les Paul/Mary Ford version, but left fans unclear which recording they wanted to honor. Somehow they listed 1960 as the year of the performance—no doubt referring to her version from the LP *Ella in Berlin*—but also commemorated Decca (the company for whom she had recorded this song in 1947, but *not* in 1960) as the label. Adding to the confusion, Ella left behind an outstanding version of the same song recorded at Carnegie Hall with Dizzy Gillespie a few weeks before the Decca session, and this lesser-known performance, which finds her exchanging licks with the trumpeter, may be the most historically important of the lot—serving as a symbolic (and perhaps actual) moment when "How High the Moon" was handed off from the boppers to the First Lady of Song.

The next year, in the same setting, Duke Ellington also featured "How High the Moon," and the contrast with Gillespie and Fitzgerald could hardly be more striking. For this high-profile concert, Duke invited Ben Webster to sit in with the band, and Webster shows that a saxophonist could push this song to its limits without borrowing anything from the modern jazz idiom. Since that time, fans have witnessed a few other attempts to wrest this song away from the beboppers and scat-singers—John Coltrane, for example, composed a piece ("Satellite") loosely based on "How High the Moon," where he tried to update the harmonic movement and create a different kind of mood. Abbey Lincoln also shook things up with her 6/8 version, mingling French and English in her adaptation of the lyrics. But for the most part, this composition has resisted tinkering, and remains today much what it was back in the 1940s: a show-off number to excite the fans with lightning-fast phrases.

RECOMMENDED VERSIONS

Benny Goodman, New York, February 7, 1940

Dizzy Gillespie (with Ella Fitzgerald), live at Carnegie Hall, New York, September 29, 1947

Stan Kenton (with June Christy and Art Pepper), New York, December 21, 1947

Duke Ellington (with Ben Webster), live at Carnegie Hall, New York, November 13, 1948

Erroll Garner, New York, October 7, 1950

Les Paul and Mary Ford, New York, January 4, 1951

Sonny Stitt (with Barry Harris), from *Burnin'*, Chicago, August 1, 1958

Ella Fitzgerald, from *Ella in Berlin*, live at Deutschlandhalle, Berlin, February 13, 1960

Joe Pass, from *Virtuoso*, Los Angeles, August 28, 1973

Abbey Lincoln (with Clark Terry and Jackie McLean), from *The World Is Falling Down*, New York, February 21–27, 1990

Ray Brown (with Joe Lovano), from *Some of My Best Friends Are . . . Sax Players*, New York (November 20–22, 1995) and Los Angeles (February 13, 1996)

How Insensitive
Composed by Antonio Carlos Jobim, with lyrics by Vinicius de Moraes (English lyrics by Norman Gimbel)

Anyone who doubts the classical music roots of Antonio Carlos Jobim need only compare the harmonic and melodic movement of "How Insensitive" with that of Chopin's prelude in E minor. The similarities are so pronounced that a few musicians have even blended the two pieces together into an almost seamless integration of works composed more than a century apart. For revealing examples, listen to guitarist Laurindo Almeida's performance of Jobim-Chopin from the 1974 live recording *The L.A. Four Scores* or George Shearing's piano arrangement from his 1985 *Grand Piano* session. Almeida introduces his demonstration of the congruent compositions by announcing: "If you copy from one, it is plagiarism. But if you copy from more than one, it is research."

Jobim certainly drew from more than one predecessor, and the rhythmic conception and emotional tone of "How Insensitive" present an inherently Brazilian sensibility, with only the most distant connection to Chopin's Warsaw roots. These more personal elements place such a powerful imprimatur on this song that the vast majority of cover versions of "How Insensitive" follow very closely the approach that the composer employed in his own performances of the piece. An odd exception is Ahmad Jamal, who presents a very driving interpretation of "How Insensitive"—out of character for both the pianist and the song. A few others have tried to transform this work into a high-speed jam number, but typically with less success than Jamal.

The song is known as "Insensatez" in Brazil and the translation of "How Insensitive" fits the melody, but is an imprecise rendering of a title that might be more accurately conveyed as "How Foolish" or "How Absurd." The music itself is deliciously understated, and serves as testimony to Jobim's skill in crafting songs that sound casual and happenstance, yet are anything but. The melody stays within a range of less than an octave, and every phrase remains within a third of its starting point. Such restraint rarely leads to hit songs, yet Jobim compensates with depth for what his songs may lack in terms of flash. This music is almost better considered as a reverie than a tune intended for airplay.

And yet . . . this song ranks among the most beloved and frequently recorded, of Jobim's works, with a strange range of artists giving it a try—including the Monkees, Iggy Pop, Liberace, William Shatner, Olivia Newton-John, Lionel Hampton, and the Fifth Dimension. In truth, many cover versions are barely listenable. If you play this song too casually, it comes across as cocktail lounge twaddle. If you play it too aggressively, or with too much Liberacian (is that a word? How about Shatnerian?) grandiloquence, it loses its emotional core. The best approach, in my opinion, is almost a kind of Method Acting channeling of intense personal recollection into the performance. For especially effective renditions, I refer you to recordings by Diana Krall, João Gilberto, and the composer himself in his 1994 duet with Pat Metheny.

RECOMMENDED VERSIONS

João Gilberto, from *The Legendary João Gilberto*, Rio de Janeiro, August 2, 1961

Stan Getz (with Antonio Carlos Jobim), from *Jazz Samba Encore*, New York, February 8, 1963

Wes Montgomery, from *Tequila*, Englewood Cliffs, New Jersey, March 17, 1966

Toshiko Akiyoshi (with Lew Tabackin and Kenny Dorham), from *Toshiko at Top of the Gate*, live at Top of the Gate, New York, July 30, 1968

Ahmad Jamal, from *At the Top: Poinciana Revisited*, live at the Village Gate, New York, 1969

Laurindo Almeida (with the L.A. Four), from *The L.A. Four Scores*, live at the Concord Pavilion, Concord, California, July 27, 1974

George Shearing, from *Grand Piano*, San Francisco, May 1985

Antonio Carlos Jobim and Pat Metheny, from *Carnegie Hall Salutes the Jazz Masters*, live at Carnegie Hall, New York, April 6, 1994

Diana Krall, from *From This Moment On*, Los Angeles, Spring 2006

How Long Has This Been Going On?
Composed by George Gershwin, with lyrics by Ira Gershwin

The challenge facing jazz musicians when playing popular songs from the 1920s is that most of them sound like quaint period pieces today. This makes them fine for deliberately retro interpretations, but somewhat resistant to fresh perspectives and adaptation to newer musical approaches. Even if one does update, say, "Sweet Georgia Brown" or "Ain't She Sweet" or "Little Orphan Annie," the resulting flavor can be a discordant postmodernism—one that has potentially damaged, or ridiculed, the song in the process of reworking it. From a Darwinian perspective, many of these once-fashionable songs are not sufficiently adaptive to survive as jazz staples today.

But then I consider "How Long Has This Been Going On?" and marvel over a composition that seems perfectly malleable to a modern sensibility. Ira Gershwin's words could easily serve as the basis for a current movie theme or pop song, the chords have an appealingly open and uncluttered feeling rare for that era of harmonic maximalism, and the melody is very soulful without the sing-song phrasing so popular during the Jazz Age. If your first introduction to this standard was Ray Charles's 1977 recording, you might have thought that it had been composed with him in mind. Or if you listen to Brad Mehldau's performance of "How Long Has This Been Going On?" from his 2000 live recording at the Village Vanguard, you might be persuaded that this is an adventurous new millennium piano piece.

I am hardly surprised that the broader public periodically rediscovers this song. The brothers Gershwin gave it its debut as part of the 1927 musical *Funny Face*. The early reception was hardly encouraging—the song was dropped from the show after two weeks. But its first revival took place soon after, when "How Long Has This Been Going On?" was picked up by Flo Ziegfeld for the successful 1928 show *Rosalie*. Peggy Lee had a minor hit with it as vocalist for the Benny Goodman band, which recorded the song a few days before Pearl Harbor. And the passing decades have hardly put a dent in this song's appeal. In 2006, an old archival tape of Ray Charles singing "How Long Has This Been Going On?" was paired with a new recording of backing tracks by the Count Basie "ghost band." The fact that Basie and Charles were no longer around to promote the music didn't stop the song from achieving the highest honor accorded to a recording nowadays: product placement on the Starbucks counter. Need I say more?

RECOMMENDED VERSIONS

Benny Goodman (with Peggy Lee), New York, November 13, 1941

Chet Baker, from *It Could Happen to You*, New York, August 1958

Carmen McRae, from *Book of Ballads*, New York, December 1–2, 1958

Ella Fitzgerald, from *Ella Fitzgerald Sings the George and Ira Gershwin Songbook*, Los Angeles, January–March 1959

Ben Webster, from *Ben and Sweets*, New York, June 7, 1962

Ray Charles, from *True to Life*, Los Angeles, 1977

Sarah Vaughan (with Oscar Peterson and Joe Pass), from *How Long Has This Been Going On?* Hollywood, April 25, 1978

Diane Schuur (with Stan Getz), from *Timeless*, Hollywood, October 12, 1986

Brad Mehldau, from *Progression: Art of the Trio, Volume 5*, live at the Village Vanguard, New York, September 22–24, 2000

I Can't Get Started

Composed by Vernon Duke, with lyrics by Ira Gershwin

It tells you something about the melting pot of Tin Pan Alley to consider that this immensely popular standard was composed by Vladimir Dukelsky, a native of Belarus who had studied at the Kiev Conservatory, and Israel Gershovitz, whose parents had first dated in St. Petersburg. We know them better as Vernon Duke and Ira Gershwin, and if you are looking for nostalgia for the Old Country in their songs, you will find none of it in this quintessentially up-to-date song about modern American life.

Well, perhaps it's more accurate to say that, *back in the Great Depression*, this song was up-to-date, with its references to the stock market crash of 1929 and military conflicts in Spain. The clever premise here is for the singer to enumerate many grand accomplishments—circumnavigating the globe or breaking par on the golf course—in each eight-bar A theme, before concluding "but I can't get started with you." The song ranks among the most popular "list songs" of the first half of the twentieth century. (Curiously enough, another "list song" with similar chord changes, "These Foolish Things," was also a big hit around this same time.)

But this song's personality has changed with the passing decades, and the words that were so timely in the 1930s now come across as quaintly passé. The lyrics work well enough in performance even today, although with a much different ambiance than they once possessed. The words also are susceptible to updating, as many singers have done over the years. I haven't heard anyone yet mention Twitter or their iPhone in modernized lyrics to "I Can't Get Started," but I don't see why they shouldn't. The music, for its part, opens with a chord progression that would later become a hackneyed staple of R&B and early rock, but it no doubt sounded much fresher in the years before World War II. The B theme is the real gem, with its constant return to the same note (a concert A) with shifting harmonies changing its flavor with each repetition.

The song had been introduced on Broadway by Bob Hope—and he later credited it with giving him the boost he needed to get a movie contract—but its fame owes more to trumpeter Bunny Berigan, whose 1937 recording of "I Can't Get Started" was a surprise hit. Perhaps if he had lived longer—his health shattered by chronic alcoholism, Berigan died at age 33—this stellar trumpeter might be better known today. Certainly he ranks among the finest soloists of his generation, and he shows off his brash, confident attack on "I Can't Get Started." Yet Berigan's singing, less impressive, may have contributed even more to the sales of this recording, with its conversational delivery so well suited to the lyrics. His recording of "I Can't Get Started" was inducted into the Grammy Hall of Fame in 1975 and has been featured in several films, including *Chinatown* and *Save the Tiger*.

Billie Holiday's recording the following year is no doubt better known among today's crop of jazz fans, and is noteworthy both for capturing Lady Day in an unusually playful mood—even back then, she was tinkering with Ira Gershwin's lyrics—and for the tenor sax contribution by Lester Young. Young only gets a brief intro and a 16-bar solo on this track, but I can't think of another jazz improviser who was more skilled at capitalizing on such short interludes than Young at this stage of his career.

The song has enjoyed a rather adventurous post-chart afterlife—much more so than one might expect given its birth as a novelty number for a comedian. Dizzy Gillespie found it suitably boppish to feature it at his first session as a leader back in early 1945, and that recording employs a number of modernistic flourishes, including a passage that would later be incorporated into the standard arrangement of "'Round Midnight." The following year Lennie Tristano, also making his first commercial recordings, offered a stunning interpretation that Gunther Schuller has compared to Louis Armstrong's "West End Blues" and Duke Ellington's "Cotton Tail"—grand claims, to be sure, but this certainly ranks among the most progressive piano performances of the era. A few years later Paul Bley tackled this same standard, also on his debut leader date.

Charles Mingus, who was a sideman at the Bley session, left behind more than a half dozen recordings of this composition—and if you think of this artist only as a bassist, bandleader, and composer, see what Mingus could do as a solo pianist on his 1963 keyboard performance of "I Can't Get Started" for the Impulse label. But even better is his combo rendition with John Handy from 1959, where you will find the bassist relying on some four-chords-to-a-bar substitute changes—a progression implied by Dizzy Gillespie's melodic lines back in 1945 and made even more explicit in the trumpeter's big band performances of "I Can't Get Started" from 1948—that are still popular today with many jazz musicians who tackle this song.

RECOMMENDED VERSIONS

Bunny Berigan, New York, August 7, 1937

Billie Holiday (with Lester Young), New York, September 15, 1938

Lester Young (with Nat King Cole and Red Callender), Los Angeles, July 15, 1942

Dizzy Gillespie, New York, January 9, 1945

Lennie Tristano, New York, October 8, 1946

Paul Bley (with Charles Mingus and Art Blakey), *from Introducing Paul Bley*, November 30, 1953

Sonny Rollins, from *A Night at the Village Vanguard*, live at the Village Vanguard, New York, November 3, 1957

Charles Mingus (with John Handy), from *Jazz Portraits: Mingus in Wonderland*, live at the Nonagon Art Gallery, New York, January 16, 1959

Stan Getz (with Kenny Barron), from *Anniversary*, live at Jazzhus Montmartre, Copenhagen, 1987

Hamiet Bluiett (with Ted Dunbar), from *Ballads and Blues*, live at the Village Vanguard, New York, February 20, 1994

Joe Lovano (with Tom Harrell), from *Live at the Village Vanguard*, live at the Village Vanguard, New York, March 12, 1994

I Can't Give You Anything but Love
Composed by Jimmy McHugh, with lyrics by Dorothy Fields

A series of successful African-American musical revues ran on Broadway during the early decades of the twentieth century, including *In Dahomey* (1903), *Abyssinia* (1906), *Bandana Land* (1908), and *Shuffle Along* (1921). But *The Blackbirds of 1928* enjoyed the longest run of them all, helped along by the popularity of this song, performed by Adelaide Hall, and the silky smooth dancing of Bill "Bojangles" Robinson, who demonstrated the staircase dance steps he would later teach to Shirley Temple in a famous cinematic moment.

More than a dozen ensembles—including those led by Duke Ellington, Paul Whiteman, and Red Nichols—recorded this song in 1928, but the most influential early jazz interpretation came the following year from Louis Armstrong. And it is truly an interpretative effort, one of the highest order. Armstrong lingers over the melody on muted trumpet for just a few opening bars, a perfunctory nod to the written composition before the real fun starts. His vocal must have been a revelation to other singers of the time, taking liberties with the melody and departing markedly from the typical rhythmic phrasing of popular music. When Ethel Waters recorded "I Can't Give You Anything but Love" with the Ellington band in 1932 she replicated Louis Armstrong's vocal note for note and even emulated the timbre of his voice. Many other vocalists no doubt also memorized this performance.

The authorship of this song is subject to dispute. Fats Waller told a journalist back in 1929 that he had sold a song that became a hit in a major show. Some years later, Gladys Redman made a hospital visit to see Andy Razaf, who had frequently collaborated with Waller, and during the conversation she asked him to sing his favorite lyrics—which he did, surprising her with a rendition of "I Can't Give You Anything but Love." The evidence here is circumstantial, enough to raise questions but insufficient to resolve them. Certainly the song bears a stylistic resemblance to Waller's best work.

"I Can't Give You Anything but Love" was played widely during the Swing Era but found few adherents among the next generation of innovators. An amateur recording of "I Can't Give You Anything but Love" was made at Minton's Playhouse in 1941 with Thelonious Monk reportedly on piano, but the arrangement is old-fashioned and gives no sign that a modern jazz lion is at the keyboard. Monk, for his part, never recorded the song again. Charlie Parker was captured playing this standard in another amateur recording from 1943, made in room 305 of the Savoy Hotel in Chicago, but he also ignored the composition in later years. Dizzy Gillespie, Miles Davis, John Coltrane, Bud Powell, Lennie Tristano, and a host of other modernists from the middle decades of the century left behind no recordings of the work.

Even when a modern jazz player did deign to tackle it, as Sonny Stitt did in his 1959 recording with Oscar Peterson, the attitude was more likely to be playful than progressive. The same can be said of Stefano Bollani's quirky rendition from 1997, which veers close to parody. Yet for playfulness, pride of place goes to Ella Fitzgerald's 1974 scat battle with Clark Terry, the latter doing his "mumbles" routine, a gem that deserves to be far better known.

If the piece's lighthearted old-timey demeanor makes it an unlikely vehicle for bop, hard bop, fusion, or avant-garde interpretations, the song does have one strong selling point—its audience appeal. The jazz artists most aligned with this standard have tended to be those with an instinct for mass-market success—from Louis Armstrong to Diana Krall—and who recognize this composition's value in live performance. Such precedents notwithstanding, the most characteristic versions of the composition in recent years have come from trad jazz bands, or artists from outside the jazz world, and I suspect you are far more likely to hear "I Can't Give You Anything but Love" at Preservation Hall than at the Village Vanguard. For an enlightening exception, however, hear

Martial Solal's solo piano treatment recorded at the latter venue in 2007—a rare updating of a standard that usually comes in retro garb.

RECOMMENDED VERSIONS

Louis Armstrong, New York, March 5, 1929

Ethel Waters (with the Duke Ellington Orchestra), New York, December 22, 1932

Teddy Wilson (with Billie Holiday), New York, November 19, 1936

Benny Goodman (with an arrangement by Fletcher Henderson), Hollywood, September 6, 1937

Benny Goodman (with Charlie Christian), New York, December 19, 1940

Sonny Stitt (with Oscar Peterson), from *Sonny Stitt Sits In With the Oscar Peterson Trio*, Paris, May 18, 1959

Ella Fitzgerald (with Clark Terry), from *Fine and Mellow*, Los Angeles, January 8, 1974

Stefano Bollani, from *Mambo Italiano*, Livorno, Italy, June 24 and September 15, 1997

Diana Krall, from *When I Look in Your Eyes*, New York, 1998

Martial Solal, from *Martial Solal Live at the Village Vanguard: I Can't Give You Anything but Love*, live at the Village Vanguard, New York, October 12, 2007

I Cover the Waterfront
Composed by Johnny Green, with lyrics by Edward Heyman

The 1932 best-selling book *I Cover the Waterfront*, which inspired this song, was written by newspaper reporter Max Miller, who literally did just that—cover the coast, as part of his beat, in search of scandals and scoops. Somehow, lyricist Edward Heyman took this phrase and managed to change its meaning to suit a love ballad, with the singer now hanging out at the docks looking for love instead of headline news. This may not have been the most challenging title to turn into a hit song—for my money, I give Paul McCartney top marks in that regard, for crafting a gold record out of the unpromising phrase "Live and Let Die"—but it certainly makes my short list. I am sorry to say that when the song was included in the 1933 film *I Cover the Waterfront*, it only appears as an instrumental, with the alchemy of the lyrics left unheard.

That said, the melody here is well prepared to fend for itself, even without a vocalist standing at dockside. I especially admire the way the phrases in the bridge alternate between high register and lower, almost as if in a call-and-response written with two singers in mind. Over the course of just seven bars, Green inserts no fewer than four octave jumps in the melody—three downward and one upward. This is breathtaking, and my only quibble is that it comes in the middle of the form, and not at the end where one normally expects song-writers to employ their most spectacular fireworks.

The song was a hit for both Joe Haymes and Eddy Duchin at the time of its initial release, and was also featured in a 1933 film clip made of Louis Armstrong in Copenhagen—an important document not just for the music but also for its glimpse into the performance demeanor of this artist at an early stage in his career. The song fell out of circulation in the late 1930s, but Artie Shaw recorded "I Cover the Waterfront" in 1941 when his career was red hot—he reportedly received $10,000 per week at the Strand during this same period, at a time when the average worker earned less than a dollar per hour—and a few months later Shaw's former vocalist Billie Holiday delivered "I Cover the Waterfront" at a session with Teddy Wilson's band.

More than anyone, Holiday ensured the staying power of this song in the jazz repertoire, and she recorded it on several later occasions. Jazz fans should seek out the version she performed at the Philharmonic Auditorium in Los Angeles in 1945, which finds her in a rare collaboration with Duke Ellington's orchestra. In Holiday's wake, the song would be embraced by many later jazz and cabaret singers, but would also continue to hold the interest of instrumentalists.

The strangest version of this song, bar none, comes from blues artist John Lee Hooker. Hooker often fought with record producers because he wanted to perform pop ballads. They were reluctant to acquiesce, and with good reason—even when playing a 12-bar blues, Hooker might end up with 13 bars on the first chorus and 14-1/2 bars on the next one; so how could he get through a 32-bar song form without a train wreck? Well, Hooker got his way, and delivered a version of "I Cover the Waterfront" that is so deviant and disconnected from the original song that the record label was justified in listing Hooker as the composer. It's a surreal departure from what normally passes for jazz, but you should listen to it anyway—if only to see if you can find the original tune hiding in the grooves.

RECOMMENDED VERSIONS

Louis Armstrong, Copenhagen, October 21–23, 1933

Artie Shaw, Hollywood, January 23, 1941

Billie Holiday, New York, August 7, 1941

Billie Holiday (with Duke Ellington), live at the Philharmonic Auditorium, Los Angeles, January 17, 1945

Lester Young (with Nat King Cole and Buddy Rich), Los Angeles, March–April 1946

Art Tatum, Los Angeles, July 13, 1949

Jackie McLean (with Mal Waldron), from *A Long Drink of the Blues*, Hackensack,
New Jersey, February 15, 1957

Henry "Red" Allen (with Coleman Hawkins), from *World on a String*. New York,
March 27, 1957

John Lee Hooker (recorded as "The Waterfront"), from *The Real Folk Blues*, Chicago,
1966

Don Byron (with Jason Moran and Jack DeJohnette), from *Ivey-Divey*, Shokan, New
York, May 23–24, 2004

I Didn't Know What Time It Was
Composed by Richard Rodgers, with lyrics by Lorenz Hart

Those great rivals of the Swing Era, Benny Goodman and Artie Shaw, both
recorded this song within a few days of each other in the fall of 1939. Goodman
enjoyed a top 10 hit with his recording, which featured a willowy vocal by Louise
Tobin, while Shaw relied on Helen Forrest to complement his clarinet lines.
Jimmy Dorsey followed up with his own version, built around Bob Eberly's
vocal, which was also a modest hit.

After this brief flurry of activity, the song was mostly forgotten by jazz
players and would not be widely covered for another decade. In 1949, George
Shearing recorded "I Didn't Know What Time It Was" with his popular quintet,
and a few months later Charlie Parker presented the song as part of his commercial project with string orchestra. These precedents no doubt encouraged
other modern jazz players to add the piece to their repertoires. But a decision by
Hollywood honchos to showcase the song in the 1957 hit film *Pal Joey*, where it
was sung by Frank Sinatra, did even more to give the tune a second wind and
ensure its popularity with the general public.

I am fascinated by the construction of the melody here, in which phrases
start on the high notes and then descend into mid- and low register. Our composer seems determined to reverse the usual formula of hit song writers, who
typically prefer to build up to dramatic high notes—based on the assumption
that listeners would rather end up in the penthouse than the basement. Yet the
constant downward motion of the melody perfectly matches the words here,
which evoke a love born in the midst of a confused, almost depressed state of
mind. When the melody makes its occasional move back to the eyrie, Hart links
the higher notes to evocative words such as "grand" or "warm"—choices that
reinforce the bipolar sensibility of the song.

I sensed a special poignancy here even before I knew about Lorenz Hart's
struggles with his own demons during the time he was working on *Too Many*

Girls, the 1939 Broadway show that launched "I Didn't Know What Time It Was." Hart's alcoholism, which would contribute to his death four years later, was increasingly out of control and evident to those who worked with him. Hart "was no fun at all," Rodgers would later write. "It was almost impossible to find him when we needed him, and this time we needed him desperately." It's hard for me to hear this song now, chronicling as it does a sense of losing track of time, the day and the place, without thinking of these behind-the-scenes turmoils.

The song adapts to a wide range of interpretative styles. When Art Blakey featured saxophonist Wayne Shorter on the number in the mid-1960s, it could serve as the springboard for a probing Coltrane-esque coda. Betty Carter frequently performed the song in concert, where she deconstructed it into an almost avant-garde art song. When the combo Sphere presented it in the 1980s they transformed the Rodgers and Hart standard into a finger-snapping groove tune. And Brad Mehldau showed that the audience might not know what time it was in, with his fanciful 5/4 trio performance from 1996.

RECOMMENDED VERSIONS

Artie Shaw, New York, November 9, 1939

Charlie Parker (with strings), New York, November 30, 1949

Peggy Lee, from *Black Coffee*, New York, April 30, 1953

Stan Getz and Gerry Mulligan, from *Getz Meets Mulligan*, Los Angeles, October 12, 1957

Art Blakey (featuring Wayne Shorter), from *Ugetsu*, live at Birdland, New York, June 16, 1963

Betty Carter, from *Betty Carter at the Village Vanguard*, live at the Village Vanguard, New York, May 16, 1970

Cassandra Wilson, from *Blue Skies*, New York, February 4–5, 1988

Sphere (featuring Kenny Barron and Charlie Rouse), from *Bird Songs*, Englewood Cliffs, New Jersey, March 12, 1988

Chick Corea, from *Expressions*, Los Angeles, 1994

Brad Mehldau, from *The Art of the Trio, Vol. 1*, Los Angeles, September 4–5, 1996

I Fall in Love Too Easily
Composed by Jule Styne, with lyrics by Sammy Cahn

This song had an almost ideal launching pad. Introduced in a high-profile Hollywood film (*Anchors Aweigh*) with an all-star cast, "I Fall in Love Too Easily" was sung on-screen by Frank Sinatra. The film, MGM's second-best-grossing release of the year, was nominated for Best Picture, and this composition also received a nomination for Best Song—losing out to another song destined for enshrinement in the jazz standard repertoire: "It Might as Well Be Spring" from *State Fair*. But Georgie Stoll, *Anchors'* musical director, did win an Oscar for Best Score. (The latter statuette got back in the news in 2001 when it was put up for auction at Butterfields. The auction house expected it to sell for $10,000 to $20,000, but in a heated bidding war it went for $156,875—later, Kevin Spacey revealed that he had purchased the award in order to return it to the Academy of Motion Picture Arts and Sciences.)

Eugenie Baird, supported by Mel Tormé and his Mel-Tones, enjoyed a modest hit with the song in the fall of 1945, but few others followed suit. Virtually no jazz recordings of this work were made for almost a decade. But Chet Baker offered up one of his dreamiest and best-known vocal performances with "I Fall in Love Too Easily" at a Los Angeles session from February 1954. Yet listeners should not overlook the trumpet solo. Richard Bock, who produced this session, once remarked to me that he thought some of Chet's finest horn work came from this early session, ostensibly arranged to highlight Baker's singing—something about the lyrical setting and the challenge of accompanying his own low-key vocal work brought out an especially tender, introspective side of the trumpet soloist.

Indeed, this song seems perfectly suited for jazz introverts. Sammy Cahn's delicate lyrics add to the effect—this is a love ballad sung by someone without a lover to sing it to. Jule Styne's melody, for its part, possesses a gentle, ruminative quality. Needless to say, this is *not* the kind of tune you belt to the back row, but rather one you deliver to yourself, or perhaps the half-filled bottle in front of you. In *Anchors Aweigh*, Sinatra sings it on an empty stage at the Hollywood Bowl, and the song's effect is all the more powerful without a cheering audience on hand. The best versions capture this same ambiance, as demonstrated by recordings by Bill Evans, Lenny Breau, and Miles Davis.

Davis kept the song in his repertoire well into his fusion years, long after he had abandoned most standards. I especially admire his 1963 recording, with Victor Feldman on piano, but it is fascinating to hear Davis at the Philharmonie in Berlin from 1969 or at San Francisco's Fillmore West in 1970, working through the same dark ballad with an electric rhythm section backing him up for an all-too-brief performance. Few later versions have pushed this song quite so far. In 1981, when Herbie Hancock reunited the mid-1960s Miles Davis rhythm section, and hired 19-year-old Wynton Marsalis to front the band, they played this song unplugged and unmodified—one sign, among many, that the Age of Fusion was coming to an end. Yet this composition brings with it an uncluttered, open feeling that makes it suitable for radical reworking into minimalist or quasi-ambient stylings. For a first-rate example of the former, listen to Patricia Barber's recording from 2000; for the latter, check out Claudia Acuña's interpretation from 2001.

I Got It Bad (and That Ain't Good)
Composed by Duke Ellington, with lyrics by Paul Francis Webster

Just look at that huge interval leap of over an octave in the middle of bar one, and you can tell that this lovely Duke Ellington melody, like many of his ballads, was composed without a singer on hand for consultation. At first glance, this composition might seem better suited to serve as a piano prelude rather than a chart-busting vocal feature. To his credit, Ellington crafted a work here that can do both.

The song dates from the most fertile period of Duke's career, those months leading up to Pearl Harbor, which found Ellington fronting his finest band, composing and recording prolifically, appearing in films, serving as sideman at small combo sessions under the leadership of his bandmates, and somehow finding the time to compose music for a full-fledged show, *Jump for Joy*, which made its premiere at the Mayan Theater in Los Angeles in the summer of 1941. Ellington had high hopes for this production, and claimed that it was the hippest thing his band ever did—so hip that a glossary of jive was included with the program. To his disappointment, the show never made it to Broadway.

But if *Jump for Joy* failed to realize its composer's ambitions, closing after three months, at least another hit song emerged from the wreckage. One of three compositions for the show written the night before he arrived in Los

Angeles, "I Got It Bad (and That Ain't Good)" would rank among Ellington's perennials, staying in the band's book as one of his most requested numbers. Even before opening night, Ellington had recorded the piece at a Hollywood session for the Victor label, and though the tune—in the studio as on stage at the Mayan Theater—served as a feature for vocalist Ivie Anderson, Johnny Hodges steals the show with a brief intro and short interlude, where the altoist shines without doing much more than stating the melody. Also pay close attention to the horn writing supporting Hodge's alto, smoky and alluring but easy for the casual listener to miss—another reminder of how some of Duke's best stuff takes place *behind* the soloist.

A song this fine was sure to be snatched up by other bandleaders. Only a month after Ellington's debut recording, Ella Fitzgerald featured "I Got It Bad (and That Ain't Good)" at a Los Angeles recording date, and around this same time Earl Hines, Stan Kenton, Jimmy Dorsey, and Bunny Berigan, among others, added the song to their bands' repertoires. In November, Benny Goodman enjoyed a modest hit with his recording of "I Got It Bad," which featured Peggy Lee and a chart by Eddie Sauter, while Ellington's recording of the song made it into the top 20 early in 1942.

Ellington's songs sometimes got saddled with subpar lyrics, but Paul Webster—who later helped write many hits and earned a stunning 16 Academy Award nominations—offered words that aptly match the ethos of Duke's melody. Even so, I tend to prefer instrumental versions of this song, and especially those featuring the inestimable Mr. Hodges. For a chance to hear him play this song on a leader date, go no further than his performance from the 1961 *Soloist* album for Verve, which finds Hodges fronting the Ellington orchestra without Duke on hand, and Billy Strayhorn filling in on piano.

If I do turn to a vocal performance, my first choices would be Nina Simone's recording from 1963 or Louis Armstrong's collaboration with the composer from 1961. I note that Armstrong, in his vocal, pays little heed to the big interval leap at the start, and recrafts the melody to suit his own vocal style. Yes, the composer is sitting right there, but, instead of making a fuss, Ellington follows (like any proper duke) the tenet of *noblesse oblige*.

RECOMMENDED VERSIONS

Duke Ellington (featuring Johnny Hodges and Ivie Anderson), Hollywood, June 26, 1941

Benny Goodman (with Peggy Lee), New York, October 2, 1941

Earl Hines (with Billy Eckstine), Chicago, October 28, 1941

Benny Carter, from *Cosmopolite*, New York, September 18, 1952

Stan Kenton (with Frank Rosolino), from *Portraits on Standards*, Chicago, July 8, 1953

Thelonious Monk, from *Thelonious Monk Plays the Music of Duke Ellington*, Hackensack, New Jersey, July 27, 1955

Louis Armstrong and Duke Ellington, from *The Great Summit*, New York, April 3, 1961

Nina Simone, from *Nina Simone Sings Ellington*, New York, 1963

Kenny Burrell, from *Stormy Monday Blues*, Berkeley, California, June 18–20, 1974

Adam Makowicz, from *Adam*, New York, 1977

Keith Jarrett, from *The Melody at Night, with You*, New Jersey, 1998

I Got Rhythm
Composed by George Gershwin, with lyrics by Ira Gershwin

This is the granddaddy of jazz tunes. "I Got Rhythm" stands out as the perennial favorite of jam session participants, time-honored and battle-tested. Styles and tendencies may go in and out of favor, but this song never falls out of fashion. Indeed, so familiar is its structure and progression that musicians don't even need to mention the title in full—the bandleader just calls out "rhythm changes" and counts in a tempo. Usually the fastest one of the evening.

We should give George Gershwin credit for putting such a lasting stamp on the jazz idiom. Or should we? On closer inspection, this song long ago separated itself from Gershwin's original conception. "Rhythm changes" are rarely played with the original "I Got Rhythm" melody these days. Instead, dozens of popular alternatives—by Duke Ellington, Lester Young, Charlie Parker, Thelonious Monk, and others—have become standards in their own right. Gershwin's initial structure for the song has also undergone transformation: jazz players found the extra tag at the end cumbersome and jettisoned it from their versions long ago. And even the chords themselves—the "changes" in "rhythm changes"—are so frequently modified and updated by jazz players that these last vestiges of the 1930 song retain only a faint resemblance to what George and Ira wrought.

The song originated in the 1930 musical *Girl Crazy*, which also produced future standards "Embraceable You" and "But Not for Me." Here the piece not only was performed by Ethel Merman, in her Broadway debut, but her delivery on opening night made her a star—creating such a frenzy of applause that she was required to give encore after encore. "I've heard honest—and even intelligent—people describe that first time they heard 'I Got Rhythm' as a 'high point in the theater,'" Merman later boasted in her autobiography, which was named *Who Could Ask for Anything More* after a line from this very song.

Gershwin's melody, with its short choppy phrases that avoid starting on down beats, must have challenged his brother Ira's wordsmithing ingenuity, but the lyricist responded with a series of striking four-syllable sentences. And jazz players were charmed from the start, especially by the suitability of the harmonic progression for improvisation. On Louis Armstrong's hit 1931 recording, he dispenses with vocals entirely—a rarity at this stage in his career—and instead exhorts his sidemen while featuring seven of them in solos. Two years later Clarence Hutchenrider stretched out for a much-admired 68-bar baritone solo on the Casa Loma Orchestra's recording of "I Got Rhythm," further demonstrating that jazz musicians valued this song less for what Gershwin wrote and more for what it might allow them to create spontaneously on the bandstand.

Red Nichols and Ethel Waters also enjoyed early hits with "I Got Rhythm," but after 1931 the song would not show up on the charts until the Happenings, a Paterson, New Jersey, group, enjoyed a surprise success with their pop makeover of the Gershwin song in 1967. Yet jazz musicians never flagged in their devotion. Wherever they performed, "I Got Rhythm" came along, fitting in with equal ease at ballrooms and nightclubs, jam sessions and private woodshedding workouts, in concert halls or on overseas tours. When Benny Goodman performed at Carnegie Hall in his historic 1938 concert, his quartet—composed of the clarinetist, Teddy Wilson, Lionel Hampton, and Gene Krupa—offered a whirlwind version of "I Got Rhythm" to their enthusiastic audience, but uptown in Harlem this same song would soon figure as a regular part of the after-hours proceedings at Minton's Playhouse and Monroe's Uptown House where the new bebop style was forged.

"I Got Rhythm" was especially popular at all-star affairs where jazz icons fraternized and jousted. The Metronome All Stars lineup that recorded the song in 1942 featured Goodman again, but this time joined by Count Basie, Benny Carter, Charlie Barnet, Cootie Williams, and J. C. Higginbotham. But an even more impressive roster showed up to play "I Got Rhythm" at the 1944 Esquire All Star concert, where the luminaries on stage included Louis Armstrong, Art Tatum, Roy Eldridge, Jack Teagarden, Barney Bigard, and Red Norvo. Equally noteworthy, a Jazz at the Philharmonic concert recorded at the Embassy Theatre in Los Angeles on April 22, 1946, presented a historic encounter between Coleman Hawkins, Lester Young, and Charlie Parker, again with "I Got Rhythm" on the agenda. Those who dismiss Young's post–World War II work as inferior simply must hear him in this setting, where Prez bests his celebrated rivals with a spirited solo that has the audience cheering phrase by phrase as he powers his way through his final chorus.

Alas, the song's chords became so famous that they eclipsed the composition itself. I have a half-dozen different fake books in front of me as I write, and none of them include "I Got Rhythm" while every other jazz standard I can name shows up in one or more of these volumes—no doubt because the compilers felt that there were so many other "rhythm songs" in these pages that it was redundant to include the original. As such exclusion might suggest, the Gershwin standard itself gradually fell off the set lists of younger, more progressive players during the postbop period, even as its harmonic progression became emblematic of the very spirit of jazz. Older players and those influenced by them continued to play "I Got Rhythm" in something approaching its original form—Stéphane Grappelli recorded at least one version in every decade from the 1930s through the 1990s—but fresh, surprising variations on this composition have become few and far between in recent years, even as players have exercised endless creativity in modifying and improvising over the underlying changes.

RECOMMENDED VERSIONS

George Gershwin (newsreel film clip), live at the Manhattan Theater (now the Ed Sullivan Theater), New York, August 1931

Louis Armstrong, Chicago, November 6, 1931

Casa Loma Orchestra (with Clarence Hutchenrider), New York, December 30, 1933

Benny Goodman Quartet, live at Carnegie Hall, New York, January 16, 1938

Metronome All Stars (with Count Basie, Benny Goodman, Benny Carter, and others), New York, January 16, 1942

Esquire All Stars (with Louis Armstrong, Art Tatum, Roy Eldridge, and others), live at the Metropolitan Opera House, New York, January 18, 1944

Jazz at the Philharmonic (with Coleman Hawkins, Lester Young, and Charlie Parker), live at Embassy Auditorium, Los Angeles, April 22, 1946

Willie "The Lion" Smith, live at Tonhalle, Zurich, December 15, 1949

Stéphane Grappelli and McCoy Tyner, from *One on One*, New York, April 18, 1990

Eric Reed, from *Pure Imagination*, New York, July 28–29, 1997

I Hear a Rhapsody
Composed by George Fragos, Jack Baker, and Dick Gasparre

Three separate artists—Charlie Barnet, Jimmy Dorsey, and Dinah Shore—scored top 10 hits with "I Hear a Rhapsody" in 1941. Bob Carroll, vocalist on the Barnet version, is seldom remembered today, but Mel Tormé has lauded this performance as a "classic . . . a virile rendition sung with great warmth." Fans nowadays are more likely to be familiar with the version recorded the following year by Frank Sinatra with the Tommy Dorsey band—but I would point listeners to the lesser-known Sinatra–Dorsey radio broadcast performance (on the show *Fame and Fortune*) from January instead of the studio version made the following month.

"I Hear a Rhapsody" had a second boost of fame a decade later. Frank Sinatra enjoyed a modest hit with his new recording of the song, and the composition was also featured in two films. Director Fritz Lang showcased "I Hear a Rhapsody" in his 1952 movie *Clash by Night* starring Barbara Stanwyck—and Marilyn Monroe in one of her first significant roles—where the song was performed by Tony Martin. "I Hear a Rhapsody" also shows up in the 1951 film *Casa Mañana*, directed by Jean Yarbrough, about a man who purchases a nightclub with the hope of turning his girlfriend into a star singer.

"I Hear a Rhapsody" started out as a slow dreamy ballad, but gradually evolved into a rapid-fire jam tune. The earliest versions tend to be introspective and understated, with most jazz renditions from the 1940s through the mid-1950s—by Erroll Garner, George Shearing, Zoot Sims, and others—keeping to a medium-slow tempo. Dave Brubeck, however, offered up a faster version with his Octet, and Jackie McLean switched from rubato to a medium-up tempo midway through his 1957 performance. But John Coltrane, who recorded the song 10 weeks after McLean, was even more influential in turning "I Hear a Rhapsody" into a fast, extroverted number.

Since that time, most jazz players have followed Trane's lead. Occasionally the more romantic side of the song emerges, as on the duet between Bill Evans and Jim Hall from 1962. But it's worth noting that both Evans and Hall recorded faster versions later in their career. I usually prefer Evans's earlier work, but in this instance I give the nod to his 1970 rendition of "I Hear a Rhapsody," recorded live at the Montreux Jazz Festival, which reveals a strident, almost funky attitude, one that only occasionally surfaced in this pianist's recordings.

Plenty of high-octane performances can be found from later decades. Keith Jarrett released two separate renditions of "I Hear a Rhapsody," both with his Standards Trio, and the song has become something of a signature piece for Italian pianist Enrico Pieranunzi, who has released several different versions on CD. Other noteworthy tracks have been provided by Chick Corea, Tom Harrell, and Lee Konitz (with Michel Petrucciani). For a lesser known, but standout performance, you are directed to Peter Erskine's live trio recording from 2009, which displays the keyboard acumen of pianist Alan Pasqua—more famous for composing the theme song for CBS Evening News and gigging with Bob Dylan, but who makes a persuasive case here for his jazz work.

RECOMMENDED VERSIONS

Charlie Barnet (with Bob Carroll), New York, October 14, 1940

Jimmy Dorsey (with Bob Eberly), New York, December 9, 1940

Duke Ellington (with Herb Jeffries and Ben Webster), Hollywood, January 15, 1941

Tommy Dorsey (with Frank Sinatra), from the NBC radio program *Fame and Fortune*, New York, January 30, 1941

Jackie McLean, from *Makin' the Changes*, Hackensack, New Jersey, February 15, 1957

John Coltrane (with Red Garland), from *Lush Life*, Hackensack, New Jersey, May 31, 1957

Bill Evans, from *Montreux II*, live at the Montreux Jazz Festival, Montreux, Switzerland, June 19, 1970

Lee Konitz and Michel Petrucciani, from *Toot Sweet*, live at Centre Musical Bosendorfer, Paris, May 25, 1982

Chick Corea (with Miroslav Vitous and Roy Haynes), from *Trio Music: Live in Europe*, live in Willisau, Switzerland or Reutlingen, Germany, September 1984

Keith Jarrett (with Gary Peacock and Jack DeJohnette), from *Standards in Norway*, live at Oslo Konserthus, Oslo, October 7, 1989

Dado Moroni and Tom Harrell, from *Humanity*, Milan, April 6, 2007

Peter Erskine (with Alan Pasqua), from *The Interlochen Concert*, live at Corson Auditorium, Interlochen, Michigan, April 8, 2009

I Let a Song Go Out of My Heart
Composed by Duke Ellington, with lyrics by Irving Mills, Henry Nemo, and John Redmond

Duke Ellington enjoyed a number one hit with "I Let a Song Go Out of My Heart" in the spring of 1938, and other bandleaders were quick to follow up with their own renditions. The same week that Ellington's song topped the charts, both Benny Goodman and Red Norvo recorded their versions, as did Hot Lips Page the following week. Each one of these releases was a top 10 hit. In May, Jimmy Dorsey recorded "I Let a Song Go Out of My Heart," and the next month Connee Boswell did the same—and her version kept the tune on the airwaves during the summer. Around this same time, the song also showed up on radio broadcasts by Count Basie, Cab Calloway, Paul Whiteman, and Charlie Barnet.

Ellington had initially presented the composition as an instrumental, drawing on a riff that Johnny Hodges played behind the melody of "Once in a While." Ellington's manager Irving Mills provided lyrics, relying on Henry Nemo, who alleged they came to his mind, *Enderby*-style, while sitting on the toilet. When Johnny Hodges recorded the song in a combo under his nominal leadership in late March, with Ellington on piano and other band regulars in tow, the song now served as a vehicle for singer Mary McHugh. Benny Goodman followed suit, promoting his star vocalist Martha Tilton on his recording, while Dorsey featured June Richmond, and Norvo relied on the considerable talents of his wife, Mildred Bailey.

I am not surprised at this composition's popularity, especially during the Swing Era, given how well it works both in dance hall and concert settings. The melody has a powerful hook in the opening phrase, with its syncopation on the word "song" and jazzy triplet to open the second measure. As noted above, Duke reportedly borrowed an idea from Hodges in writing the tune, but I suspect that he deferred to no one in his daring modulation out of the bridge, which is one of those quirky touches that this composer used to enliven even his most commercial works.

During the 1940s, few cover versions were recorded, but Ellington continued to present the song regularly in performances and broadcasts, usually as part of the medley of hits he employed to please fans who demanded to hear his more familiar numbers. The song found a new audience in the mid-1950s, via releases by Dizzy Gillespie and Stan Getz (on their 1953 *Diz and Getz* project), Thelonious Monk (from his 1955 *Thelonious Monk Plays Duke Ellington* album), and a host of other recordings by players young and old, hot and cool, East Coast and West Coast. The song has retained its popularity in more recent years, often in the context of Ellington tributes of various sorts.

RECOMMENDED VERSIONS

Duke Ellington, New York, March 3, 1938

Johnny Hodges (with Mary McHugh), New York, March 28, 1938

Red Norvo (with Mildred Bailey), New York, April 19, 1938

Benny Goodman (with Martha Tilton), New York, April 22, 1938

Hot Lips Page, New York, April 27, 1938

Dizzy Gillespie and Stan Getz, from *Diz and Getz*, Los Angeles, December 9, 1953

Thelonious Monk, from *Thelonious Monk Plays Duke Ellington*, Hackensack, New Jersey, July 27, 1955

Johnny Hodges, from *Blue Rabbit*, New York, May 15, 1963

Toshiko Akiyoshi, from *Dedications-1*, Los Angeles, July 19–21, 1976

Andy Bey, from *Ballads, Blues and Bey*, New York, May 19–20, 1995

I Love You
Composed by Cole Porter

In 1944 Bing Crosby had six songs hit the top of the charts—a record that stood for two decades until four lads from Liverpool matched it. One of Crosby's successes from that war-torn year was "I Love You," which Cole Porter wrote for the Broadway musical *Mexican Hayride*. In a strange decision, when Hollywood made a movie (with Abbott and Costello) out of this show, "I Love You" was omitted. But if the comedy duo didn't like this love song, later artists more than made up for their neglect, with performers as diverse as Frank Sinatra, John Coltrane, and Johnny Mathis offering up interpretations over the years.

The words do not rank among Porter's best, with their string of deliberate clichés—familiar prattle about birds, daffodils, the dawn—and none of the clever turns of phrase that were his trademark. Porter reportedly wrote the piece in response to a wager with his friend Monty Woolley, who doubted that the song-writer could build an effective song out of the oft-used title phrase. The resulting lyrics retain a quasi-satirical undertone, and the song could be performed ironically—although this is not how it has been typically treated in jazz circles. Rather, jazz players have embraced "I Love You" for the dramatic interval leaps in the melody and its sweet modulation in the bridge, ingredients that hold enough charm to keep this song in the jazz repertoire more than 60 years after it was written.

This song often gets the "Latin treatment"—a hit-or-miss procedure that can be the jazz equivalent of cut-rate plastic surgery. Sometimes the piece ends up enhanced, but perhaps just as often the result is unintended disfigurement. I suspect that jazz players so often opt for a propulsive rhythm on this chart because Porter inserted so many long-held notes into the melody, starting in bar one and continuing throughout the song. The melody will not swing the song on its own, and actually creates a sense of stasis. Latinizing the proceedings serves as compensation.

But at what price? The chance to hear the young Sarah Vaughan and Billy Eckstine in duet on this number, on which they collaborate in 1949, is a rare treat—ah, if only a less clichéd arrangement had been commissioned for the date! This might have been one of the defining performances of "I Love You" and, in all fairness, if you block out the listless Lester-Lannish Latin cha-cha-cha accompaniment here, the vocal performance is exquisite. Even Coltrane toys with a Latin rhythm, but only as a teaser, instead keeping to a straight 4/4 swing for most of his performance. Jackie McLean and Art Pepper do the same.

A more effective Latin arrangement comes from Ahmad Jamal, who glides over the percussion on his 1994 recording of "I Love You." And for potent reworkings that break away from traditional grooves, don't miss Bennie Wallace's 1993 treatment, on his album *The Old Songs*, or Mike Stern's 1997 trio version alongside John Patitucci and Jack DeJohnette from *Give and Take*. These renditions don't try to fight the open spaces Cole Porter built into this song, but rather rely on them to create an effective free-floating ethereal sound.

A final note: don't confuse this song with another "I Love You," composed by Harry Archer and Harlan Thompson and occasionally recorded by jazz musicians (including Coleman Hawkins and Django Reinhardt). The latter song is often listed incorrectly as written by Cole Porter. It will be easier to avoid Vanilla

Ice's song "I Love You," since it has never, to my notice, been attributed to Porter or shown up on a jazz album—and, with any luck, won't in the future.

RECOMMENDED VERSIONS

Bing Crosby, Los Angeles, February 11, 1944

Sarah Vaughan and Billy Eckstine, New York, December 22, 1949

John Coltrane, from *Lush Life*, Hackensack, New Jersey, August 16, 1957

Jackie McLean, from *Swing, Swang, Swingin'*, Englewood Cliffs, New Jersey, October 20, 1959

Art Pepper, from *Intensity*, Los Angeles, November 23 and 25, 1960

Bennie Wallace, from *The Old Songs*, January 18–20, 1993

Ahmad Jamal, from *Big Byrd: The Essence Part 2*, Paris, October 30–31, 1994

Mike Stern (with John Patitucci and Jack DeJohnette), from *Give and Take*, New York, 1997

I Mean You

Composed by Thelonious Monk and Coleman Hawkins

Coleman Hawkins assembled an impressive lineup of beboppers for the 1946 debut recording of Thelonious Monk's "I Mean You"—his cutting-edge band included Fats Navarro, J. J. Johnson, and Max Roach. But composer Thelonious Monk, despite his previous experiences working with Hawkins, is notably absent. Hank Jones handles keyboard responsibilities, and though he plays in an appropriately Monkian (or is "Monastic" the right term?) spirit, the absence of Monk himself is much to be lamented. Hawkins's advocacy of this modernistic piece must have been gratifying to its creator, but getting passed over for the recording session no doubt grated in equal measure. Monk may have been even more dismayed by the small print on the release: although the copyright application listed him as sole author, the label on the 78 rpm record credited Hawkins as co-composer.

The title makes perfect sense—not always a given in Monk's oeuvre. An emphatic quality in the melody, furthered by rhythm section accents on the back beat during the opening of the main theme, results in the perfect theme music for such an exhortation. And long before lyrics were added, Monk may well have heard the words "I mean you!" in his head as he played the last three notes of the melody. The chord changes, unlike those found in so many jazz charts of the day, are wholly original and add to the nonconformist tone of the work. The intro, unfortunately left out in some fake book lead sheets, is quite startling, beginning on a note and chord a whole step below the tonic key; it returns again as a coda and can also serve as an interlude between solos, periodically disrupting the sense of a tonal center.

More than a year and a half would transpire after the Hawkins date before Monk would record this song under his own leadership. Here he is joined by vibraphonist Milt Jackson, who had been present at the earlier session but had not played on "I Mean You." Now Jackson gets solo space, and the juxtaposition of his lithe bop-oriented lines against Monk's disjunctive chords and interjections makes for a study in contrasts. The performance is prickly, and Monk seems jumpier than usual, but an appealingly boisterous quality permeates the proceedings. Although you would never label this composer's work as "party music," this track wouldn't be out of place at some surreal rent party, blasted over the speakers at the moment when festivities veer out of control.

As was often the case with Monk's compositions, he continued to perform and record "I Mean You" regularly, serving as its loyal advocate long before it entered the standard repertoire. You can hear him playing "I Mean You" at his 1957 session with Art Blakey's Jazz Messengers, and he drew on it three months later for his album with Gerry Mulligan. An intriguing performance of the song with John Coltrane at the Five Spot, captured on an amateur recording and later released by Blue Note, shows the band stretching out for almost 14 minutes on this song and playing at a very high level.

Few other musicians covered this work until the late 1970s and early 1980s, when it got the nod from a number of high-profile jazz artists. McCoy Tyner's trio performance with Ron Carter and Tony Williams from his 1977 *Supertrios* project was widely heard and admired at the time. The Griffith Park Collection, an all-star ensemble that included Chick Corea, Freddie Hubbard, and Joe Henderson, also served as compelling advocates for "I Mean You" a few years later— I was in attendance the night they recorded this song for their *The Griffith Park Collection 2* live album and can testify to the excitement in the audience.

Since that period, "I Mean You" has remained firmly entrenched in the repertoire of jazz bands. And for good reason. More than most Monk songs, this piece can adapt to a range of interpretative postures, many of them far afield from the composer's own. The composition is amenable to a straight-ahead jam (Cedar Walton), lyrical effusions (Esbjörn Svensson), or a Latin groove (Ray Barretto), as well as a host of other perspectives.

RECOMMENDED VERSIONS

Coleman Hawkins, New York, December 1946

Thelonious Monk (with Milt Jackson), New York, July 2, 1948

Thelonious Monk (with John Coltrane), from *Live at the Five Spot—Discovery!*, live at the Five Spot, New York, September 11, 1958

McCoy Tyner (with Ron Carter and Tony Williams), from *Supertrios*, Berkeley,
    California, April 9–10, 1977

The Griffith Park Collection (with Chick Corea, Joe Henderson, and Freddie
    Hubbard), from *The Griffith Park Collection 2*, live at the Circle Star Theater, San
    Carlos, California, April 3, 1982

Cedar Walton, from *Manhattan Afternoon*, New York, December 26, 1992

Esbjörn Svensson, from *Plays Monk*, Stockholm, January 1996

Ray Barretto, from *Portraits in Jazz and Clave*, March 6–14, 1999

D. D. Jackson, from *So Far*, Montreal, May 8–9, 1999

I Only Have Eyes for You
Composed by Harry Warren, with lyrics by Al Dubin

Few jazz standards can approach the staying power and adaptability of this
song, which has been a top 20 hit for more than a half-dozen artists during
four separate decades. "I Only Have Eyes for You" started life in 1934 as a
vocal number for Dick Powell in the Busby Berkeley film musical *Dames*,
where it was used extensively—perhaps most memorably in an outlandish
sequence featuring a legion of dancers all performing while wearing Ruby
Keeler masks.

Almost immediately, the song became a staple for the "sweet bands," and
produced hits for Ben Selvin—the prolific society leader, who earned a place in
the *Guinness World Records* by recording a stunning 13,000 recordings (that's a
conservative estimate) under more than two dozen aliases—and the popular
pianist Eddy Duchin. Forty years later, Art Garfunkel relied on the same song to
prove that he could have a hit without Paul Simon on hand, and managed to
reach the top spot on the UK singles chart as well as *Billboard*'s adult contemporary chart.

Yet I suspect that the best-known version, even today, remains the Flamingos' R&B single, a modest hit from the summer of 1959. This recording never
reached higher than number 11 on the *Billboard* chart, but it became a staple of
oldies radio, showed up in various films and TV shows (e.g., *American Graffiti*,
Buffy the Vampire Slayer) and eventually found a spot (at #157) on *Rolling Stone*'s
2004 ranking of the "500 Greatest Songs of All Time."

These various recordings have their merits—and I especially like the smoky,
late-night ambiance of the Flamingos' performance. Yet they have one thing in
common: virtually no discernible jazz influence. The only major jazz star to
record "I Only Have Eyes for You" before the end of World War II was Coleman

Hawkins, who brought it into the studio in 1935 and 1944. The first recording is a sluggish affair with a Dutch band, but the latter version is an outstanding medium-fast swing interpretation, with worthy contributions from trumpeter Roy Eldridge and pianist Teddy Wilson as well as an extended, harmonically adept solo from Hawkins. I suspect that this recording played a key role in the gradual acceptance of this composition by more jazz-oriented performers over the next few years, when it was picked up by Glenn Miller, Billy Eckstine, Peggy Lee, Boyd Raeburn, George Shearing, and others.

Perhaps the absence of a clear jazz lineage may actually have given performers more latitude in their interpretations of this song. Heck, when you get a request for "I Only Have Eyes for You," you're not even sure whether it should be played in 6/8 like the Flamingos, a slow 4/4 like Garfunkel, or the loping duple beat strut of the Lettermen (who enjoyed a top 10 hit with the song in 1966). Or maybe it's best to swing it like Coleman Hawkins or treat it as a ballad à la Peggy Lee. As a result, this song has inspired more than its fair share of unconventional jazz cover versions. Even the early big band versions pushed the envelope—hear George Handy's chart for Boyd Raeburn's band or the crazy arrangement backing Billy Eckstine, both from early 1946, or Artie Shaw's use of exotic pan-global scales from his 1949 transcription recording, almost as if someone had sent him some Coltrane albums via a time machine.

Sometimes modern artists tip their hat at predecessors—for example Lester Bowie's brass evocation of the Flamingos doo-wop. But other versions seem wholly self-contained, without source or precedent. For two especially interesting (and quite dissimilar) interpretations, listen to Bobby Hutcherson's performance from 1998, with Kenny Garrett in the front line and a rhythm section of Geri Allen, Christian McBride, and Al Foster, and then compare and contrast with Jamie Cullum's neo-pop-with-electronica updating from his 2005 release *Catching Tales*.

RECOMMENDED VERSIONS

Coleman Hawkins (with Roy Eldridge and Teddy Wilson), New York, January 31, 1944

Billy Eckstine, New York, January 3, 1946

Boyd Raeburn, Hollywood, February 5, 1946

Artie Shaw, New York, December 1, 1949

Friedrich Gulda, from *Ineffable*, New York, January 12, 1965

Lester Bowie, from *I Only Have Eyes for You*, Ludwigsburg, Germany, February 1985

Bobby Hutcherson (with Kenny Garrett), from *Skyline*, New York, August 3–5, 1998

Jamie Cullum, from *Catching Tales*, London, circa 2004–5

I Remember Clifford
Composed by Benny Golson

The death of Clifford Brown in an automobile accident on the Pennsylvania Turnpike, late on a rainy night in June 1956, deprived the jazz world of an artist many felt was the finest trumpeter of his generation. Only 25 years old at the time, Brown had already put together an impressive body of work, marked by his warm tone, clarity of execution, and melodic inventiveness. The tragedy of his loss was compounded by its unexpectedness: other jazz musicians had died at a young age from drugs and dissipation, but Brown avoided narcotics, rarely drank, and enjoyed a stable home life. In fact, the accident that claimed his life took place on the second anniversary of his marriage to LaRue Anderson, a date that was also her twenty-second birthday.

Benny Golson was a close friend, and had experienced first hand Brown's formidable skills when the pair had worked together in Lionel Hampton's 1953 band. As Brown had emerged as a leading trumpeter of the new hard bop style, Golson had earned a reputation as one of the premier composers in the idiom. He was now determined to write a musical tribute to his departed colleague. He later described how he agonized over each note and that several weeks went by before he had put together a song that was both a fitting memorial and, even better, captured in some degree the musical personality of the late trumpeter.

The six-bar intro to "I Remember Clifford" could serve as the basis for a song in its own right, but it's just a teaser—starting out with an ambiguous tonal center before eventually resolving into E flat major for the main theme. This opening will later return as a coda to the form, but it also sets the tone for the melody, with its wide interval leaps and constant shifts in the pacing of the harmonies, which sometimes change every bar, sometimes twice per bar, sometimes on every beat. To Golson's credit, he had achieved a rare balance, forging a jazz composition that coheres as a whole yet also sounds like something a top-notch soloist, such as Brown himself, might improvise.

"I Remember Clifford" gained almost instant entrée into the standard repertoire. Golson envisioned the song as a feature for trumpeters—and for a time was even reluctant to perform it himself for that reason—and they were the first to embrace it. Recordings from 1957 capture Donald Byrd, Lee Morgan, and Dizzy Gillespie in separate renditions, paying tribute to Brown via Golson's ballad. Later that year, Dinah Washington—who had recorded with Brown when both had been with the EmArcy label—showcased lyrics to "I Remember Clifford" by Jon Hendricks on her album *The Queen!*, with Carmen McRae and Kenny Dorham also releasing vocal renditions of the song around this same time.

Over the next several years, other former bandmates recorded "I Remember Clifford." Quincy Jones had served in the trumpet section of Lionel Hampton's orchestra alongside Brown, and he presented a big band version of Golson's composition at a 1959 session. Art Farmer, a member of the same Hampton section, would record the song on many occasions; his best-known rendition finds Farmer alongside composer Golson on a 1960 album by their hard bop combo, the Jazztet. Sonny Rollins, who had played with Brown in the combo the trumpeter co-led with drummer Max Roach, recorded a probing, quasi-avant-garde interpretation of "I Remember Clifford" on his 1964 RCA date *Now's the Time* with Thad Jones—a rarity in its edgy approach to a song most others approach with reverence and in the spirit of how Brown himself might have played it. The contrast between Jones, who tries to bring out the lyricism of the piece, with Rollins's raw, deconstructive attitude makes this one of the least conventional—and more fascinating—versions of "I Remember Clifford" you are likely to hear.

The song reached its peak of popularity in the early 1960s, when a wide range of stylists, many of them with only the loosest ties to either Brown or Golson, presented this song in concert or in the studio. Pianist Bud Powell added it to his repertoire, but one suspects he may have been paying private tribute to his brother Richie, who had died in the same car crash that had killed the trumpeter. Stan Getz, who first played "I Remember Clifford" in the 1950s, would return to it again in the early 1960s, resurrect it for his combo with Chick Corea in the early 1970s, and record it again in duet with pianist Kenny Barron shortly before Getz's death. During this period, the song could also be heard in performances by Oscar Peterson, the Modern Jazz Quartet, and Woody Herman, among others.

This piece is not played as frequently by jazz musicians nowadays, but it is still called often enough at gigs to make it required learning for serious young players. A few artists who weren't around to see Brown perform in person have delivered memorable performances of "I Remember Clifford," ones that I think would have pleased the trumpeter. I would call particular attention to Roy Hargrove's version from 1991 and Arturo Sandoval's from 1992.

RECOMMENDED VERSIONS

Donald Byrd and Gigi Gryce, from *Jazz Lab*, New York, March 13, 1957

Lee Morgan, from *Lee Morgan Vol. 3*, Hackensack, New Jersey, March 24, 1957

Dizzy Gillespie, from *Dizzy Gillespie at Newport*, live at the Newport Jazz Festival, Newport, Rhode Island, July 6, 1957

Dinah Washington, from *The Queen!* New York, October 4, 1957

Quincy Jones, from *The Birth of a Band!* New York, May 27–28, 1959

Art Farmer, from *Meet the Jazztet*, New York, February 6–10, 1960

Sonny Rollins (with Thad Jones), from *Now's the Time*, New York, January 20, 1964

Andrew Hill, from *Mosaic Select 23: Andrew Hill Solo*, Berkeley, California, August 30, 1978

Freddie Hubbard (with Art Blakey), from *Super Live*, live at Nakano Sun Plaza Hall,
    Tokyo, February 2, 1984

Keith Jarrett (with the Standards Trio), from *Still Live*, live at Philharmonic Hall,
    Munich, July 13, 1986

Stan Getz and Kenny Barron, from *People Time*, live at Jazzhus Montmartre,
    Copenhagen, March 3–6, 1991

Roy Hargrove, from *The Tokyo Sessions*, Tokyo, December 4–5, 1991

Arturo Sandoval, from *I Remember Clifford*, New York, 1992

I Should Care
Composed by Axel Stordahl, Paul Weston, and Sammy Cahn

This pop song presents a peculiar case study in repression. The lyrics convey
ironic sentiments that are diametrically opposed to their actual signification,
unraveling romantic memes along the way, until the very last phrase, when a
glimmer of real love is allowed to shine through the callousness: "I should
care . . . and I do!" Yet the whole thing somehow coheres, a testimony to the
power of muddled thinking. For my part, when I sit down at the piano to play
this song for my own entertainment—which I do quite often—I find that I need
to sing the words in order to get full satisfaction from the experience.

The song is artfully constructed. The melody from bars 6 through 12 is all
contained with a span of four notes of the scale, an extreme compression of
range, which adds to the pensive quality of the song. The composition captures
here the ambiance of a whisper or perhaps of a soliloquy, with no unnecessary
flourishes. Then the range opens up in the later phrases, mimicking the emotional widening of the meanings at play.

I'm hardly surprised that Frank Sinatra recorded this song, which had been
introduced by his former employer Tommy Dorsey in the film *Thrill of a Romance*.
The quirky granting and withholding of emotional commitment exemplified in
the lyrics was a specialty of the Chairman of the Board. "I Should Care" demands
just such virtuosity of feeling, and Sinatra was rewarded with a top 10 hit in 1945.
But I am surprised that Sinatra didn't revisit this composition later in his
career—I can hardly imagine a song more ideally suited to his onstage persona.
I would have enjoyed hearing how he would have handled it at mid-career or late
in life.

It was left to another arch stylist to deliver the classic version of "I Should
Care." Thelonious Monk's ruminative solo piano exposition for the *Thelonious
Himself* album on Riverside is my favorite example of unaccompanied Monk,
no less impressive for dispensing with improvisation and instead settling for a

mere melody statement—but with so many pauses, hesitations, and feints that it takes the pianist more than three minutes to get through 32 bars. Monk would record a very similar interpretation of "I Should Care" seven years later, now for the *Solo Monk* album on Columbia, and though it doesn't eclipse the earlier version, the track is only a notch below its noteworthy predecessor.

This song seems to draw out unexpected interpretations. McCoy Tyner, who usually prefers the high-octane approach to any song, adopts a very subdued, melancholy tone in his solo recording from 1991. In contrast, Bill Evans, who one would expect to take it as a heartfelt ballad, turns "I Should Care" into a muscular, bop-oriented number. Bud Powell, who by rights could transform it into a bebop workhorse, takes a far gentler approach in his well-known 1947 recording, and in later years he sometimes preferred to feature "I Should Care" as a vocal number. "His choice of tunes is so closely linked to his life," Jackie McLean commented with regard to Powell, "like 'I Should Care.' And he doesn't announce it or anything like that. He just pulls the mike over and starts singing in a very quiet voice. It fits."

RECOMMENDED VERSIONS

Frank Sinatra, Hollywood, March 6, 1945

Bud Powell, New York, January 10, 1947

Hank Mobley (with Kenny Dorham), from *Mobley's 2nd Message*, Hackensack, New Jersey, July 27, 1956

Thelonious Monk, from *Thelonious Himself*, New York, April 5, 1957

Thelonious Monk, from *Solo Monk*, Los Angeles, October 31, 1964

Bill Evans, from *Bill Evans at Town Hall*, live at Town Hall, New York, February 21, 1966

John Abercrombie and John Scofield, from *Solar*, Menlo Park, California, May 1982

McCoy Tyner, from *Soliloquy*, New York, February 20, 1991

I Surrender, Dear
Composed by Harry Barris, with lyrics by Gordon Clifford

"When we were at the Cocoanut Grove, Barris wrote his great song 'I Surrender, Dear,'" Bing Crosby later recalled. "Dance bands usually played a number in straight tempo, but our recording had changes of tempo and modulations and vocal touches in several spots. This had much to do with the popularity of the song. Week after week, people demanded that we sing it: we couldn't get off without singing it several times a night." The recording stayed on the chart for 10 weeks, and was a major reason why William Paley of CBS gave Crosby a contract for a national radio show.

Crosby's 1931 recording, backed by Gus Arnheim's orchestra and featuring this stellar chart by Jimmie Greer, has its first tempo change 10 seconds into the performance, and offers up three more dramatic shifts in the pulse before the vocal enters at the one-minute mark. In the next two minutes, Crosby deals with an accompaniment that tries everything from Latin to carnival music in a quasi-postmodernist attempt to reconfigure what, on the surface, is a sentimental ballad. How odd that the recordings of this song today typically take fewer chances than Bing's debut version.

Louis Armstrong followed up with his own recording a few weeks later. He keeps the same tempo throughout, and the arrangement is hardly as creative as Greer's tour de force, but this was also a popular release primarily due to Satchmo's unconventional vocal, which at several points seems about to leave formal semantics behind and break into scat nonsense syllables. One can detect Crosby's influence here, but the effect is much like Joe Cocker emulating Ray Charles or Keith Richards learning from Robert Johnson—the end result is so different from the original that the word "imitate" is not appropriate. Armstrong, even when making it smooth and sweet as he does here, won't ever deserve the label "crooner."

Red Norvo's 1934 rendition—with an integrated band that included Teddy Wilson, Artie Shaw, and Charlie Barnet—is worth hearing. Both Shaw and his rival Benny Goodman added the song to the repertoire of their swing bands. But Coleman Hawkins's recording with the Chocolate Dandies in 1940, when he was at the peak of his fame for "Body and Soul," is the finest of the premodern jazz versions of the song. Hawkins's performance on "I Surrender, Dear" is less harmonically intricate than on that famous predecessor, but the thematic development of melodic motives is quite impressive. The recording benefits from an outstanding solo by Roy Eldridge on trumpet and unexpected but effective piano support from Benny Carter, usually known for his sax or trumpet work but showing here another side of his artistry.

Lennie Tristano's 1946 session for Keynote produced three takes of "I Surrender, Dear," and it would be hard to find a more avant-garde interpretation of any jazz standard from that year. Yet Thelonious Monk did more than anyone to keep this tune in the repertoire of jazz musicians of a more progressive persuasion, although his sideman stint with Hawkins might have been the initial cause of his attraction to the piece. Monk's 1956 solo piano version for Riverside was reportedly a spontaneous response to producer Orrin Keepnews's suggestion that Monk play something unaccompanied to fill up a few remaining minutes of studio time. The resulting take is probably the version of "I Surrender, Dear" that is most familiar to jazz pianists today.

Monk himself returned to the song eight years later when he recorded a shorter but equally idiosyncratic version for his *Solo Monk* release on the Columbia label. But the most enticing Monk performance may be the one we never had a chance to hear. This version was reportedly recorded by Jerry

Newman at one of the 1940s sessions at Minton's where, according to the standard account, bebop was born. Monk was so delighted with this amateur recording, which captured a half-hour version of "I Surrender, Dear," that he wore it out by playing it over and over again during intermissions. When Newman finally started releasing music from his personal archive, he felt this track was too damaged for public consumption. Even so, Monk fans would be justifiably eager to hear an example of early Monk that the pianist himself found so mesmerizing.

Monk's influence notwithstanding, this tune retains an old-fashioned ambiance that has limited its appeal to the younger generation of performers. This song wasn't around for the Jazz Age, but it fits the era so well that it is often used to set a 1920s tone—even Madonna has used it enhance her retro pose in the movie *Bloodhounds on Broadway* (1989). Her performance is charming from a visual standpoint, even if her phrasing is shaky. In any event, I'll take Bing over Madonna any day, and it is to Crosby's credit that his 1931 version makes the Material Girl's rendition sound dated by comparison.

RECOMMENDED VERSIONS

Bing Crosby (with Gus Arnheim's orchestra), Los Angeles, January 19, 1931

Louis Armstrong, Chicago, April 20, 1931

Red Norvo, New York, September 26, 1934

Benny Goodman (with Charlie Christian), Los Angeles, April 10, 1940

Coleman Hawkins (with the Chocolate Dandies), New York, May 25, 1940

Lennie Tristano, New York, October 8, 1946

Thelonious Monk, from *Brilliant Corners*, New York, December 7, 1956

Paul Gonsalves (with Wynton Kelly), from *Gettin' Together*, New York, December 20, 1960

Thelonious Monk, from *Solo Monk*, Los Angeles, October 31, 1964

Buddy Tate (with Tete Montoliu), from *Tate a Tete*, live at La Fontaine, Copenhagen, September 23, 1975

Paul Bley, from *Reality Check*, Copenhagen, October 24, 1994

I Thought about You

Composed by Jimmy Van Heusen, with lyrics by Johnny Mercer

Yes, art *does* imitate life. Johnny Mercer came up with the lyrics to "I Thought about You" while musing during a sleepless interlude on a long train trip. And the lyrics turned out to be about . . . someone musing during a sleepless

interlude on a long train trip. The concrete imagery—and this song is packed to
the brim with it: parked cars, moon and stars, shadows, the window shade in
the Pullman sleeper, a winding stream, the ever present railroad track, etc.—
testifies to the immediacy of the experience. Yet Mercer, ever the magician with
words, turns this ho-hum laundry list of details into one of his most intimate
love songs.

Mildred Bailey, whose 1939 vocal with the Benny Goodman band introduced
this song to many listeners, offers a playful interpretation that may unsettle
fans who are familiar with this song only as a slow, moody ballad. Bob Crosby,
who recorded the song three days later, takes a similarly lighthearted approach.
Only a few performers continued to draw on this song during the 1940s, but the
surviving recorded performances by Tommy Dorsey, Nellie Lutcher, and others
confirm that bandleaders were intent on presenting "I Thought about You" as a
swinging, dance-oriented number.

"I Thought about You" returned to the jazz repertoire in the mid-1950s, but
now as a melancholy torch song. Billie Holiday's 1954 recording, with only
Bobby Tucker's piano for accompaniment, set the tone for this new stance, and
we find a similar approach in recordings by Dinah Washington, Ella Fitzgerald,
and others from this period. Frank Sinatra still kept to the more upbeat conception of the song, but he had been with Dorsey's band in 1940 when it had been
a feature for the Pied Pipers, and he stays true to the casual, finger-snapping
spirit of that earlier treatment in his 1956 rendition for his *Songs for Swingin'
Lovers* album.

But Miles Davis would do more than any of these artists to establish "I
Thought about You" as a high-profile ballad that could serve as the centerpiece
of a concert or nightclub set. I especially admire Davis's studio recording from
1961, included on the album *Someday My Prince Will Come*, but a half-dozen
live recordings made over the next several years also testify both to the trumpeter's loyalty to the song and his ability to transfix audiences with his various
interpretations. I suspect that Davis himself had come to this song via Holiday, given the similarity in emotional tone between their treatments, and we
hear the same general attitude in exemplary later versions, such as Kenny
Burrell's 1962 collaboration with Coleman Hawkins, and Stan Getz's 1986
performance for his *Voyage* album with Kenny Barron anchoring the rhythm
section.

Players of a more recent vintage have often embraced a looser approach to
the song, as witnessed by recordings by Branford Marsalis and Uri Caine, tracks
that bear some similarity to how this piece was conceptualized back in 1939. I
rarely hear versions of "I Thought about You" that surprise me with a radically
different take on the old tune, but I give high marks to the late saxophonist Bob
Berg, who creates a whole new groove and ambient texture in his 1990 reworking of the song for his *In the Shadows* album.

RECOMMENDED VERSIONS

Benny Goodman (with Mildred Bailey), New York, October 20, 1939

Billie Holiday (with Bobby Tucker), from *Recital by Billie Holiday*, Los Angeles, September 3, 1954

Frank Sinatra, from *Songs for Swingin' Lovers*, Los Angeles, January 9, 1956

Miles Davis, from *Someday My Prince Will Come*, New York, March 21, 1961

Kenny Burrell (with Coleman Hawkins), from *Bluesy Burrell*, Englewood Cliffs, New Jersey, September 14, 1962

Stan Getz (with Kenny Barron) from *Voyage*, Menlo Park, California, March 9, 1986

Branford Marsalis (with Kenny Kirkland), from *Random Abstract*, Tokyo, August 12–13, 1987

Bob Berg, from *In the Shadows*, New York, 1990

Uri Caine, from *Live at the Village Vanguard*, live at the Village Vanguard, New York, May 23–25, 2003

I Want to Be Happy
Composed by Vincent Youmans, with lyrics by Irving Caesar

Irving Caesar wrote lyrics about happiness the way most other tunesmiths churn out songs about love and courtship. In addition to this memorable effort, his works also include "Sometimes I'm Happy," "Help Yourself to Happiness," "I'm Healthy 'Cause I'm Happy" and a song simply called "Happy." And before you cast doubts on his claims for the salubrious effects of an upbeat disposition, please note that this hale Caesar lived to the ripe age of 101.

The words here are pretty simple stuff—much of it sounds like something you might make up during your morning shower as part of an exercise in the power of positive thinking—and the Vincent Youmans melody is hardly more sophisticated. But the tune has a certain insistent élan about it, and a melody that lodges itself into an inerasable part of your cerebral cortex. This song first appeared in the 1925 hit musical *No, No, Nanette*, and I can imagine that many patrons were still trying to get "I Want to Be Happy" out of their heads months later.

The song has nothing intrinsically bluesy or jazzy about it, and the hit recordings by Vincent Lopez and Jan Garber from 1925, which reached numbers 2 and 5 on the chart, respectively, give little hint of the composition's future as a jazz standard. But if you play it with a duple feel to the pulse, you can impart some syncopated momentum to the melody line. And the tune falls easily enough under the fingers on almost any instrument, allowing the band to play it at a fast clip without too much trouble. Red Nichols does just that on his 1930 recording, which was a top 20 hit, and made clear that "I Want to Be Happy" could serve as a manic swing tune.

Glenn Miller, a sideman with Nichols at the time, was paying attention, and when he launched his own highly successful band toward the end of the decade, he brought along "I Want to Be Happy," which he featured in a hot dance arrangement. The song figured as the flip side for Miller's hit "In the Mood"— one of the biggest jukebox hits of the era. For another example of the swing potential of the song, hear Chick Webb's fanciful performance from 1937, which also includes a vocal from a very young Ella Fitzgerald, just out of her teens.

The song is susceptible to a straight jam over the changes, but can also take on a variety of attitudes, from respectful celebration of the tradition to irreverent parody. Or some performances can achieve all of the above, as on Don Byron's tour de force rendition, with pianist Jason Moran and drummer Jack DeJohnette, from his 2004 project *Ivey-Divey*. Here Byron both emulates and spoofs Lester Young's outing on the same song with similar instrumentation from 1946.

RECOMMENDED VERSIONS

Red Nichols (with Jack Teagarden), New York, February 14, 1930

Chick Webb (with Ella Fitzgerald), New York, December 17, 1937

Glenn Miller, New York, August 1, 1939

Roy Eldridge, New York, January 24, 1944

Lester Young (with Nat King Cole and Buddy Rich), Los Angeles, March–April 1946

Jo Jones, from *The Main Man*, New York, November 29–30, 1976

Don Byron (with Jason Moran and Jack DeJohnette), from *Ivey-Divey*, Shokan, New
     York, May 23–24, 2004

If You Could See Me Now
Composed by Tadd Dameron, with lyrics by Carl Sigman

The modern jazz composers of the 1940s added dozens of new standards to the jazz repertoire, but the vast majority of them were up-tempo blowing tunes. When the leading beboppers wanted to mix a slow number into their sets, they typically borrowed a familiar pop song, or at least its chord changes, and in most instances favored the same ones that had appealed to their predecessors during the Swing Era.

Yet "If You Could See Me Now" is an original modern jazz ballad, with nothing filched from the popular songs of the era—although it did recycle a distinctive phrase from a fast bop tune, namely the half-tempo coda featured in Dizzy Gillespie's "Groovin' High," first recorded in February 1945. Despite this connection and Dameron's deep roots in the modern jazz currents of the day, "If You Could See Me Now" is not an experimental or cutting-edge tune by any measure. If you listen to the debut recording, made with vocalist Sarah Vaughan fronting an orchestra assembled by Dameron, you can hear from the opening introduction—showcasing sweet strings and Freddie Webster's warm trumpet sound—that the composer was aiming for what we call, in today's quaint terminology, a "crossover hit." The same tendency was evident when Dameron revisited the song on his 1962 leader date, *The Magic Touch,* for the Riverside label. The composer led a band packed with jazz stars, but rather than inviting any of them to solo on "If You Could See Me Now," he instead opted for a pop-oriented arrangement to support vocalist Barbara Winfield.

The song was apparently written with Vaughan in mind. The lyrics are attributed to Carl Sigman, whose name also shows up on the copyright filing from June 1946. Dameron, however, claimed credit for the words in a conversation with Ira Gitler. Paul Combs, Dameron's biographer, suspects that the original draft of the lyrics came from Tadd, but that the publisher may have felt these could be improved by the input of a professional collaborator. Certainly, the end result is quite polished and not inferior to the standards set by the well-crafted pop music of the day.

Bill Evans, who can be heard accompanying Winfield on the 1962 Dameron track, brought the song to his own leader date for Riverside the following month. Evans had previously recorded "If You Could See Me Now" with Chet Baker back in 1958, but from this point on he would keep the song in the repertoire of his own trio. Baker was equally loyal to the composition—the trumpeter left behind more than a half-dozen recordings of "If You Could See Me Now."

I would also call attention to Cal Tjader's fine and little-known treatment of the piece on his *Breathe Easy* project from 1977, my favorite of his dates, which finds the vibraphonist joined by Hank Jones, Shelly Manne, and the sadly under-recorded trumpeter Allen Smith. Another gem is the 1965 *Smokin' at the Half Note* album, featuring Wes Montgomery alongside a rhythm section of Miles Davis alums—Wynton Kelly, Paul Chambers, and Jimmy Cobb. Pat Metheny has cited this as his favorite guitar solo of all time, and it is a "must hear" track for those haven't yet made its acquaintance.

RECOMMENDED VERSIONS

Sarah Vaughan (with Tadd Dameron), New York, May 7, 1946

Chet Baker, from *Chet: The Lyrical Trumpet of Chet Baker,* New York, December 30, 1958

Tadd Dameron, from *The Magic Touch,* New York, April 16, 1962

Bill Evans, from *Moon Beams*, New York, May 17, 1962

Wes Montgomery and Wynton Kelly, from *Smokin' at the Half Note*, live at the Half
    Note, New York, June 24, 1965

Cal Tjader, from *Breathe Easy*, Berkeley, California, September 14–15, 1977

Tom Harrell and Jacky Terrasson, from *Moon and Sand*, Capbreton, France,
    December 5–6, 1991

Dianne Reeves, from *The Calling*, Burbank, California, September 9–11, 2000

I'll Remember April
Composed by Gene de Paul, with lyrics by Patricia Johnston and Don Raye

When I was a very young child, I saw the Abbott and Costello movie *Ride 'Em
Cowboy* on several occasions on television, but I have no recollection of "I'll
Remember April," which was introduced in this unlikely film by Dick Foran.
But a decade later, I encountered "I'll Remember April" again—this time in a
version by pianist Erroll Garner from his landmark album *Concert by the Sea*.
And, yes, it made quite an impression on me the second time around.

I'm still not sure why so few pianists these days seem aware of Garner. I am
convinced that a young musician could build a killing style using his tricks and
techniques as a foundation—and would sound different from the pack, since
no one else appears to be exploiting this rich vein. Garner's recording of "I'll
Remember April" is a case in point, with many of his trademarks: esoteric and
almost mystical introductions that disguise the song, radical dynamic shifts at
unexpected junctures, left-hand chords employed as percussive kicks, and a
quirky way of swinging his phrases that somehow comes across as so much
happier and lighthearted than what normally passes for modern jazz. As my
aunt might say, "What's not to like?"

The song is taken at a wide range of tempos. Instrumentalists tend to play it
at a medium-fast pulse or sometimes as an outright barnburner—hear Cannonball Adderley or Stan Getz use it as a hard-swinging blowing tune. But vocalists
will typically slow it down. Carmen McRae takes it at a slow-medium pace,
Frank Sinatra is almost in ballad territory on his 1961 rendition, and Johnny
Hartman give it the full slow-mo treatment on his 1956 LP *Songs from the Heart*.

A few players have made a specialty of this song—Lee Konitz has given us
recordings in six different decades—and I can understand the appeal. The pace
of harmonic movement is unhurried, but the long form, 48 bars rather than the
standard 12- and 32-bar forms for most standards, allows for some daring modulations in the release and a sense of substance, perhaps even gravitas, to the
piece that a smart soloist can use to advantage.

RECOMMENDED VERSIONS

Richard Twardzik, from *Russ Freeman/Richard Twardzik: Trio*, Hackensack, New
 Jersey, October 27, 1954

Stan Getz (with Bob Brookmeyer), from *Stan Getz at the Shrine*, live at the Shrine
 Auditorium, Los Angeles, November 8, 1954

Carmen McRae, from *By Special Request*, New York, June 16, 1955

Erroll Garner, from *Concert by the Sea*, live at the Sunset Auditorium, Carmel,
 California, September 19, 1955

Johnny Hartman, from *Songs from the Heart*, New York, October 1955

Cannonball Adderley, from *Cannonball Enroute*, New York, March 6, 1957

Sonny Stitt and Oscar Peterson, from *Sonny Stitt Sits In with the Oscar Peterson Trio*,
 Paris, May 18, 1959

Lee Konitz, from *Motion*, New York, August 24, 1961

Frank Sinatra, from *Point of No Return*, Los Angeles, September 12, 1961

Cedar Walton, from *Naima*, live at Boomer's, New York, January 4, 1973

Keith Jarrett (with the Standards Trio), from *Tokyo '96*, live at Orchard Hall, Tokyo,
 March 30, 1996

Joe Lovano and Toots Thielemans (recorded as "On April (I'll Remember April)"),
 from *Flights of Fancy: Trio Fascination, Edition 2*, New York, June 15, 2000

Cyrus Chestnut and Eric Reed, from *Plenty Swing, Plenty Soul*, live at Dizzy's Club
 Coca-Cola, New York, March 7, 2009

I'm in the Mood for Love
Composed by Jimmy McHugh, with lyrics by Dorothy Fields

I suspect that songwriters Jimmy McHugh and Dorothy Fields were trying to
replicate the attitude of their 1927 hit "I Can't Give You Anything but Love," by
writing another extended first-person declarative sentence song title about
romance. McHugh also had success with "I Can't Believe That You're in Love
with Me" from 1926, co-written with Clarence Gaskill, so he had already staked
his career on titles too long to fit on the jukebox labels. Yet, again and again, he
managed to win against the odds.

But the circumstances were much less favorable to a hit this time around.
The Jazz Age was over and the Great Depression had arrived. And the new
tune's prominent placement in a Little Rascals comedy short film *The Pinch
Singer*, where it was sung out-of-tune by nine-year-old Carl "Alfalfa" Switzer—
who adopted it as his signature theme—didn't give quite the same push as a
featured spot on a Broadway revue.

Even so, musicians rallied around "I'm in the Mood for Love." The melody is mostly diatonic, and this context makes the three departures from the basic tonic major scale all the more striking. Except for a few touches—the chromaticism in bar five and the second half of the bridge—the song could be a nineteenth-century parlor piano tune, but these deft gestures were enough to appeal to jazz performers. Louis Armstrong's 1935 recording for Decca is the best known of the early jazz versions, and includes a vocal that stays close to the written melody (not always a given for Mr. Armstrong) and a fine trumpet solo with the usual high note climax. But the song didn't start appearing regularly in the repertoire of jazz bands until the early 1940s when Erroll Garner, Nat King Cole, and others began featuring it. Billy Eckstine enjoyed a top 20 hit with his recording from 1945.

The most important moment in this song's history as a jazz standard came about in an unexpected way. In 1949, saxophonist James Moody recorded a whirlwind improvisation on the chord changes to "I'm in the Mood for Love" on a borrowed alto sax during a session in Sweden. This variation on the original theme strayed so far from McHugh's written melody that only listeners with the most acute ears would have picked up the connection, and few would have predicted anything but an obscure fate for this recording by a little-known ex-pat artist. Yet Eddie Jefferson wrote lyrics to match the sax solo, and vocalist King Pleasure enjoyed an R&B hit in the summer of 1952 with his rendition of this version of the song, now dubbed as "Moody's Mood for Love." The complex pedigree even confused the folks at the Grammy Hall of Fame—when they honored King Pleasure's 1952 recording in 2001, they credited James Moody as the artist, although he does not perform on this track.

Since that time, this song has led a dual life in jazz. Most versions continue to reflect the original McHugh and Fields song, but a sizable minority follow in the footsteps of James Moody. Eddie Jefferson adopted the latter version of the song as his own trademark theme, and when George Benson decided to record the tune on his *Give Me the Night* LP, when he was at the peak of his smooth jazz crossover fame, he delivered it as "Moody's Mood" with a contemporary updating of King Pleasure's recording. On the other hand, when Elliott Yamin performed the song on *American Idol* in 2006 he also relied on the King Pleasure version, but judge Paula Abdul thought it was a Stevie Wonder song. She praised the choice, remarking, "That is one of the most difficult songs to sing." Her colleague Simon Cowell, however, laid it on the line, declaring "You can't win a show like this with a song like that," and advising Yamin to pick a better tune next time.

RECOMMENDED VERSIONS

Louis Armstrong, New York, October 3, 1935

Billy Eckstine, New York, October 1945

James Moody, Stockholm, Sweden, October 12, 1949

Erroll Garner, New York, January 11, 1951

King Pleasure (recorded as "Moody's Mood for Love"), New York, February 19, 1952

Louis Prima and Keely Smith, from *The Wildest Show at Tahoe*, live at Harrah's Club, Lake Tahoe, California, July 26, 1957

Eddie Jefferson (recorded as "Moody's Mood for Love"), from *The Main Man*, New York, October 9, 1977

George Benson (recorded as "Moody's Mood"), from *Give Me the Night*, Hollywood, circa 1980

Terence Blanchard, from *Let's Get Lost*, New York, January–February 2001

Impressions
Composed by John Coltrane

This simple song—a modal piece with a single chord change, a move up a half-step for the bridge—has a surprisingly intricate lineage. The most commonly offered description presents "Impressions" as John Coltrane's variant on Miles Davis's "So What," recorded for the trumpeter's *Kind of Blue* session from March 1959. Coltrane participated in the latter recording, and his "Impressions," which made its debut some two and a half years later, follows the same structure and harmonic pattern as the Davis song. But "So What" owes a debt, in turn, to Ahmad Jamal's "Pavanne," recorded in 1955—and on that track, one can hear guitarist Ray Crawford state the melody line that Coltrane would employ in "Impressions." But "Pavanne" draws on a still earlier source of inspiration: Morton Gould's *American Symphonette No. 2* from 1939, which includes an interlude that is almost identical to Coltrane's composition.

Given these precedents, "Impressions" does not so much imitate "So What," as bypass it, returning instead to an even earlier blueprint for the modal revolution in jazz. Yet Coltrane's conception of modal improvisation was also fundamentally different from that espoused by Davis. The latter had advocated restricting the choice of notes in an improvisation to the tones included in the underlying mode—in other words, the D dorian scale in the A section of "So What" and the E flat dorian scale in the B section. Coltrane would embrace a more expansive notion of modal improvisation, superimposing a variety of scales and melodic concepts over the static harmonies. Above all, a radically different ambiance permeates the modal improvisations of the two artists: *Kind of Blue* revels in the purity and austerity of a music purged of excesses and returned to first principles, while Coltrane's "Impressions," in its many incarnations, shows the tenorist's delight in constructing elaborate superstructures over the simplest foundations, and his determination to push to the tonal limits of the piece . . . and beyond.

Coltrane first recorded "Impressions" at his band's November 1961 engagement at the Village Vanguard, and it continued to show up in his performances
into the middle of the decade. These later versions are well worth hearing, and
I would call particular attention to a film clip, easily found on the Internet, of
Coltrane and Eric Dolphy performing "Impressions" on a 1961 German TV
broadcast hosted by Joachim-Ernst Berendt. As Coltrane evolved, so did "Impressions"—the well-known Village Vanguard track, for all its vitality, sounds
restrained compared to, say, his quartet's 20-minute rendition at a 1965 jazz
festival in Antibes, where the cup of Trane's horn runneth over with the entire
splintered and splayed phraseology of the era's free jazz movement.

"Impressions" retains this legacy to the current day. This is not a song typically played with nuance or restraint, but is invariably delivered with intensity
and often at great length. It is frequently employed as a display piece for virtuosic saxophony; even so, the chart is easy enough for beginners. This can be a
dangerous combination, one that encourages amateurs to emulate the icons
who defined this piece and attempt heroic feats for which they are ill prepared.
In the face of such examples, I prefer to repeat a favorite quote from art historian Edgar Wind, who once affirmed that "mediocrity which claims to be intense
has a peculiarly repulsive effect."

I've heard enough overwrought versions of "Impressions" to leave me skeptical when I see it listed on a CD sleeve. But in the hands of a world-class band,
this piece still has the power to excite and delight. Few live up to the mark set
by Coltrane himself, but here are a handful that can withstand comparison.
Wayne Shorter and Dave Liebman engage in a heated soprano sax battle over
"Impressions" at a 1987 Tokyo concert, released on both CD and video, where
they are ably supported by drummer Jack DeJohnette. DeJohnette also joins
Chick Corea and Anthony Braxton in a stirring performance of "Impressions"
recorded at a 1981 jazz festival in Woodstock, New York. Finally, McCoy Tyner
returns to the song he played so many times with Coltrane in the early 1960s on
both his 1975 *Trident* trio project with Ron Carter and Elvin Jones and his 1995
Infinity collaboration with Michael Brecker.

RECOMMENDED VERSIONS

John Coltrane, from *Impressions*, live at the Village Vanguard, New York, November
3, 1961

John Coltrane (with Eric Dolphy), video from TV broadcast, Baden-Baden, Germany,
November 24, 1961

Wes Montgomery (with Wynton Kelly), from *Complete Live at the Half Note*, live at
the Half Note, New York, June 24, 1965

McCoy Tyner (with Elvin Jones and Ron Carter), from *Trident*, Berkeley, California,
February 18–19, 1975

Anthony Braxton and Chick Corea, from *The Song Is You*, live at the Woodstock Jazz
 Festival, Woodstock, New York, September 9, 1981

Dave Liebman and Wayne Shorter, from *A Tribute to John Coltrane: Live under the
 Sky*, live at Yomiuri Land Open Theatre East, Tokyo, July 26, 1987

Art Ensemble of Chicago, from *Dreaming of the Masters Suite*, Brooklyn, January and
 March 1990

Gary Bartz (with Kenny Barron), from *There Goes the Neighborhood!* live at Birdland,
 New York, November 11–12, 1990

McCoy Tyner (with Michael Brecker), from *Infinity*, Englewood Cliffs, New Jersey,
 April 13, 1995

In a Mellow Tone
Composed by Duke Ellington, with lyrics by Milt Gabler

The leading modern jazz artists, as we have seen repeatedly in this book, often
borrowed the chord changes of preexisting pop songs for their "original" compositions. But this practice did not begin with them, and even Duke Ellington,
the preeminent jazz composer of the preceding generation, was not above lifting a particularly appealing harmonic progression for his music. A few years
before he wrote "In a Mellow Tone," Ellington had been lauded by composer
Percy Grainger, in a famous encounter at NYU, with comparisons to Delius and
Bach. Yet when Duke needed some uplifting chords for this jam-oriented song,
he left the *Well-Tempered Clavier* on the shelf and instead turned to "Rose
Room," a 1917 tune by Art Hickman and Harry Williams.

Ellington had recorded "Rose Room" in 1932, and had played a key role in
establishing it as a jazz standard. Now he grafted a new melody on to the underlying progression for his 1940 composition "In a Mellow Tone." In the process,
Duke added plenty of fresh ingredients—hear, for example, the fervent saxophone responses to Cootie Williams's trumpet solo, which will remind you of a
congregation brought to its feet by an ecstatic preacher—to make this a standout track in a year marked by many Ellington masterpieces.

Given Ellington's prolific output at the time, even first-rate songs risked getting lost in the shuffle. No other bandleader released a cover version of "In a
Mellow Tone," until Red Norvo recorded it at a V-disk session in October 1943
and Charlie Barnet (a long-standing admirer of Ellington) followed up with an
arrangement by Andy Gibson in February 1944. Norvo would also perform "In
a Mellow Tone" in a live recording made at Town Hall in 1945. Even so, another
decade would elapse before the piece started showing up frequently on jazz
records.

Several outstanding versions from the mid-1950s helped serve notice that this song could be an effective combo number, including Erroll Garner's spirited romp from 1954, Buck Clayton's recording with an all-star band from the 1956 Newport Jazz Festival, and Clark Terry's performance, in a group stacked with Ellington sidemen, from his 1957 project *Duke with a Difference*. Coleman Hawkins, who had played on the Clayton date, featured "In a Mellow Tone" on a 1957 session for Verve, and showed up as a sideman on a classic Ben Webster rendition for the same label from 1959. The latter track, a 20-minute relaxed jam on the Ellington standard, ranks as my favorite version of this much-played song.

That same year, Eric Dolphy recorded "In a Mellow Tone" as a member of Chico Hamilton's combo, but producer Richard Bock apparently felt Dolphy's approach was too advanced for the audiences of the day, and for many decades the track was kept off the market, except in an edited version released on a sampler compilation for DJs. Few other young progressive players of the era adopted the song, which was mostly heard in the repertoires of Swing Era veterans and those who emulated their styles. Even when modern-minded players tackle it— as have Charles Mingus, Rahsaan Roland Kirk, McCoy Tyner, Art Pepper, and a number of others over the years—it tends to bring out a more traditional side of their playing. When Pepper began playing clarinet again toward the end of his life, after a long hiatus, "In a Mellow Tone" was one of the songs he featured on the instrument—almost as if the return to a leading Swing Era instrument required a piece marked by the sound of that period.

Such is this composition's legacy to the present day. The chart almost forces the soloist to adapt to its intrinsic personality, and it takes some determination for an improviser to veer from the established course. The name says it all: "In a Mellow Tone" won't shake things up on the bandstand, but can still be counted on, so many decades after its debut, to impart a languorously swinging ambiance to a performance.

RECOMMENDED VERSIONS

Duke Ellington, Chicago, September 5, 1940

Red Norvo, New York, October 28, 1943

Charlie Barnet, New York, February 23–24, 1944

Erroll Garner, from *Contrasts*, Chicago, July 27, 1954

Buck Clayton (with Coleman Hawkins), from *At Newport*, live at the Newport Jazz Festival, Newport, Rhode Island, July 6, 1956

Clark Terry, from *Duke with a Difference*, New York, September 6, 1957

Coleman Hawkins, from *The Genius of Coleman Hawkins*, Los Angeles, October 16, 1957

Chico Hamilton (with Eric Dolphy), from *The Original Ellington Suite*, Los Angeles,
    August 22, 1958

Ben Webster (with Coleman Hawkins and Roy Eldridge), from *Ben Webster and
    Associates*, New York, April 9, 1959

Louis Armstrong and Duke Ellington, from *The Great Summit*, New York, April 3,
    1961

Art Pepper and George Cables, from *Goin' Home*, Berkeley, California, May 11–12,
    1982

Bob Wilber and Dick Hyman, from *A Perfect Match*, New York, August 1–2, 1997

In a Sentimental Mood
Composed by Duke Ellington, with lyrics by Irving Mills and Manny Kurtz

As with so many Ellington compositions, tracing the original sources and inspi-
rations of this song is problematic. Some accounts suggest that Ellington
adapted this piece from material provided by Otto Hardwick, who is featured on
saxophone in the band's debut recording of "In a Sentimental Mood." But this
seems to run counter to Duke's own colorful anecdote: he told of a playing after
hours in Durham, North Carolina, when a fight broke out between two women
in attendance. Ellington claimed he composed "In a Sentimental Mood" on the
spot to calm down the combatants, each one standing on a different side of the
pianist as he worked out his soothing song.

The lyrics also raise questions. "Who, may I ask, is Manny Kurtz?" Alec
Wilder has written. "We know by now of the omnipresence of Irving Mills on
the credits of Ellington songs, but had he by this time taken in a partner? I'm
bemused! Mr. Kurtz is obviously the lyric writer." We find Kurtz's name on
some 250 songs, but none with the staying power of this Ellington standard.
But Wilder goes on to suggest that this was hardly a shining moment for the
lyricist, noting that "the words certainly don't fall very fluidly." Yes, Ellington
deserves better than the string of threadbare clichés, but the melody carries us
along, and this pastiche of parlor poetry images hasn't dissuaded many singers
from adding "In a Sentimental Mood" to their repertoires.

Another angle on the song comes from a conversation with Ellington
reported by his friend Edmund Anderson:

> Once I asked him what he considered a typical Negro piece among his
> compositions. He paused a moment before he came up with "In a
> Sentimental Mood." I protested a bit and said I thought that was a very
> sophisticated white kind of song and people were usually surprised

when they learned it was by him. "Ah," he said, "that's because you don't know what it's like to be a Negro."

"In a Sentimental Mood" opens with a simple pentatonic scale, and doesn't reveal its jazz character until a single blues note in bar four adds a melancholy twinge to the proceedings. Midway through the bridge, Ellington incorporates more modernistic elements, spicing up the melody with a handful of altered tones. The composition that started out as a plaintive, but very traditional-sounding, lament, has by now taken on the trappings of a twentieth-century jazz ballad. Much of the appeal of the song comes from this contrast between the different elements here, almost as if an old spiritual were fused into a concert hall art song.

The best-known recording of this song—and deservedly so—comes from the risky pairing of Duke Ellington and John Coltrane for a 1962 date. There were many ways this cross-generational combination could have gone wrong, or resulted in fairly formulaic results. However, Coltrane adapted perfectly to the music, and Ellington reached for a different interpretation of his familiar standard, espousing a delicacy and fragility that he rarely showed in the context of his own band. The record became a favorite with critics and fans, but perhaps the most telling testimony comes from longtime Ellington associate (and Coltrane's former boss) Johnny Hodges, who remarked, "As long as I've known this song, I think Coltrane gave the most beautiful interpretation I've ever heard."

RECOMMENDED VERSIONS

Duke Ellington, April 30, 1935

Duke Ellington, from *Piano Reflections*, Hollywood, April 14, 1953

Sonny Rollins and the Modern Jazz Quartet, from *Sonny Rollins with the Modern Jazz Quartet*, New York, October 7, 1953

Art Tatum and Roy Eldridge, from *The Tatum Group Masterpieces, Vol. 2*, Los Angeles March 23 and 29, 1955

Duke Ellington and John Coltrane, from *Duke Ellington and John Coltrane*, New York, September 26, 1962

Nancy Wilson (with Hank Jones), from *But Beautiful*, Los Angeles, November 6, 1969

McCoy Tyner, from *Atlantis*, live at the Keystone Korner, San Francisco, August 31, 1974

Abdullah Ibrahim and Buddy Tate, from *Buddy Tate Meets Dollar Brand*, New York, August 25, 1977

Chris Potter (with Kenny Werner), from *Concentric Circles*, New York, December 17 and 20, 1993

In Your Own Sweet Way
Composed by Dave Brubeck

"In Your Own Sweet Way" is not just a title but could serve as a guide to the piece's performers. According to the composer the song is one that "musicians can adapt to their own uses"—in other words, play in their own sweet way. Certainly many have done just that. "One disc jockey sent me a tape of 32 versions of it," Brubeck once noted, "and another collector told me he had over 50 versions." In fact, Brubeck may have underestimated his song's impact—more than 300 cover versions have been recorded by jazz artists.

Miles Davis probably deserves as much credit as Brubeck for establishing "In Your Own Sweet Way" as a jazz standard. Miles made two recordings of the song in 1956—the first in March with Sonny Rollins in the front line, and the second in May with John Coltrane now serving as the band's saxophonist. Miles is also responsible for a creative contribution to the piece, closing the A theme with an E natural, instead of the F that Brubeck intended. The prevalence of this Davis "flat five"—which imparts a wry off-centeredness to the proceedings—in later performances is one measure of the trumpeter's influence in the dissemination of this song.

Brubeck wrote "In Your Own Sweet Way" in the early 1950s, in response to his bandmate Paul Desmond's complaint that the quartet was playing too many standards and needed to find someone to write original material. "You've got to be kidding," Brubeck responded. "I'm a composer. I can write two originals in a half hour." He proceeded to compose "In Your Own Sweet Way" and "The Waltz" in the promised time frame, winning the argument and creating a future jazz standard in the process. Brubeck held off from recording the song for some time, but in 1956 he began working with an Ampex tape recorder he had installed in his house in the Oakland Hills, and the resulting "homemade" album, *Brubeck Plays Brubeck*, includes a solo piano rendition of "In Your Own Sweet Way."

Although a few cover versions were recorded in the late 1950s, "In Your Own Sweet Way" gained more visibility in the early 1960s when several prominent jazz artists—including Stan Getz, Bill Evans, Wes Montgomery, McCoy Tyner, and Chet Baker—made recordings. A brief lull followed in the late 1960s and early 1970s, when no cover versions were released, but the song made a comeback in the middle of the latter decade, championed by Bill Evans, who performed it frequently in concert, as well as by Brubeck himself, who revived "In Your Own Sweet Way" as part of a high profile 1974 project with Anthony Braxton and Lee Konitz.

In this unusual collaboration, the composer makes the most compelling case for the inherent flexibility of his song. An odd role reversal sets in here: Brubeck seems determined to prove he is radical enough to play with Braxton, while Braxton aims to show he is traditional enough to fit in with Brubeck. The result is an inspiring partnership between artists who had much more in common than the casual jazz fan might have realized.

The song has had many well-known champions in ensuing years, especially among pianists. I would call particular attention to the lengthy trio performance—almost 18 minutes—by Keith Jarrett's "Standards Trio" that leads off the combo's six-CD live recording made at the Blue Note in June 1994. Vocal renditions are less often heard, but fitting lyrics have been provided by Iola Brubeck.

RECOMMENDED VERSIONS

Miles Davis (with Sonny Rollins), from *Collectors' Items*, Hackensack, New Jersey, March 16, 1956

Dave Brubeck, from *Brubeck Plays Brubeck*, Oakland, April 18, 1956

Miles Davis (with John Coltrane), from *Workin'*, Hackensack, New Jersey, May 11, 1956

Wes Montgomery (with Tommy Flanagan), from *The Incredible Jazz Guitar of Wes Montgomery*, New York, January 28, 1960

Bill Evans, from *How My Heart Sings!* New York, June 5, 1962

Dave Brubeck (with Anthony Braxton), from *All the Things We Are*, New York, October 3, 1974

Alan Broadbent and Gary Foster, from *Alan Broadbent/Gary Foster*, recorded live at Maybeck Recital Hall, Berkeley, California, March 14, 1993

Keith Jarrett (with Gary Peacock and Jack DeJohnette), from *At the Blue Note: The Complete Recordings*, live at the Blue Note, New York, June 3, 1994

Indiana
Composed by James F. Hanley, with lyrics by Ballard MacDonald

James Hanley was actually born in "Indiana"—a curio in American music, in which songs often boast the most misleading pedigrees. Think of Stephen Foster, the Northerner who specialized in Southern songs—no, he didn't have an old Kentucky home, and never went near the Swanee River. Recall those two best-selling modern Christmas songs, "The Christmas Song" and "White Christmas," both composed by Jewish-American songwriters, Mel Tormé and Irving Berlin, respectively, the latter of whom also gave us "Easter Parade." Ponder the incongruity of the media not only hailing a white man as the "King of Jazz" but having the gall to pick one who was actually named "Whiteman."

Consider "Georgia on My Mind," which was actually written by two gentlemen from, yes, Indiana. No surprise, then, that all this happened in the same United States that built its national anthem from a British drinking song, and where school children sing "God Save the Queen" as a patriotic American tune, with the lyrics "My Country 'Tis of Thee" grafted on to it. Ah, the joys of living in a land where everything can be turned into its opposite!

So I will be the first to celebrate James Hanley's authentic Indiana roots. Sad to say, his lyricist Ballard MacDonald was born in Portland, Oregon—a fact that didn't stop him from writing words to "Beautiful Ohio," "On the Mississippi," "She Is the Sunshine of Virginia," and this song, sometimes known by its full title "Back Home in Indiana." The latter composition is not the official state song of Indiana. That honor falls to "On the Banks of the Wabash," composed by Paul Dresser (who—applause please!—hailed from Terre Haute, Indiana) and published back in 1897. But "Back Home in Indiana" borrowed enough from this earlier song to raise accusations of plagiarism. Adding to the messy intellectual property situation, novelist Theodore Dreiser, the younger brother of Paul Dresser, claimed to have written part of "On the Banks of the Wabash." Given the embryonic nature of copyright litigation at the time, these disputes were never resolved in court.

"Back Home in Indiana" had a head start against the competition in entering the standard jazz repertoire. Recorded in 1917 by the Original Dixieland Jazz Band, this song was featured on one of the first jazz records. The disk enjoyed substantial sales as did a 1917 release by Conway's Band, a polished Sousa-style military band that embraced ragtime and various commercial dance styles. Yet while other ODJB songs were widely imitated, "Indiana" was mostly ignored by other jazz ensembles during the next decade. In later years, Louis Armstrong would frequently open performances with this piece, but he didn't adopt "Indiana" as a signature number until the 1950s. Although the Original Dixieland Jazz Band boasted of their New Orleans roots, none of the other leading Crescent City players brought the song into the recording studio before World War II.

Instead, the white jazz bandleaders associated with the Chicago and New York jazz scenes served as enthusiastic advocates. Eddie Condon revived "Indiana" for a 1928 recording, and Red Nichols's 1929 big band, which in many ways anticipated the swing music of the following decade, showcased the song in a popular version that featured two later star bandleaders: Glenn Miller, who provides the chart, and Benny Goodman, who delivers an impassioned solo that shows how closely he had studied Frank Teschemacher, featured on the earlier Condon side.

A few years later, the Casa Loma Orchestra, Benny Goodman, Harry James, and others decided that this 1917 song was sufficiently up-to-date to appeal to Swing Era dancers. Small combos, ever so gradually, also picked up on the song's potential. Chu Berry's spirited performance from 1937 was followed by renditions by other leading saxophonists. Lester Young recorded "Indiana" with Nat King Cole in 1942 and again with Count Basie in 1944—both performances warrant your attention. Perhaps more surprising, modern jazz players also latched on to the song—it shows up on several amateur recordings made at Minton's in the early 1940s when that venue was a breeding ground for the fledgling bebop movement. Bud Powell's trio performance from 1947 captures this influential artist at the peak of his creative abilities. Charlie Parker can also be heard playing "Indiana" on a number of live recordings, but he is better known for borrowing its chord changes for his own composition "Donna Lee." I suspect that many musicians of my generation first learned this progression via "Donna Lee" and only later made their way back home to the original source.

As the trad jazz revival gained momentum in the 1940s and early 1950s, the New Orleans veterans tried to reclaim this song as their own after decades of neglect. Not just Armstrong, but Sidney Bechet, Bunk Johnson, Mutt Carey, and others added it to their repertoires, but by this time "Indiana" had traveled widely. Big bands and Chicago school trad jazz ensembles continued to feature it, just as cool school star Stan Getz or hard bopper Clifford Brown could also find inspiration in the song. Jimmy Smith, Richard "Groove" Holmes, and others relied on it as a hot Hammond B-3 organ swinger—and this may be my preferred approach to "Indiana." The one jazz contingent seemingly reluctant to embrace the tune were vocalists, who have never shown much enthusiasm for it—except, perhaps, when playing concerts in Indianapolis. I would estimate that around 90 percent of the jazz recordings of "Indiana" are instrumentals.

At some point, "Indiana" got branded as an old-fashioned song. Saxophonist Zoot Sims reportedly responded to the Apollo 11 lunar landing with the comment, "Look at that! Wow! And I'm still playing Indiana!" (But playing it well—check out his 1973 recording with violinist Joe Venuti.) Today, "Indiana" can show up on the set list of almost any kind of jazz band, but the traditionalists have been the most persistent in programming the song. Occasionally a surprising track can reveal hitherto unknown dimensions of the song—hear, for example, Greg Osby's oblique reworking from 1999—but most versions nowadays are fairly predictable and not too far in spirit from what the Original Dixieland Jazz Band presented back in 1917.

RECOMMENDED VERSIONS

Original Dixieland Jazz Band, New York, May 31, 1917

Eddie Condon (with Frank Teschemacher and Gene Krupa), New York, July 28, 1928

Red Nichols (with Benny Goodman and arrangement by Glenn Miller), New York,
    April 18, 1929

Casa Loma Orchestra, New York, June 13, 1932

Chu Berry (with Hot Lips Page), New York, March 23, 1937

Lester Young (with Nat King Cole), Los Angeles, July 15, 1942

Lester Young (with Count Basie), New York, May 1, 1944

Bud Powell, New York, January 10, 1947

Louis Armstrong, from *An Evening with Louis Armstrong at Pasadena Civic Auditorium*, live at the Pasadena Civic Auditorium, California, January 30, 1951

Richard "Groove" Holmes, from *On Basie's Bandstand*, New York, April 22, 1966

Joe Venuti and Zoot Sims, from *Joe and Zoot*, New York, September 27, 1973

Dick Wellstood (with Kenny Davern), from *The Blue Three at Hanratty's*, live at Hanratty's, New York, 1981

Greg Osby, from *The Invisible Hand*, Brooklyn, September 9, 1999

Invitation
Composed by Bronislau Kaper, with lyrics by Paul Francis Webster

Few jazz listeners today will recognize the name of Polish-born Bronislaw Kaper, who joined MGM as a staff composer in 1935, one of a long list of European ex-pats who traveled to Hollywood after Hitler's rise to power. Other more famous composers may get their own star on the Hollywood Boulevard Walk of Fame—where you can see Elmer Bernstein, Max Steiner, and Alfred Newman memorialized, but not Mr. Kaper—yet none of these can match the latter's impact on the jazz idiom. In addition to "Invitation," Kaper also penned "On Green Dolphin Street" and "All God's Chillun Got Rhythm," each of which garnered more interest from jazz players than from the general public.

"Invitation" is an example of the peculiar process of "survival of the fittest" that has shaped the jazz repertoire. Few people paid attention to this song when it first showed up in the 1950 Lana Turner film *A Life of Her Own*, a box office failure that couldn't be saved by a first-class score. The song got a second chance, however, as the title theme to the 1952 film *Invitation*, a melodrama about a wealthy father hiring a husband for his terminally ill daughter, but this movie also failed to imprint the melody in the imaginations of the record-buying public—although a few months later Kaper did enjoy a major hit with "Hi-Lili, Hi-Lo," which is mostly forgotten today (not fairly, as it is a lovely waltz).

"Invitation" has survived solely because jazz musicians have enjoyed playing it. This song was probably too complex for the mass market in 1952, and it certainly is far beyond what passes for popular music today. During the course of its 48-bar form, "Invitation" uses all 12 tones as a chord root at least once, and the harmonies are thick with more higher extensions than the remodeled yuppie homes in my old neighborhood in Palo Alto. As Hesh, the record exec turned Mafia adviser, states in *The Sopranos*, "A hit is a hit, and this, my friend . . . is *not* a hit."

Even so, "Invitation" first entered the jazz repertoire shortly after its introduction as a quasi-easy-listening number. Not many jazz fans will find it worthwhile searching out the early recordings by Les Brown or George Wallington (with strings) of this composition—although Brown gets credit for keeping the song in his band's book through the 1950s and serving as its advocate before other jazz players discovered its virtues. Most of the credit goes instead to the sax players for instilling jazz *cojones* into "Invitation." I'm not surprised that John Coltrane ferreted it out for a brooding interpretation on his *Standard Coltrane* album for the Prestige label: at that stage in his career, he delighted in songs with intricate harmonic progressions, and this one fit the bill nicely. In the aftermath of Trane, we find other leading saxophonists of the day responding to "Invitation," including Stan Getz, Joe Henderson, Wayne Shorter (with Art Blakey's Jazz Messengers), and Dexter Gordon.

The song is usually taken at a medium tempo with dark hard bop overtones, but is capable of a range of interpretative angles. For his first leader date, Tom Harrell relied on "Invitation" as a fast, straight-ahead blowing number. Patricia Barber has transformed it into a torch song appropriated for a candlelit supper, while Jaco Pastorius makes it sound like a fusion-era anthem on his big band version from 1982. No, your friends and colleagues from outside the jazz inner sanctum still can't identify it, and you won't hear it in the various rock-star-turned-cabaret-singer projects that come out each year. But "Invitation" is still inviting enough to keep the jazz musicians interested, and is likely to hold on to this constituency for some time to come.

RECOMMENDED VERSIONS

John Coltrane, from *Standard Coltrane*, Hackensack, New Jersey, July 11, 1958

Art Blakey (with Wayne Shorter), from *Impulse!*, New York, June 14, 1961

Joe Henderson, from *Tetragon*, New York, May 16, 1968

Bill Evans (with Eddie Gomez), from *Intuition*, Berkeley, California, November 7–10, 1974

Tom Harrell (with Bob Berg), from *Aurora*, New York, June 24, 1976

Jack Wilson, from *Innovations*, Los Angeles, August 15–16, 1977

Jaco Pastorius, from *Aurex Jazz Festival '82: Twins I*, live at Budokan Hall, Tokyo, September 1, 1982

Patricia Barber, from *Nightclub*, Chicago, May 15–19, 2000

Roy Hargrove, from *Nothing Serious*, Los Angeles, Fall 2005

It Could Happen to You

Composed by Jimmy Van Heusen, with lyrics by Johnny Burke

Jimmy Van Heusen was a decade or two younger than the most famous of the Tin Pan Alley masters—a pantheon that includes George Gershwin, Irving Berlin, Jerome Kern, and Cole Porter—and thus was at the peak of his powers during the period when pop tunes started getting simpler and simpler. Then again, you would never guess it from his oeuvre, which includes some of the most sophisticated commercial songs of the century. He somehow managed to maintain an old-fashioned commitment to highly crafted music in an increasingly "harmony hostile" age, mostly by aligning himself with movie studios, which still supported maximalist compositions well into the age of rock, and by working with Frank Sinatra—who would record a staggering 85 compositions by this one songwriter.

"It Could Happen to You" had the good fortune to arrive on the scene when jazz was still America's popular music. I'm sure I'm not the only one who gets a kick from the contrast between the upward movement of the melody and chords with lyrics that discuss a metaphorical falling (in love) along with real stumblings and tumblings. Even nonmusicians probably pick up on this tension between words and music, if only subliminally. The song has certainly been well received among jazz players, although many other Van Heusen melodies will be more familiar to the general public. More than 500 jazz recordings have been made of "It Could Happen to You," and Dexter Gordon borrowed its chords for his popular jam tune "Fried Bananas."

The song was first heard in the film *And the Angels Sing*—a movie named after a song (never performed in the movie), but not *this* song. (Adding to the confusion, a later film was released called *It Could Happen to You*, and though the soundtrack features many fine songs from the Golden Age, they left out this Jimmy Van Heusen masterwork.) Nonetheless, the initial movie feature led to a spate of recordings, with Bing Crosby, Dinah Shore, Jo Stafford, Bob Chester, and Boyd Raeburn all promoting their versions during the summer of 1944. Stafford's version reached number 10 on the *Billboard* chart.

These early tracks present Van Heusen's song as a relaxed ballad—as do many pre-stereo jazz versions, such as those by Erroll Garner (1950), J. J. Johnson (1953), and Oscar Peterson (1955). Today, the tune is more often heard at a medium or medium-up tempo. Miles Davis played a key role in this new conception of the song, but Davis himself was probably influenced by a 45 rpm recording of "It Could Happen to You," seldom heard nowadays, made by pianist Ahmad Jamal for the Parrot label in 1954, which anticipates Miles's later approach. Further evidence for this line of influence can be found by comparing the live recording of Davis playing this song at Birdland in 1952, where he takes the song at a lugubrious pace and is not yet in command of ballads the way he would be a few years later, with his famous 1956 track. On the latter version, he doubles the tempo from this previous outing and delivers a poised, lightly swinging performance. Since that time, jazz musicians have tended to follow in Davis's footsteps.

A noticeable exception is Sonny Rollins, who not only dispensed with the strutting groove, but also got rid of the entire band. His solo version of "It Could Happen to You" from the following year is a milestone effort—one of the few jazz recordings of unaccompanied tenor sax from the decade.

The song remains especially popular with vocalists—of both jazz and cabaret variety—with close to half of the versions released in recent years coming from singers. Diana Krall's relaxed behind-the-beat rendition from 2006 is the best known of the new millennium vocal treatments. But I would call attention to the contributions of pianists, especially to recordings by Keith Jarrett from 1996, Chick Corea from 1998, and Jason Moran, alongside altoist Bunky Green, from 2004.

RECOMMENDED VERSIONS

Erroll Garner, New York, June 28, 1950

J. J. Johnson, New York, June 22, 1953

Miles Davis (with John Coltrane), from *Relaxin' with the Miles Davis Quintet*, Hackensack, New Jersey, May 11, 1956

Sonny Rollins (solo saxophone), from *The Sound of Sonny*, New York, June 11, 1957

Keith Jarrett (with the Standards Trio), from *Tokyo '96*, live at Orchard Hall, Tokyo, March 30, 1996

Chick Corea, from *A Week at the Blue Note*, live at the Blue Note, New York, December 30, 1997–January 4, 1998

Barry Harris, from *Live from New York, Vol. 1*, live at Fat Cat, New York, March 16, 2004

Bunky Green (with Jason Moran) from *Another Place*, Brooklyn, November 27–28, 2004

Diana Krall, from *From This Moment On*, Los Angeles, Spring 2006

It Don't Mean a Thing (If It Ain't Got That Swing)
Composed by Duke Ellington, with lyrics by Irving Mills

The hook here is the catchy title phrase, followed by a fusillade of syncopations—played by the horns in Duke's original conception but later usurped by countless vocalists with the incantatory words: *doo-ah, doo-ah, doo-ah, doo-ah, doo-ah, doo-ah, doo-ah, doo-ah*. Yes, that falls somewhat short of Emily Dickinson, but back in 1932, with the Swing Era still several years away, just using the word "swing" in a title was edgy, and the brashness of this performance must have stood out against the love songs and novelty tunes that accounted for most of the popular hits of the year.

The music for Ellington's most famous songs typically preceded the lyrics—often by months or years. Yet in the case of this song, I am convinced that Duke matched his melody to the pre-existing title phrase. Where did it come from? For once, Irving Mills may have earned his share of the royalty check with some creative input. David McGee, who has researched Mills's life and times, has uncovered a little known oral history with the booking agent, who describes an uneven performance by the Ellington band one night in Chicago. The band had been playing stage shows and was now struggling to adapt to the different demands of performing for a dancehall audience. Mills went backstage and confronted Ellington with the remark, "Duke, it don't mean a thing if it ain't got that swing—we got to get back into this dance routine." By Mills's account, an early version of the song was composed on the spot, in the dressing room.

This anecdote runs counter to other accounts of the song's origins. Cootie Williams also took credit for using the title as a catchphrase, and thus inspiring the resulting hit. Other sources attribute it to Bubber Miley, who left the Ellington band shortly before the debut recording of the song and would succumb to tuberculosis, at age 29, around the time it was issued. Whatever the source, the title has become an oft-repeated admonition among jazz players.

That first recording of "It Don't Mean a Thing," from February 1932, is one of Ellington's finest works of the era. The music combines the rich orchestral colors of his horn writing with a very danceable beat, but the composer still finds places to insert deft, modernistic touches—after the second chorus, Ellington reconfigures the harmonies in a daring 24-bar interlude that threatens to modulate into new tonality, maybe even a different song, before finally settling back into the original changes. Other bandleaders could record hits, or keep the ballroom patrons happy, or try for new, experimental sounds . . . but who other than Ellington so seamlessly achieves all three objectives in the same track?

The next year, Ellington took his band on a 55-day European tour, their first foray overseas, and left behind more believers in the redemptive power of swing. In the aftermath, one of the first significant cover versions of "It Don't Mean a Thing" came out of Paris, where violinist Stéphane Grappelli, in an early leader date, with guitarist Django Reinhardt as sideman, delivered a rambunctious rendition of the song, much faster than Duke's recorded version, and a revelation to jazz fans who might doubt that a band could "get that swing" in a combo without drummer or horn.

As was often the case with Ellington's songs, the composer himself was the most ambitious in reinterpreting this piece. His 1945 recording shakes things up from the outset, employing three vocalists and counterpoint (in the manner of a round, such as "Row, Row, Row Your Boat"), and drawing on a completely different set of textures and devices than in his 1932 version. In other situations,

Ellington performances of "It Don't Mean a Thing" served as a feature for male vocalists, such as Al Hibbler, Ray Nance, or Tony Watkins as well as a showcase for guest singers Ella Fitzgerald and Rosemary Clooney.

This song is more resistant to updating than most of Ellington's works. The very syncopations that were stylish in 1932 sound old-fashioned to modern-day listeners, and even the word *swing* conveys a vaguely retro sensibility, if not connotations of spouse-swapping middle-aged couples. A few forward-looking players—notably Thelonious Monk and Eric Dolphy—have recorded "It Don't Mean a Thing" over the years, but a song of this sort would hardly have fit in with the mature style of a Miles Davis or a John Coltrane. Yet in the current jazz world—dominated by tribute albums, historic recreations, and constant nods to the past—this work, so emblematic of the ethos of an earlier day, will not lack for adherents or revivals.

RECOMMENDED VERSIONS

Duke Ellington (with Ivie Anderson), New York, February 2, 1932

Stéphane Grappelli (with Django Reinhardt), Paris, October 21, 1935

Duke Ellington, New York, May 14, 1945

Thelonious Monk, from *Monk Plays Ellington*, Hackensack, New Jersey, July 21, 1955

Sidney Bechet and Martial Solal, from *Sidney Bechet–Martial Solal Quartet Featuring Kenny Clarke*, Paris, June 17, 1957

Chico Hamilton (with Eric Dolphy), from *The Original Ellington Suite*, Los Angeles, August 22, 1958

Ella Fitzgerald and Duke Ellington, from *Ella and Duke at the Côte d'Azur*, live at the Antibes Jazz Festival, Juan-les-Pins, France, July 29, 1966

Diane Schuur (with Stan Getz), from *Schuur Thing*, Hollywood and Burbank, California, April 12, 1985

Ricky Ford, from *Hot Brass*, New York, April 30, 1991

Jessica Williams, from *I Let a Song Go Out of My Heart*, Capitola, California, September–October 2000

It Might as Well Be Spring

Composed by Richard Rodgers, with lyrics by Oscar Hammerstein II

State Fair—the 1945 film that produced this popular standard—was the only Richard Rodgers and Oscar Hammerstein project that started out as a Hollywood film. No doubt, the studio would rather have been making a movie from the megahit *Oklahoma!* which was then in the early stages of its unprecedented

2,212-performance run on Broadway. But *that* intellectual property wouldn't find its way onto the silver screen for another decade. So Rodgers and Hammerstein came up with the next best thing: another bit of musical Americana—this one set in Iowa rather than Oklahoma—and cut a deal with 20th Century Fox.

The composers set one unusual condition for their participation: they insisted on writing the songs at their homes back East rather than under the watchful eyes of the West Coast movie moguls. The geographical separation may seem like a small matter, but it continues to influence the way "It Might as Well Be Spring" is performed nowadays. Richard Rodgers had written the song as a buoyant medium-tempo number, but when the studio's musical director decided to feature it as a slower ballad, the composer was merely notified in a long-distance phone call. At such a far remove from the proceedings, Rodgers was unable to impose his will. He did, however, receive a promise that, if the number flopped at the film's preview performance, the scene would be redone with the song at a faster tempo. The preview audience was enthusiastic about the slower "It Might as Well Be Spring," as was Rodgers himself when he finally saw it on the screen.

As it turned out, *State Fair* would win only one Oscar—for this lovely song. The melody is Rodgers's most ambitious, in my opinion, and the congruence with Hammerstein's words is almost uncanny. This is especially evident in the glorious hook, the dramatic phrase in bars 5–6, built out of upward interval leaps spelling out the tonic triad before settling on the flat seven. This ranks among the most inspired moments in American popular song, and it works whether sung exactly as written or jazzed up in various ways—and this passage is especially well suited to reharmonization or other creative modifications. But Hammerstein's lyric is the pièce de résistance, the words evoking the same vertigo as the spacious melody—"jumpy as a puppet on a string" and "giddy as a baby on a swing."

As Rodgers's change-of-heart about tempos might suggest, this song works in a variety of rhythmic contexts and interpretative styles. Blosson Dearie sang it in French, and Astrud Gilberto transformed it into a very understated bossa nova, one that sounds like it came straight off the beach at Copacabana. Erroll Garner takes it at the bouncy, medium tempo that Rodgers originally envisioned, while Joshua Redman, joined by Brad Mehldau, pushes the song into overdrive on his 1998 release *Timeless Tales*.

By the way, those who check songs for literal accuracy may note that a song about spring is a poor fit for a musical set at a state fair—which, as even New York–born Oscar Hammerstein realized, usually takes place at harvest time in the fall and not in the spring. But he saved the day with the wording that indicated that it wasn't actually spring, it just "might as well be spring." Score one for both poetry *and* scrupulous accuracy.

RECOMMENDED VERSIONS

Sarah Vaughan, New York, May 18, 1950

Clifford Brown, from *The Clifford Brown Quartet in Paris*, Paris, October 15, 1953

Nina Simone, from *The Amazing Nina Simone*, New York, 1959

Joe Zawinul, from *To You with Love*, New York, September 1959

Ike Quebec, from *It Might as Well Be Spring*, Englewood Cliffs, New Jersey, December 9, 1961

Erroll Garner, from *Jazz Icons: Live in '63 and '64* (DVD), Belgium, December 1963

Stan Getz (with Astrud Gilberto and Gary Burton), from *Getz Au Go Go*, New York, May 22, 1964

Sonny Stitt (with Art Blakey and the Jazz Messengers), from *In Walked Sonny*, New York, May 16, 1975

Joshua Redman (with Brad Mehldau), from *Timeless Tales*, New York, circa 1998

I've Found a New Baby
Composed by Spencer Williams and Jack Palmer

Perhaps "babe" is the equivalent term nowadays, but there is a difference in nuance that is lost in the translation. Audiences loved songs about babies in those halcyon days before the Great Depression—and not just the kind the stork leaves on the doorstep. Songwriters were more than happy to oblige them. Around the same time that "I've Found a New Baby" (sometimes called "I Found a New Baby") came out, "Baby Face" was a number one hit for Jan Garber, and "Yes, Sir, That's My Baby" propelled no fewer than five different artists on to the charts in 1925. Even Spencer Williams and Jack Palmer, composers of "I've Found a New Baby" (1926), had already enjoyed a success with "Everybody Loves My Baby" in 1924.

Spencer Williams, born in New Orleans in 1889, needed the help of Clarence Williams, born on the outskirts of that same city in 1898, in introducing "I've Found a New Baby" to jazz fans. The two artists are unrelated but often confused, the mixup amplified by their similar names, backgrounds, and occasional collaborations—for example, they share songwriting credits on the popular "Royal Garden Blues" from 1919. Clarence Williams played no role in writing "I've Found a New Baby," but brought Spencer's song into the studio for a session with the Okeh label in January 1926. That same week, Fletcher Henderson recorded the number with his Dixie Stompers, and accompanied Ethel Waters on a third version.

From the start, jazz players liked to play this song fast and fancy-free, as demonstrated on recordings by the Chicago Rhythm Kings, McKinney's Cotton

Pickers, Joe Venuti, and Sidney Bechet, among others. "I've Found a New Baby" perfectly captured the effervescent ethos of the Jazz Age, but the oom-pah high-stepping manner in which bands usually performed it must have already sounded out-of-date by the time Sidney Bechet and Tommy Ladnier made their well-known 1932 recording. But two years later, the Mills Brothers reinvented "I've Found a New Baby" and achieved a top 20 hit with their smooth, uunder-stated treatment. Charlie Christian further updated the song with an archly modernistic solo alongside Benny Goodman on a track from 1941 that would be widely studied and imitated by later guitarists.

A few other modern jazz players embraced the song around this time. Several performances of "I've Found a New Baby" by Charlie Parker have survived from the early 1940s—including a track recorded with bandleader Jay McShann in Wichita, and a version made with guitarist Efferge Ware in Kansas City in September 1942 that gives the altoist a chance to stretch out at length over the chord changes. Kenny Clarke showcased the song on his first leader date in 1938, and Dexter Gordon did the same in 1943. "I've Found a New Baby" was also the first song ever recorded by Dave Brubeck, an amateur disk reportedly made in 1942 that finds the pianist playing in an odd stride-meets-bop hybrid style—raising questions about how much bebop could a West Coast boy raised on a ranch have heard back then? Across the nation in Harlem, "I've Found a New Baby" was played at the after-hours sessions that served as the epicenter of the new modern jazz movement.

Despite these precedents, "I've Found a New Baby" soon lost its progressive cachet, and in later years was typically found in the repertoires of trad jazz or swing bands. Notable exceptions include an exciting matchup between Dizzy Gillespie and Roy Eldridge from 1954, and a Sonny Rollins session for the Con-temporary label from 1958.

The New Orleans and Chicago players and their followers have been the most loyal advocates of "I've Found a New Baby." More than two dozen rendi-tions of the song by Benny Goodman have survived—including at least one version in every decade from the 1930s through the 1980s. Sidney Bechet also kept "I've Found a New Baby" in his repertoire until the end of his life, and the song shows up in recordings by a veritable who's who of postwar trad jazz stars, including Earl Hines, Kid Ory, Eddie Condon, Art Hodes, Pete Fountain, Ralph Sutton, and many others.

This is the song's current legacy: standing out as a high-energy period piece. Even when a young lion with progressive leanings tackles the song, as did clar-inetist Don Byron for his 2004 CD *Ivey-Divey*, the treatment often comes with explicit references back to earlier jazz styles—in Byron's case the recording is dedicated to Lester Young, who featured the piece in a similar piano-drums-horn trio back in 1946.

RECOMMENDED VERSIONS

Clarence Williams Blue Five (with Bubber Miley and Eva Taylor), New York, January 22, 1926

Joe Venuti (with Eddie Lang and Jimmy Dorsey), New York, November 12, 1930

New Orleans Feetwarmers (with Sidney Bechet and Tommy Ladnier), New York, September 15, 1932

The Mills Brothers, New York, September 14, 1934

Stéphane Grappelli (with Django Reinhardt), Paris, September 29, 1937

Benny Goodman (with Charlie Christian), New York, January 15, 1941

Paul Whiteman, Los Angeles, June 5, 1942

Charlie Parker, Kansas City, September 13, 1942

Lester Young (with Nat King Cole and Buddy Rich), Los Angeles, March–April 1946

Dizzy Gillespie and Roy Eldridge, from *Roy and Diz*, New York, October 29, 1954

Sonny Rollins, from *Sonny Rollins and the Contemporary Leaders*, Los Angeles, October 20–22, 1958

Don Byron (with Jason Moran and Jack DeJohnette), from *Ivey-Divey*, Shokan, New York, May 23–24, 2004

The Jitterbug Waltz

Composed by Fats Wallers

Listeners today may not realize that this song's title was chosen with humorous intent. The jitterbug, a defining dance of the Swing Era, had nothing in common with the more stately waltz—jazz fans of the period would have laughed at the idea of merging them. In fact, jazz of any style was antithetical to the waltz meter back in 1942 when Waller introduced this transgressive song. "The Jitterbug Waltz" may not have been the first recorded jazz waltz—that honor belongs to Benny Carter's "Waltzing the Blues" from 1936—but the concept was daring for the era, and Waller's late vintage effort, recorded the year before he died, is the earliest jazz composition in 3/4 time to gain traction as a standard.

Yet the song had little impact at the time of its debut. The jazz world paid more attention to the brief waltz interlude in Duke Ellington's ambitious composition *Black Brown & Beige*, which made its debut at Carnegie Hall in January 1943, some ten months after Waller's recording. Not until waltz meter lost its stigma as an unjazzy time signature in the late 1950s and early 1960s would this catchy song find a large number of adherents. A few early cover versions—notably Art Tatum's recording from 1953—testify to the appeal of the composition. Yet for most jazz devotees of the era, the 1958 performance of "The Jitterbug Waltz" by an all-star band (including Miles Davis, John Coltrane, Bill Evans, and Phil Woods) under the leadership of Michel Legrand served as the watershed moment when this erstwhile novelty song gained credence as a vehicle for jazz improvisation. I must express disappointment, however, that Legrand's rendition switches to 4/4 time for the solos, even though several of the artists on hand rank among the most skilled interpreters of jazz in waltz time.

A wide range of artists tackled this song during the 1960s, helped along by the growing tendency for jazz players to incorporate waltz numbers as routine elements of their set lists. Eric Dolphy recorded "The Jitterbug Waltz" in 1963, and can also be heard performing it alongside Charles Mingus at a 1964 live recording from Cornell University. But the song proved equally compatible with the funk stylings of Les McCann and the Jazz Crusaders, the West Coast jazz sensibility of Vince Guaraldi, and the more traditional pianism of Earl Hines. Waller's standard lost none of its flexibility in later years, as demonstrated by two of my favorite interpretations: Rahsaan Roland Kirk's live performance at the Keystone Korner from 1973, and Greg Osby's collaboration with Andrew Hill from 1999.

Waller conceived of the song as an instrumental, but Dinah Washington performed "The Jitterbug Waltz" with lyrics by Charles Grean and Maxine Manners for her 1957 Fats Waller songbook album, and a somewhat more poetic set of words were added by Richard Maltby Jr. for the hit 1978 Broadway show *Ain't Misbehavin'*. The latter can be heard to good effect on Abbey Lincoln's *When There Is Love*, where she is accompanied by pianist Hank Jones.

RECOMMENDED VERSIONS

Fats Waller, New York, March 16, 1942

Art Tatum, from *The Art Tatum Solo Masterpieces, Vol. 3*, Los Angeles, December 28, 1953

Michel Legrand (with Miles Davis), from *Legrand Jazz*, New York, June 25, 1958

Eric Dolphy (with Woody Shaw and Bobby Hutcherson), from *Conversations*, New York, July 3, 1963

Charles Mingus (with Eric Dolphy), from *Cornell 1964*, live at Cornell University, Ithaca, New York, March 18, 1964

Rahsaan Roland Kirk, from *Bright Moments*, live at the Keystone Korner, San Francisco, June 8–9, 1973

Dizzy Gillespie (with Joe Pass), from *Dizzy's Big 4*, Los Angeles, September 19, 1974

Thomas Chapin, from *Radius*, New York, February 4, 1984

Randy Weston, from *Marrakech in the Cool of the Evening*, live at La Mamounia Hotel, Marrakech, Morocco, September 28, 1992

Abbey Lincoln (with Hank Jones), from *When There Is Love*, Paris, October 4–6, 1992

Greg Osby (with Andrew Hill) from *The Invisible Hand*, Brooklyn, September 9, 1999

Chick Corea, from *Past, Present & Future*, Los Angeles, 2001

Joy Spring
Composed by Clifford Brown

Now that more than a half-century has passed since his tragic death in an automobile accident at age 25, Clifford Brown has fallen into the unfortunate obscurity that seems to afflict many great jazz artists who never lived long enough to make stereo recordings. Jazz fans today do not enjoy listening to tracks that lack clean, crisp, seems-like-you're-in-the-same-room sound quality. The cutoff point is around 1957. If artists recorded fine music in 1958 or 1959—as did Mingus, Miles, and Monk—they are widely celebrated today, but if they left the scene in 1956, as did Clifford Brown, they risk becoming a forgotten footnote in the music's history.

Yet the new millennium jazz fans who don't know about Brownie really must acquaint themselves with this artist, who was the most breathtaking trumpeter of the mid-1950s. There's no better place to begin than with "Joy Spring," his most famous and oft-played composition. Brown left behind two studio recordings, and both are worth hearing, although I have a slight preference for the version made with Max Roach at the August 1954 sessions that did much to establish the new hard bop sound of the period.

The song is aptly named. Brown's music captures a more jubilant and optimistic worldview than one encounters with many of the later hard bop players, who aimed for an edgier and grittier sound. His trumpet technique furthered this sense of positive energy: he had a full and beautiful tone, and even at the fastest tempos hit each note cleanly and with what my old philosophy professor would call "intentionality." But not antiseptically, as with so many virtuosos: his playing is as notable for its warmth as it is for its flawless execution. The melody line of "Joy Spring" furthers this life-embracing vibe, with its phrases that constantly return to declamatory chord tones, and the modulation up a half step for the second eight bars—a common arranger's device for making a chart seem brighter and more insistent, but one that is rarely written into the lead sheet of a modern jazz combo tune.

But if casual fans often fail to recognize Brown's achievements, other trumpeters have kept the flame burning. Long after his death, "Joy Spring" would show up in memorable performances by Freddie Hubbard (joined by Harold Land, who had been on the date with Brown a quarter of a century before), Bobby Shew, and Arturo Sandoval. But the song translates well to other instruments, as demonstrated by Stan Getz's oh-so-relaxed 1981 tenor outing and Toots Thielemans's impressive adaptation of the Brownian aesthetic to chromatic harmonica from 1973.

RECOMMENDED VERSIONS

Clifford Brown, from *Jazz Immortal*, Los Angeles, July 12, 1954

Clifford Brown (with Max Roach and Harold Land), from *Clifford Brown and Max Roach*, Los Angeles, August 6, 1954

Gil Evans, from *The Complete Pacific Jazz Sessions*, New York, February 5, 1959

Toots Thielemans, from Airegin, Hilversum, Holland, January 9, 1973

Stan Getz, from *The Dolphin*, live at the Keystone Korner, San Francisco, May 10, 1981

Freddie Hubbard, from *Born to Be Blue*, Hollywood, December 14, 1981

Bobby Shew, from *Metropole Orchestra*, unidentified location, December 16, 1986, and November 24, 1988

Norma Winstone (with Jimmy Rowles), from *Well Kept Secret*, Los Angeles, October 1993

Arturo Sandoval, from *Trumpet Evolution*, Los Angeles, November 20–21, 2002

Just Friends
Composed by John Klenner, with lyrics by Sam M. Lewis

Russ Columbo's 1932 recording of this song first established it as a popular hit. But Columbo reaped few rewards from his growing fame: he was killed in a (possibly accidental) shooting a short while later at age 26. The song itself had a much happier future. The harmonic structure, a straightforward work-out that relies on a series of ii–V progressions, is more modernistic than one finds in most pop tunes from this period, and John Klenner's composition was easily adapted to the demands of the beboppers. In fact, Charlie Parker's personal favorite among his own recordings was his performance of "Just Friends" with a string orchestra—although most jazz fans today will have a hard time enjoying Bird's outing given the mood music ambiance of the arrangement.

The lyrics are a letdown. Some other songs about "friends" (for example, "A Beautiful Friendship") end up as songs about "friends with benefits," but this relationship is going downhill from the opening measure. Yet the melody and chords follow a similar downward swoop—virtually every phrase ends on a lower note than where it begins—and this uncanny alignment with the meaning of the words has doubtless contributed to the song's lasting success.

Red McKenzie—the now forgotten pioneer of the jazz comb (yes, *that* kind of comb)—recorded the song even before Columbo. Alas, he left his coiffure-care accessory in his back pocket, but does contribute a saccharine vocal. Given such precedents, I am hardly surprised that few jazz players adopted this song before Parker's famous recording. One exception was Sarah Vaughan, who recorded "Just Friends" a few months before Bird's session, also with a string orchestra as accompaniment. (Could this performance have influenced Parker's decision to use the same song on his own string date?)

One of my favorite versions comes from Parker's former employer Earl Hines, who stretched out for eight-and-a-half minutes of ecstatic improvisation on his 1977 solo piano version of "Just Friends." Lee Konitz has also put in a strong claim for ownership of this song, having recorded it on a dozen or so occasions over a period of a half-century—the place to start is his 1959 live recording at the Half Note with Bill Evans on piano. This music was long kept under wraps and tends to be neglected amidst the other celebrated sessions of that year, but has a devoted cult following for a good reason.

A few months later, John Coltrane and Cecil Taylor would pair up for a much different version of "Just Friends." This session failed to live up to the potential for fireworks promised by the first and only studio meeting between these two iconoclastic soloists. I would have liked to have heard them together in, let's say, 1965 when Trane was in a more avant-garde frame of mind; however, if that had happened they certainly wouldn't have picked "Just Friends" for the date. Taylor plays the standard with more respect for the tonal center than he would adopt in other settings, while Coltrane sticks to his own game plan and doesn't budge in the face of Taylor's more astringent conception.

I am less enthusiastic about the various vocal performances I have heard of this song over the years—I've felt that this was primarily a horn player's tune. But Tony Bennett's 1964 rendition is worth noting, if only for the remarkable band on hand: Herbie Hancock and Ron Carter (both then working with Miles Davis), Stan Getz (then at the peak of his bossa nova fame), and Elvin Jones (then with John Coltrane). It's a shame that his ensemble didn't record enough music for an entire album, but "Just Friends" and a few other gems by the same combo can be heard on Bennett's *Jazz* compilation.

RECOMMENDED VERSIONS

Red McKenzie, New York, October 15, 1931

Sarah Vaughan, New York, July 7, 1949

Charlie Parker, New York, November 30, 1949

Lee Konitz (with Bill Evans), from *Live at the Half Note*, live at the Half Note, New York, February–March 1959

Cecil Taylor (with John Coltrane), from *Coltrane Time*, New York, October 13, 1959

Sonny Rollins and Coleman Hawkins, from *Sonny Meets Hawk!*, New York, July 18, 1963

Tony Bennett (with Stan Getz and Herbie Hancock), from *Jazz*, New York, May 25, 1964

Earl Hines, from *Fatha Plays Classics*, Chicago, September 22, 1977

Dizzy Gillespie (with Oscar Peterson, Freddie Hubbard, and Clark Terry), from *The Trumpet Summit Meets the Oscar Peterson Big 4*, Hollywood, March 10, 1980

Joe Williams (with Supersax), from *In Good Company*, Hollywood, January 19–21, 1989

Just One of Those Things
Composed by Cole Porter

This Cole Porter song from the 1935 show *Jubilee* would eventually gain renown as one of the composer's signature tunes, but in the 1930s it was overshadowed by the Broadway production's other hit, "Begin the Beguine." Both are unconventional pop tunes, and take on overtones of art song. Artie Shaw would later enjoy a huge hit with "Begin the Beguine," but I consider "Just One of Those Things" the better solo vehicle. The song marries a slowly evolving melody with a propulsive underlying harmonic movement, while the lyrics offer an engaging mixture of conversational diction and high poetry.

An oft-told anecdote relates Porter's writer's block when trying to find the right three-syllable modifier for the word "wings," only to have architect Ed Tauch suggest a beautiful expedient: gossamer. The adjective could well describe the whole song, and its popularity among singers—including Frank Sinatra, Billie Holiday, Nat King Cole (who performed it both as a piano instrumental and a vocal feature), Sarah Vaughan, and Diana Krall—is well deserved. Ella Fitzgerald also left behind multiple versions, invariably including the seldom-heard verse. By all means, listen to Fitzgerald's "songbook" studio version, but her live performances are worth tracking down too, including performances from her birthday concert in Rome (1958) and her well-known live date in Berlin (1960). I'd give the nod to the Italian track if forced to settle for just one of these things.

Sinatra showcased "Just One of Those Things" onscreen and onstage. His film performance for *Young at Heart* is justly praised, but the lesser-known version from his 1959 Australian tour with a small combo (which included Red Norvo) is a gem that deserves to be better known, appealing to fans who want to hear the jazzier side of this vocalist. Tony Bennett's driving small combo rendition is even more out of character, and finds him singing with just Art Blakey's drums for accompaniment during most of the track—quite a departure for both of these artists!

Despite this song's many virtues, jazz musicians were slow to warm up to it, and didn't embrace the Porter piece until the mid-1940s. Coleman Hawkins was the first big league jazz star to record it, back in 1944 when he was navigating from a swing-oriented approach to a more modernistic style. His tenor solo is probing, and you can tell he relishes the chord changes, but Teddy Wilson makes sure that the rhythm section stays in a more traditional vein. Thelonious Monk had joined Hawkins's working band a few weeks before this session, and it is a disappointment that the saxophonist didn't bring him along for the recording.

This song seems to push musicians outside of their usual comfort zones. Django Reinhardt delivers a surprisingly beboppish solo on his fine 1947 rendition, and just a few weeks later Sidney Bechet also got a strenuous workout over the same changes. Bud Powell was at the peak of his powers when he recorded a demonic solo piano version for Norman Granz. Art Tatum sounds as if he's in a race with drummer Jo Jones on his 1957 trio performance for the same producer, but the drummer keeps his poise and maintains a relaxed sense of swing throughout, thus earning credit as one of the most *simpatico* percussionists to cross paths with the virtuoso pianist. That said, Jones does *not* succeed in holding Tatum's tempo, which accelerates markedly during the course of the track.

But my favorite performance will always remain a scintillating trio romp by Herbie Hancock, Buster Williams, and Al Foster, which took place at the grand opening of Kimball's East in Emeryville back in 1989 in front of an invited audience of jazz cognoscenti. You can't hear that version on any album, and I only wish I had snuck in a tape recorder.

RECOMMENDED VERSIONS

Coleman Hawkins, New York, May 29, 1944

Django Reinhardt, Brussels, May 21, 1947

Sidney Bechet, New York, July 31, 1947

Bud Powell, New York, February 1951

Richard Twardzik, from *Russ Freeman/Richard Twardzik: Trio*, Hackensack, New Jersey, October 27, 1954

Art Tatum (with Joe Jones and Red Callender), from *The Art Tatum Group Masterpieces, Vol. 6*, Los Angeles, January 27, 1956

Tony Bennett (with Art Blakey), from *The Beat of My Heart*, New York, October 14, 1957

Tony Scott (with Bill Evans), from *My Kind of Jazz*, New York, November 1957

Ella Fitzgerald, from *Ella in Rome: The Birthday Concert*, live at Teatro Sistina, Rome, April 25, 1958

Cannonball Adderley and Milt Jackson, from *Things Are Getting Better*, New York, October 28, 1958

Frank Sinatra (with Red Norvo), from *Live in Australia, 1959,* live at the West
 Melbourne Stadium, Melbourne, April 1, 1959

Branford Marsalis, from *Renaissance,* New York or Los Angeles, January 26–28, 1987

Hank Jones and Frank Wess, from *Hank and Frank,* New York, November 29, 2003

Just You, Just Me
Composed by Jesse Greer, with lyrics by Raymond Klages

"You know, you ain't had much pleasure out of this war," announces Private
Stagg (Lawrence Gray) to the French peasant girl Marianne (Marion Davies) in
the 1929 movie musical *Marianne.* "So I decided I'd sing for you." He holds up
a ukulele, seemingly pulled out of thin air, and launches into "Just You, Just
Me." Davies, for her part, slams the door on her would-be lover, but soon she
invites him inside and is singing "Just You, Just Me" back to the American soldier, exuding plenty of sex appeal even while struggling to maintain her *faux*
French peasant-girl accent.

I am sure the actress's boyfriend William Randolph Hearst was charmed by
the scene, and the reviewers at the more than two dozen newspapers under
Hearst's thumb were unlikely to disparage Davies's "talking movie" debut. But
this is hardly the kind of performance that launches a future jazz standard. The
hit recording, from this same period, by Ukelele Ike (Cliff Edwards), who had
also starred in *Marianne,* is tepid fare, perhaps best suited to serve as background music for a luau at the senior citizens center. Smith Ballew's society
orchestra version, also from 1929, is a somewhat jazzier effort, uplifted by the
hot breaks assigned to Jack Purvis, an Armstrong-inspired trumpeter whose
personal demons—arrests, flights from the law, attempted suicides, a stint as a
mercenary, and eventually a mysterious disappearance—prevented him from
taking full advantage of his considerable talent. Even so, few on the jazz scene
were paying attention to "Just You, Just Me," and less than a year after the film's
release, the song had fallen off the radar screens of improvisers.

But three years later, stride pianist Claude Hopkins convincingly demonstrated that Jesse Greer's composition could work as a swing dance number.
Artie Shaw and Red Norvo also bought into the idea, recording the song in 1937
and 1938, respectively; Eddie Sauter's arrangement for Norvo is especially effective. No other name bandleader would feature "Just You, Just Me" in the years
leading up to World War II, yet the song had at least abandoned its ukulele-
burdened past and become a full-fledged jazz tune.

Providing coherent lyrics to a song whose melody demands four stressed
syllables at the start of each verse is no simple task. But Mr. Klages did his

best—just you, just me . . . just us, just we, etc.—although the cuteness quotient has probably dissuaded many jazz singers from adding this composition to their set list. The idea of finding a "cozy spot to cuddle and coo" might have appealed to grandpa and grandma, but clearly doesn't cut it nowadays. Yet horn players have bought into the idea, or at least the underlying chord changes, and "Just You, Just Me" has been a favorite at jam sessions and studio dates since the mid-1940s.

The key moment in the history of "Just You, Just Me" as a jazz standard arrived with Lester Young's December 1943 recording, which became a top 10 R&B jukebox hit. The song was later adopted as a regular jam number for Young and others at Norman Granz's "Jazz at the Philharmonic" touring shows during the postwar period. The song also showed up in the repertoires of Duke Ellington, Louis Armstrong, and other leading jazz acts around this same time.

"Just You, Just Me" has been most popular among trad- and swing-oriented players, with more lindyhoppers than hard-boppers falling under its sway. Nonetheless, Thelonious Monk maintained a long-standing allegiance to this song, recording it on several occasions, relying on it to demonstrate his style during a 1954 visit to Columbia University, and even borrowing the harmonic progression for his own composition "Evidence." His eight-minute 1955 trio performance of "Just You, Just Me," alongside Oscar Pettiford and Art Blakey, is a particularly illuminating showcase of his distinctive approach to thematic improvisation.

RECOMMENDED VERSIONS

Claude Hopkins, New York, March 9, 1933

Artie Shaw, New York, October 18, 1937

Red Norvo (with an arrangement by Eddie Sauter), New York, July 26, 1938

Lester Young, New York, December 28, 1943

Duke Ellington, Hollywood, August 26, 1946

Thelonious Monk, from *The Unique*, Hackensack, New Jersey, March 17, 1956

Coleman Hawkins (with Bud Powell), from *Hawk in Germany*, live at Grugahalle, Essen, Germany, April 2, 1960

Ray Charles and Betty Carter, from *Ray Charles and Betty Carter*, Los Angeles, June 14, 1961

Abdullah Ibrahim, from *African Dawn*, Ludwigsburg, Germany, June 7, 1982

Ray Brown (with Joshua Redman), from *Some of My Best Friends Are . . . Sax Players*, New York (November 20–22, 1995) and Los Angeles (February 13, 1996)

King Porter Stomp
Composed by Jelly Roll Morton

Jelly Roll Morton, the brash New Orleans pianist and racon-teur, belongs on any short list of great jazz composers. And if you have any doubts, just track down a copy of Morton's business card from the 1920s, which proclaims "World's Greatest Hot Tune Writer," where the rest of us would insert something like "certified public accountant" or "licensed contractor." In time, Morton became as famous for his brag-gadocio as for his music—he also claimed to have invented jazz, scat singing, playing the drums with brushes, and the modern concept of the emcee. Yet his boast about his hot tunes matches my own assessment. No jazz artist before the advent of Duke Ellington put together such an impressive body of compositions as Mr. Morton.

And yet only one of his works, "King Porter Stomp," became a legitimate jazz standard. The very complexity of Morton's writing discouraged cover versions. His composi-tions usually employ several themes, embedded in long forms that are closer to ragtime than post-1920s jazz. Im-provisers tend to prefer short forms, 32 bars or fewer, and Morton rarely restricted his ambitions to such modest di-mensions. The lineage of Morton's conception is evident from his own performances of "King Porter Stomp." Mor-ton never recorded this song in a combo under his own leadership, and his solo piano renditions are very much set pieces in a pre-jazz style. In fact, Morton claimed that he wrote the piece in 1905 (others have suggested 1906 or later)—more than a decade before the first jazz recordings—back when casual listeners would have labeled a work of this sort as "ragtime."

Morton called the song a "stomp," but he admitted, "I don't know what the term 'stomp' means, myself. There wasn't really any meaning, only that people would stamp their feet." The song was named for the Florida pianist Porter King. As Morton explained to Alan Lomax, "Porter King was an educated gentleman with a far better musical training than mine and he seemed to have a yen for my style of playing. He particularly liked one certain number, and so I named it after him."

Despite its old-fashioned roots, "King Porter Stomp" not only became a hit during the Swing Era but, by some accounts, even *launched* the Swing Era. Benny Goodman's performance at the Palomar Ballroom in Los Angeles on August 21, 1935, is generally considered a "Woodstock" moment for the prewar generation, the juncture at which a new music and lifestyle emerged as a dominant cultural force. According to Goodman's own account, the band had been playing its low-key arrangement of pop songs and losing the audience's interest. He then decided to go for broke on a hotter approach and called for Fletcher Henderson's arrangement of "King Porter Stomp"—a choice greeted with an enthusiastic roar from the crowd. Goodman stuck with hot jazz from that point on, and the whole country, it seemed, was anxious to come along for the ride.

Henderson had recorded the song himself seven years before, in March 1928, and one wonders whether his choice of this tune had any connection with Morton's visit to the same studio the previous day. An even earlier recording by Henderson of "King Porter Stomp" from February 1925 was never released—all the more unfortunate given the likelihood that Louis Armstrong took a solo on the track. In the aftermath of Goodman's success, the song became a staple of working big bands across the country, with Count Basie, Chick Webb, Harry James, Glenn Miller, Jimmy Dorsey, and Cab Calloway, among others, offering up their interpretations. The composer's comment that the word "stomp" referred to the audience moving their feet was amply validated, as his song became one of the most popular dance numbers of the era.

The song fell out of vogue with most of the leading jazz stars after the 1940s. Cover versions typically were typically heard from nostalgia-oriented swing and trad acts. Yet an occasional modernist reworking—from Gil Evans, Sun Ra, or the trio Air—showed that the song that appealed so much to Porter King at the turn of the century could still charm players of a more progressive persuasion many decades later. I have a hunch, though, that Morton himself would have been especially pleased by Wynton Marsalis's 1999 recording, which makes no pretense at updating a classic for the new millennium, but instead dishes out the "plenty rhythm, plenty swing" formula that the composer himself favored. Although Marsalis's advocacy of the New Orleans tradition is well known and amply documented on record, this track is an excellent place to start for anyone who wants to hear Wynton's heritage reclamation work at its best.

RECOMMENDED VERSIONS

King Oliver and Jelly Roll Morton, Chicago, December 1924

Fletcher Henderson, New York, March 14, 1928

Fletcher Henderson (recorded as the "New King Porter Stomp"), New York, December 9, 1932

Benny Goodman, New York, July 1, 1935

Jelly Roll Morton, New York, December 14, 1939

Gil Evans (with Cannonball Adderley), from *New Bottle Old Wine*, New York, April 9, 1958

Bob Brookmeyer, from *Stretching Out*, New York, December 27, 1958

Air, from *Air Lore*, New York, May 12, 1979

Sun Ra, from *Sunrise in Different Dimensions*, life at Gasthof Mohren, Willisau, Switzerland, February 24, 1980

Wynton Marsalis, from *Mr. Jelly Lord: Standard Time, Vol. 6*, New York, January 12–13, 1999

Lady Bird

Composed by Tadd Dameron

L

Years ago, a trombonist sat in at a jam session where I was presiding over the keyboard and, during our rendition of "Lady Bird," grabbed the microphone unprompted and sang his own lyrics to the song. I was impressed by their flair, and over the ensuing weeks, tried to secure a copy of the words. Despite many promises from their author, they were never forthcoming. I still would like to get my hands on them.

That said, "Lady Bird" works perfectly well as an instrumental—albeit you will hear it less often nowadays than when I was learning the tools of the trade. Up-and-coming jazz players today take seriously the contributions of, say, a Thelonious Monk, a Charlie Parker, a Dizzy Gillespie, and this reverence will keep their compositions alive for many decades to come. But walk into a classroom of student jazz musicians and mention the name of Tadley Ewing Peake Dameron (1917–65)—Tadd Dameron, for short—and you are likely to get more than a few uncomprehending stares.

Yet, in his day, Dameron was deservedly acknowledged as a major modern jazz composer, arguably the equal of the stars of bebop when it came to songwriting and arranging. During the middle decades of the twentieth century, his compositions were jam session staples, with at least a half-dozen of his works earning a place in the standard repertoire. "Hot House" was so popular with Dizzy Gillespie—who left behind more than a dozen recordings of it—that many assumed that the trumpeter had written it, but in fact this clever reworking of "What Is This Thing Called Love?" came from Dameron's pen. His other familiar melodies include "If You Could See Me Now," "Good Bait," "Our Delight," "The Chase," "The Squirrel," "On a Misty Night," and "Lady Bird."

"Lady Bird" is a crisp 16-bar song that sounds deceptively simple. The melody, unlike many bop compositions, poses few difficulties for the aspiring player, and could be taught to a junior high jazz band. Over the years, I have relied on the typical fake book lead sheet for the song, in which the opening phrases end on a flat fifth—a device Dameron used to good effect in "Hot House" and "Our Delight"—and was disappointed to learn that the "Lady Bird" chart that Dameron submitted for copyright does not include these, and instead ends both phrases on the sixth. I abandon those flat fives with some reluctance, noting that many distinguished jazz artists share my preference, but I am ultimately swayed by the fact that early recordings substantiate Dameron's preference for the copyrighted version. Yet the meat and potatoes here lie in the chord changes. Dameron weaves a considerable amount of harmonic movement into this short form, especially with his clever turnaround, so that even a seasoned pro will find sustenance for an extended solo.

Fats Navarro, featured on Dameron's 1948 recording of "Lady Bird," is—like Dameron himself—unfairly forgotten. Had he not died at age of 26, tuberculosis combining with heroin addiction to plague his health, he might have gained recognition as one of the most accomplished jazz soloists of his generation. Certainly his tone and control, as he demonstrates alongside Dameron, are nonpareil. In contrast, Navarro's replacement in the band that Dameron took to Europe a few months later, the young Miles Davis, was destined for greatness *and* fame, although he was still working in the shadow of better-known bandleaders at this stage in his career. Davis kept "Lady Bird" in his repertoire for almost a decade, and based his own composition "Half Nelson" on the chords to the Dameron piece.

I note that cover versions of this song have become less common since Dameron's death in 1965. The older generation of modern jazz players continued to feature this song in their repertoires—check out versions by Tommy Flanagan, Hank Jones, and Dexter Gordon—and Philly Joe Jones even founded a tribute band Dameronia in the 1980s, which has operated sporadically in later years. But such efforts have merely kept the flame flickering, not burning brightly. I have a hunch, though, that a Dameron revival will take place at some point, probably spurred by a young lion with a sense of history; when it does, "Lady Bird" will be part of it.

RECOMMENDED VERSIONS

Tadd Dameron (with Fats Navarro), New York, September 13, 1948

Tadd Dameron (with Miles Davis), live at Salle Pleyel, Paris, May 8, 1949

Bud Powell, from *Piano Interpretations by Bud Powell*, New York, April 27, 1955

The Jazz Messengers (with Art Blakey and Horace Silver) from *The Jazz Messengers at the Café Bohemia*, New York, November 23, 1955

Dexter Gordon (with James Moody and Barry Harris), from *More Power!* New York, April 2, 1969

Hank Jones and Tommy Flanagan, from *Our Delights*, Berkeley, California, January 28, 1978

Dameronia (featuring Clifford Jordan), from *Live at the Theatre Boulogne-Billancourt Paris*, live at Theatre Boulogne-Billancourt, Paris, May 30, 1989

The Lady Is a Tramp
Composed by Richard Rodgers, with lyrics by Lorenz Hart

This song is a variant on the standard "list" song, but with an extra challenge for the lyricist. Every item in the list aims for a comedic angle on the main theme: namely, the low behavior of high society. Modern listeners are often unclear on the concept—puzzled why the lady is a tramp if she has dinner before eight, hates California, etc. In truth, various bits and pieces of Lorenz Hart's lyrics have aged poorly. When the singer tells about going to Harlem in ermine and pearls, the mental image is of successful rap stars, not white sophisticates out slumming.

That is the price the songwriters pay for trying to be too timely. Quips that hit the mark in the midst of the Great Depression are unlikely to get laughs in the Internet age. Yet that hasn't hurt the popularity of "The Lady Is a Tramp," which remains one of the most frequently performed Rodgers and Hart songs. Singers have helped it along by tinkering with and updating the lyrics. Almost a quarter of a century after the song's debut, Buddy Greco brought "The Lady Is a Tramp" back to the airwaves with a version packed with new stanzas and Cold War cultural references. Frank Sinatra, with whom this song is closely associated, usually kept closer to the original words, but would titillate audiences with a smattering of swear words. Hear him, on the 1959 live recording from his Australian tour, backed by Red Norvo: "She's broke—what the HELL. She hates California, because it's DAMN cold and it's damp."

The song originated in the 1937 Broadway production *Babes in Arms*, where the thin story line (one of those "C'mon kids, we'll put the show on right here" musicals) was propped up by first-rate songs. In addition to "The Lady Is a Tramp," *Babes in Arms* introduced "My Funny Valentine," "Where or When," "I Wish I Were in Love Again," and "Johnny One-Note." Yet when Hollywood made a movie of *Babes in Arms* in 1939, most of the original songs were scrapped, and "The Lady Is a Tramp" was relegated to background music.

MGM eventually made up for this egregious omission, resurrecting the song for the 1948 film *Words and Music*, a biopic about Rodgers and Hart.

The film's musical director Lennie Hayton decided to feature his wife singing "The Lady Is a Tramp." Usually nepotism in the band is a formula for disaster—but Hayton's spouse was Lena Horne. The couple, fearing a backlash to their interracial marriage, had kept their relationship a secret at the time, but filmgoers benefited from this hidden relationship. Well, not all of them: MGM made sure that Horne's performance was shot as a standalone sequence that could be snipped out of the movie when shown in the Deep South.

Only at this point, with Horne's imprimatur, did "The Lady Is a Tramp" secure its place in the jazz repertoire. Few cover versions had been recorded in the decade leading up to *Words and Music*, but in the 1950s the composition was widely adopted by jazz and pop music stars. During the song's first brief burst of renown in the 1930s, it had served as a vocal feature; now it was embraced with enthusiasm by instrumentalists. Oscar Peterson, Gerry Mulligan, and Cal Tjader recorded it on multiple occasions in the 1950s, with many others following suit in later years. Not that the singers ever forgot this "Lady," but she has always been more favored by extroverted stylists—Ella Fitzgerald, Mel Tormé, Anita O'Day—rather than moody torch singers. This sassy tune is more a vehicle for show-offs, and nothing is rarer than an *understated* vocal performance of "The Lady Is a Tramp."

The piece invites glib interpretations, but that may be inevitable for a song that made its mark with cleverness instead of passion. Even so, "The Lady Is a Tramp" has enough hooks to keep it in circulation. I especially like the abrupt two-note phrases that conclude the bridge, which hit the mark like well-timed boxing jabs, and the chords are interesting without presenting too many challenges to the novice soloist. You can garnish with gimmicks and repartee, but the "Lady" serves equally well for a straight jam.

RECOMMENDED VERSIONS

Tommy Dorsey (with Edythe Wright), New York, September 11, 1937

Lena Horne (with Lennie Hayton), from the film *Words and Music*, Culver City, California, 1948

Anita O'Day, from *The Lady is a Tramp*, Chicago, July 1952

Gerry Mulligan (with Chet Baker), from *Gerry Mulligan Quartet*, Los Angeles, January 3, 1953

Mel Tormé (with the Marty Paich Dek-Tette), from *Mel Tormé with the Marty Paich Dek-Tette*, Hollywood, January 16–18, 1956

Carl Perkins, from *Introducing Carl Perkins*, Los Angeles, 1956

Oscar Peterson, from *The Oscar Peterson Trio at the Concertgebouw*, live at the Civic Opera House, Chicago, September 29, 1957

Frank Sinatra (with Red Norvo), from *Live in Australia 1959*, live at West Melbourne Stadium, Melbourne, March 31, 1959

Buddy Greco, from *My Buddy*, live at Le Bistro, Chicago, October 15, 1959

Ella Fitzgerald, from *Ella in Berlin*, live at Deutschlandhallen, Berlin, February 13, 1960

Bill Charlap, from *Live at the Village Vanguard*, live at the Village Vanguard, New York, September 2003

Lament
Composed by J. J. Johnson

No one did more to legitimize the trombone as a modern jazz instrument than J. J. Johnson. Not every horn survived the transition from swing to bop during the middle years of the twentieth century—the clarinet, for example, has never come close to recapturing the leading role it played in many jazz bands during the late 1930s and early 1940s. Over the years, other instruments—the C-melody saxophone, the banjo, the cornet—have also struggled to retain their place in the jazz world. The trombone might easily have become another casualty, relegated to Dixieland ensembles or big band horn sections, had Johnson not shown at a decisive juncture that the big 'bone could adapt to the fleet and flashy stylings of the new idiom.

Yet as early as his high school years, Johnson also focused on writing and arranging. Johnson was a significant contributor to the Third Stream movement of the 1950s and 1960s, which aimed to merge elements of the jazz and classical traditions, and his works *Poem for Brass, Rondeau for Quartet and Orchestra*, and *Perceptions* gave notice that this consummate performer might become as well known for the work he did offstage. As it turns out, Johnson's best-known composition today is a less ambitious affair, a 32-bar ballad named "Lament."

Johnson's debut recording from 1954 testifies to the emotional pungency of the piece, and despite this trombonist's reputation for virtuosity, his approach here is understated with no wasted gestures or showy theatrics. Even so, it took another horn player to establish "Lament" as a jazz standard. Three years later, Miles Davis featured "Lament" on his high-profile collaboration with Gil Evans, *Miles Ahead*, a project that even today remains one of the biggest-selling jazz albums in the Columbia archive (now owned by Sony). Davis and Evans returned to the song for their 1961 Carnegie Hall concert, also released on LP by the Columbia label.

Most later versions emulate Davis's treatment, offering up "Lament" as a slow, wistful ballad. Few have tried to update or reconfigure this song—a wise choice, since this composition needs to be underplayed for best effect. I consider it more a test of a performer's emotional commitment rather than a vehicle for ingenuity or pyrotechnics. The best versions—by Miles Davis, Keith Jarrett, Branford Marsalis, and the composer himself—achieve just that.

By the way, fans of J. J. Johnson's composition are advised to take care before purchasing recordings of songs entitled "Lament," as there are several other jazz pieces that share this name. Apparently jazz musicians have much to lament. Chet Baker adds even more to the confusion by recording both J. J. Johnson's "Lament" on multiple occasions, as well as "Sometimes I Feel Like a Motherless Child" under the same title. Perhaps as many as a third of the jazz songs named "Lament"—recorded by Ahmad Jamal, Stan Kenton, Lester Bowie, and others—have, for all their virtues, no connection to Johnson's piece.

RECOMMENDED VERSIONS

J. J. Johnson (with Kai Winding), from *Jay & Kai*, Hackensack, New Jersey, August 24, 1954

Miles Davis (with Gil Evans), from *Miles Ahead*, New York, May 27, 1957

Miles Davis (with Gil Evans), from *Miles Davis at Carnegie Hall*, live at Carnegie Hall, New York, May 19, 1961

Milt Jackson (with J. J. Johnson), from *Jackson, Johnson, Brown & Company*, Hollywood, May 25–26, 1983

Chet Baker and Toots Thielemans, from *Chet & Toots*, live at Södra Teatern, Stockholm, February 26, 1985

Branford Marsalis, from *Renaissance*, New York or Los Angeles, January 26–28, 1987

Tommy Flanagan, from *Jazz Poet*, Englewood Cliffs, New Jersey, January 17–19, 1989

Keith Jarrett (with the Standards Trio), from *At the Blue Note: The Complete Recordings*, live at the Blue Note, New York, June 3, 1994

Laura

Composed by David Raksin, with lyrics by Johnny Mercer

David Raksin composed scores for more than 100 movies and also contributed music to several hundred television shows, but the opening notes to "Laura"—a Chopinesque phrase that evokes a haunting romantic mood—are far better known than anything else he penned in his long career. Cole Porter once claimed that "Laura" was the one song he most wished he had written.

I attribute much of the success of the 1944 film *Laura* to this melody, which can be heard in the background whenever police detective Mark McPherson (played by Dana Andrews) drifts into a reverie over lovely Laura Hunt (played by Gene Tierney) whose murder he is investigating. McPherson eventually falls in love with Laura, and since he hasn't had a chance to meet her, I can only assign responsibility to the romantic spell cast by Raksin's melody. You couldn't find a better tune to fill this role as a musical love charm.

Yet the song almost never made it into the film. Raksin was not brought in as composer until after shooting had been completed. Director Otto Preminger had originally wanted to use Gershwin's "Summertime" but couldn't secure the rights; then he focused on Ellington's "Sophisticated Lady," but Raksin argued that it wasn't right for the soundtrack. Raksin began work on the song the day after his wife walked out on him, and some have connected the charged emotions of the composition with the personal circumstances that presided over its birth.

Both the general public and jazz musicians embraced this song from the start. Many of the leading big bands of the day added "Laura" to their repertoires in 1945, as testified by recordings by Duke Ellington, Glenn Miller, Woody Herman, Harry James, Gene Krupa, Boyd Raeburn, and others. Herman's version, his first recording for the Columbia label, was so successful that the execs put a hold on releasing Harry James's version—a wise decision if we can believe claims that Herman's 78 sold a million copies. Six years later, when Charlie Parker sat in with Herman's band, the leader pulled out this song as a feature number for his illustrious guest.

Raksin's composition served as an ideal vehicle for cool school and West Coast jazz artists. Few musicians were more loyal to "Laura" than Dave Brubeck, who first recorded it with his Octet and then again with his Trio back in the 1940s, and in 1953 performed it on his well-known live recording at the College of the Pacific. Cal Tjader, who recorded "Laura" with Brubeck on the first two of those tracks, also featured it on his live recording from Carmel in 1959. Gerry Mulligan wrote an arrangement of "Laura" for Claude Thornhill in 1949, then recorded it on several occasions with his own bands, further enhancing its "cool" credentials.

Johnny Mercer's lyrics were added after the fact, in response to the popularity of the movie soundtrack theme, but nowadays it's hard for most fans of this song to think of "Laura" ever existing without the words. Alec Wilder claims he was present when the music publishers first listened to the song, and reports that they felt it was too complex to be a hit—but they changed their opinion after hearing Mercer's contribution. Wilder even goes so far as to suggest that, with less poetic lyrics, the song would never have caught on. I beg to differ, placing my bets on the intrinsic allure of the melody. Most of the jazz cover versions of "Laura" have been instrumentals, although the words clearly amplify the mood of Raksin's composition. Mercer himself often cited this work as an example of lyrics that are perfectly aligned with the emotional temperament of the music.

In its vocal version, the song was intended for a male singer, yet the best-selling jazz version on Amazon.com is Ella Fitzgerald's 1964 performance. I can't find fault with her impeccable phrasing and tone control, yet I still give the nod to Frank Sinatra's 1947 rendition, which is heartfelt in an austere way that one seldom hears on love ballads from this singer's middle or late career. And I must admit to a guilty pleasure: namely my nostalgic fondness for the very first version of "Laura" I ever heard, the campy send-off by Spike Jones. This zany chart might have killed the credibility of a lesser song—I don't think "Cocktails for Two" ever survived Jones's similarly abusive arrangement—but only added to the fame of Raksin's Hollywood classic.

RECOMMENDED VERSIONS

Woody Herman, New York, February 19, 1945

Spike Jones, Los Angeles, May 6, 1946

Frank Sinatra, New York, October 22, 1947

Charlie Parker (with Woody Herman), live at Municipal Arena, Kansas City, Missouri, July 22, 1951

Nat King Cole, from *Penthouse Serenade*, New York, July 18, 1952

Dave Brubeck, from *Jazz at the College of the Pacific*, Stockton, California, December 14, 1953

Coleman Hawkins (with J. J. Johnson), from *The Hawk Flies High*, New York, March 12, 1957

Gerry Mulligan (with Bob Brookmeyer), from *Gerry Mulligan Quartets in Concert*, live at the Hollywood Bowl, Hollywood, August 2, 1957

Cal Tjader (with Paul Horn), from *Monterey Concert*, live at the Sunset Auditorium, Carmel, California, April 20, 1959

Ella Fitzgerald, from *Ella Fitzgerald Sings the Johnny Mercer Songbook*, Los Angeles, October 20, 1964

Joe Lovano, from *On This Day at the Vanguard*, live at the Village Vanguard, New York, September 29, 2002

Patricia Barber, from *Live: A Fortnight in France*, Paris, Metz, and La Rochelle, France, March–April 2004

Lester Leaps In
Composed by Lester Young

Lester Young grew up in a great jazz city (New Orleans) and died in another (New York), but he will be forever associated in the minds of jazz fans with the Kansas City style of playing, which he helped define during his stint with the Count Basie band. Not a native son, Young nonetheless did more than anyone in establishing the Kaycee approach as a major jazz movement during the late 1930s, and a springboard for a host of more progressive players who arrived on the scene during the 1940s and 1950s. The Kansas City bands pushed the art form ahead, but in the most unassuming of manners. They emphasized a relaxed yet spirited swing in 4/4 time, and flourished while relying on a repertoire that seldom departed from blues, riff tunes, and songs built on "I Got Rhythm" chord changes.

"Lester Leaps In" combines elements of the latter two, superimposing a repeated loping melodic figure over the harmonic structure of the Gershwin standard. The debut recording from September 1939 features Young in one of his career-defining moments, delivering two full choruses capped by a dramatic stop-time interlude and followed by a series of four-bar exchanges with a coyly understated Basie. A listener seeking the essence of Kansas City swing could do much worse than spending some quality time in contemplation of this one track.

Charlie Parker clearly did just that, and his recorded output shows a careful assimilation of phrases from this particular Young solo. Parker never made a studio recording of "Lester Leaps In," but left behind stellar live performances at a 1949 Carnegie Hall concert (where he shared the stage with the composer) and at Rockland Palace in 1952. The latter is marred by poor sound quality, but includes one of the most exciting (and fastest) solos from Parker's late career. The Carnegie Hall jam is also illuminating, showing how this portmanteau piece could serve equally well for advocates of swing or bop, even when mixed together in the same ensemble.

"Lester Leaps In" has held on to its spot in the jazz repertoire, but typically as an up-tempo jam session tune: the comfortably paced swing of Young and his Kansas City cohorts replaced by a foot-on-the-accelerator quest for ultimate speed. Sax players tend to be the most loyal devotees of this piece, and it serves especially well when they confront each other head-on. Fans of tenor jousting are encouraged to check out Johnny Griffin and Eddie "Lockjaw" Davis's encounter on "Lester Leaps In" from a 1984 performance at Montmartre in Copenhagen, as well as Houston Person's studio battle with Teddy Edwards over the same changes from 1994.

RECOMMENDED VERSIONS

Count Basie (with Lester Young), New York, September 5, 1939

Jazz at the Philharmonic (with Lester Young, Charlie Parker, and Roy Eldridge), live at Carnegie Hall, New York, September 18, 1949

Charlie Parker, live at Rockland Palace, New York, September 26, 1952

Gil Evans (with Cannonball Adderley), from *New Bottle Old Wine*, New York, April 9, 1958

Illinois Jacquet (with Tommy Flanagan and Kenny Burrell), from *Desert Winds*, Englewood Cliffs, New Jersey, February 13, 1964

Johnny Griffin and Eddie "Lockjaw" Davis, from *Tough Tenors Back Again*, live at Montmartre, Copenhagen, July 10, 1984

Teddy Edwards and Houston Person, from *Horn to Horn*, Englewood Cliffs, New Jersey, December 27, 1994

James Carter (with Henry "Sweets" Edison), from *Conversin' with the Elders*, New York, October 2, 1995

Like Someone in Love
Composed by Jimmy Van Heusen, with lyrics by Johnny Burke

"Like Someone in Love" made its debut in *Belle of the Yukon*, a 1944 film about the Canadian Gold Rush. The songwriting duo of Van Heusen and Burke had just won an Oscar for "Swinging on a Star" and, sure enough, one of their tunes from *Belle of the Yukon* would also earn a nomination—but not "Like Someone in Love." Instead the now mostly forgotten "Sleigh Ride in July" was so honored, although eventually losing out to Rodgers and Hammerstein's "It Might as Well Be Spring."

Bing Crosby recorded "Sleigh Ride in July" with "Like Someone in Love" on the B side of the disk, and both songs were modest hits for him in early 1945, with "Sleigh Ride" getting the most airplay. Dinah Shore and Tommy Dorsey followed the same formula, but they only charted with "Sleigh Ride in July." Burke and Van Heusen took out an ad to promote the songs in *Billboard*, and they too gave top billing to "Sleigh Ride in July." When the Oscar nomination was announced around this same time, it simply reflected the consensus: the sleigh-ride song was the keeper, while "Like Someone in Love" seemingly lacked staying power and was destined for oblivion.

And so it was, at least until 1953, when Frank Sinatra—a longtime advocate for Jimmy Van Heusen's music—recorded "Like Someone in Love," in an arrangement by Nelson Riddle, as part of his *Songs for Young Lovers* album. Just a few weeks later, pianist Paul Bley featured the song on his debut album, *Introducing Paul Bley*, and over the next several years a number of prominent jazz artists released cover versions. Art Blakey recorded it live at Café Bohemia in 1955, and again on a 1960 studio date, the latter featuring Lee Morgan swinging over Bobby Timmon's quirky but effective on-the-beat accompaniment. Bud Powell struggled through several takes at his December 1954 session for Verve, and sounds as if he is uncertain about the chord progression—although he would later perform the song more capably in other settings. Chet Baker presented it as a vocal number in 1956, as did both Ella Fitzgerald and Blossom Dearie in 1957, and Sarah Vaughan in 1958. Around this same time, the song was also recorded by Coleman Hawkins, Sonny Rollins, and Bill Evans.

Even more surprising was the adoption of this ostensibly gentle love song as a vehicle by cutting-edge improvisers. Coltrane recorded "Like Someone in Love" at a 1957 date for the Prestige label, and again in 1958 during a sometimes tense if intriguing session under the leadership of pianist Cecil Taylor (although since reissued under the saxophonist's name). Another alternative perspective on the standard can be heard in Elmo Hope's trio performance from 1959, which mixes lyricism and dissonance in equal doses. "Like Someone in Love" also shows up in a 20-minute track recorded live at the Five Spot by Eric Dolphy and Booker Little in 1961. And if you've forgotten that Dave Brubeck was once considered an experimental player, check out his prickly and sometimes polytonal playing alongside Lee Konitz in their 1974 performance of the Van Heusen standard.

I am not surprised that this song eventually captured the hearts and minds of jazz artists. The downward motion of the bassline provides a satisfying contrast to the melody, with its upward leaps—a tension that is beautifully reflected in the lyrics. On those interval jumps, Burke inserts images—stars, wings—associated with higher places; meanwhile our starstruck lover is "bumping into things" down below. I wouldn't change a note or a word here. And though the chord changes provide a fitting platform for improvisation, this piece tempts me, when I've finished playing the melody, to return to it again, skipping the solos and savoring the craftsmanship residing in the written notes.

This composition has inspired many jazz players over the years, but the best-selling version nowadays comes from the Icelandic diva Björk, who included "Like Someone in Love" on her 1993 album *Debut*, which eventually went platinum in the United States and stayed on the charts for more than a year. Jazz fans will probably grimace at the harp accompaniment here, which is a few steps below the comping Cecil Taylor provided for John Coltrane back in 1958. But interventions from global pop stars sometimes spur interest in deserving songs, and the Björk effect may very well keep this standard current for at least a few more decades.

RECOMMENDED VERSIONS

Frank Sinatra, from *Songs for Young Lovers*, Los Angeles, November 6, 1953

Paul Bley (with Charles Mingus and Art Blakey), from *Introducing Paul Bley*, New York, November 30, 1953

Chet Baker, from *The Best of Chet Baker Sings*, Los Angeles, July 30, 1956

John Coltrane, from *Lush Life*, Hackensack, New Jersey, August 16, 1957

Sonny Rollins, from *Sonny Rollins Plays*, New York, November 4, 1957

Sarah Vaughan, from *After Hours at the London House*, live at the London House, Chicago, March 7, 1958

Cecil Taylor and John Coltrane, from *Coltrane Time*, New York, October 13, 1958

Elmo Hope, from *Elmo Hope Trio*, Los Angeles, February 8, 1959

Art Blakey (with Lee Morgan), from *Like Someone in Love*, Englewood Cliffs, New Jersey, August 14, 1960

Eric Dolphy (with Booker Little), from *Eric Dolphy at the Five Spot*, live at the Five Spot, New York, July 16, 1961

Dave Brubeck (with Lee Konitz), from *All the Things We Are*, New York, October 3, 1974

Steve Grossman, from *Way Out East, Vol. 2*, Milan, July 24, 1984

Art Farmer (with Clifford Jordan), from *Ph.D.*, New York, April 3–4, 1989

Tony Monaco (with Bruce Forman), from *East to West*, Columbus, Ohio, September 2005

Limehouse Blues

Composed by Philip Braham, with lyrics by Douglas Furber

No, "Limehouse Blues" is not a real blues—which would require a 12-bar structure and an acceptable blues chord progression to make the grade. Nor can I imagine a rough-and-tumble blues musician in the early 1920s deciding to sing about Limehouse, an area in London on the north bank of the Thames. Cotton blues, yes. Sugarcane and catfish, maybe. But the lime kilns of old London town are a stretch.

In truth, this song by Douglas Furber and Philip Braham, which originated in the 1921 West End production *A to Z*, is actually far closer to jazz than to the blues, and stands out as not only the first significant British jazz standard, but also one of the first popular songs anywhere to incorporate jazzlike phrasing into its melodic construction. Just compare it to some of the other hits of that period—such as Henry Burr's recording of "My Buddy," Lambert Murphy's rendition of "I Dream of Jeannie with the Light Brown Hair," or Fanny Brice's "Second-Hand Rose"—and you will get a sense of the paradigm shift then underway in the music business.

Jazz musicians usually take "Limehouse Blues" at a brisk pace, but Ellington slowed it down to a medium-tempo amble for his 1931 recording, a top 20 hit for the band, which almost sounds like it could serve as a soundtrack for a cowboy movie given the horse-trot beat he employs. Other versions of the era—by Fletcher Henderson, Joe Haymes, the Casa Loma Orchestra, Bert Ambrose, and others—throw caution to the wind, presenting "Limehouse Blues" as a race-course for jazz thoroughbreds. The latter track, built on a fine Sid Phillips arrangement, may come as a shock to those jazz fans who doubt that a band of Brits could swing so crisply, circa 1935.

The French were not far behind, with the Quintette du Hot Club de France delivering a spirited performance of "Limehouse Blues" nine months later. Guitarist Django Reinhardt thrives on the frenetic pace, but his colleague Stéphane Grappelli steals the show, delivering one of the most driving solos of his early career. Yet pride of place among the early swing band versions belongs to Fletcher Henderson, whose September 1934 recording of "Limehouse Blues" features a propulsive rhythm, impressive section work, and a felicitous chart by Benny Carter.

"Limehouse Blues" fell out of favor during the bebop era, at least among younger musicians, but in later years a handful of memorable performances testified to its continuing ability to inspire top-notch performances. Cannonball Adderley performs it alongside John Coltrane at a little-known session held a few weeks before the saxophonists started work on *Kind of Blue* with Miles Davis. If the latter project was meditative chamber jazz, this earlier pairing is a sax battle, plain and simple. Another duel of the horns, from 1980, finds Phil Woods and Lew Tabackin engaged in fierce combat over this same terrain. Yet the biggest surprise came around this time, when Sun Ra—the avant-garde bandleader who claimed to have originated on the planet Saturn—dipped into the Limehouse for a strange atonal intergalactic piano extravaganza before bringing in his Orchestra—excuse me, *Arkestra*—for a deliciously retro tribute to an old jazz workhorse.

RECOMMENDED VERSIONS

Duke Ellington, Camden, New Jersey, June 16, 1931

Casa Loma Orchestra, New York, February 24, 1934

Fletcher Henderson, New York, September 11, 1934

Bert Ambrose, London, August 8, 1935

Quintette du Hot Club de France (with Django Reinhardt and Stéphane Grappelli), Paris, May 4, 1936

Sidney Bechet (with Willie "The Lion" Smith), New York, September 13, 1941

Benny Goodman (with Mel Powell), New York, October 28, 1941

Sonny Rollins (with Percy Heath and Connie Kay), from *Sonny Rollins and the Big Brass*, live at the Music Inn, Lenox, Massachusetts, August 3, 1958

Cannonball Adderley (with John Coltrane), from *Cannonball Adderley Quintet in Chicago*, Chicago, February 3, 1959

Anita O'Day, from *Mello'day*, Los Angeles, January–February 1979

Sun Ra, from *Sunrise in Different Dimensions*, live at Gasthof Mohren, Willisau, Switzerland, February 24, 1980

Phil Woods and Lew Tabackin, from *Phil Woods/Lew Tabackin*, New York, December 10, 1980

Charlie Hunter, from *Public Domain*, Brooklyn, no date given (CD released in 2010)

Liza
Composed by George Gershwin, with lyrics by Ira Gershwin

Accounts of the opening night performance of this song, at the premiere of Flo Ziegfeld's musical revue *Show Girl*, tell of Al Jolson standing up from his seat in the third row and singing a chorus of "Liza"—much to the surprise of everyone, apparently even composer George Gershwin. Jolson was not a member of the cast (although his wife, Ruby Keeler, had a starring role), but he became closely associated with "Liza," soon recording a version that was a top 10 hit. The moment, as described, seems like something contrived for a Hollywood movie, and in fact turned into one—it is featured prominently in the 1946 biopic *The Jolson Story*.

Was Jolson trying to upstage his wife, ostensibly the featured vocalist on this number? Or, perhaps, nudge out of the way Nick Lucas, who sang "Liza" with her on stage? Or was Jolson just so hungry for the limelight that he couldn't help grandstanding in such dramatic fashion? Probably none of the above. Jolson and Ziegfeld must surely have planned this crowd-pleasing gesture—devised during rehearsals, which Jolson frequented, and designed to extract maximum publicity from Jolson's recent marriage to Keeler (promoted on the billing as Ruby Keeler Jolson). This interpretation is substantiated by the calculated repetition of the supposedly spontaneous intervention: Jolson continued to sing "Liza" from the audience throughout the initial Boston run of *Show Girl* and during the first week of New York performances. If Gershwin was upset, he did a good job of hiding it. Certainly he knew from his "Swanee" (1919) what Mr. Jolson's support could do to boost royalties.

The crisp harmonic movement of "Liza," accentuated by the chord tones in the melody, is distinctly jazzy. Gershwin had toyed with this progression for some time: hints of it can be heard in a short work from 1923, "Sixteen Bars without a Name," which was reworked into a violin piece, "Short Story," in 1925.

Gershwin may have continued to tinker with the song destined to be "Liza" while working on *East Is West*, a *Madame Butterfly*–ish show slated for launch in late 1927 or early 1928. But that production proved too costly to stage, and the brothers Gershwin along with their embryonic song moved on to *Show Girl*—a musical put together in such a rush that Ziegfeld advised his star composer to pull old material out of his trunk. "Liza (All the Clouds'll Roll Away)"—the song's full title is rarely used by jazz players—proved to be the only lasting hit from the high-profile revue.

Show Girl caught the attention of jazz fans from the start, but not so much for "Liza" or Jolson, rather due to the participation of the Duke Ellington band. Ziegfeld added $1,500 per week into the budget to cover the cost of featuring the hot Cotton Club ensemble in his show—an important milestone in the integration of Broadway productions. The band did not perform on "Liza," and Ellington would not record it until many years later, but other jazz groups gradually adopted the Gershwin composition. Art Tatum, who first recorded "Liza" in 1934, even enchanted the composer with his virtuoso reworking of the piece. Oscar Levant, in his frank, witty book *A Smattering of Ignorance*, describes a visit he paid to a California nightclub with Gershwin, where Tatum was holding court. "To George's great joy," Levant writes, "Tatum played virtually the equivalent of Beethoven's 32 variations on his tune 'Liza.' Then George asked for more."

Piano players have taken the lead in keeping this song in the jazz repertoire. In its early years, James P. Johnson and Fats Waller played it as a Harlem stride showpiece. Teddy Wilson also recorded it on many occasions, and may have spurred Benny Goodman to feature it as a combo number. In later years, "Liza" rarely showed up outside the set list of trad and swing bands, but Thelonious Monk recorded it both in trio and quartet settings, and in 1978 Herbie Hancock and Chick Corea relied on it as the centerpiece of their much-publicized US "dueling pianos" tour.

The song has fallen out of favor in more recent years, and when it is played by jazz musicians it is usually taken at breakneck speed—hear, for example, Bill Charlap's race-to-the-finish-line version from 2005. Charlap is very much in the tradition of playing "Liza" for fun and fireworks, initiated by Tatum and continued by Corea, Hancock, and others. Yet this composition, originally conceived as a medium-tempo love song, can work at a much more leisurely pulse, even as a slow ballad, and might benefit nowadays from treatments that brings out nuances lost when the pulse rises above 250 beats per minute.

RECOMMENDED VERSIONS

Art Tatum, New York, August 24, 1934

Fletcher Henderson (with Benny Carter), New York, September 25, 1934

Red Norvo, Chicago, March 22, 1937

Chick Webb, New York, May 3, 1938

James P. Johnson, New York, May 1945

Django Reinhardt and Stéphane Grappelli, London, February 1, 1946

Sonny Stitt, from *Kaleidoscope*, New York, February 1, 1951

Thelonious Monk, from *The Unique*, Hackensack, New Jersey, March 17, 1956

Chris Connor (with Joe Newman), from *Chris Connor Sings the George Gershwin Almanac of Song*, New York February 1, 1957

Donald Lambert, from *Classics in Stride*, Warren, New Jersey, 1960

Herbie Hancock and Chick Corea, from *An Evening with Herbie Hancock and Chick Corea in Concert*, live at an unidentified U.S. location, February 1978

Bill Charlap, from *Plays George Gershwin: The American Soul*, New York, February 7, 2005

Lonely Woman
Composed by Ornette Coleman

Fans of experimental music seeking "Free Jazz" standards have few choices. The avant-garde players who emerged in the late 1950s and shook up the jazz scene of the 1960s and 1970s found little sustenance in the existing standard repertoire. Almost everything about these old songs was anathema to them: the rigid 32-bar forms, the tonally centered progressions, the conventional bar lines, the lyrics about romance and courtship. They almost universally rejected the existing standards and seemed indifferent, perhaps even hostile, to the idea of adding new ones of their own devising.

But one generation's heretics often become the next generation's saints, and the canonization process in jazz invariably demands the assimilation of new pieces into the standard repertoire. Ornette Coleman, the most visible champion of the jazz avant-garde, presented challenges to later jazz artists who wanted to play his songs, but they were not insurmountable obstacles. A few of his compositions have been recorded in cover versions often enough to stake out a place on the periphery of the jazz repertoire, but they rarely come in plug-and-play charts ready at hand in the standard fake books.

"Lonely Woman" is a case in point. On the original recording, the drums are keeping strict time, and the bass follows a loose AABA form . . . but horn players Ornette Coleman and Don Cherry refuse to recognize the bar lines that most jazz musicians view as milestones to mark their progress through a tune. The song lacks defined chord changes—no harmony instrument is present on the track—but some are implicit or at least not out of character with the mood of the piece. This wavering between tonal clarity and ambiguity adds to the excitement of the composition, and soloists who tackle this unconventional song are at liberty to apply the phraseology of chord-based, modal, or atonal improvisational techniques, as the spirit moves them.

Denny Zeitlin, for example, starts out his 1965 live recording of "Lonely Woman" by translating the horn lines of Coleman and Cherry from the original 1959 recording to the piano; but then, as he constructs his solo, he gradually adopts different harmonic personalities—ones that are essentially pianistic in nature and depart in varying degrees from the composer's initial vision. When other mainstream keyboardists interpret the song—such as John Lewis with the Modern Jazz Quartet from 1962 or Marian McPartland on her album *Twilight World* from 2007—the piece takes on more subtle shadings, and the dictates of freedom are balanced against a more acute formalism. In a far different vein, Branford Marsalis and Kenny Kirkland engage in an intensely rhapsodic 16-minute exposition on the 1987 album *Random Abstract*, one that has more romanticism than harmolodics in its sinews, but is equally successful in its realization as more free-form renditions. And by the time John Zorn has finished his reworking of this song for his 1989 *Naked City* CD, "Lonely Woman" sounds ready to appear on the soundtrack of a James Bond spy film.

These varied interpretations serve to disprove the often-heard lament that avant-garde music may move outside the chords but is less skilled in moving beyond a very narrow emotional range—proving capable, in the words of its critics, of expressing only harsher sentiments. In each of these recordings, "Lonely Woman" retains a haunting lyricism, very much in keeping with the musical moods found in the American popular song tradition, even if the means employed are radically different. Just as surprising is this composition's flip-flop of the typical rules of engagement for improvisers: it's easy to take a tonal jazz song and play it from an atonal perspective, but this Coleman song provides the much rarer case of an avant-garde jazz classic that can also be brought inside the chord changes . . . or linger on the border between freedom and form.

RECOMMENDED VERSIONS

Ornette Coleman, from *The Shape of Jazz to Come*, Hollywood, May 22, 1959

Modern Jazz Quartet, from *Lonely Woman*, New York, January 25, 1962

Denny Zeitlin (with Charlie Haden), from *Shining Hour*, live at the Trident, Sausalito, California, March 22–24, 1965

Lester Bowie (with Julius Hemphill), from *Fast Last*, New York, September 10, 1974

Old and New Dreams (with Don Cherry, Dewey Redman, Charlie Haden, and Ed Blackwell), from *Old and New Dreams*, Oslo, August 1979

Branford Marsalis (with Kenny Kirland), from *Random Abstract*, Tokyo, August
    12–13, 1987

John Zorn (with Bill Frisell), from *Naked City*, New York, 1989

JD Allen, from *In Search of*, New York, August 1998

Love for Sale
Composed by Cole Porter

Many songs have overcome nonmusical obstacles in gaining acceptance and popularity, but few tunes faced a stiffer challenge than "Love for Sale." For decades, radio stations refused to allow its lyrics on the air. The song, which made its debut in the 1930 Broadway musical *The New Yorkers*, is sung from the perspective of a Prohibition-era prostitute, and composer Cole Porter did not mince his words in presenting "appetizing young love for sale." Charles Darnton, the reviewer for the *Evening World*, accused the song of being "in the worst possible taste." The *Herald Tribune* called it "filthy."

Porter, perhaps in a mood of defensiveness, claimed that it was his favorite among the songs he had composed. "I can't understand it," he griped. "You can write a novel about a harlot, paint a picture of a harlot, but you can't write a song about a harlot." Perhaps most revealing: audience outrage subsided after the Broadway production shifted the setting of the song to Harlem, in front of the Cotton Club, and assigned the number to African-American vocalist Elizabeth Welch instead of Kathryn Crawford, a white singer.

Bandleader Fred Waring and vocalist Libby Holman had some success with their respective recordings of the song, despite the problems with airplay—in truth, the scandal associated with the composition may have served to boost sales. Yet jazz artists seldom turned to "Love for Sale" until the late 1940s and early 1950s. Billie Holiday recorded a definitive version, and her persona as a troubled diva who, by her own account, was working as a prostitute when this song first came out, gave her a kind of credibility that few singers would want to match. Despite her advocacy, vocalists long avoided this song. During this period a jazz fan was more likely to encounter the Porter tune in instrumental arrangements by Erroll Garner, Sidney Bechet, Art Tatum, or even Charlie Parker, who recorded it as part of a Cole Porter tribute project for the Verve label shortly before his death. And when brave female singers tackled the song—for example, Ella Fitzgerald, who was almost forced to cover it for her Cole Porter songbook album—they typically fell short of the verisimilitude established by Lady Day in her interpretation of "Love for Sale."

Cannonball Adderley recorded a well-known version for his 1958 project *Somethin' Else*—a rare date that found Miles Davis working as a sideman. Here, the Porter tune is turned into a jaunty hard-bop chart, and the transformation works perfectly. The roles were reversed a few months later when Davis brought what was arguably his finest group—the same all-star ensemble that would record *Kind of Blue*—into the studio and called "Love for Sale" on the spur of the moment. This version, which features first-rate solos by each of the horn players and some of the most forceful piano work of Bill Evans's early career, would be hard to surpass, but it has not been widely heard, largely because it remained unreleased for many years, a straggler track kept off the better-known Davis albums. Yet only a few days later, avant-gardist Cecil Taylor took even more liberties with Porter's standard, on a recording that commemorates one of this mordant musician's few attempts to cover a Broadway song.

By the 1960s, the taboo associated with "Love for Sale" had faded, and it became entrenched in the repertoires of jazz players. And for good reason. The opening theme is suitable for vamps of all stamps, from Latin to funky, and the release offers effective contrast both rhythmically and harmonically. A tension in tonality is evident from the outset: this song in a minor key nonetheless starts on a major chord, and seems ready to go in either direction during the course of Porter's extended form. A composition of this sort presents many possibilities, and can work either as a loose jam or bear the weight of elaborate arrangement.

RECOMMENDED VERSIONS

Erroll Garner, Hollywood, June 10, 1947

Billie Holiday, from *Solitude*, Los Angeles, circa May 1952

Charlie Parker, from *Charlie Parker Plays Cole Porter*, New York, December 10, 1954

Ella Fitzgerald, from *Ella Fitzgerald Sings the Cole Porter Songbook*, Los Angeles, February 8, 1956

Cannonball Adderley (with Miles Davis), from *Somethin' Else*, Hackensack, New Jersey, March 9, 1958

Miles Davis, from *Circle in the Round*, New York, May 26, 1958

Cecil Taylor, from *Love for Sale*, New York, April 15, 1959

Eddie Harris (with Cedar Walton), from *The In Sound*, New York, August 30, 1965

Buddy Rich (with an arrangement by Pete Myers), from *Big Swing Face*, live at Chez Club, Hollywood, February 22, 1967

Wallace Roney (with Ravi Coltrane and Geri Allen), from *Munchin'*, Englewood Cliffs, New Jersey, June 6, 1993

Jacky Terrasson, from *Alive*, live at the Iridium Jazz Club, New York, June 14, 1997

Lover

Composed by Richard Rodgers, with lyrics by Lorenz Hart

Jeanette MacDonald gave this waltz its debut in the 1932 film *Love Me Tonight*, where she sings it to a horse—and, unbeknownst to her, Maurice Chevalier, who remains hidden out of sight. Waltzes were well known to the general public at the time, but you wouldn't guess it from listening to the leading jazz stars— at least back during the Great Depression—and when they have played "Lover" over the years they have usually changed the meter to a fast 4/4.

In his book *American Popular Song*, Alec Wilder expresses puzzlement over this composition's commercial success, wondering why non-musicians would find it appealing. "For it is only a series of chromatic intervals made palatable by an interesting chord progression which, however, once the pattern is established, telegraphs its punches." His is a harsh verdict but one that matches my own response. The predictable unfolding of "Lover" seems more suited to a practice-room exercise than a public performance.

Yet the public has enjoyed a long-standing love affair with "Lover." In 1953, "Lover" climbed to the number 3 spot on the *Billboard* chart on the strength of Peggy Lee's hard-driving rendition. Almost exactly 20 years earlier, Paul Whiteman had also enjoyed a number 3 hit with the song, albeit in a much different arrangement—one that kept to the original 3/4 time ignored by most later jazz bands. (It's interesting to note that when Whiteman re-recorded "Lover" in 1956, he abandoned the waltz time and embraced the fast 4/4 approach— just at the point when other bandleaders were returning to his initial 3/4 conception.)

Even before Peggy Lee gave this song a fever, Gene Krupa turned "Lover" into a hot and fast drum feature, and his 1945 recording is one of his finest post-Goodman moments. Stan Kenton hints at the waltz feel in his rubato intro, but soon his band is also dashing ahead at a blistering 4/4 pulse. The contrast is even starker in Les Paul's recording, which presents a dainty waltz rendition before galloping off in swing time, but this performance is even more interesting for Paul's multitracking, reverb, and tape-speed modifications, which could fool you into believing that the guitarist had secured his own Moog synthesizer back in 1948. Charlie Parker also stays true to the speedy "Lover" routine in his 1952 recording, and it stands out as the most viscerally exciting of all the tracks he made with strings.

What surprise could a jazz musician add after these precedents? Perhaps the most shocking would be a return to straight waltz treatments of "Lover," and in the mid-1950s Dave Brubeck, Paul Desmond, Gerry Mulligan, and Max Roach did just that. Brubeck presents a relaxed and lyrical treatment on his *Jazz: Red, Hot and Cool* album, the antithesis of the Krupa-Kenton-Parker-Lee formula, and Paul Desmond captures an even more low-key mood on his 1957 pairing with Gerry Mulligan on "Lover." Max Roach's performance of "Lover" from that same year proffers a hard swinging 3/4 that few bands of that period could have matched. Over the next decade, jazz waltzes would become prevalent, but in 1957 other drummers must have marveled at Roach's ability to retain such rhythmic drive while playing in a meter that many still associated with Vienna and "The Blue Danube."

Nonetheless, in the jazz world, speed usually wins out in the end. In more recent decades, those looking for a slow and gentle "Lover" will be mostly disappointed. On recordings by Wynton Marsalis, Tom Harrell, Kenny Garrett, George Coleman, and others, this song is treated as a virtuosic showpiece, and listeners might assume that it dates from the bebop era, and not from 1932.

RECOMMENDED VERSIONS

Paul Whiteman, New York, April 4, 1932

Gene Krupa, New York, September 26, 1945

Stan Kenton (with Vido Musso and Kai Winding), Hollywood, March 31, 1947

Les Paul, Hollywood, March 22, 1948

Charlie Parker, from *Charlie Parker with Strings: The Master Takes*, New York, January 22, 1952

Peggy Lee (with Gordon Jenkins), from *Lover*, New York, April 28, 1952

Dave Brubeck (with Paul Desmond), from *Jazz: Red, Hot and Cool*, live at Basin Street, New York, July 23, 1955

Max Roach, from *Jazz in 3/4 Time*, New York, March 21, 1957

Kenny Garrett (with Mulgrew Miller), from *Introducing Kenny Garrett*, Englewood Cliffs, New Jersey, December 28, 1984

Tom Harrell (with Hal Galper), from *Open Air*, Copenhagen, May 26, 1986

Wynton Marsalis (with Marcus Roberts), from *Standard Time, Vol. 2: Intimacy Calling*, New York, September 1987–August 1990

Bill Charlap, from *'S Wonderful*, New York, December 26, 1998

Lover, Come Back to Me
Composed by Sigmund Romberg, with lyrics by Oscar Hammerstein II

Few composers of jazz standards took a more roundabout path to a songwriting career than Sigmund Romberg. Born in Nagykanizsa in present-day Hungary in 1887, Romberg studied engineering in Vienna and served in the military before moving to the United States in 1909. Even in this new setting, his prospects were meager—in the New World he worked in a pencil factory earning seven dollars a week before finally securing work as a café pianist. Eventually he formed his own orchestra, which focused on salon music in the European tradition, and in time his compositions attracted the interest of the Shubert brothers, who helped launch Romberg's Broadway career.

Romberg seemed determined to stand out as the least Americanized of the many Broadway composers who were immigrants or the children of immigrants, and followed the unconventional formula of emulating what he had heard back in Vienna in his youth. While others were assimilating the sounds of jazz or Tin Pan Alley, Romberg looked instead to the works of fellow Hungarian composer Franz Lehár, most famous for his operetta *The Merry Widow*, and other Old World role models. This very unjazzy formula led to successes with Romberg's adaptation of Franz Schubert's *Das Dreimäderlhaus*, launched on Broadway in 1921 as *Blossom Time*, which ran for 592 performances, as well as Romberg's follow-up efforts *The Student Prince* (1924), the longest-running Broadway show of the decade, *The Desert Song* (1926), and *The New Moon* (1928). In later years, Romberg became more skilled at emulating the conventional songwriting style associated with American musicals, but ironically found less success the more he adjusted to contemporary trends.

Romberg wrote two songs that have survived as jazz standards: "Softly, as in a Morning Sunrise" and "Lover, Come Back to Me," both from *The New Moon*. This show enjoyed a lengthy run on Broadway, and inspired two movie adaptations—both of which made significant alterations to the original story but retained "Lover, Come Back to Me." Yet anyone watching Grace Moore singing this song in the 1930 adaptation, reset in Russia, or Jeanette MacDonald, star of the 1940 version, delivering their chirpy, squeaky clean renditions, would have put long odds against this tune ever gaining a following among jazz musicians.

The composition was recorded by a few jazz bands in 1929 following its debut, and was even a modest hit for Paul Whiteman at the time, but then fell out of favor. "Lover, Come Back to Me" only gained traction among improvisers after its resurrection in the 1940 Hollywood remake of *The New Moon*. Yet, as recordings by Coleman Hawkins (1943), Lester Young (1946), and others testify, the preferred approach now was to speed up the tempo, purge the piece of its original quality as a lament for a lost lover, and turn it into a light, swinging jam number. Billie Holiday resisted this trend on her 1944 recording, which still stays true to Oscar Hammerstein's lyrics and their melancholy significations, but by the time she had recorded "Lover, Come Back to Me" with Oscar Peterson and Paul Quinichette in 1952, she too had bought into the faster and flashier conception of the song.

In its new guise, Romberg's work could be adopted for heated horn battles—as in Dizzy Gillespie's high stakes game of one-upmanship with Stan Getz from 1956, John Coltrane's 1958 treatment alongside Donald Byrd, or the Zoot Sims/Al Cohn sax duel recorded live at the Half Note in 1959. By the close of this period, the song's transformation was complete. Since that time, the standard has typically been treated as a set of blowing changes, chosen by musicians for demonstrations of speed and virtuosity or *mano a mano* combat with bandstand rivals.

That works for me. Each of these performances is viscerally exciting and testifies to the adaptability of the song and appeal of the harmonic progression. But this approach categorically does *not* work for a vocalist. The song, in its modern jazz guise, is bright and full of energy, while Hammerstein's lyrics convey something much different. Perhaps if someone came up with new words—"Lover, Let's Go on a Rollercoaster," or "Lover, Press that Pedal to the Metal"—singers could perform this song with the same verve and gusto that animate the horns. Until that day arrives, this song remains the property of the instrumentalists, or those rare vocalists who are willing to slow it down and resuscitate lyrics that lose their meaning when presented at warp speed.

RECOMMENDED VERSIONS

Paul Whiteman, New York, February 7, 1929

Andy Kirk, New York, December 13, 1937

Artie Shaw, New York, January 17, 1939

Coleman Hawkins, New York, December 18, 1943

Billie Holiday (with Eddie Heywood), New York, April 8, 1944

Lester Young, Los Angeles, January 18, 1946

Dizzy Gillespie (with Stan Getz), from *For Musicians Only*, Los Angeles, October 16, 1956

John Coltrane (with Donald Byrd), from *Black Pearls*, Hackensack, New Jersey, May 23, 1958

Zoot Sims and Al Cohn, from *Jazz Alive! A Night at the Half Note*, live at the Half Note, New York, February 6–7, 1959

Shelly Manne (with Art Pepper and Bill Watrous), from *Hollywood Jam*, Hollywood, May 4, 1981

Makoto Ozone, from *Nature Boys*, Los Angeles, October 4–5, 1995

Lover Man
Composed by Jimmy Davis, Ram Ramirez, and James Sherman

Nowadays they are called "one-hit wonders"—isolated successes by artists whose first chart-climbing song is also their last. Jimmy Davis, a soldier, had presented an early version of this piece to Billie Holiday before he was sent to Europe. She never saw him again, and he never enjoyed another comparable songwriting success (and do not confuse him with the Jimmie Davis who is listed as composer of "You Are My Sunshine" and later became governor of Louisiana). The same is true of pianist Rogelio "Ram" Ramirez, who worked with a wide range of jazz and blues acts over a lengthy career but remains best known for his contributions to this song. The third collaborator, Swing Era pianist and singer James Sherman, also found his claim to fame here, although both Davis and Ramirez downplayed Sherman's contribution to the now-famous composition.

Billie Holiday, in contrast, is anything but a one-hit wonder, yet "Lover Man" would be her last release to receive significant jukebox plays and crossover sales during her lifetime. Although "Lover Man" had been published in 1942, Holiday couldn't record it until 1944 due to the musicians' union strike that plagued the entertainment industry during the war years. When she finally got her chance, she insisted on performing the piece with strings rather than a standard jazz combo. The result is a more pop-oriented approach than one finds on other Holiday releases, but the record-buying audience responded enthusiastically. Jazz fans may prefer the singer's lesser-known live recordings of the song, for example tracks from the *Just Jazz* radio broadcast from June 1949 or her October 1951 performances at the Storyville Club in Boston.

Among more forward-looking jazz fans of the late 1940s, Sarah Vaughan's recording of "Lover Man" was even more influential than Lady Day's. But Vaughan had an unfair advantage: she was supported by the leading bebop artists of the day, with Charlie Parker providing obbligato accompaniment and Dizzy Gillespie contributing a solo—this track was the only vocal number at a session that also produced definitive versions of "Salt Peanuts" and "Hot House." Lennie Niehaus recalls studying Vaughan's "Lover Man" and using both the vocal and trumpet line in one of his early bebop charts. French classical composer Henri Dutilleux has also cited this recording when asked about jazz works that he found inspiring.

A year later, Charlie Parker recorded "Lover Man" at a session under his own leadership, and the resulting track stands out as the most controversial jazz release of the era. Parker had been drinking heavily in the period leading up to the date and was suffering from a host of physical disorders—often unable to score heroin, he would consume up to a quart of whiskey a day, or drink port, or take Benzedrine or whatever else he could lay his hands on. He arrived at the studio late and in a haggard, torporific state; a doctor who was on hand surmised that the altoist was suffering from alcoholism and malnutrition, and gave Parker six tablets of phenobarbital. Producer Ross Russell decided to proceed with the session, even though he needed to hold up Parker from behind during the recording of "Lover Man"—and, as the track makes clear, Bird still veered off microphone. That night Parker suffered a nervous breakdown at his hotel, was taken off by police, and eventually held for six months at Camarillo State Hospital. When he learned that "Lover Man" had been released, the altoist was angry, and though some have praised the recording, I find it painful to listen to the slurred phrasing and anguished sounds coming from the horn on this infamous track.

Parker's precedent notwithstanding, "Lover Man" has remained one of the most popular saxophone ballads. Most of the leading bop and postbop alto saxophonists—including Sonny Stitt, Phil Woods, Cannonball Adderley, Art Pepper, and Charles McPherson—have tried their hand at it. Lee Konitz has been an especially tireless proponent of "Lover Man." Recordings capture him performing the song on more than thirty occasions, but I would call particular attention to his 1953 rendition with Stan Kenton, my favorite ballad track by Konitz—here he offers up an ideal balance between the emotional and cerebral. Another memorable horn encounter finds Sonny Rollins matching up with Coleman Hawkins on an extended version of "Lover Man," and though slow numbers usually don't serve as effective vehicles for tenor battles, the give-and-take on this performance is riveting.

RECOMMENDED VERSIONS

Billie Holiday, New York, October 4, 1944

Dizzy Gillespie (with Sarah Vaughan), New York, May 11, 1945

Charlie Parker, Hollywood, July 29, 1946

Billie Holiday, live at Billy Berg's, Hollywood, June 2, 1949

Stan Kenton (with Lee Konitz), from *Sketches on Standards*, Hollywood, January 28, 1953

Johnny Griffin (with Wynton Kelly), from *Introducing Johnny Griffin*, Hackensack, New Jersey, April 17, 1956

Sonny Rollins and Coleman Hawkins, from *Sonny Meets Hawk!* New York, July 15, 1963

Thelonious Monk, from *The Complete London Collection*, London, November 15, 1971

Bill Evans and Stan Getz, from *But Beautiful*, live at the Jazz Middelheim festival, Antwerp, August 16, 1974

Jimmy Giuffre, Paul Bley, and Steve Swallow, from *Fly Away Little Bird*, New York, April 25, 1992

Lullaby of Birdland
Composed by George Shearing

In 1952, Morris Levy was ready to launch a radio program to promote his flourishing nightclub Birdland, and needed a theme song that could be played every hour on the hour. He sent the sheet music of his proposed number to pianist

George Shearing, who grumbled that he could write a much better song. A few days later, Shearing sat down to dinner at his home in Old Tappan, New Jersey, and was a few bites into his steak before he jumped up and hurried to the piano. The whole song had come to him almost in a flash, and within ten minutes Shearing had worked out the entire piece. The composer would later quip: "Since then I've been back to the same butcher several times and asked him if he could manage a repetition of that steak."

Levy accepted Shearing's song—on condition that the clubowner be granted publishing royalties. But in this instance, the bossman may well have earned his cut of the action. Levy kept "Lullaby of Birdland" on the airwaves, and when name jazz acts played at Birdland, they frequently performed the club's theme song. Indeed, one marvels at a standard by a modern jazz pianist that would be covered by artists as diverse as Duke Ellington (who kept it in his band's repertoire for more than a decade), Paul Bley (who inserted bits of polytonality into his treatment of it), Pérez Prado, and Lil Hardin Armstrong. The song has traveled far, and Shearing enjoyed telling of a French version whose title, when translated back into English, was rendered as "Lullaby of the Land of the Birds."

Shearing has always been a bit of a puzzle. At the keyboard he could do almost anything he put his mind to—as demonstrated by his various recordings of "Lullaby," over the years, in a daunting range of styles; yet the question remains of what it was he really wanted to achieve as an artist. He earned his best sales with a sound that veered dangerously close to elevator music, and even his finest work seems to convey the facile elegance of a player who didn't want to work up a sweat. But just when one was tempted to dismiss Shearing as a shallow popularizer, he would deliver some very deep performance that would show the levels this artist was capable of reaching.

To my mind, "Lullaby of Birdland" represents the more homogenized Shearing. His lesser-known composition "Conception" is not only a more interesting work, but one of the best modern jazz charts of the era. I would also favor other of the pianist's forgotten efforts—"How's Trix," "The Fourth Deuce," "Consternation"—over this jazzy jingle for a nightclub. By comparison with these more probing works, the melodic development of "Lullaby of Birdland" comes across as staid and formulaic.

That said, the song has inspired some noteworthy cover versions, as one would expect with a piece so widely performed: Stan Getz's interpretation, made only a short while after Shearing issued his own debut recording; Sarah Vaughan's rendition on a date with Clifford Brown; and—a recording that Shearing picked as his favorite take on his own song—a jaunty outing by Erroll Garner.

RECOMMENDED VERSIONS

George Shearing, New York, July 17, 1952

Stan Getz, from *The Getz Age*, New York, December 19, 1952

Erroll Garner, from *Erroll Garner at the Piano*, February 27, 1953

Ella Fitzgerald, from *Lullabies of Birdland*, New York, June 4, 1954

Sarah Vaughan (with Clifford Brown and Herbie Mann), from *Sarah Vaughan with Clifford Brown*, December 16, 1954

Duke Ellington, from *Piano in the Background*, Hollywood, June 20, 1960

Jaki Byard, from *Hi-Fly*, New York, January 30, 1962

Paul Bley, from *The Nearness of You*, Copenhagen, November 21, 1988

Lee Konitz, Brad Mehldau, Charlie Haden, and Paul Motian, from *Live at Birdland*, live at Birdland, New York, December 2009

Lush Life
Composed by Billy Strayhorn

"Lush Life" ranks among the most sophisticated jazz ballads—whether one considers its intricate harmonic palette, its elaborate structure, or just its world-weary lyrics. Even the key—D flat—was an uncharacteristic choice for a jazz chart, reinforcing the sense that this was an art song, not a pop tune. Given these ingredients, one wonders if it is really possible that Billy Strayhorn composed "Lush Life" while still a teenager? Friends recall him singing parts of it a cappella as early as 1933, when the composer would have been 17 or perhaps had just turned 18. Yet a frightening maturity seems to inform this piece from its musing opening verse to its final held high note.

When Strayhorn completed it in 1936, the song's working title was "Life Is Lonely"—a pithy summary of the defining mood of the composition. The use of the word "gay" in the lyrics may be significant—Strayhorn being that greatest of rarities at the time, a gay jazz musician who did not disguise his sexual preference. Scholars have debated the semantic resonance of the term "gay" back in the Great Depression as well as the likelihood that Strayhorn would deliberately play on its double meaning. The word shows up again in his composition "Something to Live For" from this same period—in both contexts open to double entendre interpretation. In a song already rich with multiple meanings—even the title "Lush Life" can be taken two ways—the hypothesis that a coded additional level of signification resides in the lyrics cannot be resolved with any finality; yet even if Strayhorn intended this, I suspect he also felt confident that his song lost little in its overall impact when heard by audiences who missed the innuendo.

The song itself stayed in the closet far too long—not receiving its public debut until Ellington's 1948 Carnegie Hall concert. Here, Strayhorn accompanied singer Kay Davis in a duet rendition; strangely, Ellington introduced "Lush Life" as a new composition and described this segment of the concert as an "extra added thought." The audience responded with enthusiasm, and Strayhorn played with great passion during his brief solo interlude. Yet "Lush Life" was rarely revisited by Ellington after that and was never featured in a commercial recording by the full band.

Certainly the song is not an easy vehicle for a soloist, but that can hardly explain Ellington's reluctance to showcase this gem—a perfect composition, in my opinion, one in which the melodic phrases, harmonies, and poetic sentiments are each unconventional yet sublime. Add to this the sheer audacity of writing a love song that denounces romance with such vehemence—to a degree that no other song that I am aware of, from any genre, has matched—yet still shows such a sadly broken heart beneath. If I were allowed to steal a single song from the twentieth century and make it my own, without question it would be "Lush Life."

Fortunately, others stepped in to embrace a composition that Ellington felt disinclined, for whatever reason, to promote. Only one artist took the plunge in the 1940s—Nat King Cole, who performed "Lush Life" with great sensitivity—and in the early 1950s the song's biggest supporter was an unlikely one, Swing Era trumpeter Harry James, who recorded "Lush Life" on four separate occasions. In the middle of the decade, a number of prominent singers took up the cause of "Lush Life," including Carmen McRae (1956), Sarah Vaughan (1956), and Ella Fitzgerald (1957), contributing to the gradual acceptance of the Strayhorn song as a standard, still little known among the general public but now showing up occasionally on the bandstand.

These earlier precedents pale in comparison with the influence of John Coltrane in giving prominence to "Lush Life." Coltrane left behind two recordings of the song. The first comes from a 1958 session and finds the tenorist stretching out in a 14-minute version that gives Coltrane (as well as trumpeter Donald Byrd and pianist Red Garland) a chance to solo. But most listeners prefer the shorter performance from 1963, on which Coltrane is joined by vocalist Johnny Hartman in an exquisite rendering of the Strayhorn song. This track is a perennial favorite with listeners—a survey from 2011 found fans placing it at #32 in a survey to determine the most "quintessential" jazz performances—and rightly so.

Coltrane and Hartman cast a long shadow over all later attempts to perform "Lush Life." Sometimes the debt to them is acknowledged openly—as in Kurt Elling's tribute from 2009—but even when unspoken it still hovers over the proceedings. The most successful versions of this song in the post-Trane era have usually been the most understated. Stan Getz, who frequently performed "Lush Life" in concert, felt no compulsion to improvise over the changes, and could mesmerize audiences with a simple, heartfelt melody statement. Joe

Henderson is even more austere in his 1991 treatment, dismissing the band and performing Strayhorn's ballad on unaccompanied tenor sax.

RECOMMENDED VERSIONS

Billy Strayhorn and Kay Davis, live at Carnegie Hall, New York, November 13, 1948

Nat King Cole, New York, March 29, 1949

Carmen McRae, from *Blue Moon*, New York, March 29, 1956

John Coltrane (with Donald Byrd), from *Lush Life*, Hackensack, New Jersey, January 10, 1958

John Coltrane and Johnny Hartman, from *John Coltrane and Johnny Hartman*, Englewood Cliffs, New Jersey, March 7, 1963

Stan Getz, from *Captain Marvel*, New York, March 3, 1972

Joe Henderson, from *Lush Life: The Music of Billy Strayhorn*, Englewood Cliffs, New Jersey, September 3–8, 1991

Kurt Elling from *Dedicated to You: Kurt Elling Sings the Music of Coltrane and Hartman*, live in the Allen Room at Frederick P. Rose Hall, New York, January 21, 2009

Mack the Knife
Composed by Kurt Weill, with lyrics by Bertolt Brecht (English lyrics by Marc Blitzstein)

I often cringe when I hear this song, perhaps a subliminal holdover from a bad trio gig from years ago. During the course of our regular Saturday engagement, the cook—the cook!—would stroll out from the kitchen and insist on singing with the band. He then would proceed to deliver "Mack the Knife" in a campy, exaggerated Louis Armstrong voice. Needless to say, the audience would go bonkers, cheering and screaming in a way that they never did for our intelligent mix of hard bop, modal, and other jazz esoterica. Go figure! In many instances, our man in the white puffy hat would be emboldened and demand to do another Louis Armstrong imitation, usually a version of "Sweet Georgia Brown" enhanced with his own quasi-obscene lyrics. At the end of that engagement, I gave a fatal dagger thrust to "Mack the Knife" and haven't played it since.

Clearly others do not share my aversion. A host of famous recordings have kept this song—sometimes also recorded under the name "Moritat" (which cheerily translates as "murderous deed")—in the standard repertoire. Even so, "Mack the Knife" was slow in finding an audience outside of Europe, where it made its debut in the 1928 Berlin production *Die Dreigroschenoper* (*The Threepenny Opera*), an adaptation by Bertolt Brecht and Kurt Weill of John Gay's *The Beggar's Opera* from 1728. The Brecht and Weill work was widely translated and first appeared on a US stage in 1933, closing after only a dozen performances. But two decades later, a popular off-Broadway engagement at the Theater de Lys (now the Lucille Lortel Theatre) in Greenwich Village turned *The Threepenny Opera* and "Mack the Knife" into an American success story. The show ran, with only a brief hiatus, until 1961—a total stint of more than 2,700 performances. Marc Blitzstein's translation (one of at least eight English versions) toned down the more unseemly references in the lyrics, paving the way for Mack's rehabilitation as a jukebox success, but earning the translator the nickname "Marc the Knife" for his considerable excisions.

Jazz musicians were paying attention. In 1956, Louis Armstrong's spirited vocal performance of "Mack the Knife" reached number 20 on the *Billboard* chart. Lotte Lenya, Weill's wife and leading vocal interpreter, was a guest in the studio when it was recorded, and though her attempt to engage in a jazz duet with Armstrong proved a failure and was never released, he tackled it on his own and offered up a peculiar tribute—even including Lenya's name in his list of Mack's conquests. Several instrumental recordings of the song garnered airplay around this time, including singles by Dick Hyman and Les Paul, both of which surprisingly recapture some of the flavor of the original German version of this work. But Bobby Darin's huge hit recording of "Mack the Knife" outstripped all these predecessors, holding on to the top spot on the Hot 100 for nine weeks in 1959 and earning the singer a Grammy for Record of the Year.

The following year, Ella Fitzgerald put her own lasting stamp on this song, forgetting the lyrics but making up new ones on the spot during a live recording from Berlin, the same city where the song had made its debut some 32 years earlier. Fitzgerald would deliver more polished versions in later concerts, but producer Norman Granz decided to release this beguiling performance as a single—and was rewarded with a hit that spent 14 weeks on the chart and earned the singer Grammy Awards for both the record and the specific track.

The two-beat feel to this composition makes it an unlikely vehicle for modern jazz, but that didn't stop Sonny Rollins from featuring "Moritat" on his well-known 1956 *Saxophone Colossus* project. The song also shows up on Wayne Shorter's debut leader date from 1959, where it serves as an effective vehicle for some Coltrane-esque sax fireworks. But these updatings tend to be exceptions. Although cutting-edge players occasionally take a stab at this song even today, "Mack" typically prefers to associate with trad jazz musicians, who find that this German import mixes well with their various New Orleans– and Chicago-bred standards.

RECOMMENDED VERSIONS

Hans Schindler and the Haller Revue Jazz Orchestra, Berlin, January 1929

Louis Armstrong, from *Satchmo the Great*, New York, September 28, 1955

Dick Hyman, from *The Unforgettable Sound of the Dick Hyman Trio*, New York, circa 1955

Sonny Rollins (with Tommy Flanagan), from *Saxophone Colossus*, Hackensack, New Jersey, June 22, 1956

Anita O'Day (with an arrangement by Jimmy Giuffre), from *Cool Heat*, Los Angeles, April 7, 1959

Wayne Shorter (with Lee Morgan), from *Introducing Wayne Shorter*, New York, November 10, 1959

Ella Fitzgerald, from *Ella in Berlin*, live at Deutschlandhalle, Berlin, February 13, 1960

Kenny Garrett (with Mulgrew Miller), from *African Exchange Student*, New York, 1990

Arturo Sandoval (with Clark Terry), from *Swingin'*, New York, January 6–9, 1996

Nicholas Payton (with Dr. John), from *Dear Louis*, New York, September–October 2000

Maiden Voyage
Composed by Herbie Hancock

In accounts of jazz during the tumultuous 1960s, the limelight tends to shine most brightly on John Coltrane, Miles Davis, and Ornette Coleman as the towering figures who pushed the music forward. Yet the creative strides made by Herbie Hancock during the decade are equally impressive. In fact, it would be hard to find another figure from the annals of jazz who came further or covered more ground during any ten-year slice of the music's history.

At the start of this period, Hancock was studying with Chicago pianist Chris Anderson and taking classes at Grinnell College. He didn't even make his debut leader date, *Takin' Off*, until 1962. But the name of this project was an apt one, with Hancock seemingly moving to a higher level with each passing year, not only releasing a series of stunning—and constantly evolving—projects under his own name, but also playing a key role in most of Miles Davis's albums of the era, and serving as sideman on more than 30 projects for the Blue Note label. Yet Hancock also shows up on other classic dates for RCA, Columbia, Verve, CTI, and Atlantic during the course of the decade. And all this recording happened during a period of constant touring and live performing, again both as sideman and leader. By the end of the decade, Hancock had embraced electric keyboards and a cutting edge fusion of jazz, rock and funk elements that would exert enormous influence during the 1970s. The scope and quantity of all this music making is overwhelming, but the consistency and sheer ingenuity of his keyboard work—even on the casual sessions that most journeyman players toss off with little thought—continually stand out amidst this massive oeuvre.

Yet if I had to pick a single session to encapsulate this period of Hancock's career, I would highlight the *Maiden Voyage* album released by Blue Note at almost the midpoint of the decade. The title track never received the airplay of Hancock's "Watermelon Man," which was a top 10 hit in an arrangement by Mongo Santamaría, but it is equally memorable and far less conventional. The economy of means is striking. Relying on only four suspended chords and a melody consisting mostly of high held notes, the song conveys a floating, unresolved quality that is countered by an urgent rhythmic figure that provides the hook for the whole endeavor.

Although there are precedents—the heavy reliance on suspended chords was a trademark of McCoy Tyner's piano work during this same period, and uncluttered structures had been a trademark of modal jazz since the late 1950s—Hancock creates something new here, a composition that seems to define its own terms of engagement. Yet it is characteristic of Hancock's work of this period that, by the time he got to his next leader projects, he had moved on to something else—a film soundtrack to a Michelangelo Antonioni film (*Blow Up*) and an intriguing combo album (*Speak Like a Child*) featuring flugelhorn, alto flute, and bass trombone. And these two were also just way stations on to the next new thing on Hancock's busy agenda.

The original recording from *Maiden Voyage* is the place to start in appreciating this composition, and that track is enlivened not just by Hancock's contribution but also features one of Freddie Hubbard's most-admired trumpet solos. Hancock made a number of later recordings of this work—I especially like his solo performance recorded in Japan in 1974 but, sad to say, the *Dedication* album on which it was released, was kept off the market in the United States and remains the pianist's least well-known leader date from the era. Two early cover versions—by Bobby Hutcherson and Denny Zeitlin—are also noteworthy. But the most provocative reworking of "Maiden Voyage" comes from Robert Glasper, who offers a mashup of the Hancock standard with Radiohead's "Everything Is in Its Right Place" on his *In My Element* CD.

RECOMMENDED VERSIONS

Herbie Hancock, from *Maiden Voyage*, Englewood Cliffs, New Jersey, March 17, 1965

Bobby Hutcherson, from *Happenings*, Englewood Cliffs, New Jersey, February 8, 1966

Denny Zeitlin, from *Zeitgeist*, Hollywood, March 18, 1967

Herbie Hancock, from *Dedication*, Tokyo, July 29, 1974

Leny Andrade (with Fred Hersch), from *Maiden Voyage*, New York, December 21–22, 1993

Dianne Reeves and Geri Allen, from *Bob Belden's Shades of Blue*, New York, December 7, 1994

Robert Glasper, from *In My Element*, New York, September–November 2006

The Man I Love

Composed by George Gershwin, with lyrics by Ira Gershwin

This song had a long, troubled history before becoming a hit. "The Man I Love" initially appeared in the 1924 musical *Lady Be Good*, where it served as a feature for Adele Astaire—but only lasted a week before getting yanked from the show. The tune was recycled in 1927 for *Strike Up the Band*, but that production never made it to New York, and when the musical was retooled and revived in 1930 the song was no longer part of it. "The Man I Love" was next assigned to the 1928 Flo Ziegfeld show *Rosalie* but was cut before opening night (and, if Ira Gershwin can be believed, wasn't even heard in rehearsals before getting axed). At this point, the Gershwins' publisher Max Dreyfus, in a desperate gesture, convinced the composers to take a one-third reduction in their royalty rate as an incentive for bandleaders to release "The Man I Love" on record.

This last-gasp strategy worked, and four different recordings of "The Man I Love"—by Marion Harris, Sophie Tucker, Fred Rich, and Paul Whiteman—were top 20 hits in 1928. The latter version features a dramatic arrangement by Ferde Grofé and includes a sax interlude by Frankie Trumbauer, best known for his collaborations with Bix Beiderbecke but here delivering one of his better solos from his stint with the Whiteman orchestra. The composition also became closely associated with torch singer Helen Morgan, and Gershwin himself gave her much of the credit for its eventual popularity; but, strange to say, she made no commercial recording of this signature song.

Benny Goodman brought the piece back into the limelight almost a decade later, enjoying a hit with his 1937 quartet recording of "The Man I Love." Goodman continued to feature the work in a variety of settings—with a combo at Carnegie Hall in 1938, in an Eddie Sauter big band arrangement from 1940, with his bop-oriented band from the late 1940s, with symphony orchestra in the 1950s, with various pick-up bands in later decades—for the rest of his career. But equally influential in jazz circles was Coleman Hawkins's 1943 recording, which finds the tenorist constructing a harmonically expansive solo that ranks among the finest sax improvisations of the era. Over the next 18 months, more than two dozen cover versions of "The Man I Love" were recorded—more than in the entire decade leading up to Hawk's session.

This song's popularity has never waned in later years. The hand-me-down that couldn't find a home in a Broadway show eventually became one of Gershwin's most beloved and recorded compositions. British composer and musicologist Wilfrid Mellers would extol "The Man I Love" as the "most moving pop song of our time." Others have been equally lavish in their praise. "This is the music of America," proclaimed Gershwin's friend and patron Otto Kahn. "It will live as long as a Schubert lieder."

In truth, the melodic material employed here is quite simple—many of the phrases merely move up and down a half or full step before concluding up a minor third. Gershwin employs this device no fewer than 15 times during the course of a 32-bar song. Yet the repetition of this motif contrasts most markedly with the constant movement in the song's harmonies. The contrast gives added emphasis to Gershwin's repeated use of the flat seven in the vocal line, an intrinsically bluesy choice that transforms what might otherwise sound like a folkish nineteenth-century melody into a consummate Jazz Age lament.

RECOMMENDED VERSIONS

Paul Whiteman (with Frank Trumbauer), New York, May 16, 1928

Benny Goodman (with Teddy Wilson, Lionel Hampton, and Gene Krupa), live at Carnegie Hall, New York, January 16, 1938

Billie Holiday (with Lester Young), New York, December 13, 1939

Coleman Hawkins, New York, December 23, 1943

Lester Young (with Nat King Cole and Buddy Rich), Los Angeles, March–April 1946

Art Tatum, live at the Shrine Auditorium, Los Angeles, April 2, 1949

Miles Davis (with Thelonious Monk and Milt Jackson), from *Miles Davis and the Modern Jazz Giants*, Hackensack, New Jersey, December 24, 1954

Art Pepper (with Red Garland), from *Art Pepper Meets the Rhythm Section*, Los Angeles, January 19, 1957

Mary Lou Williams, from *Live at the Cookery*, live at the Cookery, New York, November 1975

Fred Hersch, from *Heartsongs*, New York, December 4–5, 1989

Herbie Hancock (with Joni Mitchell and Wayne Shorter), from *Gershwin's World*, New York (March–April 1998) and Los Angeles (June 1998)

Manhã de Carnaval

Composed by Luiz Bonfá, with lyrics by Antônio Maria (English lyrics by Carl Sigman)

This song shows up under a confusing array of names on jazz recordings. Often it is called "Manhã de Carnaval," or the English translation of that title, "Morning of the Carnival." In the late 1960s, it was redubbed "A Day in the Life of a Fool," with English lyrics by Carl Sigman, and generated a modest hit for Jack Jones as well as a host of cover versions under its new title. In addition, it has been frequently recorded as "The Theme from *Black Orpheus*"—although I have sometimes heard people use that name to refer to the "Samba de Orfeu."

which is another popular song from that film by the same composer. To add to the bewilderment, George Jones enjoyed a country and western hit in 1972 entitled "A Day in the Life of a Fool," which is a completely different tune, and one that you will never hear a Carioca singing in public or private.

I wouldn't be surprised if the identity of the composer has also caused confusion over the years. Many jazz fans probably assume this song was written by Antonio Carlos Jobim, given its similarity in style and conception to the bossa nova pieces that Jobim created during this same period. In fact, Jobim also composed music for the 1959 film *Black Orpheus* (*Orfeu Negro*) in which "Manhã de Carnaval" made its debut. But Luiz Bonfá, a guitarist from Rio de Janeiro and occasional songwriter, is the source of this oft-recorded tune, which turned out to be the most popular piece on a soundtrack album that still remains, so many years later, a worldwide best-seller.

The song is now entrenched in the jazz repertoire, but it took some time before non-Brazilians mastered the bossa nova rhythm that is now second nature to jazz players. Vince Guaraldi recorded "Manhã de Carnaval" for his best-selling 1963 album *Jazz Impressions of Black Orpheus*, but adopted a straight swing with walking bass support more akin to West Coast jazz than the hot new thing from Rio. A few months later, Dizzy Gillespie tried for a generic Latin beat on his rendition of "Manhã de Carnaval," and although he captures a dance rhythm that eludes Guaraldi, he makes the bossa sound like something out of one of those Havana casinos that Castro had recently shut down. Stan Getz presents a more characteristically Brazilian sensibility in his version, recorded three months later, and delivers a first-rate solo, but the big band chart here sometimes weighs down the proceedings.

These recordings have their virtues, but for a more authentic bossa nova of the period you are directed to João Gilberto's performance from 1959 or Sérgio Mendes's 1963 recording, eventually released on the *Quiet Nights* LP, but unfortunately kept off the market until after the bossa fad had faded. The composer also introduced his personal interpretation to US audiences at a November 1962 Carnegie Hall concert that was recorded and released commercially.

Before long, jazz players had assimilated the nuances of the style, and most recordings of "Manhã de Carnaval" made post-1965 reflect either a firm command of the idiom or a deliberate attempt to subvert it. My favorites include Paul Desmond's live recording at Toronto's Bourbon Street club, McCoy Tyner's collaboration with Freddie Hubbard from 1980, and Tuck Andress's extravagant solo guitar rendition from his 1990 *Reckless Precision* project.

RECOMMENDED VERSIONS

João Gilberto, from *The Legendary João Gilberto*, Rio de Janeiro, July 2, 1959

Vince Guaraldi, from *Jazz Impressions of Black Orpheus*, San Francisco, November 1961 and February 1962

Dizzy Gillespie, from *New Wave*, New York, May 1962

Stan Getz (with an arrangement by Gary McFarland), from *Big Band Bossa Nova*, New York, August 27, 1962

Luiz Bonfá, from *Bossa Nova at Carnegie Hall*, live at Carnegie Hall, New York, November 21, 1962

Sérgio Mendes, from *Quiet Nights*, New York, 1963

Paul Desmond (with Ed Bickert), from *Live*, live at Bourbon Street, Toronto, October 25–November 1, 1975

Art Pepper (with Cal Tjader and Clare Fischer), from *Tokyo Debut*, live at Yubin Chobin Hall, Tokyo, April 5, 1977

McCoy Tyner (with Freddie Hubbard), from *4X4*, Englewood Cliffs, New Jersey, May 28, 1980

Tuck Andress, from *Reckless Precision*, Menlo Park, California, 1990

Mean to Me
Composed by Fred E. Ahlert, with lyrics by Roy Turk

Billie Holiday was saddled with many second-rate songs during her visits to the recording studio, especially in the early days of her career, yet her ability to infuse real feeling into the typically ersatz emotion of the proffered lyrics makes virtually every one of her releases from this period worthy of attention. Often her interpretation is the only reason why listeners today would pay any attention to these compositions, and in some instances she took a song that might otherwise have gone by the wayside and established it as a standard.

"Mean to Me" is a case in point. This number is a strange hybrid, half torch song and half novelty tune, with the main hook deriving from the double meaning of "mean." Billie Holiday was not the first to sing it. The Dorsey brothers had been involved in several recordings from 1929. Annette Hanshaw, in February of that year, tackled it at a sprightly pace, and three weeks later, Ruth Etting, accompanied by many of the same musicians, slowed it down considerably and recrafted "Mean to Me" as a sentimental parlor song. The latter version was a million-seller, helped along by "Button Up Your Overcoat" on the flip side. But after the stock market crash in October, "Mean to Me" fell out of favor— audiences were looking for more upbeat songs as the economy faltered—with only a handful of new jazz versions circulating before Teddy Wilson decided to resurrect it as a feature for Holiday at his band's May 1937 session.

Holiday was 22 years old at the time, yet the emotional maturity she brought to "Mean to Me" belied her young years. The result was a top 10 hit for Wilson, and a definitive version of the song, its cutesy attitudes not completely extinguished but now anchored in a plausible sense of heartbreak. Holiday was aided and abetted by her longtime collaborator, saxophonist Lester Young who, for his part, would record an exquisite instrumental version of the same song a decade later in a trio setting with Nat King Cole on piano and Buddy Rich manning the drums.

"Mean to Me" owes most of its subsequent popularity to singers, who have periodically brought it back to the public's attention. At one of her first sessions, Sarah Vaughan adopted a more assertive stance on "Mean to Me" than Holiday, coming across as a lady who could definitely be mean in return. She was helped in her attempts to modernize the song by a dream bebop lineup, which included Dizzy Gillespie, Charlie Parker, and Max Roach. Vaughan would record "Mean to Me" on several subsequent occasions, including a 1961 session with Count Basie. The following year Ella Fitzgerald included "Mean to Me" on her Grammy-winning *Ella Swings Brightly with Nelson* album for Verve. But the most widely heard later version must be, hands down, Diana Ross's rendition for the Billie Holiday biopic *Lady Sings the Blues*. The soundtrack reached the top spot in the *Billboard* album chart in April 1973, and introduced a new generation of listeners to "Mean to Me."

The song survives today, but less on its own merits than as a Holiday tribute or period piece. Yet this composition is not without its potential for clever reworkings and updatings. Back in the early 1960s, the Modern Jazz Quartet showed that the piece could inspire fanciful counterpoint, and Betty Carter offered such a quirky, personal interpretation on her *Modern Sound* project from this same period, that one ever-so-briefly forgets Holiday's looming shadow. I am also quite taken with Curtis Counce's hard bop arrangement of this song from 1957, which deserves to be far better known. But these are exceptions to the more mundane approaches to "Mean to Me" that predominate—so much so that this jazz song may end its life more at home with cabaret performers and those deliberately retro singers who would rather evoke the past than update its legacy.

RECOMMENDED VERSIONS

Annette Hanshaw (with Tommy Dorsey and Jimmy Dorsey), New York, February
    20, 1929

Teddy Wilson (with Billie Holiday and Lester Young), New York, May 11, 1937

Sarah Vaughan (with Dizzy Gillespie and Charlie Parker), New York, May 25, 1945

Woody Herman (with Bill Harris), live at Carnegie Hall, New York, March 25, 1946

Lester Young (with Nat King Cole and Buddy Rich), Los Angeles, March–April 1946

Curtis Counce (with Harold Land), from *Carl's Blues*, Los Angeles, September 3,
    1957

Betty Carter, from *Modern Sound*, New York, August 18, 1960

Count Basie and Sarah Vaughan, from *Count Basie/Sarah Vaughan*, New York, January 10–12, 1961

Ella Fitzgerald (with an arrangement by Nelson Riddle), from *Ella Swings Brightly with Nelson*, Los Angeles, November 13, 1961

Modern Jazz Quartet, from *The Sheriff*, New York, May 16, 1963

Diana Ross, from the soundtrack to *Lady Sings the Blues*, Hollywood, 1972

Carmen McRae (with Clifford Jordan), from *Any Old Time*, New York, June 23, 1986

Meditation
Composed by Antonio Carlos Jobim, with lyrics by Newton Mendonça

"Meditation"—or "Meditação" as it was originally known in Brazil—enjoyed some airplay during the height of the bossa nova craze, but never quite achieved hit status. Charlie Byrd's single reached number #66 on the *Billboard* Hot 100 in March 1963, and Pat Boone's recording (with English lyrics by Norman Gimbel) placed briefly at #91 that same month. Three years later, Claudine Longet's dreamy rendition of the song, which found her singing the lyrics in French (by Eddy Marnay) and English, got no higher than #98. Stan Getz, who made other bossa nova songs into hit records, might well have done better, but he steered clear of this song even as he recorded so many other Jobim compositions. Despite this lackluster start, "Meditation" has found favor with musicians and earned a place in the standard jazz repertoire.

The song is aptly titled. Even the chord progression possesses a calming, centering quality. After the first two bars, with its lulling tonic major, Jobim moves down a half step for his next chord; those familiar with the harmonic pyrotechnics of this songwriter will now expect some elaborate modulation, but instead—surprise!—the composer returns back to the same hypnotic tonic major. The overall effect is of a song circling in on itself. The melody itself adds to the meditative effect, alternating between long, lingering phrases built on the sixth, perhaps the most relaxing of the scale tones outside the chord notes themselves, and a series of gently descending phrases in half-steps played in a rhythm of three notes against two beats.

The reflective quality is so pronounced that performers will have a hard time imposing a different personality on this song. Even a flashy jazz extrovert such as Oscar Peterson seemed to realize this, paring away at the excesses of his style and taking a decidedly contemplative angle in his reading of this work, and a similarly chastened approach can be heard from Dexter Gordon on his 1969 recording of "Meditation." Such examples notwithstanding, "Meditation" has typically been found in the repertoires of artists known for their sense of understatement. Excellent examples can be found on recordings by Paul Desmond, Blossom Dearie, and Harry Allen.

RECOMMENDED VERSIONS

João Gilberto, from *The Legendary João Gilberto*, Rio de Janeiro, March 28, 1960

Charlie Byrd, from *Bossa Nova Pelos Passaros*, New York, October 5, 1962

Sérgio Mendes, from *Quiet Nights*, New York, 1963

Oscar Peterson, from *Soul Español*, Chicago, December 12–14, 1966

Blossom Dearie, from *Soon It's Gonna Rain*, London, late 1967

Dexter Gordon (with Barry Harris), from *More Power!*, New York, April 4, 1969

Paul Desmond, from *Like Someone in Love*, live at Bourbon Street, Toronto, March 29, 1975

Ray Brown (with Gene Harris), from *The Red Hot Ray Brown Trio*, live at the Blue Note, New York, November–December 1985

Harry Allen, from *Eu Não Quero Dançar—I Won't Dance*, New York, December 18–19, 1997

Memories of You
Composed by Eubie Blake, with lyrics by Andy Razaf

Eubie Blake's 100th birthday in 1983 was a major event, covered by newspapers and TV reporters. Too bad that the dates didn't align with census data, passport info, social security files, and other official documents—all of which placed Blake's birth in 1887, not 1883. So Mr. Blake only lived to the ripe age of 96. But his importance in American music is still secure, even if he never arrived at the century mark. In particular, his song "Memories of You"—introduced on Broadway as part of *Lew Leslie's Blackbirds of 1930*—is a much beloved standard that has stood the test of time. It remains popular with stride and swing players, and is susceptible to sly modern updating (hear Monk's version) as well. Certainly this tune has appeared in some surprising places over the years: for example, backing a montage during Johnny Carson's final appearance on *The Tonight Show* or showing up at the White House where Blake himself played it for President Jimmy Carter.

The song is also noteworthy for establishing a new instrument in the jazz band. Louis Armstrong was recording "Memories of You" for the Okeh label and noticed a strange metal contraption in the studio, a kind of modified xylophone with aluminum bars instead of wooden ones. The vibraharp, as it was called then—nowadays, the "vibes" is the common appellation—was used by NBC Radio, which shared the studio, for their station identification: *"N-B-C"*— *ding, dong, ding*. Armstrong turned to Lionel Hampton, the drummer on the session, and asked: "Can you play it?" "I was a young kid, full of confidence," Hampton later recalled, "and I said, 'Sure.'" Hampton saw that the layout of the notes was the same as a keyboard, so he performed an ad lib imitation of Armstrong's famous solo on "Cornet Chop Suey." Armstrong was floored. "Come on," he said, "we going to put this on a record." The next take of "Memories of You" was the first recording of the vibes on a jazz tune.

Benny Goodman may have done even more than Armstrong in establishing "Memories of You" as a widely played jazz standard. The Casa Loma Orchestra, a role model for Goodman's hotter style, had already proven that this song could serve as a suitable platform for Swing Era jazz—and Sonny Dunham contributed such a confident, fluid solo that, in the words of one critic, "for the rest of his career he owned the song, much in the way Bunny Berigan owned 'I Can't Get Started.'" Yet it would be hard to top the lineup Goodman showcased for his 1939 sextet session, when the clarinetist's lyrical improvisation was followed by fluent solos by Lionel Hampton (again putting his stamp on this tune) and the young guitar sensation Charlie Christian. Goodman featured this song a few weeks later at the *Spirituals to Swing* Carnegie Hall concert, and kept the number in his repertoire for the rest of his life; his discography includes more than two dozen versions of "Memories of You," and his cumulative contributions in royalty checks to Eubie Blake must have amounted to a sizable income. When the song had a second wind in the mid-1950s, Goodman was again an instigator—it was featured in the 1956 biopic *The Benny Goodman Story* and became a hit for the vocal group The Four Coins. Their version stayed on the *Billboard* chart for four months and reached as high as #22. Goodman's recording with Rosemary Clooney did even better, peaking at #20.

But you won't really know this song unless you hear it played by a first-rate trad-style piano player. Eubie Blake obliged on a number of occasions—he liked to close out his sets with his famous tune, and did so to good effect amidst an all-star lineup of keyboardists, at the New School for Social Research in April 1972. Art Tatum recorded "Memories of You" as part of his solo piano project for Norman Granz, and though the first half of his performance is a rubato exercise in baroque excess, he delivers some great slow stride once he falls into tempo. One of my favorite versions finds Jaki Byard, a modernist who deeply understood the stride tradition, performing "Memories of You" on an unfairly forgotten Prestige session with Rahsaan Roland Kirk from 1968.

But for combining the traditional and transgressive in the same performance it would be hard to top Mingus and Monk, who both recorded Blake's song in the late 1950s. Mingus featured it on both his combo recording *East Coasting* and his quirky but surprisingly accomplished solo keyboard album

Mingus Plays Piano. Monk, who was schooled on stride before he strayed from the Harlem school, delivered a classic solo rendition at a Riverside session from 1956. These two artists became all the more influential after their deaths, and their advocacy no doubt remains a major reason why this very old-fashioned song is still fodder for jazz players in the new millennium.

RECOMMENDED VERSIONS

Louis Armstrong, Los Angeles, October 16, 1930

Casa Loma Orchestra, New York, December 1, 1937

Benny Goodman (with Lionel Hampton and Charlie Christian), New York, November 22, 1939

Art Tatum, from *The Art Tatum Solo Masterpieces, Vol. 5*, Los Angeles, December 28, 1953

Benny Goodman (with Rosemary Clooney), from *Date with the King*, New York, November 14, 1955

Thelonious Monk, from *The Unique*, Hackensack, New Jersey, March 17, 1956

Charles Mingus, from *East Coasting*, New York, August 1957

Jaki Byard (with Rahsaan Roland Kirk), from *The Jaki Byard Experience*, New York, September 17, 1968

Eubie Blake, from *Jazz Piano Masters*, live at the New School for Social Research, New York, April 10, 1972

Jessica Williams, from *More for Monk*, Capitola, California, 2002

Fred Hersch, from *Alone at the Vanguard*, live at the Village Vanguard, New York, December 5, 2010

Milestones
Composed by Miles Davis

Consider this piece as a warm-up for the modal explorations of *Kind of Blue*, which Miles Davis recorded the following year. "This was the first record where I started to write in the modal form and on 'Milestones,' the title track, I really used that form," Davis would later explain. "When you play in this way, you can go on forever. You don't have to worry about changes. . . . You can do more with the musical line. The challenge here, when you work in the modal way, is to see how inventive you can become melodically."

Around this time, Davis had conceived the idea for modal improvisation after seeing a New York performance of the Ballet Africaine from Guinea. The excitement of the rhythms here was married to a more static harmonic base—Davis was especially impressed by the use of the thumb piano, an instrument that can only play within a single mode, lacking the ability to adjust to the different scales of modern Western music. What others would see as a limitation struck Davis as a liberating alternative to the formulas of chord-based improvisation. "I think a movement is beginning in jazz away from the conventional string of chords, and a return to emphasis on melodic rather than harmonic variation," Davis noted in an interview with Nat Hentoff from 1958. "There will be fewer chords but infinite possibilities as to what to do with them."

Yet modern-day newcomers to *Milestones* expecting to hear anticipations of the more introspective mood of *Kind of Blue* may be surprised at the intensity and drive of Davis's February 1958 album. As the title track demonstrates, modal jazz doesn't need to sacrifice energy along with the chord changes—a learning that John Coltrane (who is featured here) took with him to his classic 1960s quartet.

The stir caused by *Kind of Blue* no doubt also contributed to the popularity of "Milestones," as more and more jazz artists decided to try their hand at modal improvisation. Bill Evans recorded the number at his influential live Village Vanguard date in 1961. A few months later, Mark Murphy added lyrics to "Milestones" for his *Rah* album, and the following year Gerald Wilson recorded a big band arrangement of the piece with his L.A.-based ensemble. Other notable cover versions include Wynton Kelly's performance at the Half Note from 1965 and Herbie Hancock's little-known 1977 trio version with Ron Carter and Tony Williams.

Miles himself kept this song in his repertoire at least until the late 1960s, and continued to redefine how "Milestones" was performed. His various interpretations should be the starting point for anyone trying to come to grips with this song's essence and potential. A recording made in Antibes in 1963 finds him taking it at around 340 beats per minute—a significant acceleration from his studio recording—and, in general, trying to push this song to its limits. By the close of the decade, Davis had brought the tempo back down, but had now electrified and funkified the number to accommodate his fusion sound of that era.

Note: Davis previously composed and recorded a different song called "Milestones" in 1947. This "Milestones," sporadically covered by musicians in later years (you can find it on recordings by Joe Henderson, Paul Motian, Booker Little, and others), is not a modal piece and reflects more the bebop idiom that Davis was mastering at the time. But the existence of an alternative "Milestones" does occasionally cause confusion among fans, and I've even encountered a well-known jazz critic expounding on the modal structure of this chord-based work.

RECOMMENDED VERSIONS

Miles Davis (with John Coltrane and Cannonball Adderley), from *Milestones*, New
    York, February 4, 1958

Bill Evans (with Scott LaFaro and Paul Motian), from *The Complete Village Vanguard
    Recordings, 1961*, live at the Village Vanguard, New York, June 25, 1961

Miles Davis, from *Miles Davis in Europe*, live at the Festival du Jazz, Antibes, France,
    July 27, 1963

Wynton Kelly, from *Complete Live at the Half Note*, live at the Half Note, New York,
    August 17, 1965

Miles Davis (with Wayne Shorter and Chick Corea), from *Live in Berlin 1969*, live at
    the Montreux Jazz Festival, Montreux, Switzerland, July 1969

Herbie Hancock (with Ron Carter and Tony Williams), from *Herbie Hancock Trio*,
    San Francisco, July 13, 1977

The Candid Jazz Masters (with Claudio Roditi, Donald Harrison, Ricky Ford, and
    Kenny Barron), from *For Miles*, live at Birdland, New York, November 29–30,
    1991

Horace Tapscott and Sonny Simmons, from *Among Friends*, Longwy, France, July
    28, 1995

Gerald Wilson, from *New York, New Sound*, New York, February 25–26, 2003

Misterioso
Composed by Thelonious Monk

"Misterioso" was the first original 12-bar blues recorded by Thelonious Monk,
and is one of the most unusual—both by Monk's own standards and those of
the jazz world in general. The song's melody follows a predictable pattern and
is played in a steady on-the-beat rhythm, without any syncopation or rests. No
previous jazz song sounded anything like it, and the more obvious precedents
are classical novelty numbers (for example, Leroy Anderson's *The Syncopated
Clock* from 1945) or perhaps the practice-room scales and workouts that piano
students employ to improve finger independence. The melody proceeds unflag-
gingly up and down, doggedly pursuing its pattern in an uninterrupted string
of eighth notes, each scale tone followed by its counterpart a major or minor
sixth higher.

    Needless to say, these are not your usual ingredients for jazz, and one might
think that, despite the name, a song of this sort would come across as more
tedious than mysterious. Yet by marrying this relentless pattern to a 12-bar
blues structure and mixing in bits of chromaticism, Monk creates something

surreal, a Czerny exercise from an alternative universe. The song puts obvious constraints on jazz players—for amusement, listen to different jazz drummers trying to swing this unsyncopated melody—but it also inspires a different attitude toward the blues form, making it, in this instance, less a generic progression for blowing familiar licks and riffs and more an extension of Monk's own idiosyncratic sensibility.

As was often the case with Monk's pieces, the composer was involved in many of the key early recordings. "Misterioso" first appears at Monk's Blue Note session from July 2, 1948, which finds the pianist playing sly cat-and-mouse games with vibraphonist Milt Jackson. Almost a decade would elapse before a major jazz artist would record a cover version of "Misterioso," but when Sonny Rollins did so in 1957, he took the unusual step of bringing two pianists to the date—both Monk and Horace Silver, who divvy up keyboard responsibilities and find a way to make this unusual job-sharing concept work. The following year, Monk recorded a more freewheeling version of "Misterioso" with Johnny Griffin at the Five Spot, and he would continue to feature the song in various contexts up to and including his final studio session in London from 1971.

This song inspires more than its share of reverential versions, with musicians applying various Monk signature sounds in quasi-rote emulation. But this piece is also conducive to radical reconfigurations, as testified by the world music adaptations by Tito Puente (from the 1996 album *Special Delivery*) and Anthony Brown's Asian-American Orchestra (from the 2000 project *Monk's Moods*). Also, jazz fans should not miss Ornette Coleman's rare rendition of a Monk song from *Naked Lunch* of 1991, more a mash-up of two distinct sensibilities than a true cover, but a fascinating example of one master paying tribute to another while still asserting his own musical personality.

RECOMMENDED VERSIONS

Thelonious Monk (with Milt Jackson), New York, July 2, 1948

Sonny Rollins (with Thelonious Monk, Horace Silver, and J. J. Johnson), from *Sonny Rollins, Vol. 2*, New York, April 14, 1957

Thelonious Monk (with Johnny Griffin), from *Misterioso*, live at the Five Spot, New York, August 7, 1958

Carla Bley and Johnny Griffin, from *That's the Way I Feel Now*, New York, 1984

Ran Blake, from *Epistrophy*, Milan, April 19–20, 1991

Ornette Coleman, from *Naked Lunch*, London, August 12–19, 1991

Tito Puente, from *Special Delivery*, New York, June 11–12, 1996

Anthony Brown's Asian-American Orchestra (with Steve Lacy), from *Monk's Moods*, Berkeley, California, April 20 and August 28, 2000

Misty

Composed by Erroll Garner, with lyrics by Johnny Burke

How fitting that many people have learned about this song in recent decades from Clint Eastwood's film *Play Misty for Me* (1971)—for which Eastwood reportedly paid $25,000 for the right to use Garner's tune. I say fitting, because most jazz musicians, I suspect, only play this song in response to a request, just as in Eastwood's film, his directorial debut by the way, which features an obsessed fan repeatedly phoning a radio deejay to ask for "Misty." Garner's ballad is certainly well written, and the ascending melody line entering the bridge, spanning more than an octave over the course of three bars, makes for high drama, but "Misty" has suffered from too many saccharine cocktail-piano versions over the years. Even the great jazz players struggle to reclaim its dignity nowadays.

Garner's original recording from 1954 is too baroque for my taste. This pianist was at his best in medium and medium-fast tempos, where his sense of swing and dynamics was nonpareil. But for ballads, Garner often settled for an overwrought sentimentality in which the jazz content is minimal. Compositions such as "Nightwind," "Solitaire," and "Passing Through," are so dreamy that one can't help thinking Garner wrote them with hopes of crossing over to a pop-oriented, nonjazz audience. "Misty" did just that, rising to fame via Johnny Mathis's 1959 recording, which reached #12 on the *Billboard* pop singles chart. Both Mathis's and Garner's recordings were eventually inducted into the Grammy Hall of Fame.

The song was almost cut from Mathis's *Heavenly* album—but the singer had told Garner, whom he had known since he was 13, that he would record "Misty." The studio execs wanted to substitute a Broadway show tune, but Mathis fought to keep "Misty," if only to avoid the embarrassment of reneging on his promise. Subsequent events more than validated his advocacy: "Misty" would become Mathis's signature song and would help propel *Heavenly* to the top spot in the *Billboard* album chart.

With lyrics added by Johnny Burke—who had also been a reluctant participant in this hit-making process, only writing words at the insistence of his pianist and transcriber, Herb Mesick—"Misty" was now a pop standard, and jazz musicians belatedly took notice. Count Basie recorded it while Mathis's version was still on the chart, and Ella Fitzgerald followed suit a short while later at her celebrated 1960 Berlin concert; but give Sarah Vaughan credit for adding "Misty" to her repertoire even before Mathis's hit single. She featured it at a 1958 Paris session, backed by a Quincy Jones arrangement, and performed it regularly in later years.

My favorite instrumental versions include Ahmad Jamal's 1965 trio outing, with its funky undercurrent; Richard "Groove" Holmes's up-tempo organ romp; and Wes Montgomery's live recording at the Half Note with Wynton Kelly on piano. Among more recent recordings, I would call attention to Steve Turre's version of "Misty" from 1999; this would be well worth hearing if only for Turre's effective use of plunger mute on his trombone solo, but the addition of Ray Charles as a sideman on a jazz combo track definitely adds to the appeal.

The Eastwood film might have given "Misty" some renewed respectability in the 1970s, but Ray Stevens more than offset that with his countrified hit takedown from 1975—a follow-up to his chart-busting "The Streak" from the previous year. Stevens insisted that he and his bandmates "weren't making fun of it, just having fun with it," but the result was pure cornball. Stevens won a Grammy and gave jazz musicians one more reason to steer clear of this tune. But in vain, because audience members still ask, "Play 'Misty' for me."

RECOMMENDED VERSIONS

Erroll Garner, from *Contrasts*, Chicago, July 27, 1954

Sarah Vaughan (with an arrangement by Quincy Jones), from *Vaughan and Violins*, Paris, July 7, 1958

Johnny Mathis, from *Heavenly*, New York, April 1959

Count Basie, from *Dance Along with Basie*, New York, December 30–31, 1959

Hank Crawford, from *More Soul*, New York, October 7, 1960

Wes Montgomery (with Wynton Kelly), from *Complete Live at the Half Note*, live at the Half Note, New York, June 24, 1965

Richard "Groove" Holmes, from *Soul Message*, Englewood Cliffs, New Jersey, August 3, 1965

Ahmad Jamal, from *Heat Wave*, Washington, D.C., February 17–18, 1966

Carmen McRae (with Shirley Horn on piano), from *Sarah—Dedicated to You*, New York, October 12–14, 1990

Steve Turre (with Ray Charles), from *In the Spur of the Moment*, New York, August 14, 1999

Moment's Notice
Composed by John Coltrane

Did John Coltrane think that casual listeners would notice that all 12 notes of our well-tempered scale show up as roots during the first 16 bars? Probably not. But he did know that the saxophonists who followed in his wake—no small crew, that—would be painfully aware of how quickly the chords were flashing by, and how unusual the harmonic landscape was in comparison with other songs of the day.

No, it's not as taxing as "Giant Steps," the obstacle course that Coltrane would launch on the world two years later, but "Moment's Notice" is still luxuriating in the harmonic maximalism that characterized this stage in the tenorist's evolution. Almost any melodic phrase or scale you rely on for soloing over bar one is unlikely to work for bar two—and this unsettling discontinuity continues for most of the song. Shortly before the final turnaround, Coltrane lets the improviser relax for a brief spell with only one chord change per bar blocking the road ahead. But this is merely time for a deep breath before the form returns to the top, and the battle begins all over again.

So it's a good workout, the musical equivalent of a full circuit around the Nautilus gym. And if you want to hear how it's supposed to be done, just put on Coltrane's debut recording of "Moment's Notice" from his Blue Note album *Blue Train*. Note that this is the *only* place to hear John Coltrane perform "Moment's Notice," because he never recorded it again, either in concert or in the studio—perhaps he concluded that it wasn't especially well suited for public performance. But other jazz artists adopted it in turn, incorporating "Moment's Notice" into the standard repertoire—increasingly so since the mid 1970s.

McCoy Tyner, a mainstay in Coltrane's finest working bands, never had the chance to record "Moment's Notice" with the composer, but he made up for it with his spirited rendition, alongside Ron Carter and Tony Williams, from his 1977 *Supertrios* project. In more recent years, a number of pianists have embraced this song with enthusiasm, as demonstrated on recordings by Fred Hersch (a track that, surprisingly, showed up in a demo disk used to highlight the sound systems in BMWs), Harry Connick Jr. (who mixes bits of stride with his 'Trane bag), and Dave Burrell (who gives it the full stride treatment), among others.

Even so, I usually prefer to hear "Moment's Notice" with a horn player in the band. Saxophonist George Coleman, whose harmonically driven approach to improvisation makes him a perfect exponent of this kind of song, displays his acumen on the aptly named *Playing Changes* album, recorded at Ronnie Scott's in 1979. Mark Turner, in contrast, is less married to the chords and much more playful on his fine outing as a member of Billy Hart's band for the drummer's 2005 *Quartet* project (also compare with Turner's 1994 performance from his *Yam Yam* leader date). Best of all, Arturo Sandoval invites Michael Brecker to join him in "Moment's Notice" from his 1996 *Swingin'* project, which finds both in fine form.

RECOMMENDED VERSIONS

John Coltrane, from *Blue Train*, Hackensack, New Jersey, September 15, 1957

McCoy Tyner (with Ron Carter and Tony Williams), from *Supertrios*, Berkeley, California, April 9–10, 1977

Dexter Gordon (with George Cables), from *Manhattan Symphonie*, New York, May 2, 1978

George Coleman, from *Playing Changes*, live at Ronnie Scott's Club, London, April 19–20, 1979

Fred Hersch, from *The Fred Hersch Trio Plays . . .*, Astoria, New York, February 16–17, 1994

Mark Turner (with Brad Mehldau and Kurt Rosenwinkel), from *Yam Yam*, New York, December 12, 1994

Arturo Sandoval (with Michael Brecker), from *Swingin'*, New York, January 6–9, 1996

Billy Hart (with Mark Turner and Ethan Iverson), from *Quartet*, Easton, Connecticut, October 2005

Mood Indigo
Composed by Duke Ellington and Barney Bigard, with lyrics by Irving Mills

Finally a Duke Ellington song that is easy on the singers! So many of his melodies ("Sophisticated Lady" "I Got It Bad (and That Ain't Good)" "Do Nothin' Till You Hear from Me") are filled with leaping and skipping intervals that sound as though they were written at the piano, and not necessarily with vocalists in mind. But "Mood Indigo" strikes me as a song that might have been composed while singing in the shower or humming during a lazy afternoon stroll. It only requires a little more than an octave range, and the phrases move with the rightness and directness that I associate more with hymns and folk music than with big band charts—at least until the B section, when Duke offers a sprightly contrast to his melancholy main theme.

As is often the case with Ellington, the intellectual property comes with a complicated lineage. Barney Bigard claimed that he had written much of the piece and had learned it in turn from his teacher, New Orleans pioneer Lorenzo Tio. Bigard eventually sued to get a share of the royalties. The song may have been performed by A. J. Piron's band, in which Tio played, before Duke ever recorded it. Ellington's own account describes him composing "Mood Indigo" in 15 minutes while waiting for his mother to finish cooking dinner the evening before an important broadcast. The debut radio performance generated enthusiastic fan mail, and Duke's manager Irving Mills seized the opportunity by adding lyrics. Or did he? Mitchell Parish, under contract to Mills, later asserted that he was the author of the now well-known words. Even the original name of the song is open to debate: the record label initially released it as "Dreamy

Blues," but Bigard insisted that Ellington himself had called it "Mood Indigo" from the start.

Yet anyone who doubts Ellington's decisive role here need only look at his arrangements. His 1930 debut recording features a pared-down seven-piece band, but even here Duke adds his signature by scoring the melody for muted trumpet and muted trombone joined by clarinet playing in the low register. This type of smoky texture, with the low instruments playing the high notes and vice versa, is classic Ellington misdirection. Within a few weeks, he had recorded the piece for three separate labels, and the Victor release of "Mood Indigo" proved to be his first big hit.

Even so, I give the nod to the Ellington band's magnificent 15-minute version of "Mood Indigo" recorded 20 years later for his *Masterpieces by Ellington* release. At this key juncture in the evolution of recording technology, long-playing albums were making it possible for jazz performers to present extended compositions that would never have fit on the side of a 78, previously the dominant format for recorded music. Ellington seized the opportunity by featuring Billy Strayhorn's transformation of "Mood Indigo" into an elaborate series of variations on a theme—over the course of an unprecedented 17 choruses, the band moves through three different keys and adapts to a range of rhythmic settings (including waltz time, then still a rarity in jazz).

The song has been frequently covered by other artists. As is often the case with Ellington's compositions, "Mood Indigo" is performed with a bit too much reverence for my tastes. But some surprises are out there lurking in the jazz bins, for example, Thelonious Monk's quirky interpretation from 1955, Nina Simone's ambitious reworking from 1957, and Charles Mingus's playful and pulse-changing rendition from 1959 (one of several recordings the bassist left behind of this piece). This song was also a frequent choice for guest artists when they sat in with Ellington—an impressive 1962 track finds Coleman Hawkins delivering a lengthy and harmonically advanced solo with the composer at the piano. When this performance was recorded, the jazz world was in a progressive state of mind, but the old-timers were still capable of creative reinvention of past masterpieces, as this version makes clear.

"Mood Indigo" has never lacked for admirers. As early as 1931, a newspaper reviewer compared it with Gershwin's *Rhapsody in Blue*, and in more recent years the piece has been included on a list of the 100 most important American musical works of the twentieth century by National Public Radio, and also inducted into the Grammy Hall of Fame. Despite these honors, "Mood Indigo" shows up less often on the bandstand in the current day, and when it does it is often packaged as a ho-hum interlude in the midst of an "Ellington medley." More flamboyant facets of Ellingtonia—Tizol's "Caravan" or Strayhorn's "Lush Life"—are perhaps better suited for bravura performances in the modern age of academically trained jazz stars. But this song, with its quasi-spiritual profundity, does not sound old-fashioned by any means, and still can serve as a vehicle for jazz of great emotional depth.

RECOMMENDED VERSIONS

Duke Ellington, New York, October 14, 1930

Jimmie Lunceford, New York, September 4–5, 1934

Duke Ellington, from *Masterpieces by Ellington*, New York, December 18, 1950

Thelonious Monk, from *Thelonious Monk Plays Duke Ellington*, Hackensack, New Jersey, July 27, 1955

Nina Simone, form *Little Girl Blue*, New York, 1957

Charles Mingus, from *Shoes of the Fisherman's Wife*, New York, November 13, 1959

Duke Ellington and Coleman Hawkins, from *Duke Ellington Meets Coleman Hawkins*, Englewood Cliffs, New Jersey, August 18, 1962

Clark Terry and Bob Brookmeyer (with Hank Jones), from *Gingerbread Men*, New York, 1966

Marcus Roberts, from *Alone with Three Giants*, New Orleans, June 4–5, 1990

More Than You Know
Composed by Vincent Youmans, with lyrics by Billy Rose and Edward Eliscu

Musicians probably don't get many requests for this song nowadays, but after Barbara Streisand sang it in the film *Funny Lady*, it enjoyed a brief flurry of popularity among a nonjazz audience. I'm sure I'm not the only musician who took advantage of this, engaging the requestor as an unwitting straight man. Fan: "Do you know 'More Than You Know'?" Pianist's response: "Buddy, that's an oxymoron." For the full effect, the response should be said in the voice of Willie "The Lion" Smith with a cigar dangling from the lower lip.

This song seemed ill-fated from the start, and not just because of the bad wisecracks its title inspired. It started out in the show *Great Day*, which lasted a not-so-great month on Broadway, closing after a 30-day run in 1929. It didn't help that the show opened right before the stock market crash that set off the Great Depression. Metro-Goldwyn-Mayer purchased the movie rights to *Great Day*, but the film fared no better than the stage version, with production halted after eight weeks when star Joan Crawford rebelled against the "baby talk" she was asked to recite in her performance of a Southern belle. The original plan was to resume shooting after fixing the script, but this never happened. A follow-up attempt to revive *Great Day* in 1934 as a feature for Jeanette MacDonald also went nowhere.

Yet three tunes from the failed musical managed to survive the debacle, with "More Than You Know," "Without a Song," and the title number "Great Day" testifying to the quality of Youmans's contributions and explaining why Hollywood came knocking even after the abbreviated Broadway run. In 1930, Ruth Etting had a hit record with "More Than You Know," as did Mildred Bailey in 1937. In 1936, at the peak of his fame, Benny Goodman recorded it with his trio, and three years later Teddy Wilson, pianist on that date, would call on "More Than You Know" at a session under his own leadership, where it served as a showcase for Billie Holiday.

The song maintained is popularity during the 1940s, with many of the biggest bands of the day (Basie, Goodman, James, Kenton, Dorsey, Goodman) embracing it, most often as a vehicle for a female singer, but occasionally as an instrumental. As modern jazz slowly nudged the swing bands aside, "More Than You Know" held its position in the jazz repertoire. The song retained its popularity with vocalists, but a number of leading modern jazz tenor saxophonists also helped solidify its jazz credentials. Sonny Rollins recorded a well-known version with Thelonious Monk on piano in 1954, and was still playing "More Than You Know" more than a half-century later, as demonstrated on a gripping live performance from a concert in Toulouse, France included in the tenorist's 2008 release *Road Shows*. Dexter Gordon also recorded the song in different settings, invariably to good effect. I recommend both his 1975 recording with orchestra and his live performance at Carnegie Hall from 1978—the latter includes what might be the best recorded solo by pianist George Cables, who avoids the glibness that sometimes undermines his work and reaches for some concert-hall effects possibly inspired by the august surroundings.

The song reveals its basic personality in the pickup beats, with a yearning upward-moving motif that is developed over the next 16 bars with a precision that hardly diminishes the fragile emotional content of the piece. In the bridge there are no fewer than eight different downward-moving phrases, most of them positioned against minor chords. When the main melody returns, it's almost as if a ray of sunlight has broken through an ominous cloud cover. I can't think of another song where the contrast between the two sections is so artfully handled to produce a poignant holistic effect.

RECOMMENDED VERSIONS

Benny Goodman Trio (with Teddy Wilson and Gene Krupa), Chicago, April 24, 1936

Mildred Bailey (with Ben Webster), New York, November 9, 1936

Billie Holiday (with Teddy Wilson), New York, January 30, 1939

Sonny Rollins (with Thelonious Monk), from *Moving Out*, Hackensack, New Jersey, October 25, 1954

Coleman Hawkins, from *The Hawk Relaxes*, New York, February 28, 1961

Dexter Gordon (with an orchestra conducted and arranged by Palle Mikkelborg), from *More Than You Know*, Copenhagen, February 21–23, 1975

Joe Pass, from *Joe Pass at the Montreux Jazz Festival 1975*, live at the Montreux Jazz Festival, Montreux, Switzerland, July 17–18, 1975

Dexter Gordon (with George Cables), from *Live at Carnegie Hall*, live at Carnegie Hall, New York, September 23, 1978

Claudia Acuña, from *Rhythm of Life*, New York, October 3–5, 2001

Sonny Rollins, from *Road Shows, Vol. 1*, live at La Halle aux Grains, Toulouse, France, May 15, 2006

Muskrat Ramble
Composed by Kid Ory, with lyrics by Ray Gilbert

In an unexpected turnabout, this traditional jazz tune reached its largest audience at Woodstock, where Country Joe McDonald performed the melody, with new words attached, as an antiwar chant. *And it's one, two, three, what are we fighting for?* . . . Audience members can be heard singing along—perhaps they remembered the melody from their parents' Dixieland jazz albums—but Country Joe is less than pleased. He gripes to the assembled masses: "Listen, people, I do not know how you expect that we ever stop the war if you cannot sing any better than that."

Kid Ory, the 72-year-old trombonist, had reason to gripe too. His composition had just shared the largest stage in the land, alongside Hendrix and Joplin, and he had nothing to show for it. His daughter Babette Ory claims that his dying request was for her to go after the person who had infringed his intellectual property. Eventually she attempted just that, but not until more than 30 years had elapsed. For a while, Country Joe was subject to a $150,000 fine if he sang his version of the song, known as "I-Feel-Like-I'm-Fixin'-to-Die Rag," in public. But the case was ultimately decided against Ory—largely because the claim had not been made in a timely enough manner.

I feel some sympathy for Ory's family, but his own rights to this song are far from rock solid. The trombonist claimed he had composed "Muskrat Ramble" in Los Angeles in 1921, inspired by an exercise in a music method book, and that Lil Armstrong came up with the name. Yet Louis Armstrong asserted that he was the true composer of the tune, and Ory only supplied the title, while Sidney Bechet traces the origin of the composition, or at least the second theme of Woodstock fame, back even further to the turn-of-the-century jazzman Buddy Bolden. Bolden, in turn, may have borrowed the melody from the preexisting folksong "The Old Cow Died and the Old Man Cried." Adding to the complexity, Ray Gilbert was later awarded a third of the royalties in compensation for the lyrics he wrote to "Muskrat Ramble" in 1950.

After his well-known debut recording of the piece, Louis Armstrong put the song aside for more than two decades. "Muskrat Ramble" managed to survive the transition to the Swing Era, showing up in big band arrangements performed by Lionel Hampton, Woody Herman, and a few others, while Roy Eldridge recorded a hot combo arrangement in December 1939. But the traditional jazz revival of the 1940s did more than anything to bring the piece back to the attention of jazz fans. West Coast traditionalists, notably Lu Watters and Turk Murphy, featured the song prominently throughout the decade, while genuine New Orleans pioneers, such as Louis Armstrong, Sidney Bechet, and Ory, also showcased the composition during this same period.

Modernists have rarely tried to update "Muskrat Ramble." When you find an occasional cover version from a forward-looking jazz icon—such as Mingus's 1965 performance at UCLA—the attitude is usually playful or even tongue-in-cheek. And, in truth, this song so perfectly captures the good-times ambiance the general public associates with New Orleans jazz that it's probably best for musicians just to go along for the ride. I doubt the melody of "Muskrat Ramble" will again find itself on a stage in front of a half million listeners, but even in an intimate venue this song retains the same appeal that got the audience singing along at Woodstock.

RECOMMENDED VERSIONS

Louis Armstrong (with Kid Ory), Chicago, February 26, 1926

Lionel Hampton, New York, July 21, 1938

Lu Watters (with Turk Murphy), San Francisco, March 29, 1942

Kid Ory (with Jimmy Noone and Zutty Singleton), Los Angeles, March–July 1944

Sidney Bechet (with Sidney de Paris and Vic Dickenson), New York, December 20, 1944

Muggsy Spanier (with Pee Wee Russell), New York, March 1–3, 1945

Pete Fountain, from *Standing Room Only*, live at the French Quarter Inn, New Orleans, 1965

Charles Mingus, from *Music Written for Monterey, 1965 Not Heard . . . Played Live in Its Entirety at UCLA*, live at Royce Hall, Los Angeles, September 25, 1965

Harry Connick Jr., from *25*, New York, October 2–9, 1992

My Favorite Things

Composed by Richard Rodgers, with lyrics by Oscar Hammerstein II

This song was immensely popular in the 1960s due to its prominence in the successful Broadway show *The Sound of Music* (1959), as well as the 1965 film version, which was the top grossing movie of the decade and, after adjusting for inflation, the third biggest box-office hit of all time. I was a very young child at the time of the film's release, but I can attest that even the kindergarten set knew about "My Favorite Things," which seemed especially suited for children. In the film adaptation, it is even sung by Julie Andrews to the youngsters in her charge.

Even so, "My Favorite Things" must have struck many musicians at the time as an unlikely jazz vehicle. I have a hard time believing that, without the intervention of John Coltrane, this composition would have made much headway on the jazz bandstand. But in this instance, the advocacy of one famous saxophonist proved sufficient. Give Coltrane credit for the depth of his commitment to the Rodgers and Hammerstein song. His initial studio recording, from 1960, was 14 minutes long, taking up more than a third of the successful album named after the tune. The following year, he brought "My Favorite Things" with him on the road, and surviving recordings from five different European countries find him working over the song at length, with Eric Dolphy joining in on the proceedings. The song also shows up on later Coltrane recordings made at Birdland, the Newport Jazz Festival, the Half Note, and the Village Vanguard, among other locales. As Coltrane evolved, during the final years of his life, so did his interpretation of "My Favorite Things," and he played the piece—now stretched to more than a half hour in duration—on his last live recording, from a concert at the Olatunji Center of African Culture in Harlem, a few weeks before his death in 1967.

Then again, how much did Coltrane really like this composition? Despite his stated praise, he displayed no interest in soloing over the chord changes in any of his various performances—after a perfunctory melody statement, he invariably pushes the composition's structure and harmonies aside, and works over an endlessly repeating 6/8 vamp. In truth, his approach to "My Favorite Things" is little different from his later transformation of other well-known songs into preambles for minor key vamps in 6/8 time, such as "Chim Chim Cheree" or "Greensleeves." Whether the composer listed on the album sleeve is Richard Rodgers or "traditional" is hardly important here. The driving force, the source of inspiration and perspiration, is John Coltrane, who takes a sing-song Broadway show tune and turns it into a springboard for advanced modal improvisation.

In the aftermath of Coltrane, a few jazz artists returned to the song itself and performed "My Favorite Things" with the inclusion of a conventional solo over chord changes—hear, for example, Bill Evans in 1963 or Dave Brubeck in 1965.

But more emblematic of this song's place in the repertoire are the edgier versions, such as Sun Ra's 1977 rendition—in which the musicians seem undecided about whether to follow Rodgers's harmonies or Coltrane's vamp, and end up with strange hybrid, tossing out the bridge but gradually coalescing around a progression possibly traceable back to a Broadway show.

Among *my* favorite things are two versions that feature former members of Coltrane's band playing this song in very different settings: McCoy Tyner's solo piano rendition from his 1972 *Echoes of a Friend* project, and Elvin Jones's 1994 trio outing in the company of guitarist John McLaughlin and organist Joey DeFrancesco. I would also recommend Stanley Jordan's interpretation from 1986, which manages to capture Coltrane-esque intensity without a rhythm section, relying only on Jordan's unconventional fret-tapping guitar attack.

RECOMMENDED VERSIONS

John Coltrane, from *My Favorite Things*, New York, October 21, 1960

Bill Evans, from *The Solo Sessions, Vol. 1*, New York, January 10, 1963

John Coltrane, from *One Up, One Down*, live at the Half Note, New York, May 7, 1965

McCoy Tyner, from *Echoes of a Friend*, Tokyo, November 11, 1972

Sun Ra (with John Gilmore), from *Some Blues But Not the Kind That's Blue*, New
     York, October 14, 1977

Stanley Jordan, from *Standards, Vol. 1.*, New York, October 1986

John McLaughlin (with Elvin Jones and Joey DeFrancesco), from *After the Rain*, New
     York, October 4–5, 1994

George Coleman, from *I Could Write a Book*, New York, January 8–9, 1998

My Foolish Heart

Composed by Victor Young, with lyrics by Ned Washington

In 1949 Hollywood released the first—and, as it turned out, the last—authorized movie version of a story by reclusive author J. D. Salinger. But by the time Samuel Goldwyn and company had finished tinkering with Salinger's 1948 tale "Uncle Wiggily in Connecticut," there wasn't much recognizable from the original left on the screen. The film was lambasted by critics, and though Salinger avoided public comment, one can perhaps deduce his views from the opening paragraph of his classic 1951 novel *The Catcher in the Rye*. Here the narrator, Holden Caulfield, mentioning his brother D. B., remarks: "Now he's out in Hollywood, D. B., being a prostitute. If there's one thing I hate, it's the movies. Don't even mention them to me."

Yet when Academy Award time came around, the title song to *My Foolish Heart*—the new name given by the studio to its film adaptation of Salinger's story—was nominated for an Oscar, losing out to "Baby, It's Cold Outside." In 1950 more than a half-dozen versions of "My Foolish Heart" found a place on the charts, including sentimental treatments by Billy Eckstine and Gene Ammons. But after a few months, the song was put aside by musicians, with no jazz cover versions recorded during the following five years.

The song's revival started on March 29, 1956, when, after this hiatus, both Carmen McRae (in New York) and André Previn (in Los Angeles) recorded "My Foolish Heart" on the same day. A few months later Ray Brown brought the song with him to a session for the Verve label, and over the next several years "My Foolish Heart" gained a few more admirers in the jazz community. Lionel Hampton, Bob Crosby, Ted Heath, Maynard Ferguson, and other bandleaders of various styles and generations made recordings of it.

Yet Bill Evans's trio performance, alongside Scott LaFaro and Paul Motian, from their June 1961 live recording at the Village Vanguard, stands out as the most influential version of "My Foolish Heart." Few jazz artists dared to take songs at such a slow tempo back then, with Evans's treatment hovering around 50 beats per minute (by comparison, Coleman Hawkins's well-known ballad performance on "Body and Soul" is twice as fast). Far from tensing up at such a snail's pace, as other even top-tier rhythm sections might have done at the time, this trio allows the song to breathe and for the underlying beat to flow in waves rather than advance in clearly delineated pulses. This would be one of the last times this trio would play together—LaFaro would be killed in an automobile accident a few days later—but this recording testified to a new conception of rhythm and space, one that other musicians would study and emulate in the coming years.

This was especially evident in the work of later pianists, but other instrumentalists were not immune to Evans's influence. A shared aesthetic vision can be sensed, for example, on Gary Burton's solo vibraphone version of "My Foolish Heart" from his 1968 project *Country Roads and Other Places*, John McLaughlin's interpretation on his 1978 *Electric Guitarist* album, and Lenny Breau's treatment from that same period. The song became associated with a certain sensibility, even more than most jazz standards, serving as a vehicle for an open, uncluttered approach to improvisation, and an introspective tone more attuned to inner states of being than finger-snapping patrons at the bar.

Evans himself made a number of later recordings of "My Foolish Heart," keeping the song on his set list until the very end of his life. Few of these hold many surprises, but on his pairing with Tony Bennett from 1975 the pianist is forced to adapt to another forceful presence in the studio, and the give-and-take makes for a fresh reading of a familiar song. In more recent years, "My Foolish Heart" has rarely been heard in novel or uncharacteristic interpretations, but two riveting live versions can be found in Kurt Elling's impassioned reworking from 1999, and an equally exhilarating collaboration between Ahmad Jamal and George Coleman from 2000.

RECOMMENDED VERSIONS

Billy Eckstine, New York, December 14, 1949

Gene Ammons, Chicago, May 2, 1950

Bill Evans (with Scott LaFaro and Paul Motian), from *Live at the Village Vanguard*, live at the Village Vanguard, New York, June 25, 1961

Gary Burton, from *Country Roads and Other Places*, New York, September 27, 1968

Tony Bennett and Bill Evans, from *The Tony Bennett/Bill Evans Album*, Berkeley, California, June 10–13, 1975

John McLaughlin, from *Electric Guitarist*, New York, January 1978

Lenny Breau, from *The Complete Living Room Tapes*, Maine, circa 1978–79

Bobby Hutcherson (with McCoy Tyner), from *Solo/Quartet*, Hollywood, February 1–2, 1982

Kurt Elling (with Laurence Hobgood), from *Live in Chicago*, live at the Green Mill, Chicago, July 14–16, 1999

Ahmad Jamal (with George Coleman), from *Olympia 2000*, live at the Olympia, Paris, November 6, 2000

My Funny Valentine
Composed by Richard Rodgers, with lyrics by Lorenz Hart

The song made its debut in Rodgers and Hart's *Babes in Arms*, a 1937 Broadway production that ran for eight months and produced more lasting hits than any other show by this duo. "My Funny Valentine" must have seemed an unlikely love song at the time—how many romantic tunes announce that the beloved's appearance is "laughable" and "less than Greek"?—but was destined to become one of the most frequently recorded ballads of the century.

Two jazz trumpeters have staked their claim to this song: Miles Davis and Chet Baker. Usually Baker is accused of following in Davis's footsteps, but in this instance Chet had the first and longest association with the standard. He first recorded it with Gerry Mulligan in 1952, but probably had already been performing it for some time. "Gerry made a lot of money with songs that Chet already played for years, like 'My Funny Valentine' and 'Bernie's Tune,'" tenorist Teddy Edwards has commented. "Chet was playing them way before he met Gerry." And Baker continued performing "My Funny Valentine" long after he left Mulligan—around 40 different recorded versions can be found in his discography.

Few other jazz musicians were playing "My Funny Valentine" in the early 1950s. But after Chet's success with the song, both as an instrumental and vocal feature, others quickly jumped on the bandwagon. More jazz versions of "My Funny Valentine" were recorded in 1954 than in the 1930s and 1940s combined. These include a rendition by Charlie Parker in an uncharacteristic pairing with the Stan Kenton band (in a hot Latin-and-swing arrangement), as well as recordings by Sarah Vaughan, Ben Webster, and Artie Shaw and His Gramercy Five. Around this same time, Frank Sinatra highlighted the song as the lead-off track on his classic LP *Songs for Young Lovers*, recorded in late 1953 and released in 1954—a key milestone in bringing this ballad out of the jazz subculture and onto the record players of mainstream America.

By the time Miles Davis recorded the Rodgers and Hart standard at an October 1956 session for the *Cookin'* release on Prestige, he was late to the Valentine's Day party. Davis shows his affinity with the composition on this track, but the rhythm section is a bit too pushy for my tastes, and doubles up the tempo as soon as the trumpet solo is over. If you are only planning to check out one Miles Davis version, I would suggest either the live recording from Philharmonic Hall (now known as Avery Fisher Hall) in 1964, which is my favorite recording of this oft-played tune, or his performance from the Plaza Hotel in 1958 during Bill Evans's brief tenure with the trumpeter's band.

This song, for all its popularity, can come across as lugubrious without a first-rate soloist leading the way. The chord changes rehash a familiar progression—Ellington used a similar formula, consisting of a descending bassline combined with a static minor chord, in the opening bars of "In a Sentimental Mood" and "It Don't Mean a Thing (If It Ain't Got That Swing)," to cite just two examples—and the modulation into the relative major for the bridge is as predictable as a heart-shaped box of candy on February 14. But Rodgers builds to a fine climax in an otherwise simple melody, and knows when to throw in the high E flat for dramatic effect. For my money, this is the hook in the water—a grand gesture that turned what might have been a forgettable song into a cherished standard.

RECOMMENDED VERSIONS

Gerry Mulligan (with Chet Baker), from *Gerry Mulligan Quartet*, live at the Black Hawk, San Francisco, September 2, 1952

Frank Sinatra, from *Songs for Young Lovers*, Hollywood, November 5–6, 1953

Sarah Vaughan, from *The Rodgers and Hart Songbook*, New York, February 10, 1954

Chet Baker (vocal), from *Chet Baker Sings*, Los Angeles, February 15, 1954

Charlie Parker (with Stan Kenton), from *Kenton and Bird*, live at the Civic Auditorium, Portland, Oregon, February 25, 1954

Ben Webster, from *Sophisticated Lady*, New York, March 30, 1954

Artie Shaw and His Gramercy Five, from *Artie Shaw And His Gramercy Five, Vol. 3*, Hollywood, June 1954

Miles Davis, from *Cookin'*, Hackensack, New Jersey, October 26, 1956

Miles Davis (with Bill Evans), from *Jazz at the Plaza*, live at the Plaza Hotel, New York, September 9, 1958

Miles Davis, from *My Funny Valentine*, live at Philharmonic Hall, New York, February 12, 1964

Herbie Hancock (solo piano) from *The Piano*, Tokyo, October 25–26, 1978

Keith Jarrett (with Jack DeJohnette and Gary Peacock), from *Still Live*, live at Philharmonic Hall, Germany, July 13, 1986

Roy Hargrove, from *Emergence*, Hollywood, June 16–17, 2008

My Old Flame

Composed by Arthur Johnston, with lyrics by Sam Coslow

"My Old Flame" was written for Mae West to perform in the 1934 movie *Belle of the Nineties*. West is remembered today as a risqué sex symbol who tweaked the prudish sensibilities of the prewar era, rather than as a jazz vocalist; but she had paid close attention to blues singers Ma Rainey and Bessie Smith in crafting her own onstage demeanor. And she was a stickler for surrounding herself with the right accompanists—in the film she is supported by Duke Ellington's band. The studio execs initially balked at the extra expense of bringing in a name band, but West insisted on Ellington. Even after agreeing to her request, the honchos at Paramount tried to persuade West to allow white actors to serve as stand-ins onscreen for the black musicians playing on the soundtrack, but the actress again stood her ground.

The song is an intriguing one, jolting the listener from the very start when the opening phrase drops down to linger on the flat 7 in bar two. This song may be written in a major key, yet the psychological tone of "My Old Flame" definitely tends toward the minor mode, and I wonder if the song might have been more popular if it had made its debut in some noir film that better matched its mood. The harmonic movement is extreme, yet the song itself comes across as lazy and unrushed. This combination—of indolence and intricacy—is an odd one, but casts a certain charm over performances of the standard.

Six weeks after participating in the filming with West, Ellington recorded "My Old Flame" with Ivie Anderson handling vocal duties. Yet Guy Lombardo, not Ellington, enjoyed the greatest popular success with "My Old Flame" at this time—his recording, a textbook example of what musicians call a "Mickey Mouse" arrangement, climbed as high as #7 in the country during the early summer of 1934. The song was soon forgotten by jazz players, at least until the early 1940s when both Benny Goodman and Count Basie recorded it. Cover versions were fairly common during the war years—I especially admire Billie Holiday's treatment from 1944.

Charlie Parker recorded "My Old Flame" for the Dial label in 1947, and the track ranks among the most moving ballad performances of his career. A few modern jazz players followed his example, but I suspect that more might have done so if not for Spike Jones's devastating parody of the song, which came out around the same time as Bird's 78. Poor Sam Coslow, who had hated the results when Jones had deconstructed his cherished song "Cocktails for Two" ("a "noisy, slapstick, grotesque novelty . . . the worst possible taste, desecrating what I felt was one of my most beautiful songs"), had to withstand the onslaught again when "My Old Flame," another collaboration with Arthur Johnston, got a similar treatment. Jones turned a romantic lament into a maniacal first-person narrative about sending up one's old flame in flames, performed in a crazed faux Peter Lorre voice. The song survived as a love ballad, but just barely.

In the 1950s, "My Old Flame" found its greatest allegiance from members of the cool school. Miles Davis, who sounded tentative and strained playing the song alongside Parker in 1947, recorded it again in 1951, and revealed the strides he had made toward formulating his own mature ballad style during the intervening four years. Other recordings from the decade find Stan Getz, Gerry Mulligan, Chet Baker, the Modern Jazz Quartet, Zoot Sims, and other artists on the cooler side of the jazz spectrum putting their stamp on the song. Toward the end of the decade, Stan Kenton adopted "My Old Flame," relying on a beautifully brooding Marty Paich chart that stayed in his band's book for years.

"My Old Flame" has retained its popularity in the jazz world—more versions have been recorded in the last decade than in the 1930s and 1940s combined. This longevity is all the more striking when one considers the relatively low profile of the composers—indeed, Coslow eventually left songwriting behind to focus on stock market analysis and publishing during the final decades of his life. So this tune gets no boost from theme albums devoted to its creator, or from the Broadway revivals and other historic associations that keep other old melodies in circulation. The appeal here comes solely from the composition itself, a melancholy and evocative work that ranks among the most well-crafted songs of its era.

RECOMMENDED VERSIONS

Mae West (with Duke Ellington), from the film *Belle of the Nineties*, Hollywood, March 24, 1934

Duke Ellington (with Ivie Anderson), Hollywood, May 9, 1934

Count Basie (with Lynne Sherman), New York, September 24, 1941

Benny Goodman (with Peggy Lee), New York, October 2, 1941

Billie Holiday, New York, March 25, 1944

Spike Jones, Los Angeles, October 7, 1947

Charlie Parker (with Miles Davis), November 4, 1947

Miles Davis, from *Dig*, New York, October 5, 1951

Chet Baker (with Russ Freeman), from *Jazz at Ann Arbor*, live at the University of Michigan, Ann Arbor, Michigan, May 9, 1954

Stan Kenton (with arrangement by Marty Paich), from *Back to Balboa*, Balboa Beach, California, January 20, 1958

Sarah Vaughan (with Joe Pass), from *How Long Has This Been Going On?* Hollywood, April 25, 1978

Sonny Rollins, from *Old Flames*, New York, July–August 1993

Enrico Pieranunzi (with Charlie Haden and Paul Motian), from *Special Encounter*, Rome, March 6–8, 2003

My One and Only Love
Composed by Guy Wood, with lyrics by Robert Mellin

This is the only song composed by Guy Wood to gain acceptance as a jazz standard—and who would have thought that a British tunesmith who wrote music for Captain Kangaroo could come up with such a majestic ballad? It reminds me of a handful of other popular jazz tunes—"In a Sentimental Mood," "Someone to Watch over Me"—that place their hook in a rapturous opening phrase that rises over an octave. Needless to say, you won't find that formula in many songs currently in rotation on the radio.

"My One and Only Love" is inextricably linked to John Coltrane, who left behind an exquisite recording of the song in the company of vocalist Johnny Hartman—a classic track that never seems to fall out of favor among jazz fans. In this instance, I concur with the consensus, and find myself frequently returning to this poignant performance. But another saxophonist, Charlie Ventura, is responsible for establishing "My One and Only Love" as a legitimate jazz ballad a full decade before Coltrane recorded it.

The song had struggled in its first incarnation, released under the name "Music from Beyond the Moon" in 1947. With new lyrics by Robert Mellin, it served as the B side of Sinatra's hit recording of "I've Got the World on a String" from 1953. At this point, Ventura saw its jazz potential and adopted it as a tenor feature. Ventura is mostly forgotten nowadays, and even knowledgeable jazz fans would be surprised to learn that the readers of *Downbeat* picked him as the best tenor saxophonist in jazz back in 1945—just three years after Gene Krupa discovered him while he was working in a shipyard. Those who want to understand Ventura's popularity need merely hear what he does with "My One and Only Love" in his 1953 recording.

Almost every tenorist of note has tackled it, and any short list of memorable versions needs to acknowledge renditions by Sonny Rollins (who recorded it a year after Coltrane), Ben Webster (who performed it at his celebrated 1954 session with Art Tatum), Michael Brecker, and Joshua Redman. Yet the song is limber enough to bend to a wide range of approaches, and not always with a horn on hand. For examples of this, check out Susana Raya's lovely 2009 reinterpretation in Spanish, to guitar accompaniment, as "Mi Verdadero Amor," which can be found on the Internet, or Cassandra Wilson's adaptation of "My One and Only Love" into a fast, swinging tune on her 1988 *Blue Skies* CD.

RECOMMENDED VERSIONS

Charlie Ventura, from *Charlie Ventura's Open House*, New Orleans, October 12, 1953

Art Tatum and Ben Webster, from *The Tatum Group Masterpieces, Vol. 8*, Los Angeles, September 11, 1954

John Coltrane, from *John Coltrane and Johnny Hartman*, Englewood Cliffs, New Jersey, March 7, 1963

Sonny Rollins (with Herbie Hancock), from *The Complete RCA Victor Recordings*, July 2, 1964

Chick Corea, from *Now He Sings, Now He Sobs*, New York, March 14, 1968

McCoy Tyner, from *Atlantis*, live at the Keystone Korner, San Francisco, August 31, 1974

Michael Brecker, from *Michael Brecker*, New York, late 1986 or early 1987

Cassandra Wilson, from *Blue Skies*, New York, February 4–5, 1988

Joshua Redman, from *Spirit of the Moment*, live at the Village Vanguard, March 21–26, 1995

Sting, from the soundtrack to *Leaving Las Vegas*, 1995

Mark Murphy, from *Once to Every Heart*, Berlin, 2001–2

Kurt Elling, from *Dedicated to You*, live in the Allen Room at Frederick P. Rose Hall, New York, January 21, 2009

Susana Raya, YouTube video performed in Spanish as "Mi Verdadero Amor," Amsterdam, June 19, 2009

My Romance

Composed by Richard Rodgers, with lyrics by Lorenz Hart

When I sit down at the piano to play for my own enjoyment, this song is frequently at my fingertips. The beginning is deceptively simple, just a major scale moving upward from the third. The second eight bars shift to yearning interval leaps and the contrast is quite effective, while the final eight, with their four repeated high notes and lovely harmonic motion, offer an impassioned and almost operatic conclusion. Others might have been surprised when Mario Lanza recorded this song, but I can understand why a singer of his pedigree—with one foot in the concert hall and the other in the commercial music world—would have found it appealing.

The lyrics, which enumerate all the things a lover doesn't need (real estate, background music, a waterfront view, etc.), threaten to collapse into an overly cute list. But Rodgers's subdued melody imparts a heartfelt dignity to the whole, and makes the romance here more plausible than Hart's words, on their own, might deserve.

The song first showed up in the 1935 Broadway production *Jumbo*, a strange cross between a musical and a circus. Paul Whiteman's band played the music, and Jimmy Durante shared the stage with (among other performers) a live elephant. Both Durante and (presumably a different) elephant made the leap to the screen, 27 years later, for the 1962 movie version. Doris Day got assigned the song for the film—a less-than-jazzy diva, and a better choice than Jumbo, but hardly the singer to bring this composition to the attention of improvisers.

Jazz musicians were slow in warming up to "My Romance." Very few versions were recorded until the 1950s. Dave Brubeck's 1952 solo piano version made clear the potential for harmonic games implicit in Rodgers's chord progression, and probably led other piano players to add this song to their repertoires. But Bill Evans had even greater impact with this song. He recorded it on numerous occasions, starting with his first leader date on the Riverside label in 1956 and continuing to the 1980 live version recorded eight days before his death at the Keystone Korner in San Francisco. My favorite—and the best known—of Evans's performances comes from that magical Village Vanguard session on June 25, 1961, an inspired day of music making and the last recording date for this pianist's most influential trio.

After the release of this recording, "My Romance" became entrenched in the jazz repertoire. On Keith Jarrett's debut recording session, as a member of Art Blakey's Jazz Messengers, he offers up a mind-expanding solo on "My Romance," and though he recorded it again almost 30 years later with his Standards Trio, I still prefer the boundary-pushing 20-year-old versus the veteran a few months shy of his fiftieth birthday. Jessica Williams's solo version from 1977 is another standout performance and one of my preferred renditions of the song—alas, fans will have a hard time tracking down this long out-of-print track.

"My Romance" has never enjoyed the crossover renown of many other Richard Rodgers songs, but in recent years it increasingly shows up when rock-pop stars want to go retro. Carly Simon has probably reached more people with this song than Bill Evans, Keith Jarrett, and Dave Brubeck combined. Simon's former husband James Taylor's own romance with Simon might not have fulfilled the promise of the lyrics, but he has also recorded it, and their son Ben, maintaining the peculiar family connection with the song, later performed it on a Ralph Lauren fragrance commercial. Other high profile advocates include Cybill Shepherd, Sammy Davis, Jr. and Roberta Flack. Generally jazz players depart when pop stars stake out a song, but "My Romance" is resilient enough to maintain its jazziness even in the face of incursions from commercial artists.

RECOMMENDED VERSIONS

Dave Brubeck, from *The Dave Brubeck Quartet*, San Francisco, September 1952

Bill Evans (with Scott LaFaro and Paul Motian), from *The Complete Village Vanguard Recordings, 1961*, live at the Village Vanguard, New York, June 25, 1961

Ben Webster (with Hank Jones), from *Ben and "Sweets,"* New York, June 7, 1962

Art Blakey (with Keith Jarrett), from *Buttercorn Lady*, live at the Lighthouse, Hermosa Beach, California, January 1966

Jessica Williams, from *Portraits*, Baltimore, May 16, 1977

Warne Marsh, from *A Ballad Album*, Holland, April 7, 1983

Tuck & Patti, from *Tears of Joy*, Menlo Park, California, 1988

N

Naima
Composed by John Coltrane

A musicologist might divide John Coltrane's career into three distinct phases. During the course of the first period, which culminated around 1960, the chord changes got more and more complex. In the second phase, the chords got simpler and simpler—as demonstrated in vamp numbers and modal vehicles such as "My Favorite Things" and "Impressions." And in the final stage, chords became wholly optional, jettisoned when necessary in Coltrane's quest for musical self-enlightenment and liberation. A word to the wise: as is true of all artists, but perhaps preeminently so with Coltrane, later is not necessarily better.

"Naima" is Coltrane's great ballad composition from the high point of the first period, and may be the most perfectly realized piece of songwriting from this musician's pen. The other intricate bits of harmonic legerdemain from this phase—"Moment's Notice," "Countdown," "Giant Steps"—might have represented major milestones in jazz performance, but still retain the flavor of études, not so much songs as workout regimens to ensure the fitness and adroitness of the soloist. "Naima" in contrast wears its complexity lightly, and impresses more by its serenity and sheer beauty than for the demands it imposes on the band.

"Naima," named after the saxophonist's first wife, sounds deceptively simple—which it, most assuredly, is not. The bassline is built on repeated notes, creating what musicians call a "pedal point" (the term derived from the use of sustained tones played on the pedals of the organ), with only a shift up a fifth during the bridge. But over this static anchor, Coltrane constructs a lush harmonic superstructure marked by ingenious ways of creating tension and release.

The melody itself is austere, a call to prayer or meditation that makes no attempt to borrow pop-song hooks or modern jazz phraseology.

I believe that this spiritually-infused quality to "Naima" explains why this song stayed in Coltrane's repertoire long after he had stopped performing "Giant Steps" and other signature compositions from his early period. He returned to "Naima" again and again, as documented on various live recordings—with Eric Dolphy in 1961; overseas with his classic quartet in 1962, 1963, and 1965; and even amidst his 1966 band with new wife Alice Coltrane joining him on stage. The song evolved into something quite different from Coltrane's original hymnlike conception from 1959, but always retained a certain transcendental grandeur.

The resiliency that this composition revealed in its various reinterpretations by Coltrane continued to ensure its staying power after his death. Many of Carlos Santana's rock-oriented fans were less than pleased by his 1972 collaboration with John McLaughlin, on which the duo perform "Naima" on acoustic guitars, but this track has worn well with the years. Other creative transformations find "Naima" presented by David Grisman on mandolin amid an all-strings band, and turned into an electric-rock jam tune by Derek Trucks. A number of lyricists have added words, not surprisingly, given the inherent loveliness of the melody.

Despite these precedents, this song will remain, first and foremost, a saxophone number, with particular appeal for those (their numbers are legion) who have studied and assimilated Coltrane's legacy. Representative examples can be found on the tracks listed below by Dave Liebman, Steve Grossman, and James Carter. Another sax rendition, a little-known gem, comes from John Handy's recording of the song from June 1967—and, yes, the date here is correct. Although producer John Hammond released it as a posthumous tribute to Coltrane, this "Naima" was actually recorded three weeks before the tenorist's death during Handy's engagement at the Village Gate in New York.

RECOMMENDED VERSIONS

John Coltrane, from *Giant Steps*, New York, December 2, 1959

John Coltrane, from *Afro Blue Impressions*, live at Auditorium Maximum, Berlin, November 2, 1963

John Handy (with Bobby Hutcherson and Pat Martino), from *New View*, live at the Village Gate, New York, June 28, 1967

John McLaughlin and Carlos Santana, from *Love, Devotion, Surrender*, New York, October 1972

McCoy Tyner, from *Echoes of a Friend*, Tokyo, November 11, 1972

David Grisman, from *Quintet '80*, Berkeley, California, 1980

David Liebman and Richard Beirach, from *Double Edge*, Copenhagen, April 21, 1985

Steve Grossman (with Cedar Walton), from *Love Is the Thing*, Milan, May 1985

James Carter (with Hamiet Bluiett), from *Conversin' with the Elders*, New York,
    February 5, 1996

Nardis
Composed by Miles Davis

The title is a bit of a mystery. Miles was known for names that made sense when
spelled backward—he later recorded "Selim" and "Sivad"—but those who have
explained this song as the trumpeter's tribute to jazz vocalist Ben Sidran, who
was a 14-year-old in Racine, Wisconsin when it was first recorded, are grasping
at straws. I am more inclined to accept Bill Crow's third-hand account of Miles
overhearing a fan requesting a song from an uncooperative Bill Evans, who allegedly replied: "I don't play that crap . . . I'm an artist." Add a slight New Jersey
accent to that last phrase, and you arrive at something similar to "n'ardis." Until
a better hypothesis comes to light, this one will have to do.

Miles had written the composition "Nardis" for a session on which he was
neither leader nor performer, but was headed by his sideman at the time, altoist
Cannonball Adderley. The harmonic movement was unconventional, and Davis
was unhappy with the way the band tackled his new song. Indeed, he must have
given up on the piece entirely, because he never recorded it with his own group.
But after the session, Davis complimented pianist Bill Evans, stating that he
had been the only musician at the session to play "Nardis" the right way. Evans,
for his part, kept the song in his repertoire—and it stayed there for the rest of
his life. Some have even speculated that Evans was the actual composer, but the
pianist gave credit to Davis for the piece, although Evans is more closely associated with it.

In fact, you could trace Evans's entire career by studying his different interpretations of this composition over the years, documented by more than 30 recordings. When Evans played "Nardis" as a sideman on Cannonball's album,
the song is just a tad faster than a ballad, gliding by at 110 beats per minute.
With Scott LaFaro and Paul Motian in 1961, Evans still underplays while floating
over the ground rhythm, which is now closer to 160 beats per minute. Listeners
can hear a greater sense of urgency in his eight-minute 1968 live recording of
"Nardis," made alongside Eddie Gomez and Jack DeJohnette at the Montreux
Jazz Festival. But this track still keeps to a medium tempo and an aesthetic vision aligned to Evans's initial conception of the song. In contrast, during the
final months of his life, Evans relied on "Nardis" as a daring up-tempo vehicle

bristling with raw energy. His trio often stretched out for more than 15 minutes on the number, which would typically serve as the centerpiece of their sets. I usually prefer Evans's work from the 1950s and 1960s over his late-period efforts—which sometimes strike me as jittery and uncentered, but I make an exception in the case of "Nardis." The performances from the last year of his life are well worth hearing, encompassing some of the most probing and unpredictable efforts from this band.

Although Evans, in these final days, showed that "Nardis" could be a slashing and dashing piece of almost demonic intensity, many of the best cover versions by other artists take on a more subdued cast. George Russell's recording from 1961 offers up a cerebral arrangement, with the front line—Eric Dolphy on bass clarinet, Don Ellis on trumpet, and David Baker on trombone—mixing in counterpoint, dissonance, call-and-response, and other devices in a large-scale reinvention of the Davis standard. Ralph Towner's solo guitar track from 1979 is at the other end of the spectrum, purged of clever arranging tricks but equally powerful in its emotional currents, rhapsodic and introspective by turns. Jacky Terrasson, on his trio performance from 2002, goes still further in his paring down of the song, offering a sparse, moody version that is even slower than Adderley's debut performance from 1958.

RECOMMENDED VERSIONS

Cannonball Adderley, from *Portrait of Cannonball*, New York, July 1, 1958

Bill Evans (with Scott LaFaro and Paul Motian), from *Explorations*, New York, February 2, 1961

George Russell (with Eric Dolphy and Don Ellis), from *Ezz-Thetics*, New York, May 8, 1961

Richard Davis (with Joe Henderson), from *Fancy Free*, Berkeley, California, June 30–July 1, 1977

Ralph Towner, from *Solo Concert*, live at Limmathaus, Zurich, October 1979

Bill Evans, from *The Paris Concert* (Edition Two), Paris, November 26, 1979

Jacky Terrasson, from *Smile*, Pompignan, France, June 12–21, 2002

Nature Boy
Composed by eden ahbez

The tunesmiths who created the golden age of American popular song had their quirks and idiosyncrasies, but eden ahbez demands pride of place as the most eccentric of them all. Twenty years before the first hippies showed up on college campuses, ahbez had already perfected a lifestyle that mixed Eastern mysticism, natural foods, long hair, and a constant quest for self-enlightenment. He reportedly lived on just three dollars a week, and his conversation was dotted with grand pronouncements. Here's a taste: "When I was young I dreamed of a boy searching for God. Now I am old and I dream of God searching for a boy." He preferred to spell his name using all lowercase letters, proclaiming that capital letters should be reserved for God and Infinity.

This orphan from Brooklyn—where he was born as George Alexander Aberle in 1908—was an unlikely composer of hit material, especially when he chose to write about his own "natural" lifestyle. But ahbez had grand plans for "Nature Boy" and showed up backstage after a Nat King Cole performance in Los Angeles, where he attempted to interest the singer's manager in this peculiar song. Cole was intrigued with the piece, and when he started playing it in concert was struck by the enthusiastic response. But before he could make a record, Capitol Records execs needed to find and get permission from the composer, who lived outdoors with no known address. The manhunt ended when ahbez was discovered camped out underneath the letter "L" in the Hollywood Sign.

The song more than fulfilled Cole's and Capitol's expectations, rising to #1 on the *Billboard* chart during the summer of 1948, and remaining there for eight weeks. A host of other famous singers followed up with hit versions of their own. "Nature Boy" was a charted single for Frank Sinatra, Dick Haymes, and Bobby Darin. The composer was written up in *Time* and *Newsweek*, but it's fair to say that success neither spoiled him nor softened his eccentricities. (For evidence, you are pointed toward ahbez's 1960 leader date, *Eden's Island*, which was ahead of its time, and always will be.)

"Nature Boy" took on greater relevance during the 1950s and 1960s, as the rest of society struggled to catch up with ahbez's alternative lifestyle. I find it fitting that John Coltrane embraced this composition at the very moment in his career when he was lingering at the brink between tonal and atonal styles of playing. This is, after all, a song about liberation from the conventional, and who better to put that into practice than Mr. Coltrane, circa 1965? The saxophonist's studio and live recordings from that period find him using the composition as a springboard for lengthy improvisations over static harmonies and a queasy, churning rhythmic undercurrent. Pianist McCoy Tyner maintains only a loose allegiance to various E minor voicings during the solos, and even this slack discipline of the chord-change-that-doesn't-change is more structure than the tenorist can accept, as he superimposes clashing and clanging melodic ideas and kaleidoscopic modal colors.

So many years later, "Nature Boy" is still a deep and deeply moving song. If a performer can rise to the occasion of delivering it—and it requires a certain poise and earnestness to do so convincingly—audiences can be left reeling in the aftermath. That said, a composition that aspires to such Delphic heights invites controversy, ridicule, and parody, as has certainly been the case with "Nature Boy." Red Ingel's Unnatural Seven released their rival recording, "Serutan Yob" (spell it backward to unlock the mystery)—on the Capitol label, no less—shortly after Cole enjoyed his hit with the song, and spurred much laughter with their cutting takeoff. And when contestant Casey Abrams presented "Nature Boy" in a straight jazz arrangement on *American Idol* in 2011, he earned a tumultuous standing ovation from the audience but was widely dissed in the blogosphere and among web chatterers for the sheer strangeness of the proceedings.

Less amusing were accusations and litigation launched by Herman Yablokoff, who claimed that ahbez had plagiarized his song "Shvayg, Mayn Harts" ("Hush, My Heart")—charges that reportedly resulted in a cash settlement from ahbez. Yet an even earlier source for part of the melody can be found. Just compare "Nature Boy" with the second movement of Antonín Dvořák's Piano Quintet No. 2 in A, Op. 81 from 1887.

RECOMMENDED VERSIONS

Nat King Cole, Los Angeles, August 22, 1947

Miles Davis (with Charles Mingus), from *Blue Moods*, New York, July 9, 1955

John Coltrane, from *The John Coltrane Quartet Plays*, Englewood Cliffs, New Jersey, February 18, 1965

Milt Jackson (with Oscar Peterson), from *The Milt Jackson Big 4*, live at the Montreux Jazz Festival, Montreux, Switzerland, July 17, 1975

George Benson, from *In Flight*, Hollywood, August–November 1976

Art Pepper (with Tommy Flanagan), from *Straight Life*, Berkeley, California, September 21, 1979

Kurt Elling, from *The Messenger*, Chicago, July 1994–December 1996

Enrico Rava and Ran Blake, from *Duo en Noir*, live at the Südbahnhof, Frankfurt, September 23, 1999

The Nearness of You
Composed by Hoagy Carmichael, with lyrics by Ned Washington

"The Nearness of You" was a top 10 hit for Glenn Miller during the summer of 1940. But "hit" is a relative term and, for Hoagy Carmichael, nothing composed after his fortieth birthday was likely to match the remarkable successes of "Star Dust" (1927) or "Georgia on My Mind" (1930)—two of the most popular

American songs of the twentieth century. "The Nearness of You" peaked at #5, inspired a few other bands to add it to their repertoire for a while, and then faded from view before the end of the year.

If you follow many of the standard references and discographies, you might gather that Dizzy Gillespie's 1947 Carnegie Hall concert was the high-profile moment that brought this song back into the jazz repertoire. But the surviving recording of the concert shows that Gillespie actually performed the Tadd Dameron chart "Nearness," which bears no relation to Carmichael's "The Nearness of You." The latter composition didn't start showing up on jazz recordings until later in the decade and the early 1950s, when a handful of cover versions were released. George Shearing recorded "The Nearness of You" in London in 1948 in a languorous trio arrangement (but even better is his 1960 collaboration with singer Nancy Wilson); Sarah Vaughan followed up in 1949 and Woody Herman began featuring a Ralph Burns arrangement of the song in 1950. A surviving tape of a radio broadcast from 1951 captures Charlie Parker performing the song as a guest soloist with the Herman band in a concert from Kansas City.

The return of "The Nearness of You" to the pop charts in 1953, in a sugary version by Bob Manning backed by an orchestra led by Monty Kelly (of 101 Strings fame), helped propel the song back into the public's consciousness. More than a dozen jazz versions of "The Nearness of You" were recorded over the next two years, including renditions by Gerry Mulligan (both with Chet Baker and, a few months later, with Bob Brookmeyer), Stan Getz (also with Brookmeyer), Lionel Hampton, Gene Krupa, and others. Louis Armstrong and Ella Fitzgerald performed it for their 1956 collaboration. The song has been firmly entrenched as a jazz standard since that time.

"The Nearness of You" is less overtly jazzy than other Hoagy Carmichael compositions, without the intervallic theatrics of "Star Dust" or "Skylark" or the invitation to bluesiness of "Georgia on My Mind." But the song conveys a sense of intimacy and heartache that even these grand showpieces can't surpass. The melody unfolds so naturally that you can imagine the composer coming up with it in a single burst of inspiration, and Ned Washington's lyrics are almost uncanny in how comfortably they match and amplify the emotional sensibility of the music.

A number of jazz artists seeking a larger crossover audience have relied on this song in more recent decades, and their success testifies to the durability of such a well-wrought composition. Two of the most interesting are Norah Jones's interpretation from her mega-seller (a staggering 20 million copies sold) *Come Away with Me*—with "The Nearness of You" standing out as her jazziest performance from the album—and Michael Brecker's 2000 pairing with James Taylor. On the latter track, a world-class combo (including Herbie Hancock and Pat Metheny) presents a very effective arrangement that artfully mixes jazz and pop sensibilities.

RECOMMENDED VERSIONS

Glenn Miller, New York, April 28, 1940

Sarah Vaughan, New York, December 21, 1949

Charlie Parker with the Woody Herman Orchestra (with an arrangement by Ralph Burns), live at the Municipal Arena, Kansas City, Missouri, July 22, 1951

Gerry Mulligan (with Bob Brookmeyer), from *Pleyel Jazz Concert, Vol. 1,* live at Salle Pleyel, Paris, June 1, 1954

Louis Armstrong and Ella Fitzgerald, from *Ella and Louis,* Los Angeles, August 16, 1956

George Shearing and Nancy Wilson, from *The Swingin's Mutual,* New York, July 6, 1960

Johnny Hodges, from *Wings and Things,* Englewood Cliffs, New Jersey, July 27, 1965

Warne Marsh, from *A Ballad Album,* Monster, Holland, April 7, 1983

Michael Brecker and James Taylor (with Herbie Hancock), from *Nearness of You: The Ballad Book,* New York, 2000

Steve Turre (with James Carter and Mulgrew Miller), from *TNT,* November 9–10, 2000

Norah Jones, from *Come Away with Me,* New York and Shokan, New York, circa 2001

Nice Work If You Can Get It
Composed by George Gershwin, with lyrics by Ira Gershwin

Here we find that felicitous marriage of jazzy melody and brisk American diction that is characteristic of the Gershwin brothers' finest work. A British peer might say, "It would be suitable employment if one could secure it," but the Yank simply declares: "Nice work if you can get it."

Which makes it all the more surprising to learn that Ira Gershwin picked up the title from an English magazine, and the song was written for a movie, *A Damsel in Distress,* based on a novel by British author P. G. Wodehouse. Indeed, Gershwin's great Anglophile tunes "A Foggy Day (in London Town)" and "Stiff Upper Lip" come from the same film. But, coming full circle, Wodehouse's tale is about an American songwriter named George. So allow me to view this tune as an autobiographical exercise of sorts. In the film, the song accompanies a famous Fred Astaire dance that involved an early use of the zoom lens in the context of a continuous take.

Tommy Dorsey made the first jazz recording of "Nice Work If You Can Get It" three weeks after the release of the movie, delivering a very danceable arrangement well suited to the Swing Era tastes of the day. Billie Holiday recorded the song with the Teddy Wilson Orchestra the following month, and their version reached #20 on the chart. This is in an odd affair, with Wilson setting up a surprisingly old-fashioned, almost ragtime-ish, feel to the performance. But when Holiday starts singing, she resists the traditional two-beat pulse and captures a more modern sensibility. Even so, one senses that her perspective on this song is at cross-purposes with the bandleader's.

The beboppers adopted this song at a very early stage. It seems to have been a frequently called tune at Minton's Playhouse, the Harlem nightclub closely connected with the rise of modern jazz. Jerry Newman captures Thelonious Monk performing a quirky and avant-garde-ish "Nice Work" on a 1941 amateur recording from Minton's. You would be hard pressed to find a more daring jazz recording from this period. Monk revisited the song in a similar spirit for his October 1947 trio session for Blue Note, and it showed up again on his very last studio project, made for the Black Lion label in London in November 1971.

Art Tatum recorded the standard at his justly praised July 1949 session for Capitol, and showed once again that he was a marvelous interpreter of George Gershwin's music—no wonder Gershwin himself was one of Tatum's admirers. Other memorable keyboard versions of this song include Erroll Garner's brief but spirited rendition from 1968 and Jessica Williams's solo performance from her 1992 live recording at the Maybeck Recital Hall.

Virtually every jazz vocalist of note has tackled "Nice Work" at one point or another. Mel Tormé's collaborations with Marty Paich are much prized by fans of the Velvet Fog (as this singer was sometimes called), and their version of "Nice Work" from 1956—with its modulations, interpolations, and palpitations—ranks among their better moments. Not to be outdone, Frank Sinatra brought Count Basie and company along for a fast, swinging 1962 treatment. Ella Fitzgerald, for her part, secured the services of André Previn for her 1983 recording on Pablo.

The tune has been mainstreamed over the years, even showing up on the opening credits for the late-1990s sitcom *Cybill*, starring Cybill Shepherd. Certainly, Gershwin's changes are still capable of surprises. Paul Motian's version from his *On Broadway* project—where he is joined by Joe Lovano, Bill Frisell, and Charlie Haden—captures a bracingly postmodern sensibility. Nonetheless, it's sobering to consider that Monk's version of this song from back in 1941 sounds more modernistic than the vast majority of current-day renditions you will hear.

RECOMMENDED VERSIONS

Tommy Dorsey, New York, October 14, 1937

Billie Holiday (with Teddy Wilson), New York, November 1, 1937

Thelonious Monk, live at Minton's Playhouse, New York, May 4, 1941

Thelonious Monk, New York, October 24, 1947

Art Tatum, Los Angeles, July 13, 1949

Mel Tormé (with Marty Paich), from *Mel Tormé Sings Fred Astaire*, Hollywood, November 1956

Frank Sinatra (with Count Basie), from *Sinatra-Basie*, Los Angeles, October 2, 1962

Erroll Garner, from *Erroll Garner Plays Gershwin and Kern*, New York, February 5, 1968

Ella Fitzgerald (with André Previn), from *Nice Work If You Can Get It*, New York, May 23, 1983

Paul Motian (with Joe Lovano, Charlie Haden, and Bill Frisell), from *On Broadway, Vol. 2*, New York, September 1989

Jessica Williams, from *Live at Maybeck Recital Hall, Vol. 21*, live at the Maybeck Recital Hall, Berkeley, California, February 16, 1992

Night and Day
Composed by Cole Porter

Fred Astaire later noted that *Gay Divorce*, which now sounds like the name of a ballot initiative rather than a Broadway musical, "came to be known as the 'Night and Day' show." When Hollywood made it into a movie—changing the title to *The Gay Divorcee* to placate the censors at the Hays Office—"Night and Day" was the only original Cole Porter tune to make the transition to the silver screen. Astaire was skeptical about the song and show at first, but Porter was skilled at matching his melodies to the dancer's narrow vocal range. The end result was not only a perfect vehicle for Astaire, but also one of the top ten ASCAP-revenue producing songs of all time.

I wonder if Porter's unusual chord change into the second theme, which moves up a minor third rather than the more common shift of a fourth, was designed to ensure that the high notes here weren't too high for his star performer. Or perhaps we can take at face value Porter's claim to have been inspired by the Islamic call to prayer he heard during a trip to Morocco. The vocal leaps required are not child's play the range here is four notes beyond the octave— but still quite manageable for most singers. In any event, the shift imparts a piquant flavor to the whole and represents the moment when a song that might have been ho-hum reaches for greatness. The elongated 48-bar form and lopsided couplets of the lyrics enhance the ecstatic flow of the music.

Swing bands were the first to see jazz potential in this song, with Benny Goodman, Artie Shaw, Tommy Dorsey, and the Casa Loma Orchestra standing out as early adopters of "Night and Day." Django Reinhardt, with his 1938 recording, confirmed that the song was also suitable for small combo performance. But Frank Sinatra did more than anyone to imprint Cole Porter's song into the collective American consciousness—although, for the record, Porter didn't like Sinatra covering his tunes because of the liberties the vocalist took with the words. Sinatra "was so excited you almost believed he had never recorded before," conductor Alex Stordahl later recalled. "I think this was the turning point in his career." Sinatra would record "Night and Day" again in the 1950s, 1960s, and 1970s, yet never surpass the innocence and passion conveyed on this early vintage performance.

Jazz fans have no shortage of high-octane versions of this song to enjoy. Teddy Wilson's Keystone transcriptions from 1939 and 1940 include a finely etched solo rendition, while Mary Lou Williams offered up a more swinging interpretation five years later. Bill Evans adopted a much different attitude on his 1958 trio outing, and his acerbic reworking of the standard will surprise those who associate this pianist only with a tranquil impressionism. Among sax versions, Sonny Rollins and Stan Getz both recorded standout tracks within a few days of each other in 1964, and Joe Henderson did the same five months later. Yet this litany of tenorists would be incomplete without the inclusion Eddie "Lockjaw" Davis, a fiercely inventive soloist who often gets forgotten amidst his more progressive contemporaries, but put in as strong a claim as any to this song. Check out, for a persuasive example of Lockjaw's sax heroics, his 1962 version, which will give you a sense of why this player was so formidable in a horn battle.

RECOMMENDED VERSIONS

Django Reinhardt (with the Quintette du Hot Club de France), London, January 31, 1938

Teddy Wilson, New York, circa 1939–40

Frank Sinatra, Hollywood, January 19, 1942

Mary Lou Williams, New York, August 10, 1944

Red Norvo (with Charles Mingus and Tal Farlow), Los Angeles, May 3, 1950

Art Tatum and Roy Eldridge, from *The Tatum Group Masterpieces, Vol. 2*, Los Angeles, March 29, 1955

Eddie "Lockjaw" Davis, from *Goin' to the Meeting*, New York, May 1, 1962

Stan Getz (with Bill Evans), from *Stan Getz & Bill Evans*, New York, May 6, 1964

Sonny Rollins, from *The Standard Sonny Rollins*, New York, June 24, 1964

Joe Henderson (with McCoy Tyner), from *Inner Urge*, Englewood Cliffs, New Jersey, November 30, 1964

Joe Pass, from *Virtuoso*, Los Angeles, August 28, 1973

Michel Petrucciani, from *Pianism*, New York, December 20, 1985

Kenny Garrett, from *Trilogy*, New York, 1995

Night in Tunisia
Composed by Dizzy Gillespie and Frank Paparelli

The earliest recording of this song gives little indication of its exciting future. Composed by Dizzy Gillespie during his stint at Kelly's Stables on 52nd Street with Benny Carter's band, the piece was first recorded by Sarah Vaughan under the title "Interlude," and comes across in this incarnation as more an exotic atmosphere piece than a modern jazz anthem. But by the time Gillespie recorded it with Boyd Raeburn's band in January 1945, the tempo had picked up considerably, the arrangement was brassier and sassier, and an ecstatically nervous energy propels the performance forward.

Earl Hines later claimed that he came up with the name "A Night in Tunisia," but Gillespie rebuts this, noting that he had performed the song under its eventual title before joining Hines's band. For the record, the trumpeter insisted that the work should be called "Night in Tunisia," but most have ignored this reasonable request, adding a prefatory article to the name ("A Night in Tunisia"). Frank Paparelli is usually credited as co-composer, but Gillespie adds a footnote to this as well, insisting that Paparelli played no role in writing the song, but was given a piece of the action in exchange for transcribing some Gillespie solos for publication.

Art Blakey later told a colorful story of Gillespie composing the piece on a desktop improvised from a garbage-can lid. Dizzy, in contrast, recalls first devising the chords during a break from the filming of a Maxine Sullivan "soundie" (an early predecessors of the music video). Whatever its origins, the song is a marvel. The melody is catchy, and the harmonic movement in the interlude leading up to the solo break deserves to be studied in conservatory composition classes. During my experiences teaching the niceties of bebop to college students, I found that they often still recalled this song long after they had forgotten "Donna Lee," "Ornithology," and other modern jazz standards.

Gillespie plays an exhilarating solo on his 1946 recording for Victor—the version of this song that was later inducted into the Grammy Hall of Fame. Yet Charlie Parker eventually staked his own claim to "Night in Tunisia," with some 20 recordings documenting his zeal in performing it. On the occasions when Bird and Dizzy gigged together (Town Hall in 1945, Carnegie Hall in 1947, Massey Hall in 1953), the altoist took the featured four-bar break that introduces the first solo. His most memorable outing, however, transpired with Miles

Davis rather than Gillespie on trumpet, at Parker's 1946 Hollywood session for the Dial label. Bird's execution of the break, not just the blistering speed but his masterful placement of rhythmic accents in the midst of the maelstrom, thrilled me the first time I heard it as a teenager and still does today.

With such rich precedents, later versions of this song often strike me as anticlimactic. Yet Clifford Brown's extended solo from his jam session appearance at Music City in Philadelphia is worthy of inclusion on any short list of classic performances, as is Sonny Rollins's live renditions at the Village Vanguard two years later. Shortly before his death, Fats Navarro performed "Night in Tunisia" at a Birdland engagement that was captured on an amateur recording. The sound quality is abysmal, but Navarro's contribution is riveting. Art Blakey, who was a sideman on this gig, sometimes turned the Gillespie song into a drum feature with his Jazz Messengers. His discography includes more recorded versions than Parker, and almost as many Gillespie himself. Many of these are worth hearing, but Blakey's 1960 recording with Lee Morgan and Wayne Shorter in the band is a good place to start.

RECOMMENDED VERSIONS

Sarah Vaughan (released under the title "Interlude" or "Love Was Just an Interlude"), New York, December 31, 1944

Boyd Raeburn (with Dizzy Gillespie), New York, January 26, 1945

Charlie Parker and Dizzy Gillespie, live at Town Hall, New York, June 22, 1945

Dizzy Gillespie, New York, February 22, 1946

Charlie Parker, Hollywood, March 28, 1946

Charlie Parker and Dizzy Gillespie, live at Carnegie Hall, New York, September 29, 1947

Fats Navarro, live at Birdland, June 30, 1950

Bud Powell, New York, May 1, 1951

Charlie Parker and Dizzy Gillespie, from *Jazz at Massey Hall*, live at Massey Hall, Toronto, May 15, 1953

Clifford Brown, from *The Beginning and the End*, live at Music City, May 31, 1955

Sonny Rollins, the "evening take" from *A Night at the Village Vanguard, Vol. 1*, live at the Village Vanguard, New York, November 3, 1957

Art Blakey (with Lee Morgan), from *A Night in Tunisia*, Hackensack, New Jersey, August 14, 1960

Dexter Gordon (with Bud Powell), from *Our Man in Paris*, Paris, May 23, 1963

Mary Lou Williams, from *Live at the Keystone Korner*, live at the Keystone Korner, San Francisco, May 8, 1977

Donald Harrison (with Christian Scott), from *Real Life Stories*, New York, November 4–6, 2001

Night Train

Composed by Jimmy Forrest

Jimmy Forrest's recording of this song stayed on the R&B chart for 20 weeks in 1952, and held on to the top spot for almost two months. Buddy Morrow also enjoyed a hit recording of the song around this same time. A decade later James Brown put "Night Train" back on to the charts, with his record rising to #5 on the R&B rankings and #35 on the *Billboard* Hot 100.

Although Forrest is credited as composer, little in this piece is original, and most of it can be traced back to the Ellington band, where Forrest briefly worked in the late 1940s. The familiar opening riff from "Night Train" can be heard on Johnny Hodges's 1940 recording of "That's the Blues Old Man," credited to Hodges and Irving Mills. The ensuing boogie-oriented theme can be found on Duke Ellington's "Happy-Go-Lucky Local," the fourth movement of his *Deep South Suite* from 1946, where composer credits are shared by Ellington and Billy Strayhorn. Ellington, himself no stranger to the benefits of borrowing musical ideas, pursued legal action in this instance, and his suit was settled out of court, the terms undisclosed.

But give Forrest credit for adding a few elements, including a very clever integration of the sax and drum parts and a memorable tenor solo, often imitated note-for-note in later cover versions. Ellington's piece, despite its bluesy elements, is one of the more avant-garde jazz works of its day, and was unlikely to earn many spins on the jukebox. In contrast, Forrest finds a meeting point between jazz and rhythm-and-blues, anticipating in his own way the hard bop movement that would dominate the jazz scene a short while later.

Various lyrics have been added to this song. The earliest set of words was written by Oscar Washington and Lewis Simpkins (the latter, by *coincidence*, an owner of the label that released the Forrest recording) in 1952. James Brown, for his part, just reels off a list of cities—ostensibly, the stops on the night train itinerary. Around 1960, vocalist Eddie Jefferson contributed his own (and generally superior) words for a different take on "Night Train," and he kept the song in his repertoire for the rest of his life. It is presented in a very swinging arrangement by Slide Hampton with a solo contribution by Hamiet Bluiett on Jefferson's 1977 project *The Main Man*.

Few jazz standards have come from rhythm-and-blues bands, and I suspect many improvisers still scorn "Night Train" the way a wine connoisseur would scoff at a jug of muscatel. For a time, "Night Train" had a reputation as a song more suited to strip clubs than jazz clubs. Yet the song lives on in the jazz repertoire because it works like a charm in performance—even or especially when the musicianship on the bandstand is less than virtuosic—energizing the audience in a manner that compositions with finer pedigrees often fail to match.

RECOMMENDED VERSIONS

Jimmy Forrest, Chicago, November 27, 1951

Buddy Morrow, Hollywood, April 12, 1952

James Brown, from *Live at the Apollo*, recorded live at the Apollo Theater, New York, October 24, 1962

Oscar Peterson, from *Night Train*, Los Angeles, December 16, 1962

Eddie Jefferson (with Hamiet Bluiett), from *The Main Man*, New York, October 9, 1977

Dirty Dozen Brass Band, from *Live: Mardi Gras in Montreux*, live at the Montreux Jazz Festival, Montreux, Switzerland, July 1985

World Saxophone Quartet, from *Rhythm and Blues*, New York, November 1988

Now's the Time
Composed by Charlie Parker

Four years after Charlie Parker recorded "Now's the Time," the melody showed up on a jukebox R&B hit by Paul Williams called "The Hucklebuck." "The Hucklebuck" would also be a big seller for Roy Milton, Lucky Millinder (who recorded it as "D-Natural Blues") and, years later, Chubby Checker, each version earning jukebox spins with the same catchy blues riff. Audience appeal was helped along by a lascivious dance of the same name. In one of the funniest moments from *The Honeymooners*, Art Carney teaches Jackie Gleason how to dance "The Hucklebuck"—track this TV show clip down on YouTube, and enjoy Carney's dancing and Gleason's reaction, while marveling at the convoluted path of dissemination that, over the course of a decade, brought this cultural meme from Charlie Parker's horn to Ralph Kramden's apartment.

Since Williams's "The Hucklebuck" was released on the same label as Parker's record, and relied on the same producer, Teddy Reig, you might think that the connection between the two songs would be noticed and that authorship would be assigned to the originator. Instead, Andy Gibson—who had already "composed" the aforementioned "D-Natural Blues" as a work-for-hire for Millinder—received songwriting credit on Williams's hit record. Millinder later sued, unsuccessfully, for a share of the royalties, but Parker never entered the legal fray.

Yet Bird's original song has enjoyed more lasting success than the assorted R&B knockoffs. Over the years, "Now's the Time" has been covered by many prominent jazz saxophonists, but the first to do so would be 20-year-old John Coltrane, who is captured taking a fluid two-chorus solo on "Now's the Time" in the company of some Navy musicians at a semiprofessional recording session held in Hawaii in 1946. Coltrane's alto work here shows an allegiance to Parker that is far less evident in his mature output.

When Sonny Rollins, Coltrane's great rival for sax supremacy, recorded the song in the 1960s, he brought a top-notch band into the studio—Herbie Hancock, Ron Carter, and Roy McCurdy—and left behind two very different takes of this song. The best-known version is the four-minute track featured as the opening cut on his *Now's the Time* album. But Rollins fans are advised to seek out the 16-minute alternate take, a far more discursive and unpredictable exploration of Parker's composition, which can be found on the *Sonny Rollins & Co. 1964* release.

"Now's the Time" figures prominently on many Parker tribute recordings—including Sonny Stitt's *Stitt Plays Bird*, Supersax's *Chasin' the Bird*, and Roy Haynes's *Birds of a Feather*—and in other gatherings where bebop is on the agenda. Yet this composition is one of the least bop-oriented of the modern jazz songs that came to the fore during the 1940s. Although Parker was capable of writing intricate bebop melody lines, he sometimes stepped back from his more progressive leanings and drew on his Kansas City jazz roots in crafting simpler, bluesier compositions—of which "Now's the Time" is a case in point. Musicians who don't feel quite yet ready to tackle "Confirmation" or "Donna Lee" will find this a far less intimidating entry point into Parker's oeuvre.

By the way, my favorite memory of this song comes from neither recording nor performing but from a teaching gig. At the summer camp conducted each year by the Stanford Jazz Workshop, founder Jim Nadel instituted an annual tradition in which all the faculty members and students in the program would, at the exact same moment, stop whatever they were doing and join together in a communal rendition of "Now's the Time": 200 or more performers, of all ages and levels of ability, bombarding the classrooms and corridors of the Braun Music Building with their simultaneous tribute to Bird. Even after several years of participating in this event, I never lost the feeling that we were all doing something deeply subversive—which may, after all, be exactly the right attitude for propagating Parker's legacy.

RECOMMENDED VERSIONS

Charlie Parker, New York, November 26, 1945

John Coltrane, Hawaii, July 13, 1946

Art Blakey (with Clifford Brown and Horace Silver), from *A Night at Birdland, Vol. 2*, live at Birdland, New York, February 21, 1954

Sonny Stitt (with John Lewis and Jim Hall), from *Stitt Plays Bird*, New York, January 29, 1963

Sonny Rollins, from *Sonny Rollins & Co. 1964*, New York, January 24, 1964

Eddie Jefferson (with James Moody), from *Body and Soul*, New York, September 27, 1968

Roy Haynes (with Roy Hargrove and Kenny Garrett), from *Birds of a Feather: A Tribute to Charlie Parker*, New York, March 26–27, 2001

Nuages
Composed by Django Reinhardt

Django Reinhardt's most famous composition "Nuages" was a wartime effort, first recorded a few months after the Germans occupied Paris. This was a difficult time for Reinhardt. His colleague in the Quintette du Hot Club de France, Stéphane Grappelli, had taken residence in London for the duration of the war, but Reinhardt, after briefly abandoning Paris for the South of France, returned to the French capital. Here he resumed his music career and familiar role as the leading light of Parisian jazz—a dicey proposition given the Nazis' animosity to that type of music. Reinhardt was granted permission to perform in public, but was required to submit his song selections to the *Propagandastaffel*, the official censorship bureau, in advance of each concert.

Reinhardt arranged his new song for a reconfigured combo relying on clarinet, then in the ascendancy in Swing Era bands, rather than Grappelli's violin. He first tackled "Nuages" during a visit to the studio in October 1940 but was unhappy with the results; later, at a December session he adopted a slower tempo, added a second clarinet, and delivered both a classic jazz performance and a commercial hit. "Nuages" sold 100,000 copies and would prove to be the most celebrated record in Reinhardt's career. With "La Marseillaise" banned by the new overseers, many adopted this nostalgic melody, with its wistful evocation of a bygone better time, as an alternative national anthem.

The song, as it is usually played, evokes a dreamy mood. Yet Reinhardt's December 1940 recording adds a strident eight-bar intro that has more in common with Stravinsky than traditional jazz. Later recordings tend to omit this avant-garde setup in the song, which is a shame—it is well worth retaining, if only for the shock value when the band settles into the impressionistic main theme. Yet even Reinhardt learned to do without it.

Although Europeans had jumped on the jazz bandwagon almost from the start, and could boast of their own cadre of homegrown performers, with Django and his "Nuages" one hears something even more prepossessing: a fresh conception of jazz that moves beyond the imitation of role models from America. From this starting point one traces a genealogy leading to many of the major European jazz talents of the current day. Today every major city on the continent has its distinctive jazz bands drawing on local cultural traditions for inspiration, but before Django this type of self-confident European jazz was all but unknown.

As subsequent events have shown, this song knows no geographical borders. In recent years, Detroit-born James Carter has adapted "Nuages" to the bass sax in a performance that threatens to blow out the woofer in your stereo speakers. British guitarist Allan Holdsworth slyly updates the composition on his 1994 recording *None Too Soon*, and for his 2006 release *Welcome to the Instrumental Asylum*, Australian guitarist Ben Rogers performs Reinhardt's song in a raw electric version, with hints of blues, heavy metal, and surf music. There are quite a few ingredients on that list, and none of them relating to Django's Gypsy and European roots, but such unconstrained hybridization is one more sign that this old song still has something new to say.

RECOMMENDED VERSIONS

Django Reinhardt (with the Quintette du Hot Club de France), Paris, December 13, 1940

Sidney Bechet, from *Rendez-vous avec Sidney Bechet et André Réwéliotty*, Paris, May 28, 1953

Paul Desmond, from *Pure Desmond*, New York, September 24–26, 1974

Oscar Peterson and Stéphane Grappelli, from *Skol*, live at Tivoli Hall, Copenhagen, July 6, 1979

Benny Carter, from *Elegy in Blue*, Los Angeles, May 18–19, 1994

Allan Holdsworth, from *None Too Soon*, North County, San Diego, California, October 1994

James Carter, from *Chasin' the Gypsy*, New York, circa 2000

Ben Rogers, from *Welcome to the Instrumental Asylum*, Elsternwick, Australia, January 20, 2005

O

Oh, Lady Be Good!
Composed by George Gershwin, with lyrics by Ira Gershwin

I've never, ever heard anyone use the phrase "lady be good" in conversation, although I have been tempted to try it out on my wife over breakfast some morning, just to gauge the response. I am assured that back in the 1920s, this admonition, while explicitly asking the lady in question to be *good*, actually signaled a request for her to be somewhat *bad*.

In any event, I'm convinced that much of the lasting appeal of this standard derives from the snappy, slangy pertness of the words. When the song made its debut in the 1924 show *Lady, Be Good!* (note the insertion of the comma—the producer's attempt to soften the cheekiness of Ira Gershwin's rejoinder), many tunesmiths were still writing sentimental ballads and mushy romantic fare little different from what parlor pianists had been pounding out in the late nineteenth century. But the Gershwins were determined to change all that, and just as George had an ear for the innovations of jazz, his brother Ira listened for the new vernacular twists in the spoken language of the day. In "Oh, Lady Be Good!" both came together to create a brash, new song—one that could hardly have been written only a few years before.

Gershwin's tempo directions state that "Oh, Lady Be Good!" should be played "slow and gracefully." If you want to get a sense of Gershwin's original conception, track down Cliff "Ukulele Ike" Edwards's recording from 1925, which traipses ahead at a leisurely 130 beats per minute and captures a sweet, plaintive quality that rarely comes across in later cover versions. Jazz musicians, for their part, have wanted to play this song at a much faster pace. Early jazz band recordings—such as Paul Whiteman's hit version from 1924—tend to take it at a danceable medium tempo.

And by the time Django Reinhardt recorded it, almost exactly a decade later, the pulse had accelerated further.

The song was destined to become a hard-swinging staple of the big bands, but three small combo performances from the mid-1930s, each presenting a leading horn player of the day, helped to establish "Oh, Lady Be Good!" as a jazz standard. Lester Young's rendition alongside Count Basie from 1936 remains the best known of these nowadays, and includes one of his most studied and emulated sax solos, but Coleman Hawkins's London recording from 1934 and Benny Goodman's trio outing from 1936 also captured the attention of jazz fans and other musicians.

From that point onward, the Gershwin tune would remain a staple of jam sessions and record dates. The rise of bebop and other new styles may have somewhat diminished its luster but could not dislodge it as an important song that all jazz players need to know. Charlie Parker clearly paid close attention to Lester Young's famous solo on "Oh, Lady Be Good!" and left us a memorable live recording of it alongside Young himself in Los Angeles in 1946. The only artist to match, and perhaps surpass, Young's advocacy of this song is Ella Fitzgerald. Her 1946 recording was a last-minute addition to a studio date, with an arrangement worked out on the spot and the song captured in a single take, yet this pull-out-the-stops performance, built around the vocalist's scat-singing pyrotechnics, ranks among her most popular efforts. Fitzgerald often delivered very similar interpretations in later years, but on her 1959 Gershwin songbook project she offers a true ballad performance of "Oh, Lady Be Good!" and also includes the brooding verse, an opening that contrasts effectively with the main of the body of the song but is usually omitted by jazz artists.

The song continues to be widely played in jazz circles, but rarely by the fashionable players of the day. Like many standards from the 1920s, this one risks marginalization as a period piece, relied on to evoke the spirit of a bygone era rather than reflect the musical tastes of the current era. Yet the song still can serve as an inspiring springboard for a jam, and performers who call on "I Got Rhythm" in those freewheeling contexts might want to consider this other Gershwin standard as an occasional alternative.

RECOMMENDED VERSIONS

Paul Whiteman, New York, December 29, 1924

Cliff "Ukelele Ike" Edwards, New York, January 1925

Coleman Hawkins, London, November 18, 1934

Django Reinhardt (with the Quintette du Hot Club de France), Paris, December 28, 1934

Benny Goodman (with Teddy Wilson and Gene Krupa), Chicago, April 27, 1936

Lester Young (with Count Basie), Chicago, November 9, 1936

Jazz at the Philharmonic (with Charlie Parker and Lester Young), live at Philharmonic Auditorium, Los Angeles, January 28, 1946

Ella Fitzgerald (with Bob Haggart), New York, May 19, 1947

Lee Konitz and Gerry Mulligan (with Chet Baker) from *Konitz Meets Mulligan*, Los Angeles, January 25, 1953

Ella Fitzgerald, from *Ella Fitzgerald Sings the George and Ira Gershwin Songbook*, Los Angeles, January 5–8, 1959

Sonny Stitt, Harry "Sweets" Edison, and Eddie "Lockjaw" Davis, from *Sonny, Sweets and Jaws*, live at Bubba's, Fort Lauderdale, Florida, November 11, 1981

Regina Carter (with Kenny Barron), from *Rhythms of the Heart*, New York, November–December 1998

Old Folks

Composed by Willard Robison, with lyrics by Dedette Lee Hill

Few things are rarer in the realm of popular music than a hit song about old age and the imminence of death. Yet composer Willard Robison built his legacy on unconventional tunes of this sort—not just "Old Folks," but also "Don't Smoke in Bed" (a hit for Peggy Lee in 1948) and "It's Never Too Late to Pray." In addition to finding musical accompaniment to end-of-life musings, Robison also pushed further into the aural afterlife, as documented in his song "The Devil Is Afraid of Music" and his tribute work "The Band Upstairs," which envisions the postmortem music making of great jazz players who have passed on, including Fats Waller, Bix Beiderbecke, and Bunny Berigan.

Robison relied on a variety of lyricists for his songs, which were often marked by a lonesome world-weariness mixed with ample doses of nostalgia and small-town Americana. "Old Folks," with words by Dedette Lee Hill—the wife and sometime collaborator of Billy Hill, a tunesmith who specialized in cowboy songs—is a character sketch of an elderly man who has taken on that nickname. "Everyone knows him as Old Folks," as the song states in its opening phrase. The lyrics must have struck listeners as quaintly anachronistic even back in the 1930s, with their references to the Civil War and Gettysburg Address. Nowadays audiences will probably scratch their heads in befuddlement when the singer mentions that no one can remember whether Old Folks fought for the "blue or the gray." But the song retains its appeal and place in the standard repertoire, even as its references grow more and more outdated, largely due to its muted poignancy.

"Old Folks" enjoyed a brief flurry of commercial success in late 1938 and early 1939. Larry Clinton's release, featuring vocalist Bea Wain, was a top 10 hit, while Mildred Bailey and Bing Crosby also recorded "Old Folks" around this time, and Benny Goodman and Fats Waller performed it on radio broadcasts. Very few cover versions were made in the 1940s, although Don Byas's rendition from 1946 set the stage for the song's adoption by other horn players during the 1950s. Ben Webster, who first recorded "Old Folks" in 1951, would serve as the most tireless advocate for the composition—he continued to rely on it as a ballad feature for the rest of his career, and left behind more than a dozen recordings of the song. Charlie Parker's 1953 interpretation is perhaps the best-known version of "Old Folks" from the decade, but this is not one of Bird's shining moments, his alto stylings weighed down by obtrusive and campy contributions from the Dave Lambert Singers.

The song has produced other jazz curios along the way. An amateur recording of a practice session at Eric Dolphy's home, made in 1954, finds the altoist working through "Old Folks" with trumpeter Clifford Brown making an unexpected appearance as pianist. A Jimmy Giuffre recording from 1958 showcases the leader playing "Old Folks" on four overdubbed tenor saxophones—an attempt to recreate his famous "four brothers" sound as a one-man horn section. That same year, Fred Katz tried to turn "Old Folks" into a vehicle for jazz cello.

These versions may delight or amuse, but Miles Davis's recording of "Old Folks," from his 1961 project *Someday My Prince Will Come*, remains the most familiar jazz interpretation of this standard. Because of a misleading album cover, many fans have long assumed that John Coltrane plays sax on this track. In truth, Hank Mobley handles the tenor duties here. But don't let Trane's absence deter you from listening—this is one of Davis's most moving ballad performances, and as close as you will come to a definitive version of "Old Folks."

RECOMMENDED VERSIONS

Mildred Bailey, New York, September 14, 1938

Don Byas, New York, May 17, 1946

Ben Webster, Los Angeles, December 27, 1951

Gene Ammons, New York, March 24, 1952

Max Roach (with Booker Little), from *Award-Winning Drummer*, New York, November 25, 1959

Miles Davis, from *Someday My Prince Will Come*, New York, March 20, 1961

Carmen McRae, from *Carmen McRae at the Great American Music Hall*, live at the Great American Music Hall, San Francisco, June 15–17, 1976

Henry Butler (with Freddie Hubbard), from *Fivin' Around*, Los Angeles, 1986

Keith Jarrett (with the Standards Trio), from *Standards in Norway*, live at Oslo Konserthus, Oslo, October 7, 1989

Oleo
Composed by Sonny Rollins

Miles Davis's *Bags' Groove* album, recorded for the Prestige label in 1954, is less often heard by jazz fans nowadays than the trumpeter's projects for Columbia from the second half of the decade. Yet every one of the original compositions featured at this session became a jazz standard, including three jam-oriented Sonny Rollins works: "Airegin," "Oleo," and "Doxy."

Rollins was only 23 at the time of this date, but few young players of any era could boast of such a star-studded musical education and apprenticeship. While still in high school, Rollins gigged in a band alongside Jackie McLean and Kenny Drew. At age 18, he recorded alongside Fats Navarro as a member of Bud Powell's Modernists, whose music foreshadowed the coming hard bop sound of the 1950s. Other early projects found him in the company of Charlie Parker, Thelonious Monk, Miles Davis, and the Modern Jazz Quartet. The year after this session, Rollins would join the Clifford Brown-Max Roach Quintet, arguably the most exciting modern jazz combo of the period.

Even after Miles formed a new band with John Coltrane, "Oleo" stayed in Davis's repertoire. The trumpeter recorded it on his *Relaxin'* album from 1956, returned to it again when Bill Evans joined the band in 1958, performed it at Carnegie Hall in 1961, and was still playing it at the Plugged Nickel in 1965. The propagation continued from there: Bill Evans recorded "Oleo" on his *Everybody Digs Bill Evans* album from 1958—those who don't hear Evans's debt to pianist Lennie Tristano in his later work merely need listen to this early effort to trace the connection. A little-known and peculiar John Coltrane session from around this time finds the tenorist performing "Oleo" alongside teenage tuba player Ray Draper. A live recording from 1961 captures Coltrane's occasional bandmate Eric Dolphy also in fine form working over the changes to "Oleo."

Sonny Rollins was on sabbatical from the jazz world at the time, but he too put his personal stamp on "Oleo" again and again, as documented by a series of live performances captured on tape in 1959 and from 1962 to 1965. His interpretation of the song evolved in tandem with his own playing—nowhere more impressively than on the 25-minute version of "Oleo" recorded by Rollins alongside Don Cherry in 1962. Few of Rollins's solos from any period can surpass this extended outing in terms of sheer bravado and avant-garde risk taking.

The song itself is simple enough: a 32-bar chart based on "I Got Rhythm" changes, with a bop-oriented line for the A theme, and no set melody for the B section. But the flexibility and familiarity of the underlying harmonic structure have no doubt kept "Oleo" popular with jazz musicians over the years, and more than a half-century after its debut it remains one of the most frequently played "rhythm changes" tunes both at informal jam sessions and public performances. Noteworthy recordings of the song include Keith Jarrett's trio performance from Montreux, Horace Tapscott's prickly reworking alongside Billy Hart and Ray Drummond, and Brad Mehldau's duet with Joel Frahm, the latter putting a new spin on "Oleo" by taking it at half the usual tempo.

RECOMMENDED VERSIONS

Miles Davis (with Sonny Rollins and Horace Silver), from *Bags' Groove*, Hackensack, New Jersey, June 29, 1954

Miles Davis (with John Coltrane, Bill Evans, and Cannonball Adderley), from *Jazz at the Plaza*, live at the Plaza Hotel, New York, September 9, 1958

John Coltrane (with Ray Draper), from *Like Sonny*, New York, November 1958

Bill Evans, from *Everybody Digs Bill Evans*, New York, December 15, 1958

Eric Dolphy, from *Eric Dolphy in Europe, Vol. 1*, live at Berlingske Has, Copenhagen, September 8, 1961

Sonny Rollins (with Don Cherry), from *Our Man in Jazz*, live at the Village Gate, New York, July 29–30, 1962

Jeremy Steig (with Denny Zeitlin), from *Flute Fever*, New York, 1963

Pat Martino, from *Desperado*, New York, March 9, 1970

James Carter, from *Jurassic Classics*, New York, April 16–17, 1994

Horace Tapscott, from *Thoughts of Dar es Salaam*, New York, June 30 and July 1, 1996

Keith Jarrett (with the Standards Trio), from *My Foolish Heart*, live at Auditorium Stravinski, Montreux, Switzerland, July 22, 2001

Joel Frahm and Brad Mehldau, from *Don't Explain*, Pipersville, Pennsylvania, December 8, 2001

On a Clear Day

Composed by Burton Lane, with lyrics by Alan Jay Lerner

The melodies of American popular music got more compact during the mid-1960s—a trend that has continued, largely unabated, until the present day. The vocal range required for performing top 40 material became narrower and narrower, and the melodies increasingly avoided wide interval leaps in favor of repeated notes and phrases that moved up or down in steps or half-steps. If tunesmiths of earlier decades had sometimes aspired to create popular music that approached concert-hall fare in complexity and sophistication—indeed, Gershwin had even made the leap from Tin Pan Alley to the opera house—the hit makers of the Vietnam era aspired instead to composing contemporary works that sounded like old folk songs or rhythm-and-blues riffs.

Apparently no one told Burton Lane and Alan Jay Lerner of the changes afoot. They worked on their new musical *On a Clear Day You Can See Forever*, which opened on Broadway on October 17, 1965, as if the old rules were still in effect. The #1 record of the year, according to *Billboard*, would be "Wooly Bully," but Burton Lane, who had been writing for musical revues since the early 1930s, was still following the same maximalist aesthetic he had brought to *Finian's Rainbow* (1947)—his best-known Broadway production but just a dim memory to audiences attending this new show. Reviewers' reactions to *On a Clear Day You Can See Forever* were mixed, with the *New York Times* noting the cumbersome nature of the big production numbers—no doubt true given the emerging zeitgeist—and the show closed eight months later. It was hardly a flop, but given Alan Jay Lerner's successes with *My Fair Lady* (whose movie version had recently swept eight Oscars) and *Camelot* (literally the defining musical of the Kennedy administration), the response was a disappointment.

Yet the title song was a gem. This ecstatic bit of music making is a through-composed work of 34 bars that changes its harmonic personality at every point when you might expect a repeat. The development of the opening motif—a triumphant arpeggiated figure that moves up to the ninth before settling on the major seventh—creates a sense of continuity that makes this elaborate work flow naturally from start to finish. This opening gambit is also the hook in the song, the catchy line that plants the title deep in the listener's memory banks.

Even so, this was a far more intricate song than most of the radio audience was willing to accept at this juncture in history. Johnny Mathis had the best results at the time of the song's initial release, but his single got no higher than #98 on the *Billboard* Hot 100. Robert Goulet's release stalled out at #119. Barbra Streisand, who starred in the movie version of the show a few years later, ranked no better than #82 when she put "On a Clear Day" on the flip side of her performance of "Didn't We." The public had spoken . . . and they preferred "Wooly Bully" and others of its ilk.

But jazz musicians liked what they heard. More than 20 different jazz versions of "On a Clear Day" were recorded in 1966, and the song retained its popularity among improvisers long after most of the general public forgot about it. Just as striking was the range in ages and stylistic allegiances of the artists who picked up on the song in later years. Bud Freeman, the white Chicagoan who made his reputation back in the 1920s, recorded "On a Clear Day," as did bebopper Sonny Stitt, big band idol Harry James, and Kansas City jazz pioneer Jay McShann. Some took it slow and Chopin-esque (as George Shearing did in his 1980 recording), or dished it out funky and soulful (as on Stanley Turrentine's 1966 tenor-and-organ album *Let It Go*). Others combined extremes in the same performance, as did Bill Evans in his solo piano recording from 1968, which starts out as a dreamy meditation but evolves into a cerebral linear improvisation.

The lyrics are no doubt the most modern thing about the song. The themes of self-awakening and personal redefinition were very much part of the 1960s ethos and are no less current nowadays. The sentiments here veer a little bit too much toward trite aphorisms, a New Age mantra in 4/4 time, but the chords and melody give the words more vitality on the bandstand than they possess on the written page. In any event, the versatility of "On a Clear Day," combined with the inherent virtues of such a well-crafted piece, have given this song staying power—all the more remarkable when one considers how few pop hits from the mid-1960s onward have found a lasting place in the jazz repertoire.

RECOMMENDED VERSIONS

Stanley Turrentine (with Shirley Scott), from *Let It Go*, Englewood Cliffs, New Jersey, April 6, 1966

Oscar Peterson, from *Girl Talk*, Villingen, Germany, November 1967

Bill Evans, from *Alone*, New York, September–October 1968

Sarah Vaughan, from *Live in Japan*, live at Sun Plaza Hall, Tokyo, September 24, 1973

Eddie "Lockjaw" Davis (with Tommy Flanagan), from *Straight Ahead*, Los Angeles, May 3, 1976

Carmen McRae (with Dizzy Gillespie), from *At the Great American Music Hall*, live at the Great American Music Hall, San Francisco, June 15–17, 1976

George Shearing (with Brian Torff), from *On a Clear Day*, live at the Concord Pavilion, Concord, California, August 1980

Martial Solal, from *Solitude*, Paris, April 29–30, 2005

On Green Dolphin Street

Composed by Bronislaw Kaper and Ned Washington

"On Green Dolphin Street" (often simplified to "Green Dolphin Street" by musicians and fans) illustrates the sometimes unexpected sources of the standard jazz repertoire. The song first appeared in a mostly forgotten film of the same name from 1947, which earned an Academy Award nomination for its soundtrack—but *not* for the music, merely for Douglas Shearer's sound recording. (The Oscar winner for best song that year was "Zip-a-Dee-Doo-Dah"— almost the antithesis of jazz standard material—from Disney's *Song of the South*, an animated feature so embarrassing in its racial stereotyping that the company has never released it on the home video market.)

In truth, "On Green Dolphin Street" was not hit parade material, and never found much favor with the broader public, although the movie was a box-office success in its day. Yet jazz musicians eventually embraced it because of its engaging chord changes, which alternate between eight bars of floating pedal point and eight bars of rapid harmonic movement. Even so, the song would never have become widely played without the example set by Miles Davis, who recorded the piece in 1958.

Only a few jazz artists (Tommy Dorsey, Urbie Green, Chet Baker) had interpreted this song before Miles, but the version that probably spurred on the trumpeter was the 1956 recording by Ahmad Jamal, whose repertoire choices were often mimicked by Davis during this period. Jamal's performance, with its artful use of space and dynamics, anticipates Davis's later rendition, especially with its shifting rhythmic textures. But Davis added something new to the mix—specifically three illustrious sidemen named John Coltrane, Cannonball Adderley, and Bill Evans, each of whom imposed his own personality on the proceedings.

This ability of "On Green Dolphin Street" to accommodate widely varying interpretations has kept it in the jazz repertoire long after other songs of the era have gone by the wayside. For examples of this flexibility, compare the different stances adopted by reed players Eric Dolphy, Eddie "Lockjaw" Davis, Sonny Rollins, Stan Getz, and Albert Ayler (the latter acknowledges a few of the chord changes but just plows through most of them as if they don't exist). My favorite transgressive version comes from Anthony Braxton, who stretches the song without avoiding its harmonic implications on his 2003 live track from France.

Vocalists occasionally tackle this song, but the lyrics suffer from shallowness. If you fell in love, would you sing about your beloved or just her address? Singers who insist in going down this path are perhaps best advised to adopt a tone of hip nonchalance, which adds some plausibility to this paean to a place. A good example can be found on Mark Murphy's 1961 recordings for his *Rah* album.

RECOMMENDED VERSIONS

Ahmad Jamal, from *Count 'Em 88*, Chicago, September–October 1956

Miles Davis, from *'58 Miles*, New York, May 26, 1958

Bill Evans, from *On Green Dolphin Street*, New York, January 19, 1959

Wynton Kelly, from *Kelly Blue*, New York, March 10, 1959

Eric Dolphy, from *Outward Bound*, New York, April 1, 1960

Mark Murphy, from *Rah*, New York, September 19, 1961

Albert Ayler, from *Holy Ghost: Rare & Unissued Recordings (1962–70)*, Helsinki, June 30, 1962

Sonny Rollins, from *Sonny Rollins on Impulse!* Englewood Cliffs, New Jersey, July 8, 1965

Eddie "Lockjaw" Davis, from *Leapin' on Lenox*, Vallauris, France, July 20, 1974

Anthony Braxton, from *20 Standards*, live at the Nevers Jazz Festival, Nevers, France, November 13, 2003

On the Sunny Side of the Street
Composed by Jimmy McHugh, with lyrics by Dorothy Fields

Lew Leslie was about as Caucasian as you can get—he was born not far from the Caucasus Mountains back in Russia under Czar Alexander III—but he made his mark bringing African-American entertainment to white audiences, most notably at the Cotton Club and via his various *Blackbirds* revues. Yet, for his *International Revue* from 1930, Leslie tried something different: an all-white production. The audience was distinctly unimpressed, and the costly show closed after only 12 weeks. But two songs from *International Revue* became standards: "Exactly Like You" and "On the Sunny Side of the Street." Ted Lewis released the first hit version of the latter tune and his recording, made the month the show debuted, reached #2 on the chart. Harry Richman, who was featured in the *International Revue*, enjoyed his own top 20 success with the song a short while later.

Yet black performers ultimately played the key role in establishing the jazz credentials of the tunes from Leslie's all-white production. Louis Armstrong's performance from Stockholm in October 1933 is preserved on one of the first live jazz recordings, but the poor sound quality will discourage any but the most fanatic Satchmo fans. (You can even hear what sounds like a telephone conversation in the background—I guess that's what happened back in the day when you phoned in the performance to a remote recording device.) Armstrong's studio recording from November 1934 is the better-known version, and at six minutes—originally covering both sides of a 78 rpm disk—gives the trumpeter a chance to present his full band arrangement. Other memorable performances from this era come from Coleman Hawkins, Chick Webb (featuring trumpeter and vocalist Taft Jordan), and Don Redman, the latter relying on an appealing dance-oriented swing chart. Lionel Hampton's recording also became a top 10 hit—and inspired Bing Crosby to hire Hampton's band for the singer's later recording of the song.

TV host Steve Allen and others have conjectured that the "sunny side" of this song refers to African Americans who passed as white. Certainly the lyrics are open to this interpretation, yet this theory hardly fits with the origins of this song as a feature for performers such as Richman and Lewis. Indeed, Richman's early work as a blackface performer and Lewis's assimilation of jazz mannerisms seem to flip-flop this account—the actual lineage of this song tells us more about whites borrowing the trappings of black culture. In this regard, conspiracy theorists might find more cause for cogitation in the persistent rumors that Fats Waller actually wrote the music to "On the Sunny Side of the Street," but sold the rights in a behind-the-scenes transaction—and was later so mad when the song became a hit, that he wouldn't allow it to be played at his home. One would think that a composer as skilled as Jimmy McHugh wouldn't need to buy someone else's work, yet the melody does sound plausibly Wallerian. And what should we conclude from the fact that Fats made a test recording of "On the Sunny Side of the Street" for RCA on December 15, 1937, but when he returned the following day for a formal recording session, he declined to perform it? Nor did he ever play it at any other commercial recording session. A grudge over royalties would be a plausible explanation for this behavior.

The song retains a certain old-fashioned sensibility that makes it more suitable for nostalgia than modernistic jazz stylings. Among the beboppers, only Dizzy Gillespie showed any enthusiasm for "On the Sunny Side of the Street," and it stayed in his repertoire for a number of years; but he tended to view it as a crowd-pleasing novelty tune rather than as a vehicle for his trumpet pyrotechnics. Even on his much-admired *Sonny Side Up* project, which found the trumpeter alongside Sonny Stitt and Sonny Rollins, Gillespie breaks up what could have been a heated jam encounter with a lighthearted vocal. A more interesting, but less well-known, modern jazz performance of the standard comes from a benefit concert organized by Barry Ulanov and broadcast on the radio in 1947. Here Gillespie trades fours with Charlie Parker and puts aside his antics in clear determination to give as good as he gets; Lennie Tristano and John LaPorta follow up with solos of their own that are both very edgy in their hints of polytonality. Yet neither Parker nor Tristano ever played the song at a commercial session, and it is equally absent from the discographies of Thelonious Monk, Bud Powell, and most of the other jazz progressives of the era.

Recordings of this song from recent decades tend to possess a quaint retro quality, and the song remains a favorite among trad jazz players. Yet the composition is not completely resistant to updating. Terence Blanchard provides a slick reharmonization and a different rhythmic feel on his 2001 recording of "Sunny Side" with Cassandra Wilson. And in 2003, Cyndi Lauper released a delightful zydeco version of the song for her *At Last* CD, which was a top 40 album in the United States and Australia—showing that performers outside of the jazz idiom sometimes take the most chances in reinventing the old songs.

RECOMMENDED VERSIONS

Chick Webb (with Taft Jordan), New York, December 20, 1933

Coleman Hawkins, New York, March 8, 1934

Louis Armstrong, Paris, November 7, 1934

Lionel Hampton, New York, April 26, 1937

Don Redman, New York, May 28, 1937

Charlie Parker and Dizzy Gillespie (with Lennie Tristano), from the *Bands for Bonds* broadcast, New York, September 20, 1947

Dizzy Gillespie (with Sonny Rollins and Sonny Stitt), from *Sonny Side Up*, New York, December 19, 1957

Duke Ellington (with Johnny Hodges), from *The Great Paris Concert*, live at the Olympia, Paris, February 23, 1963

Terence Blanchard (with Cassandra Wilson), from *Let's Get Lost*, New York, January–February 2001

Cyndi Lauper, from *At Last*, New York and New Jersey, circa 2003

Once I Loved

Composed by Antonio Carlos Jobim, with lyrics by Vinicius de Moraes (English lyrics by Ray Gilbert)

Jazz is a style of music best suited for extroverts. Even at its birth in New Orleans, the music stood out for its brashness, and during the appropriately named Jazz Age evolved into the preferred lifestyle soundtrack for those who partied perhaps a *wee bit too much*. Jazz has calmed down some since then—and needed to, in order to make its peace with places like Juilliard and Lincoln Center—but only in the smallest degree. Something at the very heart of the music, hard to define but palpable in every successful performance, still resists limitations and curtailment.

Even so, there are a handful of songs in the standard repertoire that convey a sense of introspection and quiet soul-searching. For the most part, they are slow pieces, delicate ballads that sacrifice rhythmic drive in exchange for a ruminative self-questioning. But "Once I Loved" is that rarity—a melancholy soliloquy that shouldn't be played too slowly. The composition works best at a medium tempo, almost as if the lingering nostalgia of the lyrics needs to tussle with the forward momentum of the bossa nova beat.

I am not surprised that Frank Sinatra was heard to mutter, after recording this song in collaboration with the composer: "I haven't sung so soft since I had the laryngitis." Sinatra himself was one of those celebrated extroverts who have served as the most ardent ambassadors for jazz among the general public, and his singing style was hardly an obvious match with the understated bossa nova idiom. Yet he returned again and again to Jobim's songs, even featuring the composer on a high-profile TV special, and Sinatra's ability to adapt to such uncharacteristic material was impressive. I'll admit that, for many years, I avoided listening to the Sinatra-Jobim tracks, fearing a mismatch driven by marketing considerations rather than a real meeting of musical minds. But their partnership on "Once I Love" (and other numbers) is much more *simpatico* than I could have envisioned if I hadn't actually heard the unimpeachable results.

Sinatra clearly deserves credit for the popularity of this song. Even during the height of the bossa nova craze, which peaked around 1964–65, "Once I Loved" was not widely known and it is conspicuously missing from most of the bossa nova theme albums of the day. But after Sinatra's 1967 recording, the song became one of Jobim's best-known and most-covered compositions.

The song gets stretched even further in McCoy Tyner's 1975 album *Trident*. This album brought the pianist together with drummer Elvin Jones and bassist Ron Carter in one of the most aggressive trio projects of the era. Tyner briefly tinkles on celeste to start and end the track, but otherwise needs the weightier piano sound to match the energy level of his cohorts. The performance ultimately succeeds, although listeners will find it hard to detect the song's Brazilian origins in all the tumult.

Such precedents notwithstanding, the most characteristic renditions of this composition don't manhandle it quite so much. For his 1994 recording, tenorist Joe Henderson relies solely on the guitar accompaniment of Oscar Castro-Neves, and though he takes the song much faster than most performers, he keeps true to the spirit of the piece. Shirley Horn's recording from 1988 is another standout example of how a jazz performer can get inside such a fragile song. But, above all, the quintessential versions of "Once I Loved" come from the Brazilian artists who first established the song, composer, Antonio Carlos Jobim and, especially, his most sublime interpreter, guitarist-vocalist João Gilberto.

RECOMMENDED VERSIONS

João Gilberto (recorded as "O Amor Em Paz"), from *The Legendary João Gilberto*, Rio de Janeiro, August 16, 1961

Antonio Carlos Jobim, from *The Composer of Desafinado Plays*, New York, May 10, 1963

Frank Sinatra, from *Francis Albert Sinatra & Antonio Carlos Jobim*, Hollywood, February 1, 1967

McCoy Tyner, from *Trident*, Berkeley, California, February 18–19, 1975

Hal Galper, From *Dreamsville*, New York, March 3, 1986

Shirley Horn, from *Close Enough for Love*, New York, November 14–16, 1988

Joe Henderson (with Oscar Castro-Neves), from *Double Rainbow*, New York, November 5–6, 1994

One Note Samba
Composed by Antonio Carlos Jobim, with lyrics by Newton Mendonça (English lyrics by Antonio Carlos Jobim)

As noted already, one of the most striking changes in popular music over the last half-century has been a radical simplification in the melodic line. The extreme example, of course, is rap music, where melody is abandoned entirely in favor of a spoken or semispoken chant. But even when vocalists deliver a real melody nowadays, phrases are often built on repeated notes, with perhaps a few small intervallic steps thrown in to avoid complete stasis. Years ago, some critics griped that George Gershwin relied too heavily on repeated notes in his pop tunes, but compared to, say, the works of Jay-Z and Eminem—or even Bruce Springsteen and Kurt Cobain—Gershwin's compact melodies seem full of movement.

This is a historical development susceptible to statistical measurement, and I would be curious to see a trendline charting the intervallic motion in hit songs over the course of the passing decades. I suspect it would follow the same pattern as a line tracing the sales of typewriters or slide rules during those same years. Whatever the causes, we definitely live in an age of anorexic melodies.

But back when Antonio Carlos Jobim wrote "One Note Samba" (known in Portuguese as "Samba de Uma Nota Só") the idea of writing such static phrases was seen as a novelty—or perhaps a challenge, since the music industry still held on to the notion that recording a monotonous melody was tantamount to commercial suicide. The subject had even been chronicled in the 1937 Rodgers and Hart song "Johnny One Note," whose lamentable protagonist would find his name turned into a slang term for anyone boring and fixated on a single point.

Jobim was perfectly equipped to meet this challenge head-on, if only for the expansive harmonic palette he invariably brings to his songs. Yet even Jobim refuses to be limited to just one note, no matter what the song's title promises. He actually uses two notes in the verse, and in the bridge lets loose with extravagant scales, almost as if the deprivation of the first 16 bars had been too much to bear. True to form, Jobim underpins his constrained melody with a rich tapestry of chords, ensuring that "One Note Samba" is anything but monotonous. I especially like the coda, where Jobim avoids the return to the expected opening note, and instead holds on to the tonic in the melody, meanwhile finding a new progression to drive the song to its final resolve.

Stan Getz brought the song to the public's attention with its inclusion on the hit *Jazz Samba* LP. Before the decade was out, the whole jazz establishment had seemingly discovered "One Note Samba," not just the expected Latin jazz advocates such as Herbie Mann and Dizzy Gillespie, but even the Duke and Count and other nobility of the old regime. Ellington's 1969 performance, a seldom-heard track, is fascinating for the leader's daring pianism, which pays little attention to how everyone else was playing bossa nova, instead drawing on drones, ostinato effects, and other elements that seem to come from a different Brazil of Ellington's own invention.

But the song has been most warmly embraced by practitioners of cool jazz. Laurindo Almeida, the Brazilian guitarist who first came to the notice of jazz fans when he joined the Kenton band in 1947, sometimes strikes me as lacking the light touch required by the bossa nova style, but his performance of this piece with the Modern Jazz Quartet from 1964 is exquisite and highly recommended. I would also call attention to Harry Allen, one of the few new millennium tenorists to maintain allegiance to a Lesterian-Getzian paradigm in the face of more fashionable role models. He has recorded "One Note Samba" on several occasions to good effect and proves that it can serve as an effective no-frills blowing number.

Even so, this song has never quite dislodged its reputation as a novelty tune. The lyrics don't help, merely calling attention to the novelty—*I have used up all the scale I know*, etc. Yet there is enough magic in this song to compensate both for the lackluster words and, of course, the maddening musical lipogram that is the impetus of the whole endeavor. I don't think "One Note Samba" has many surprises left for us, but it still works as a change-up pitch that can add variety to a performer's set list.

RECOMMENDED VERSIONS

João Gilberto, from *The Legendary João Gilberto*, Rio de Janeiro, April 4, 1960

Stan Getz, with Charlie Byrd, from *Jazz Samba*, Washington, D.C., February 13, 1962

Dizzy Gillespie (with Leo Wright), from *New Wave*, Juan-les-Pins, France, July 24, 1962

Modern Jazz Quartet and Laurindo Almeida, from *Collaboration*, New York, July 21, 1964

Duke Ellington, from *Live and Rare*, New York, September 3, 1969

Ella Fitzgerald (with Toots Thielemans and Zoot Sims), from *Ella Abraça Jobim/ Sings the Antonio Carlos Jobim Songbook*, Hollywood, September 17–19, 1980 and March 18–20, 1981

Harry Allen, from *Once Upon a Summertime*, New York, February 1–2, 1999

One o'Clock Jump
Composed by Count Basie, Eddie Durham, and Buster Smith

No, the US Copyright Office won't let anyone file a claim on the 12-bar blues. But if anyone deserves credit for teaching the blues how to swing, it would be Bill Basie and his Kansas City colleagues. This number, like so many other

Basie tunes—such as "Jumpin' at Woodside" or the chronologically related "Two o'Clock Jump"—sounds as if it sprang spontaneously from a jam session, so effortlessly does the band fall into its riffs. And, in truth, more than a little of this song was borrowed from swing tunes already circulating in the jazz world. Yet with works such as "One o'Clock Jump," Basie and company deserve recognition for bringing the loose ambiance of the after-hours club into the organized world of the modern big band, offering a different perspective on the blues than one heard from his New York and Chicago contemporaries.

The song was originally called "Blue Balls," but a radio announcer in Little Rock deemed that title too risqué to introduce on the airwaves, and the time of the broadcast was adopted as a last-minute replacement. The Basie band members had originally treated the song as something of a joke, little more than a series of conventional phrases disrupted by an unexpected key change. But the original framework, literally created on the bandstand by Buster Smith, served as the impetus for a crowd-pleasing chart, crafted with the assistance of Eddie Durham, (the uncredited) Oran "Hot Lips" Page, and Basie himself. The song eventually proved so popular that the Basie band would perform it three or four times every evening.

Basie's debut recording of "One o'Clock Jump" from 1937 would serve as a blueprint for many of the later riff blues that enlivened the ballrooms of America during the following decade. But a song of this sort is only as strong as the cadre of soloists who add their improvisational acumen to the proceedings, and here the track is enlivened by the contrasting sax styles of Herschel Evans (a would-be star who was dead from heart disease, 18 months later, at age 29) and Lester Young, the former robust and declamatory, the latter lithe and elusive. But the bandleader is not to be outdone here, and Basie's introduction and opening solo showcase his supple blues sensibility with a hint of boogie, and he finishes with a flair when the band modulates suddenly from F to D flat—not a typical key for the blues—where it remains for the rest of the song.

Many of the major bandleaders of the period—Duke Ellington, Benny Goodman, Chick Webb, Glenn Miller, Jimmy Dorsey, and others—added "One o'Clock Jump" to their repertoires, and the song became as much a signature theme for the Swing Era as for Basie himself. Goodman featured it at his historic 1938 Carnegie Hall concert, with Basie (who was on hand as a guest performer that evening) serving as a spectator. Even New Orleans pioneers paid attention, and both Louis Armstrong and Sidney Bechet recorded "One o'Clock Jump" in the early 1940s. The modern jazz players also benefited from Basie's example, perhaps most notably when the young Charlie Parker headed off to the Ozarks during the summer of 1937 for the intense practice sessions that would transform him into an alto legend—and brought along Basie's "One o'Clock Jump" as one of the records he used to inspire his daily regimen.

This song is not called on the bandstand quite so often nowadays, although when jazz musicians are put in the (now rare) situation of playing for dancers, "One o'Clock Jump" still has a role to play. And if the composition fails to excite the younger jazz artists of our day, it has become something larger, a cultural meme, a symbol of an era and way of life. As such, it shows up in unexpected places, in films such as *The English Patient* and *Harlem Nights* or in the repertoire of the rock band Rush. Given this lineage, few were surprised when the Recording Industry Association of America and the National Endowment for the Arts included Basie's "One o'Clock Jump" on their roster of "Songs of the Century."

RECOMMENDED VERSIONS

Count Basie (with Lester Young), New York, July 7, 1937

Benny Goodman, live at Carnegie Hall, New York, January 16, 1938

Red Garland, from *At the Prelude*, live at the Prelude Club, New York, October 2, 1959

Duke Ellington, from *The Reprise Studio Recordings*, Chicago, November 29, 1962

Illinois Jacquet, from *With Milt and Jo*, Paris, January 12, 1974

Count Basie (with Joe Pass and Milt Jackson), from *Kansas City Five*, Burbank, California, January 26, 1977

Frank Wess and Harry "Sweets" Edison, from *Dear Mr. Basie*, live at Kan'i Hoken Hall, Tokyo, November 1989

Ornithology
Composed by Charlie Parker and Benny Harris

This Charlie Parker composition has always puzzled me. The melody line to "Ornithology" is, for the most part, cussedly diatonic, with little of the chromaticism or color tones that were the boppers' trademark. You will find more jazz content in many Irving Berlin or Jerome Kern songs from the 1920s. One might be tempted to attribute this retrograde element to Benny Harris, Parker's (sometimes uncredited) co-composer, but the opening phrase comes straight from Parker's 1942 solo on "The Jumping Blues," recorded when he was a member of Jay McShann's band. This motif may have an even earlier source, given its similarity to a line played by Lester Young on his 1936 solo on "Shoe Shine Boy." Given these antecedents, "Ornithology" is perhaps best viewed as a sign of Bird's Kansas City jazz roots, rather than a talisman of his forward-looking ambitions.

As for the chord changes, they are lifted from the 1940 Broadway song "How High the Moon." However, no deception was intended: Parker and other bebop composers openly admitted to relying on borrowed harmonic progressions for many of their most famous works. Yet modern jazz performers usually substituted a more interesting melody rather than, as in this instance, such a formulaic one.

Charlie Parker more than makes up for these hand-me-downs with his solo contributions. More than 40 versions of Parker playing "Ornithology" have survived, most of them poorly recorded bootlegs of live performances, but the place to start is his studio rendition for Dial, made in Hollywood in March 1946. This performance was later inducted into the Grammy Hall of Fame, and with good reason. Parker was in top form, and not just on this track—this session also produced definitive versions of "Yardbird Suite," "Moose the Mooche," and "Night in Tunisia."

Few besides Parker fanatics are familiar with the amateur recordings Dean Benedetti made of the saxophonist's music at the Hi-De-Ho Club in Los Angeles in March 1947, but "Ornithology" was a regular number in Bird's set list at the time, and Parker usually stretched out for three full choruses. Unfortunately, Benedetti only recorded Parker's solos, leaving out the melody statement and other players' improvisations; even so, these tracks capture the altoist at the high point of his career and are worthy of close attention. A live performance from Boston in 1952 is equally compelling: the sound quality is better, Parker takes a long, ingenious solo, and the rhythm section is a dream lineup of Charles Mingus, Roy Haynes, and Dick Twardzik.

Few today can appreciate how influential this music was at the time. Parker not only stood out as the dominant role model for younger jazz musicians of the period, but even the older generation was taking note, as demonstrated by Coleman Hawkins's breakneck recording of "Ornithology" from 1949—indeed, he plays the composition even faster than Bird. If the great Coleman Hawkins felt pressured to live up to Parker's demonstrated virtuosity, imagine how lesser talents reacted at the time. For the most part, musicians have relied on "Ornithology" to show off their bop prowess, and versions by Bud Powell, Sonny Stitt, and Dizzy Gillespie are very much in the spirit of Parker's original conception.

Sometimes deference for the composer and the idiom can lead to surprising end points—listen to Supersax perform Parker's music scored for a full sax section for an extreme example of jazz hagiography. But the old bop staples can also serve in more contemporary settings: hear, for example, Anthony Braxton's performance of "Ornithology" on contrabass clarinet, which, true to the name of the song, sounds like a bird call for some unwieldy feathered creature who can no longer fly. Within a few bars, you will definitely know you aren't in Kansas (City) anymore.

RECOMMENDED VERSIONS

Charlie Parker, Hollywood, March 28, 1946

Charlie Parker, live at the Hi-De-Ho Club, Los Angeles, March 9, 1947

Bud Powell, New York, August 9, 1949

Coleman Hawkins, live at Maison du Peuple, Lausanne, Switzerland, December 3, 1949

Charlie Parker, live at the Hi-Hat Club, Boston, December 14, 1952

Stan Getz (with Bob Brookmeyer), live at the Hi-Hat Club, Boston, March 8, 1953

Babs Gonzales (recorded as "The Boss Is Back"), from *All That Jive*, New York, October 9, 1953

Sonny Stitt, from *Stitt Plays Bird*, New York, January 29, 1963

Anthony Braxton, from *In the Tradition, Vol. 1*, Copenhagen, May 29, 1974

Supersax, from *The Japanese Tour*, live at the Sun Palace, Tokyo, Winter 1975

Dizzy Gillespie, from *Bird Songs—The Final Recordings*, live at the Blue Note, New York, January 23, 1992

Our Love Is Here to Stay

Composed by George Gershwin, with lyrics by Ira Gershwin

Movie mogul Samuel Goldwyn brought together the best talents he could find for his immodestly named production *The Goldwyn Follies* (1938), which would be his first Technicolor release. But George Gershwin wasn't his initial choice for composer. Goldwyn wanted to create a cinematic equivalent of the annual revues staged by Flo Ziegfeld on Broadway, and hoped to hire Irving Berlin, who had written music for several of the *Ziegfeld Follies*. When Berlin proved unavailable, the producer settled on the Gershwin brothers. Not without reservations: when George played some of the songs he had written for Goldwyn and his staff, the producer wondered aloud why this expensive talent couldn't write more memorable melodies the way Irving Berlin did. Oscar Levant later noted that this tense moment marked one of the few times he ever saw his friend Gershwin genuinely offended.

This song has proven to be a lasting hit, but Goldwyn may have had good reason for his hesitancy—*The Goldwyn Follies* was a bomb at the box office, and failed to recoup its massive (for the time) budget of $2 million. "Our Love Is Here to Stay" was given cursory treatment in the movie and would not receive a suitable cinematic setting until the 1951 film *An American in Paris*, in which Gene Kelly sings it to Leslie Caron. George Gershwin, for his part, did not live to see either of these movies, dying in July 1937 at age 38, following surgery to treat a brain tumor, some seven months before the premiere of *The Goldwyn Follies*.

Confusion surrounds the song's title. The original name was "It's Here to Stay," but then became "Our Love Is Here to Stay." Finally, the piece was published as "Love Is Here to Stay," although Ira Gershwin remained dissatisfied with this title. For many years he hesitated to tinker with such a well-known work, but finally, with the publication of *The George and Ira Gershwin Songbook* in 1960, he had the song listed as "Our Love Is Here to Stay."

The song enjoyed a brief flurry of popularity with jazz musicians around the time of its debut, and Red Norvo's recording alongside his wife Mildred Bailey was a top 20 hit in March 1938. But "Our Love Is Here to Stay" fell out of favor with swing bands during the 1940s. The composition gradually gained the status of a jazz standard during the course of the 1950s, helped along by Gene Kelly's song-and-dance routine.

A number of fine instrumental versions have been recorded over the years, but singers have done the most to establish the jazz credentials of "Our Love Is Here to Stay," with Dinah Washington, Billie Holiday, and Ella Fitzgerald standing out as key interpreters. To my mind, this melody is so intimately entangled with Ira Gershwin's words—I especially like the geologic allusions ("the Rockies may crumble, Gibraltar may tumble") that set off the final boast of love's permanence—that you can't really comprehend the majesty of this song unless you have heard it in a first-rate vocal rendition.

Like so many Gershwin songs, this one seems to find new life with each generation. In addition to *The Goldwyn Follies* (1938) and *An American in Paris* (1951), "Our Love Is Here to Stay" gained further exposure from *Lady Sings the Blues* (1972) and *When Harry Met Sally* (1989). And if you hear it on the radio nowadays, Rod Stewart, Natalie Cole, or Smokey Robinson might be delivering Gershwin's timeless melody. Jazz players don't turn to this song as often as they once did, but it still enjoys a prominent spot in the repertoire. Among modern jazz interpretations, I would call attention to three piano interpretations: by Jaki Byard (1971), Marcus Roberts (1994), and Michel Camilo (2004).

RECOMMENDED VERSIONS

Red Norvo (with Mildred Bailey), New York, January 21, 1938

Dinah Washington, from *Dinah Washington in the Land of Hi-Fi*, New York, April 24, 1956

Billie Holiday, from *All or Nothing at All*, Los Angeles, January 8, 1957

Louis Armstrong and Ella Fitzgerald, from *Ella and Louis Again*, Los Angeles, July 23, 1957

Ella Fitzgerald, from *Ella Fitzgerald Sings the George and Ira Gershwin Songbook*, Los Angeles, January 5–8, 1959

Ben Webster (with Hank Jones), from *See You at the Fair*, New York, March 11, 1964

Jaki Byard, from *Parisian Solos*, Paris, July 29, 1971

Marcus Roberts, from *Gershwin for Lovers*, Tallahassee, Florida, 1994

Susannah McCorkle, from *Hearts and Minds*, New York, March 28–30, 2000

Michel Camilo, from *Solo*, New York, May 11–13, 2004

Out of Nowhere
Composed by Johnny Green, with lyrics by Edward Heyman

In 1928 Johnny Green graduated from Harvard, still in his teens when he received his degree. In college, he had majored in economics, and after taking his diploma he moved on, at his father's prodding, to a job as a Wall Street stockbroker—an impressive start for a promising young man, but not a typical launching pad for a great for a great American songwriter. Yet only a few months later, Green had forgotten bonds and stocks and instead written "Body and Soul." And even before leaving college, Green had rustled up a summer job writing for Guy Lombardo's band, laying the groundwork for his later music career.

Lombardo would feature "Out of Nowhere" at New York's Roosevelt Grill, but the big hit version came in May of 1931 from Bing Crosby, the public's favorite singer at that moment in time—an astounding 10 of the top 50 records of the year featured Crosby as either leader or sideman. The crooner's vocal on "Out of Nowhere" lacks the unaffected, conversational quality that he would bring to other performances relying instead on touches of Al Jolson that modern listeners may find overly theatrical. Yet the audiences of the period were enthusiastic, and this recording topped the charts for three weeks running. The song got additional help from Crosby's onscreen performances in the films *Dude Ranch* and *Confessions of a Co-Ed*. That same spring, Leo Reisman—a violinist and bandleader who specialized in tepid dance arrangements—also enjoyed a top 10 hit with "Out of Nowhere."

Despite the song's initial success, the jazz world didn't pay much attention to "Out of Nowhere" until Coleman Hawkins recorded it in Paris six years later—a version that finds Benny Carter offering a caressing, behind-the-beat melody statement on trumpet and Django Reinhardt anchoring the rhythm section. Hawkins, however, is the featured artist here, taking a low-key stance during his first half-chorus, a coy, hesitating approach out of character for this artist; but he makes up for it over the next 48 bars, with a breathless and baroque manipulation of motives that sounds far less dated nowadays than most other tenor offerings from the period. So carried away by the song, Hawkins uses up all of the 78 "disk space" and the track ends as he concludes his solo, with no time for a final melody recapitulation.

I'm not surprised that Hawkins revived this tune. The harmonic construction is quite sophisticated, even by the high standards of the day. As early as the third bar, Green offers a fakeout, apparently laying the groundwork for a modulation up a half step . . . then settles back instead into the tonic key. Casual listeners would hardly notice anything unusual here, but chord-change wonks find such feints appealing, and in the late 1930s, Hawkins was the wonkiest of them all, except for perhaps Art Tatum, who also enjoyed performing "Out of Nowhere." The more cerebral the improviser, the more likely that this song shows up on the set list—or perhaps just the chords, as for example on Lennie Tristano's piece "317 East 32nd Street."

Before the close of the 1930s, a number of name bandleaders—including Artie Shaw, Ella Fitzgerald, and Harry James—had made recordings of "Out of Nowhere." The song's placement in the 1945 movie *You Came Along*, where it was delivered by Helen Forrest, also gave it a boost with the general public. Indeed, the song—sometimes known as "You Came Along (from Out of Nowhere)"—even inspired the title for this movie, perhaps best known today for Ayn Rand's work on its screenplay. Tommy Dorsey enjoyed a modest hit with "Out of Nowhere" around this same time—his version peaked at number 20 in September 1945.

But when I think of "Out of Nowhere," the first artist who comes to mind is Charlie Parker. During my apprenticeship years, I immersed myself in Parker's music, and was struck by how often the amateur recordings of his live performances found him playing this composition, which must have been one of his favorite standards. His best-known recording of it comes from a November 1947 session for the Dial label, but more than two dozen versions of Bird playing "Out of Nowhere" have survived.

The most intriguing example, however, of Parker working over these changes comes from his performance of Gerry Mulligan's "Roundhouse"—which borrows its chords from "Out of Nowhere"—at a 1953 concert with a Washington, D.C., big band. Parker had apparently never played this arrangement before, and no one told him that the chart modulated from the key of G to E flat after the first chorus. To add to the drama, Bird takes a flashy solo break leading into the modulation, and is charging ahead on all cylinders when he suddenly realizes that the tonal center has shifted out from under him. It's breathtaking to hear how Parker pauses for just a second, absorbs what has happened, and then takes off in full flight in the new key as if this had been just the mildest road bump.

RECOMMENDED VERSIONS

Bing Crosby, Los Angeles, March 30, 1931

Coleman Hawkins (with Django Reinhardt and Benny Carter), Paris, April 28, 1937

Ella Fitzgerald, New York, June 29, 1939

Teddy Wilson (with Lena Horne), New York, September 16, 1941

Art Tatum, New York, January 20, 1947

Charlie Parker, New York, November 4, 1947

Dave Brubeck (with Paul Desmond), from *Jazz Goes to College*, live at the University of Cincinnati, Cincinnati, Ohio, March 1954

Pee Wee Russell (with Ruby Braff and Vic Dickenson), from *Portrait of Pee Wee*, New York, February 18–19, 1958

Joe Williams and Harry "Sweets" Edison, from *Together*, live at The Cloister, Los Angeles, February 1961

Eddie "Lockjaw" Davis and Zoot Sims (with Oscar Peterson), from *The Tenor Giants*, Geneva, October 17, 1975

Fred Hersch, from *Dancing in the Dark*, Astoria, New York, December 3–4, 1992

Over the Rainbow
Composed by Harold Arlen, with lyrics by E. Y. Harburg

It's hard for the 1939 film *The Wizard of Oz* to retain its allure for children in an age of extravagant computer-generated special effects. When my oldest son was a young boy, I took him to a screening of the film at a local movie theater—but it failed to hold his interest, and he asked me to take him home before the end of the first hour. Yet when I was a youngster, every child I knew was intimately familiar with *The Wizard of Oz*, which CBS broadcast once each year in an event of quasi–Super Bowl importance for the under-10 crowd. I still remember my awe when I learned that the father of one of my kindergarten classmates had helped paint the yellow brick road as part of his work as a studio hand at MGM. I could hardly have been more astonished if he had told me his dad was an astronaut or a secret agent.

So I knew "Over the Rainbow," the emotional centerpiece of *The Wizard of Oz*, long before I understood anything about jazz and the techniques of song-writing. Only years later could I comprehend how carefully Harold Arlen and Yip Harburg had constructed the effects that came across so naturally and un-affectedly in Judy Garland's delivery of the song: how the opening octave leap in the melody, which then settles down into the major seventh, matches the journey over the rainbow related in the lyrics; how the repetitions in the release lull and hypnotize the listener before the dramatic return of the main melody; how yearning and homesickness, central to the drama of the song, are stitched into its inner workings.

These virtues gave "Over the Rainbow" a viability outside of the preteen audience and a staying power that, for all the success of the film, would have hardly been possible with a less well-crafted composition. A few years before, Shirley Temple had been given prime vocal features with songs that would be popular with the nursery-room set—"On the Good Ship Lollipop" (1934), "Animal Crackers in My Soup" (1935), etc.—but they never managed to make the transition to the dance halls of the Swing Era. But "Over the Rainbow" was quickly adopted by the leading jazz bands, and before the end of 1939 the song had entered the repertoires of Benny Goodman, Artie Shaw, and Glenn Miller, among others. Miller's version—recorded even before the film's release—was a #1 hit for his band, with both Judy Garland and Bob Crosby also enjoying top 10 successes with "Over the Rainbow" at this same time.

"Over the Rainbow" has never fallen out of favor among jazz players, and has inspired some very creative performances over the years. It has served as a virtuoso keyboard showpiece for Art Tatum, a forward-looking big band chart for Boyd Raeburn, and a jangly electric-guitar solo feature for Stanley Jordan. Dave Brubeck has noted that his 1952 Storyville performance of the song is one of his favorites among his own recordings, and I don't think it is going too far to see this version, which completely reworks the harmonic structure without employing a single jazz syncopation, as anticipating the later concert-hall improvisation style associated with the ECM label. Four years later, Sonny Rollins drew on Arlen's chord changes, but changed the meter, for his composition "Valse Hot." And more than 50 years after it first charmed the public, singer Eva Cassidy could still make "Over the Rainbow" sound newly minted, as demonstrated on her recording, a posthumous hit for the singer, from 1992.

But the jazz world has no special claim on this composition, and it retains its popularity with listeners of all ages and backgrounds. Indeed, I can't imagine any other song matching the many honors awarded to this Arlen-Harburg gem. When the Recording Industry Association, with help from the National Endowment for the Arts, conducted a poll of experts and music lovers in 2001 to determine the most important American songs of the previous century, Judy Garland's recording of "Over the Rainbow" topped the list. Even deeply ingrained cultural artifacts such as "Take Me Out to the Ballgame," "White Christmas," and "God Bless America" couldn't dislodge it from the premier spot. The song was also picked as the greatest movie theme ever by the American Film Institute, and in that survey it beat out "As Time Goes By" and "Singin' in the Rain."

And yet "Over the Rainbow" was almost deleted from the movie, after studio head Louis B. Mayer griped that it slowed down the film, and—horrors!—was sung by Judy Garland *in a barnyard*! Fortunately for us, Arlen and executive producer Arthur Freed were able to convince Mayer to keep "Over the Rainbow" in the final cut—their arguments helped by the fact that the song was used extensively in instrumental references throughout the film and behind the title credits, and thus would require a major overhaul of the soundtrack were it removed.

RECOMMENDED VERSIONS

Glenn Miller, New York, July 12, 1939

Judy Garland (with Victor Young and His Orchestra), Hollywood, July 28, 1939

Boyd Raeburn, Los Angeles, June 3, 1946

Bud Powell, New York, May 1, 1951

Dave Brubeck, from *Jazz at Storyville*, live at Storyville, Boston, October 12, 1952

Art Tatum, from *The Art Tatum Solo Masterpieces, Vol. 6*, Los Angeles, December 28, 1953

Ray Charles (with an arrangement by Marty Paich), from *Ingredients in a Recipe for Soul*, Los Angeles, July 10, 1963

Stanley Jordan, from *Stolen Moments*, live at the Blue Note, Tokyo, November 7–9, 1990

Eva Cassidy, from *The Other Side*, Glendale, Maryland, July 1992

Keith Jarrett, from *La Scala*, live at Teatro Alla Scala, Milan, February 13, 1995

Peace

Composed by Horace Silver

Horace Silver built his career on catchy groove tunes performed by a series of stellar bands under his leadership—
groups that inevitably thrived at medium and medium-fast
tempos. Here was Silver's forte: inviting rhythms at which
fingers snap along or toes tap on the backbeat; melodies
with hooks as big as a cartoon pirate's prosthesis; and a
clean, crisp ensemble sound that got funky without ever
sounding too textured, too busy. Silver's own piano technique would never inspire comparisons to Art Tatum or
Oscar Peterson, but when he dug into these mid-range
funk-and-gospelish tunes, his playing had a certain rightness about it that made you forget what other pianists might
be doing at different nightclubs in other cities.

If Silver had a weakness, however, it came at slower
tempos. One sometimes sensed his impatience playing ballads. His keyboard attack had none of the sentimental flourishes or gentle ripples that other pianists rely on in these
settings. He most assuredly did not "tickle the ivories" (ugh!
a phrase I abhor); he gave them a spankin' instead, one
which skipped the ticklin' foreplay. Jazz bachelors of the day
quickly learned that, for a dose of lovey-dovey when the gal
of your dreams is coming over for dinner, you didn't put
Horace Silver's Greatest Hits on the hi-fi. Silver didn't do
lovey-dovey.

True to form, when this artist finally delivered his ballad
masterpiece, it wasn't about love and courtship, it was about
peace and serenity. And this ode to tranquility sounds so
natural and unaffected, one might think that these kinds of
meditative mood pieces were Silver's stock-in-trade. But
none of the other Silver songs that have earned a place in
the standard repertoire bears the slightest resemblance to

"Peace." And even here, Silver is a reluctant jazz pacifist—during the course of his solo, he prods bassist Gene Taylor and drummer Louis Hayes to double up the pulse with a series of licks more suitable for a faster tune. The rest of the band mostly resists these attempts to change the ambiance, and ultimately peace does reign supreme.

Perhaps the most striking aspect of this song is its renunciation of the usual tricks of the songwriters' trade. You won't find a single catchy melodic motif here, no surprising interlude, no harmonic shift that takes the piece in an unexpected direction. Instead the soloist cycles through a series of gentle resolving chords, mostly following a familiar ii-V formula, before settling unobtrusively into the tonic key of B flat. The whole effect is to avoid effects, to create a circular motion that is calming rather than overtly jazzy. The placid mood and unconventional ten-bar structure—both reminiscent of Miles Davis's "Blue in Green," which was released some 12 days before Silver recorded "Peace"—mask the turnaround, so that the composition returns to the beginning of the form without the usual dominant chord to herald the change.

Doug Carn has provided lyrics that snugly fit Silver's musical reverie. For an especially moving vocal rendition, check out Bobby McFerrin's performance from his eponymous debut album, which finds him doing something that he rarely has done since—sing a standard straight, with a direct, unaffected delivery of the words. Once you hear him do it here, you will wish he performed standards in this manner more often.

By the way, you will occasionally hear a jazz musician play a song under the title "Peace" that bears no resemblance to the Horace Silver composition. In those instances, you are probably encountering a different "Peace" piece, one with the same title written by Ornette Coleman. I am not suggesting that Mr. Silver resented the confusion, but I do note that, a short while later, he named one of his compositions "Lonely Woman"—thus appropriating the title of one of Coleman's most famous works.

RECOMMENDED VERSIONS

Horace Silver, from *Blowin' the Blues Away*, Englewood Cliffs, New Jersey, August 29, 1959

Chico Freeman, from *Spirit Sensitive*, New York, September 1979

Bobby McFerrin, from *Bobby McFerrin*, Los Angeles or New York, 1982

Chet Baker, from *Peace*, New York, February 23, 1982

Alan Broadbent, from *Live at Maybeck Recital Hall, Vol. 14*, Berkeley, April 21, 1991

Ian Shaw (with Billy Childs and Paul Bollenback), from *A World Still Turning*, New York, June 2003

Mulgrew Miller, from *Live at Yoshi's, Vol. 1*, live at Yoshi's, Oakland, July 22–23, 2003

The Peacocks
Composed by Jimmy Rowles

The jazz repertoire became increasingly resistant to change during the mid-1970s. Only a few years before, *The Real Book* (circa 1971)—an illegal but vastly influential compilation of lead sheets circulated first among Berklee students and eventually all over the jazz world—had given comparable emphasis to current-day compositions and classic material from the previous decades. But this open attitude of the early 1970s had all but disappeared by the close of the decade, and a calcified approach to the repertoire set in, one that continues to the present day.

Yet Jimmy Rowles's "The Peacocks" managed to defy the trend. Within a few months of Jimmy Rowles's first recording of this composition in April 1974, the song was picked up by a number of high-profile jazz artists. Stan Getz recorded it with Bill Evans at a jazz festival in Belgium, and followed up by producing a Rowles album for the Columbia label, on which he sat in with the composer on "The Peacocks." Evans also added it to his repertoire and left behind a number of recordings. A decade later, the song received a further boost when Herbie Hancock performed it with Wayne Shorter for the soundtrack for the film *'Round Midnight*.

The popularity of this ballad among jazz musicians is well deserved. The haunting open theme is countered by a slyly dissonant and almost Monkish melody in the bridge. This combination of lyricism and abstraction is powerful, almost a left-brain-meets-the-right-brain kind of creation. Because of the fluttery phrases in the melody, this piece works especially well on sax or piano—less so on other instruments: hence you won't hear quite as many trumpet or trombone versions. For those who knew Rowles, the composition is especially evocative of his quirky (and peacock-ish?) personality.

RECOMMENDED VERSIONS

Bill Evans and Stan Getz, from *But Beautiful*, Antwerp, August 16, 1974

Jimmy Rowles (with Stan Getz), from *The Peacocks*, New York, July 1975

Bill Evans, from *You Must Believe in Spring*, Hollywood, August 23–25, 1977

Herbie Hancock and Wayne Shorter, from the soundtrack to *'Round Midnight*, Paris, July 1–12, 1985

Fred Hersch, from *Sarabande*, New York, December 4–5, 1986

Branford Marsalis (with Herbie Hancock), from *Renaissance*, New York, December 31, 1986

Esperanza Spalding, from *Junjo*, Westwood, Massachusetts, April 2005

Pennies from Heaven
Composed by Arthur Johnston, with lyrics by Johnny Burke

Songs about money were popular during the Great Depression. But this one probably brought in the most pennies of them all. Bing Crosby's recording of "Pennies from Heaven," also featuring the Jimmy Dorsey band, was the biggest hit of 1936, holding on to the top spot for ten weeks. The success was supported by Crosby's starring role in a film of the same name—which was also noteworthy for the appearance of Louis Armstrong (at Crosby's insistence). The tune was nominated for an Academy Award but lost out to "The Way You Look Tonight." No disgrace there—especially when you consider that Cole Porter's "I've Got You Under My Skin" was another also-ran that year.

Armstrong recorded his own version of "Pennies from Heaven" two weeks after Crosby, but Bing, far from being territorial, joined in on the proceedings. Armstrong would keep this song in his repertoire for the rest of his career—a video captures him performing it with absolute authority at a Newport tribute concert in his honor shortly before his death. Inspired by Crosby and Armstrong's successes, other jazz players soon added the song to their set lists, and over the next 12 months Billie Holiday, Count Basie, and Louis Prima recorded "Pennies from Heaven," and it showed up on radio broadcasts by Duke Ellington and Django Reinhardt.

Despite these precedents, "Pennies from Heaven" soon fell by the wayside, and few jazz recordings of it were made after 1937, until the song took off again following World War II—at first as a trad jazz vehicle, even though the tune had not been around back in the early days of New Orleans and Chicago jazz. For his famous Town Hall concert in 1947—a historic moment in focusing audience and media attention on early jazz styles—Armstrong featured it, and once again played a key role in establishing "Pennies from Heaven" as a popular jazz piece. Modern jazz players eventually embraced it, with Bird, Dizzy, and other leading beboppers performing the song at one time or another.

Memorable later versions include Louis Prima's exciting if somewhat unhinged 1957 reworking (*shoobie-doobie . . . sunshine and ravioli . . . pizzioli . . .*)— which served up more "*Penne* from Heaven" than "Pennies from Heaven"; Stan Getz's collaboration with Oscar Peterson from later that same year; and Frank Sinatra's performance with Count Basie from 1962. The song has inspired both parody and tribute, including Steve Martin's lugubrious revival of it for the film *Pennies from Heaven* (yes, again, a movie named for the song) from 1981, which was based in turn on Dennis Potter's BBC series of the same name. But my favorite adaptation is "Benny's from Heaven," a very funny take-off popularized by Eddie Jefferson and James Moody, which turned the venerable standard into a song about uncertain paternity during those distant days before DNA testing.

RECOMMENDED VERSIONS

Bing Crosby with Jimmy Dorsey and His Orchestra, Los Angeles, August 4, 1936

Louis Armstrong, Los Angeles, August 17, 1936

Billie Holiday (with Teddy Wilson), New York, November 19, 1936

Count Basie (with Jimmy Rushing), New York, January 21, 1937

Louis Armstrong, live at Town Hall, New York, May 17, 1947

Jimmy Raney (with Sonny Clark), from *Jimmy Raney Quartet*, Paris, February 6, 1954

Louis Prima, from *The Call of the Wildest*, Hollywood, January 31, 1957

Stan Getz with Oscar Peterson, from *Stan Getz and the Oscar Peterson Trio*, Los Angeles, October 10, 1957

Frank Sinatra with Count Basie, from *Sinatra-Basie*, Los Angeles, October 3, 1962

Dave Brubeck (with Paul Desmond), from *The Dave Brubeck Quartet at Carnegie Hall*, live at Carnegie Hall, New York, February 22, 1963

Eddie Jefferson, from *The Main Man*, New York, October 9, 1977

Harry Allen, from *Harry Allen Meets John Pizzarelli Trio*, New York, December 18–19, 1995

Perdido
Composed by Juan Tizol, with lyrics by Ervin Drake and Hans Lengsfelder

"Perdido" in Spanish means "lost," and this simple jam tune could easily have been lost in the shuffle of the Duke Ellington band's remarkable output from the early 1940s. This was the golden age for Ellington, a period of peak creativity during which the bandleader seemed capable of delivering pathbreaking recordings every month. His biggest obstacles came solely from constant nonmusical stumbling blocks that threatened to derail his band—not just the outbreak of war (Pearl Harbor occurred four days after Duke first recorded "Perdido" as part of a transcription intended solely for radio broadcast), or the departure of ailing bassist Jimmy Blanton a few weeks before that, but also an ASCAP dispute with radio broadcasters in 1941 and the musicians' union strike against record labels in 1942. In this environment, Ellington's challenge was hardly composing or arranging, but just getting a song recorded, released, and heard on the airwaves.

In a narrow window between the ASCAP moratorium and the AFM strike, Ellington recorded both "Perdido" and "C Jam Blues" at the same Victor session—curiously enough, these were the two simplest hit songs from his entire career. "Perdido" is so bare bones that Ellington's biographer James Lincoln Collier has argued that you can't really classify it as a song. Yet its popularity among musicians no doubt stems from its ease of use. The main theme employs just a handful of notes and three chords, while the bridge harmonies are a familiar retread from "I Got Rhythm." A horn player could figure it out in a New York minute, even without a lead sheet on hand. As for swing fans, they had an insatiable appetite for repetitive riff-based dance tunes during this period, and few fit the recipe more completely than "Perdido." Ellington's recording of the song reached #21 on the chart during the spring of 1943.

Words were not grafted on to "Perdido" until 1944, and are no more elaborate than the tune itself. I do give the lyricists credit for trying to add ethnic flavor to a song whose only "Latin" element was a Spanish title—although I will leave you to judge whether the sombrero/bolero rhymes here represent an enhancement to a straight instrumental version. A more important enhancement was a countermelody, dating back to around the same time that words were added, which became a staple in later years. Often used in the out chorus, this alternative riff has been attributed to a number of players, including Benny Harris and Tadd Dameron. For the earliest recorded example, check out Stuff Smith's performance with Billy Taylor and Ted Sturgis from Town Hall in June 1945, where it emerges shortly before the four-and-a-half-minute mark.

Despite its unpretentious attitude, this song has enjoyed some of its finest moments under the auspices of Carnegie Hall. Charlie Parker and Ella Fitzgerald joined in a "Perdido" jam there as part of a Jazz at the Philharmonic concert from September 1949, just as two years earlier Flip Phillips and Illinois Jacquet put the audience into a frenzy with their sax battle on the same song on the same stage. Sarah Vaughan recorded it at Carnegie Hall as part of her 1954 performance there with the Count Basie band, and Charles Mingus relied on "Perdido" for his all-star jam at Carnegie Hall in 1974.

The reason this song figures at so many all-star dates is its very simplicity. When horn players engage in combat, "Perdido" is the jazz equivalent of neutral territory, where all parties are equally at home and no one has an edge. Charlie Parker and Gillespie jousted on it at their celebrated 1953 Massey Hall concert with Charles Mingus, Bud Powell, and Max Roach. Ben Webster, who served as soloist on "Perdido" back in his Ellington days, continued to call it when matching up with other name players in later years. An especially provocative pairing finds Webster taking on Don Byas in an outing on "Perdido," a familiar carryover from home when the two American ex-pats met up for a session in Villingen, Germany. A few weeks later, Oscar Peterson recorded

"Perdido" in the same location for his *My Favorite Instrument* album, a solo piano outing that ranks among this artist's best efforts.

RECOMMENDED VERSIONS

Duke Ellington, Chicago, January 21, 1942

Stuff Smith (with Billy Taylor), live at Town Hall, New York, June 9, 1945

Illinois Jacquet and Flip Phillips, live at Carnegie Hall, New York, September 27, 1947

Charlie Parker and Ella Fitzgerald (with Jazz at the Philharmonic), live at Carnegie Hall, New York, September 18, 1949

Dave Brubeck (with Paul Desmond), from *Jazz at Oberlin*, live at Oberlin College, Oberlin, Ohio, March 2, 1953

Dizzy Gillespie and Charlie Parker, from *Jazz at Massey Hall*, live at Massey Hall, Toronto, May 15, 1953

Randy Weston, from *Berkshire Blues*, New York, October 14, 1965

Ben Webster and Don Byas, from *Ben Webster Meets Don Byas*, Villingen, Germany, February 1, 1968

Oscar Peterson, from *My Favorite Instrument*, Villingen, Germany, April 1968

Charles Mingus, from *Mingus at Carnegie Hall*, live at Carnegie Hall, New York, January 19, 1974

Michel Camilo, from *Thru My Eyes*, Stamford, Connecticut, October 30–November 2, 1996

Poinciana

Composed by Nat Simon, with lyrics by Buddy Bernier

And what exactly, you ask, is a Poinciana? The name of the gal back home? An exotic island in the South Seas? A horse running in the fourth race at Del Mar? None of these, but rather the *delonix regia*, a tree native to Madagascar notable for its shade and bright flowers—striking blossoms that earn it the name of "flame tree."

There aren't many songs—especially ones so passionate—devoted to trees. For my part, I would prefer to pretend that this song is really about the girl back home, the daughter of a botanist, perhaps, who gave her an arboreal name. But composers Simon and Bernier make it hard for me to persist in this illusion. They based the song on a Cuban folk tune named "Cancion del Arbol," which translates as—yes, you guessed it!—"Song of the Tree."

In the jazz world, "Poinciana" is inextricably linked with Ahmad Jamal, whose successful recording of the composition from 1958 helped keep his album *Ahmad Jamal at the Pershing: But Not for Me* on the *Billboard* chart for more than two years. But the song long predates Jamal's interpretation, and was composed back in 1936. Glenn Miller performed it in the late 1930s, Benny Carter enjoyed a modest hit with "Poinciana" in February 1944, and Bing Crosby did the same the following month. Carter's version is especially interesting, with its strange groove, half Latin and half-R&B—a stark contrast to the pop-oriented approach Miller had adopted in his treatment.

Around this time, a number of name bandleaders embraced "Poinciana" and it shows up on live broadcasts by Duke Ellington, Jimmy Dorsey, Jack Teagarden, and other jazz stars of the era. Jazz cover versions were less common in the late 1940s and early 1950s, but "Poinciana" never completely fell off the radar screens of improvisers. Charlie Parker quotes the melody in a 1950 recording of "Ornithology," while Gerry Mulligan and Chet Baker are captured on record performing "Poinciana" during their celebrated stint at the Haig, a launching pad for the West Coast sound, in 1953. Other recordings that predate Jamal's success include versions by Erroll Garner, Lennie Niehaus, Red Callender, and George Shearing.

But Jamal eclipsed these precedents with a vamp-based arrangement that superimposed the pianist's unhurried phrasing over an insistent, appealing beat—so appealing that his "Poinciana" earned repeated jukebox plays and dance-floor loyalty at a time when modern jazz had largely abandoned these public platforms for crossover success. In ensuing years, a number of quirky jazz hit singles would be built on vamps—a short while later Dave Brubeck would storm the charts with "Take Five," Vince Guaraldi would do the same with "Cast Your Fate to the Wind," and Lee Morgan would follow up with "The Sidewinder"—each one following in the footsteps of "Poinciana," with repeated figures and hypnotic rhythm-based hooks.

Even after Jamal redefined "Poinciana," the song enjoyed a surprisingly varied career. It has been popular with vocal groups, as demonstrated in recordings by the Four Freshman and the Manhattan Transfer. It has appeared on albums devoted to musical exotica, getting the full Les Baxter "bring-the-Third-World-to-your-bachelor-pad" treatment, and has also been adapted for big bands, Afro-Cuban ensembles, and easy listening orchestras. But I am still under Jamal's sway, and feel "Poinciana" is best served by small combo versions that avoid the mood music baggage and let the song swing. For three striking examples, check out Shelly Manne's fast romp in straight 4/4 walking time from his 1959 performance at the Black Hawk, Sonny Rollins's hot work on soprano sax backed by George Cables's electric piano from 1972, and Keith Jarrett's convivial trio rendition from 1999.

RECOMMENDED VERSIONS

Benny Carter, San Francisco, October 25, 1943

Lennie Niehaus (with Hampton Hawes), from *The Quintets*, Los Angeles, January 20, 1956

Ahmad Jamal, from *Ahmad Jamal at the Pershing: But Not for Me*, live at the
Pershing Lounge, Chicago, January 16, 1958

Shelly Manne, from *Live at the Black Hawk 1*, live at the Black Hawk, San Francisco,
September 22, 1959

Booker Ervin, from *That's It*, New York, January 6, 1961

Ahmad Jamal, from *At the Top: Poinciana Revisited*, live at the Village Gate, New
York, 1969

Sonny Rollins (with George Cables), from *Sonny Rollins' Next Album*, New York, July
14, 1972

McCoy Tyner, from *McCoy Tyner and the Latin All-Stars*, New York, July 29–30, 1998

Keith Jarrett (with the Standards Trio), from *Whisper Not*, live at the Palais des
Congrès, Paris, July 5, 1999

Polka Dots and Moonbeams

Composed by Jimmy Van Heusen, with lyrics by Johnny Burke

I adore the music, but the lyrics make me cringe. The phrase "pug-nosed dream"
as a term of endearment would be bad enough if Johnny Burke had included it
once, but he finds reason to say it three times during the course of 32 bars. I
suspect he is aiming for a rhyme with "moonbeams," but it doesn't work on that
account either—both due to the conflicting syllabic accent and the mixing of
singular and plural. In any event, the result is a lyric that is cutesy and clumsy
married to a stately melody that has genuine moments of grandeur.

That said, I do play this song fairly often when seated at the piano. And
when I do, I play it fairly straight, not making many changes with the original
harmonies. The economy, almost simplicity, of means employed here by Van
Heusen does not detract from the emotional power of this song, even though
the melody is mostly diatonic with few marked leaps, and the chords in the
bridge are almost the same as those in the main theme, just transposed up a
major third. This folksy quality fits in with the supposed setting of the song—a
country dance in a garden—so much so that, at moments, I could almost be
convinced that this was a nineteenth-century parlor tune slightly updated for
modern audiences.

All the more surprising, then, that urban sophisticate Frank Sinatra, specialist in big-city songs, played the key role in establishing this pastoral piece
in the public's imagination. His onstage persona seems at odds with such an
old-timey song. Yet his recording with the Tommy Dorsey band was the first
Sinatra song to reach the *Billboard* chart—setting off a string of successes,
which included 23 top 10 hits just during his short stint with that popular big

band. He puts about as much sincerity into the words as they can bear, and avoids the tell-tale irony that would be a trademark of his mid- and late-career work.

A few later singers have been brave enough to tackle this song, including Ella Fitzgerald and Sarah Vaughan, while Sinatra himself revisited it in the early 1960s. Cassandra Wilson gets the top marks from me, for the daring altered metrics of her 1988 version from her fine *Blue Skies* album. But most jazz renditions have come from instrumentalists, who don't need to worry about keeping a straight face each time the "pug-nosed dream" comes around. Bill Evans kept this song in his repertoire for many years, but my preferred version by him is the first, recorded for his 1962 *Moon Beams* project on the Riverside label. Pianist Elmo Hope tackled the song on a 1956 session, and benefited from having John Coltrane, Donald Byrd, and Hank Mobley on hand; yet after Trane's rise to fame, Hope was dealt the ignominious fate of having his project reissued with Coltrane listed as leader, and the pianist relegated to a sideman's credit.

Certainly the men in suits have a high opinion of the value of this song. When Jean Bach was preparing her celebrated 1995 short film *A Great Day in Harlem* for release, she wanted to include Lester Young's performance of "Polka Dots and Moonbeams" in the soundtrack but changed her plans when the publisher demanded $100,000—which would have represented a substantial portion of her $500,000 budget, and far more than Young made even in his peak earning year. For his last tour, the iconic tenor saxophonist was paid $500 per week—which suggests that, with four years of steady work, and spending nothing on himself, Young might have been able to secure the rights to one of his own recordings.

RECOMMENDED VERSIONS

Tommy Dorsey (featuring Frank Sinatra), New York, March 4, 1940

Lester Young, New York, September 17, 1949

Sarah Vaughan, from *Swingin' Easy*, New York, April 2, 1954

Elmo Hope (with John Coltrane), from *Informal Jazz*, New York, May 7, 1956

Count Basie (with Lester Young), from *Count Basie at Newport*, live at the Newport Jazz Festival, Newport, Rhode Island, July 7, 1957

Wes Montgomery, from *The Incredible Jazz Guitar of Wes Montgomery*, New York, January 28, 1960

Bill Evans, from *Moon Beams*, New York, June 5, 1962

Ella Fitzgerald, from *Fine and Mellow*, Los Angeles, January 8, 1974

Cassandra Wilson (with Mulgrew Miller), from *Blue Skies*, New York, February 4–5, 1988

Prelude to a Kiss

Composed by Duke Ellington, with lyrics by Irving Gordon and Irving Mills

In the late 1930s, the musical tastes of the American public had finally caught up with Duke Ellington. The Swing Era was in full force, and the music industry (as well as their customers) displayed an insatiable appetite for hot riff-based tunes to serve as accompaniment to drinking and dancing. Ellington was eminently equipped to give the public exactly what it wanted—he had almost invented this kind of music—yet at this juncture he does the *exact opposite*. The Duke uses his fame and greater artistic freedom to become more ambitious, more experimental, less beholden to the formulas of swing music. As I survey his work from the late 1930s and early 1940s, I constantly encounter recordings that seem to defy almost every rule of the music business, or even the jazz tradition, aspiring rather to some new aesthetic standards of Ellington's own creation. Yet—and here is the marvel of it all—he continued to enjoy enormous commercial success and fame, even broadening his audience and appeal, despite the surprises he kept throwing at his fans.

"Prelude to a Kiss" from 1938 is a case in point. The descending chromatic melody line of the opening theme is more suited to classical music than jazz, and is devoid of anything resembling a Tin Pan Alley hook. The meat-and-potatoes are the thick harmonies, which are a joy to play on the piano but unlikely to cause a sensation on the dance floor. And if you had any doubts about Ellington's ambivalence to commercial considerations, consider that he recorded this composition as an ethereal instrumental on August 9, 1938, but let his sideman Johnny Hodges take credit for the more successful vocal version two weeks later. By the way, the lyrics grafted on to Ellington's songs rarely approach the exquisite artistry of the music, but I especially like the words here, in particular the phrase about a "Schubert tune with a Gershwin touch," which is about as apt a way of describing this song as one could contrive.

As with so many of Ellington's compositions, "Prelude to a Kiss" owes a debt to a band member. Otto Hardwick is credited with contributing to the melody, yet the end result bears the strong stamp of Ellington's personality and comes across as very much in keeping with Duke's affinity for mood pieces. His fingerprints remain when others interpret this song, and most of the cover versions from later decades—even when strong individualists such as McCoy Tyner and Steve Lacy are involved—remain faithful to the spirit of Ellington's original inspiration.

Jazz fans who want a rare behind-the-scenes look at how a star performer crafts an interpretation of this song can compare Billie Holiday's studio version from August 23, 1955 with the surviving (and now commercially available) tape of her rehearsal the previous day with only Jimmy Rowles accompanying on piano. And, after that, if you are still looking for something stronger in your cup of Ellingtonia, I would push you in the direction of Latin jazz artists Tito Puente and, especially, Chilean vocalist Claudia Acuña. The latter's 1999 reinterpretation of this standard takes some invigorating twists and turns, and could work as a prelude to many things, some of them bolder than a kiss.

RECOMMENDED VERSIONS

Duke Ellington, New York, August 9, 1938

Johnny Hodges, New York, August 24, 1938

Duke Ellington, from *Piano Reflections*, April 13, 1953

June Christy and Stan Kenton, from *Duet*, Los Angeles, May 5, 1955

Billie Holiday (with Benny Carter), from *Velvet Mood*, Los Angeles, August 23, 1955

McCoy Tyner (with Ron Carter and Tony Williams), from *Supertrios*, Berkeley, April 9–10, 1977

Phil Woods, from *Live from New York*, live at the Village Vanguard, New York, October 7, 1982

Mal Waldron and Steve Lacy, from *Sempre Amore*, Milan, February 17, 1986

Tito Puente, from *Un Poco Loco*, San Francisco, January 1987

Claudia Acuña, from *Wind from the South*, New York, 1999

Matthew Shipp, from *Pastoral Composure*, New York, January 6, 2000

Rhythm-a-ning

Composed by Thelonious Monk

The title refers to Gershwin's "I Got Rhythm," which provides the harmonic underpinning to this song, as it has to so many other "original" jazz compositions. But if most borrowers of spare changes try to obscure the connection to an older song with a new title, Monk proudly announces that he is "rhythm-a-ning." This wasn't the only time this composer served up a new title as a clue to the old one. His "Evidence," based on "Just You, Just Me," was initially called "Justice" ("Just us"). When he recorded his adaptation of Coleman Hawkins and Sir Charles Thompson's "Stuffy," it was released as "Stuffy Turkey." Even the venerable gentleman in the title to the nursery song "This Old Man" stayed around in Monk's version, which was released as "That Old Man."

But more than just the chords were hand-me-downs in "Rhythm-a-ning." Most of the A theme comes from Mary Lou Williams's 1936 chart "Walkin' and Swingin'" for the Andy Kirk band. And anyone who thinks this may be mere coincidence should compare Monk's "Hackensack" with Mary Lou Williams's arrangement of "Lady Be Good." Looks like Monk the composer was doing some "Mary-a-ning" as well as "Rhythm-a-ning."

But the genealogy gets even more complex here. Long before Monk made his first recording of "Rhythm-a-ning," this same "Walkin' and "Swingin'" riff showed up on "Pagin' Dr. Christian" (sometimes called "Meet Dr. Christian"), attributed to guitarist Charlie Christian and recorded at Minton's in 1941. It can also be heard on Al Haig's "Opus Caprice," first recorded in 1950, and Sonny Stitt's "Symphony Hall Swing" from 1952. Monk's presence at Minton's, back in 1941, might earn him some claim for the Christian piece, or possibly suggest he borrowed the motif from the guitarist and not from Williams. But Mary Lou Williams's clear precedence, by a half-decade, in the chain of recordings, strengthens her claim as the originator if this ever went to a jury of jazz peers.

Despite these forerunners, Monk's eventual debut recording of "Rhythm-a-ning" in 1957, on a session alongside Art Blakey, is anything but anticlimactic. Blakey, who invariably managed to inspire this pianist to first-rate performances, adopts a more assertive stance here than on Monk's Blue Note work. This is Blakey's leader date, and he calls a faster tempo for "Rhythm-a-ning" than the composer probably would have picked. At the outset, Monk offers an intro that realigns the melody even before it has been formally stated. After the head, Monk is assigned first solo, and he adapts to the hard bop ethos established by the leader, delivering a more driving solo than usual but still with his trademark sound and personality. I only wish it had lasted longer—and it sounds as if the rest of the band is just as surprised as me when Thelonious drops out after just two choruses. Later Monk griped that the record was fine, but the drummer couldn't keep time. More likely, he was peeved at being forced to play his song at Blakey's brisk beat.

In fact, Blakey keeps a fairly steady pulse here, catty comments notwithstanding, but on Monk's next recording of "Rhythm-a-ning," in a collaboration with Gerry Mulligan recorded three months later, the tempo does slow down when Monk solos. I suspect that Mulligan counted in the tempo here and, like Blakey, took this song somewhat faster than the composer wanted. A more holistic performance can be heard on the 1958 live album made at the Five Spot, *Thelonious in Action*, which finds Monk supported by Roy Haynes on drums and joined by saxophonist Johnny Griffin. Griffin claims most of the solo space, and Monk doesn't get his chance to shine until six minutes into the track, but when his time comes, he is wholly in command—he develops a probing, off-balance pattern during his second chorus that sounds like something carefully hatched in his practice time. And in the third chorus . . . Monk returns to this same musical idea. It's an intriguing interlude that probably could work as a standalone piece or inspire a big band chart.

This song, like many other Monk pieces, has made up for early obscurity, gradually gaining in popularity over the decades. Few musicians recorded cover versions during the 1960s (Art Pepper and Eddie "Lockjaw" Davis stand out as notable exceptions), and "Rhythm-a-ning" failed to make the cut for inclusion in *The Real Book* when that work was compiled in the early 1970s. Later in that decade and throughout the 1980s, the song started figuring more often in set lists and on recordings, and today is firmly entrenched in the standard repertoire.

Oddly enough, for a composition that found Monk borrowing most of its constituent elements from other sources, the end result bears the distinctive marks of his musical persona. Nonetheless, the ascendancy of "Rhythm-a-ning" since the composer's death has no doubt been helped along by the never-failing appeal of "I Got Rhythm" changes among jazz players. Indeed, performances of "Rhythm-a-ning" too often find the soloists forgetting Monk after the opening melody statement, treating this as one more excuse for a "Rhythm" jam. But when played in the right spirit, "Rhythm-a-ning" can be something much more, as demonstrated most clearly on Monk's own recordings of the work.

RECOMMENDED VERSIONS

Art Blakey (with Thelonious Monk), from *Art Blakey's Jazz Messengers with Thelonious Monk*, New York, May 15, 1957

Thelonious Monk (with Johnny Griffin and Roy Haynes), from *Thelonious in Action*, live at the Five Spot, New York, August 7, 1958

Art Pepper (with Conte Candoli and Wynton Kelly), from *Gettin' Together*, Los Angeles, February 29, 1960

Don Cherry, Steve Lacy, and Mal Waldron, from *Interpretations of Monk*, live at Wollman Auditorium, Columbia University, New York, November 1, 1981

Chick Corea (with Miroslav Vitous and Roy Haynes), from *Trio Music*, Los Angeles, November 1981

McCoy Tyner, from *Double Trios*, New York, June 9, 1986

Esbjörn Svensson, from *Plays Monk*, Stockholm, January 1996

Branford Marsalis (with Joey Calderazzo), from *Metamorphosen*, Durham, North Carolina, August 25–27, 2008

'Round Midnight
Composed by Thelonious Monk and Cootie Williams, with lyrics by Bernie Hanighen

Miles Davis's celebrated performance of "'Round Midnight" at the 1955 Newport Jazz Festival stands out as the most important moment in the history of this song, and did more than any of the composer's own renditions to establish it as a jazz standard. Was Monk pleased? Not in the least. Davis shared a ride back home from the festival with the composer, who told the trumpeter that he hadn't played the piece correctly. The two jazz icons got into a heated argument, and Monk ordered the driver to stop the car, and got out. "We left Monk standing there where you catch the ferry," Davis later recalled, "and drove back to New York."

The audience had a different opinion. "Everybody went crazy," Davis bragged. "It was something. I got a standing ovation. When I got off the bandstand everyone was looking at me like I was a king or something—people were running up to me offering me record deals." This performance led to the trumpeter's contract with Columbia, and on his debut for the label, *'Round about Midnight,* he shared with record-buyers the same intensely moody performance that had captivated the audience at Newport. The marvel here is that Davis delivers a definitive performance without even taking a solo—just a chiaroscuro melody statement, haunting and succinct, with a few deft alterations and embellishments.

The song had led a subterranean life for more than a decade before Miles recorded it for Columbia, and its genealogy is especially convoluted. Monk copyrighted it in 1943 under the name "I Need You So," with forgettable lyrics added by his neighbor Thelma Elizabeth Murray. Some time after the end of World War II, Coleman Hawkins recorded a two-part solo saxophone improvisation for the Selmer corporation, known as "Hawk's Variation," which was released as a demo to help promote their new line of horns. This was the first recording of solo jazz saxophone—even before Hawk's famous "Picasso"— and it is interesting to note that the second variation is an improvisation over the chord changes of Monk's tune. Still earlier, Ellington alum Cootie Williams had recorded "'Round Midnight," apparently at the urging of his pianist Bud Powell. Williams, like Miles, saw the song's value as a trumpet feature.

Williams also initiated a long history of tinkering with this composition. He inserted a strident interlude that later artists have preferred to ignore, and used it as a pretext to add his name as co-composer. New lyrics by Bernie Hanighen were written around this same time—even though Williams performed this song as an instrumental—and these, unlike Williams's interpolation, have often been featured in cover versions. Nevertheless, some performers still prefer to omit "'Round Midnight" from their Monk tribute recordings, because Monk's estate must share royalties with these collaborators.

Other parties have also put their marks on the song. "All the guys who play ''Round Midnight' use my introduction and they use my ending," Dizzy Gillespie later boasted. Miles, for his part, added a very effective interlude, in addition to his modification of the harmonies. Not everyone looks favorably on these attempts to improve the original. "Thelonious Monk wrote ''Round Midnight,' but his changes were so complex that most musicians couldn't play them," Branford Marsalis has commented. "Then Miles Davis found a lot simpler way of playing it and that's the version everyone plays today. Nobody's gonna do that to Beethoven or Bach."

But even the alterations get altered on this song. I remember an illegal fake book that came into my hands when I was a teenager, which offered two lead sheets for "'Round Midnight"—one giving the Miles Davis chords, and the other laying out the "West Coast chord changes." As a native Californian,

I wondered whether I needed to learn this alternative progression—but was skeptical, since I had never played with any musician on the Coast who used the "West Coast changes." I still haven't. Jazz players must all be New Yorkers at heart.

In truth, this is one of the few Thelonious Monk songs that makes it easy for performers to infuse their own personality into the music. Other Monk standards—such as "Epistrophy" or "Well You Needn't" or "Straight, No Chaser"—almost force the musician to take on the mannerisms of the composer. I have heard even great stylists get flummoxed when playing Monk: they end up losing their own identity and wallow around in Monk's second-hand wardrobe. "'Round Midnight," in contrast, can be played as a straight jazz-pop ballad—or in any number of other ways—without losing the essence of the song. For that reason, performers with little apparent affinity for Monk's idiosyncratic techniques, from June Christy to Bill Evans, have been able to cover this song without budging from their usual *modus operandi*.

But you won't really comprehend "'Round Midnight" if you don't hear Monk perform it. Fortunately he left behind more than two dozen recorded versions. I would call particular attention to the Blue Note version from 1947 and the solo piano recording for Riverside made a decade later—the latter sometimes packaged with some 20 minutes of illuminating outtakes.

RECOMMENDED VERSIONS

Cootie Williams, New York, August 22, 1944

Dizzy Gillespie, Glendale, California, February 6, 1946

Thelonious Monk, New York, November 21, 1947

Miles Davis, from *'Round about Midnight*, New York, September 10, 1956

Thelonious Monk, from *Thelonious Himself*, New York, April 1957

Barry Harris, from *Chasin' the Bird*, New York, May 31 and August 23, 1962

Betty Carter (with an arrangement by Oliver Nelson), from *'Round Midnight*, New York, December 6, 1962

Sarah Vaughan, from *Sarah Sings Soulfully*, Los Angeles, May 29, 1963

Dexter Gordon (with Woody Shaw and George Cables), from *Homecoming*, live at the Village Vanguard, New York, December 11–12, 1976

Wayne Shorter (with Herbie Hancock), from *Jazz at the Opera House*, live at the War Memorial Opera House, San Francisco, February 22, 1982

Bobby McFerrin (with Herbie Hancock) (from the soundtrack to the film *'Round Midnight*), Paris, August 20–21, 1985

James Carter, from *The Real Quietstorm*, New York, October–November 1994

Royal Garden Blues
Composed by Clarence Williams and Spencer Williams

No, the composers aren't brothers. Yet you might make that assumption when you learn that both were born in the environs of New Orleans a few years apart, and both were successful African-American songwriters steeped in the jazz idiom of the day—each comprehending the value of intellectual property at a time when other black artists would sell the rights to hit songs for a few dollars. And both made the journey—following the pathway of jazz itself—from New Orleans to Chicago (where the Royal Gardens Café, which gave its name to this song, was located) and on to New York.

But this song would travel even further. The influential French modernist composer Darius Milhaud had heard jazz in Harlem in 1922, and when he returned to France he composed *La création du monde*, inserting melodic elements reminiscent of "Royal Garden Blues" into this avant-garde work. Soon after, composer Spencer Williams also made his way to Paris, and brought his jazz-oriented music to the Folies Bergère, where it was performed by Josephine Baker. Such proselytizing efforts were not without their impact: nowadays, "Royal Garden Blues" is more likely to show up in the repertoire of European trad jazz bands than on the set lists of improvisers back stateside.

In America, both the Original Dixieland Jazz Band and Mamie Smith enjoyed hit records with "Royal Garden Blues" in 1921. Smith didn't sing on her record, instead featuring her accompanists, known as the Jazz Hounds, in an instrumental performance—Ethel Waters would do the same a few months later—but this hardly lessens the distinction of this track, which many consider the first genuine jazz recording by a black band. Yet of all the early recorded versions, Bix Beiderbecke's performance from 1927 is the one most often heard these days.

Although the tune is now considered a staple of New Orleans jazz, African-American musicians from that city were slow to embrace "Royal Garden Blues." Jelly Roll Morton, King Oliver, and Freddie Keppard never recorded it, but Bunk Johnson and the revivalists took "Royal Garden Blues" on board and helped establish it as one of the most frequently recorded jazz standards from the 1940s onward. Sidney Bechet and Kid Ory didn't record it until the World War II years, around a quarter of a century after it was composed. Bechet, however, made up for lost time, leaving behind more than two dozen recorded versions. Louis Armstrong waited until 1947 before adding "Royal Garden Blues" to his band's repertoire.

Swing Era bandleaders were also paying attention to the song during the 1940s. Benny Goodman recorded a sextet version in 1940 with Charlie Christian and Count Basie in the band. The song also shows up in two mind-expanding big band treatments of the postwar years: Duke Ellington's performance of a Billy Strayhorn arrangement of "Royal Garden Blues" in 1946, and Gil Evans's chart for Claude Thornhill from 1949. A brash modern jazz treatment can also be heard on Bud Shank and Bill Perkin's 1955 collaboration for the Pacific Jazz label, where the front line is supported by a rhythm section of Hampton Hawes, Red Mitchell, and Mel Lewis—gatekeepers who prevent any elements of trad jazz from encroaching on the beat.

But in more recent decades, "Royal Garden Blues" has lost the piquancy that inspired a modernist such as Milhaud or Strayhorn to turn to it for inspiration. When Branford Marsalis, Don Byron or other leading players perform this work, they are usually in a mood more playful than experimental. But even these sly updatings tend to be rare events. If you encounter this song nowadays, it is likely to come from a Dixieland band, who will probably sound as if they are auditioning for a gig at the Royal Gardens Café back in the 1920s.

RECOMMENDED VERSIONS

Mamie Smith's Jazz Hounds (without Mamie Smith), New York, January 1921

Original Dixieland Jazz Band, New York, May 25, 1921

Bix Beiderbecke, New York, October 5, 1927

Benny Goodman (with Charlie Christian), New York, November 7, 1940

Edmond Hall's Blue Note Jazzmen (with James P. Johnson and Sidney de Paris), New York, November 29, 1943

Sidney Bechet (with Bunk Johnson), live at the Savoy Café, Boston, March 25, 1945

Duke Ellington (with an arrangement by Billy Strayhorn), Hollywood, September 3, 1946

Claude Thornhill (with an arrangement by Gil Evans), New York, July 1949

Bud Shank and Bill Perkins (with Hampton Hawes), from *Bud Shank-Bill Perkins*, Los Angeles, May 2, 1955

Louis Armstrong, from *Ambassador Satch*, Milan, December 19–20, 1955

Bobby Hackett, from *Creole Cookin'*, New York, January 30, 1967

Branford Marsalis, from *Royal Garden Blues*, New York, March 18–20 and July 2, 1986

Don Byron, from *Bug Music*, Astoria, New York, May 1996

Ruby, My Dear
Composed by Thelonious Monk

Around 1937 or 1938, Thelonious Monk began dating Rubie Richardson, an attractive young neighbor of West Indian descent. The relationship was complicated by the hostility of her parents—Monk was not allowed to come to her house, and needed to meet his new girlfriend on the corner. The pianist was interested in marriage, but never got quite that far, although years later, Monk's wife Nellie told his biographer Robin D. G. Kelley: "There were only two women in his life—me and Rubie." The relationship eventually wound down after Richardson moved to Washington, D.C. in 1942.

In October 1945, Gil Fuller registered a copyright on behalf of Monk for the pianist's composition "Manhattan Moods," which a few months later took on the name "Ruby, My Dear." Monk must have been pleased with the work, because he played it for Alfred Lion when he auditioned for the Blue Note label, and the song was recorded at his October 24, 1947 session for that company. This composition, more than most of Monk's pieces, had potential for crossover success, with its very singable melody and satisfying harmonic movement. But from the outset of this track, which he opens with a jarring whole-tone run, Monk showed that this song, at least in his hands, would be no conventional love ballad.

Few paid attention at the time. "Ruby, My Dear" would eventually gain popularity with jazz musicians, but except for an amateur recording of Charlie Parker toying with it, no one else would record the song during the remainder of the decade. In 1953, Kenny Dorham covered the piece for a session on the Debut label, removing Monk's passing chords in order to present a more streamlined ballad conception. But almost two years would pass before another jazz musician would record it, and "Ruby, My Dear" wouldn't show up with any frequency at studio sessions until the 1960s.

Monk himself remained a tireless advocate of this piece even before others caught on. He recorded it with Coleman Hawkins and revisited it a few weeks later on the *Thelonious Monk with John Coltrane* album—both from 1957. "Ruby, My Dear" shows up again on a 1958 live recording from the Five Spot with John Coltrane, and on Monk's outstanding 1959 solo piano session in San Francisco. The cumulative impact of these performances can hardly be overstated, and these many decades later, Monk's interpretations remain touchstones for others tackling "Ruby, My Dear."

Among later recordings, I especially admire James Moody's probing rendition with Kenny Barron from 1966, McCoy Tyner's trio outing with Elvin Jones and Ron Carter from his 1975 *Trident* session, and Mal Waldron's duet with Jim Pepper from 1988. I am often skeptical about efforts to turn Monk's works into vocal numbers, but Carmen McRae's reconfiguration of this song into "Dear Ruby" strikes me as a fitting realization of the composer's vision, one that I suspect Monk would have appreciated.

RECOMMENDED VERSIONS

Thelonious Monk, New York, October 24, 1947

Kenny Dorham, "Ruby, My Dear (Take 2)" from *Kenny Dorham Quintet*, New York, December 15, 1953

Thelonious Monk (with John Coltrane), from *Thelonious Monk with John Coltrane*, New York, July 1957

Thelonious Monk, from *Thelonious Alone in San Francisco*, San Francisco, October 21, 1959

James Moody (with Kenny Barron), from *Moody and the Brass Figures*, New York, October–November 1966

McCoy Tyner (with Elvin Jones and Ron Carter), from *Trident*, Berkeley, February 18–19, 1975

Hank Jones, from *Bebop Redux*, New York, January 18–19, 1977

Paul Motian (with Joe Lovano, Geri Allen, and Bill Frisell), from *Monk in Motian*, New York, March 1988

Carmen McRae (recorded as "Dear Ruby"), from *Carmen Sings Monk*, New York, April 1988

Mal Waldron and Jim Pepper, from *Art of the Duo*, Munich, April 5, 1988

Marilyn Crispell, from *Live in San Francisco*, recorded live at New Langton Arts, San Francisco, October 20, 1989

S

St. James Infirmary
Traditional

No doubt many New Orleans tourists wander around the French Quarter in hopes of finding the St. James Infirmary, the location memorialized in the famous old jazz song—where Louis Armstrong, Jack Teagarden, and others saw their baby stretched out on "a long white table, so sweet, so cold, so fair."

Unfortunately they are in the wrong city, even the wrong continent, according to the most common current interpretation of this song's meaning. To find the real St. James Infirmary, they would need to travel to London, where a St. James Hospital was established before the Norman invasion to house "fourteen leprous maiden sisters." And even if they made the trek to the original site, they would no doubt be disappointed to encounter a palace, established by King Henry VIII in the 1530s, instead of an infirmary. Somehow "St. James *Palace* Blues" just doesn't seem to have the same potential for jazz immortality.

But this song, better than any other standard, makes clear the oft-forgotten folkloric roots of jazz. Few listeners today are aware of the deep connection between British ballads and the music of the American South, yet Cecil Sharp, the researcher whose efforts helped spur the English folksong revival, actually did his most important fieldwork in Tennessee, Kentucky, Virginia, and North Carolina—where he found singers who knew more of the old English songs than anyone in the ballads' land of origin. By the same token, scholar Stephen Calt, in his research into the origins of puzzling phrases found in early blues recordings, discovered that many are variants of British expressions that had never made their way into wider American speech patterns, but somehow persisted in African-American communities. In short, black American culture has deep European, as well as African, roots.

"St. James Infirmary" must possess a similarly convoluted lineage. It has been traced back to "The Unfortunate Rake" and other related ballads. As sung by A. L. Lloyd on his 1956 recording *English Street Songs*, the words describe the scene:

> As I was a-walking down by St. James Hospital,
> I was a-walking down by there one day,
> What should I spy but one of my comrades
> All wrapped up in flannel though warm was the day.

In this version, the young man is dying of venereal disease—hardly a topic for a hit song nowadays—but in other versions the protagonist is a young lady "led astray." Elsewhere the story morphed into a song about a dying gambler, or in "The Streets of Laredo" tells of a cowboy with a gunshot wound in his breast.

The path from leprous maidens to Louis Armstrong is a murky one at best—and some still dispute the Old World connections of this jazz song—but after the trumpeter's 1928 recording, the dissemination of "St. James Infirmary" is easily traced. A little over a year later, both King Oliver and Duke Ellington recorded "St. James Infirmary," just a day apart, both at New York sessions. Irving Mills, Ellington's perspicacious manager, even secured the copyright for himself (using his pseudonym Joe Primrose)—his application filed the year *after* Armstrong's recording and a few centuries after the original St. James Infirmary closed its door.

Cab Calloway enjoyed great success with his 1930 recording of "St. James Infirmary"—it will come as no surprise that Irving Mills was Mr. Calloway's manager at the time. "St. James Infirmary" also helped inspire Calloway's signature hit "Minnie the Moocher," which borrows elements of the earlier song. Artie Shaw enjoyed a top 20 hit with "St. James Infirmary" 12 years later, with a version that featured Hot Lips Page as vocalist. This two-part recording covered both sides of a 78, with a looser instrumental jam on the flip side of the vocal. "St. James Infirmary" was also a signature song for Jack Teagarden, who recorded it on more than 20 occasions. Most later jazz versions are derivative and formulaic, yet a few gems can be found in the mix. New Orleans native Nicholas Payton even gets into a quasi-Coltranish modal groove on his 1995 interpretation.

The song has become a well-traveled cultural meme by now and, as such, shows up in the least expected places. It has been covered by the Doors, Janis Joplin, Tom Jones, the Ventures, and other unlikely performers of traditional material. Back in the debut season of *Saturday Night Live*, Lily Tomlin sang it while seated atop the piano with the band dressed as nurses. Tomlin won't make anyone forget Armstrong or Teagarden, but her dark humor focused attention on the peculiarity, at least within the American popular music tradition, of a love song delivered to a corpse.

RECOMMENDED VERSIONS

Louis Armstrong, Chicago, December 12, 1928

King Oliver, New York, January 28, 1930

Duke Ellington, New York, January 29, 1930

Cab Calloway, New York, December 23, 1930

Jack Teagarden (with Ben Webster), New York, December 15, 1940

Artie Shaw (with Hot Lips Page), New York, November 12, 1941

Jimmy Smith, from *Monster*, Englewood Cliffs, New Jersey, January 19–20, 1965

Nicholas Payton, from *Gumbo Nouveau*, New York, November 28–30, 1995

Evan Christopher, from *The Road to New Orleans*, Newport Beach, California, 2002

Anat Cohen, from *Clarinetwork: Live at the Village Vanguard*, live at the Village
    Vanguard, New York, July 5, 2009

St. Louis Blues
Composed by W. C. Handy

W. C. Handy is sometimes called the Father of the Blues. Yet when Handy moved to Mississippi in 1903 to take a job as bandleader, he was unfamiliar with blues music, more interested in Sousa-style marches than vernacular African-American song forms. Around this time, Handy heard his first blues—performed by a guitarist at a train station in Tutwiler who accompanied his singing by playing on the strings with a knife. Handy was struck by the music, but more as a curiosity than a source of inspiration. A short while later, Handy was jolted into recognition of the commercial potential of blues music when, while entertaining at a dance, his slick, well-rehearsed band was upstaged by an untutored local trio who played blues on guitar, bass, and mandolin. "A rain of silver dollars began to fall," Handy later recalled. "The dancers went wild. Dollars, quarter, halves—the shower grew heavier. . . . There before the boys lay more money than my nine musicians were being paid for the entire engagement."

Handy's embrace of the blues can be dated back to this singular event, and within a few days he had written arrangements of blues songs for his band. Yet he would not compose his most famous blues song, "St. Louis Blues," until he was 40, a full decade after his first exposure to the music. This composition is only partially a blues, the standard 12-bar form followed by a 16-bar strain incorporating a habanera rhythm, a distinctive Cuban element that adds to the exoticism and appeal of "St. Louis Blues." Today, few jazz composers would mix a blues stanza and a 16-bar song form in the same composition, but the striking contrast between the two themes—not just in length, but even more in rhythmic and tonal flavor—no doubt served as the key hook that ensured widespread popularity for this unconventional piece.

Few songs have been more popular than "St. Louis Blues." I've been told that only "Silent Night" was recorded more frequently during the first half of the twentieth century. In the United States, more than a dozen artists enjoyed hits with "St. Louis Blues" in the years leading up to World War II, including Louis Armstrong, Bessie Smith, the Original Dixieland Jazz Band, Cab Calloway, Benny Goodman, and the composer W. C. Handy himself. Many of these recordings rank among the finest works of these respective artists. Bessie Smith is joined by Armstrong on her 1925 recording, and she delivers one of the most moving vocal performances of the era. Armstrong adopted the song as his own at a 1929 session, and quickly turned "St. Louis Blues" into a signature number—he would leave behind more than 50 renditions of this piece, which invariably received an enthusiastic response from his audiences. I call particular attention to his nine-minute recording, complete with new lyrics and extended solos, from his 1954 album *Louis Armstrong Plays W.C. Handy*—which also includes noteworthy contributions from Barney Bigard and Trummy Young. But others infused their own mojo into this piece. Cab Calloway holds a high G for eight bars and engages in some of the most uninhibited scat singing on record on his 1930 performances of the song.

"St. Louis Blues" was equally popular overseas. Long before British rockers "discovered" the blues in the 1960s, the Handy standard found favor in the United Kingdom, and in some unlikely locales: Edward VIII requested the tune from his Scottish pipers at Balmoral Castle, Prince George and Princess Marina of Greece danced to it at their 1934 wedding, and Queen Elizabeth called it one of her favorite songs.

"St. Louis Blues" held even greater significance in other countries, where it became something of an anthem in the geopolitical conflicts of the era. Ethiopian soldiers adopted the song as a battle hymn in their fight against fascist invaders. Django Reinhardt made several recordings of "St. Louis Blues" in Paris in the 1930s, but after the German occupation the performance of this song, and other American jazz tunes, became a dicey matter. The Nazi authorities didn't actually ban jazz itself, but rather aimed to stop the import of American culture—hence a charade emerged in which jazz tunes from the United States were given new French titles. "Take the A Train" was now "L'attaque du train," "Tiger Rag" became " La rage du tigre," and "St. Louis Blues" took on the mellifluous name "La tristesse de saint Louis"—a canonization in which Louis Armstrong now shared as much, or even more, than Louis IX. As such, performances of the Handy song took on symbolic valence as a rallying call and a gesture of resistance amid the glamour and frivolity of Parisian nightlife.

Given this legacy, "St. Louis Blues" has become more than a work of popular music and takes on the aura of a historical artifact. This has led to a certain museum-piece quality to most later performances of the Handy standard. Indeed, the composer himself put a damper on creative interpretations. Dizzy Gillespie's big band performance from 1949, a true bebop updating of "St. Louis Blues" with a dose of Charlie Parker's "Parker's Mood" included in Budd Johnson's chart, was kept off the market for several years because of Handy's objections. Gillespie would record "St. Louis Blues" again, but not until a few months after Handy's death. Coincidence or deliberate rebuff? You be the judge. But most other modern jazz players tended to bypass the piece entirely. Many consider "St. Louis Blues" the quintessential jazz song, but you will seek in vain for recordings of it by Miles Davis, Thelonious Monk, John Coltrane, Charles Mingus, Lennie Tristano, and many other leading post-1950s jazz artists.

Yet a work this iconic inevitably invites some bold reworkings. Gil Evans's 1957 arrangement, featuring saxophonist Cannonball Adderley, is even more daring than Gillespie's treatment. Bob Brookmeyer's big band chart, recorded by the Thad Jones/Mel Lewis Orchestra in 1968, is equally clever, transforming the composition while remaining true to its essential emotional temperament. Greg Osby and Nicholas Payton mix up traditional and avant-garde elements in their irreverent reworking of the standard from their *St. Louis Shoes* CD. In sharp contrast, Herbie Hancock's 1998 recording, with Stevie Wonder on harmonica and vocals, is a finger-snapping exercise in funk that, with a little promotion, might have brought Mr. Handy's famous song back to the charts in a stunning new guise.

RECOMMENDED VERSIONS

W. C. Handy, New York, March 1923

Bessie Smith (with Louis Armstrong), New York, January 14, 1925

Fats Waller (on pipe organ), Camden, New Jersey, November 17, 1926

Louis Armstrong, New York, December 13, 1929

Cab Calloway, New York, July 24, 1930

Django Reinhardt, Paris, September 9, 1937

Earl Hines (recorded as "Boogie Woogie on St. Louis Blues"), New York, February 13, 1940

Dizzy Gillespie, New York, April 14, 1949

Louis Armstrong (with Barney Bigard and Trummy Young), from *Louis Armstrong Plays W. C. Handy*, Chicago, July 13, 1954

Gil Evans (with Cannonball Adderley), from *New Bottle Old Wine*, New York, April 9, 1958

Dave Brubeck (with Paul Desmond), from *The Dave Brubeck Quartet at Carnegie Hall*, live at Carnegie Hall, New York, February 22, 1963

Thad Jones/Mel Lewis Orchestra (with an arrangement by Bob Brookmeyer), from *Monday Night*, live at the Village Vanguard, New York, October 17, 1968

Herbie Hancock (with Stevie Wonder), from *Gershwin's World*, New York and Los Angeles, March–June 1998

Greg Osby (with Nicholas Payton), from *St. Louis Shoes*, Brooklyn, January 22–23, 2003

St. Thomas
Composed by Sonny Rollins

The composer's mother, Valborg Solomon Rollins, had been born on the island of St. Thomas in the Caribbean, but immigrated to New York, where she worked as a domestic. She played a lasting role in her son's musical development, purchasing a saxophone for him when he was 13, and paying for his 25-cent lessons on the horn. But the influence that resulted in the composition "St. Thomas" dates from an even earlier period in the artist's life.

Among Rollins's earliest childhood recollections is a memory of his mother singing a calypso song from her native St. Thomas. At age 25, in the studio to record his *Saxophone Colossus* album for Prestige, Rollins drew on this tune from his youth as inspiration for his song "St. Thomas." Although the record label assigned composer credit to Rollins, the melody comes from a well-known traditional song of the West Indies. Pianist Mal Waldron, five years older than Rollins, knew the song as "The Carnival," while Randy Weston, whose grandfather was born in Jamaica, even recorded the piece a year before Rollins, under the name "Fire Down There."

But Rollins's version would be the one to capture the imagination of the jazz world. His debut recording is fascinating in its contrast between the loose energy of the song's beat, both relaxing and insistent, and the rigorous logic of Rollins's improvised lines. Listen to his development of a two-note motif in his first two solo choruses, and marvel at a musical mind that can do so much with so little. Rollins would showcase other calypso-tinged works (such as "Don't Stop the Carnival" or "Brown Skin Girl") over the years, but none would match the popularity of "St. Thomas," which would remain a core part of Rollins's repertoire—at least a dozen different recordings capture him in action over these changes—and become his best-known piece. The popularity of the song among other jazz players is no doubt due to both its ease of use—"St. Thomas" presents few challenges to soloists—and to its appeal to listeners.

A certain informality permeates the proceedings even when "St. Thomas" is featured in a concert hall or arranged for big band. It's best to retain the Caribbean sensibility of the song—and jazz players have tended to resist their urge to tinker when dealing with this piece, which is still typically presented with a similar attitude and tempo to the one Rollins imparted to it back in 1956. But the song does invite performers to stretch out and explore its possibilities at length. For an especially exciting example, check out Joshua Redman's 18-minute rendition of "St. Thomas" from the *Blues for Pat* release, which captures the saxophonist in a 1994 performance alongside Pat Metheny, Christian McBride, and Billy Higgins.

RECOMMENDED VERSIONS

Sonny Rollins (with Tommy Flanagan), from *Saxophone Colossus*, Hackensack, New Jersey, June 22, 1956

Hampton Hawes, from *The Green Leaves of Summer*, Los Angeles, February 17, 1964

Eric Kloss (with Pat Martino), from *Life Force*, Englewood Cliffs, New Jersey, September 18, 1967

Jim Hall and Ron Carter, from *Alone Together*, live at the Playboy Club, New York, August 4, 1972

Monty Alexander, from *Monty Alexander in Tokyo*, Tokyo, January 22, 1979

Branford Marsalis, from *Renaissance*, live at Concerts by the Sea, Redondo Beach, California, January 25, 1987

David Murray, from *South of the Border*, New York, May 23–25, 1992

Bill Holman (with the SWR Big Band), from *Jazz in Concert*, live at the Liederhalle, Stuttgart, Germany, July 3, 1993

Joshua Redman (with Pat Metheny) from *Blues for Pat*, live at an unidentified location, San Francisco, 1994

Satin Doll
Composed by Duke Ellington and Billy Strayhorn, with lyrics by Johnny Mercer

When America's musical tastes changed in the 1950s, not many big bands were left to deal with the fallout. The survivors considered themselves lucky to have gigs, and few expected to enjoy radio hits. The week "Satin Doll" was recorded, the number one song in America was "The Doggie in the Window," sung by Patti Page, and when fans got tired of that, they next raised Percy Faith's "The

Song from Moulin Rouge" to the top spot. Rock and roll hadn't yet begun its avalanche, but the exhaustion of the commercial music world that would make it inevitable was already evident.

In this environment, Duke Ellington managed to secure a record contract with Capitol, a label well known for its clout with disk jockeys, and at his debut session delivered a hit song. "Satin Doll" lingered briefly at #27 on the chart in June 1953, then left the rankings after only three weeks. By Ellington's standards, this was a modest success at best, yet none of his later songs—and Duke would continue to make records for another two decades—would do so well.

No, this wasn't Ellington's finest work; not even his best work from the early 1950s. One week after recording "Satin Doll," he returned to the studio to perform the lovely "Reflections in D," a solo piano piece that deserves to be far better known. And not long before he had crafted his exquisite *Harlem Suite*, one of the most appealing and ambitious projects of his career. But neither of those works was suitable for jukebox play, whereas "Satin Doll" served as the ideal soundtrack for that second or third round of drinks at the local watering hole. Loud and simple enough to cut through the noisy banter, bright enough to enliven the good times, "Satin Doll" was less intricate than, say, "Sophisticated Lady" or "Prelude to a Kiss," but perhaps, for that very reason, better suited to the tastes of the era.

As in so many other instances, Ellington's role in composing the piece has been a matter of discussion and dispute. In a surprising posthumous lawsuit, the heirs of Billy Strayhorn and Duke Ellington engaged in legal jousting, with the former eventually getting a share of royalties for Strayhorn's contribution to the harmonization of the song. One wonders what the two artists themselves would have thought of this litigation, given the smooth give-and-take that characterized their professional relationship over a period of three decades.

The song easily falls into a very danceable beat, and if the ballrooms of the Swing Era had still dominated urban nightlife the way they had just a few years earlier, "Satin Doll" might have enjoyed far more traction. As it stood, few jazz artists recorded cover versions until the second half of the decade, when Ella Fitzgerald, Billy Taylor, and Eddie "Lockjaw" Davis each brought "Satin Doll" into the studio. By the close of the 1950s, the song had clearly entered the standard repertoire, helped along by the addition of lyrics. In the 1960s a host of leading jazz artists from a variety of camps recorded it. But even when their treatments were appealing, they rarely rocked the boat. For example, McCoy Tyner's recording from his 1963 leader date *Nights of Ballads and Blues* ranks among my favorite treatments of "Satin Doll," but is almost entirely purged of the modal stylistic devices you would have heard if you had caught this pianist playing with the John Coltrane quartet during that same period. Most later versions follow in this same tradition, swinging and pleasant enough but unlikely to shake up the students at Berklee.

Ellington rarely had the opportunity to work with the leading lyricists of his day. But Johnny Mercer, who had helped found the Capitol label back in 1942, was invited to provide suitable lyrics for "Satin Doll"—replacing an earlier set of words, never recorded, by Billy Strayhorn, who had drawn the song's title from his pet name for his mother. The idea of pairing Ellington and Mercer must have seemed a dream match-up, but the short melodic phrases of "Satin Doll" didn't give the lyricist much to work with, and his attempt to update Duke with hip lingo is too cute for its own good. The song starts out with the cringe-inducing line *cigarette holder which wigs me*, and never recovers. I generally prefer vocalists to deliver a lyric straight and with plenty of feeling, but this tune is one in which a certain flippant irreverence may be just the ticket. Fitting examples were recorded by Ella Fitzgerald at the Crescendo Club in 1961, Blossom Dearie at Ronnie Scott's in 1966, and Mr. Mercer himself, on his 1974 recording *My Huckleberry Friend*.

RECOMMENDED VERSIONS

Duke Ellington, from *Capitol Sessions 1953–55*, Hollywood, April 6, 1953

Ella Fitzgerald, from *Ella in Hollywood*, live at the Crescendo Club, Los Angeles, May 11–12, 1961

McCoy Tyner, from *Nights of Ballads & Blues*, Englewood Cliffs, New Jersey, March 4, 1963

Blossom Dearie, from *Blossom Time at Ronnie's*, live at Ronnie Scotts, London, circa March 1966

Oscar Peterson and Clark Terry from *Oscar Peterson & Clark Terry*, Los Angeles, May 18, 1975

Joe Sample (with Ray Brown and Shelly Manne), from *The Three*, Los Angeles, November 28, 1975

Dewey Redman (with Joshua Redman), from *African Venus*, New York, December 11, 1992

Hank Jones (with Richard Davis and Elvin Jones), from *Someday My Prince Will Come*, New York, May 12–13, 2002

Scrapple from the Apple
Composed by Charlie Parker

The young Charlie Parker clearly enjoyed improvising over the chord changes to Fats Waller's "Honeysuckle Rose." The earliest surviving recording of the future jazz star, an amateur disk made in Kansas City when he was still in his teens, finds him imposing his burgeoning bebop vocabulary on the song. A few months later Parker took an impressive 32-bar solo on "Honeysuckle Rose" on a recording made with the Jay McShann band.

When Parker and other beboppers started writing new, more arcane melodies to graft on to existing popular songs, "Honeysuckle Rose" was an inevitable candidate for a transplant. Yet almost seven years elapsed between the altoist's performance of the Waller song with McShann and the recording of his own adaptation under the name "Scrapple from the Apple." Parker modified the harmonies in the process of updating the song, inserting the bridge chords from "I Got Rhythm" in the place of Waller's original progression. This has caused occasional confusion on the bandstand—hear, for example, Wardell Gray's hesitancy over the chords in the opening measures of the bridge during his solo choruses alongside Parker at a Boston live date from 1951.

Parker's composition never quite supplanted Waller's, but during the 1950s the leading jazz saxophonists of the younger generation were increasingly likely to opt for "Scrapple from the Apple" over "Honeysuckle Rose." Recordings from the second half of the decade find an impressive roster of modern jazz horn players—Stan Getz, Sonny Stitt, Phil Woods, Lee Konitz, Bud Shank, Cecil Payne, Tony Scott, and others—recording the Parker tune. I can understand the appeal to up-and-coming improvisers during this period. The ii-V cadence and the circle of fifths were key building blocks of modern jazz, and "Scrapple from the Apple" offers a brisk but not too taxing workout in these required subjects.

As different harmonic conceptions came to the fore in the 1960s and 1970s, "Scrapple from the Apple" continued to be performed but could no longer stand out as cutting edge in the midst of modal, free, fusion, and other styles. While various jazz trends have come and gone, this song has mostly kept true to its original inspiring vision, and is almost always played at the same moderately fast tempo without fancy arrangements or other adornments. Success or failure here, as with most Charlie Parker compositions, rests on the shoulders of the soloist, and when world-class players tackle "Scrapple from the Apple" it still can be exhilarating to hear.

By the way, the "scrapple" in the title is a concoction of pork trimmings, cornmeal, and flour, shaped into a loaf, then sliced and fried. Connoisseurs of pork dishes assure me that it contains every part of the pig except the oink.

RECOMMENDED VERSIONS

Charlie Parker, New York, November 4, 1947

Phil Woods (with Red Garland), from *Sugan*, New York, July 19, 1957

Lee Konitz (with Bill Evans and Warne Marsh), from *Live at the Half Note*, live at the
   Half Note, New York, February–March 1959

Sonny Stitt (with Oscar Peterson), from *Sonny Stitt Sits In with the Oscar Peterson Trio*, Paris, May 18, 1959

Dexter Gordon (with Bud Powell), from *Our Man in Paris*, Paris, May 23, 1963

Sonny Criss (with Tal Farlow and Cedar Walton), from *Up, Up and Away*, Englewood Cliffs, New Jersey, August 18, 1967

Tom Harrell (with Kenny Garrett and Kenny Barron), from *Moon Alley*, Englewood Cliffs, New Jersey, December 22, 1985

Secret Love

Composed by Sammy Fain, with lyrics by Paul Francis Webster

After the mid-century mark, new jazz standards increasingly came from Hollywood movies, and often those with little jazzy about them. "Secret Love" is a case in point, arriving on the scene via the 1953 proto-feminist Western film *Calamity Jane*, where it was introduced by Doris Day, who starred in the title role. Jazz artists rarely took their cues from Westerns in general or from Doris Day in particular, but this catchy, forthright song sold itself. It won the Oscar for Best Original Song, and Day's version rose to the top of the *Billboard* chart, inspiring a number of successful cover versions in its wake.

"Secret Love" is one of the few love songs that can be played at a fast tempo without losing its romantic attitude—no doubt because the lyrics, which recommend shouting a once hidden love from the highest hills, almost demand a boisterous delivery. In my mind, "Secret Love" is the "Do ask! Do tell!" advocacy song par excellence. Frankly, I'm surprised that more jazz singers don't program this number as a set opener or closer, since it comes equipped with both fireworks and pathos. Yet few jazz artists embraced "Secret Love" until the late 1950s when versions from Ahmad Jamal, Count Basie, Maynard Ferguson, and Toots Thielemans, among others, set the tone, and proved that it was cool to cover a Doris Day hit. Jazz singers were the last to take it on board, but early 1960s recordings by Dinah Washington (with a very funky Quincy Jones arrangement), Billy Eckstine, and Nancy Wilson finished the process of rehabilitation.

My favorite version, hands down, finds 20-year-old Keith Jarrett making his big league debut as a member of Art Blakey's Jazz Messengers, and deconstructing this Hollywood tune as if it were *Finnegans Wake* and he were there to defend his dissertation. Brad Mehldau, however, reminds us in his 2000 adaptation, that this composition still works as a slow ballad. His radical departure from song form in the solo section might be overlooked by casual listeners, but reveals an alternative way of improvising on standards, developing the melodic motives rather than simply following the chord changes.

RECOMMENDED VERSIONS

Ahmad Jamal, from *Ahmad's Blues*, live at the Spotlight Club, Washington D.C., September 6, 1958

Count Basie, from *Dance Along with Basie*, New York, December 30–31, 1959

Dinah Washington (with an arrangement by Quincy Jones), from *Tears and Laughter*, New York, August 16, 1961

Art Blakey (with Keith Jarrett), from *Buttercorn Lady*, live at the Lighthouse, Hermosa Beach, California, January 1966

Dexter Gordon (with Hampton Hawes), from *Blues à la Suisse*, live at the Montreux Jazz Festival, Montreux, Switzerland, July 7, 1973

Al Cohn, from *Rifftide*, Monster, Holland, June 6, 1987

Brad Mehldau, from *Progression: Art of the Trio, Vol. 5*, New York, September 22–24, 2000

The Shadow of Your Smile
Composed by Johnny Mandel, with lyrics by Paul Francis Webster

"The Shadow of Your Smile" first arrived on the scene via the soundtrack of *The Sandpiper*, a high-profile 1965 film starring Hollywood's most beloved couple of the era, Richard Burton and Elizabeth Taylor. The movie didn't live up to its all-star lineup, and the only Oscar it garnered was for this Johnny Mandel song, which also earned a Golden Globe and a Grammy.

Mandel wisely enlisted jazz trumpeter Jack Sheldon to deliver the melody, and Sheldon—an artist capable of bathos or pathos, depending on the occasion—showed why many prefer him as a balladeer rather than as a comedian. (Little known fact: this trumpeter starred in his own sitcom, the short-lived *Run, Buddy, Run*, from 1966.) Mandel also held the baton for Tony Bennett's hit recording of "The Shadow of Your Smile," recorded a few weeks after the release of *The Sandpiper*—however, before you buy a download make sure you *aren't* getting Bennett's 2006 reworking in "Spanglish" with Colombian rocker Juanes by mistake. Before 1965 was out, more than a dozen jazz artists had covered the song.

I wouldn't change a note in this composition, which may be Mandel's finest moment. The melody moves with a stately emotional logic, as if each succeeding phrase builds from some syllogism of the heart established by the previous notes. Yet this mood is best undersold—as much as I admire this composition, if it is played too forcefully it comes across as overwrought and insincere. Unlike some songs, which benefit from fireworks in the final bars, this one requires a more measured build-up. The lyrics are better whispered rather than declaimed.

For these reasons, some of the finer versions of "The Shadow of Your Smile" come from performers with a knack for understatement. No one would ever confuse Astrud Gilberto with Ella or Sarah, but her intimate delivery is perfectly suited for the song. Bill Evans also possessed the right temperament, and recorded Mandel's piece both in the studio (back when he was experimenting with piano multitracking for the Verve label) and in live performance. Even a brash virtuoso such as Oscar Peterson figured that he needed to show some restraint when playing it, and his recording shines—I especially like his intro, which other pianists should consider "borrowing." In contrast, Sonny Stitt and Eddie Harris, for all their talents, forget the shadow in "The Shadow of Your Smile"—a song that stubbornly resists funkification—and the results, whether intentionally or not, come across as kitschy and parodic. Then Lou Donaldson comes along, supported by Dr. Lonnie Smith on organ, and just when you expect threadbare soul jazz clichés, he delivers a very sensitive reading.

The retrospective nature of the lyrics, which celebrate a love past rather than a current passion, perhaps endears this song to performers in their golden years. Benny Carter recorded a fine version a few weeks before he turned 88, as did Hank Jones at age 83 and Lionel Hampton at 82. And as a septuagenarian, Jack Sheldon, who first introduced the song at age 33, revisited "The Shadow of Your Smile" for his 2006 recording *Listen Up*.

RECOMMENDED VERSIONS

Johnny Mandel (with Jack Sheldon), from the soundtrack to *The Sandpiper*, Hollywood, April 1965

Wes Montgomery, from *Bumpin'*, Englewood Cliffs, New Jersey, May 18, 1965

Astrud Gilberto, from *The Shadow of Your Smile*, Los Angeles, June 3, 1965

Tony Bennett (with Jimmy Rowles and an arrangement by Johnny Mandel), from *The Movie Song Album*, September 26, 1965

Hampton Hawes, from *I'm All Smiles*, live at Mitchell's Studio Club, Los Angeles, April 30 and May 1, 1966

Oscar Peterson, from *Blues Etude*, Chicago, May 4, 1966

Bill Evans, from *Further Conversations with Myself*, New York, August 9, 1967

Lou Donaldson (with Blue Mitchell and Dr. Lonnie Smith), from *Mr. Shing-a-Ling*, Englewood Cliffs, New Jersey, October 27, 1967

Benny Carter, from *New York Nights*, live at Iridium, New York, June 22–24, 1995

Hank Jones (with Elvin Jones), from *Someday My Prince Will Come*, New York, May 12–14, 2002

Shine

Composed by Ford Dabney, with lyrics by Cecil Mack and Lew Brown

I'm sure many jazz fans misunderstand the title of this song, assuming that it's just another of the innumerable popular songs drawing on the imagery of sunlight. Turn on the radio and wait long enough and you'll hear an example. *You are the sunshine of my life, yeah!* Others, realizing that "shine" long served as a derogatory term for African-Americans, may cringe at the thought that this is one more degrading example of what were known as "coon songs"—stereotype-ridden novelty tunes that demeaned the blacks who performed them, or sometimes served as vehicles for white entertainers in blackface.

But the story behind this song is more complex. Instead of blackface, the composition's origins found it associated with cross-dressing (more on that later). And there was an actual man named Shine, or perhaps Kid Shine, who inspired the song—a victim of the white mob and police violence during the New York race riot of August 1900. The same individual may also have served as the model for the character Shiny in James Weldon Johnson's 1912 novel *The Autobiography of an Ex-Colored Man*—a brilliant young classmate of the narrator who earns recognition for his eloquence and scholarly ambitions.

The song, published in 1910, was originally called "That's Why They Call Me Shine" and was popularized in the traveling black show *His Honor the Barber*. The number served as a feature for Aida Overton Walker, who performed it dressed in male attire and in impersonation of her husband George W. Walker, a successful comedy performer of the day. After he fell ill in 1909, Aida would often wear her husband's costumes and play his roles in loving tribute to her spouse. The surviving sheet music for the song features a photo of her wearing a man's suit and hat.

The words can be read as a call for racial tolerance, but framed in a stoic acceptance of the abusive epithets hurled at blacks.

> *So when these clever people call me shine or coon or smoke*
> *I simply smile then smile some more and vote them all a joke.*

Louis Armstrong left these words out of his celebrated recording of "Shine" from 1931, and in any event the vocal is overshadowed by his virtuosic trumpet work. Armstrong's recordings from this period—often neglected by fans who tend to focus on the Hot Fives and Hot Sevens from the 1920s, or his popular hits from the 1960s—contain many of the finest solos of his career, and this one ranks with the best of them. Around this same time, Armstrong was filmed performing "Shine" in the short film *A Rhapsody in Black and Blue*, shown in movie theaters during the late summer of 1932. But the value of this rare footage of the young Armstrong in performance is marred by the strange and demeaning setting—Armstrong's is featured in a dream sequence that requires him to wear a leopard skin and perform surrounded by soap bubbles.

Such undignified moments did much to fuel criticism of Armstrong as a too accommodating participant in racially insensitive entertainment for white America. Armstrong may well have come to agree with this verdict, at least in part. He dropped "Shine" from his repertoire after the early 1940s, avoiding it in later decades even when reviving so many other hits of younger days. Similarly, Ella Fitzgerald recorded "Shine" in 1936, but never again in later years.

Even so, such precedents were sufficient to establish "Shine" as a jazz standard, helped along by the composition's suitability as a hard-swinging dance number. And "Shine" shows up in strange and surprising places. Bing Crosby changes the words around for his 1931 recording of "Shine," where he is joined by the Mills Brothers—*Shines away your blues—eee! Why don't you shine, start with your shoes—eee!* Lionel Hampton tackled the song in 1937, renaming it as "Piano Stomp"—a hot track that finds him setting his vibraphone aside and demonstrating his percussive two-fingered piano technique, albeit in a style that is almost identical to how he would have played this song on vibes. For a while, "Shine" even emerged as an anthem for white tenor sax disciples of Lester Young, as demonstrated on recordings by Stan Getz, Al Cohn, and Zoot Sims.

But few modern jazz players followed up on these leads, and nowadays the song rarely travels beyond the world of trad jazz players, who typically present it as an instrumental with the controversial words kept under wraps. It is perhaps worth noting that the majority of versions recorded in recent years come from traditional bands operating outside of the United States—in Oslo, Barcelona, London, Sydney, and other far-flung locations. In this manner, a song that has fallen off the radar screens of the major stars of American jazz continues to shine, albeit outside the music's land of origin.

RECOMMENDED VERSIONS

Louis Armstrong, Los Angeles, March 9, 1931

Bing Crosby (with the Mills Brothers), New York, February 29, 1932

Ella Fitzgerald, New York, November 19, 1936

Lionel Hampton (recorded under the name "Piano Stomp"), Hollywood, August 16, 1937

Jack Teagarden (with Ben Webster), New York, December 15, 1940

Bunk Johnson, New Orleans, October 2, 1942

Benny Goodman (with Red Norvo and Mel Powell), New York, August 29, 1945

Stan Getz, from *West Coast Jazz*, Los Angeles, August 15, 1955

Al Cohn and Bob Brookmeyer, from *The Al Cohn Quintet*, New York, December 3–4, 1956

Willie "The Lion" Smith, from *The Legend of Willie "The Lion" Smith*, New York, August 21, 1957

Joe Venuti and Zoot Sims, from *Joe Venuti and Zoot Sims*, New York, May 1975

Wild Bill Davison and Ralph Sutton, from *Together Again!* Copenhagen, May 23, 1977

Stéphane Grappelli and Martial Solal, from *Olympia 1988*, live at the Olympia, Paris, January 24, 1988

Skylark
Composed by Hoagy Carmichael, with lyrics by Johnny Mercer

If I had to rank jazz ballads on the emotional impact of their melodies, on their capability of sinking me into a sweet reverie, Hoagy Carmichael's "Skylark" would be a contender for the top spot on the list. Carmichael had already proven 15 years earlier with "Star Dust" that he could construct a pop song from probing jazz phrases and still manage to generate a mega-hit. With "Skylark" he offered another telling example. The melody grows more daring as it develops. The motif in bar six is very much akin to what a jazz trumpeter might play, and the ensuing turnaround is not just a way of getting back to the beginning, as with so many songs, but a true extension of the melody, which pushes all the way to the end of the form.

The B theme is just as good as the A theme, and even more jazz-oriented. Commentators have suggested that "Skylark," much like this composer's "Star Dust," represented an attempt to capture the essence of 1920s-era Bix Beider-becke's improvising style in a song—and, in fact, Carmichael first developed the piece as part of his unrealized plans for a Broadway musical about Beider-becke. But, to my ears, the bridge to "Skylark" reminds me of the manner in which a 1940s-era Coleman Hawkins would solo on a ballad. Whatever the gen-esis, the end result of these various ingredients is an expression of feeling so natural and unforced that casual listeners won't notice the technical aspects, only the potent mood created by the finished song.

Johnny Mercer makes a substantial contribution with his words. Mercer's widow claimed that it took him a year to find the right phrases to match Carmi-chael's convoluted melodic line—lyric expressions that some have seen as a reflection of Mercer's romantic longings for Judy Garland, with whom he had recently had a torrid affair—but, by the lyricist's own account, he tossed off the words in less than a half hour. He couldn't make headway until he came up with a title, and then one day Mercer saw the word "Skylark" on a billboard or a book—*not*, he insisted, in Percy Bysshe Shelley's famous poem "Ode to a Sky-lark." After that impetus, he explained, the rest of the song came to him quickly. Both accounts may be true: the germination period often was long with a Mer-cer lyric, while the actual pen-and-paper work might be brief. In any event, I wouldn't change the smallest morpheme or phoneme of the final product.

I can easily understand why jazz musicians took an immediate hankering to "Skylark." A half-dozen major bands recorded it within a few weeks of its intro-duction. Glenn Miller enjoyed a top 10 hit with his performance of the Carmi-chael standard in the spring of 1942, and three other versions reached the top 20 that same year. The song made few inroads with the beboppers, and in gen-eral "Skylark" has proven fairly resistant to attempts to update or reconfigure its musical personality. But the inherent appeal of the composition has kept "Skylark" in the jazz repertoire.

Among later interpretations, I would call attention to the composer's per-formance from 1956 fronting a band consisting of some of the leading West Coast jazz players of the day. Jimmy Rowles, who plays piano on that date, resurrected "Skylark" for his 1975 leader project *The Peacocks*, where he per-formed it with Stan Getz, then delivered another duet version on his 1977 *Tenorlee* date with Lee Konitz. Michael Brecker's 1997 recording is also a stand-out interpretation.

Despite these solid horn-player outings, "Skylark" needs to be heard with Johnny Mercer's lyrics to be fully appreciated. In your quest for significant vocal renditions, good starting points would include Billy Eckstine's recording, made with the Earl Hines band when the song was new, and (fast-forwarding more than a half-century) accomplished performances by Cassandra Wilson and Mark Murphy.

RECOMMENDED VERSIONS

Glenn Miller (with Ray Eberle), New York, January 8, 1942

Harry James (with Helen Forrest), New York, January 29, 1942

Earl Hines (with Billy Eckstine), New York, March 19, 1942

Lee Konitz, from *Lee Konitz at Storyville*, live at Storyville, Boston, August 6, 1954

Hoagy Carmichael (with Art Pepper), from *Hoagy Sings Carmichael*, Los Angeles, September 10, 1956

Art Blakey (with Freddie Hubbard), from *Caravan*, New York, October 24, 1962

Stan Getz and Jimmy Rowles, from *The Peacocks*, New York, October 1975

Cassandra Wilson, from *New Moon Daughter*, New York, 1995

Michael Brecker, from *Two Blocks from the Edge*, New York, December 20–23, 1997

Mark Murphy, from *Once to Every Heart*, Berlin, 2001–2002

Smile

Composed by Charlie Chaplin, with lyrics by John Turner and Geoffrey Parsons

Musicians will be the first to acknowledge the importance of a soundtrack to the success of a motion picture. But when Charlie Chaplin began work on his film *Modern Times* (1936), all matters relating to the sound of the movie took on even greater significance than usual. Chaplin was belatedly coming to grips with the shift from silent to sound films—a change that had ended the careers of many movie stars of his generation. Even though audiences were now accustomed to "all singing, all talking, all dancing" cinematic entertainment, Chaplin felt that his on-screen persona "the Tramp" should remain mute. He believed, more-over, that film was essentially a pantomimic medium, owing its impact to the fact that audiences had a greater and more immediate comprehension of action over words. Given these views, seemingly so anachronistic almost a decade after the first talkies, critics and fans would pay especially close attention to how he reconciled them with the possibilities and expectations generated by the new cinema technologies.

For *Modern Times*, Chaplin brought in small doses of sound into a film still largely beholden to the aesthetic values of the silent movie era. Chaplin worked directly with Alfred Newman on the score, for which the actor-director com-posed the song "Smile." It figures as an instrumental in the film. The lyrics, although they seem to espouse a comedian's personal philosophy—celebrating the power of lightheartedness in the face of adversity—did not come from Chaplin but were contributed years later by John Turner and Geoffrey Parsons, a duo who typically focused on adapting foreign-language songs into English.

Don't be confused by early jazz recordings of a song called "Smile"—released, for example, by Paul Whiteman (with Bix Beiderbecke in the band), Fred Elizalde, and Hoagy Carmichael. That is a different composition, written by Donald Heywood. Chaplin's song didn't emerge as a popular standard until 1954 when, with lyrics now attached, Nat King Cole enjoyed a top 10 hit with "Smile." Around the same time Capitol released Cole's single, Duke Ellington—perhaps coincidentally recording for the same label—also put his imprimatur on "Smile" in a pensive big band arrangement that features the leader's piano, Ray Nance's violin, and Harry Carney's baritone sax, but never strays far from the original melody.

Bop and post-bop players mostly stayed on the sidelines until the early 1960s, when Dexter Gordon and Kenny Dorham featured this song on leader dates. A few years later, the trad jazz crowd also staked a claim, with "Smile" showing up in the repertoire of various Dixieland bands, while in ensuing decades, the song adapted just as easily to the gypsy jazz stylings of Biréli Lagrène, the fusion-oriented sound of David Sanborn, and the rough-and-tumble pianism of McCoy Tyner.

This song's most salient quality, namely its old-fashioned sentimentality, also presents a challenge to jazz performers, who can easily find their renditions slipping into a maudlin shallowness. Some performers confront this risk straight on, aiming for a hypersensitive interpretation that tries to give full force to the emotional content of the lyrics—an approach that risks mawkishness, but when done successfully (as by Tony Bennett, who aims for a scrupulous realism in his various renditions) can be quite effective. Others, such as Brad Mehldau or Jacky Terrasson, modify the song's harmonies or rhythms to impart a more modern edge to "Smile." Still others, such as Dexter Gordon and Kenny Dorham, have treated Chaplin's legacy as a set of blowing changes for a no-frills jam.

Plenty of smile-inducing jazz versions have been recorded, but this piece has been so warmly embraced by artists in other genres, that it has largely lost its character as a jazz song. If younger listeners are familiar with it, it is probably due to Michael Jackson, who recorded it for his 1995 *HIStory* album and presented it in concert as a tribute to the late Princess Diana. The composition, which was reportedly Jackson's favorite song, was sung at his own memorial service by his brother Jermaine, again bringing "Smile" back to the public's attention. But the sheer range of artists who have performed "Smile"—Eric Clapton, Djavan, Lyle Lovett, Judy Garland, Trini Lopez, Elvis Costello, and Diana Ross, to name just a few—testifies to the composition's appeal to audiences across genres, generations, and geographical borders.

RECOMMENDED VERSIONS

Nat King Cole, from *Ballads of the Day*, Hollywood, July 27, 1954

Duke Ellington, from *The Complete Capitol Sessions 1953–1955*, Hollywood, September 1, 1954

Dexter Gordon, from *Dexter Calling*, Englewood Cliffs, New Jersey, May 9, 1961

Tony Bennett (with Tommy Flanagan and an arrangement by Al Cohn), from *The Movie Song Album*, New York, December 27, 1965

Sonny Criss, from *Portrait of Sonny Criss*, Englewood Cliffs, New Jersey, March 23, 1967

Jimmy Rowles and Ray Brown, from *Tasty!* San Francisco, October 22, 1979

Kenny Burrell (with Cedar Walton), from *Sunup to Sundown*, New York, June 10–12, 1991

Biréli Lagrène, from *Standards*, Paris, June 1992

Chick Corea, from *Expressions*, Los Angeles, 1994

Jacky Terrasson, from *Smile*, Pompignan, France, June 12–21, 2002

Brad Mehldau, from *Anything Goes*, New York, October 8–9, 2002

Smoke Gets In Your Eyes

Composed by Jerome Kern, with lyrics by Otto Harbach

Jerome Kern initially struggled to find the right beat for this composition. He originally conceived of it as incidental music for *Show Boat*, where it would support a tap dance performed before the curtain during a scene change. But the interlude was cut from the production, and in 1932 Kern considered a different use, this time recasting the melody as a march theme for NBC's planned made-for-radio musicals. When NBC put that project on hold, the song was again shuttled aside. Finally, lyricist Otto Harbach made the suggestion that, with a change of some of the note lengths, the song might serve as a vocal feature for their 1933 show *Roberta*.

"Smoke Gets in Your Eyes" saved the day, its popularity drawing audiences to a musical that had received poor reviews and lost money in its first few weeks on the stage. By January 1934, only two months after the New York opening, the *Herald Tribune* proclaimed that "Smoke Gets in Your Eyes" had "swept the dance floors, radio studios and glee clubs of the country," and that *Roberta* was now "profiting immeasurably by a sudden outburst of public whistling, humming and crooning of its score." Eventually another Kern composition from this production, "Yesterdays," would also emerge as a jazz standard, but there was never any doubt which song the general public preferred. In 1934, Paul Whiteman enjoyed a number one hit with "Smoke Gets in Your Eyes," and three other artists also released successful recordings of the song.

Modern-day musicians tend to perform this song as a languid ballad, but in earlier days it was typically presented as a medium-tempo dance tune—an approach that can be heard on the spirited early hit versions by Paul Whiteman and Leo Reisman, as well as later treatments by Tommy Dorsey (1937), Benny Goodman (1941), and many other swing bands. Shortly before his death, Glenn Miller showcased a slower, dreamier conception of "Smoke Gets in Your Eyes"—check out his wistful and beautifully recorded (at Abbey Road Studios in London) interpretation from 1944, made not for commercial release but for use in propaganda broadcasts into Nazi-occupied territories. This is the "mood music" conception of "Smoke Gets in Your Eyes" familiar to modern listeners, and gradually adopted by jazz musicians.

Occasionally a jazz player opts for a pricklier interpretation. Thelonious Monk recorded "Smoke Gets in Your Eyes" twice in 1954, the first time with a combo at a session for the Prestige label, and a month later in a solo piano arrangement at a Paris date that must have been in violation of the pianist's contract with his US label. The Prestige track is better known nowadays, but I find the rest of the band sounding tentative and the horns hidden by the sound mix.

I prefer the looser, unaccompanied version from France, where the pianist seems especially relaxed and playing as if for his own enjoyment. This treatment retains the lyrical quality we associate with the song, but leavened by Monk's characteristic humor and irreverence.

Despite these precedents, most of the credit goes to the Platters for how we hear "Smoke Gets in Your Eyes" today. This vocal group—which mixed elements of R&B and doo-wop with traditional sounds more akin to the Mills Brothers and the Ink Spots—had a penchant for taking old songs such as "Harbor Lights," "My Prayer," and "To Each His Own" and putting them back on the charts in refreshed vocal versions. For their interpretation of "Smoke Gets in Your Eyes," they brought the tempo down to 120 beats per minute (compared to Whiteman's 170 back in 1933), and supported their vocals with a low-key orchestral arrangement marked by harp flourishes and soothing strings. Jerome Kern, who had passed away in 1945, was no longer around to complain about musicians taking liberties with his songs, but his widow expressed dismay about this respected song now mutating into *rock and roll*. Record buyers, however, approved of the new version, which neither rocks nor rolls, yet still climbed to the top spot on the charts both in the United States and in Britain. There is no evidence of Eva Kern returning the royalty checks that must have poured in.

And continue to do so. This song remains popular with the general public long after other hits from the 1930s have been forgotten. Jazz musicians, for their part, tend to prefer other Kern compositions. And I don't blame them. I enjoy hearing this song, but more for the statement of Kern's sweeping melody rather than as a platform for jazz improvisation. Certainly jazz musicians haven't forgotten "Smoke Gets in Your Eyes," and a few more cover versions are released every year. Even so, when I hear the musicians strike up this familiar tune, I usually assume that it's the result of an audience request and not a decision by the performers on the bandstand.

RECOMMENDED VERSIONS

Paul Whiteman, New York, November 3, 1933

Teddy Wilson, Chicago, April 7, 1941

Benny Goodman (with Helen Forrest), New York, June 4, 1941

Glenn Miller, London, November 30, 1944

Thelonious Monk, from *Solo 1954*, Paris, June 7, 1954

Clifford Brown, from *Clifford Brown with Strings*, New York, January 19, 1955

Cannonball Adderley, from *African Waltz*, New York, May 9, 1961

Archie Shepp (with Horace Parlan), from *Black Ballads*, Monster, Holland, January 13, 1992

Kurt Elling (with Laurence Hobgood), from *Live in Chicago*, live at the Green Mill, Chicago, July 14–16, 1999

Norma Winstone (with the NDR Big Band), from *It's Later Than You Think*, Hamburg, September 2004

So What
Composed by Miles Davis

Who would think that Miles Davis's most widely heard melody would be performed by the bass player in the band? Yet, as the opening track to Davis's best-selling *Kind of Blue*, "So What" is not only well known but often serves as an introduction to jazz to the many fans who start their collection with this famous album. The dialogue between bassist Paul Chambers, who plays a series of interrogative phrases, and the horns—who reply with two crisp chords each time—was unlike anything else in the jazz repertoire circa 1959. Even today, this is the only widely played jazz standard with a melody line that never rises above middle C.

But the harmonic structure, not the melody, was even more of a shocker at the time this recording was first released. Davis was exploring the potential of improvisation based on modes rather than chord changes. In the case of "So What," this meant that the soloist was assigned a single scale for the A section of the song—a D dorian scale, which consists of the white notes on the piano—and needed to construct a solo from only those tones. During the B section of the song, from bars 17 through 24 of the repeating 32-bar form, a different mode, an E flat dorian scale, was employed.

When compared to the bop and pop tunes that most jazz groups played at the time, this represented a dramatic simplification of means. The structure of most jazz standards requires the soloist to change scales constantly, and even those scales are frequently modified with passing tones, blue notes, and other alterations. Modal jazz, at least in its original incarnation, dispensed with all these in favor of an austere minimalism. If jazz were a battle—and it more than occasionally feels that way on the bandstand—Davis had suddenly announced an end to the arms race, putting aside the missiles and warheads to grapple instead with the musical equivalent of sticks and stones.

Miles had already experimented with this pared-down approach in his 1958 recording of "Milestones," and some would trace this concept even further back to Ahmad Jamal—an admitted role model for Davis at the time—who had recorded a somewhat similar piece in 1955, which was based in turn on a classical composition by Morton Gould. (See the entry on "Impressions" for more on this.) Yet this convoluted genealogy should not distract attention from the fact that *Kind of Blue* marked the decisive moment when modal playing first became an influential force in the jazz world.

Yet almost from the start, musicians chafed against these restrictions. When altoist Sonny Stitt played this song with Miles, he mixed in plenty of chromatic tones from outside the assigned modes to "spice up" the tune. Most jazz musicians who play "So What" today do the same. When jazz musicians talk about a modal song nowadays, they often mean a composition with very few chord changes—a paucity that allows them to impose *many* modes on top of a simple harmonic structure. And here is the irony of the whole situation: *Kind of Blue* is lauded as the most important album of its time, yet Miles's concept of limiting the selection of notes has been given an emphatic thumbs down by posterity.

Miles himself recorded this song on many other occasions, and these later tracks are well worth hearing. Gil Evans provided an orchestral arrangement for the 1959 TV special *The Sound of Miles Davis*, a chart that was subsequently featured on the trumpeter's 1961 live recording at Carnegie Hall, and the contrast between bass and band is even more pronounced with a larger ensemble on hand. When Davis brought in a younger crop of sidemen in 1963, he continued to play "So What" regularly in concert, but his rhythm section of Herbie Hancock, Ron Carter, and Tony Williams constantly sought out ways of making familiar songs sound newly hatched. The much-lauded live recordings of Davis's band at the Plugged Nickel in Chicago from Christmas week in 1965 include a blistering version of "So What" that races along at 350 beats per minute, almost half again as fast as the original studio version. Even before the close of the melody, the horns are playing unexpected call-and-response games, and then the soloists stretch out at length in a 14-minute version of "So What" that ranks as one of the most compelling demonstrations of virtuoso combo playing of the era.

"So What" has frequently been covered by other artists, but has also been imitated in new songs that closely mimic Davis's original. John Coltrane's "Impressions," famous in its own right, follows the same harmonic and formal structure of "So What." Other modifications of the tune include Eddie Jefferson's very clever lyrics to "So What"—not only to the melody of the song, but also to Miles's entire trumpet solo. Jefferson uses the words to offer a free-form commentary on Mr. Davis, remarking on everything from his aloof performance mannerisms to the fit of his wardrobe. It is a peculiar, albeit entertaining, bit of doggerel. But the strangest "So What" knockoff comes courtesy of Andy Baio, who released a chiptune version of the entire *Kind of Blue* album in 2009, featuring a clever reenactment of the original track, complete with solos, as it might have sounded if played on an old Nintendo video game system. Baio secured rights to all the songs, and released the project under the name *Kind of Bloop*—only to get sued for a huge sum because his pixel art cover was derived from the original cover photograph on *Kind of Blue*.

I enjoy these sly homages to a now famous track. Yet many of the best versions of "So What" diverge sharply from Davis's original conception. I give high marks to George Benson's gut-bucket guitar and organ treatment from 1971, the adventurous reworking by Jeremy Steig and Denny Zeitlin from their collaboration on Steig's *Flute Fever* album back in 1963, and George Russell's 1983 funkified big band reworking of the song. Yet for sheer bravado it would be hard to top the 9/4 East-and-West version of "So What" arranged by Bob Belden for his 2008 *Miles from India* release, which brings together chanting, mridangam, kanjira, and Ron Carter's raga-and-rollish accompaniment to the proceedings, all in support of Chick Corea's adventurous piano work.

RECOMMENDED VERSIONS

Miles Davis, from *Kind of Blue*, New York, March 2, 1959

Miles Davis (with Gil Evans), from *Miles Davis at Carnegie Hall*, live at Carnegie Hall, New York, May 19, 1961

Jeremy Steig (with Denny Zeitlin), from *Flute Fever*, New York, 1963

Miles Davis, from *The Complete Live at the Plugged Nickel 1965*, live at the Plugged Nickel, Chicago, December 23, 1965

Eddie Jefferson, from *Body and Soul*, New York, September 27, 1968

George Benson, from *Beyond the Blue Horizon*, New York, February 2–3, 1971

George Russell, from *So What*, live at Emmanuel Church, Boston, June 18, 1983

Chick Corea, Ron Carter and others, from *Miles from India*, no date or location given, CD released in 2008

Softly, as in a Morning Sunrise
Composed by Sigmund Romberg, with lyrics by Oscar Hammerstein II

This song has been transformed over the years into a sleek, versatile jazz piece, but its origins were far from promising. "Softly, as in a Morning Sunrise" was originally performed as a melancholy tango in the 1928 operetta *The New Moon*, and the hit recording by bandleader Nat Shilkret from that period, built around an overwrought vocal by Franklyn Baur, incorporates minimal jazz content. The 1930 film version didn't help matters by changing the setting from New Orleans to Czarist Russia, and the 1940 remake was no jazzier—Nelson Eddy's performance of "Softly, as in a Morning Sunrise" while wearing a wig and shining a pair of shoes was unlikely to grab the attention of hot music fans of any persuasion.

Yet by that time, clarinetist Artie Shaw had already taken the song onboard—although less for its adaptability to Swing Era conventions, I suspect, and due more to Shaw's constant search of unconventional or exotic-sounding pieces. Shaw retains the brooding temperament of the original, but ditches the tango rhythm in favor of straight 4/4 swing time. A few other bandleaders tried out the song over the next few years—both Benny Goodman and Woody Herman performed it on radio broadcasts—but by the 1950s, the Romberg composition had been forgotten by jazz players and seemed unlikely to mount a comeback.

Yet "Softly, as in a Morning Sunrise" did come back, and largely due to the suppleness and flexibility of the song. Instead of drawing on what the piece had been, jazz artists found inspiration in visions of what it might become. The Modern Jazz Quartet turned Romberg's song into a vehicle for canonic counterpoint, and other cool school players adopted it in their wake. Its dark minor key ambiance also made "Softly" a suitable vehicle for hard bop players of the period, as demonstrated in recordings by Sonny Rollins, Sonny Clark, and Lee Morgan. But even more important—indeed, decisive, in my opinion—the song's fairly simple chord progression, which keeps returning to the tonic minor, gave it a quasi-modal flavor. John Coltrane draws on this latter quality in his Village Vanguard recording from 1961—a track that set the stage for the current conception of "Softly, as in a Morning Sunrise" as a platform for advanced jazz phraseology.

However, I must admit disappointment—and some amazement—that Coltrane did not return to this composition again in later years. The harmonic structure would seem to have been an ideal springboard for his later modal-meets-free-jazz approach, and I would have been interested to hear how Trane might have tackled the song in the mid-1960s. Yet other explorers of the outer reaches of tonality stepped into the breach, with Eric Dolphy and Albert Ayler offering up their own iconoclastic interpretations. At the same time, "Softly, as in a Morning Sunrise" continued to inspire more traditional renditions. A host of Lester Young disciples—Al Cohn, Zoot Sims, Stan Getz—had recorded the song before Coltrane adopted it, and many continued to do so in later years with little alteration in their basic approach. Buddy DeFranco looked back even further, to the song's pre-modern roots as a clarinet showpiece, and others offered trad, Latin, or smooth jazz arrangements.

Despite this varied history, the continued popularity of this song derives primarily from its modal leanings, which makes it an ideal platform for improvisers who aim for edginess, neither playing the changes straight nor abandoning them completely. For examples, check out David Liebman's recording from 1996, Freddie Hubbard's rip-roaring 18-minute performance captured live at the Keystone Korner in 1982, and Nick Brignola's outing from 1989 (backed by Kenny Barron, Dave Holland, and Jack DeJohnette), the latter enlivened by constant modulations into unexpected keys.

RECOMMENDED VERSIONS

Artie Shaw, New York, November 17, 1938

The Modern Jazz Quartet, from *Concorde*, Hackensack, New Jersey, July 2, 1955

Al Cohn (with Hank Jones), from *Cohn on the Saxophone*, New York, September 29, 1956

Sonny Clark, from *Sonny Clark Trio*, New York, October 13, 1957

Sonny Rollins (with Elvin Jones and Wilbur Ware), from *A Night at the Village Vanguard*, live at the Village Vanguard, New York, November 3, 1957

John Coltrane, from *Live at the Village Vanguard: The Master Takes*, live at the Village Vanguard, New York, November 2, 1961

Larry Young (with Woody Shaw and Joe Henderson), from *Unity*, Englewood Cliffs, New Jersey, November 10, 1965

Freddie Hubbard, from *Above and Beyond*, live at the Keystone Korner, San Francisco, June 17, 1982

Nick Brignola, from *On a Different Level*, Englewood Cliffs, New Jersey, September 25, 1989

David Liebman (with Richie Beirach), from *Quest*, New York, December 28–29, 1996

Solar

Composed by Miles Davis

Miles Davis is listed as composer on the 1963 copyright registration for "Solar," but almost fifty years later an acetate disk was found in the Library of Congress featuring guitarist Chuck Wayne playing a virtually identical song entitled "Sonny" (named for trumpeter Sonny Berman). This unreleased recording, from 1946, casts serious doubt on Davis's authorship—an ironic state of affairs, since the notes to "Solar" are inscribed on his tombstone. But Davis did improve the turnaround, and changed the first chord from major to minor. These additions have perhaps contributed to the song's frequent appearance at jam sessions, student lessons and gigs.

The appeal here is a song that adopts the 12 bar form of the blues, but with chord changes that are more boppish than bluesy. The shift from minor to major in the fifth bar makes it clear that "Solar" is not a minor blues—although the opening hints that it might be. The ambiguity in tonality accentuates the modernistic personality of this composition. In fact, a performer could conclude this song by resolving on a major chord and hardly generate a ripple of surprise among the audience.

As he sometimes did with other famous compositions—"Blue in Green," "Flamenco Sketches," "E.S.P."—Davis never recorded "Solar" again after the initial session that introduced the song. Frankly, I would have enjoyed hearing what Davis's band of a decade later might have done with this compact tune. No other jazz band covered "Solar" until trombonist J. J. Johnson recorded it more than two years after Miles. Bill Evans, however, played a key role in disseminating this piece, performing it on his influential Village Vanguard live date from June 1961. I suspect that Evans's version, better known than Davis's original, served as this piece's introduction to many jazz players who added "Solar" to their repertoires in later years.

I especially enjoy Joanne Brackeen's riveting quasi-modal approach to this song from 1976, and Keith Jarrett's trio rendition from 1992—which reunited the pianist with drummer Paul Motian, a member of Jarrett's 1970s band and also part of the Bill Evans trio that recorded "Solar" more than 30 years before. Yet the leading advocates for "Solar" today are students and jazz educators, who appreciate the benefits of a compositional structure that is both rich and succinct. Perhaps the greatest testimony to this is found on the YouTube, where more than 100 videos of student and amateur performances of "Solar" can be seen.

RECOMMENDED VERSIONS

Miles Davis, from *Walkin'*, Hackensack, New Jersey, April 3, 1954

J. J. Johnson (with Hank Jones), from *J Is for Jazz*, New York, July 25, 1956

Chet Baker (with Al Haig), from *Chet Baker in New York*, New York, September 1958

Bill Evans, from *Sunday at the Village Vanguard*, live at the Village Vanguard, New York, June 25, 1961

Joanne Brackeen, from *New True Illusion*, Weesp, Holland, July 15, 1976

Keith Jarrett (with Gary Peacock and Paul Motian), from *At the Deer Head Inn*, live at the Deer Head Inn, Delaware Water Gap, Pennsylvania, September 16, 1992

Loren Stillman, from *Cosmos*, Brooklyn, February 2, 1996

Michel Camilo, from *Spirit of the Moment*, New York, circa 2006

Solitude
Composed by Duke Ellington, with lyrics by Eddie DeLange and Irving Mills

Those who believe great artists must wait for the fickle cooperation of the muse will be disappointed in the biography of Duke Ellington, a man who created a long list of masterpieces on a tight schedule, and usually faced with an imminent deadline. "Solitude" is a case in point. Ellington was literally at the recording session when he composed it. "When I did 'Solitude,'" he later explained to Stanley Dance, "I was one number short, and I wrote it in twenty minutes standing up against the glass enclosure of RCA's record studio in Chicago."

Ellington often embellished his anecdotes, but this one has the ring of authenticity, and no one has stepped forward to counter it. Even the recording his band made that day in Chicago reflects a tentativeness that substantiates the players' unfamiliarity with the music. In time, they would come to know this song very well—Ellington left behind more than 100 recorded performances of "Solitude," sometimes just a cursory nod in a medley, at other points a full-scale reworking, but the piece never left his set list for long. He performed it solo, in a trio, in instrumental renditions, and in vocal versions of various sorts—compare Ivie Anderson's forthright interpretation (1940), Ellington's whimsical treatment involving four vocalists (1945), and the loose and relaxed meeting-of-the-masters collaboration with Louis Armstrong handling the words (1961).

"Solitude" is better suited to vocal delivery than many of Ellington's other melodies, with their keyboard-inspired leaps and turns, and the lyrics are among the most poetic of the after-the-fact collaborations that Mills arranged for his star artist. Billie Holiday recorded "Solitude" on several occasions in the 1940s and 1950s, and the song proved to be an effective vehicle for her, with the world-weariness of the words matching to an almost disturbing degree her late-career persona. But "Solitude" also received endorsements from the high-profile instrumentalists of the era, with Thelonious Monk, Sonny Rollins, and John Coltrane (as sideman on a Red Garland date) all tackling it during the mid-1950s.

Ellington often pushed his own songs even further than the ostensibly more modern musicians who covered them in later years. On the 1962 *Money Jungle* album, where he performs "Solitude" alongside Charles Mingus and Max Roach, the composer takes more chances than either Monk or Coltrane did on their surprisingly cautious cover versions. I wish more jazz artists today would reinvent Ellington's songs as boldly as the composer did himself. For the most part, "Solitude" serves as a tribute piece nowadays, often played in an overly respectful manner that captures more the sound than the spirit of this forward-looking jazz pioneer.

RECOMMENDED VERSIONS

Duke Ellington, Chicago, January 10, 1934

Benny Goodman, New York, September 11, 1934

Duke Ellington (with Ivie Anderson), New York, February 14, 1940

Duke Ellington, New York, May 15, 1945

Billie Holiday, from *Solitude*, Los Angeles, circa April 1952

Thelonious Monk, from *Thelonious Monk Plays Duke Ellington*, Hackensack, New
Jersey, July 27, 1955

Sonny Rollins, from *Way Out West*, Los Angeles, March 7, 1957

Red Garland (with John Coltrane), from *High Pressure*, New York, December 13, 1957

Louis Armstrong and Duke Ellington, from *The Great Summit*, New York, April 3, 1961

Duke Ellington (with Charles Mingus and Max Roach), from *Money Jungle*, New
York, September 17, 1962

Jaki Byard, from *To Them—To Us*, Milan, May 27, 1981

Gary Burton and Rebecca Paris, from *It's Another Day*, New York, May 1993

Matthew Shipp (with Mat Maneri), from *By the Love of Music*, New York, August 5,
1996

Someday My Prince Will Come
Composed by Frank Churchill, with lyrics by Larry Morey

A vocalist doesn't need to be a *jazz* singer to introduce a future standard—as
tunes given their debut by Cher ("Alfie"), Doris Day ("Secret Love"), and Jimmy
Stewart ("Easy to Love") make clear. Even so, few hep cats would have figured
that Snow White could step out of her fairy tale and establish a popular jazz
song. Yet "Someday My Prince Will Come," from the 1937 animated film *Snow
White and the Seven Dwarfs*, made the leap. Ms. White had some help, of
course—from Adriana Caselotti who served as the voice for the cartoon diva
(yes, there was lip-syncing back in the Great Depression), but even more from
a catchy score contributed by Frank Churchill and Larry Morey.

Walt Disney realized that the songs were a major hook for his feature, and
the marketing of a soundtrack album in conjunction with the release of the film
represented the first time this had been done for an American movie. The
American Film Institute later recognized "Someday My Prince Will Come" as
one of the 100 greatest movie songs, where it shows up at #19. Little in
Churchill's background suggested he had such a sophisticated tune inside
him—his biggest prior hit had been for the Three Little Pigs ("Who's Afraid of
the Big Bad Wolf?"), an even less glamorous vocal act than Snow White and her
dwarfs, and he never enjoyed a comparable success in later life.

Miles Davis's 1961 recording of "Someday My Prince Will Come" is the best-
known jazz interpretation of the composition, and there is much to admire on
this track: Wynton Kelly's coy piano intro over Paul Chamber's pedal point,
which masks the waltz time until the band is into the melody statement; Miles's

sensitive solo; and the contrasting sax stylings of Hank Mobley and John Coltrane. Coltrane's solo appears unexpectedly here, arriving after a recapitulation of the melody that suggests the song is over; his much more aggressive stance is often interpreted, with the benefit of hindsight, as a knockout victory of Trane over Mobley, one that prefigures the latter's departure from the Davis band and the former's rise to stardom.

This Davis recording represented my introduction to this song, and it actually came as a surprise to me during my teen years when, after I had performed it for a group of people one day, somebody came up to me and mentioned that it had originated in a Walt Disney animated feature. Until that moment, I had no realization why people of my age, who rarely recognized jazz songs, seemed familiar with this tune. I had a vague recollection of seeing the Disney film during my childhood, but the song clearly made little impression on me at the time. I also only learned at a late date that Dave Brubeck, not Miles Davis, had been the first jazz star to appreciate the jazz potential of the composition—back with his 1957 *Dave Digs Disney* project. Even a garden-variety jazz waltz was a rarity during this period, but Brubeck's mid-solo alternation between 3/4 to 4/4 was an especially daring technique for the time.

The harmonic movement is quite pleasing on this song, and even though the melody is mostly chord tones, they are often juicy notes—for example, a sharp five against an augmented chord in the second bar—that give this cartoon song some extra bite. Even avant-garde players who sometimes dispense with the chord changes entirely—such as Paul Bley (who plucks the strings inside the piano on this song), Sun Ra, and Anthony Braxton—have been enticed by this progression. The composition has proven especially popular with pianists. Herbie Hancock and Chick Corea highlighted it when they shared the stage on a 1978 concert tour, and both recorded it on their own in later years. Oscar Peterson left behind seven recorded versions, and Bill Evans more than a dozen, the last one performed less than two weeks before his death in 1980.

RECOMMENDED VERSIONS

Dave Brubeck (with Paul Desmond), from *Dave Digs Disney*, New York, June 30, 1957

Bill Evans, from *Portrait in Jazz*, New York, December 28, 1959

Miles Davis, from *Someday My Prince Will Come*, New York, March 20, 1961

Oscar Peterson and Milt Jackson, from *Reunion Blues*, Villingen, Germany, July 1971

Herbie Hancock, from *The Piano*, Tokyo, October 25–26, 1978

Paul Bley, from *Jazz 'n (E)motion: Films*, Pernes-les-Fontaines, France, April 5, 1997

Fred Hersch and Bill Frisell, from *Songs We Know*, San Francisco, circa 1998

Enrico Pieranunzi, from *Live in Paris*, live at Le Duc des Lombards, Paris, April 22–24, 2001

Someone to Watch over Me
Composed by George Gershwin, with lyrics by Ira Gershwin

Ah, the power of the pentatonic scale. This sequence of notes—the easiest example for nonmusicians to find is the series of black notes on the piano—is arguably the most appealing and certainly the most universal melodic motif in human history. Archaeologists have excavated ancient instruments tuned to the pentatonic scale, and its influence can be traced around the world, from Indonesian gamelan music to the Scottish bagpipes, from Africa to the Andes. Countless hit songs, from "Oh! Susanna" by Stephen Foster to "My Girl" by the Temptations, have built their hooks on this scale, and its potency is far from exhausted today.

Jazz, with its obsession with blues notes and the higher intervals of the scale, might seem resistant to such a simple device, yet many popular jazz standards draw strength from pentatonic melody lines. The opening of "Someone to Watch over Me" simply states the pentatonic scale—interestingly enough, Ellington uses the exact same phrase to open his "In a Sentimental Mood," only shifting the tonal center from major to minor.

"Someone to Watch over Me" first appeared in the 1926 Broadway production *Oh, Kay*, where Gertrude Lawrence sang it while clutching a rag doll that Gershwin had purchased in a Philadelphia toy store. The song was written with a fairly fast tempo in mind—quite a contrast from its typical ballad interpretation nowadays. Lawrence's recording, which reached number two on the chart in 1927, is taken at an animated medium pulse, while Gershwin's own recording from this period, which also sold well, moves forward at an even quicker pace. Not many performers today play "Someone to Watch over Me" at the speed the composer preferred, but a lasting reminder can be seen in the marking "scherzando" (meaning light and playful), which can still be seen on the sheet music.

The song found few advocates in the jazz world, at least at first. But Eddie Condon had been present in the studio in 1939 when Lee Wiley had recorded it with only Fats Waller accompanying on organ. Condon must have been impressed, since he added it to his repertoire in the mid-1940s, at a point when Gershwin's piece had been largely forgotten by the public Over the next several years, a number of leading jazz stars began featuring "Someone to Watch over Me," yet even at this point interpretations differed radically, with Coleman Hawkins presenting it as a slow romantic number, Artie Shaw swinging it at a medium-fast tempo, and Art Tatum transforming it into a virtuoso piano rhapsody.

This song has retained its popularity since that time, and it is especially favored by vocalists, both for its audience appeal and easy range—if they can hit the open seven notes of the melody, they won't find anything higher or lower in the rest of the song. Even jazz interlopers such as Sting, Rod Stewart, Art Garfunkel, Linda Ronstadt, and Willie Nelson have brought this standard, much older than any of them, into the studio. Among jazz divas, Ella Fitzgerald's performance from her monumental Gershwin songbook project may be the best-known interpretation, but I would point listeners in the direction of an even more poignant earlier recording of the song by Fitzgerald, made for the Decca label with only pianist Ellis Larkins for support. I am less than thrilled with the saccharine accompaniment for Sarah Vaughan (1957), Nancy Wilson (1963), and Chet Baker (1955), but the vocals here are emotionally charged and earn a place on the roster of classic versions of the Gershwin standard. Among more recent performances, I highly recommend the solo piano renditions by Keith Jarrett and Brad Mehldau.

RECOMMENDED VERSIONS

Lee Wiley (with Fats Waller on organ), New York, November 15, 1939

Coleman Hawkins, Los Angeles, March 9, 1945

Artie Shaw, Hollywood, July 17, 1945

Art Tatum, live at the Shrine Auditorium, Los Angeles, April 2, 1949

Ella Fitzgerald (with Ellis Larkins), New York, September 12, 1950

Chet Baker, from *Chet Baker Sings and Plays*, Los Angeles, February 28, 1955

Sarah Vaughan, from *Sarah Vaughan Sings George Gershwin*, New York, March 20, 1957

Nancy Wilson, *Yesterday's Love Songs/Today's Blues*, Los Angeles, October 9, 1963

Oscar Peterson, from *My Favorite Instrument*, Villingen, Germany, April 1968

Keith Jarrett, from *The Melody at Night with You*, New Jersey, 1998

Brad Mehldau, from *Live in Tokyo*, live at Sumida Triphony Hall, Tokyo, February 13, 2003

Song for My Father
Composed by Horace Silver

The hard bop movement of the 1950s and 1960s forced almost every performer to double as a composer. Instead of recording familiar standards or relying on outsiders to develop the band's repertoire—as so many previous jazz stars had done—this new generation of players mostly relied on their own pieces to fill their albums. These might feature simple head arrangements or more elaborate horn parts—but, in either case, the end results emphasized content over form, energy over refinement. At times, the songs came across more as excuses for a blowing date than as finely crafted works intended to last for the ages.

Then we have Horace Silver, the most consistently creative of the hard bop composers and an artist whose allure was almost inseparable from the appealing songs he wrote for his band. In truth, there was no single "Horace Silver style," and a list of his most popular works would include funky groove tunes, gentle mood pieces, vamp songs, outings in 3/4 and 6/8 time, Latin workouts of various stripes, up-tempo jam numbers, and examples of almost any and every other kind of approach congruent with the hard bop aesthetic. Yet a consistent set of values underpinned all of these efforts: Silver's best work was invariably marked by an economy of means in which excesses were pared away, an inviting sense of rhythmic momentum and, above all, supple melody lines that stuck in your head long after you first heard them.

At least a half-dozen Silver songs have gained some following as jazz standards, but his most popular composition is, without question, "Song for My Father." This work also represented a personal return to the roots for the pianist. During his childhood, Silver had been exposed to the Cape Verdean music his father, John Tavares Silver, played on violin and guitar. The elder Mr. Silvers had long prodded his son to draw on this heritage for his jazz work, but the pianist resisted the notion. Yet, after touring Brazil in 1964, where Silver was exposed to the bossa nova sounds that were so popular during that era, he decided to write a song that combined a Cape Verdean melody, akin to something his father would play, with a bossa nova beat. To make the tribute complete, Silver dedicated the song to his father, and put the elder Mr. Silver's photo on the cover of the resulting album.

This song would become Silver's signature theme. "Song for My Father" is perfectly realized on its debut recording from 1964—a track, aided by Joe Henderson's solo contribution, that remains the definitive performance of the work and one of the cornerstones of the Blue Note label. In the aftermath of Silver's hit, other jazz musicians would offer up cover versions of the song, but these hardly measure the impact of this tune, which is more likely to show up at a jam session or student performance than in the recording studio. It has inspired knockoffs: trumpeter Dave Douglas, who played with Silver's band from 1987 to 1990, recorded "Song for My Father-in-Law," and the jazz-oriented hip-hoppers Us3 transformed the original version into "Eleven Long Years." But if listeners of a later generation, when first hearing "Song for My Father," find the opening riff vaguely familiar, it is probably because Steely Dan borrowed the catchy vamp for their hit single "Rikki Don't Lose That Number."

RECOMMENDED VERSIONS

Horace Silver (with Joe Henderson), from *Song for My Father*, Englewood Cliffs,
New Jersey, October 26, 1964

George Benson, from *Talkin'*, New York, November 1968

Richard "Groove" Holmes, from *As Blue as They Want to Be*, New York, February 28, 1991

Dee Dee Bridgewater, from *Love and Peace*, Paris, December 1994

Michel Camilo, from *Through My Eyes*, Stamford, Connecticut, October 30–November 2, 1996

Orrin Evans (with JD Allen), from *Easy Now*, Brooklyn, April 27, 2004

The Song Is You
Composed by Jerome Kern, with lyrics by Oscar Hammerstein II

I am often impatient with self-referential art. You know that famous drawing of the hand drawing a hand that, in turn, is drawing the initial hand? It gives me the creeps. By the same token, I am suspicious of novels that are about writing novels, movies about making movies, poems about writing poems. A survey of poems in *The New Yorker* found that 27 percent of them mention poetry—and I was surprised the damage assessment wasn't higher, given the self-referential nature of our age. But the worst, by far, is the song about composing songs. Barry Manilow may very well "write the songs," but that doesn't mean I want to hear him croon about it.

So "The Song Is You" has a big smudge against it from the start, at least in my book. Yet the melody here is so propulsive and catchy, each phrase inviting the next, that I must begrudgingly grant my approval. And even the lyrics work, holding off the proclamation that the "song is you" until the very end, where the buildup and surprise value overcome the potential for cliché. When presented by the right vocalist—Frank Sinatra, for example, who recorded it on more than a half-dozen occasions—this song about a song can actually be a spellbinder.

"The Song Is You" originated in the 1932 Broadway production *Music in the Air*, Jerome Kern and Oscar Hammerstein's follow-up to the duo's immensely popular *Show Boat*. Two years later, the show and the song found their way into movie theaters with the release of the film version of *Music in the Air*, which featured Gloria Swanson and John Boles. But "The Song is You" did not enter the jazz repertoire until the 1940s when it gained newfound popularity due to the advocacy of Mr. Sinatra, whose performances inspired both fans and imitators.

Jazz musicians typically take this tune at a brisk pace, but it also works at slower tempos, and in a wide range of interpretive moods. June Christy can deliver it as a languorous ballad or Art Blakey can turn the changes into a high-speed slalom. Both approaches prosper. This versatility came to the fore in the 2003 movie *The Saddest Music in the World*, which won a Genie Award (a Canadian Oscar-type award for film music) for Christopher Dedrick, who created nine different versions of "The Song Is You" for the score. And if you are still looking for more, and prefer your saxophone straight and in large doses, check out Lee Konitz's unaccompanied 1974 version of "The Song Is You," which presents close to 20 minutes of unadulterated horn microsurgery on the Kern standard on its initial release, but later came out in an unedited version twice the length—some 39 minutes of solo alto on this one song.

RECOMMENDED VERSIONS

Frank Sinatra, Hollywood, January 19, 1942

Charlie Parker, New York, December 30, 1952

Clifford Brown, from *The Clifford Brown Quartet in Paris*, Paris, October 15, 1953

Gerry Mulligan and Chet Baker, from *Reunion*, New York, December 3–17, 1957

Anita O'Day, from *Anita O'Day at Mr. Kelly's*, live at Mister Kelly's, Chicago, April 27, 1958

Nancy Wilson (with the Gerald Wilson Orchestra), from *Yesterday's Love Songs—Today's Blues*, Los Angeles, October 8–10, 1963

Lee Konitz (unaccompanied), from *Lone-Lee*, Copenhagen, August 15, 1974

Art Blakey, from *In This Korner*, live at the Keystone Korner, San Francisco, May 8, 1978

Keith Jarrett (with the Standards Trio), from *Still Live*, live at Philharmonic Hall, Munich, July 13, 1986

Joe Lovano, from *Celebrating Sinatra*, New York, June 2–3, 1996

Sophisticated Lady
Composed by Duke Ellington, with lyrics by Irving Mills and Mitchell Parish

In 1952, *Downbeat* conducted a survey of 50 celebrities to determine their favorite Duke Ellington recordings, with each respondent allowed to name five titles. "Sophisticated Lady" showed up on 15 ballots and thus tied for first place (with "Mood Indigo"). The results did not specify which version of "Sophisticated Lady" was favored by these fans, but the well-known 1933 recording by Ellington, which stayed on the charts for 16 weeks and peaked at #3, is the most likely candidate. Yet the brilliant 11-minute version that Ellington had released a few months before the poll—taking advantage of the new LP format to offer extended versions of his familiar hits—must have found a few adherents as well.

From the start, this song had many admirers, especially among the more daring musicians of the day. The great keyboard virtuoso Art Tatum, newly arrived in New York, recorded his solo piano version of "Sophisticated Lady" just one month after Ellington's own studio performance—and you can tell from his piano explorations how deeply Tatum was intrigued by the structure of this composition. That same spring, two other leading jazz artists, Don Redman and Glen Gray with the Casa Loma Orchestra, recorded versions of "Sophisticated Lady," and both these performances charted in the top 20.

One admirer even became Ellington's collaborator. At the very first meeting between Billy Strayhorn and Duke Ellington, the bandleader asked his future colleague to sit down at the piano and play something. Strayhorn acquiesced, and offered an uncanny imitation of how Ellington played "Sophisticated Lady." Then he proclaimed: "Now this is the way I would play it"—at which point he changed keys, pushed the tempo, and added more and more modifications to the song as he went along. Ellington immediately called for Harry Carney, baritone saxophonist and trusted associate, then asked Strayhorn: "Can you do that again?" Soon after, Strayhorn was writing for the Ellington band.

Ellington described "Sophisticated Lady" as a musical portrait of the cosmopolitan women who worked as teachers during his youth—ladies who would spend the academic year with students but head off to Europe in the summer. The melody has been attributed to band members Lawrence Brown and Otto Hardwick—with Brown contributing the A theme and Hardwick coming up with the B theme. On the initial recording both men were included in the composer credits, but they later sold their rights for a flat payment of $15 each. Subsequent releases list only Ellington, who provided the harmonic underpinning, and his manager Irving Mills, with Mitchell Parish of "Star Dust" fame helping with lyrics.

The song is hard on singers—its interval leaps are more suited to the piano than the human voice—and its four-to-the-bar chord changes tend to force improvisers into predictable patterns. Pianist Lou Levy summed up the challenges in his mock toast: "Here's to all the guys who died coming out of the bridge of 'Sophisticated Lady.'" Some may even think that "Sophisticated Lady" is too sophisticated for its own good—decades after he composed it, Ellington still felt compelled to answer charges that it was not sufficiently "black." "As far back as 1933, when I said I was playing Negro music, some critics complained, 'Sophisticated Lady is not Negro music,'" Ellington wrote in an article for Music Journal in 1962. "But the fact remains that Sophisticated Lady is Negro music—it's the Negro I know, and my interpretation."

Although I admire this work, I prefer hearing it in settings that emphasize the composition, rather than rely on it as a launching pad for improvisation. The melody is perfectly matched to the harmonic movement, while solos over these changes often strike me as somewhat awkward. Little wonder that even Ellington himself, when he recorded his lengthy version in 1950, kept returning over and over again to the melody. By the same token, when Billy Eckstine brought "Sophisticated Lady" back to the charts in the late 1940s, no instrumental solos were found necessary; and when Thelonious Monk recorded his memorable interpretation in 1955, he too rarely strayed far from Ellington's famous melodic line.

RECOMMENDED VERSIONS

Duke Ellington, New York, February 15, 1933

Art Tatum, New York, March 21, 1933

Don Redman, New York, April 26, 1933

Casa Loma Orchestra, New York, June 5, 1933

Billy Eckstine, Los Angeles, April 27, 1947

Duke Ellington, from *Masterpieces by Ellington*, New York, December 18, 1950

Thelonious Monk, from *Thelonious Monk Plays Duke Ellington*, Hackensack, New Jersey, July 27, 1955

Spud Murphy, from *Gone with the Woodwinds*, Los Angeles, August 16, 1955

Charles Mingus, from *The Great Concert of Charles Mingus*, live at Salle Wagram, Paris, April 17, 1964

Toots Thielemans (with Fred Hersch), from *Only Trust Your Heart*, April–May 1988

Chick Corea, from *Chick Corea Akoustic Band*, New York, January 2–3, 1989

The Vanguard Jazz Orchestra, from *Can I Persuade You?* New York, January 4–5, 2001

Soul Eyes
Composed by Mal Waldron

The name of the late Mal Waldron may hardly register with young jazz fans today, and he rarely shows up on lists of significant jazz pianists of the late 1950s and early 1960s. But his impact during that period could be felt in an impressive range of settings—albeit usually as a sideman supporting a far better-known bandleader. He worked as accompanist to Billie Holiday in the final stages of her career and anchored the all-star band that performed with her on CBS in 1957—a setting where, in a manner emblematic of his career, he can be heard but barely seen. Around this same time, Waldron performed on Charles Mingus's *Pithecanthropus Erectus* and on a number of sessions with Jackie McLean and other artists. A few years later he held the piano spot in the seminal Eric Dolphy and Booker Little band that recorded at the Five Spot. On the 1957 album that produced "Soul Eyes," Waldron was the main creative force behind the project, but even here he was shortchanged: on the cover his name is listed after the four horn players on the date. A recent jazz book of some repute refers to the recording as "a leaderless date . . . by Mal Waldron"—not intended as a putdown, I am sure, but this oxymoronic credit sadly confirms the unjust destiny of an artist relegated to obscurity even at his most glorious moment.

But Waldron did have some good luck when he recorded the latter album, released as *Interplay for Two Trumpets and Two Tenors*. One of those tenors turned out to be John Coltrane, then in the early stages of redefining the role of the saxophone in modern jazz. Over the next five years, the jazz world forgot "Soul Eyes"—not a single cover version was recorded during that period—but Coltrane remembered the song, and revived it at a June 1962 session for the Impulse label. This rendition remains the best-known version of "Soul Eyes" and serves as an illuminating example of the tenorist's midcareer ballad style. I especially admire the tension McCoy Tyner instills in the proceedings by implying a 6/8 time against the underlying slow 4/4 during parts of the opening and closing melody statement—a trademark technique that you will hear in other slow numbers recorded by this band during the early 1960s.

Yet this high-powered advocacy by the most prominent jazz combo of the day did little to advance the prospects for "Soul Eyes," at least immediately, and few other artists picked up on the song until the late 1970s and early 1980s. When things finally changed, the impetus came from a surprising direction—namely the avant-garde contingent, a group of jazz renegades previously disinterested in enshrining works in the standard repertoire, but then in the process of softening rough edges and digging into more traditional song forms. Over the course of several years, "Soul Eyes" was recorded by Rashied Ali, Archie Shepp (both on his own leader date and in collaboration with vocalist Karin Krog), and Marion Brown—at a point when few mainstream artists were showcasing this piece.

Mal Waldron's 1978 solo piano performance—included in the CD reissue of his *Moods* album—shows how the composer interpreted his most famous work during this period. That said, I don't hear this song as a keyboard-oriented composition. Ballads with melodies that rely on so many long-held notes—such as Billy Strayhorn's "Chelsea Bridge," Wayne Shorter's "Infant Eyes," or this work—are clearly better suited for horn players. During the 1980s, a number of them took up the mantle: Michael Brecker can be heard performing "Soul Eyes" with the band Steps Ahead on a live album from 1980, while Art Farmer demonstrated his affinity for the piece on his *Azure* and *Soul Eyes* albums, recorded in 1987 and 1992 respectively. Stan Getz added the song to his repertoire around this same time, and recorded it in several different settings during the final years of his life.

"Soul Eyes" can fill the role of a high drama ballad, but also works when adapted in other ways. I see that one of the jazz education outfits has issued a play-along album with this composition featured as a bolero, and other rhythmic concepts are equally applicable here. Finally, singers should take note: Waldron also wrote lyrics to "Soul Eyes," which are rarely performed but well matched to the temperament of the music.

RECOMMENDED VERSIONS

John Coltrane, Mal Waldron, and others, from *Interplay for Two Trumpets and Two Tenors*, New York, March 22, 1957

John Coltrane, from *Coltrane*, Englewood Cliffs, New Jersey, June 19, 1962

Karin Krog and Archie Shepp, from *Hi-Fly*, Oslo, June 23, 1976

Mal Waldron, from *Moods*, Ludwigsburg, Germany, May 8, 1978

Steps Ahead (with Michael Brecker), from *Smokin' in the Pit*, live at the Pit Inn, Tokyo, December 14–16, 1980

Stan Getz, from *Bossas and Ballads: The Lost Sessions*, Hollywood, March 1989

Art Farmer, from *Soul Eyes*, live at the Blue Note, Fukuoka, Japan, May 1991

David Murray and Mal Waldron, from *Silence*, Brussels, October 5–6, 2001

Speak Low
Composed by Kurt Weill, with lyrics by Ogden Nash

From a jazz perspective, this song had an unpromising pedigree from the start. The music came from a German composer who had first learned songwriting from Engelbert Humperdinck (no, not *that* Engelbert Humperdinck, but rather the opera-writing one who was a hot property back in 1890). The lyrics were penned by a writer who made his reputation publishing nonsense verse. And the first hit record came under the baton of Guy Lombardo, leader of the sweetest-of-sweet bands and a strong candidate for the least hip musician of the twentieth century.

Yet "Speak Low" bears none of the ominous genetic markers of this inauspicious lineage. Unlike Weill's even better-known "Mack the Knife," "Speak Low" does not sound like a European cabaret song, but comes across as a sleek, streamlined American-flavored tune, a plug-and-play number ready for jazz improvisation straight out of the box. The melody, built on short, choppy phrases, mixing in three-against-two rhythms and spacious intervals, seems written with jazz horn players in mind.

In fact, the song was composed for Broadway, where it was performed by Mary Martin and Kenny Baker in the successful 1943 musical *One Touch of Venus*. After Guy Lombardo enjoyed his top 10 hit in the spring of 1944, a few jazz bandleaders showcased the song, but typically on radio broadcasts rather than at formal record dates. A V-disc from December 1943 captures Sinatra performing "Speak Low"—but this would be his sole recording of it—and Woody Herman made a transcription recording featuring vocalist Frances Wayne a few weeks later. By late spring, the song had fallen off the radar screens of both musicians and the general public, even though *One Touch of Venus* continued its Broadway run until February 1945.

"Speak Low" got a second chance with the 1948 movie version of *One Touch of Venus*. Although Sinatra had been mentioned as a possible star for the film, the movie instead featured his future wife Ava Gardner, who sings "Speak Low" onscreen with Dick Haymes, although her vocal was dubbed by Eileen Wilson. Claude Thornhill was the only name jazz bandleader to feature the Weill song around this time, but Gerry Mulligan—arranger and saxophonist with Thornhill—brought "Speak Low" with him to the West Coast a short while later and recorded it alongside Chet Baker in their popular L.A. quartet. Several leading jazz divas of the mid-1950s—Billie Holiday, Sarah Vaughan, Carmen McRae— gave the composition the last needed boost to ensure its staying power as a standard, its disreputable sweet-band past now forgotten.

Singers have continued to favor this composition, but the lyrics aren't the main attraction here. Admittedly even the finest poet would find it challenging to fit words to Weill's abbreviated melodic phrases, most lasting four notes or less. Ogden Nash might seem an ideal candidate to do so—his light verse is often quite compact (he famously wrote the shortest poem in history, called "Fleas," its entire text reading "Adam / Had 'em"). Strangely enough, our lyricist opts to borrow from Shakespeare. You will find Don Pedro, toward the beginning of *Much Ado about Nothing*, declare: "Speak low, if you speak love." Most of the remainder (of Nash's lyrics, *not* Shakespeare's play) consists of clichés about the brevity of love—time is late, the curtain is coming down, tomorrow arrives too soon, etc.

The chord changes, in contrast, are well suited for improvisation. If you have any doubts, listen to John Coltrane's exuberant solo, made as a sideman on a Sonny Clark date from 1957. Some of the more impactful renditions from later years follow this formula of matching a premier saxophonist with a top-notch pianist, notably Charles Lloyd's recording with Keith Jarrett from 1966, Bill Evans's studio encounter with Warne Marsh and Lee Konitz from 1977, and Joe Farrell's 1979 date with guest sideman Chick Corea.

RECOMMENDED VERSIONS

Frank Sinatra, New York, December 5, 1943

Gerry Mulligan (with Chet Baker), from *Gene Norman Presents the Original Gerry Mulligan Tentet & Quartet*, Los Angeles, May 7, 1953

Sonny Clark (with John Coltrane) from *Sonny's Crib*, Hackensack, New Jersey,
September 1, 1957

Sarah Vaughan, from *After Hours at the London House*, live at the London House,
Chicago, March 7, 1958

Charles Lloyd (with Keith Jarrett and Jack DeJohnette), from *The Flowering*, live at
Aulaen Hall, Oslo, October 29, 1966

Bill Evans (with Lee Konitz and Warne Marsh), from *Crosscurrents*, Berkeley,
February 28–March 3, 1977

Joe Farrell (with Chick Corea), from *Skateboard Park*, Los Angeles, January 29, 1979

Donny McCaslin, from *Exile and Discovery*, Brooklyn, November 18, 1997

Spring Can Really Hang You Up the Most
Composed by Tommy Wolf, with lyrics by Fran Landesman

I suspect that many jazz fans, upon learning that this song is attributed to Tom
Wolf, conclude that the composer is one of the two better-known Tom Wolfes,
either the novelist who wrote *You Can't Go Home Again* or else the white-suited
bon vivant associated with the so-called New Journalism of the 1960s and 1970s.
After all, Truman Capote wrote the lyrics for Harold Arlen's "A Sleepin' Bee,"
and Ken Kesey performed as warm-up band for the Grateful Dead, extracting
"music" from a device of his own invention—the so-called Thunder Machine,
which combined the fender from a T-Bird with a smoke machine, piano strings,
and other incongruous elements. So why couldn't Kesey and Capote's friend
Mr. Wolfe turn out to have the *right stuff* for songwriting?

But Tommy Wolf (without the "e") never enjoyed the fame of these other
Wolfes, pursuing a modest career more suited for sheep's clothing. Yet he was
an exceptional songwriter—in my opinion, one of the most talented of his
generation. A few of his compositions have survived at the periphery of the
jazz repertoire, none of them widely known among the general public but
prized by musicians for their poetry and sophistication. In this regard, Wolf
benefited enormously from the contributions of lyricist Fran Landesman, who
wrote the words for his best songs. The two met by chance when Landesman
and her husband stopped by the Jefferson Hotel in St. Louis where Tommy
Wolf was playing piano, and struck up a conversation with the musician that
led to collaborations on a number of fronts. One evening in 1951, Landesman
gave Wolf a poem, which he set to music, initiating a songwriting partnership
that reached its high point with their work on the 1959 Broadway musical *The
Nervous Set*.

"Spring Can Really Hang You Up the Most" began in response to a peculiar challenge Landesman had set herself: to restate, in the hip lingo of a jazz musician, the sentiments T. S. Eliot expressed in the opening line to his poem "The Waste Land." That phrase ("April is the cruelest month . . .") was transformed into "Spring Can Really Hang You Up the Most." Wolf constructed a poignant melody that gave emotional depth to Landesman's arch lyrics. There is much to admire here, with both the main theme and bridge sustaining the poignancy of the piece; but I especially like Wolf's clever alteration in the final restatement of the A theme, which briefly hints at a modulation down a fifth before returning back to the tonic key.

George Shearing, who heard Wolf perform this song during a visit to St. Louis, was so impressed that he brought a tape of the duo's work back with him to New York, where he passed it on to Jackie & Roy, a popular husband and wife jazz act who were on the lookout for fresh, contemporary material. They featured "Spring Can Really Hang You Up the Most" on a 1955 album, and over the next few years a few other singers picked up on the tune. In 1961, it showed up on studio dates by Ella Fitzgerald, Mark Murphy, and Julie London, and has stayed in the jazz repertoire ever since.

At one point, the lyrics make playful reference to "Spring Is Here." But in its serpentine motion this piece reminds me of still another cherished "spring" standard by Richard Rodgers: "It Might as Well Be Spring." I wouldn't be surprised to learn that Wolf used the earlier song as a role model. In any event, Wolf and Landesman created something here that rises above their ambitions for a hipster's ode to spring. It works as a dramatic-monologue-turned-ballad that can serve as the emotional centerpiece of a public performance or can work just as well as a melancholy reverie that the pianist at the bar plays to an empty room before calling it quits for the night.

This Wolf and Landesman composition has been favored more by singers than instrumentalists over the years, and clearly you don't get the full impact of the piece if you don't hear the words. Yet the melody is lovely enough to stand on its own. As a result, it has been adopted by horn players with a taste for deep ballads—most notably Stan Getz, who recorded it on several occasions. You can hardly find a starker contrast in settings than between the full orchestra version from Getz's 1963 *Reflections* project and his minimalist duet on the same song with pianist Albert Dailey from 20 years later, yet both interpretations are essential recordings of this song.

Tommy Wolf had the bad fortune of being born a few decades too late, when the kind of craftsmanship he brought to his songs was falling out of fashion in favor of simpler, more raucous material. Yet I wouldn't be surprised to see a revival of interest in his music someday. He wrote a number of other finely etched songs that jazz musicians would find it worthwhile learning. In addition to this song, I would suggest those unacquainted with his music to check out

"The Ballad of the Sad Young Men," "I'm Always Drunk in San Francisco" (think of it as a seedier alternative to Tony Bennett's most famous hit) and—his nod in direction of that *other* Wolfe—"You Can't Go Home Again."

RECOMMENDED VERSIONS

Jackie Cain and Roy Kral, from *Storyville Presents Jackie and Roy*, Los Angeles, May 1955

Ella Fitzgerald, from *Clap Hands, Here Comes Charlie*, Los Angeles, June 22, 1961

Mark Murphy, from *Rah*, New York, September 15, 1961

Stan Getz, from *Reflections*, New York, October 21–22, 1963

Carmen McRae, from *Bittersweet*, New York, May 20, 1964

Hampton Hawes and Martial Solal, from *Key for Two*, Paris, January 1968

Betty Carter, from *The Audience with Betty Carter*, live at the Great American Music Hall, San Francisco, December 6–8, 1979

Stan Getz and Albert Dailey, from *Poetry*, Irvington, New York, January 12, 1983

Cassandra Wilson, from *Loverly*, New York, August 13–17, 2007

Spring Is Here
Composed by Richard Rodgers, with lyrics by Lorenz Hart

Many of Richard Rodgers's compositions tempt me into wishing he had written art songs for the concert hall instead of—okay, in addition to—tunes for Broadway productions. The stage of the Shubert Theater, where this song made its debut in *I Married an Angel* in 1938, would seem more suited to high-energy singing to the lofty back row, rather than the intimate and almost pastoral sentiments of "Spring Is Here." Yet somehow Rodgers and Lorenz Hart managed to put nuance and introspection into a genre often given to grand theatrics. And the box office didn't suffer: the show ran for 338 performances, and *I Married an Angel* made the leap to movie screens four years later.

Everything contributes to a hushed and gentle tone in this song. The melody starts low, with a rolling motif that drops even lower when it is restated, transposed down a third, four bars later. Rodgers builds up to a high note in bar 16, but only gradually over the course of four sumptuously languid bars. Yet when he gets to the end of the song, he opts instead for a gradually descending melody line. I just don't see this subdued approach coming out of the Broadway playbook, but am chastened by the composer's daring and success. More to the point, I am deeply moved by this song, which doesn't sound the least bit dated to my ears these many years later.

"Spring Is Here" had modest success during its Broadway run, but jazz performers did not record this work with any regularity until the 1950s, when piano players took the lead in promoting it. In June 1950, both Dave Brubeck and Erroll Garner recorded their versions of the song, but no other jazz players followed suit until 1953, when George Shearing and Oscar Peterson also taped their renditions. Peterson actually delivers a vocal on his recording, and if you suspected that his piano playing was influenced by Nat King Cole, wait until you hear how he sings. At the close of the decade, Andrew Hill made an unexpected selection of this low-key standard, so out of character with his prickly school of pianism, for his debut album. By that time, "Spring Is Here" had become a jazz staple and a song that aspiring players needed to learn.

Some have tried to turn this Rodgers and Hart standard into a free-wheeling jam chart—hear Coltrane's 1958 recording for a good example—but I tend to prefer the chamber jazz interpretations of Ahmad Jamal and Bill Evans, which get closer to the essential mood of this piece. And as if aiming to prove my point about the concert hall destiny of this song, Miles Davis brought "Spring Is Here" with him to Carnegie Hall in 1961 where, fronting an orchestra conducted by Gil Evans, he delivered a glorious interpretation.

By the way, Rodgers and Hart wrote another song with the same title for the 1929 show *Spring Is Here*. But this flashier song seems to be heralding a different season, and is almost never heard nowadays.

RECOMMENDED VERSIONS

Erroll Garner, New York, June 28, 1950

Ahmad Jamal, from *Chamber Music of the New Jazz*, Chicago, May 23, 1955

Cannonball Adderley, from *Sophisticated Swing*, New York, February 11, 1957

John Coltrane, from *Standard Coltrane*, Hackensack, New Jersey, July 11, 1958

Andrew Hill, from *So in Love*, Chicago, 1959

Bill Evans, from *Portrait in Jazz*, New York, December 28, 1959

Miles Davis (with Gil Evans), from *Miles Davis at Carnegie Hall*, live at Carnegie Hall, New York, May 19, 1961

Denny Zeitlin, from *Mosaic Select: The Columbia Studio Trio Sessions*, Los Angeles, March 18, 1967

Warne Marsh, from *A Ballad Album*, Monster, Holland, April 7, 1983

Kenny Barron and Charlie Haden, from *Night and the City*, live at Iridium, New York, September 20–22, 1996

David Murray (with Roland Hanna), from *Seasons*, Brooklyn, August 3, 1998

Star Dust

Composed by Hoagy Carmichael, with lyrics by Mitchell Parish

The official title is "Star Dust"—two separate words that even the composer was unable to define but found ever so appealing. Yet almost everybody, Mr. Carmichael included, later compressed them into "Stardust." His friend Stu Gorrell, who would also contribute lyrics to "Georgia on My Mind," suggested the evocative title, a neologism that somehow perfectly captured the mood of Carmichael's song.

The composer claimed the melody came to him while looking up at the night sky, thinking of a girl—he then ran to find a piano to work it out before the inspiration left him. His biographer Richard Sudhalter has documented a more gradual and less colorful process of composition. Judging by the song itself, Carmichael's artistic vision was spurred less by a romantic attachment and more by his friend, cornetist Bix Beiderbecke. The latter's spirit and style of improvisation seem infused in the intricate phrases that make "Star Dust" arguably the most melodically complex hit song in the history of American music.

Jazz players, as a matter of course, find inspiration for their solos in pop songs, but how many pop songs take their inspiration from a jazz solo? "The verse," Mel Tormé has noted, "rambles up the scale and down, resembling nothing so much as an improvisational cornet solo." Then he adds: "It is one of the most bittersweet examples of 'lost love' ever written. I will sing it until I die." True to his word, on his last recorded performance—for an A&E television special—Tormé showcased this song. Two weeks later, he suffered a stroke and never returned to the concert stage.

Carmichael's initial recording, made on Halloween in 1927, will surprise listeners with a much faster beat than one hears in later performances—but is largely in keeping with conventional practice during an era in which ballads, except for slow blues, were rarely attempted by jazz players. The dreamy ambiance of the song was enhanced by the lyrics, but these weren't added until 1929, when Mitchell Parish took the composer's explanation of the song's origins—a person gazing up at the stars while thinking about a lover—and turned them into poetic lines that come across as overwrought when read on the page but sound ever so right when coupled with Carmichael's melody. Parish later claimed he could have supported himself just off the royalties from this one song, which amounted to a million dollars during his lifetime. But Parish's boss, Irving Mills, publisher of the work, also contributed to the song's success, using his connections in the jazz world to ensure that "Star Dust" was widely recorded.

The Chocolate Dandies, with Don Redman and Lonnie Johnson in the band, were the first to cover Carmichael's song, and they follow the composer in offering an extroverted, moderately fast interpretation. But by the time Louis Armstrong recorded "Star Dust" on November 4, 1931—the day Buddy Bolden died, by the way—the more reflective approach to this song was already evident. Bing Crosby's version of "Star Dust" was a top 10 hit that same year, as were recordings by several other prominent artists over the next decade. One gauge of the song's extraordinary popularity can be seen in the Victor label's unprecedented release of two versions of "Star Dust" on the same disk—with Benny Goodman on the A side and Tommy Dorsey on the B side. Goodman offered a faster instrumental arrangement, while Dorsey opted for a more meditative vocal version . . . and, yes, both became top 10 hits in June 1936.

By the early 1940s, one might have thought that "Star Dust" had run its course, but Artie Shaw brought the song back to prominence with his recording, which sold in bountiful copies during the first weeks of 1941. "The greatest clarinet solo of all time" was Buddy DeFranco's description of Shaw's achievement. And I concur in giving Shaw the nod over his rival Goodman in this instance. But Shaw was not alone in championing the song. This same month Dorsey had his second success with "Star Dust"—his version with Frank Sinatra finding a receptive audience. Three months later Glenn Miller enjoyed his own hit record with the now pervasive song. Looking over this astonishing track record, I can only surmise that the composition's extreme complexity, normally the death knell for commercial success, here had the opposite effect, at least once "Star Dust" had gotten over the hump of first exposure to the public: the intricate interval leaps in the melody kept it sounding fresh after many repetitions, where a simpler song might have seemed insipid within a few hearings.

A few weeks after Shaw made his popular recording of "Star Dust," an equally memorable version was captured in concert, but would remain unknown to jazz fans for many years. The live recording, made by two enthusiastic jazz fans, of Duke Ellington's November 1940 appearance in Fargo, North Dakota, is now much prized by music lovers but wasn't made available commercially until 1964. Ben Webster's performance of "Star Dust" so delighted the tenorist that he repeatedly asked Jack Towers, who had helped make the recording, for personal copies in later years.

"Star Dust" never really fell out of favor, but Nat King Cole gave it a new boost with his 1956 recording for his *Love Is the Thing* album, which was a number one album in both the United States and United Kingdom—achieving gold status in 1960 and platinum in 1992. During the 1960s and 1970s, several hundred versions of "Star Dust" were recorded, mostly by jazz performers. Yet even during the age of rock, a handful of artists—Frank Sinatra, Willie Nelson, Johnny Mathis, Carly Simon—achieved crossover success with the song.

I suspect that this state of affairs may have changed in more recent years. Many, perhaps a majority, of casual music fans nowadays might not even recognize the song to which their parents and grandparents courted, romanced, and wed. Even within the jazz world, "Star Dust" has taken on a decidedly retro flavor, favored by the older generation of performers or those on a nostalgia kick. But I don't count out this now venerable composition by any means. In the hands of the right player, who can rise to its demands (expressive rather than merely technical), "Star Dust" can still wow audiences and serve as the highlight of an album or concert.

RECOMMENDED VERSIONS

Hoagy Carmichael, Richmond, Indiana, October 31, 1927

The Chocolate Dandies (with Don Redman and Lonnie Johnson), New York, October 13, 1928

Louis Armstrong, Chicago, November 4, 1931

Benny Goodman (with an arrangement by Fletcher Henderson), April 23, 1936

Chu Berry and Roy Eldridge, New York, November 10, 1938

Artie Shaw, Hollywood, October 7–8, 1940

Tommy Dorsey (with Frank Sinatra), Hollywood, November 11, 1940

Nat King Cole (with an arrangement by Gordon Jenkins), from *Love Is the Thing*, Hollywood, December 19, 1956

John Coltrane, from *Stardust*, Hackensack, New Jersey, December 26, 1958

Dave Brubeck and Paul Desmond, from *1975: The Duets*, New York, September 15–16, 1975

Willie Nelson, from *Stardust*, Southern California, December 3–12, 1977

George Shearing and Mel Tormé, from *Top Drawer*, San Francisco, March 1983

Jaki Byard, from *Changes of Life*, New York, January 30–31, 1996

Star Eyes

Composed by Gene de Paul, with lyrics by Don Raye

Charlie Parker was not the first jazz musician to record this song—several big bands had added it to their repertoire in the early 1940s. But the song had fallen by the wayside before the close of World War II, and no jazz artist had brought it to a recording session for more than five years when Bird resuscitated it for his 1950 Verve studio date. His performance—accompanied by Hank Jones, Ray Brown, and Buddy Rich—turned "Star Eyes" into a standard, and many later versions even borrow the distinctive intro he used on that occasion.

Parker had probably heard the song in the film *I Dood It*, the 1943 comedy that had introduced "Star Eyes" to the public. Certainly there was enough hot music in the movie—with Lena Horne, Jimmy Dorsey, and Hazel Scott on hand—to appeal to the young altoist; and even if he missed the film, Parker must have heard Dorsey's subsequent recording, which was a top 10 hit. Parker, for his part, later acknowledged Dorsey as an early influence, and it is not hard to hear the connection between Dorsey's recording and Parker's later rendition.

The song has proven worthy of its second life as a jazz staple. The harmonic personality shifts back and forth between a major and minor sensibility, ultimately resolving into the former, and nicely aligning with the affirmation of romantic optimism in Don Raye's lyrics. The words come close to echoing the clichés of previous "star" songs—from "Star Dust" to "When You Wish upon a Star"—but are imbued with a whimsical enough tone to make these references seem cute rather than parasitical. The melody is first rate, evoking a jazz sensibility with its alternating measures of half notes and eighth notes and the majestic clarion phrase that concludes the final A theme.

Although I am fond of several piano interpretations, especially Art Lande's hard-to-find solo outing from 1977, the saxophonists have tended to be the most active in keeping "Star Eyes" in the repertoire. Virtually all of the leading post-Parker altoists—including Cannonball Adderley, Jackie McLean, Art Pepper, Phil Woods, Sonny Stitt, and Lee Konitz—have offered up their interpretations. Next-generation saxophonists, such as Vincent Herring and Chris Potter, have also turned frequently to "Star Eyes." But even today this song is played in a manner similar to the way Parker tackled it back in 1950—thus the tune that started as a big band hit from a Hollywood movie seems to have found its ultimate destiny as a medium- or up-tempo bebop anthem.

RECOMMENDED VERSIONS

Jimmy Dorsey, for the soundtrack to the film *I Dood It*, Hollywood, November 10–24, 1942

Charlie Parker, New York, March–April 1950

Lennie Niehaus, from *Quintets and Strings*, Los Angeles, March 30, 1955

Art Pepper, from *Art Pepper Meets the Rhythm Section*, Los Angeles, January 19, 1957

Tina Brooks, from *Minor Move*, Hackensack, New Jersey, March 16, 1958

Cannonball Adderley, from *The Cannonball Adderley Quintet Plus*, New York, May 11, 1961

McCoy Tyner, from *Nights of Ballads and Blues*, Englewood Cliffs, New Jersey, March 4, 1963

Art Lande, from *The Eccentricities of Earl Dant*, Berkeley, February 1977

Phil Woods (with Hal Galper), from *Birds of a Feather*, New York, August 11–12, 1981

Vincent Herring, from *The Days of Wine and Roses*, New York, June 17–18, 1994

Jackie McLean (with Cedar Walton), from *Nature Boy*, New York, June 12, 1999

Chris Potter, from *Gratitude*, New York, September 27–28, 2000

Stella by Starlight
Composed by Victor Young, with lyrics by Ned Washington

I was much taken with this composition in my early twenties, and found its construction very compatible with my conception of modern jazz. So I was quite shocked to discover one day that my mother, who almost never paid attention to music of any sort, not only knew the song but could sing all the words. I was crestfallen—and immediately tempted to abandon "Stella" for an even more modern lady, one that would not meet with Mom's approval.

Back then, I didn't even known this song *had* words. I had assumed that, like so much of Victor Young's music, it had come from a film score, where it had served as an instrumental background to the story on the screen. I later learned that I was partially correct. In its original form, in the 1944 movie *The Uninvited*, the melody lacked lyrics, although it had a name—in a key scene Roderick (played by Ray Milland) is at the piano, when Stella (Gail Russell) asks him what song he is playing. He replies, "It's a serenade—'To Stella by Starlight.'" When lyrics were added later, Ned Washington must have struggled to fit that phrase against the resistant notes of Young's melody. As a result, the title phrase "Stella by Starlight" makes only a single appearance in the words, squeezed in midsentence some 20 bars into the form. After that, both Stella and her starlight disappear from view.

The structure is conventional in length, with the melody filling up the expected 32 bars. But everything else about it breaks the rules. Instead of the usual repeats found in American popular song, "Stella by Starlight" is a masterpiece of through-composed misdirection. At bar eight, where one would normally get a repeat of the A theme in most Tin Pan Alley songs, we *do* go to the tonic chord, but this is actually its first appearance in the piece. We might now expect that the repeat will come in bar 16, but here Young has another surprise in store—a gut-wrenching modulation, in which the melody is held on an altered note of the chord for a full bar. The final eight bars are as close as we will get to a recapitulation of the main theme, but even here Young tinkers with his melody and chords, only lingering on the familiar opening motif for two bars before heading off toward a different path to a final resolve.

This bold framework, which violates our ingrained expectations, was precisely what made me embrace "Stella by Starlight" as an essentially modernistic composition—so much so, that I kept it in my core repertoire, even after my mother sang the words to me on that unhappy day. In all honesty, I still have trouble understanding the appeal of such a hook-free art song among the general public. I suspect that, as with David Raksin's "Laura," its prominent placement in an emotionally charged film imprinted a melody, which under normal circumstances would have been too complex for the Hit Parade, into the deep memory banks of the moviegoers. In any event, a maudlin rendition of "Stella by Starlight" by Harry James became a minor hit in the spring of 1947, and Frank Sinatra's recording from July of that year also generated considerable airplay.

Yet, by the end of the 1940s, "Stella by Starlight" had been put aside by jazz musicians. Two sax recordings from 1952 brought it back to the forefront of the jazz repertoire. Charlie Parker performed it with strings at a high-profile studio session in January, and at the end of the year Stan Getz recorded a sweet-toned and very Lester Young–ish version of "Stella by Starlight" with his combo. More than a dozen jazz cover versions were released over the next two years, and this song has never fallen out of favor since then.

A number of well-known players, especially those with an affinity for cool jazz, have found recurring inspiration in this song. Chet Baker, who learned the song while playing with Getz on the West Coast, recorded it again and again—his debut recording, made at the University of Michigan in 1954, and his final one, from a celebrated Tokyo concert in 1987, are both worth hearing. Getz, for his part, held on to "Stella by Starlight" over the decades, leaving behind recordings of the song that span 35 years. Bill Evans recorded "Stella by Starlight" with Miles Davis in the 1950s, and with his own group in the 1960s, 1970s, and 1980s. Davis kept it in his band's regular repertoire until he went electric in the late 1960s. Jim Hall performed it with Chico Hamilton's band at the outset of his career, featured it on his fist leader date *Jazz Guitar* from 1957, and recorded it again, alongside Chris Potter, more than 40 years later.

For my part, "Stella by Starlight" was the first song I called when I went into the studio to make my debut album. Let me dedicate that one, in retrospect, to Mom, who taught me an unexpected lesson in what the song was really about.

RECOMMENDED VERSIONS

Charlie Parker (with strings), from *Charlie Parker with Strings: The Master Takes*, New York, January 1952

Stan Getz, from *Stan Getz Plays*, New York, December 12, 1952

Miles Davis (with John Coltrane and Bill Evans), from *'58 Miles*, New York, May 26, 1958

J. J. Johnson, from *Proof Positive*, New York, May 1, 1964

Joe Pass, from *Virtuoso*, Los Angeles, August 28, 1973

McCoy Tyner (with Jack DeJohnette and Eddie Gomez), from *Supertrios*, Berkeley, April 11–12, 1977

Jimmy Giuffre, from *Dragonfly*, Southbury, Connecticut, January 14-15, 1983

Chet Baker, from *Chet Baker in Tokyo*, live at Hitomi Kinen Kodo, Tokyo, June 14, 1987

Jim Hall and Chris Potter, from *Jazzpar Quarter + 4*, live at Holbaek Jazzklub,
      Copenhagen, April 3, 1998

Stolen Moments
Composed by Oliver Nelson

Oliver Nelson's career was betwixt and between, straddling divides in the music world, and thus making it difficult for critics to pigeonhole him in a convenient category. In his early twenties, Nelson focused on alto saxophone, apprenticing in Louis Jordan's R&B-oriented band and later working in jazz ensembles led by Erskine Hawkins, Louie Bellson, and others. Then in the 1960s, he gravitated to tenor sax on his own leader dates and various sideman projects. As the decade progressed, Nelson performed less and devoted his attention to composing and arranging. After his move to Los Angeles in 1967, he became entrenched in a range of commercial projects, composing music for a host of TV shows and working with a number of top-drawer pop and soul acts. At the time of his death from a heart attack in 1975, the 43-year-old musician was largely forgotten by the jazz world.

Well, not entirely forgotten. Over the years, I have found that many jazz fans own one Oliver Nelson album, and invariably the same one—his remarkable 1961 release *The Blues and the Abstract Truth*. Even today, it remains one of the best-selling jazz albums on the market, and for a good reason. Here Nelson served as leader of one of the finest jazz combos ever to enter a recording studio, with Eric Dolphy and Freddie Hubbard joining him in the front line, and the rhythm section featuring Bill Evans, Paul Chambers and Roy Haynes. For the opening track, Nelson drew on his composition "Stolen Moments," a querulous hard bop chart that makes full use of the horns on hand with its rich spread-out voicings. After the 16-bar melody statement, the band settles into a minor blues form during the solos.

For some reason, most lead sheets (from *The Real Book* and elsewhere) as well as some recordings leave out a clever hook in the song—its brief resolve into the tonic major in bar four of the melody, one of many interesting twists in Nelson's original chart. Indeed, "Stolen Moments" sounds almost painfully sophisticated, yet the reliance on the blues form for the solos makes it fairly easy to perform, even for a mid-level student band.

The song had originally appeared as "The Stolen Moment" on Eddie "Lockjaw" Davis's big band 1960 project *Trane Whistle*. But Nelson's version of the song on his own leader date, five months later, will remain forever the definitive version of "Stolen Moments." It is a consummate performance, and belongs on any short list of the most important jazz tracks of the era. Nonetheless, others have been inspired by Nelson's piece and have delivered noteworthy interpretations. Ahmad Jamal performs "Stolen Moments" on *The Awakening*, my favorite of his midcareer albums. Mark Murphy added his own lyrics for his popular 1978 recording of the Nelson song, while Carmen McRae and Betty Carter rely on a different set of words, contributed by Ann Fischer, for their 1987 collaborative project.

But the strangest vocal recording of this song comes from Frank Zappa's *Broadway the Hard Way* album. Here Zappa introduces "a very nice man named Sting" to the cheering audience, and the latter delivers a fervent version of the Police song "Murder by Numbers" while the band plays "Stolen Moments" in the background. You might dismiss this as a mere novelty, but Zappa's rock ensemble dishes up a first-class performance of the Nelson standard, and Sting seems quite enlivened by the proceedings.

RECOMMENDED VERSIONS

Eddie "Lockjaw" Davis (recorded as "The Stolen Moment"), from *Trane Whistle*, New York, September 20, 1960

Oliver Nelson (with Eric Dolphy, Bill Evans, and Freddie Hubbard), from *The Blues and the Abstract Truth*, Englewood Cliffs, New Jersey, February 23, 1961

Herbie Mann (with Chick Corea), from *Standing Ovation at Newport*, live at the Newport Jazz Festival, Newport, Rhode Island, July 3, 1965

Ahmad Jamal, from *The Awakening*, New York, February 2–3, 1970

Mark Murphy, from *Stolen Moments*, San Francisco, June 1, 1978

Carmen McRae and Betty Carter, from *The Carmen McRae/Betty Carter Duets*, live at The Great American Music Hall, San Francisco, January 30, 1987

Frank Zappa and Sting (recorded as part of "Murder by Numbers"), from *Broadway the Hard Way*, live at the Auditorium Theater, Chicago, March 3, 1988

Joe Locke and Kenny Barron, from *But Beautiful*, New York, August 1991

Stompin' at the Savoy
Composed by Edgar Sampson, Benny Goodman, and Chick Webb, with lyrics by Andy Razaf

This song, a cross between a pop tune and a riff-based jam chart, ranks among the most beloved dance numbers of the Swing Era. Its appeal has diminished among jazz fans today—for whom a song about a dance hall that closed more than a half-century ago holds little fascination. But even in its reduced state, "Stompin' at the Savoy" possesses enough pizzazz and recognition to retain its place in the standard repertoire.

The dance hall in question is the Savoy Ballroom, once the ultimate destination for lindy-hoppers and a landmark on Lenox Avenue in Harlem. And you can measure the extent of the stompin' by the fact that the owners needed to replace the maple dance floor every three years during the ballroom's heyday. The jitterbug originated at this nightspot, as did this song, forever linked with drummer Chick Webb, who led the house ensembles and would take on all comers—from Count Basie to Benny Goodman—in the most famous "battles of the bands" of the era. Webb died in his mid-thirties, and his personal contributions have been unfairly forgotten—in my opinion, he was the most exciting jazz drummer of his day—but the song remains.

Despite the multiple credits, Edgar Sampson—then a saxophonist with Webb's band—was the creative mind behind this catchy tune. The composition was originally an instrumental, but Andy Razaf later added words, which valiantly attempt to justify a love song for a sole proprietorship housed between 140th and 141st Streets. A few famous jazz singers have tried to deliver these lyrics with conviction, but most have wisely passed on them. Even though Ella got her start in Chick Webb's band, she avoided this song in later years, until Louis Armstrong enlisted her service in a now classic duet performance.

This piece may have failed as a vocal feature, but worked like a charm in a dance hall. And also at a jam session—pianist Nadi Qamar once told me the implausible tale of a marathon jam at Brother's, a Los Angeles after-hours club during the post–World War II era, during which musicians played "Stompin' at the Savoy" for two days straight. He claimed that he and the other musicians would take breaks, while others filled in for them, and after resting up, return to the bandstand to keep the song going.

Most cover versions today adopt a deliberately old-fashioned pose, but occasionally the song moves into the modern mainstream. I was happy to see Dave Holland and John Scofield tackle the tune on a 2002 recording, but wonder if that would have happened if the leader of the date had not been Roy Haynes, who was old enough to have heard fellow drummer Chick Webb live back when this song was new. I don't expect this piece to come back into the forefront of the repertoire—the way, for example, that "Caravan" (another mid-1930s big band number) has done in recent years—but the song's virtues should not be sold short. The changes are conducive for a blowing date, and even a young fan who has never encountered it before may be humming "Stompin' at the Savoy" after a single hearing. Certainly when a swinging dance number is needed in a pinch, a bandleader will be glad that the musicians on hand know how to play it.

RECOMMENDED VERSIONS

Chick Webb, New York, May 18, 1934

Benny Goodman, Chicago, January 24, 1936

Esquire All Stars (with Coleman Hawkins, Art Tatum, Jack Teagarden, and Roy
    Eldridge), live at the Metropolitan Opera House, New York, January 18, 1944

Art Tatum, from *The Art Tatum Solo Masterpieces, Vol. 5*, Los Angeles, December 29,
    1953

Clifford Brown and Max Roach, from *Brown and Roach, Incorporated*, Los Angeles,
    August 5, 1954

Art Pepper, from *Modern Art*, Los Angeles, December 28, 1956

Louis Armstrong and Ella Fitzgerald, from *Ella and Louis Again*, Los Angeles, July
    23, 1957

Eddie Daniels (with an arrangement by Peter Herbolzheimer), from *Swing Low
    Sweet Clarinet*, Frankfurt, November 8–12, 1999

Roy Haynes (with Dave Holland and John Scofield), from *Love Letters*, New York,
    May 23–24, 2002

Stormy Weather
Composed by Harold Arlen, with lyrics by Ted Koehler

Although plenty of instrumentalists have tackled "Stormy Weather" over the
years, it remains primarily a vocal feature, and many distinguished American
singers of the twentieth century have tried to put their stamp on it. Devotees still
debate who really "owns" this song. The two leading candidates: Lena Horne,
who sang "Stormy Weather" in the 1943 film of the same name, and Ethel Waters,
whose recording from 1933 has been honored by the Grammy Hall of Fame and
was one of the first "culturally, historically, or aesthetically important" performances enshrined in the Library of Congress's National Recording Registry.

Both divas offered classic interpretations, with Waters bringing out more of
a blues sensibility, while Horne delivers a finely etched torch song. If forced to
save up one for my stormy day, I would opt for Horne's rendition—if you
haven't seen it already, check out her riveting performance from the film, which
is readily accessible on the web; but Waters may actually get closer to what
Arlen and Koehler intended with this song, which was an evocation of black
vernacular music spruced up for the audience at the Cotton Club. To add to the
effect, Waters sang it against a log cabin backdrop—typical of the ersatz Southern rusticity regularly practiced at this Harlem nightspot—with a blue spotlight
on the singer.

These songwriting partners wrote music for eight Cotton Club revues in the early 1930s, and were expected to deliver material for a new production every six months. "Stormy Weather" was originally composed with Cab Calloway in mind, but by the time the *Cotton Club Parade of 1933* was ready for its debut, the Hi-De-Ho man was gone and responsibility for the song fell to Waters. Yet even before Waters recorded the song, composer Arlen made his own recording— and proved (here as elsewhere in his career) to be a persuasive interpreter of his oeuvre. William Zinsser, who later wrote extensively on standards, recalls that Arlen's plaintive vocal on this recording, brought home by his parents, was what first inspired his passion for the American popular song.

Arlen's version was a hit, as was Waters's and Duke Ellington's recording with Ivie Anderson. When Ellington made a short film featuring the song in May 1933, he introduced "Stormy Weather" by calling it "the most popular composition in recent years"—a fitting claim given the many successful versions that dominated the airwaves during the Great Depression.

Yet other contenders also deserve consideration here. We need to take into account Billie Holiday, who left behind an uncharacteristically lighthearted studio version of this melancholy song at a 1952 session, and an outstanding (if sonically inferior) live recording from Carnegie Hall in 1955, which finds her accompanied by Lester Young and Count Basie (on organ). Frank Sinatra gave us several studio recordings of "Stormy Weather," which span 40 years. On what may be his darkest and most brooding album, *No One Cares* from 1959, Sinatra delivers a powerful lament, with help from an ambitious Gordon Jenkins chart. Many other leading vocalists—including Louis Armstrong, Billy Eckstine, Ella Fitzgerald, Judy Garland, Betty Carter, Dinah Washington, Mel Tormé, Sarah Vaughan, Tony Bennett, and Joni Mitchell—have recorded their own personal interpretations.

The melody, with its upward interval leaps—evocative of someone checking out the stormy skies?—effectively captures the yearning sentiments of the lyrics. The latter strike me as a bit awkward with their self-conscious imitation of phrases one might find in an old blues song or even a spiritual—*can't get my poah self togethuh*—but the great singers pull it off, usually by reaching for the dramatic elements in words that, delivered too casually, might make a modern-day listener cringe.

Even among instrumental versions of this song, I prefer those with more gravitas. Charles Mingus's 1960 recording, which opens with an extended bass-and-sax duet with Eric Dolphy, is perhaps the best example, and bears comparison with the celebrated vocal versions of this popular song.

RECOMMENDED VERSIONS

Harold Arlen, New York, February 28, 1933

Ethel Waters, New York, May 3, 1933

Duke Ellington, New York, May 16, 1933

Lena Horne, from the soundtrack to the film *Stormy Weather*, Hollywood, January 1943

Billie Holiday (with Lester Young and Count Basie), from *Broadcast Performances, Vol. 2*, live at Carnegie Hall, New York, May 6, 1955

Frank Sinatra, from *No One Cares*, Los Angeles, March 24, 1959

Billy Eckstine, from *Once More with Feeling*, New York, 1960

Charles Mingus (with Eric Dolphy), from *Mingus*, New York, October 20, 1960

Mary Lou Williams, from *Live at the Keystone Korner*, live at the Keystone Korner, San Francisco, May 8, 1977

Woody Shaw (with Steve Turre), from *Imagination*, New York, June 24, 1987

Straight, No Chaser
Composed by Thelonious Monk

Jazz musicians frequently rely on the 12-bar blues progression for their compositions, but too often the opening and closing melody statements are merely formulaic—a simple riff which is little more than an excuse for a jam over familiar chords. Only a handful of jazz artists have been able to craft blues that sound like fully realized compositions, with personalities so defined that they retain their character even in the midst of the solos. Parker, Ellington, and Mingus were each capable of this feat, constructing blues that resisted the generic tendencies of the form, and artfully crystallized their own musical visions. But Thelonious Monk was preeminent in this regard, composing blues that bore the full weight of his ambitions, and which demand a rare degree of humility from those who want to perform them successfully.

"Straight, No Chaser" made its studio debut at Monk's July 23, 1951, Blue Note session, where he was joined by Milt Jackson and Sahib Shihab. Monk had just recorded with Jackson three weeks earlier, and at the end of his second chorus here, he quotes from "Misterioso," another Monk blues that he had brought to the previous session. Jackson had seemed a bit rattled by Monk's comping on "Misterioso," but sounds more comfortable on "Straight, No Chaser." Yet the melody on this blues is, if anything, even quirkier. Monk deconstructs a simple blues lick, and by displacing it in unpredictable ways—the flat third sometimes arrives on beat one, elsewhere on beat two, or a half-beat later, or on beat three or beat four—gives the piece a start-and-stop quality that is wholly original and unapologetically strident.

Not many other musicians were game to play this kind of blues, and no cover versions were recorded during the five years following Monk's launch of "Straight, No Chaser." Monk himself was the next to include it on an album, for his 1957 session with Gerry Mulligan. Miles Davis also adopted the song the following February for his *Milestones* project, which featured an 11-minute blowing version of the song. Cannonball Adderley recorded "Straight, No Chaser" exactly one month later at a session for EmArcy (which features a very Monkish solo from his brother Nat), and three months after that Miles and Cannonball, along with John Coltrane and Bill Evans, performed the song at the Newport Jazz Festival. These high-profile associations gave the composition great visibility in the jazz community, and by the early 1960s, "Straight, No Chaser" was showing up on recordings by a wide range of jazz artists—including Buddy Rich, Marian McPartland, Quincy Jones, Dave Grusin, Buddy DeFranco, and Shelly Manne—many of them with only the loosest connection to Thelonious Monk.

The more interesting performances of this song retain the spirit of Monk's original conception. Gil Evans's 1959 chart is an especially effective realization, helped along by the presence of saxophonist Steve Lacy. Keith Jarrett—who is not the first pianist one thinks of as an interpreter of Monk—delivers a very convincing rendition on his 1991 *Bye Bye Blackbird* trio project, one that is not in the least imitative but still shows insight into the distinctive character of the piece. Let me also call attention to two fine versions by lesser-known artists that you could easily miss. Bobby Timmons recorded a very clever version of "Straight, No Chaser" in 1967, with its own unique stop-and-start twists and a terrific chart by Tom McIntosh. Jessica Williams is also a very effective interpreter of Monk, and on the recording of her 1995 piano recital at the University of Victoria she presents a 15-minute version of "Straight, No Chaser" that warrants your closest attention—Williams even throw in a bit of "Misterioso," just the way the composer did back in 1951.

RECOMMENDED VERSIONS

Thelonious Monk, New York, July 23, 1951

Thelonious Monk and Gerry Mulligan, from *Mulligan Meets Monk*, New York, August 12, 1957

Miles Davis (with John Coltrane and Cannonball Adderley), from *Milestones*, New York, February 4, 1958

Cannonball Adderley (with Nat Adderley), from *Cannonball's Sharpshooters*, New York, March 4, 1958

Gil Evans (with Steve Lacy), from *Great Jazz Standards*, New York, early 1959

Bobby Timmons, from *Got to Get It*, New York, November 21, 1967

Kenny Barron, from *Green Chimneys*, Monster, Holland, July 9, 1983

Keith Jarrett (with the Standards Trio), from *Bye Bye Blackbird*, New York, October
12, 1991

Jessica Williams, from *The Victoria Concert*, live at the University of Victoria,
Victoria, Canada, September 15, 1995

Struttin' with Some Barbecue
Composed by Lil Hardin Armstrong

Louis Armstrong's famous "Struttin' with Some Barbecue" is credited to his
wife, accompanist, and sometime employer of the period, Lil Hardin. But if you
think the trumpeter was grateful, think again. The two battled over the rights to
the composition, although Armstrong eventually gave way . . . but only after she
filed a lawsuit—yes, a custody battle, but over a tune instead of a child. Although
Armstrong lost out to his former spouse, he still refused to acknowledge her
authorship. As late as 1967, Satchmo was still telling people that he came up
with the idea for the song while eating some barbecue ribs with drummer Zutty
Singleton. With more than 600 recordings to its credit, this song has certainly
proven that it was worth the battle.

The melody is mostly built from chord tones, in some instances actually
spelling out the entire chord—an approach in keeping with Hardin's keyboard
style and thus reinforcing her claim to the song. But the repeated use of the
major seventh, instead of the flat seventh so common in the blues-oriented
repertoires of New Orleans bands, imparts a more carefree, relaxed ambiance
to the proceedings—and one can see this trademark sound as evidence of Armstrong's authorship. "The man loved that major seventh, frequently used it in
his improvisations and gravitated towards songs that were built around it—
such as 'When It's Sleepy Time Down South,'" remarks Armstrong expert
Ricky Riccardi. "Lil might have had something to do with the verse or the cute
Hot Five arrangement of 'Struttin' with Some Barbecue,' but I think it reeks of
Louis."

Although Armstrong recorded "Struttin' with Some Barbecue" on numerous occasions, his first version is the most famous. The ensemble's sound
is still shaped by the conventions of early New Orleans jazz, but something new
has also entered the mix—an emphasis on the individual soloist, whose improvisational skills now take center stage. And for "Struttin' with Some Barbecue,"
Armstrong steps forward in that heroic role, setting an example that would be
followed by the later leading soloists of small combo jazz.

The closest anyone came to eclipsing this version was Armstrong himself. His 1938 version is faster and more virtuosic, showing off his high notes. Here the piece is in F (rather than A flat as on the 1927 recording), but the band modulates to B flat before his final choruses, allowing Satchmo to cap off the performance with a bravura high D. Less flamboyant, but equally interesting, are the modernistic flourishes in the arrangement (by Chappie Willet) and Armstrong's horn part, both of which include elements that anticipate the coming bebop revolution. This "Struttin'" was looking ahead, not behind.

Other jazz artists didn't start covering this song until the mid-1940s, and it only became entrenched as a standard with the trad jazz revival. Dixieland bands tended to play it in F rather than A flat, suggesting that they were taking their cue from the later Armstrong performances rather than the Hot Five original. Fans are more familiar with the latter, but trumpeters as different in temperament as Maynard Ferguson and Bobby Hackett have cited the 1938 rendition as one of their personal favorites.

Most modern versions of this song have been deferential rather than exploratory, yet some artists have put a new spin to the old song. Gil Evans recorded his arrangement just a few weeks before he began working with Miles Davis on *Porgy and Bess*, and took a number of unconventional steps, including assigning the melody to tuba(!) and featuring Cannonball Adderley in a hot, bop-oriented solo. A few years later, Paul Desmond recorded "Samba with Some Barbecue" with a Brazilian jazz accompaniment in a version that also includes a very pleasing Herbie Hancock two-chorus solo. Anat Cohen has followed in this tradition, mixing up Armstrong's tune with "Samba de Orfeu" in a New Orleans-meets-Rio arrangement.

Armstrong tribute recordings often draw on this now-venerable song, and artists of varying predilections and affinities have interpreted it in novel ways, yet the majority of cover versions have been recorded by trumpeters, who remain its most loyal fans. For my part, I prefer hearing this song played for fun and entertainment rather than with too much obeisance. Certainly those who associate the music of the Big Easy with parties and good times will find a suitable soundtrack to their New Orleans fantasies in this number. Nonetheless, one of the most moving memorials came amidst mourning from pianist Earl Hines—with whom Armstrong had a productive if sometimes contentious relationship—who recorded "Struttin' with Some Barbecue" in a solo piano version two weeks after the trumpeter's death.

RECOMMENDED VERSIONS

Louis Armstrong, Chicago, December 9, 1927

Louis Armstrong, Los Angeles, January 12, 1938

Gil Evans, from *The Complete Pacific Jazz Sessions*, New York, May 21, 1958

Ed Thigpen (with Herbie Hancock and Kenny Burrell), from *Out of the Storm*, Englewood Cliffs, New Jersey, April 18, 1966

Paul Desmond (recorded as "Samba with Some Barbecue"), from *Summertime*, New York, November 20, 1968

Earl Hines, from *My Tribute to Louis*, Wisconsin, July 18, 1971

The Marsalis Family, from *A Jazz Celebration* (Marsalis Music), New Orleans, August 4, 2001

Anat Cohen, from *Noir*, New York, August 2006

Summertime
Composed by George Gershwin, with lyrics by DuBose Heyward

The experts have disputed endlessly on how to classify this song. Gershwin himself thought he had composed a lullaby. Composer and song scholar Alec Wilder, for his part, refused to consider "Summertime" in his book *American Popular Song* because, in his opinion, it belonged to the world of opera. Others have tried to show a connection between Gershwin's composition and the spiritual "Sometimes I Feel Like a Motherless Child" or link it to blues-oriented songs such as W. C. Handy's "St. Louis Blues." Musicologist Peter Van der Merwe, in contrast, has suggested that the piece has more in common with the music of Antonín Dvořák, while Wayne Shirley of the Library of Congress has argued that the main harmonies of "Summertime" are derived from the "Tristan chord" (F, B, D#, and G#) of Richard Wagner. Then again, both the original 1935 production of *Porgy and Bess* and the 1942 revival took place on Broadway, where the connection with American musical theater would have been more obvious.

Note that no one on this laundry list has even hinted that "Summertime" is primarily a jazz song. Jazz musicians, for their part, were slow in appreciating the potential of this piece (although they would later take quite a fancy to it). In the late 1930s, at the height of the Swing Era, few big bands showed any interest in "Summertime," except for Bob Crosby, who relied on it as a theme song. The two most compelling jazz recordings from this decade come from small combo sessions by Billie Holiday and Sidney Bechet, but though these are much cherished nowadays, they had little influence at the time in convincing other name bandleaders to embrace "Summertime." That would not happen until the 1942 revival of *Porgy and Bess* proved that Gershwin's "folk opera"—now pared down and made less operatic—could also be a commercial success.

As a result, the cover versions of "Summertime" increased markedly after the end of the American Federation of Musicians strike that curtailed recording from 1942 until 1944. Artie Shaw, who had appeared on Billie Holiday's 1936 recording, revived the song with his own band for a very bluesy 1945 performance, which features an arrangement by Eddie Sauter and a well-known plunger mute solo by Roy Eldridge. Duke Ellington, who had expressed reservations about *Porgy and Bess* on its debut—bluntly arguing that it "does not use the Negro musical idiom" and suggesting that Gershwin had "borrowed from everyone from Liszt to Dickie Wells' kazoo band"—had also come around by this time; he featured "Summertime" at his December 1943 Carnegie Hall concert and returned to it periodically in later years. Ellington's strident trio performance of "Summertime" from 1961 deserves to be far better known, and sounds as if the pianist were intent on proving that he could still be cutting edge in the midst of the increasingly avant-garde jazz environment of the day.

More than 400 jazz cover versions of "Summertime" were recorded during the 1950s and 1960s. Among the best known are Miles Davis's performance from his *Porgy and Bess* project with Gil Evans, but I must admit to disappointment that Davis, the consummate ballad player of his era, delivers the song in a perky, medium-tempo arrangement on this, his sole studio recording of the song, rather than return to the thoughtful intimacy of Gershwin's original conception. The only other jazz interpretation of "Summertime" from the period to match Davis's in crossover appeal is Louis Armstrong and Ella Fitzgerald's collaboration, recorded exactly one year earlier—and here these two artists, both known to show more than a little irreverence in their interpretations, stick surprisingly close to the composer's vision of a Catfish Row lullaby.

Later arrangements have been even more varied, and Gershwin's composition has been interpreted in every possible manner. No baby will be lulled to sleep by Albert Ayler's sax shrieks and moans, which repeatedly move inside and outside of the chord changes and bend the notes until they are torn off the staff lines. Joshua Redman, supported by Brad Mehldau, has pushed "Summertime" ahead in a lopsided 5/4 time. Eddie Jefferson, for his part, has added hip and ironic new lyrics—*Your daddy is rich, your mamma don't care, your sister's got dough to go any ol' where.* And if you want to hear "Summertime" handled in whatever other manner—salsa, hip-hop, country and western, reggae, you name it—there is a recording out there for you waiting somewhere.

By the way, if you call this song at a jam session, be sure to confer on the key before counting in the tempo. The original Gershwin score is written in B minor, but the song is often played by jazz musicians in A minor nowadays. Young sax tyros may want to emulate John Coltrane, who takes it all the way down in a very dark-sounding D minor. A trumpeter who has memorized Miles Davis's famous solo will come out swinging in B flat minor. And any trad jazz player who learns "Summertime" from the famous Sidney Bechet record will opt for G minor.

RECOMMENDED VERSIONS

Billie Holiday, New York, July 10, 1936

Sidney Bechet, New York, June 8, 1939

Artie Shaw (with Roy Eldridge), Hollywood, April 17, 1945

Louis Armstrong and Ella Fitzgerald, from *Porgy and Bess*, Los Angeles, August 18, 1957

Miles Davis (with Gil Evans), from *Porgy and Bess*, New York, August 18, 1958

John Coltrane, from *My Favorite Things*, New York, October 24, 1960

Duke Ellington, from *Piano in the Foreground*, Hollywood, March 1, 1961

Bill Evans, from *How My Heart Sings*, New York, May 17, 1962

Art Blakey (with Sonny Stitt and McCoy Tyner), from *A Jazz Message*, New York, July 16, 1963

Joshua Redman (with Brad Mehldau), from *Timeless Tales (for Changing Times)*, New York, circa 1998

Greg Osby (with Nicholas Payton), from *St. Louis Shoes*, Brooklyn, January 22–23, 2003

Sweet Georgia Brown

Composed by Ben Bernie and Maceo Pinkard, with lyrics by Kenneth Casey

You've probably never heard of Brother Bones and his Shadows. And the good Brother's combination of playing the bones—originally cow ribs that he secured at the slaughterhouse—while whistling with his old God-given puckeroo is hardly a recipe for a hit recording. But if you are familiar with the song "Sweet Georgia Brown," you have no doubt encountered Brother Bones's 1949 recording, which was picked up as a theme song by the Harlem Globetrotters three years later. As the Globetrotters trotted the globe, they brought this recording with them. Devotees of the bones—may their numbers increase!—will tell you that this track ranks as one of the ten most widely heard recordings in history.

The song had already been around a quarter of a century by the time it showed up on the hardwood. Ben Bernie, who composed the tune along with Maceo Pinkard and Kenneth Casey, also enjoyed the first hit recording of "Sweet Georgia Brown"—his rendition, surprisingly swinging for a white hotel dance band of the era, was the number one song in America for more than a month during the summer of 1925. Ethel Waters and Isham Jones also enjoyed big sellers with their versions later that year. Jones was again involved when "Sweet

Georgia Brown" returned to the charts seven years later, but now as accompanist for crooner Bing Crosby. The song enjoyed another burst of airplay in the late 1940s, when both Joe Liggins and the aforementioned Brother Bones earned hits with their R&B-oriented versions.

During the mid-1930s, a number of outstanding jazz recordings were made of this composition but most of them came out of Europe. Coleman Hawkins recorded "Sweet Georgia Brown" in Paris, helped along by Benny Carter (on trumpet) and Django Reinhardt, who dominates the rhythm section—listen to it the first time for the horn contributions, but then play it again to savor the sweet fury of the guitar accompaniment. In December 1937, Reinhardt followed up with a duet recording alongside violinist Stéphane Grappelli, and a month later performed "Sweet Georgia Brown" with his Quintette du Hot Club de France at a London session. Other tracks from various bands in Paris, London, and Brussels testify to the popularity abroad of this American song, even before the Globetrotters took it on their Grand Tour.

The song stayed in the jazz repertoire throughout the big band era and was quickly adopted by the beboppers. The very first recording of Charlie Parker and Dizzy Gillespie—made in Room 305 of the Savoy Hotel in Chicago in 1943—captures them playing "Sweet Georgia Brown." Bud Powell's trio performance from 1950 may be even more noteworthy, a high-speed outing that ranks among the most exciting bop piano recordings of the era. Another trio track from this period finds vibraphonist Red Norvo joined by guitarist Tal Farlow and bassist Charles Mingus in an uninhibited workout that—like this combo's entire output—deserves greater recognition. Miles Davis borrowed the chord changes of "Sweet Georgia Brown" for his composition "Dig," a regular part of his repertoire during the early 1950s, and Thelonious Monk did the same for his "Bright Mississippi."

The popularity of this progression among jazz musicians is well warranted. The harmonies, which move leisurely from dominant chord to dominant chord, are ideal for supporting blues and funk licks of every denomination; and the final resolution offers a pleasant surprise since the tonic chord doesn't appear in the first 12 bars of the song, an opening that proves in retrospect to be a masterful exercise in misdirection. Finally, thanks to endless proselytizing by a world-famous group of itinerant basketball players, the song is invariably recognized and greeted with enthusiasm by audiences everywhere, no matter how modest their jazz expertise.

Even so, "Sweet Georgia Brown" has gradually turned into a period piece. Close to 500 recordings were made during the 1950s and 1960s, but increasingly the song fell into the domain of trad jazz bands, with cutting-edge players only occasionally giving it a chance. Not much has changed in the intervening years. Certainly the composition is capable of updating and reconfiguration—if you doubt it, check out Denny Zeitlin's drastic reharmonization from 2003. For the most part, though, if you hear this song at the jazz club nowadays, the treatment will be painfully quaint or tongue-in-cheek.

RECOMMENDED VERSIONS

Ben Bernie and His Hotel Roosevelt Orchestra, New York, March 19, 1925

Ethel Waters, New York, May 13, 1925

Cab Calloway, New York, July 9, 1931

Bing Crosby (with the Isham Jones Orchestra), Chicago, April 23, 1932

Coleman Hawkins (with Benny Carter and Django Reinhardt), Paris, April 28, 1937

Django Reinhardt (with the Quintette du Hot Club de France), London, January 31, 1938

Art Tatum, live at Monroe's Uptown House, New York, September 16, 1941

Charlie Parker and Dizzy Gillespie, Chicago, February 15, 1943

Bud Powell, New York, February 1950

Red Norvo (with Charles Mingus and Tal Farlow), Chicago, circa 1950

Anita O'Day, from *Jazz on a Summer's Day*, live at the Newport Jazz Festival, Newport, Rhode Island, July 7, 1958

Oscar Peterson, from *Live at the Blue Note*, live at the Blue Note, New York, March 16, 1990

Denny Zeitlin, from *Slickrock*, Brooklyn, August 23–24, 2003

'S Wonderful
Composed by George Gershwin, with lyrics by Ira Gershwin

George and Ira Gershwin's *Funny Face* seemed destined for failure even before it arrived on Broadway. The show was in such bad shape before its Philadelphia world premiere that opening night needed to be delayed, and the eventual debut was received with little enthusiasm. Attendance soon fell off, and as the musical comedy went on the road, the producers desperately tinkered with every aspect and detail during a six-week crisis period of (in Ira Gershwin's words) "recasting, rewriting, rehearsing, recriminating—of rejoicing, there was none." By the time *Funny Face* arrived in Wilmington, Delaware, virtually every performance brought with it more modifications. Along the way, "almost enough scenery and costumes were discarded," reported *The New York Times*, "to outfit another musical show."

Yet miracles sometimes happen on Broadway, and not just in the final act: *Funny Face* proved to be a hit when it opened in New York, running for 244 performances and spurring a London production. Hollywood picked it up for a film adaptation, although not until three decades had elapsed, and then much of the plot was changed. Only four songs were retained from the original show—one of these was "'S Wonderful," a tune that would almost become more closely associated with dancers than jazz musicians. Onstage, it served as a vehicle for Adele and Fred Astaire, and the latter also danced to "'S Wonderful" in the movie adaptation of *Funny Face*, where his partner is Audrey Hepburn, some 30 years younger than her leading man. When the song appeared in the 1951 film *An American in Paris*, Gene Kelly delivered the vocals and accompanying tap dance.

Gershwin assisted the hoofers by writing a song easy on the vocal cords. The melody stays within a range of less than an octave and is built largely on repeated notes, chord tones, and modest intervallic leaps—along with plenty of rests. If Frank Sinatra, as has been commonly reported, swam laps underwater to help him deliver long phrases without taking a breath, he could have prepared for this song with a toddler's wading pool. "Its verse is a monotony of imitative phrases which no amount of adroit harmony can leaven," is the perhaps overly harsh verdict of song connoisseur Alec Wilder.

Benny Goodman recorded a pristine quartet rendition with Teddy Wilson and Lionel Hampton in 1938, but "'S Wonderful" didn't figure prominently in the jazz repertoire until the mid-1940s. Coleman Hawkins is joined by Roy Eldridge and, again, Teddy Wilson on his excellent 1944 performance. Another former Goodman pianist, Mel Powell, would be closely associated with this song, recording it in the 1940s and 1950s, and featuring it again during his brief return to jazz in the 1980s, after a long hiatus as a classical composer.

Few Gershwin songs have shown themselves so capable of reinvention, reinterpretation, and—yes, finally!—rejoicing. "'S Wonderful" has worked as a swing, bop, or trad chart; as stride or Latin; hot or cool. A half-century after the Gershwins wrote it, the song was recast as a bossa nova tune by João Gilberto—and the very low-key qualities that Wilder castigated make it effective in this different idiom. You might even think that Antonio Carlos Jobim composed it, not Gershwin, based on how singers such as Diana Krall tackle it today.

RECOMMENDED VERSIONS

Frankie Trumbauer, New York, April 27, 1936

Benny Goodman (with Teddy Wilson and Lionel Hampton), Chicago, October 12, 1938

Coleman Hawkins (with Roy Eldridge and Teddy Wilson), New York, January 31, 1944

Artie Shaw, New York, January 9, 1945

Herbie Nichols, New York, March 6, 1952

Lennie Tristano (with Lee Konitz), from *Live at the Confucius Restaurant 1955*, live at the Sing Song Room of the Confucius Restaurant, New York, June 11, 1955

João Gilberto, from *Amoroso*, New York and Los Angeles, November 17–19, 1976, and January 3–7, 1977

Mel Powell (with Benny Carter and Louie Bellson), from *The Return of Mel Powell*, live on the SS *Norway*, Caribbean Sea, October 21, 1987

Diana Krall, from *The Look of Love*, Hollywood, June 3–4, 2001

T

Take Five
Composed by Paul Desmond

"Take Five" may be the most unlikely hit record of its era. It became the first instrumental modern jazz single on the *Billboard* Hot 100 to sell a million copies—and was also one of the last. Even more peculiar, the song was written in 5/4, a meter that had never been used before in American popular music and had hardly existed in jazz before Dave Brubeck recorded "Take Five." To add to the obstacles, the suits at the record label were opposed to releasing "Take Five" as a single, until Goddard Lieberson, the president of Columbia Records, prodded them into issuing it.

In truth, even the composer had little faith in "Take Five." Brubeck had asked Paul Desmond, alto saxophonist with his quartet, to write a piece for *Time Out*, an album that would focus on jazz songs in unusual time signatures. Desmond toyed with two different concepts for a song in 5/4—the first was a minor key melody over a vamp, while the second was a major key pattern over shifting harmonies. Desmond eventually took Brubeck's advice, and combined these two contrasting themes into a single song. But he remained skeptical. "I still think, basically, it was a dubious idea at best. . . . I thought it was kind of a throwaway. I was ready to trade the entire rights of 'Take Five' for a used Ronson electric razor."

Yet the song's success is far from inexplicable. When jazz songs become popular hits, they often feature catchy vamps played by the rhythm section—as witnessed, for example, by Mongo Santamaría's "Watermelon Man," Ahmad Jamal's "Poinciana," Lee Morgan's "The Sidewinder," and Cal Tjader's "Soul Sauce." Brubeck followed this formula with his comping on "Take Five." Although some have griped that he should have taken more chances with the 5/4 groove—as he would do in later performances of the song—instead of staying within the confines of a repeated vamp, this very conservatism no doubt proved the key ingredient in turning an experimental concept into a hit single. The solos are played over the vamp, with the bridge used only for the opening and closing melody statements.

But even instrumental hit songs require words. In a 1961 letter to his father, Emil Breitenfeld, Desmond enlisted his help in writing lyrics to "Take Five" in anticipation of the quartet's recording with vocalist Carmen McRae. Dad apparently failed to deliver, since a short while later McRae did the date singing words provided by Dave Brubeck with assistance from his wife Iola. These lyrics were later adopted by Al Jarreau for his popular recording of "Take Five" from his Grammy-winning 1977 project *Look to the Rainbow*, which introduced a new generation of fans to this song.

Although some no doubt considered this song a novelty at the time of its initial release, Brubeck and Desmond have been vindicated by the subsequent dissemination of the unusual meters they championed back in the 1950s. The 5/4 meter is far more widely used by jazz musicians nowadays, and I suspect that, for many of them, this was the first 5/4 piece they learned. Sad to say, student and semi-professional bands often add this to their set list before they really have a good grasp of odd metrics, and as a result you are likely to hear far too many lackluster versions of "Take Five." It has certainly shown up in some very unjazzy settings over the years—rapped over and sampled, played by marching bands and sung by choirs. Desmond's biographer Doug Ramsey tells of finding a carved music box in a small shop off a main street in Prague that, when opened, played the opening bars of "Take Five." And I am sure I will hear it on a cell phone ringtone someday soon. But though the song may have lost much of its capacity to surprise, given its taken-for-granted familiarity, it still can delight.

And do some good deeds too. When Paul Desmond passed away in 1977, his will stipulated that royalties from this song and his other compositions go to the American Red Cross. Since then, the Red Cross has received more than $6 million from Desmond's bequest. The Red Cross has reciprocated by naming a training room in its Washington, D.C., headquarters after the alto saxophonist.

RECOMMENDED VERSIONS

Dave Brubeck (with Paul Desmond), from *Time Out*, New York, July 1, 1959

Dave Brubeck (with Paul Desmond), from *At Carnegie Hall*, live at Carnegie Hall, New York, February 22, 1963

George Benson, from *Bad Benson*, Englewood Cliffs, New Jersey, May 29–30 and June 20, 1974

Paul Desmond (with Ed Bickert), from *Live,* live at Bourbon Street, Toronto, October 25–November 1, 1975

Al Jarreau, from *Look to the Rainbow,* January–February 1977

Carmen McRae, from *Upside Down,* live at the Montreux Jazz Festival, Montreux, Switzerland, July 22, 1982

Tito Puente, from *Mambo Diablo,* San Francisco, May 1985

Anthony Braxton, from *20 Standards,* live at Teatro Filarmonico, Verona, Italy, November 17, 2003

Take the A Train
Composed by Billy Strayhorn

How could the Ellington band adopt a signature theme song not written by Ellington? But the battle between ASCAP and radio stations in the early 1940s forced Duke to keep his ASCAP-represented songs off the airwaves. Duke had been using "Sepia Panorama" as his theme, but now needed a substitute. Fortunately his frequent collaborator Billy Strayhorn—who was not an ASCAP member and thus not restricted by the ban—helped keep the band on the radio with his contributions to the orchestra's repertoire, including "Take the A Train."

Strayhorn had been working on the piece as early as 1939, but was hesitant about presenting it to Ellington because he feared that it sounded like the type of song that Fletcher Henderson, an Ellington rival, might use. The lyrics were reportedly inspired by the directions Strayhorn needed to follow for his first New York meeting with Duke—instructions that included the admonition "take the A train." Ellington's decision to adopt the song as his new theme was validated by its immense success. His February 1941 recording stayed on the chart for seven weeks, and soon the tune was picked up by other bandleaders.

Within the next year the song showed up in the repertoires of Glenn Miller, Cab Calloway, Stan Kenton, and others. Not all of the Ellington imitators, however, were playing close attention—at least if we can believe the perhaps apocryphal tale of Lawrence Welk introducing Strayhorn's classic as follows: "Now we're going to play the song, 'Take a Train.'" In a different version of this anecdote, the garbled title is attributed to club owner Billy Berg. In either case, the story testifies to the fame of the song, which was so popular that even the least hip folks were expected to know it.

The hook in the melody stems from its willingness to land emphatically on the flat fifth—the most modern and unstable of the blue notes—in the opening phrase. The effect is jarring but in an uplifting way, and demonstrates that what most Tin Pan Alley composers might have dismissed as excessive dissonance could, in the context of the Ellington band, serve as the most memorable moment in a hit song.

Ellington couldn't help tinkering with his collaborator's efforts, and at the band's 1948 Carnegie Hall concert he presented a different version of "A Train" under the name "Manhattan Murals," with his own name listed as co-composer. The revised chart is full of surprises and dramatic effects and proved, once again, that Ellington himself could be more radical in reinventing his band's material than the modern jazz players who covered these same works.

"Take the A Train" remains a favorite among musicians and fans, and has become so well known that many outside the jazz arena—from Charlie Watts of the Rolling Stones to the rock-pop band Chicago—have tried it on for size. Like other Ellington-Strayhorn standards, "Take the A Train" is often interpreted with reverent fidelity as a period piece, yet some have managed successful reconfigurations. Clifford Brown and Max Roach mounted a hot hard bop takeover of the tune in 1955, and even do a better job than the Duke at mimicking the sound of an actual train. Among the various solo piano versions, Michel Petrucciani's riveting boogie-woogie arrangement rises far above the usual clichés of that idiom, while Sun Ra's live performance in Italy from 1977 manages somehow to respect the original spirit of the composition while gradually layering on various avant-garde elements, eventually ending with a pedal-to-the-metal explosion that threatens to derail the proceedings. But no tour of "Take the A Train" is complete if it doesn't include composer Billy Strayhorn's own performance, captured in an elegant arrangement with strings from 1961.

RECOMMENDED VERSIONS

Duke Ellington, Hollywood, February 15, 1941

Cab Calloway, New York, July 3, 1941

Bob Wills and His Texas Playboys, San Francisco, August 30, 1947

Duke Ellington (performed under the title "Manhattan Murals"), live at Carnegie Hall, New York, November 13, 1948

Clifford Brown/Max Roach Quintet, from *A Study in Brown*, New York, February 23, 1955

Billy Strayhorn, from *The Peaceful Side of Billy Strayhorn*, Paris, May 1961

Sun Ra, from *Piano Recital*, live at the Teatro La Fenice, Venice, November 24, 1977

Joe Henderson, from *Lush Life: The Music of Billy Strayhorn*, Englewood Cliffs, New Jersey, September 3–8, 1991

Michel Petrucciani, from *Solo Live*, live at Alte Opera, Frankfurt, February 27, 1997

Tea for Two
Composed by Vincent Youmans, with lyrics by Irving Caesar

The popularity of this tune among jazz musicians is a bit of a puzzle—the melody is monotonous and akin to a second-rate nursery song. In fact, I would rather play "Mary Had a Little Lamb" or "On the Good Ship Lollipop": at least those melodies won't stick in your head like a chronic migraine. The chord changes to "Tea for Two" are your typical ii-V fare, and the B theme sounds suspiciously similar to the A theme, almost as if musical phrases were being rationed and recycled in a time of shortage. Of the lyrics, the less said the better.

Give lyricist Irving Caesar credit for admitting, years later in an interview with Steve Allen, that the words were just supposed to be temporary fillers, replaced later by something more profound. But no later fixing took place—or was needed: the song and its musical, *No, No, Nanette*, were successes, and both would be revived periodically in future years. Even so, the show had a hidden cost: a fanciful—and possibly true—legend claims that producer Harry Frazee raised money for *No, No, Nanette* by selling Babe Ruth, then a player for Frazee's Boston Red Sox, to the Yankees. For this reason alone, those Boston-bred Berklee College of Music students ought to insist on a perpetual boycott of this tune.

Yet "Tea for Two" has enjoyed widespread popularity, not just with the general public—no accounting for their tastes, after all—but even in highbrow circles. Dmitri Shostakovich scored a very dainty arrangement of it, and it even got him in trouble with Soviet Union authorities for its *decadent Western influences*. Piano virtuoso Vladimir Horowitz developed his own version of the song, which was recorded but never released. Put these beside the more than 700 jazz recordings and you would need a massive tea set to serve all the famous artists who have put their stamp on the Vincent Youmans tune.

Art Tatum featured the song as a keyboard showpiece when he arrived in New York and recorded a bravura solo version at his celebrated March 1933 session for the Brunswick label. At a now-legendary cutting contest, he relied on this number to beat into submission an all-star assembly of New York's finest jazz pianists, including Fats Waller, James P. Johnson, and Willie "The Lion" Smith. "When Tatum played 'Tea for Two' that night, I guess that was the first time I ever heard it really played," the great James P. later recalled. Tatum's recording does little to persuade me of the significance of the song, but does show what a formidable pianist Tatum was at age 23.

Fats Waller clearly wasn't shaken enough to hand the song over to Tatum, and offered up his own solo version in 1937—an uncharacteristically graceful and subdued performance from this often raucous performer. That same year, Benny Goodman performed it with an all-star quartet and Django Reinhardt recorded it in Paris. In fact, Reinhardt tackled "Tea for Two" on five separate occasions in the period leading up to World War II. My favorite is his 1937 solo version, with its impressive reworking of the song's underlying harmonies.

I suspect that the ease with which this song is adapted to ulterior purposes is what keeps it in the jazz repertoire. The best jazz versions have a certain extravagance about them. Mark Levine has recorded an Afro-Cuban version (under the name "Te Para Dos") that might make you think that the composers had written it with a *montuno* in mind. And for other subversive examples, just listen to Dave Brubeck's bold conception of the standard from his first trio session for the Fantasy label, Bud Powell's blistering version recorded the following year, or Thelonious Monk's quirky interpretation from 1963.

Even more intriguing than the version Monk recorded, however, was the one he might have made three months earlier, when both the high priest of bop and the famous concert pianist Vladimir Horowitz were present at Columbia's New York studio on the same day. This was the occasion when Horowitz recorded his never released version of "Tea for Two." I enjoy speculating on what might have happened if Monk had joined Horowitz in a duet to show him how it should be played.

RECOMMENDED VERSIONS

Art Tatum, New York, March 21, 1933

Benny Goodman (with Lionel Hampton, Teddy Wilson, and Gene Krupa), New York, February 3, 1937

Fats Waller, New York, June 11, 1937

Django Reinhardt, Paris, December 28, 1937

Dave Brubeck, San Francisco, September 1949

Bud Powell (with Ray Brown and Buddy Rich), New York, June–July 1950

Thelonious Monk from *Criss Cross*, New York, February 26, 1963

Norma Winstone, from *Somewhere Called Home*, Oslo, July 1986

Mark Levine (recorded as "Te Para Dos"), from *Isla*, Berkeley, California, 2002

Tenderly
Composed by Walter Gross, with lyrics by Jack Lawrence

During a chance encounter at a publisher's office in 1946, Margaret Whiting told Jack Lawrence about a fantastic melody she had heard that was begging for suitable words. She brought Lawrence to the nearby offices of the Musicraft label, where pianist and record executive Walter Gross sat at the keyboard and played the piece, a winsome waltz with wide, yearning intervals. The song was hardly hit material—then as now, few waltzes showed up on the *Billboard* charts—and must have seemed more like a parlor piano piece than a jukebox number. But Lawrence asked for a lead sheet, and found that the song's melody stayed in his head over the following days.

He soon returned to Gross with the words to the song, which he had now christened "Tenderly." But the composer was unimpressed. Alec Wilder would later gripe that the melody is a poor fit with the title word, since it forces the singer to put an unnatural stress on the last syllable of the word: *ten-der-leeee*. Gross, for his part, had a different complaint: he thought the name was better suited to serve as directions to the performer—*play this song tenderly*—than a formal title. He dismissed Lawrence with some curt words, and that seemed to put an end to the matter.

Yet Lawrence continued to perform the song for publishers, and eventually managed to convince Gross to accept an offer with E. H. Morris Music. A short while later, Sarah Vaughan's vocal recording and an instrumental version by Randy Brooks introduced audiences to the unconventional pop song, and over the next several years, a number of popular jazz musicians—Woody Herman, Harry James, Erroll Garner—embraced "Tenderly." In 1952 Rosemary Clooney enjoyed a surprising crossover success with the song, achieving a million seller with her version of the waltz. The following year, "Tenderly" showed up in the MGM film *Torch Song*—where it was ostensibly sung by the unlikely torch singer Joan Crawford (although vocals were actually provided behind the scenes by India Adams).

The song has been adopted as a virtuoso piano showpiece, recorded multiple times by Art Tatum, Oscar Peterson, Phineas Newborn Jr., Paul Smith, and other similarly extroverted keyboardists. The song also works for jazz singers, Wilder's reservation notwithstanding, as demonstrated by Nat King Cole, or on the popular 1956 pairing of Ella Fitzgerald and Louis Armstrong (with Ella's clever parody of Satchmo at the end). Finally "Tenderly" has enjoyed underground success as a platform for more avant-garde players—hear, for example, Eric Dolphy's solo sax version from 1960, or the titanic 1994 performance by David S. Ware (joined by Matthew Shipp), whose fractious sparring comes across as a deliberate renunciation of the title.

And "Tenderly" doesn't need to stay in waltz time. A number of artists—including Dexter Gordon, Bud Powell, Gary Burton, and Mongo Santamaría—have shown that this composition also works in a range of 4/4 beats, and my friend Jeff Sultanof tells me he has a killing chart of "Tenderly" in 7/4 on his shelf, waiting for the right orchestra to come along and play it.

RECOMMENDED VERSIONS

Sarah Vaughan, New York, July 2, 1947

Woody Herman (with Gene Ammons and Bill Harris), Los Angeles, July 20, 1949

Rosemary Clooney, New York, November 21, 1951

Art Tatum, from *The Art Tatum Solo Masterpieces, Vol. 3*, Los Angeles, December 28, 1953

Louis Armstrong and Ella Fitzgerald, from *Ella and Louis*, Los Angeles, August 16, 1956

Eric Dolphy, from *Far Cry*, Englewood Cliffs, New Jersey, December 21, 1960

Oscar Peterson, from *À la Salle Pleyel*, live at Salle Pleyel, Paris, March 17, 1975

David S. Ware (with Matthew Shipp), from *Earthquation*, New York, May 4–5, 1994

Gary Burton, from *Departure*, New York, September 20–22, 1996

There Is No Greater Love
Composed by Isham Jones, with lyrics by Marty Symes

Isham Jones (the first name is pronounced with a long "i" as in ice) is a mostly forgotten figure in American music, yet in his day this contemporary of Paul Whiteman led one of the finest dance bands in the nation. During the course of the 1920s, Jones ranked among the biggest-selling recording artists with seven #1 hits to his credit. Yet if jazz fans now recognize the name today, it is probably due to Jones's connection with Woody Herman, who took over the band after the leader retreated (temporarily, as it turned out) from the music world at the dawn of the Swing Era. Yet, to some degree, Jones had helped bring about this shift in the public's taste, with his incorporation of blues-based material in his band's repertoire, his adoption of a streamlined, jazz instrumentation in place of the sugary violins of earlier dance orchestras, and the perfectionism that led him to fill his band with first-rate jazz talent. Jones never sought a reputation as a leader of a hot band, and even objected to the term "jazz," preferring that his work be called "American dance music," but his contributions to the jazz idiom are nonetheless significant.

Jones was also a talented arranger and composer, and his legacy lives on in the jazz world through his songs, including "It Had to Be You," "On the Alamo," "The One I Love (Belongs to Somebody Else)," and "There Is No Greater Love." For the debut recording of the latter song, Jones assigned the vocal to 22-year-old Woody Herman, whom he had hired because the young man was a triple threat: singer, dancer, and saxophonist. But Herman had not seen himself as a ballad singer until Jones recast him in that mold. Audiences responded favorably to the young vocalist, and "There Is No Greater Love" was a top 20 hit in April 1936.

Duke Ellington recorded the song around this same time, but few jazz band-leaders except for Herman kept this piece in their repertoires during the next decade. Yet in February 1947 Herman made a new recording of "There Is No

Greater Love," and a week later Billie Holiday also recorded the song. In May, Holiday featured the composition at a Carnegie Hall concert, and over the next several years "There Is No Greater Love" occasionally appeared on bandstands and at studio sessions. But Miles Davis's recording of "There Is No Greater Love" from November 1955 and Sonny Rollins's version from his 1957 trio project *Way Out West* were more influential than any of these precedents in entrenching this piece in the set lists of modern jazz players.

The song is typically played at a relaxed medium tempo, but adapts easily to other pulses. The melody unfolds with a sense of pleasing inevitability—as is often the case with Isham Jones's compositions, which tend to avoid drama and surprising shifts, instead satisfying the ear with the natural, unaffected way the phrases connect to one another. This holistic quality to "There Is No Greater Love" also allows it to maintain its inner logic even when subjected to radical reworkings. For some sense of the range of possible approaches, compare the avant-garde treatment of the Circle ensemble—comprised of Chick Corea, Anthony Braxton, Dave Holland, and Barry Altschul—from their 1971 *Paris Concert*, with the dueling saxes of Sonny Stitt and Gene Ammons from a decade earlier, and the chamber jazz duet of Stan Getz and Kenny Barron from a decade later.

If younger fans recognize the song nowadays, credit is mostly due to the late British chanteuse Amy Winehouse, who featured "There Is No Greater Love" on her million-selling 2003 album *Frank*. That release is aptly named—hence the parental advisory warning label on the cover—but her ballad treatment of the Isham Jones standard is prim and inoffensive, and very much in the spirit of Dinah Washington and Billie Holiday.

RECOMMENDED VERSIONS

Isham Jones (with Woody Herman), New York, February 3, 1936

Duke Ellington, New York, February 27, 1936

Billie Holiday, live at Carnegie Hall, New York, May 24, 1947

Dinah Washington, from *Dinah Jams*, Los Angeles, August 14, 1954

Miles Davis, from *Miles*, Hackensack, New Jersey, November 16, 1955

Sonny Rollins, from *Way Out West*, Los Angeles, March 7, 1957

Sonny Stitt and Gene Ammons, from *Boss Tenors*, Chicago, August 27, 1961

Miles Davis, from *Four and More*, live at Philharmonic Hall, New York, February 12, 1964

Circle (with Chick Corea and Anthony Braxton), from *Paris Concert*, live at the Maison de l'ORTF, Paris, February 21, 1971

Woody Shaw (with Cedar Walton), from *Setting Standards*, Englewood Cliffs, New Jersey, December 1, 1983

Stan Getz and Kenny Barron, from *People Time*, live at Jazzhus Montmartre, Copenhagen, March 3–6, 1991

Vincent Herring (with Wallace Roney and Mulgrew Miller), from *Simple Pleasure*, Englewood Cliffs, New Jersey, March 21, 2001

There Will Never Be Another You
Composed by Harry Warren, with lyrics by Mack Gordon

In the first few measures of this song, the vocalist mentions an interest in seeing "someone new," and a few bars later the passionate declarations of love are interrupted to muse on "other lips" the singer might kiss. Okay, I'm no expert on seduction techniques, but somehow these asides don't strike me as advancing the cause.

So I advise against using this song on a date. But using it on the bandstand is another matter entirely. The long phrases with their sweeping movement, the contrast between the ascending triumphalism in the melody and the downward push of the bassline, and—yes—even the words, with their brazen enumeration of other songs, other seasons, others lips, impart an irresistible momentum to the proceedings that keep listeners engaged in the drama through the entire form.

The composition originally came from *Iceland*, the 1942 movie and not the country. In the film—built around the skating talents of Sonja Henie, the three-time Olympic champion—the composition was given its debut by Joan Merrill, better known at the time for patriotic songs than love ballads. Controversy ensued: men in Iceland protested the movie, objecting to its premise that local Icelandic women preferred US Marines over Nordic males. In all the ice and hubbub, few paid attention to the music. Even though the Academy of Motion Picture Arts and Sciences nominated 10 compositions per year back in those days for the Oscar for Best Song, this future standard did not make the cut. For the record, Harry Warren had 11 other songs nominated over the years, and won three Oscars, but got nothing for this gem.

Woody Herman recorded "There Will Never Be Another You" around the time of the film's release, but his performance only lingered on the chart for a single week before disappearing—even Herman soon dropped the song from his repertoire. Few jazz versions appeared until the early 1950s, when Lionel Hampton, Sonny Stitt, Lester Young, and Stan Getz each recorded "There Will Never Be Another You." The first version of the song I heard, during my adolescent years, featured Nat King Cole, and I was quite captivated at the time. Listening to it again, I demur at Nelson Riddle's sugar-coated arrangement, but he does leave a little space for Nat's piano, while Cole's delivery of the lyrics still strikes me as divine. Chet Baker's recording from 1954 is another crossover classic, and ranks among his most popular vocal performances.

This song has been interpreted in a wide range of styles, and though it is most often performed as a slow-to-medium number with a straight swing tempo, it also works at faster pulses, where it can serve as a springboard for casual jams or more intense horn battles. For that matter, Matthew Shipp has shown, with his 2008 recording, that the Warren-Gordon standard can even cross over into the realm of atonal energy jazz. At the opposite extreme, Chris Montez—a local hero who grew up in my old neighborhood—somehow managed to transform this song into a top 40 pop hit in 1966, with a production that could almost serve as a textbook example of mid-1960s pop-rock. Other artists have borrowed the chord changes for their own compositions, notably Horace Silver for his "Split Kick" and John Scofield for "Not You Again."

RECOMMENDED VERSIONS

Lionel Hampton, New York, January 26, 1950

Lester Young (with Oscar Peterson), from *Lester Young with the Oscar Peterson Trio*, New York, November 28, 1952

Chet Baker, from *Chet Baker Sings*, Los Angeles, February 15, 1954

Lee Konitz (with Lennie Tristano), from *Live at the Confucius Restaurant 1955*, live at the Sing Song Room, Confucius Restaurant, New York, June 11, 1955

Nat King Cole, from *Nat King Cole Sings for Two in Love*, Hollywood, August 25, 1955

Hampton Hawes, from *Four*, Los Angeles, January 27, 1958

Tony Bennett and Count Basie, from *In Person!* New York, December 30, 1958

Sonny Rollins (with Don Cherry), from *Our Man in Jazz*, New York, February 20, 1963

Woody Shaw (with Kenny Garret) from *Solid*, New York, March 24, 1986

Modern Jazz Quartet (with Freddie Hubbard), from *Modern Jazz Quartet and Friends*, New York, June 27, 1992

Matthew Shipp, from *Harmonic Disorder*, Brooklyn, August 2008

These Foolish Things
Composed by Jack Strachey, with lyrics by Holt Marvell (Eric Maschwitz)

The British are the masters of "list songs." Gilbert & Sullivan composed several quite flamboyant examples, even one often simply called "I've Got a Little List," and in later years everyone from John Lennon to Pink Floyd tried their hand at the concept. But here Jack Strachey and lyricist Eric Maschwitz (working under the name Holt Marvell) take the list recipe, usually best suited for a novelty song, and turn it into a romantic ballad. The approach could easily come across as contrived or overly cutesy—as with "I Can't Get Started," another list love song that arrived on the scene around the same time—but the attitude, nostalgic and melancholy in tone, imparts a depth of feeling here that few other list songs have achieved.

"These Foolish Things" was featured in the 1936 London musical *Spread It Abroad*, and was received with so little initial fanfare that Maschwitz's agent deemed it unworthy of publishing—thus renouncing a royalty stream that would still be going strong today. Yet in 1936, five different recording artists were able to achieve hit records with "These Foolish Things." Benny Goodman reached the top of the chart with his release, featuring vocalist Helen Ward and an arrangement by Jimmy Mundy. Goodman would record the piece in a combo version four years later, during the brief spell when electric-guitar sensation Charlie Christian was with his band. Goodman's longtime clarinet rival, Artie Shaw, also recorded "These Foolish Things" on a 1952 session for Decca, and years later called attention to this performance as "the best thing I ever did in my life."

But a Goodman sideman would eventually put the most lasting stamp on this song. Pianist Teddy Wilson entered the studio two weeks after Goodman in the company of singer Billie Holiday, who delivered what will always be, in my opinion, the definitive vocal rendition of "These Foolish Things." This version was also a top 10 hit, and showcases Lady Day in a brisk upbeat mood that counters her prevalent image as a troubled purveyor of sad songs. For a more pensive treatment, listen to Holiday's 1952 recording, which brings out the torch song aspects of this popular standard.

Lady Day's closest competition comes from Nat King Cole, who tackled this song repeatedly in a variety of settings—both as a vocal feature and instrumental, leader and sideman (with Lester Young and Charlie Parker, no less), in combos or as a solo pianist. Another loyal exponent, Art Pepper, kept this song in his repertoire from his early days to the end of his career, leaving behind more than a half-dozen recordings. The version taped live at the Village Vanguard in July 1977 is especially poignant.

RECOMMENDED VERSIONS

Benny Goodman (with Helen Ward and an arrangement by Jimmy Mundy), New York, June 15, 1936

Billie Holiday (with the Teddy Wilson Orchestra), New York, June 30, 1936

Benny Goodman Sextet (with Charlie Christian and Lionel Hampton), Los Angeles, June 11, 1940

Billie Holiday, from *Solitude*, Los Angeles, May 1952

Thelonious Monk, from *Thelonious Monk Trio*, New York, December 18, 1952

Artie Shaw, from *Did Someone Say a Party?* New York, July 2, 1953

Sauter-Finegan Orchestra, from *Directions in Music*, New York, April 22, 1957

Nat King Cole, from *Just One of Those Things*, Los Angeles, July–August 1957

Johnny Hartman, from *Hartman for Lovers*, New York, September 22, 1964

Art Pepper, from *Friday Night at the Village Vanguard*, live at the Village Vanguard, July 29, 1977

Hamiet Bluiett, from *Makin' Whoopee*, Upper Marlboro, Maryland, March 5–21, 1996

Enrico Pieranunzi, from *Ballads*, Rome, June 17 and July 18, 2004

They Can't Take That Away from Me

Composed by George Gershwin, with lyrics by Ira Gershwin

This song offers an extreme example of George Gershwin's use of repeated notes in his melodic phrases, but in this instance the lyricist may be the culprit. The original melody had only three to start the song, but Ira begged for two more to make room for his words. Otherwise "the way you wear your hat" or "sip your tea" would have been squeezed into "the way you [fill in a one-syllable verb]." Smooch? Smoke? Cook? Hardly enough syllabic space there for courtship and romance. Fortunately George listened to his older brother, and the result is one of their most effective collaborations.

The relaxed phrases were no doubt written with a specific singer in mind. Fred Astaire may not be mentioned in any list of influential vocalists, and his singing has rarely gotten more than passing acknowledgment from jazz insiders, yet he seemed to be on hand when many popular standards were introduced. In the case of "They Can't Take That Away from Me," from the 1937 film *Shall We Dance*, Astaire doesn't even get to add some dance steps—he just sings it to Ginger Rogers on the foggy deck of a ferry, nary a bandy twist or heel click to lighten the mood.

George Gershwin was reportedly unhappy with the song's placement in the movie—he felt that it was treated as a throwaway without a proper plug. But the composer was pleased by Astaire's recording of his piece for the Brunswick label, which was the #1 hit in the nation the week the film came out. Gershwin also took considerable pride in Irving Berlin's praise of "They Can't Take That Away from Me" as a song destined to last.

The composition was nominated for an Oscar, but somehow lost to Harry Owens's "Sweet Leilani" from *Waikiki Wedding*. Can we request a revote? Yet Berlin's prediction has been more than adequately validated. Even before the film's release, the song showed up on the music stands of bands led by Benny Goodman, Count Basie, Tommy Dorsey, and other jazz stars of the day. Less than three weeks after Astaire made his own recording of the song, Billie Holiday came into the studio to wax her version for the Vocalion label, and this proved to be one of her more popular releases of the era—Lady Day's vocal more than compensating for the turgid rhythm section. But the song soon fell out of favor, and only a handful of jazz cover versions were released until the end of World War II.

Artie Shaw recorded "They Can't Take That Away from Me" during his productive summer of 1945, a period that found him in the studio making dozens of tracks over the span of a few weeks. Victor had planned to issue it at the time, with "Our Love Is Here to Stay" on the flip side, but then canceled the release, so it never found an audience until the advent of LPs. Yet it is one of Shaw's standout performances from this busy period.

The main reason why this song came back into the limelight was because Astaire—that man again!—revived it for his 1949 film *The Barkleys of Broadway*, where he does get to dance to the Gershwin number in formal attire with the lovely Ginger Rogers as his partner. A few months later, Charlie Parker performed the song as part of his "Bird with Strings" endeavor, where the first 15 seconds are gripping, the best moment of this whole session, and make you wish that the rest of the project had been as good. Soon after, Dizzy Gillespie recorded the Gershwin composition for his Dee Gee label, and used it as a vehicle for some aggressive double-time playing after the languid melody statement—but even better than the studio recording is the trumpeter's live performance at Salle Pleyel in February 1953. Around this same time, Oscar Peterson, Mary Lou Williams, Art Tatum, and Stan Getz further validated the jazzworthiness of the song, and it has remained a core part of the repertoire ever since.

This Gershwin standard remains primarily a feature for singers. Certainly the best-known jazz recording—from the winning mid-1950s collaboration of Louis Armstrong and Ella Fitzgerald—showcases it in that context. But some lesser-known instrumental renditions demonstrate the tune's adaptability as a jam song for horn players. For two compelling examples, track down Stanley Turrentine's 1992 performance from *More Than a Mood*, where he fronts a rhythm section of Cedar Walton, Ron Carter, and Billy Higgins, and then proceed on to Lester Young's recording on clarinet, alongside Hank Jones and Harry "Sweets" Edison, from 1958. The latter, made just a year before Young's death, is as moving a closing statement as you will find from Prez's late-career output.

RECOMMENDED VERSIONS

Fred Astaire (with Johnny Green's Orchestra), March 14, 1937

Billie Holiday, New York, April 1, 1937

Artie Shaw, Hollywood, July 14, 1945

Charlie Parker (with strings), New York, July 5, 1950

Mary Lou Williams, from *The London Sessions*, London, January 23, 1953

Dizzy Gillespie, from *Pleyel Jazz Concert 1953*, live at Salle Pleyel, Paris, February 9, 1953

Louis Armstrong and Ella Fitzgerald, from *Ella and Louis*, Los Angeles, August 16, 1956

Lester Young (with Hank Jones and Harry "Sweets" Edison), from *Laughin' to Keep From Cryin'*, New York, February 8, 1958

Stanley Turrentine, from *More Than a Mood*, New York, February 13, 1992

Marcus Roberts, from *Gershwin for Lovers*, Tallahassee, Florida, 1994

Things Ain't What They Used to Be
Composed by Mercer Ellington, with lyrics by Ted Persons

Here's an oddity: an Ellington standard *not* composed by *Duke* Ellington. Instead his son Mercer contributed this popular tune to his father's band. But the story behind the song is more a matter of economics than nepotism. In 1941, Ellington's music was kept off the radio because stations were in a battle over royalties with ASCAP. But works composed by Mercer or Duke's frequent collaborator Billy Strayhorn were not impacted, since neither (unlike the band-leader) were ASCAP members. Since things truly weren't like they used to be, Ellington was in a situation where giving his son a boost was also a smart business move.

The Ellington orchestra would not make a studio recording of "Things Ain't What They Used to Be" until after the strike was settled. But Duke also organized small combo sessions during this period under the nominal leader-ship of his star soloists, and in this setting his son's tune made its debut at a Johnny Hodges date from July 1941. Ellington also performed "Things Ain't What They Used to Be" for the 1943 film *Cabin in the Sky*, although in a trun-cated version with no camera shots of the band. The song gained another boost of cinematic fame that same year when "Things Ain't What They Used to Be" appeared in a short movie by the Columbia studio starring former Ellington sideman Cootie Williams. Contrary to some accounts, bop pianist Bud Powell does not play on this clip, but it does feature a vocal by Eddie "Cleanhead" Vinson.

Lyrics by Ted Persons are sometimes heard, but this song is most often played as an instrumental. The composition, occasionally known as "Times A-Wastin'," is based on a straightforward 12-bar blues form, but the riff melody is memorable and effective. A consummate blues player, Hodges continued to stake his claim to this piece in later years. He is lead-off soloist when the Ellington band performed "Things Ain't What They Used to Be" at Carnegie Hall in December 1944, and on the studio recording for Victor from the following May.

Yet Ellington also relied on this song in intimate settings when no horn player was around. I especially enjoy his trio performance from his 1953 *Piano Reflections* project—pay attention to the games he plays with the last note of each phrase of the melody, sometimes slamming it home staccato, or else letting the tone linger, or bringing the dynamics down to pianissimo. Ellington returned to "Things Ain't What They Used to Be" on his 1972 duet project with Ray Brown, *This One's for Blanton*.

Ellington's own example notwithstanding, this song's melody is usually delivered in a perfunctory manner, and the tune is treated as little more than a pretext for soloing over blues changes. It works well at a jam session, which is the most typical context in which it is heard. A persuasive example can be heard on the Grammy Award-winning album *Oscar Peterson Jam*, recorded at the Montreux Jazz Festival in 1977, where the pianist is joined by Dizzy Gillespie, Eddie "Lockjaw" Davis, and Clark Terry.

Terry also contributes to a much different version of "Things Ain't What They Used to Be" at a 1961 date ostensibly under the leadership of bassist Buell Neidlinger but now usually marketed as a session by avant-gardist Cecil Taylor. From the outset, the clash between the horns and Taylor's jarring piano work could hardly be more unsettling, and Terry's solo finds Neidlinger sticking doggedly to the blues chord changes while the keyboardist doesn't so much alter the harmonies as trample them underfoot.

Finally, let me recommend Charles Mingus's 1959 performance of the Ellington blues, included in his *Shoes of the Fisherman's Wife* album. This track also has moments of Dionysian excess, but with Mingus always exerting firm control when needed—dictating a stop-time interlude, changing the rhythmic groove, stepping in to solo, and, in general, pushing and prodding the band to a classic performance.

RECOMMENDED VERSIONS

Johnny Hodges, Hollywood, July 3, 1941

Duke Ellington, New York, May 30, 1945

Duke Ellington, from *Piano Reflections*, Hollywood, April 14, 1953

Charles Mingus, from *Shoes of the Fisherman's Wife*, New York, November 13, 1959

Cecil Taylor, from *Jumpin' Pumpkins*, New York, January 10, 1961

Duke Ellington and Ray Brown, from *This One's for Blanton*, Las Vegas, December 5, 1972

Oscar Peterson (with Dizzy Gillespie, Clark Terry, and Eddie "Lockjaw" Davis), from
    Oscar Peterson Jam/Montreux 77, live at the Montreux Jazz Festival, Montreux,
    Switzerland, July 14, 1977

Gene Harris, from *Live at Town Hall, New York City*, live at Town Hall, New York,
    September 23, 1989

Keith Jarrett (with the Standards Trio), from *The Cure*, live at Town Hall, New York,
    April 21, 1990

Tiger Rag
*Composed by Nick La Rocca, Eddie Edwards, Henry Ragas, Tony Sbarbaro,
and Larry Shields, with lyrics by Harry DeCosta*

Who, in their right mind, would want to "hold that tiger"—as the words of this
song repeatedly urge listeners to do—and why would you write a composition
about it? Yet the very outrageousness of the concept explains much of the initial appeal of this song, one of the oldest jazz standards and among the first to
be preserved on record. Those of the modern day who learn about jazz in
schools or documentaries, get a valuable reminder via "Tiger Rag" of the brash,
counterculture attitudes with which this style of music first came to the fore.
The phrase "holding a tiger by the tail" has meant, at least since the late nineteenth century, engaging in a very dangerous pursuit—and that was exactly the
attitude with which this exciting hybrid music from New Orleans arrived on
the scene.

The Original Dixieland Jazz Band made the first recording of "Tiger Rag"
back in 1917, but it was their follow-up attempt from the next year that turned
this song into a huge game-changing hit. The track may not rank among the
greatest of early jazz performances, but definitely succeeds in conveying the
transgressive essence of the new musical style from New Orleans. The band
members also copyrighted the song, although many claims and counter-
claims have been made about its actual origins. Jelly Roll Morton boasted
that he adapted "Tiger Rag" from a French quadrille. Bits and pieces of evidence also point to Achille Baquet, Jack Carey, and others as originators of all
or part of the song. Some performers have copyrighted the same (or almost
identical) tune under a different name to avoid generating royalties for the
ODJB, a group seen by many as white usurpers of the innovations of
African-Americans.

Others merely borrowed the chord changes—no one with more success
than Duke Ellington. He turned the New Orleans standard into his thinly dis-
guised "Whispering Tiger" in the mid-1930s, and drew on the underlying

harmonies in a variety of other settings, such as his "Daybreak Express" (1933) and "Braggin' in Brass" (1938). But Ellington also recorded "Tiger Rag" in its more-or-less original form. He featured it in a two-part recording with his Cotton Club band from 1929 and still found it worth playing a few months before his death in 1974.

Louis Armstrong used the harmonies from "Tiger Rag" for his "Hotter Than That" from 1927, but he too also recorded the original song—for the first time in May 1930, but at least 30 other performances have been preserved. The version to hear comes from a little-known live recording, made at a concert in Sweden from 1959. Here Armstrong must have found the fountain of youth by the shores of Lake Malaren: he and his cohorts play "Tiger Rag" for almost 10 minutes—the initial rendition is followed by four encores, with the trumpeter taking a solo each time. Armstrong, who was approaching his sixtieth birthday, is caught up in the audience's exuberance and soon starts reaching for high notes that one might have thought were no longer in his range, meanwhile inserting allusions to everything from operatic arias to his own classic performances from the past. This belongs in that small set of tracks to play for your friends who don't think they like jazz—put it on and watch them become true believers before your eyes.

A host of other leading jazz stars found inspiration in this song. Paul Whiteman enjoyed a top 10 hit with his recording of "The New Tiger Rag" in 1930, and the following year the Mills Brothers rose to stardom when their million-selling vocal arrangement of the song was the top hit in the nation for a month. Piano virtuoso Art Tatum relied on "Tiger Rag" to assert his dominance of the keyboard when he first arrived in New York, and featured the song on his debut solo piano recording from 1932. Ray Noble also enjoyed a hit with his 1933 recording of the song. During the Swing Era, "Tiger Rag" continued to find advocates among big band leaders—Benny Goodman and Glenn Miller were especially fervent in their support—even though this type of multithemed rag-oriented song was increasingly falling out of favor among younger jazz players.

Yet the strangest performance of "Tiger Rag" in my collection, hands down, comes from a 1947 radio broadcast sponsored by the US Treasury to sell bonds. Barry Ulanov had enlisted an all-star bebop combo—which featured Charlie Parker, Dizzy Gillespie, and Lennie Tristano—to engage in a "battle of the bands" with a trad jazz group. The modernists decided to deconstruct "Tiger Rag," playing it in a bop arrangement at a blistering tempo. None of these musicians ever recorded "Tiger Rag" again, in any setting, and this sole track testified to the peculiar yet exhilarating sound of the venerable New Orleans song turned into a swashbuckling modern jazz chart.

But this track is a glaring outlier. For later leading-edge jazz performers—whether beboppers or hard-boppers, cool players or soul jazz exponents, free or fusion advocates—"Tiger Rag" has held little appeal. How far the once mighty song had fallen! Among the first jazz compositions to be released on record, "Tiger Rag" stood out as the archetypal hot number of its day, almost as central to the music as "Body and Soul" or "Summertime" would be to a later generation of improvisers. But after the midpoint of the century, "Tiger Rag" stagnated. I hear some fresh stirrings in a couple of versions from the 1950s—by Les Paul and Raymond Scott—but after that point, a long dry spell set in, and one struggles to find a rendition of "Tiger Rag" that isn't a rehash, retread, or rerun. It didn't help the song's cachet among jazz artists that "Tiger Rag" became a signature showpiece for Liberace, or that André Kostelanetz turned it into an easy listening song.

Yet a few rumblings of creativity from the new millennium prove that the "Tiger" has not become totally domesticated. I call attention to two versions by New Orleans natives. An odd if uplifting Juilliard-comes-to-the-backwoods mood permeates the collaboration of Mark O'Connor and Wynton Marsalis on their 2002 recording of "Tiger Rag" from the violinist's *In Full Swing* release. And Nicholas Payton offers an invigorating reinterpretation on his *Dear Louis* project from 2000.

RECOMMENDED VERSIONS

Original Dixieland Jazz Band, New York, March 25, 1918

Bix Beiderbecke (with the Wolverine Orchestra), Richmond, Indiana, June 20, 1924

Duke Ellington, New York, January 8, 1929

Louis Armstrong, New York, May 4, 1930

Paul Whiteman (recorded as "The New Tiger Rag"), New York, July 25, 1930

The Mills Brothers, New York, October 3, 1931

Art Tatum, New York, March 21, 1933

Benny Goodman (with Mel Powell), New York, August 29, 1945

Charlie Parker, Dizzy Gillespie, and Lennie Tristano, from the *Bands for Bonds* radio broadcast, New York, September 20, 1947

Les Paul and Mary Ford, Oakland, New Jersey, circa 1951–1952

Raymond Scott, from *At Home with Dorothy and Raymond*, New York, November 3, 1956

Louis Armstrong, from *Louis Armstrong in Scandinavia, Vol. 4*, live at Konserthuset, Stockholm, January 16, 1959

Nicholas Payton, from *Dear Louis*, New York, September–October 2000

Mark O'Connor (with Wynton Marsalis), from *In Full Swing*, New York, August 26–30, 2002

Time after Time
Composed by Jule Styne, with lyrics by Sammy Cahn

"It's a man's song," the composer Jule Styne once remarked of his work "Time after Time." "When a woman sings it, it is drained of all its power, so to speak. The girls can't do it." I'm not sure I agree—Sarah Vaughan, one of the first vocalists to record this song, delivered a convincing rendition on a 1946 Teddy Wilson session, and other divas (Ella, Dinah, Carmen, Anita, etc.) followed suit in later years.

Then again, the women got their ultimate rejoinder when Cyndi Lauper released another song named "Time after Time," which became a #1 hit in 1984 and was subsequently covered by Miles Davis. Despite this high-profile advocacy, Lauper's composition has yet to become as popular in jazz circles as Styne's, but it's catching up . . . and when a patron at the nightclub requests "Time after Time" nowadays, odds are two-to-one that the lady's tune, also a fine jazz vehicle, is the one being sought. By the way, I think that Lauper's composition might be difficult for a male singer to deliver effectively. So take that, Jule Styne!

Styne's song was not written for just any man, but for Frank Sinatra, who brought "Time after Time" to the public's attention in the 1947 film *It Happened in Brooklyn*. Here, with the singer seated at the keyboard (and André Previn, who two decades later would marry Frank's ex Mia Farrow, providing piano accompaniment behind the scenes), Sinatra has the unenviable task of singing this love song to Jimmy Durante. This version is not as poised as the studio recording Sinatra made of "Time after Time" in 1946, but best of all is his 1957 recording for Capitol, where he is supported by a dramatic Nelson Riddle chart.

This song has inspired some unusual cover versions over the years—compare recordings by Plácido Domingo and Screamin' Jay Hawkins, and try to decide which is the most unsettling—but it is ultimately a composition best served when the screamin' is held in check and the wistful qualities inherent in Styne's melody and Cahn's words come to the fore. The lyrics risk banality—how lucky I am to love you, et cetera—but the stutter-step rhyming of "time" with "I'm" in the middle of the run-on sentence that opens this composition serves to draw the listener into the song, as does the music, which sounds almost through-composed, despite the repeat after bar 16. Indeed, few popular songs flow so effortlessly from the first bar to the final note—Styne helping matters along by curtailing the use of rests in the melody.

He probably had in mind Sinatra's breath control and smooth legato phrasing—the singer's lasting legacies from his apprenticeship with Tommy Dorsey, whose trombone playing Sinatra admired for these very qualities—when composing this piece. In any event, the end result is a song best served up by jazz players who have a fluid and effortless quality to their delivery. For superior examples, check out Stan Getz's recording of "Time after Time" from 1957 or Paul Desmond's collaboration with Jim Hall on this tune from 1959. Hall once cited Desmond's closing phrases on his restatement of the theme here as a quintessential example of the altoist's ability to craft improvised melodies to rival the original. If you haven't heard it, you would do well to make its acquaintance.

RECOMMENDED VERSIONS

Teddy Wilson (with Sarah Vaughan), New York, November 19, 1946

Chet Baker, from *Chet Baker Sings*, Los Angeles, February 15, 1954

Stan Getz, from *Award Winner*, Hollywood, August 2, 1957

Frank Sinatra, from *This Is Sinatra, Vol. 2*, Hollywood, November 25, 1957

John Coltrane, from *Stardust*, Hackensack, New Jersey, December 26, 1958

Paul Desmond (with Jim Hall), from *First Place Again*, New York, September 5–7, 1959

Joe Morello (with Phil Woods and Gary Burton), from *It's about Time*, New York, June 6, 1961

Freddie Hubbard (with Ricky Ford and Kenny Barron), from *The Rose Tattoo*, Englewood Cliffs, New Jersey, December 9–10, 1983

Ian Shaw, from *The Echo of a Song*, live at Ronnie Scott's, London, June 12–13, 1996

Cedar Walton, from *One Flight Down*, Englewood Cliffs, New Jersey, April 7, 2006

Tin Roof Blues
Composed by Paul Mares, Ben Pollack, Mel Stitzel, George Brunies, and Leon Roppolo

Although "Tin Roof Blues" ranks among the most popular traditional jazz songs, closely linked in listeners' minds with the early days of jazz, many of the leading New Orleans players did not embrace it until fairly late in life. Sidney Bechet didn't record "Tin Roof Blues" until he was in his fifties, although it then became a core part of his repertoire. The same is true of Louis Armstrong, whose recordings of this piece all date from the 1950s and 1960s. Jazz revivalists hailing from the West Coast—such as Lu Watters, Turk Murphy, and Bob Crosby—actually recorded this song before Armstrong, Hines, and many other pioneers ever acknowledged its importance.

The earlier history of this song is marked by controversy, which may have some bearing on the reluctance of first-generation jazz stars to embrace it. The piece was first recorded by the New Orleans Rhythm Kings in 1923 in a performance that, in the words of historian Samuel Charters, "could be considered the stylistic source of almost all the small-band white jazz that followed in [the Rhythm Kings'] wake." Yet some have raised questions of plagiarism, pointing out similarities with Richard M. Jones's "Jazzin' Babies Blues," recorded by King Oliver shortly after the NORK session, or to other traditional New Orleans songs.

There is a loose affinity, in the second themes, between the Jones and NORK compositions, which both rely on a repeated descending four-note chromatic motif; but in the Jones piece the melody gets its bluesy bite from sliding over the flat third, while, in "Tin Roof Blues" the lick incorporates the more exotic flat five. I'm not sure that I would go so far as to subscribe to Martin Williams's rejoinder that "having lived with both pieces on records for some twenty-plus years now, I confess that the only real similarity I hear between them is that they are both 12-bar blues." Yet the kinship here is more like the slight resemblance between cousins, not the striking congruence of identical twins. Historians of American music can cite a number of early twentieth-century songs that incorporated similar phrases—Williams, for his part, calls attention to Ollie Powers's "Play That Thing" from 1923—but it was recorded after the New Orleans Rhythm Kings track.

In contrast to these various allegations, the New Orleans Rhythm Kings' trombonist George Brunies recalls that the song originated during the band's famous engagement at the Friar's Inn, where it was originally known as "The Rusty Rail Blues." After publisher Walter Melrose secured the rights, in exchange for a $500 advance, the song was rechristened as "Tin Roof Blues" and was recorded by the band at its March 13, 1923 session for the Gennett label in Richmond, Indiana.

Most recordings of this song follow a familiar formula. "Tin Roof Blues" is, today, pretty much what it was a half-century ago, a token of respect for the past rather than a leap (or even a half-hearted step) into the future. You know that small-print disclosure in advertisements, the one that says *results may vary?* Well, the opposite is true with "Tin Roof Blues"—the results don't vary, at least not much. Even when a player schooled in modern ways addresses the song (a rarity), such as Jaki Byard did on his 1981 recording session from *To Them—To Us*, the proceedings aren't too far afield from what you might hear from Art Hodes or Willie "The Lion" Smith.

By the way, "Tin Roof Blues" served as the basis for the 1954 pop song "Make Love to Me"—a number one hit for Jo Stafford. For the Stafford release, no fewer than eight individuals are listed as composer, including each member of the New Orleans Rhythm Kings and Walter Melrose—and all this for a simple twelve-bar blues, with a melody that, in the opinion of some commentators, none of them wrote.

RECOMMENDED VERSIONS

New Orleans Rhythm Kings, Richmond, Indiana, March 13, 1923

Jelly Roll Morton, piano roll, Cincinnati, June–July, 1924

King Oliver, New York, June 11, 1928

Sidney Bechet, New York, January 21, 1949

Lu Watters and His Yerba Buena Jazz Band, live at Hambone Kelly's, El Cerrito, California, June–July, 1950

Louis Armstrong, from *The California Concerts*, live at the Crescendo Club, Los Angeles, January 21, 1955

Al Hirt (with Pete Fountain), from *At the Jazz Band Ball*, live at Dan's Pier 600, New Orleans, 1957

Herb Ellis (with Stan Getz and Roy Eldridge), from *Nothing But the Blues*, Los Angeles, October 11, 1957

Manny Albam, from *Something New, Something Blue*, New York, May 15, 1959

Jaki Byard, from *To Them—To Us*, Milan, May 27, 1981

Flip Phillips (with Kenny Davern), from *Mood Indigo*, Oslo, August 9, 1987

The Very Thought of You

Composed by Ray Noble

Horn players step aside; the vocalists own this song. The dozen best-selling versions on Amazon.com all feature famous singers, with one exception—and that track is a karaoke instrumental designed to back up amateur vocalists. The most popular performance remains Nat King Cole's oh-so-slow rendition, which has no shortage of admirers a half-century after it was recorded, despite the elevator-ish strings. This was also the first version I ever heard of this tune, when it arrived at the Gioia household as part of a mail-order set of Nat King Cole albums that my parents purchased (probably at my insistence) around the time of my twelfth birthday.

Composer Ray Noble enjoyed a #1 hit with "The Very Thought of You," featuring Al Bowlly on vocals, which stayed atop the chart for five weeks in 1934. Bing Crosby also had some success with the song at the time, but his fairly brisk tempo and a jarring and long-held high note at the end of the track—an unexpected choice for the usually low-key Mr. Crosby—will probably leave most modern-day listeners dissatisfied. My bet is that a focus group today would prefer Harry Connick Jr. at 70 beats per minute over Bing at twice that speed by a landslide.

In general, interpretations of this song have gotten slower and slower with the passing years. Billie Holiday did more than anyone to establish "The Very Thought of You" as a jazz standard with her medium-tempo 1938 performance, a musical gem that also includes a choice solo by Lester Young on clarinet. The previous year Young, playing tenor sax, had performed alongside Benny Goodman, then not just a name clarinetist but the most popular musician in America, on a Holiday session; but now Prez seemed determined to take center stage as the anti-Goodman on clarinet, a plaintive melodicist, who could make do with only a fraction of the notes that the King of Swing required.

The bebop maestros of the 1940s and 1950s had little interest in this sentimental song. Charlie Parker played it at gigs during a brief spell when vocalist Earl Coleman was performing with his band, but never brought it into the studio, and Dizzy Gillespie left behind a single recording, with strings, from a Paris date in 1953. The song works well on piano, yet Monk, Powell, and Tristano never touched it as far as I can tell. The same can be said for trumpeters Clifford Brown, Miles Davis, and Fats Navarro.

At the close of the 1950s, jazz cover versions started to proliferate, as did pop vocal renditions. Nat King Cole recorded his interpretation in 1958, and Ella Fitzgerald, Sarah Vaughan, and Frank Sinatra did the same in 1962, although the latter track, featuring a thoughtful Robert Farnon arrangement, was only released in Britain at the time. Horn players increasingly embraced the standard, and during this same period Pee Wee Russell, Eddie "Lockjaw" Davis, Earl Bostic, and Johnny Hodges climbed on the bandwagon. The song has never lagged in popularity since that time, and later recordings of note include performances by Sonny Rollins, Wynton Marsalis, and Brad Mehldau.

Jazz players have no lock on this song, and few standards have attracted a more eclectic group of advocates. Even back in the 1960s, this song produced crossover hits for R&B singer Little Willie John and pop-rocker Ricky Nelson—the latter relying on a backbeat big enough to register on the Richter scale. Among recording artists who have released versions of "The Very Thought of You" in more recent years, we find Elvis Costello, Rod Stewart, Aaron Neville, Neil Sedaka, Albert King, and Paul McCartney (in a duet with Tony Bennett). With advocates like these, this standard will remain a popular request, and not just among jazz audiences.

RECOMMENDED VERSIONS

Ray Noble (with Al Bowlly), London, April 21, 1934

Billie Holiday (with Lester Young), New York, September 15, 1938

Dizzy Gillespie (with strings), from *Jazz in Paris: Dizzy Gillespie and His Operatic Strings*, Paris, February 22, 1953

Nat King Cole (with the Gordon Jenkins Orchestra), from *The Very Thought of You*, Hollywood, May 1958

Pee Wee Russell (with Buck Clayton and Tommy Flanagan), from *Swingin' with Pee Wee*, Englewood Cliffs, New Jersey, March 29, 1960

Sarah Vaughan (with Barney Kessel), from *Sarah Plus Two*, Los Angeles, August 7–8, 1962

Sonny Rollins, from *Love at First Sight*, Berkeley, California, May 9–12, 1980

Diane Schuur, from *Deedles*, Seattle, December 6, 1984

Wynton Marsalis (with Ellis Marsalis), from *Standard Time, Vol. 3: The Resolution of Romance*, New York, circa 1990

Harry Connick Jr., from *Only You*, Hollywood, May 13–22, 2003

Brad Mehldau, from *Brad Mehldau Trio Live*, live at the Village Vanguard, New York, October 11–15, 2006

Cassandra Wilson, from *Loverly*, Jackson, Mississippi, 2007

W

Waltz for Debby
Composed by Bill Evans, with lyrics by Gene Lees

Upon completing a three-year stint in the US Army in January 1954, Bill Evans headed to Florida, where his parents had moved after his father's retirement. Here Evans acquired a grand piano and practiced zealously, trying to rebuild his confidence, shaken by the accumulated negative feedback dished out by musicians who had been prodding him to play more like the fashionable jazz pianists of the day. He also visited his brother Harry in Baton Rouge, and spent time with his niece Debby, whom he would take to the beach. Around this time, Evans wrote what would be his most famous composition, a gentle, introspective waltz, and named it after Debby—but at a stage in his development when he had no assurances it would ever be recorded or heard beyond the confines of his practice sessions.

In July 1955, Evans made the move to New York, and when he had the opportunity to record an album for the Riverside label the following year, he featured the waltz he had written for his niece in an all-too-brief track. The performance lasts a mere 80 seconds; even so, the solo piano format here gives us a chance to hear the song in a style and setting that probably reflects how it sounded when he first composed it during his period of seclusion from the jazz scene. A follow-up session with Cannonball Adderley, six months later, presented Evans with another opportunity to record "Waltz for Debby," now in a combo setting. This rendition starts with a solo statement of the melody, before settling into an animated 4/4 pulse—so there isn't much waltz in this version of "Waltz for Debby."

The definitive performance of the composition was still to come, and arrived with Evans's engagement at the Village Vanguard on June 25, 1961—where his producer Orrin

Keepnews had arranged to tape the pianist's exceptional trio of the period, an ensemble that found Evans demonstrating uncanny rapport with drummer Paul Motian and bassist Scott LaFaro. As it turned out, this would be the trio's last recording—LaFaro would be killed in a car accident just 11 days later. The loss was devastating to the pianist, both personally and artistically. Evans would never have a better band, in my opinion, and their recordings from the Village Vanguard would exert a powerful influence on the next generation of jazz rhythm sections. Although Evans would record "Waltz for Debby" on more than a dozen later occasions, the 1961 track remains the best known and most widely imitated of his many performances of the piece.

As he had done alongside Cannonball Adderley, Evans switches to 4/4 for the solos. This is one of the incongruities of this song: Evans was probably the most adept jazz pianist of his day at playing jazz waltzes, yet he preferred to improvise in 4/4 meter when playing his own famous jazz waltz. But there were exceptions. I especially enjoy Evans's 1975 collaboration with Tony Bennett, not just for the vocalist's touching delivery of Gene Lees's lyrics to "Waltz for Debby," but also because this track gives us a rare chance to hear the pianist solo over the changes in 3/4. Evans's partnerships with other headline artists—pairings that became increasingly rare with the passing years—often forced him out of his comfort zone; but, as the Bennett project substantiates, this creative tension could spur the pianist to his freshest mid- and late-career work.

Oscar Peterson would seem an unlikely champion of Evans's music in general or this song in particular—one finds little in common when comparing the keyboard conception, phrasing, and rhythmic sensibility of these two artists. Yet Peterson was one of the first jazz pianists to add "Waltz for Debby" to his repertoire, and he continued to perform it in concert for many years, although more often as part of a medley in the 1980s and 1990s. Peterson's work from his 1962 *Affinity* project is notable not only for his thoughtful performance of "Waltz for Debby," but also for surprising signs of how Evans's example had inspired Peterson to try a more interactive trio approach with his own band. For this project, Peterson consciously aimed for a different kind of sonic balance, in which bass and drums play a less static supportive role—even the miking and volume of the different instruments in the final mix reflected this shift. The change would not be a lasting one: Peterson's domineering approach to the piano was hardly conducive to nuanced dialogues with cohorts. But the very fact that he made the experiment was testimony to how deeply Evans had changed the rules of the game.

The song has traveled widely over the years. In addition to the lyrics in English by Gene Lees, the song's Swedish incarnation with words by Beppe Wolgers was validated by the composer himself in his recording with vocalist Monica Zetterlund. A number of guitarists—Ralph Towner, John McLaughlin,

Jim Hall—have shown that this composition is just as suited to the six strings as to piano. Don Sebesky earned a Grammy for his orchestral arrangement from 1997, and the Grammy voters took note again in 2008, when Gary Burton and Chick Corea performed "Waltz for Debby" on the duo's *The New Crystal Silence*, which won that year's award for the best jazz instrumental album.

Perhaps the only sour note here is the frequent misspelling of "Debby" as "Debbie"—roughly 20 percent of the cover versions of this song, by my estimate, get the name wrong.

RECOMMENDED VERSIONS

Bill Evans, from *New Jazz Conceptions*, New York, September 27, 1956

Cannonball Adderley (with Bill Evans), from *Know What I Mean?* New York, March 13, 1961

Bill Evans (with Scott LaFaro and Paul Motian), from *Live at the Village Vanguard*, live at the Village Vanguard, New York, June 25, 1961

Oscar Peterson, from *Affinity*, Chicago, September 25, 1962

Tony Bennett and Bill Evans, from *The Tony Bennett/Bill Evans Album*, Berkeley, California, June 10–13, 1975

Ralph Towner, from *Open Letter*, Oslo, July 1991 and February 1992

John McLaughlin, from *Time Remembered*, Milan, March 25–28, 1993

Don Sebesky (with Joe Lovano and Tom Harrell), from *I Remember Bill: A Tribute to Bill Evans*, New York, June and August 1997

Chick Corea and Gary Burton, from *The New Crystal Silence*, live at Bjornsonhuset, Molde, Norway, July 2007

Watermelon Man
Composed by Herbie Hancock

Almost exactly a year after Herbie Hancock recorded this song he would go into the studio for his first session as a member of Miles Davis's band. "Watermelon Man," with its simple melody and funky vamp, was nothing like the forward-looking music he would make with Miles over the next several years. Yet before the decade was over, Davis would have changed courses and embraced the high-strutting groove music that Hancock had been exploring on his Blue Note debut back in '62. Miles even performed "Watermelon Man" toward the end of his life—the event, which featured an all-star band, was captured on a memorable video.

By then, "Watermelon Man" would be a popular hit. But this was due less to Hancock than to Mongo Santamaría, who enjoyed a huge success with the song. Santamaría's jukebox version of "Watermelon Man" reached as high as #10 on the pop chart in 1963. When the song was inducted into the Grammy Hall of Fame in 1998, it was Santamaría's track, not Hancock's, that got the nod.

The work is a 16-bar blues. The hook comes from stretching out the final line of the standard 12-bar blues form for four extra bars with a break at the end of the form. The tune is easy to play, and as result has made inroads with many nonjazz bands. It has even crossed over into the insular world of electric blues—where it has been covered by artists (such as Buddy Guy, Albert King, and Little Walter) who rarely perform compositions by jazz musicians.

Hancock tried reworking the song in a fusion format for his 1973 *Head Hunters* release. Generally jazz composers play their hit songs faster and faster as the years go by, but Hancock bucked the trend here and went after an elusive slow funk sound. The result was so different from his 1962 version as to almost be another composition entirely, but was just as effective. Bill Summers was able to recreate the sound of African Hindewhu music with a beer bottle on this track—an appropriation lamented by ethnomusicologists, who tried to recast this as a robbery of intellectual property. But it's hard not to be dazzled by the cleverness and audacity of Summers's achievement.

The song has traveled widely and undergone many other changes over the years. "Watermelon Man," in its various incarnations, has been frequently sampled by hip-hoppers. Jon Hendricks added words for his 1963 version, and different lyrics were later contributed by Gloria Lynne. "Watermelon Man" was even adopted as a theme song for ATA Airlines. Yet how odd that, in an illustrious career, Herbie Hancock's most famous song came from the first track of his very first leader date, made back when he was an unknown young pianist from Chicago.

RECOMMENDED VERSIONS

Herbie Hancock (with Dexter Gordon), from *Takin' Off*, Englewood Cliffs, New Jersey, May 28, 1962

Mongo Santamaría, from *Watermelon Man!* New York, December 17, 1962

Gerald Wilson (with Teddy Edwards), from *Feelin' Kinda Blues*, Los Angeles, December 2, 1965

Erroll Garner, from *Up in Erroll's Room*, New York, March 19, 1968

Buddy Guy, from *Hold That Plane*, New York, 1970

Herbie Hancock, from *Head Hunters*, San Francisco, September 1973

Miles Davis, from *Black Devil*, live at Grande Halle de la Villette, Paris, July 10, 1991

Wave
Composed by Antonio Carlos Jobim

When I was first learning jazz harmony, I was taught by my elders to limit my use of diminished chords—the conventional wisdom was that they imparted an "old-fashioned" sound to a song and could usually be replaced by a more stylish altered dominant voicing. Yet in the second bar of "Wave," Jobim not only gets a hip, up-to-date attitude out of a diminished chord, but he even spells out the entire chord in the melody line. Then in the bridge, Jobim recycles the same changes he used a few years before in "One Note Samba," but again he gets away with the transgression just through the sheer sense of rightness to his overall construction.

"Wave" did not arrive on the scene until after the bossa nova fad was over, so it never received the crossover airplay of some other Jobim tunes. Yet it is even more popular with musicians than many of that composer's hits. Certainly the song has its famous advocates. Sinatra recorded "Wave" in 1969, and hit a low E flat, which is reportedly his lowest note on record. Jobim wrote both English and Portuguese lyrics to "Wave," but it is somewhat more difficult to sing than most of his pieces—however Sarah Vaughan has delivered a slow and sultry version that shows that "Wave" can work even with most of the Brazilian flavor removed from the arrangement.

Jobim is one of my favorite composers, but few of his works show such flexibility—usually they demand a straight bossa treatment and sound like parodies or half-baked postmodern mashups when dealt with in any other way. McCoy Tyner presents another example of this adaptive quality in his rhapsodic trio performance of "Wave," alongside Ron Carter and Tony Williams, from his 1977 *Supertrios* project. I suspect that Tyner may have been inspired by Ahmad Jamal's trio recording of this same song from 1970, an uncharacteristically aggressive outing from this often understated player.

The composer has left us a handful of recordings of "Wave," of which his 1967 rendition from the hit album of the same name remains the best known, but jazz fans may also want to hear the more intimate version recorded by Jobim with an all-star band in São Paulo in 1993. And with this song, as with so many Jobim compositions, João Gilberto offers the closest thing to a definitive vocal performance, which can be heard on his 1977 release *Amoroso*.

RECOMMENDED VERSIONS

Antonio Carlos Jobim, from *Wave*, Englewood Cliffs, New Jersey, May–June 1967

Frank Sinatra, from *Sinatra and Company*, Hollywood, February 11, 1969

Ahmad Jamal, from *The Awakening*, New York, February 2–3, 1970

Sarah Vaughan, from *Live in Japan*, live at Sun Plaza Hall, Tokyo, September 24, 1973

Paul Desmond, from *Live*, live at Bourbon Street, Toronto, October 25–November 1, 1975

João Gilberto, from *Amoroso*, New York, November 17–19, 1976, and Hollywood, January 3–7, 1977

McCoy Tyner (with Ron Carter and Tony Williams), from *Supertrios*, Berkeley, California, April 9–10, 1977

Antonio Carlos Jobim, from *Antonio Carlos Jobim and Friends*, live at the São Paulo Free Jazz Festival, São Paulo, September 27, 1993

Fred Hersch and Bill Frisell, from *Songs We Know*, San Francisco, circa 1998

The Way You Look Tonight

Composed by Jerome Kern, with lyrics by Dorothy Fields

Fred Astaire introduced this Oscar-winning song in the 1936 film *Swing Time*, but—in a departure for this celebrated song-and-dance man—didn't show his feet once. He is seated at the piano for the scene and sings it to Ginger Rogers who, in an even less elegant posture, is in the bathroom with shampoo in her hair. The *New York Times* wasn't impressed, panning Jerome Kern's music for the film as "merely adequate or worse. Neither good Kern or good swing." Audiences were more enthusiastic, and Astaire's recording of "The Way You Look Tonight" became a #1 hit in October 1936.

Much of the impetus behind *Swing Time*—and certainly behind the selection of the movie's name, which had been a late choice—was to take advantage of the public's obsession for anything and everything labeled as "swing" during this period. Benny Goodman's huge success on the West Coast the previous year had launched the so-called Swing Era, and anyone with even the loosest connection to hot jazz was trying to take advantage of the craze. Jerome Kern, born in 1885, was hardly the right person to champion the new sound—back in the 1920s, he had led a crusade to stop jazz bands from "distorting" his songs, and had actually proclaimed that there was nothing original or inherently American about jazz music. Now even Kern was trying to get into the swing of swing jazz, but with unclear results. One of his other compositions for the Astaire movie had been ridiculed by Astaire's rehearsal pianist Hal Borne for its corny syncopations, and Kern was involved in heated behind-the-scenes conflicts over the suitability of his music.

Perhaps this history explains the peculiar construction of "The Way You Look Tonight"—in which there are not only *no syncopations*, but every melody note is played on the beat! This almost seems like a negation of swing. Who would have predicted a happy future for this composition as a jazz standard?

Yet it's worth noting that the Kern piece with the most similar rhythmic phrasing, "All the Things You Are"—which is almost a darker, more melancholy twin of "The Way You Look Tonight"—ranks as the most popular piece by this composer among jazz musicians. Maybe songs of this sort succeed because they can serve as a Rorschach test for improvisers, allowing—indeed forcing!—performers to find their own paths to jazziness amidst the on-the-beat chord tones.

Dorothy Fields later said that she cried the first time she heard Kern's melody, so moved was she by the beauty of the tune. William Zinsser has pointed out that her lyrics begin with a convoluted run-on sentence of 26 words that takes more than a dozen bars to complete. Yet Fields's contribution conveys a certain emotional logic, which may even be accentuated by the rambling quality of her syntax. Kern's structure is equally elongated, with both the A and B themes stretching out for 16 bars and the form capped by an extra four-bar tag at the end.

Ten weeks after movie's release, Teddy Wilson went into the recording studio with hopes of capitalizing on the success of the new Kern song, and brought along 21-year-old vocalist Billie Holiday. Wilson and company take the piece at a much faster pace than Astaire, and focus mostly on instrumental solos—the performance is half over before Holiday sings a note. Often Holiday's stamp of approval would lead other singers to add a song to their repertoire, but she apparently had little effect in this instance. No major jazz star would record the song during the remainder of the decade, and the Kern composition would not return to the charts until Mr. Wilson's former employer, Benny Goodman, released "The Way You Look Tonight" in a 1942 feature for vocalist Peggy Lee—a lullaby version that finds Mel Powell tinkling on a celeste and the rhythm section playing at a whisper.

The following year Frank Sinatra recorded a contemplative interpretation of the song on a V-disc, but his brasher treatment from a 1964 session with Nelson Riddle is the performance everyone remembers these days—this rendition has become the most widely heard version of the Kern tune, used for TV commercials (to sell Michelob beer, Chase credit cards), emulated on *American Idol*, and regurgitated by Sinatra impersonators of all stripes.

With a melody consisting entirely of quarter notes, half notes, and whole notes, this song is almost begging for up-tempo treatment, if only to impart a sense of momentum to phrases that each seem bunkered in their own bar. I could even imagine that, under slightly different circumstances, this tune might have evolved into a favored blowing number akin to "Cherokee," an ultra-fast song employed by boppers to end their sets. Charlie Parker occasionally played the Kern composition in just that manner, but never in a studio session; however, his recording of "Klaustance" relies on the chord changes from "The Way You Look Tonight"—and since the performance jumps right into the solos from the outset of the track, I assume that the Kern melody was deliberately left out of the arrangement as a cost-saving measure or to avoid the wrath of the jazzophobic composer. An amateur recording made at the Onyx Club on 52nd Street in 1948 captures Parker soaring in a full-fledged performance of "The Way You Look Tonight," and the altoist improvises here at top form; but the muffled audio quality and abysmal mix—it sounds as if a cheap recording device were placed between Tommy Potter's bass and Max Roach's drum kit—will dissuade all but the most avid Bird devotees from this music.

More sonically satisfying examples of the hot side of "The Way You Look Tonight" can be found on recordings by Clifford Brown, Tina Brooks, and, best of all, Johnny Griffin's 1957 album *A Blowing Session*, which also features John Coltrane, Hank Mobley, Lee Morgan, and Art Blakey in a dream hard bop lineup. Given Jerome Kern's distaste for jazz players tampering with his tunes, he probably would have turned off the record player before the end of the first chorus, maybe even phoned his lawyer. But fans of saxophony will want to hear this battle, which is less well known than the "Tenor Madness" session pitting Coltrane against Rollins from the previous year, but every bit as exciting.

RECOMMENDED VERSIONS

Billie Holiday (with Teddy Wilson), New York, October 21, 1936

Benny Goodman (with Peggy Lee), New York, March 10, 1942

Charlie Parker, live at the Onyx Club, New York, July 6, 1948

Dave Brubeck (with his Octet), San Francisco, July 1950

Art Blakey (with Clifford Brown), from *A Night at Birdland, Vol. 2*, live at Birdland, New York, February 21, 1954

Sonny Rollins (with Thelonious Monk), from *Thelonious Monk and Sonny Rollins*, Hackensack, New Jersey, October 25, 1954

Mel Tormé (with the Marty Paich Dektette), from *Mel Tormé Sings Fred Astaire*, Hollywood, November 1956

Johnny Griffin (with John Coltrane), from *A Blowing Session*, Hackensack, New Jersey, April 6, 1957

Tina Brooks, from *Minor Move*, Hackensack, New Jersey, March 16, 1958

Frank Sinatra, from *Frank Sinatra Sings Days of Wine And Roses, Moon River, and Other Academy Award Winners*, Los Angeles, January 27, 1964

Tete Montoliu, from *Music for Anna*, live at La Boite, Barcelona, October 6–7, 1992

Taylor Ho Bynum and Eric Rosenthal, from *Cenote*, Boston, November–December 2000 and February 2001

Well, You Needn't
Composed by Thelonious Monk

The song's title reportedly came from Charles Beamon, an aspiring vocalist and the cousin of the composer's sister-in-law Geraldine Smith. Monk could do little to help the man's singing career but offered to name a song for him. Beamon's reply was "Well, you need not," a demurral that Monk, true to his word, adopted as the title.

Back in February 1944, a version of this song was copyrighted under the title "You Need 'Na." Teddy McRae, who handled the filing, listed himself as co-composer, much to Monk's dismay. Such practices were not uncommon and, as we have seen, many jazz standards find freeloaders grabbing a share of the royalty checks. But Monk was shrewd enough to make a few alterations, and when he finally recorded the song in 1947 he listed it under a new title with his name as sole composer.

Few other jazz artists recorded "Well, You Needn't" in the early years following its debut. In a noteworthy exception—especially when one considers how rarely he performed any of Monk's songs—Charlie Parker can be heard playing "Well, You Needn't" on an amateur recording made by Dean Benedetti at the Onyx Club in July 1948. As with the Kern track described above, the sound quality here is terrible—Benedetti had set up his equipment in a storage room below the bandstand, through which he drilled a hole to place a microphone, apparently near Max Roach's drum kit. Even so, it is fascinating to hear the leading altoist of modern jazz tackle this piece at a time when few others paid any notice to it. Bird attacks it with obvious relish, spurred on by the aggressive comping of the composer, who is sitting in on piano.

Miles Davis can't be heard on this track, although he was no doubt present that evening as a member of Parker's combo and may even have been on the stand when it was recorded. But when the first studio cover version of "Well, You Needn't" was recorded—albeit not until 1954—Davis was the bandleader. This performance is less poised, however, than the trumpeter's later recordings of the composition, notably his version with John Coltrane from 1956 and a 1961 track made at the Black Hawk.

In the early 1960s, other jazz artists were finally taking notice of this song, as demonstrated on recordings by Cannonball Adderley, Eddie "Lockjaw" Davis, Bud Shank, Chet Baker, and Phineas Newborn Jr. I suspect that Miles Davis had more impact than Monk on this brief flurry of interest. I am not surprised that, when the song dropped from Davis's repertoire in the mid-1960s, cover versions of "Well, You Needn't" also fell out of fashion—although Monk featured it regularly in concert during that same period. Very few recordings can be found from the late 1960s and early 1970s; Monk's music was perhaps seen as too prickly for the fusion movement whose sound set the tone for the era. But shortly before Monk's death in 1982, "Well, You Needn't" began showing up again with increasing frequency on jazz albums and in live performances, and has maintained its popularity ever since.

The melody, as with many of Monk's best works, comes across as both catchy and unsettling. The lopsided phrases of the main theme arrive with a real kick, whether played fast or slow, and the relentless logic of the bridge— which plays off a simple idea built on chord tones, which Monk moves up and down in half-steps—testifies to the composer's ability to impart a querulous, experimental quality to something that is little more than a playful extension of an elementary pattern.

RECOMMENDED VERSIONS

Thelonious Monk, New York, October 24, 1947

Charlie Parker (with Thelonious Monk), live at the Onyx Club, New York, July 11, 1948

Miles Davis (John Coltrane), from *Steamin'*, Hackensack, New Jersey, October 26, 1956

Thelonious Monk (with Coleman Hawkins and John Coltrane), from *Monk's Music*, New York, June 26, 1957

Miles Davis (with Hank Mobley), from *In Person, Saturday Night at the Blackhawk, San Francisco*, live at the Black Hawk, San Francisco, April 22, 1961

Cannonball Adderley, from *The Cannonball Adderley Quintet Plus*, New York, May 11, 1961

Herbie Hancock (with Wynton Marsalis), from *Quartet*, Tokyo, July 28, 1981

Don Pullen, from *Don Pullen Plays Monk*, New York, October 11, 1984

Charles McPherson, from *First Flight Out*, New York, January 25–26, 1994

Ron Carter (with Javon Jackson and Gonzalo Rubalcaba), from *Mr. Bow Tie*, New York, February 17–18, 1995

What Is This Thing Called Love?
Composed by Cole Porter

I find the title phrase a little awkward, akin to those *Jeopardy!* quiz show answers that, the TV host incessantly reminds us, "must be stated in the form of a question." Yet Cole Porter later claimed that the title served as the key to whole composition, inspiring a haunting melodic line. The music and words came together so easily, he later recounted, it was almost as if they wrote themselves.

The song received a warm welcome virtually from its debut in the 1929 musical revue *Wake Up and Dream*, and several bandleaders—Leo Reisman, Ben Bernie, and Fred Rich—enjoyed hit recordings with the song in 1930. Reisman's performance is notable for featuring Ellington trumpeter, Bubber Miley, a rare example of an integrated society dance band from the era. James P. Johnson recorded a solo piano version the very next day, and gave the song a swinging stride treatment, but this was a rare jazz adaptation of a composition that generally was dressed up in tepid dance arrangements until the late 1930s.

Artie Shaw enjoyed a hit with his 1938 recording of "What Is This Thing Called Love?" and Tommy Dorsey put the song back on the chart in 1942. This period marks the true beginning of the Porter song's history as a jazz standard. Before the close of World War II the composition would be covered by Art Tatum, Sidney Bechet, Lena Horne, Nat King Cole, and, recording the day before the end of hostilities, Billie Holiday.

Three months earlier, Dizzy Gillespie and Charlie Parker had made the debut recording of Tadd Dameron's "Hot House"—based on the chords to "What Is This Thing Called Love?"—testifying to the appeal of this song, or at least its underlying harmonies, for the new generation of jazz modernists. For a spell, Dameron's reworking was more popular than Porter's original with the young progressive players of the day, and other musicians also constructed their own melodic variations on top of these changes. Lee Konitz borrowed the chords for his "Subconscious-Lee," and Fats Navarro for his "Barry's Bop." Some years later, Bill Evans relied on Porter's progression for his "These Things Called Changes," as did John Coltrane for "Fifth House," although throwing in his trademark substitute harmonies in the process. But the strangest transformation of Porter's song during the postwar era no doubt comes from guitarist Les Paul, who achieved a top 20 hit in 1948 with an eerie electric-guitar treatment that could have served as the soundtrack to a Cold War sci-fi film.

In the 1950s a number of leading jazz stars offered fresh treatments of "What Is This Thing Called Love?" Dave Brubeck's Octet delivered a quasi-avant-garde arrangement on the ensemble's 1950 recording for the Fantasy label, replete with many unexpected ingredients, including a shift into 3/4 for part of the final chorus—much different in flavor from the understated version of the same song the pianist made with his quartet fifteen years later. Charlie Parker recorded "What Is This Thing Called Love?" with a big band two years after Brubeck, and the results are spirited enough, but I would have been intrigued to hear what Bird might have done as featured soloist with this same Octet arrangement. Charles Mingus also adopted an unconventional approach as part of the aptly named *The Jazz Experiments of Charles Mingus* album from 1954, mixing equal doses of Dameron's "Hot House" with Porter's standard.

For the most part, modern-day performers of this song have been less interested in clever arrangements, and more focused on sheer speed. The version recorded by the Clifford Brown/Max Roach quintet in 1956 is emblematic of the song's most familiar role in the modern jazz repertoire, as a fast, swinging number perfect for opening or closing a set (or, in this case, an LP). Sonny Rollins, a member of the Brown-Roach combo, presented an up-tempo version of "What Is This Thing Called Love?" (not surprisingly as a set opener) on his well-known live recording at the Village Vanguard. You will hear a similar off-to-the-races conception of the song on recordings by Stan Getz, Cannonball Adderley, J. J. Johnson, Art Pepper, Woody Shaw, Kenny Garrett, Vincent Herring, and many others.

Even so, this old song is still capable of taking on new guises. Occasionally these come via dissonance and tough love—as Matthew Shipp shows on his solo piano version from 2009. But sometimes the most unexpected twist comes from returning to the roots, as Bobby McFerrin demonstrates on his 1986 duet recording alongside Herbie Hancock, which brings "What Is This Thing Called Love?" back to its initial conception as a medium-slow love song.

RECOMMENDED VERSIONS

Leo Reisman (with Bubber Miley), New York, January 20, 1930

James P. Johnson, New York, January 21, 1930

Artie Shaw, New York, September 27, 1938

Tommy Dorsey (with Connie Haines), Hollywood, December 22, 1941

Billie Holiday, New York, August 14, 1945

Dave Brubeck (with his Octet), San Francisco, July 1950

Charlie Parker, New York, March 25, 1952

Charles Mingus (with Thad Jones), from *The Jazz Experiments of Charles Mingus*, New York, December 1954

Clifford Brown and Max Roach, from *Clifford Brown and Max Roach at Basin Street*, New York, February 16, 1956

Sonny Rollins, from *A Night at the Village Vanguard*, live at the Village Vanguard, New York, November 3, 1957

Cannonball Adderley, from *At the Lighthouse*, live at the Lighthouse, Hermosa Beach, California, October 16, 1960

Woody Shaw (with Gary Bartz), from *United*, New York, March 7, 1981

Bobby McFerrin and Herbie Hancock, from *The Other Side of 'Round Midnight*, Paris, February 1986

Matthew Shipp, from *4D*, New York, May 17, 2009

What's New?

Composed by Bob Haggart, with lyrics by Johnny Burke

Many listeners who were introduced to this song via Linda Ronstadt's triple-platinum 1983 album *What's New* had only the vaguest notion of the jazz lineage of the composition. Yet even most jazz fans, I suspect, are unaware that "What's New?" originally came from a band and composer best known as exponents of white Dixieland music, that least hip of jazz idioms. As one exponent of this style of performance lamented to me: "When people ask me, 'Do you play cool jazz?' I tell 'em, 'No, I play un-cool jazz'"—an unfair assessment of trad jazz, no doubt, but a not uncommon one among opinion leaders in the music world.

In time, this song earned its coolness credentials, via performances by Billie Holiday, John Coltrane, Miles Davis, and others. But it started out as an instrumental entitled "I'm Free," recorded in 1938 by Bob Crosby's band, for which composer Bob Haggart worked as bassist, composer, and arranger. If not for this song, Haggart would be remembered today as a specialist in Dixieland and novelty numbers, most notably "Big Noise from Winnetka" and "South Rampart Street Parade." But "What's New?" is something else, a noir ballad, set in a major key but with the sensibility of the minor mode.

Indeed, you could resolve this song in C minor, rather than C major (and Crosby's band seems on the verge of doing just that on the debut recording, before opting for a more uplifting finale), and it might be an even better match with the personality of the song—not just the musical sensibility but also the lovelorn sentiments of the lyrics by Johnny Burke. Words were added after the song's debut, but so closely match the emotional tone of the melody that one could easily imagine Haggart constructing his song with them in mind.

Not everything pleases me here. The bridge is essentially a transposition of the main theme, a device songwriters occasionally fall back on but which typically strikes me as the musical equivalent of a TV rerun—a visitation here of what's old in a song that's supposed to be about what's new. Yet the harmonic movement is satisfying, and the touches of chromaticism in the melody impart a dreamy Chopinesque flavor to the proceedings.

Both Miles Davis and Charlie Parker played this song in live performance, but neither recorded it in the studio on a leader date. Better known among jazz fans today are versions by Billie Holiday—it is one of her most moving late-career recorded performances—and John Coltrane, who offered a restrained treatment on his popular *Ballads* album. The song is almost always played at a slow pulse, but Woody Shaw shakes things up with a brittle, up-tempo treatment alongside Cedar Walton on his *Setting Standards* release from 1983. And Cecil Taylor shows, on his live 1962 recording of the song, that no matter your own thoughts on what's new, he probably had something newer in mind.

RECOMMENDED VERSIONS

Bob Crosby (recorded as "I'm Free"), Chicago, October 19, 1938

Helen Merrill (with Clifford Brown), from *Helen Merrill*, New York, December 24, 1954

Billie Holiday (with Benny Carter), from *Velvet Mood*, Los Angeles, August 25, 1955

John Coltrane, from *Ballads*, Englewood Cliffs, New Jersey, September 18, 1962

Cecil Taylor (with Jimmy Lyons and Sunny Murray), from *Nefertiti, the Beautiful One Has Come*, live at Café Montmartre, Copenhagen, November 23, 1962

Dexter Gordon, from *Our Man in Amsterdam*, live at the Paradiso, Amsterdam, February 5, 1969

Betty Carter, from *'Round Midnight*, live at Judson Hall, New York, December 6, 1969

Modern Jazz Quartet, from *The Last Concert*, live at Avery Fisher Hall, New York, November 25, 1974

Woody Shaw (with Cedar Walton), from *Setting Standards*, Englewood Cliffs, New Jersey, December 1, 1983

Bennie Wallace (with Lou Levy), from *The Old Songs*, Hollywood, January 18–20, 1993

When the Saints Go Marching In
Traditional

Casual fans assume that New Orleans musicians love playing this song. But nothing could be further from the truth. Even back in the 1960s, the Preservation Hall Jazz Band would perform "St. James Infirmary" for a dollar tip, but insisted on five bucks before honoring a request for "When the Saints Go Marching In." Who could blame them? Even if the musicians were blasé, the tourists love it and, since they didn't consider their visit to the Big Easy complete until they had heard it played by a *real jazz musician*, they would invariably fork over the cash.

In fact, not a single New Orleans jazz musician recorded this song during the 1920s and early 1930s. Jelly Roll Morton, King Oliver, Freddie Keppard, and a who's who of other New Orleans legends never performed it in a recording studio. And even Louis Armstrong—the jazz artist most closely associated with this song—didn't tackle it until his late thirties, almost 16 years after he left New Orleans. He finally introduced this traditional hymn to jazz fans at a 1938 session in New York for the Decca label, and his version of the now familiar tune was a top 10 radio hit the following year. "Saints" stayed in Armstrong's repertoire the rest of his life—he eventually left behind around 60 versions on record and film.

Even at the start, a bit of hokum was apparent. "Sisters and brothers, this is Reverend Satchmo getting ready to beat out this mellow sermon for you," Armstrong proclaims during the introduction to his debut recording. "My text this evenin': 'When the Saints Go Marching In' . . ." Armstrong knew the song from his time at the Waif's Home, where he had been institutionalized as a youngster. As a member of the brass band, he would have played this song for funerals—it would be performed as a dirge (rarely done nowadays) on the way to the cemetery, and in a more boisterous style on the way back. When Armstrong recorded it as a jazz song, audiences loved it, but his sister told him that his adaptation was inappropriate and sacrilegious.

The composition, of disputed authorship and possibly originating in the Bahamas, came into its own as part of the traditional jazz revival movement that flourished during the years following World War II. Trumpeter Bunk Johnson, a darling of the revivalists, embraced the song, recording it several times during the mid-1940s, and many others followed suit. By the close of the decade, "When the Saints Go Marching In" was established as a jazz standard, with most listeners assuming it had always been part of the repertoire. Yet more jazz versions of this song were recorded in 1949 and 1950 than in all the preceding years put together.

The song has by now traveled far beyond the confines of jazz, with recordings by Elvis Presley, the Beatles, Bruce Springsteen, and Fats Domino, among others, testifying to its universal appeal. I suspect that serious jazz fans have mostly lost interest, and dismiss this tune as just a cliché, holding no more surprises for devotees. Yet even the most jaded will find a version to their liking if they look in some unlikely places—for example, Jimmy Smith's soul jazz version from 1964 (which eerily anticipates Lee Morgan's hit recording of "The Sidewinder" from later that year) or Nicholas Payton's quasi-Brazilian reworking from 1995. Perhaps the only thing you won't hear nowadays is a somber traditional version suitable for an honest-to-God funeral. For that, you are advised to bypass all the jazz performances and check out the Paramount Jubilee Singers' rendition from November 1923—the very first recording of this song—which is sung with plenty of feeling, and no tip required.

RECOMMENDED VERSIONS

Paramount Jubilee Singers, New York, November 1923

Louis Armstrong, New York, May 13, 1938

Bunk Johnson, New York, December 19, 1945

Sidney Bechet, New York, January 21, 1949

Jimmy Smith, from *Prayer Meetin'*, Englewood Cliffs, New Jersey, February 8, 1963

Sweet Emma and Her Preservation Hall Jazz Band, from *Sweet Emma*, live at
Tyrone Guthrie Theater, Minneapolis, October 18, 1964

Nicholas Payton, from *Gumbo Nouveau*, New York, November 28–30, 1995

Wycliffe Gordon (with Marcus Printup and Eric Reed), from *In the Cross*, Brooklyn,
New York, December 12, 2003, and Augusta, Georgia, January 2–3, 2004

Whisper Not
Composed by Benny Golson

While gigging at Storyville in Boston with Dizzy Gillespie's band, Benny Golson
would visit the deserted club during the daytime hours, seat himself at the
piano keyboard, and work on new compositions. "Whisper Not" came to him so
easily during one of these working sessions—taking a mere 20 minutes to
write—that Golson doubted its value. But Gillespie heard the piece and wanted
to play it with the band. Other musicians quickly picked up on it, and before
Golson had the chance to record it with his own combo, Lee Morgan and Thad
Jones had also featured it with their own groups.

The song's ease of conception is reflected in its unlabored flow. The phrases
succeed each other with a rigorous logic that, if not for the occasional blue note,
would be more characteristic of a classical prelude than a hard bop chart. The
harmonic movement grabs the listener's attention by alternating between a
whole-step bassline and a conventional circle of fifths progression, both familiar enough in jazz songs but combined here in a fresh manner. As with Golson's best work, "Whisper Not" manages to convey both elegance and subtle
funkiness.

Leonard Feather contributed lyrics, and showed no threat of putting Cole
Porter out of business. But these have occasionally shown up on recordings—
most notably as the title track from Ella Fitzgerald's collaboration with Marty
Paich from 1966. Anita O'Day's performance from 1962, which reunites her
with former Krupa bandmate Roy Eldridge, further confirms this piece's suitability as a vocal number.

But "Whisper Not" is more often presented as an instrumental, typically in
the context of a hard bop-oriented combo. I especially admire Shelly Manne's
performance from 1959, as part of the live Black Hawk recordings that captured
some of the best work of the drummer's career. Art Blakey also demonstrated
an affinity with "Whisper Not," and kept it in his band's book long after Golson
had departed. But the place to start here is with the composer himself, who has
given us more than a dozen recorded renditions of the song, both as sideman

and leader. Indeed, the piece has become so closely associated with its instigator that, 50 years after its debut, Benny Golson gave it marquee billing on his "Whisper Not Tour."

RECOMMENDED VERSIONS

Lee Morgan (with Horace Silver and Hank Mobley), from *Lee Morgan, Vol. 2*, Hackensack, New Jersey, December 2, 1956

Dizzy Gillespie (with an arrangement by Benny Golson), from *Birk's Works*, New York, April 8, 1957

Benny Golson (with Art Farmer), from *New York Scene*, New York, October 14, 1957

Art Blakey (with Lee Morgan and Benny Golson), from *1958 Paris Olympia*, live at the the Olympia, Paris, December 17, 1958

Shelly Manne, live at the Black Hawk, *Shelly Manne and His Men at the Black Hawk, Vol. 3*, live at the Black Hawk, San Francisco, September 23, 1959

Anita O'Day (with Roy Eldridge and Gene Harris), from *Anita O'Day and the Three Sounds*, New York, October 12–15, 1962

Ella Fitzgerald (with an arrangement by Marty Paich), from *Whisper Not*, Los Angeles, July 20, 1966

Keith Jarrett (with the Standards Trio), from *Whisper Not*, live at Palais des Congrès, Paris, July 5, 1999

Willow Weep for Me
Composed by Ann Ronell

While an undergraduate at Radcliffe, Ann Ronell interviewed George Gershwin for a student publication. She confessed her own songwriting aspirations to the composer, who offered encouragement and asked her to look him up in New York after her graduation. She did just that in 1927, and Gershwin directed her toward a career on Broadway, where Ronell was soon working as a rehearsal pianist and vocal coach. Yet her attempts to sell her own songs met with resistance—no doubt aggravated by Ronell's status as a woman in a male-dominated sector of the entertainment industry. But her "Baby's Birthday Party" proved to be a modest hit, finally opening doors for the young composer.

During her first year at Radcliffe, Ann Ronell had been struck by the loveliness of the willow trees on campus, and this simple observation became the subject of an intricate song. Ronell took "Willow Weep for Me" to Irving Berlin's publishing company, but Berlin's associate Saul Bornstein expressed sharp criticism of the piece—especially its rhythmic complexity and its dedication to George Gershwin. Even after "Willow Weep for Me" became a hit, Ronell continued to hear from naysayers—one publisher telling her, some 30 years later, "If I walked into an office today with 'Willow Weep for Me,' I'd never be able to sell it."

But when Irving Berlin himself heard the song, he was enthusiastic, and helped get "Willow Weep for Me" on the radio. Paul Whiteman and Ted Fio Rito both had hit recordings with the song in December 1932. Whiteman's version may surprise modern listeners by its radical conception of the pulse, which includes sporadic bursts of double time (implicit in Ronell's composition but rarely emphasized to such a degree by later interpreters) and an effective stop-time interlude.

Stan Kenton's recording from 1946 was popular with disk jockeys and jazz fans, and helped to establish "Willow Weep for Me" as a jazz standard. June Christy, who handles vocal duties here, is remarkably unflustered by Pete Rugolo's demonstrative arrangement, and would even adopt the tune as one of her signature pieces. But "Willow Weep for Me" did not lack for other high-profile advocates. Frank Sinatra recorded Ronell's song on his *Only the Lonely* album from 1958—an LP that the singer later picked out as his personal favorite among his releases. Seven years later, in January 1965, the British pop duo Chad & Jeremy reached #15 on the *Billboard* Hot 100 with a very different treatment of the song.

I most closely associate "Willow Weep for Me" with pianist Art Tatum, who featured it frequently in performances during the last decade of his life. Tatum's introduction is occasionally borrowed by later performers—I've heard Hank Jones, Phineas Newborn, and others rely on it. Tatum's precedent has no doubt convinced many later pianists that "Willow Weep for Me" is primarily a virtuoso piece requiring a generous application of arpeggios and sweeping runs. But the song is equally effective as a vehicle for understated soulfulness—hear Red Garland's trio version from 1956 if you have doubts. I find it worth noting that Oscar Peterson, one of the most accomplished technicians in the history of jazz, avoided Tatumesque fireworks when performing "Willow Weep for Me" and instead opted for a hard-grooving funkiness.

Yet still other interpretations have emerged with this multifaceted composition. Bob Brookmeyer's arrangement for the Thad Jones/Mel Lewis Orchestra offers an inspiring example of how a visionary arranger can revitalize an old song. And for a cranky but brilliantly realized experiment, check out Phil Woods's attempt to blend "Willow Weep for Me" with Miles Davis's "All Blues"— a recording which features top-notch alto work from Woods and a beast of a piano solo from Jaki Byard.

RECOMMENDED VERSIONS

Paul Whiteman (with Irene Taylor), New York, November 17, 1932

Stan Kenton (with June Christy), Hollywood, July 25, 1946

Art Tatum, live at the Shrine Auditorium, Los Angeles, April 2, 1949

Red Garland, from *Groovy*, New York, December 14, 1956

Frank Sinatra, from *Frank Sinatra Sings for Only the Lonely*, Hollywood, May 29, 1958

Thad Jones/Mel Lewis Orchestra (with an arrangement by Bob Brookmeyer), from *Presenting Thad Jones/Mel Lewis and The Jazz Orchestra*, New York, May 6, 1966

Phil Woods (with Jaki Byard), from *Musique du Bois*, New York, January 14, 1974

Oscar Peterson and Harry "Sweets" Edison, from *Oscar Peterson and Harry Edison*, Los Angeles, December 21, 1974

Dorothy Donegan, from *The Many Faces of Dorothy Donegan*, Antibes, France, July 22, 1975

Andy Bey, from *Ballads, Blues and Bey*, New York, May 19–20, 1995

Bennie Wallace (with Kenny Barron), from *The Nearness of You*, New York, June 23–24, 2003

Yardbird Suite

Composed by Charlie Parker

The Yardbird in question is Charlie "Yardbird" Parker (the nickname is usually abbreviated to Bird), and the "suite" mentioned in the title is actually a straightforward 32-bar song. That said, Parker did not require longer forms to display his acumen, and was able to infuse considerable innovation into the simple compositional structures he inherited from Tin Pan Alley composers. Indeed, the title here is no doubt intended as a playful reference to Igor Stravinsky's imposing work, the *Firebird Suite* (*Suite de L'Oiseau de Feu*).

Parker's songs, once commonly called at jam sessions and gigs, are somewhat less popular with jazz musicians nowadays. But even at this far remove, his pathbreaking efforts of the 1940s still cast a long shadow over the art form. Fashions may change, but any serious improviser still must come to grips with Parker sooner or later, and "Yardbird Suite" is a good place to begin. This song has one of the easiest bebop melody lines to play, and is usually taken at an ambling medium or medium-fast tempo that stands in stark contrast to the rapid-fire showpieces that make up much of the bebop repertoire. "Yardbird Suite" is mid-level Parker, somewhat more challenging than his blues pieces, but far less daunting than "Ko-Ko" or "Donna Lee."

Unlike many of Parker's compositions, "Yardbird Suite"—first recorded by the altoist in Hollywood in 1946 as part of his historic work for the Dial label comes with an original set of chord changes, rather than the borrowed pop song harmonies. Some have suggested, incorrectly, that Parker borrowed the chords from Earl Hines's "Rosetta," but the progressions are markedly different.

Gil Evans was one of the first arrangers to adopt bop songs for big band format, and he showcased "Yardbird Suite" in a forward-looking chart for Claude Thornhill's band—performed in December 1947 at a session that also featured 20-year-old altoist Lee Konitz. Konitz seemed focused on showing here how little he deferred to Parker's precedent, and exudes a rare degree of confidence for a young player defying the leading role model of the day.

In truth, the composition has few tell-tale bop mannerisms in its melody line, and as such can be adapted to other performance styles with ease. Jimmy McGriff has funkified it, Joe Lovano has turned it into a waltz, and both Eddie Jefferson and Bob Dorough have added lyrics. (In fact, Parker himself—in an uncharacteristic gesture—wrote his own sentimental words to the song, which he originally called "What Price Love.") Long after Parker's death, Jay McShann, who had been Bird's boss back in the 1930s, recorded a version that sounds more like old Kansas City jazz than bebop—not so surprising when one considers that McShann had performed the song with the composer back in Kaycee in the early 1940s.

Even so, the most characteristic performances of this standard come from artists deeply schooled in the modern jazz idiom, with especially notable versions recorded by Frank Morgan, Hampton Hawes, and Dodo Marmarosa, each of whom had played alongside Bird, and evoke his legacy in their interpretations.

RECOMMENDED VERSIONS

Charlie Parker, Hollywood, March 28, 1946

Claude Thornhill (with Lee Konitz and an arrangement by Gil Evans), New York, December 17, 1947

Bob Dorough, from *Devil May Care*, New York, October 1956

Hampton Hawes, from *Four*, Los Angeles, January 27, 1958

Dodo Marmarosa, from *Complete Studio Recordings*, Chicago, May 4, 1962

Eddie Jefferson, from *Come Along with Me*, New York, August 12, 1969

Jimmy McGriff, from *Fly Dude*, New York, 1972

Jay McShann, from *The Man from Muskogee*, Toronto, June 4, 1972

Frank Morgan, from *Yardbird Suite*, Berkeley, California, January 11–12, 1988

Joe Lovano (with Esperanza Spalding), from *Bird Songs*, New York, September 7–8, 2010

Yesterdays

Composed by Jerome Kern, with lyrics by Otto Harbach

Jerome Kern had high hopes for his 1933 musical based on Alice Duer Miller's novel *Gowns by Roberta*, a love story where romance comes to fruition in a Paris dress shop. But the show received a tepid response at its Philadelphia opening in October, and frantic last-minute changes—new costumes, new sets, and a shortened title (now simply *Roberta*)—did little to help matters in New York the following month. But gradually word of mouth overcame unfavorable reviews. Ticket sales picked up over the holiday season, *Roberta* eventually lasted for 295 performances, and was transformed into a successful Hollywood film in 1935. The show was brought to movie theaters a second time in 1952, under the name *Lovely to Look At*. And later came to television audiences in a high profile NBC broadcast from 1969—the latter featuring Bob Hope, who had starred in the original 1933 production.

Many commentators attribute the turnaround after *Roberta*'s dismal opening to the appeal of a single song, "Smoke Gets in Your Eyes," a timeless pop standard that would produce #1 hits for Paul Whiteman (in 1934) and the Platters (in 1959). "Yesterdays," from the same show, also enjoyed some success with the general public—Leo Reisman's very unjazzy recording was popular in the closing days of 1933—but would never match the other song's staying power or crossover appeal. In most years, "Smoke Gets in Your Eyes" has outsold "Yesterdays" by roughly a ten-to-one margin.

Yet jazz musicians have tended to prefer "Yesterdays," recording it far more often than "Smoke Gets in Your Eyes," although, based on my experience, the latter generates more requests from the audience. "Yesterdays," put simply, is a much better vehicle for improvisation, even if it lacks the grandiloquent melody of its more popular companion. It is more compact, sounding simple while still employing the rapid harmonic motion so characteristic of this composer's better works. The downward movement in the bass line is especially satisfying, countering the upward motion in the melody—the combination of these contrary impulses in bars 5–7 provides, in my opinion, the most memorable hook in the song.

Horn players soon appreciated the jazz potential in "Yesterdays." Artie Shaw and Coleman Hawkins were early adopters, and both kept the song in their repertoires for many years. But Art Tatum initiated another tradition in the 1940s by transforming "Yesterdays" into an extravagant piano showpiece—and a host of later keyboardists followed in his wake, presenting elaborate variations on the Kern song. Even normally incisive linear players such as Bud Powell and Hampton Hawes fell under Tatum's sway, and decorated their arrangements of this song with dramatic two handed gestures. Over the years, pianists who have wanted to establish their credentials as advanced technicians—such as Oscar Peterson, Lennie Tristano, Adam Makowicz, Paul Smith, and Dorothy Donegan—have inevitably found themselves drawn to this song. And performers on other instruments also came to embrace "Yesterdays" as a vehicle for showy pyrotechnics—on the much-publicized drum battle between Buddy Rich and Max Roach from 1959, the two percussionists engaged in fierce stick-to-stick combat on this very piece. The song also showed up when Sonny Rollins matched up with Coleman Hawkins in the studio in 1963, and when Stéphane Grappelli encountered Yehudi Menuhin in 1976, Kern's standard serving duty both in friendly collaborations and feisty confrontations.

But this song doesn't need to be played solely for ostentation or one-upmanship. Erroll Garner, who recorded "Yesterdays" on many occasions, found the soulfulness hidden inside the Kern tune—just listen to Garner's irresistible 1973 performance, on his unfairly forgotten *Magician* project, for a prime example. Keith Jarrett opts for an unhurried delivery on his trio outing from 2001. In contrast, David S. Ware and Matthew Shipp replace all the typical licks with buzzing, braying, and a general sense of pandemonium on their unsettling treatment from 1991.

RECOMMENDED VERSIONS

Coleman Hawkins, New York, February 16, 1944

Art Tatum, live at the Shrine Auditorium, Los Angeles, April 2, 1949

Bud Powell, New York, February 1950

Artie Shaw (with Hank Jones), from *The Last Recordings: Rare and Unreleased, Vol. 1,* Hollywood, June 1954

Charles Mingus (with Hampton Hawes), from *Mingus Three,* New York, July 9, 1957

Buddy Rich and Max Roach, from *Rich vs. Roach,* New York, April 7–8, 1959

Sonny Rollins and Coleman Hawkins, from *Sonny Meets Hawk!* New York, July 15, 1963

Erroll Garner, from *Magician,* New York, October 30, 1973

Stéphane Grappelli and Yehudi Menuhin, from *Tea for Two,* London, October 28–30, 1977

Tom Harrell (with Kenny Werner), from *Sail Away,* Paris, April 26, 1991

David S. Ware (with Matthew Shipp), from *Flight of I,* New York, December 10–11, 1991

Keith Jarrett (with the Standards Trio), from *Yesterdays,* live at the Metropolitan Festival Hall, Tokyo, April 30, 2001

You Don't Know What Love Is
Composed by Gene de Paul, with lyrics by Don Raye

Gene de Paul and Don Raye collaborated on three timeless jazz standards from the early 1940s—"You Don't Know What Love Is," "Star Eyes," and "I'll Remember April"—each of which succeeded despite placement in three of the most cornball slapstick comedies of the period. "I'll Remember April" first appeared in Abbot and Costello's goofy western *Ride 'Em Cowby* (1942), "Star Eyes" made its debut in Red Skelton's *I Dood It* (1943), while "You Don't Know What Love Is" had the least propitious start of them all. It was composed for Abbott & Costello's war effort comedy *Keep 'Em Flying* (1943)—the trailer was actually turned into a recruitment film for the military—but removed from the movie before release. While other songs of the period enjoyed the advocacy of Frank Sinatra or Bing Crosby or some glamorous starlet, this one ended up on the cutting-room floor, not good enough to hold on to its screen time, where it was sung by Carol Bruce in the role of a USO hostess.

In truth, few popular standards were less suitable for inclusion in a comedy movie. "You Don't Know What Love Is" ranks among the darkest, most melancholy ballads in the jazz repertoire, and characteristic performances bring out an almost anguished sensibility from the melody. Don Raye references the blues explicitly in the lyrics—*You don't know what love is until you've learned the meaning of the blues*—and the harmonic progression congruently invites the rawest minor blues licks. On the other hand, more than a few performers have tried to deliver "You Don't Know What Love Is" in a glib or casual manner—usually a failed strategy. More than most, this song reserves its riches for artists who step away from the prepared patterns and practice-room licks, and instead put something of their own emotional core into their phrases.

The song got a second chance on the screen in 1942, when it was included in *Behind the Eight Ball*. Again the setting was a comedy, this time featuring the Ritz Brothers, and the vocalist was still Carol Bruce. But even before this revival, jazz artists had started taking notice of the tune. In the final months of 1941, "You Don't Know What Love Is" was recorded by Ella Fitzgerald, Benny Goodman, Earl Hines, Harry James, and other bandleaders—in each instance, serving as a feature for a vocalist. The following April, Louis Armstrong performed "You Don't Know What Love Is" on a West Coast broadcast, again as a vocal number, but by then the song was already falling out of favor—only a handful of jazz cover versions would be made over the next decade.

When the song finally returned to prominence among jazz players, trumpeters were now its most ardent champions. Chet Baker recorded "You Don't Know What Love Is" with strings in 1953 and as a vocal number in 1955. Miles Davis performed it on a 1954 date for the Prestige label, and Thad Jones also brought it into the studio a few months later. By the second half of the decade the song had become a staple of jazz recordings and live performances. Sonny Rollins sealed the deal by showcasing the standard on his high-profile *Saxophone Colossus* album from 1956. Among later recordings of note, I would call attention to three seminal tracks from the early 1960s: Lennie Tristano's solo piano outing from *The New Tristano*, John Coltrane's lyrical interpretation from his *Ballads* project, and Eric Dolphy's extended flute workout from his *Last Date* release.

RECOMMENDED VERSIONS

Ella Fitzgerald, New York, October 28, 1941

Earl Hines (with Billy Eckstine), New York, November 17, 1941

Miles Davis, from *Walkin'*, Hackensack, New Jersey, April 3, 1954

Chet Baker, from *Chet Baker Sings and Plays*, Los Angeles, March 7, 1955

Sonny Rollins, from *Saxophone Colossus*, Hackensack, New Jersey, June 22, 1956

Lennie Tristano, from *The New Tristano*, New York, Autumn 1961

John Coltrane, from *Ballads*, Englewood Cliffs, New Jersey, November 13, 1962

Eric Dolphy, from *Last Date*, live at the VARA Studio, Hilversum, Holland, June 2, 1964

Freddie Hubbard, from *Outpost*, New York, March 16–17, 1981

Roy Hargrove (with Antonio Hart), from *Approaching Standards*, New York, 1994

You Go to My Head
Composed by J. Fred Coots, with lyrics by Haven Gillespie

In 1934, this same songwriting duo collaborated on "Santa Claus Is Coming to Town," which endeared itself to Mom and Dad by getting countless youngsters to move from the naughty to nice cohort group. Four years later, some of those nice kids had grown up, but I'm confident few parents encouraged their headstrong teens to follow the lead of the new Gillespie-Coots hit "You Go to My Head." This song was a paean to romantic infatuation, packed with similes relating love to booze; in the course of a few bars—musical ones, that is, not those called "Dew Drop Inn"—we get references to champagne, burgundy, and a kicker of julep. Indeed, this song comes closer than any tune I know to capturing in musical form the feeling of losing control.

If the words were a bit too sophisticated for the kids, so was the music. "You Go to My Head" is an intricately constructed affair with plenty of harmonic movement. The song starts in a major key, but from the second bar onward, Mr. Coots seems intent on creating a feverish dream quality tending more to the minor mode. The release builds on the drama, and the final restatement holds some surprises as well. The piece would be noteworthy even if it lacked such an exquisite coda, but those last eight bars convey a sense of resigned closure to the song that fittingly matches the resolution of the lyrics.

Four artists had hit records with this song during the summer of 1938. Larry Clinton's version was the biggest success, reaching as high as #3, but Teddy Wilson, Billie Holiday, and Glen Gray's Casa Loma Orchestra each enjoyed placement in the top 20 with their releases. The song fell out of circulation during the early 1940s, but was widely covered during the second half of the decade, with artists from a range of stylistic camps—including Dizzy Gillespie, Gene Krupa, Lena Horne, Coleman Hawkins, Dave Brubeck, Artie Shaw, and Lennie Tristano—bringing their individual talents to bear on it.

Vocalists tend to take this song at a "deep ballad" tempo, sometimes so extremely slow that they test the competence of the rhythm section to maintain a sense of swing while moving along at less than 40 beats per minute. Check out the recordings by Betty Carter and Shirley Horn for examples of how this can work when the instrumentalists on hand match the skill of the singer. In contrast, Bill Evans—whom one might expect to linger over the chart—delivers a simmering hard bop treatment on his 1962 *Interplay* album, helped along by Jim Hall and Freddie Hubbard.

Dave Brubeck and Paul Desmond take a different approach in their 1952 duet performance from Storyville, mixing romanticism and cerebral deconstruction in equal doses. Desmond had such fondness for this recording that when he and Brubeck reunited for a duet project in 1975, he wanted to showcase "You Go to My Head" again, and the song served as the emotional centerpiece of the resulting album. Both versions are worth hearing, but the earlier track is especially revealing of the simpatico relationship between these two artists, and is my favorite performance from their work for the Fantasy label.

RECOMMENDED VERSIONS

Casa Loma Orchestra (with Kenny Sargent), New York, February 24, 1938

Billie Holiday, New York, May 11, 1938

Coleman Hawkins (with Milt Jackson), New York, December 1946

Dizzy Gillespie (with Johnny Hartman), Chicago, May 6, 1949

Dave Brubeck and Paul Desmond, from *Jazz at Storyville*, live at Storyville, Boston, October 12, 1952

Bill Evans (with Freddie Hubbard and Jim Hall), from *Interplay*, New York, July 16, 1962

Betty Carter, from *It's Not about the Melody*, New York, 1992

Shirley Horn (with Joe Henderson and Elvin Jones), from *The Main Ingredient*, Washington, D.C., May 15–18, 1995

Dianne Reeves (with Nicholas Payton), from *A Little Moonlight*, New York, December 4–10, 2002

You Stepped Out of a Dream
Composed by Nacio Herb Brown, with lyrics by Gus Kahn

During the early 1940s, "You Stepped Out of a Dream" was best known as a theme song for actress Lana Turner, the leading Hollywood femme fatale of the period. The song had received prominent placement in the 1941 film *Ziegfeld Girl*, where Turner neither sings nor dances to the number, but merely promenades down a staircase in an extravagant costume amid a bevy of similarly clad chorus girls, while Tony Martin handles the vocal duties. Turner would never record the song, but the connection stuck—no doubt because she fit many guys' idea of precisely what they would like to see stepping out of their dreams.

Kay Kyser enjoyed a modest hit with the song at the time of its initial release, and recordings by Glenn Miller (featuring Ray Eberle and the Modernaires) and Guy Lombardo were also popular. These renditions came with little jazz content, but the song captured the attention of musicians, no doubt due to the unusual chord progression, which captures an appealingly exotic flavor while still serving as a suitable framework for improvisation. As early as 1941, George Shearing recorded "You Stepped Out of a Dream" in London, and American ex-pat Teddy Weatherford did the same in Calcutta.

Yet this song didn't become a widely played standard until the 1950s. Recordings by Dave Brubeck and Stan Getz from 1950 helped demonstrate the jazz potential of the piece, while later crossover efforts by Nat King Cole and the Four Freshmen kept the song in the consciousness of the general public. Sonny Rollins's combo performance from 1957 stands out as one of his best efforts of the period, and must have inspired a number of other saxophonists to add the song to their set lists; over the next several years, many of the leading tenorists of the day—including Dexter Gordon, Eddie "Lockjaw" Davis, Warne Marsh, Teddy Edwards, Brew Moore, and Archie Shepp—were captured on tape performing it.

"You Stepped Out of a Dream" has retained its place in the repertoire, although I note that, in more recent years, it has been more popular with singers than horn players. The melody, which stays within an octave range (albeit a widely used fake book lead sheet shows the tune ending on a high E that you will rarely hear in actual performance), makes few demands on vocalists with its long-held notes and few wide interval leaps. The lyrics are a bit of a sentimental mish-mash—praising the lips, the eyes, the smile, etc.—but built on the same clichés that always seem to find a ready audience. A few pop-oriented crooners (Peter Cincotti, Art Garfunkel) have tackled the number. Even so, I can hardly imagine a song of this complexity ever returning to the charts.

RECOMMENDED VERSIONS

Glenn Miller (with Ray Eberle), New York, January 17, 1941

George Shearing, London, December 9, 1941

Dave Brubeck, San Francisco, May 1950

Lennie Niehaus, from *Vol. 1: The Quintets*, Los Angeles, July 9, 1954

Barney Kessel, from *Kessel Plays Standards*, Los Angeles, September 12, 1955

Sonny Rollins (with J. J. Johnson), from *Sonny Rollins, Vol. 2*, New York, April 14, 1957

Dexter Gordon (with Sonny Clark), from *A Swingin' Affair*, Englewood Cliffs, New Jersey, August 29, 1962

McCoy Tyner, from *Fly with the Wind*, Berkeley, California, January 19–21, 1976

Shirley Horn, from *You Won't Forget Me*, June–August 1990

Stefon Harris, from *Black Action Figure*, New York, February 14–15, 1999

Johnny Griffin and Martial Solal, from *In and Out*, Paris, June 29–July 1, 1999

You'd Be So Nice to Come Home To
Composed by Cole Porter

Clearly, the redoubtable Mr. Porter never learned that you shouldn't end a sentence with a preposition. And "you'd" is no doubt the most inelegant of contractions. By the way, could you find a more namby-pamby modifier than "nice"? But, as a jazz player might say, the whole title phrase swings—may I say "swings nicely"?—and provides an excellent reminder of Porter's knack for invigorating poetic sentiments with colloquial English. The words of the song, written almost at the exact midpoint of World War II, must have echoed the sentiments of countless soldiers—and I suspect many quoted the title directly in their letters back home.

In fact, at an early stage the song had the cumbersome working title "You Would Be So Wonderful to Come Home To," and other names under consideration by the composer included "Someone to Come Home To" or "Something to Keep Me Warm." But when Porter completed the song on the last day of April 1942, it had the title by which it is now known, and early the following year it made its debut in the film *Something to Shout About* (dang, another concluding preposition!), for which it earned an Oscar nomination. Porter was disappointed, nonetheless, with the lukewarm public response to the film, which he dubbed "Something to Cry About."

Dinah Shore enjoyed a hit record with "You'd Be So Nice to Come Home To," but jazz musicians were hardly enthusiastic, and more than a decade elapsed before the song became a familiar standard. Singer Helen Merrill featured it on her 1954 EmArcy session, with Clifford Brown contributing a superb solo that threatens to outshine the vocal, and a number of prominent saxophonists adopted it over the next several years. Coleman Hawkins and Ben Webster rely on "You'd Be So Nice to Come Home To" for their 1957 tenor confrontation, and Zoot Sims and Al Cohn do the same on their 1960 project *You 'n Me.* Lee Konitz first recorded "You'd Be So Nice to Come Home To" in 1953, and would perform it on a half-dozen later albums. During this same period Cannonball Adderley, Sonny Stitt, Herb Geller, and Art Pepper also brought Porter's song to the studio.

In his autobiography *Straight Life*, Pepper describes the song and session in heroic—if perhaps exaggerated—terms: "I was going to have to play on a messed up horn. And I was going to have to play with Miles Davis's rhythm section. They played every single night, all night. I hadn't touched my horn in six months." Pepper arrived at the studio without knowing what songs to call, and relied on Red Garland's suggestion to start off with this Cole Porter tune, even though Pepper barely knew the melody. Yet his confident and incisive solo on the resulting track is completely convincing, and ranks among my favorite performances by this artist.

Cecil Taylor's recording of "You'd Be So Nice to Come Home To," made a few months earlier, takes a completely different approach to the song. This was the pianist's first commercial recording session, and he was still trying to find a way to express his radical new conception of jazz via the standard repertoire. At times on this album, Taylor seems hindered in his creativity by the harmonic structures implied in the bassline, but on the Cole Porter piece he dispenses with the rest of the band, and finally sounds completely free and unfettered in a solo piano outing. Forty seconds into the track, he breaks away dramatically from the basic structure of the composition, and over the course of the next nine minutes delivers one of the most avant-garde jazz performances of its day.

RECOMMENDED VERSIONS

Helen Merrill (with Clifford Brown), from *Helen Merrill*, New York, December 22, 1954

Cecil Taylor, from *Jazz Advance*, Boston, September 14, 1956

Art Pepper, from *Art Pepper Meets the Rhythm Section*, Los Angeles, January 19, 1957

Coleman Hawkins and Ben Webster, from *Coleman Hawkins Encounters Ben Webster*, Los Angeles, October 16, 1957

Al Cohn and Zoot Sims, from *You 'n Me*, New York, June 1 and 3, 1960

Nina Simone, from *Nina Simone at Newport*, live at the Newport Jazz Festival, Newport, Rhode Island, June 30, 1960

Jo Stafford (with Ben Webster), from *Jo + Jazz*, Los Angeles, August 1, 1960

Lee Konitz (with Elvin Jones), from *Motion*, New York, August 24, 1961

Jim Hall (with Paul Desmond and Chet Baker), from *Concierto*, April 16 and 23, 1975

David Murray, from *Love and Sorrow*, New York, September 14-17, 1993

Joey DeFrancesco, from *Singin' and Swingin'*, Hollywood, January 24–25, 1999

Dick Hyman and Randy Sandke, from *Now & Again*, New York, June 16–17, 2004

After You've Gone

3   Alec Wilder, a connoisseur of classic popular music, has called:
Alec Wilder, *American Popular Song: The Great Innovators,
1900–1950*, edited by James T. Maher (New York: Oxford
University Press, 1972), 26.

Ain't Misbehavin'

5   "I believe that great song, and the chance I got to play it": This
and the quotes below from reviewers can be found in the
context of an excellent discussion of the song's role in
Armstrong's career in Terry Teachout, *Pops: A Life of Louis
Armstrong*, (New York: Houghton Mifflin Harcourt, 2009),
137–38.

All the Things You Are

16   Alec Wilder, mulling over this verdict: Alec Wilder, *American
Popular Song: The Great Innovators, 1900–1950*, edited by James
T. Maher (New York: Oxford University Press, 1972), 79.

Bags' Groove

28   "Monk never did know how to play behind a horn player":
Miles Davis and Quincy Troupe, *Miles: The Autobiography* (New
York: Simon & Schuster, 1989), 187.

Blue Moon

40   "an innocent young girl saying—or rather singing—her
prayers": Richard Rodgers, *Musical Stages* (New York: Random
House, 1975), 160.

42   "No, no, no, no, no! Not like that, Mel!": Mel Tormé, *It Wasn't
All Velvet* (New York: Kensington, 1988), 164.

Body and Soul

46   "It's funny how it became such a classic": John Chilton, *The
Song of the Hawk* (Ann Arbor: University of Michigan Press,
1990), 163.

Chelsea Bridge

60   "From the moment I heard 'Chelsea Bridge'": David Hajdu,
Lush Life: A Biography of Billy Strayhorn (New York: Farrar,
Straus & Giroux, 1996), 87.

Come Sunday

66 **"the most exquisite moments of music ever heard on a concert stage":** Leonard Feather, from the accompanying essay to *The Duke Ellington Carnegie Hall Concerts: January 1943* (Prestige 34004–2).

67 **"This encounter with Mahalia Jackson had a strong influence on me":** Duke Ellington, *Music Is My Mistress* (New York: Doubleday, 1973), 256.

Confirmation

70 **Parker's "most beautiful composition":** Donald Maggin, *Dizzy: The Life and Times of John Birks Gillespie* (New York: HarperCollins, 2005), 188.

Darn That Dream

75 **"hodge-podge of Shakespeariana":** Quoted in Stephen Bourne, *Butterfly McQueen Remembered* (Lanham, Md.: Scarecrow, 2008), 42.

76 **praises the spirit of "sophistication and chance-taking":** Alec Wilder, *American Popular Song: The Great Innovators, 1900–1950*, edited by James T. Maher (New York: Oxford University Press, 1972), 444.

Desafinado

79 **"We had a lot of samba music and Stan Getz used to bug me to death":** Dizzy Gillespie with Al Fraser, *To Be or Not . . . to Bop* (New York: Doubleday, 1979), 431.

Donna Lee

86 **"Donna Lee" was "the first tune of mine that was ever recorded":** Miles Davis and Quincy Troupe, *Miles: The Autobiography* (New York: Simon & Schuster, 1989), 103–4.

Don't Get Around Much Anymore

91 **Johnny Hodges—who, according to Rex Stewart:** Rex Stewart, *Boy Meets Horn*, edited by Claire P. Gordon (Ann Arbor: University of Michigan Press, 1991), 190.

Easy to Love

96 **"I'll write Jewish tunes":** Richard Rodgers, *Musical Stages* (New York: Random House, 1975), 88.

97 **"If ever there was a song that shouldn't have a note changed":** Alec Wilder, *American Popular Song: The Great Innovators, 1900–1950*, edited by James T. Maher (New York: Oxford University Press, 1972), 243.

Falling in Love with Love

112 **"considerable monotony":** Alec Wilder, *American Popular Song: The Great Innovators, 1900–1950*, edited by James T. Maher (New York: Oxford University Press, 1972), 209.

Fascinating Rhythm

113 **Aaron Copland lavished high praise:** From Aaron Copland, "Jazz Structure and Influence" (1927), included in *Aaron Copland: A Reader: Selected Writings: 1923–1972*, edited by Richard Kostelanetz (New York: Routledge, 2004), 86.

Georgia on My Mind

122 **"Why don't you write a song called 'Georgia'?":** Hoagy Carmichael, *The Stardust Road and Sometimes I Wonder: The Autobiographies of Hoagy Carmichael* (New York: Da Capo, 1999), 216.

God Bless the Child

130   "One night I met Holiday when she was off from work": Donald Clarke, *Wishing on the Moon: The Life and Times of Billie Holiday* (New York: Viking, 1994), 191.

Have You Met Miss Jones?

140   "the most eagerly awaited musical of all times": Richard Rodgers, *Musical Stages* (New York: Random House, 1975), 187.

141   **Steve Kuhn, who worked briefly with Coltrane during this period:** For more on this, see Lewis Porter, *John Coltrane: His Life and Music* (Ann Arbor: University of Michigan Press, 1998), 146.

Honeysuckle Rose

143   "You don't remember the melody?": Ed Kirkeby, *Ain't Misbehavin': The Story of Fats Waller* (New York: Dodd, Mead, 1966), 123.

145   **Dan Morgenstern has suggested that the composer:** Liner notes to Fats Waller, *"Oh Mercy! Looka Here," His Piano . . . His Rhythm—1935 & 1939* (Honeysuckle Rose Records HR 5000-1, 5000-2, 5000-3).

Hot House

146   "There was never anybody who played any closer than we did": Dizzy Gillespie with Al Fraser, *To Be or Not . . . to Bop* (New York: Doubleday, 1979), 232.

146   "I believe that the history of jazz will remember as an essential date": Included and translated by Alyn Shipton in his *Groovin' High: The Life of Dizzy Gillespie* (New York: Oxford University Press, 1999), 169.

I Didn't Know What Time It Was

163   "It was almost impossible to find him when we needed him": Richard Rodgers, *Musical Stages* (New York: Random House, 1975), 192.

I Got Rhythm

167   "I've heard honest—and even intelligent—people": Ethel Merman and Pete Martin, *Who Could Ask for Anything More* (New York: Doubleday, 1955), 82.

I Hear a Rhapsody

169   "classic . . . a virile rendition sung with great warmth": Mel Tormé, *My Singing Teachers* (New York: Oxford University Press, 1994), 80.

I Should Care

181   "His choice of tunes is so closely linked to his life": From Ira Gitler, *The Masters of Bebop: A Listener's Guide* (New York: Da Capo, 2001), 111.

I Surrender, Dear

181   "When we were at the Cocoanut Grove": Bing Crosby, as told to Pete Martin, *Call Me Lucky* (New York: Da Capo, 1993), 104.

If You Could See Me Now

187   **Pat Metheny has cited this as his favorite guitar solo of all time:** Ben Ratliff, "Pat Metheny: An Idealist Reconnects with His Mentors," *New York Times*, February 25, 2005.

Impressions

192   "mediocrity which claims to be intense has a peculiarly repulsive effect": Edgar Wind, *Art and Anarchy* (New York: Knopf, 1964), 71.

In a Sentimental Mood

195   "Who, may I ask, is Manny Kurtz?": Alec Wilder, *American Popular Song: The Great Innovators, 1900–1950*, edited by James T. Maher (New York: Oxford University Press, 1972), 414.

195   "Once I asked him what he considered a typical Negro piece among his compositions": Quoted in Derek Jewell, *Duke: A Portrait of Duke Ellington* (New York: W. W. Norton, 1977), 57–58.

196   "As long as I've known this song": Quoted in J. C. Thomas, *Chasin' the Trane: The Music and Mystique of John Coltrane* (New York: Doubleday, 1975), 155.

In Your Own Sweet Way

197   "One disc jockey sent me a tape of 32 versions of it": Dave Brubeck, "Standard Time" (a letter to the editor), *Jazz Times*, December 1994, 10.

197   "You've got to be kidding," Brubeck responded. "I'm a composer": From an interview with Len Lyons, included in Len Lyons, *The Great Jazz Pianists: Speaking of Their Lives and Music* (New York: William Morrow, 1983), 109.

It Don't Mean a Thing (If It Ain't Got That Swing)

205   David McGee, who has researched Mills's life and times: From email correspondence between the author and David McGee, September 28–29, 2010. McGee draws on an oral history with Irving Mills, conducted by Stephen Lesser for the William E. Wiener Oral History Library of the American Jewish Committee on April 9, 1975.

King Porter Stomp

220   "I don't know what the term 'stomp' means, myself": Alan Lomax, *Mister Jelly Roll* (Berkeley: University of California Press, 1973), 121.

Laura

229   Cole Porter once claimed: Matt Schudel, "'Laura' Composer David Raksin Dies," *Washington Post*, August 11, 2004, B4.

Liza

237   Oscar Levant, in his frank, witty book: Oscar Levant, *A Smattering of Ignorance* (New York: Doubleday, 1940), 196.

Love for Sale

240   "You can write a novel about a harlot": William McBrien, *Cole Porter* (New York: Knopf, 1998) 137.

Lover

242   "For it is only a series of chromatic intervals": Alec Wilder, *American Popular Song: The Great Innovators, 1900–1950*, edited by James T. Maher (New York: Oxford University Press, 1972), 189.

Lullaby of Birdland

248 **"Since then I've been back to the same butcher several times"**: George Shearing, *Lullaby of Birdland: The Autobiography of George Shearing* (New York: Continuum, 2004), 138.

The Man I Love

256 **British composer and musicologist Wilfrid Mellers would extol**: Wilfrid Mellers, *Music in a New Found Land* (London: Barrie and Rockliff, 1964), 388.

256 **"This is the music of America"**: Philip Furia, *Ira Gershwin: The Art of the Lyricist* (New York: Oxford University Press, 1997), 42.

Memories of You

263 **Armstrong turned to Lionel Hampton, the drummer on the session:** Lionel Hampton with James Haskins, *Hamp* (New York: Warner, 1989), 38.

263 **"for the rest of his career he owned the song"**: Marc Myers, "Sonny Dunham: Memories of You," *JazzWax* (http://www.jazzwax.com/2009/10/sonny-dunham-memories-of-you.html), October 14, 2009.

Milestones

264 **"This was the first record where I started to write in the modal form"**: Miles Davis and Quincy Troupe, *Miles: The Autobiography* (New York: Simon & Schuster, 1989), 225.

265 **"There will be fewer chords but infinite possibilities"**: Nat Hentoff, "An Afternoon with Miles Davis," *The Jazz Review*, Vol.1, no.2 (December 1958), 12.

My Funny Valentine

280 **"Gerry made a lot of money with songs that Chet already played"**: *Chet Baker: His Life and Music* by Jeroen de Valk (Berkeley, Calif.: Berkeley Hill Books, 1989), 41.

My Old Flame

283 **"noisy, slapstick, grotesque novelty"**: Sam Coslow, *Cocktails for Two: The Many Lives of Giant Songwriter Sam Coslow* (New York: Arlington, 1977), 145.

Nardis

290 **"I don't play that crap . . . I'm an artist"**: Bill Crow, *Jazz Anecdotes: Second Time Around* (New York: Oxford University Press, 2005), 164. The anecdote is related here as something Andy Farber told to Joe Gianono. Miles makes no mention of the song in his autobiography.

Nature Boy

292 **"When I was young I dreamed of a boy searching for God"**: Quoted in Pearl Rowe, "To Nature Boy, Life Needn't Be Capitalized," *Los Angeles Times*, July 24, 1977.

Night and Day

298 **Sinatra "was so excited you almost believed he had never recorded before"**: Peter J. Levinson, *Tommy Dorsey: Livin' in a Great Big Way* (New York: Da Capo, 2006), 151.

Once I Loved

317 **"I haven't sung so soft since I had the laryngitis"**: From the liner notes to *Francis Albert Sinatra & Antonio Carlos Jobim* (Reprise 1021).

Perdido

336 **Ellington's biographer James Lincoln Collier has argued that you can't really classify it as a song:** James Lincoln Collier, *Duke Ellington* (New York: Oxford University Press, 1987), 235.

'Round Midnight

345 **"We left Monk standing there":** Miles Davis and Quincy Troupe, *Miles: The Autobiography* (New York: Simon & Schuster, 1989), 191.

346 **"All the guys who play ''Round Midnight' use my introduction":** Dizzy Gillespie with Al Fraser, *To Be or Not . . . to Bop* (New York: Doubleday, 1979), 489.

346 **"Thelonious Monk wrote ''Round Midnight,' but his changes":** Richard Ouzounian and Ashante Infantry, "Marsalis Heeds Music's Message," *Toronto Star*, June 27, 2009 (www.thestar.com/entertainment/music/article/656763).

Ruby, My Dear

350 **"There were only two women in his life—me and Rubie":** Robin D. G. Kelley, *Thelonious Monk: The Life and Times of an American Original* (New York: Free Press, 2009), 51.

St. James Infirmary

353 **some still dispute the Old World connections of the jazz song:** See Robert W. Harwood, *I Went Down to St. James Infirmary* (Kitchener, Ontario: Harland Press, 2008) for the most complete account of this controversy.

St. Louis Blues

354 **"A rain of silver dollars began to fall":** W. C. Handy, *Father of the Blues: An Autobiography* (New York: Da Capo, 1991), 77.

Smoke Gets in Your Eyes

371 *Herald Tribune* **proclaimed that "Smoke Gets in Your Eyes" had "swept the dance floors":** Gerald Bordman, *Jerome Kern: His Life and Music* (New York: Oxford University Press, 1980), 341.

Solitude

379 **"When I did 'Solitude,'" he later explained to Stanley Dance, "I was one number short":** Stanley Dance, *The World of Duke Ellington* (New York: Charles Scribner's Sons, 1970), 271.

Sophisticated Lady

387 **Then he proclaimed, "Now this is the way I would play it":** David Hajdu, *Lush Life* (New York: Farrar, Straus & Giroux), 1996, 50.

387 **"As far back as 1933, when I said I was playing Negro music":** Duke Ellington, "Where Is Jazz Going?" originally published in *Music Journal*, March 1962, pp. 31, 96; reprinted in *The Duke Ellington Reader*, edited by Mark Tucker (New York: Oxford University Press, 1993), 324–26.

Star Dust

396 **His biographer Richard Sudhalter has documented a more gradual:** Richard M. Sudhalter, *Stardust Melody: The Life and Music of Hoagy Carmichael* (New York: Oxford University Press, 2003), 106.

396 **"The verse," Mel Tormé has noted, "rambles up the scale":** Mel Tormé, *My Singing Teachers* (New York: Oxford University Press, 1994), 121.

397 **"The greatest clarinet solo of all time":** Whitney Balliett, *Barney, Bradley and Max: 16 Portraits in Jazz* (New York: Oxford University Press, 1989), 196.

Stormy Weather

406 **William Zinsser, who later wrote extensively on standards:** William Zinsser, *Easy to Remember: The Great American Songwriters and Their Songs* (Jaffrey, N.H.: David R. Godine), 2001, 59.

Struttin' with Some Barbecue

409 **"The man loved that major seventh":** Ricky Riccardi's comment here is from email correspondence with the author, May 5, 2011.

Summertime

412 **Duke Ellington, who had expressed reservations about *Porgy and Bess*:** See Edward Morrow, "Duke Ellington on Gershwin's Porgy," originally published in *New Theater*, December 1935, 5–6; reprinted in *The Duke Ellington Reader*, edited by Mark Tucker (New York: Oxford University Press, 1993), 114–17. I note that Ellington tried to distance himself from these comments about Gershwin after they appeared in print, but their harshness may be less a matter of misquoting and more a reflection of the fact that Ellington thought he was speaking off the record.

'S Wonderful

415 **"recasting, rewriting, rehearsing, recriminating—of rejoicing, there was none":** Howard Pollack, *George Gershwin: His Life and Work* (Berkeley: University of California Press, 2006), 407–8.

416 **"Its verse is a monotony of imitative phrases":** Alec Wilder, *American Popular Song: The Great Innovators, 1900–1950*, edited by James T. Maher (New York: Oxford University Press, 1972), 139.

Take Five

418 **"I still think, basically, it was a dubious idea at best":** From a 1976 interview with Radio Canada, quoted in Doug Ramsey, *Take Five: The Public and Private Lives of Paul Desmond* (Seattle: Parkside, 2005), 207.

Tea for Two

422 **"When Tatum played 'Tea for Two' that night":** Maurice Waller and Anthony Calabrese, *Fats Waller* (New York: Schirmer, 1977), 96–98.

Tenderly

424 **Alec Wilder would later gripe that the melody is a poor fit:** Alec Wilder, *American Popular Song: The Great Innovators, 1900–1950*, edited by James T. Maher (New York: Oxford University Press, 1972), 515.

These Foolish Things

429 **"the best thing I ever did":** Tom Nolan, *Three Chords for Beauty's Sake: The Life of Artie Shaw* (New York: W. W. Norton, 2010), 279.

Time after Time

437 **"It's a man's song"**: Mark Steyn, *Mark Steyn's American Songbook, Volume One* (Woodsville, N.H.: Stockade, 2008), 71.

Tin Roof Blues

438 **"could be considered the stylistic source"**: Samuel Charters, *A Trumpet around the Corner: The Story of New Orleans Jazz* (Jackson: University Press of Mississippi, 2008), 198.

439 **"having lived with both pieces on records for some twenty-plus years now"**: Martin Williams, *Jazz in Its Time* (New York: Oxford University Press, 1989), 31.

The Way You Look Tonight

449 **"merely adequate or worse"**: Gerald Bordman, *Jerome Kern: His Life and Music* (New York: Oxford University Press, 1980), 359.

Willow Weep for Me

461 **"If I walked into an office today with 'Willow Weep for Me' "**: Tighe E. Zimmers, *Tin Pan Alley Girl: A Biography of Ann Ronell* (Jefferson, N.C.: McFarland, 2009), 20.

You'd Be So Nice to Come Home To

472 **"I was going to have to play on a messed up horn"**: Art and Laurie Pepper, *Straight Life: The Story of Art Pepper* (New York: Schirmer, 1979), 192.

INDEX

Page ranges in **bold** indicate the main discussion for a song.